The
Politics
of # Exclusion

The
Politics
of
Exclusion

Michael N. Danielson

Columbia University Press
New York   1976

Library of Congress Cataloging in Publication Data

Danielson, Michael N
  The politics of exclusion.

  Includes bibliographical references and index.
  1. Discrimination in housing—United States.
2. Suburbs—United States.   3. Housing policy—United
States.   4. Metropolitan areas—United States.   I. Ti-
tle.
HD7293.D26   301.5'4   76-7609
ISBN 0-231-03697-3 cloth
ISBN 0-231-08342-4 paper

Columbia University Press
New York—Guildford, Surrey

Copyright © 1976 Columbia University Press
Printed in the United States of America

For Jessica and Jeffrey
two very special suburbanites

Preface

Many people have had a hand in the preparation of this study. To begin at the beginning, Charles F. Westoff, Professor of Sociology at Princeton University, stirred the initial thought of examining the impact of local housing and land use policies on population distribution while he was serving as the executive director of the Commission on Population and the American Future. Out of these conversations came support from the Commission for an exploratory paper on "Differentiation, Segregation, and Political Fragmentation in the American Metropolis." [1]

Among those who read the paper, a number suggested expansion into a longer study. Particularly helpful at this stage were the comments of a colleague at Princeton, Professor Marguerite R. Barnett. Encouragement also came from Bernard Gronert of Columbia University Press.

Support from the Ford Foundation under a grant for the Project on State and Local Government, which I directed during the academic year 1972–73, permitted the collection and analysis of most of the research materials used in expanding the initial study into the present volume. Among the many people at the Ford Foundation who lent a hand in one way or another, particularly helpful were Mitchell Sviridorf, Louis Winnick, William J. Grinker, Thomas V. Seessel, and Robert W. Chandler. My colleagues on the Project on State and Local Government, John M. Bayne and Alan M. Hershey, also pitched in from time to time to help with interviewing and collecting materials. More generally, our numerous discussions of exclusion, responsiveness, and equity in American society helped clarify my thinking on a number of important points. [2]

Research assistance from the Woodrow Wilson School of Public and International Affairs permitted the better part of two summers to be devoted to the writing of this volume.

Yoma Ullman worked for two years collecting and digesting materials, keeping the bibliography straight, and suggesting clearer ways to say all sorts of things. Her help was invaluable. Sharon Naeole did much of the initial research on the judicial aspects of the study. She also performed yeoman service in the development of the materials dealing with the New York Urban Development Corporation, open-housing groups, and metropolitan housing plans. David Jones spent a good part of the summer of 1972 interviewing in the Detroit, Dayton, St. Louis, and Twin Cities area. Hamilton Candee was a particularly responsible undergraduate research assistant during the summer of 1974. David Smith spent many frustrating hours in the bowels of Firestone Library trying to locate elusive references.

A number of librarians at Princeton were helpful to me and the people who worked with me on the project. I especially thank Rosemary Little and her colleagues in the Public Administration Collection, and Margorie Blake and the staff at the Woodrow Wilson School Library.

Many people were involved in the typing of the various incarnations of the manuscript. Most of the burden for the final version rested with Barbara Keller, who produced excellent copy under sometimes trying circumstances. Assisting with the typing at one time or another were Lucille Crooks, Ruth Dilley, and Mary Robertson.

My friend and colleague, W. Duane Lockard, Professor of Politics at Princeton, read the entire manuscript and provided a variety of useful comments and suggestions. Another friend and sometime collaborator, Walter F. Murphy, McCormick Professor of Jurisprudence at Princeton, helped me avoid some pitfalls in my venture into the world of judicial politics. In addition, parts of the manuscript profitted from thoughtful reading by Bruce Ackerman, a member of Governor Brendan Byrne's staff who worked closely with me on land-use and housing policies in New Jersey, by Jameson W. Doig, Jr., Professor of Politics and Public Affairs at Princeton, by Lawrence Goldman, good friend and former member of Edward J. Logue's staff at the New York Urban Development Corporation, and by my wife, Patricia S. Danielson. Much of the manuscript also was read by the students in Public Affairs 530, a graduate seminar on "Problems in Urban Development" which focused on suburban housing, land-use, and environmental issues during the Spring Term of 1975. The discussions and comments that resulted from the work of the seminar are reflected throughout the volume. David L. Morell, of Princeton's Center for Environmental Studies and a former land-use specialist for the U.S. Environmental Protection Agency, taught this seminar with me and made a particularly useful contribution.

Bernard Gronert, David Diefendorf, and their colleagues at Columbia University Press were helpful, encouraging, and relevant throughout the process of turning a mass of material into what is contained between these covers. They also were much better at making deadlines than the author.

Of the scores of others who provided information, insights, assistance, and time, I am particulary indebted to: Herbert J. Franklin of The Potomac Institute's Metropolitan Housing Program, whose work constitutes an invaluable source to anyone working in this field; Ernest Erber, Aileen Hernandez, and Edward Holmgren of the National Committee Against Discrimination in Housing; Edward J. Logue, Daniel L. Miller, and others at the New York Urban Development Corporation; Richard F. Babcock, of Ross, Hardies, O'Keefe, Babcock & Parsons, Chicago, Illinois; Kale Williams and Harry Gottlieb of the Leadership Council for Metropolitan Open Communities, Chicago, Illinois; Paul Davidoff of Suburban Action Institute, White Plains, New York; and various staff members at the Miami Valley Regional Planning Commission, Tri-State Regional Planning Commission, Delaware Valley Regional Planning Commission, East-West Gateway Coordinating Council, Association of Bay Area Governments, Atlanta Regional Council, and Northeast Illinois Planning Commission.

MICHAEL N. DANIELSON

Princeton, New Jersey
May 1976

Contents

Chapter One □ The Separated Society   1

Chapter Two □ Suburban Autonomy   27

Chapter Three □ Zoning for Fewer People   50

Chapter Four □ Excluding Subsidized Housing   79

Chapter Five □ Unequal Odds   107

Chapter Six □ Latent Interests with Limited Clout   130

Chapter Seven □ Exclusion and the Courts   159

Chapter Eight □ Opening the Suburbs
from Washington   199

Chapter Nine □ Fair Shares for the Metropolis   243

Chapter Ten □ The Reluctant Partner   279

Chapter Eleven □ Whither an Open Society   323

Notes   359

Index   427

The
Politics
of Exclusion

Chapter One

The Separated Society

To a greater degree than in other modern societies, urbanization in the United States has separated people spatially along economic and social lines. Nowhere in urban America is the heterogeneity encompassed by a metropolis reproduced in its local jurisdictions and neighborhoods. Instead, the forces of urban growth and change have produced significant income, class, ethnic, and racial variations among the many disparate communities which comprise a metropolitan area. These settlement patterns have been reinforced by a fragmented system of local government which separates cities from suburbs and suburbs from one another, thus institutionalizing the diversity of a complex urban society. Within this decentralized political system, public policies have played a central role in the development of a spatially differentiated metropolis in which blacks are separated from whites, the poor from the more affluent, the disadvantaged from economic and educational opportunity, and local jurisdictions with the greatest public needs from communities which possess the greatest share of the public resources.

Among the various components of the American federal system, local governments have had the most direct influence on spatial differentiation and residential segregation. In every state but Hawaii, local jurisdictions bear the primary responsibility for the regulation of housing, land use, and urban development. Zoning laws, building codes, subdivision regulations, and other powers permit local governments to determine whether housing can be built in a particular area, the amount of land that must be used for a new housing unit, the size and nature of the units, and the construction materials and methods. Local participation or consent is required for most subsidized housing programs, and this enables localities to determine the availability and location of lower-income projects. In addition, local governments influence the availability of land for all kinds of development through the provision of streets, water and sewer lines, and other public facilities. Throughout urban America, these powers have been used by local governments to increase housing costs, restrict housing opportunities, and otherwise reinforce the spatial separation of the metropolitan population along social and economic lines. Lower-income and minority groups have been excluded from much of the metropolis because the construction of apartments and subsidized housing has been blocked in many jurisdictions, the use of mobile homes has been widely prevented, and almost any kind of residential development has been foreclosed in some communities.

Exclusionary policies have played a major role in shaping the residential patterns of both cities and suburbs. In the cities, apartments have been kept out of areas dominated by single-family homes. City governments commonly have used their control over the location of subsidized housing to exclude lower-income groups from more affluent area. The success of these policies in cities is indicated by the existence of enclaves for the well-to-do, by the maintenance of large middle-class areas of single-family homes, and by the concentration of most subsidized housing in lower-income and black neighborhoods.

Local governmental actions which limit access, however, tend to be most significant in the suburbs.[1] More Americans live in suburbs than in either central cities or outside metropolitan areas. Most of the nation's population growth occurs at the periphery of metropolitan areas, where vacant land is available for residential development. Between 1960 and 1970, suburbs accounted for 81 percent of the population growth in metropolitan areas and 72 percent of all the housing added to the metropoli-

Table 1.1. Population in Cities, Suburbs, and Outside
Metropolitan Areas, 1970

	Total (000)	Percent
Total Population	203,212	100.0
Cities	63,797	31.4
Suburbs	75,622	37.2
Outside Metropolitan Areas	63,793	31.4

Source: U.S. Department of Commerce, Social and Economic Statistics Administration, Bureau of the Census, Statistical Abstract of the United States 1974 (Washington: U.S. Government Printing Office, 1974), p. 17.

tan stock.[2] Except for the newer cities of the South and West, which encompass large amounts of undeveloped land, central cities have run out of room to grow, even in the outer neighborhoods which have accounted for most of their residential development in recent years. Suburbs, on the other hand, can expand indefinitely into the rural hinterland which awaits development, unless checked by the outward spread of another metropolitan area, natural obstacles, economic constraints such as rising energy costs, or public policies designed to constrain urban sprawl. The comparative advantage of suburbs with respect to the availability of land for housing development led the President's Committee on Urban Housing to conclude in 1968 that "regardless of the extent to which the nation chooses to tear down the central cities and rebuild them, a large share of the new housing, including subsidized housing, developed in the coming decade will have to be located outside of central cities." [3]

Suburbia is also the locus of most commercial and industrial development in the metropolis. Approximately three-quarters of all new industrial plants in metropolitan areas were located in the suburbs during the 1960s. In the fifteen largest metropolitan areas, suburban employment increased by 3.1 million between 1960 and 1970, while the number of jobs in the central cities dropped by 836,000. Chicago alone lost 229,000 jobs, 220 factories, and 760 retail establishments during the decade, while suburban areas gained almost 600,000 jobs.[4] In 1973, as many people were employed in the suburbs of these fifteen areas as in the cities.[5]

Table 1.2. Employment in the Chicago SMSA, 1960–1970

Place of Work	1960	1970	Change	% Change
Chicago	1,578,036	1,348,880	−229,156	−14.5
Suburban Cook County	405,159	745,468	340,309	84.0
Other Suburban Counties	300,592	545,308	244,716	81.4

Source: Pierre de Vise, "The Wasting of Chicago," Working Paper II.14, Chicago Regional Hospital Study (Oct., 1972), Table 1.

Suburbanization shows no signs of abating, although the rising cost of energy is likely to slow the outward spread of urban development somewhat. Relatively few Americans prefer to live in cities—only 18 percent according to a 1972 survey.[6] At least two-thirds of the nation's population growth over the last quarter of the century is expected to occur in suburbs, resulting in approximately 45 percent of the population living in suburbia by the year 2000. In the future, as during the past thirty years, "the vast majority of new homes, new apartments, new shopping centers, new schools, new streets, new parks, new roads, new highways, new public buildings, new factories, new sewer and water systems, and other new structures built in the United States" will be located in the suburbs.[7]

As a result of these developmental trends, the suburbs are where governmental actions have the greatest impact on housing. Not only are opportunities for exclusion greater in suburbs than in cities, but so are the prospects for success. Most suburban jurisdictions are small and have relatively homogeneous populations, which makes it easier to secure consensus on exclusionary policies than is commonly the case in larger and more heterogeneous cities. As a consequence, suburban jurisdictions have been more successful than other local governments in establishing and maintaining exclusionary policies.

For these reasons, the primary focus of this volume is the politics of exclusion in the suburbs. The remainder of this chapter examines the roots and significance of suburban exclusion in the context of the development of the spatially differentiated and politically fragmented American metropolis. The chapters which follow analyze the role of the suburban political system in fostering and facilitating exclusionary behavior, the nature and effect of exclusionary policies in the suburbs, and the activities of other governmental institutions—including the states, the national government, metropolitan agencies, and the courts—which condition, sanction, reinforce, modify, or negate local governmental policies affecting housing and land use in the suburbs.

The suburbs, of course, cannot be examined in isolation from central cities. They were spawned by the cities. Their political character and exclusionary aims have been shaped in large part by political and social developments in the city. Although the linkages between city and suburb have steadily weakened in the wake of the decentralization of jobs and other activities, the actions of each constantly affect the other. This is particularly the case with suburban policies which influence the housing and employment opportunities of those who live in the city. Lower-income and minority groups are more concentrated in central cities than would be the case if suburbs permitted more lower-cost and subsidized housing to be built within their boundaries. Suburban exclusion also intensifies the segregation of schools in metropolitan areas, widens the gap in the quality of education and other public services between city and suburbs, and magnifies the tax burdens borne by residents of older cities. Unemployment and welfare problems in the city are exacerbated by the inaccessibility of more and more suburban jobs to lower-income city dwellers. And the concentration of disadvantaged citizens in older cities undermines most efforts to strengthen the tax base, attract middle- and upper-income residents, and otherwise revitalize the decaying center of the metropolis.

The Differentiated Metropolis

Until well into the nineteenth century, social and economic differences were not markedly reflected in the residential pattern of most American cities. Since walking was the principal mode of transportation for all but the wealthy, city dwellers were forced to live close to their place of work, and "most areas of the new big city were a jumble of occupations, classes, shops, homes, immigrants, and native Americans." [8] This undifferentiated settlement pattern was radically altered by a succession of transportation innovations which freed residential development from the constraints imposed by the necessity to walk to work. By opening more and more land for housing, improvement in accessibility greatly accelerated the spread of urban development at progressively lower densities. Enhanced mobility combined with the vast increase in the scale of the metropolis to sort urban dwellers out along economic and social lines.

Once this process began, income came to play an increasingly important role in determining where people lived. The affluent were in the best position to take advantage of the territorial expansion of the metropolis. New housing along the urban periphery generally was more expensive than that available in the older sections of the city; and commuting expenses almost always were higher in the newer neighborhoods. Differences in the costs of various kinds of new housing reinforced spatial separation along economic lines. Because of the common practice of building large amounts of uniformly priced housing in a particular city neighborhood or suburban community, the degree of physical separation involved often was considerable.

Until the advent of subsidized housing programs, most lower-income families were dependent on older dwellings, which became available as former occupants moved outward to better neighborhoods. As with new housing, variations in the costs of used housing in different sections of the metropolis tend to subdivide people further on the basis of income. The least attractive housing filters down to the lowest-income groups.

Most of this housing is located in the central city, and its availability largely accounts for the concentration of the poor in central cities. Not much older rental housing is available to filter down outside the urban core. Exceptions are smaller cities scattered around many of the larger metropolitan areas, some older suburbs whose housing stock has deteriorated, and rural slums encompassed by the spread of urban growth.

Reinforcing this pattern of income differentiation has been the widespread desire of urban dwellers to separate themselves from lower-income and minority groups. In the past as in the present, most of those moving outward have been seeking social separation from the lower classes as well as better housing and more spacious surroundings. Middle-class families commonly equate personal security, good schools, maintenance of property values, and the general desirability of a residential area with the absence of lower-income groups. Given these concerns, residents of middle-class areas rarely are content to rely solely on economic factors to separate them from the poor. Instead, they seek to use the local political system to exclude those whose presence threatens to undermine the quality of life in their neighborhood. High standards for home building and land-use controls are widely employed to preclude the construction of inexpensive housing in developing areas. Rigorous enforcement of local housing codes severely limits housing opportunities for less affluent families in middle-class neighborhoods. Further intensifying concentration of the poor in the urban core is the widespread resistance of the outer areas to public housing, almost all of which, as a result, has been located in the inner city.

Spatial separation also is enhanced by the importance of housing to social status in the United States. As a study prepared for the U.S. Department of Housing and Urban Development in 1972 emphasized, "housing choice is *par excellence* a decision involving perceptions of status." [9] Where one lives tells the rest of society a great deal about one's income, socio-economic background, and "success." Safeguarding status usually is seen in terms of keeping out those whose presence would detract from the desirability of an area. As Brian J. L. Berry and Katherine B. Smith point out:

> The bases of segregation reside in two fundamental traits of American culture: aggressive, achievement-oriented mobility and protective, home-related territoriality.
> Earnings must be spent on the best possible homes and material posses-

sions in the best possible neighborhoods. Any increase in job or financial status must be matched by a move to a better neighborhood. "Downgrading" of the neighborhood through entry of those of lower status must be fought, and if it cannot be contained, one must flee to avoid the inevitably resulting loss of status.[10]

Fears of lower-income groups and the loss of status implied by their presence tends to be expressed in collective rather than individual terms. Throughout the development of the differentiated metropolis, those ethnic and racial minorities whose ranks included large numbers of poor people have been the prime targets of exclusionary practices. The barriers erected by more established groups to protect their neighborhoods combined with poverty, ethnic rivalries, and ties of language, custom, and religion to produce ethnic clustering in the rapidly growing cities of the late nineteenth and early twentieth centuries. Over time, however, ethnic influences on residential patterns receded as immigrants and their offspring moved up the economic ladder and outward from the urban core in search of newer housing in more attractive neighborhoods. In the process, most were assimilated into broader social groupings. With rising incomes, the dispersal of residences and jobs across the metropolitan landscape, the dilution of ethnic identification, and the fading of ethnic prejudices, ethnicity has had declining impact on the territorial separation of the urban population.

In sharp contrast to the waning significance of ethnicity is the persistence of race as a potent influence on urban settlement patterns. Black Americans have not been able to move out of the urban core in the same fashion, or with as wide a range of choices, as white ethnics. These differences were underscored in the report of the National Advisory Commission on Civil Disorders in 1968:

The later phases of Negro settlement and expansion in metropolitan areas diverge sharply from those typical of white immigrants. As the whites were absorbed by the larger society, many left their predominantly ethnic neighborhoods and moved to outlying areas to obtain newer housing and better schools. Some scattered randomly over the suburban area. Others established new ethnic clusters in the suburbs, but even these rarely constituted solely members of a single ethnic group. As a result, most middle-class neighborhoods—both in the suburbs and within central cities—have no distinctive ethnic character, except that they are white.

Nowhere has the expansion of America's urban Negro population followed this pattern of dispersal.[11]

Instead, after half a century of rapid urbanization of the nation's black population, blacks remain the most spatially differentiated group in the modern metropolis. Within the older cities, the vast majority of blacks live in racially segregated neighborhoods.[12] Less than five percent of the population of the suburbs was black in 1970, compared with over 21 percent of the residents of the central cities. Black movement to the suburbs increased rapidly during the 1960s, from around 20,000 per year in the early part of the decade to approximately 200,000 annually in the latter years, but most of these blacks moved to suburban areas immediately adjacent to black neighborhoods in the central city.[13] In the Cleveland area, for example, black migration to the suburbs has primarily been an extension of the black ghetto eastward across the city line into East Cleveland, Shaker Heights, and Warrensville, which together housed over 80 percent of the metropolitan area's suburban blacks in the late 1960s.[14] East Cleveland's population of 43,000 was 60 percent black in 1970, compared with less than three percent ten years earlier. In 1970, only 20 percent of the blacks in the Philadelphia suburbs lived in "ra-

Table 1.3. Metropolitan Population, by Race, 1970

	Total (000)	White (000)	Black (000)	Percent Black
Metropolitan Areas	139,419	120,579	16,771	11.1
Central Cities	63,797	49,430	13,140	20.6
Suburbs	75,622	71,148	3,630	4.8

Source: U.S. Bureau of the Census, Statistical Abstract of the United States 1974, p. 17.

cially dispersed residential situations (census blocks with fewer than 40% black)."[15] In the Washington area, three-fourths of the increase in the black suburban population during the 1960s occurred in Prince Georges County, primarily in neighborhoods adjacent to black sections of the District of Columbia.[16]

As a result of these settlement patterns, most suburbs have only a handful of black residents, while a few have large minority populations. Almost 7,000 of the 10,000 blacks in Southern California's Orange County resided in Santa Ana in 1970, compared with 170 in Anaheim and 41 in Newport Beach, where they comprised 0.1 percent and 0.08 percent of the population respectively. In northern New Jersey, 89 percent of Essex County's 72,000 black residents in 1970 lived in East Orange, Orange, and Montclair—all older suburbs bordering on New-

Table 1.4. Black Proportion of the Population
of the Suburbs of Essex County, New Jersey, 1970

Municipality	Total Population	Black Population	Percentage Black
East Orange	75,471	40,099	53.1
Orange	32,566	11,630	35.7
Montclair	44,043	11,932	27.1
North Caldwell	6,425	414	6.4
Cedar Grove	15,582	725	4.7
Irvington	59,743	2,345	3.9
South Orange	16,971	583	3.4
Belleville	34,643	856	2.5
Bloomfield	52,029	914	1.8
Maplewood	24,932	428	1.7
Verona	15,067	235	1.6
Nutley	32,099	498	1.6
Glen Ridge	8,518	102	1.2
Caldwell	8,719	100	1.1
West Orange	43,715	471	1.1
Essex Fells	2,541	22	.9
Millburn	21,307	180	.8
Livingston	30,127	96	.3
West Caldwell	11,887	33	.3
Roseland	4,453	7	.2
Fairfield	6,731	8	.1
Total	547,569	71,678	13.1

Source: U.S. Department of Commerce, Bureau of the Census, Census of Population: 1970;
General Population Characteristics, Final Report Pc(1)-B32, New Jersey (Washington: U.S.
Government Printing Office, 1971), pp. 116–19.

ark. Fifteen of the 237 suburban municipalities in the Chicago area accounted in 1970 for 83 percent of the 128,300 blacks living in the suburbs. Moreover, as Pierre de Vise has pointed out, the Chicago area's "entire 10-year gain of 50,800 suburban blacks [during the 1960s] occurred in these 15 suburbs." [17]

Underlying the racial bifurcation of the metropolis are income differences between blacks and whites, the reluctance of blacks and especially whites to live in integrated neighborhoods, and a ubiquitous set of discriminatory practices which exclude blacks from most white residential areas. In 1970, the median income for all black families in metropolitan areas was $7100, compared to $11,200 for white families. In the same year, one out of every four blacks living in metropolitan areas fell below the federally defined poverty line, while only one in thirteen white metropolitan residents was classified as poor. Because black incomes tend to be lower than those of whites, blacks are more dependent on the older housing stock of the metropolis, which is concentrated in the inner city and older suburbs. Relatively low incomes also mean that blacks are disproportionately affected on strictly economic grounds by rising housing costs and exclusionary practices which limit the availability of inexpensive dwelling units.

Like whites, blacks who move to the suburbs tend to have higher incomes than those who remain in the city.[18] As indicated in Table 1.5, however, blacks and whites with similar incomes are not found in the same proportions in the suburbs. In 1970, almost half of all white families with incomes under $5,000 lived outside central cities, compared with less than 20 percent of the black families with similar economic situations. Over 60 percent of all whites earning between $10,000 and $15,000 were in the suburbs, while less than a quarter of the blacks in the same income bracket lived beyond the city limits. Even among those with incomes of more than $25,000, the proportion of whites in the suburbs is nearly double that of blacks. Albert I. Hermalin and Reynolds Farley estimate that if black families were represented in the suburbs to the same extent as whites with similar incomes, the proportion of black households in the suburbs in 1970 would have increased "from 16

Table 1.5. Proportion of Metropolitan Population in Suburbs by Race and Total Family Income, 1972

Total Family Income	Percent in Suburbs	
	Whites	Blacks
Under $5,000	50.6	15.5
$5,000–$8,999	56.1	20.2
$9,000–$11,990	60.2	20.5
$12,000–$14,999	62.7	26.3
$15,000–$24,999	66.7	25.5
$25,000 and over	66.5	32.1

Source: U.S. Bureau of the Census, Statistical Abstract of the United States 1974, p. 385.

to 43 percent, a proportion much nearer the white figure of 57 percent in the suburban ring." [19] A detailed analysis of residential movement and income in the Philadelphia area revealed that "in general, black residential patterns are relatively insensitive to income in contrast to white patterns." According to Phoebe Cottingham,

not only is the white rate of suburbanization higher than the black rate, regardless of income, but it is also much more sensitive to white family income. The higher up the income scale, the more likely a white family will move from the central city to the suburbs; for the black family, there is only a slight increase in the proportion selecting . . . the suburbs with increases in income.[20]

Some blacks who could afford to move to the suburbs undoubtedly remain in the central city because they prefer to live in black neighborhoods. Among lower-income families surveyed in Dayton, Ohio, 61

Table 1.6. Residential Preferences of Lower-Income
Families in Dayton, Ohio, by Race

Location Preferred	% Whites	% Blacks
Own City Neighborhood	43	61
Suburb	53	34
Indifferent	4	5

Source: Nina Jaffe Gruen and Claude Gruen, Low and Moderate Income Housing in the Suburbs: An Analysis for the Dayton, Ohio Region (New York: Praeger Publishers, 1972), p. 26.

percent of the blacks preferred their own city neighborhoods to a suburban location, while 53 percent of the whites opted for a move to the suburbs.[21] The significance of these preferences for the differentiation of the metropolitan population along racial lines, however, is extremely difficult to gauge as long as housing options are more limited for blacks than for whites at the same economic level. As a civil rights leader in Indianapolis explains: "When the pressure for movement is on, blacks—because of their inability to exercise options—move in the same direction. This implies to people in the white community that all black people want to live together, and this is not necessarily true. The reason for concentration . . . is that it is the only option." [22]

Options are limited because most whites do not want to live in the same neighborhood with blacks. Large numbers of whites identify almost all blacks with poverty, crime, broken families, and other undesirable characteristics of lower-class populations. As one study notes: "Many white Americans confuse socioeconomic class differences with race. Consequently, class characteristics are often attributed to race." [23] Racial stereotypes and negative collective judgments are reinforced by the legacy of three hundred years of slavery, segregation, discrimination, and racial hostility which has left a disproportionate number of blacks poor, employed in low status jobs, dependent on public welfare, badly educated, housed in slums, addicted to dangerous drugs, and involved in violent crimes. As a consequence of these attitudes and realities, the arrival of blacks in a neighborhood is widely perceived as threatening white families with a loss of status, declining property values, deteriorating public schools, substandard public services, and other disruptive changes. To foreclose these developments, whites seek to exclude blacks. When they fail and blacks begin to move into a neighborhood or school district, those whites who are able to flee usually escape, producing the rapid transition of neighborhoods and schools from white to black. White flight, in turn, fuels the fears of other whites in the path of blacks moving outward in search of better housing and schools, thus insuring the continued racial differentiation of the metropolis.

In response to white opposition to black neighbors, home builders, realtors, and financial institutions have systematically discriminated against blacks in order to maintain segregated housing markets. As Donald L. Foley notes, "the planning, actual production, and subsequent sale and resale or rental of housing is a complex set of subprocesses with innumerable constraints, regulations, and negotiations among various parties at sequential points." [24] Each step in this process tends to be tainted by discriminatory practices. A study of limitations on the access of blacks to suburban housing in the San Francisco area concluded that "every routine act, every bit of ritual in the sale or rental of a dwelling unit can be performed in a way calculated to make it either difficult or impossible to consummate a deal." [25] Information concerning housing opportunities usually is not available to blacks and whites on the same basis. Realtors commonly steer blacks away from white areas. Delays, deception, and hostility plague the efforts of blacks to rent or buy in white areas. Blacks are more likely to face limitations on credit, or to be unable to secure mortgages if they seek housing outside "black" areas. Opportunities normally available to whites, such as second mortgages or flexibility in meeting contract deadlines, are frequently withheld from blacks. The net effect of these practices has been the creation of what Chester W. Hartman calls "two separate housing submarkets at all rent and price levels: a highly restricted market for racial minorities, and an open, free-choice market for the white majority." [26]

Efforts by the private sector to limit housing opportunities for blacks have been reinforced by public policy at all levels of government. After examining the impact of governmental activities on housing patterns, the U.S. Commission on Civil Rights concluded that "when much of what now constitutes the Nation's metropolitan areas was built, racial exclusion was expressly endorsed and implemented by Federal and many State and local governments, as well as by all components of the private sector." [27] Racial zoning was used by localities to exclude blacks until outlawed by the U.S. Supreme Court in 1917.[28] Restrictive covenants attached to deeds and enforceable in the courts were widely used to limit black access to white residential areas prior to 1948 when the Supreme Court ruled against further judicial enforcement.[29] During the 1930s and 1940s, federal mortgage insurance programs respected covenants and other restrictive devices designed to preserve the racial homogeneity of neighborhoods.

Responding to the desire of their white constituents to exclude blacks, local governments generally are silent partners in the web of racial discrimination which characterizes the private housing market almost everywhere in urban America.[30] Most suburbs have not enacted fair-housing ordinances; and where local laws have been adopted, they tend to be ineffective. Even when local political backing exists for fair-housing efforts in the suburbs, enforcement is difficult in the face of discriminatory practices which are usually subtle and hard to document. Moreover, in the typical suburban setting where most residents tacitly endorse private housing practices which exclude blacks, public support for fair housing is meager and positive commitment on the part of local officials is rare.

As a result of these circumstances, low visibility and a passive approach characterize most suburban fair-housing and human-relations agencies. In the Dayton metropolitan area, where a number of suburbs created human-relations commissions in the wake of racial conflict in 1967, only two had held hearings four years later. According to the chairman of one inactive commission, "We've never even had a complaint. I don't think anyone knows we exist." [31] The desire of many suburbs for low visibility for their open-housing efforts was illustrated in another Dayton suburb when its human-relations commision sought to distribute literature throughout the metropolitan area indicating that the community welcomed all races, only to be instructed by the municipal council to dispense the material only within the community.

Many suburbs also seek to limit housing opportunities for blacks more directly. Some jurisdictions have attempted to exclude blacks by upgrading housing codes and enforcing them strictly in order to raise the cost of older and less expensive housing. According to the Greater St.

Louis Committee for Freedom of Residence, "occupancy permits are racially oriented" in transitional neighborhoods in the St. Louis area. "After a certain number of blacks move in, people become concerned and they [seek to] control it by instituting [stricter housing] ordinances."[32] As pointed out in the next chapter, suburban governments have employed zoning changes, urban renewal, and other public-works projects to eliminate housing occupied by blacks in their communities. And, as discussed in detail in chapter 4, suburban antipathy to blacks has been a major factor in the widespread resistance to subsidized housing in the suburbs.

Like almost everything in American society, racial attitudes are in flux, although the implications of these changes on housing opportunities for most blacks are far from clear. Whites are more aware of racial discrimination in housing than in education, employment, or law enforcement, with half of all whites in a recent survey acknowledging that blacks are discriminated against in housing.[33] Approximately seven out of ten whites indicated their willingness in 1972 to live in a neighborhood with blacks of roughly the same income and educational level. The other side of this coin, of course, is the substantial number of whites who oppose living near blacks on purely racial grounds. Considerably fewer whites, about one in two, in a recent survey, would be willing to share their neighborhood with lower-income blacks.[34] Moreover, the close identification of low income blacks with subsidized housing programs increases white opposition to such efforts. The depth of racially motivated concerns about status, property values, and personal security led the authors of a wide-ranging survey of attitudes to conclude that "no set of public issues affecting the status of nonwhite minorities was more complex, controversial and farther from solution in mid-1972 than those determining where low-income families could live and work."[35]

All of these private and public attitudes and actions combine to create an atmosphere which deters most blacks from seeking housing in the white suburbs. Confronted with higher prices and hostility, to say nothing of the possibility of harassment and violence in some suburban jurisdictions, many blacks conclude that black neighborhoods offer the only viable housing options available in the segregated metropolis. As Pierre de Vise asks; "How many whites would move to the suburbs at the price of ostracism, insults, and vandalism?"[36]

Political Fragmentation

The political separation of city and suburb is not the product of "natural" forces which caused the city to cease to expand and independent suburban jurisdictions to grow up around the urban core. Until the last decades of the nineteenth century, and much later in many cities, the steady exodus from the urban core typically was not accompanied by creation of politically independent suburbs. Quite the contrary, local political jurisdictions in the path of the decentralizing urban population commonly were swallowed up by the city. Milton Kotler has described the process in Philadelphia:

> Germantown originated as a chartered town of Quaker immigrants, founded concurrently with Philadelphia to its south. Germantown continued as a political unit until it was annexed by Philadelphia without the consent of its residents in the consolidation of 1854. After 171 years of independent growth, that neighborhood lost its political self-rule. . . . In 1854, twenty-eight cities, towns, and boroughs lost their local government and were incorporated into the city of Philadelphia. The present day neighborhoods of Philadelphia can be traced to these original political units.[37]

Through annexation, cities extended their jurisdiction to encompass established communities, newly settled neighborhoods, and undeveloped land at the urban periphery. New areas usually welcomed annexation because the city was the only source of urban services. Cities, for their part, were eager to expand. The American credo assured city fathers that growth was good—to be bigger was to be better. Few cities could resist an expansion program that promised to bolster its image, expand the tax base, enhance the local economy, enlarge opportunities for political rewards, and enrich speculators, developers, and utility operators. Cincinnati's growth was typical of the era, as it expanded from six to twenty-one square miles between 1850 and 1880, and then annexed another twenty-eight square miles over the next thirty years.

As the spreading city sorted itself out along income, ethnic, and racial lines, however, political as well as spatial separation from the inner city became increasingly attractive in the middle-class neighborhoods. Independence promised neighborhood control over taxes and services, a homogeneous local political system responsive to community interests, an end to involvement with the city's complex politics and costly problems, and a more effective means of excluding the lower classes. Reinforcing the desire for autonomy was the rise of the political machine, whose strength was rooted in the lower-income and ethnic wards in the core of the differentiated metropolis. Opposition to the machine came primarily from the middle-class neighborhoods on the city's rim. "The boss," as Richard C. Wade notes, "fed on the problems and predicaments of the old congested center of the city while reform committees grew on the fears and anxieties of the new residential neighborhoods." [38]

Resistance to annexation and demands for local autonomy in the outer neighborhoods became more insistent as immigrants poured into the city and machines consolidated their grip on the governmental machinery. At issue was the question of whether the urban community should maintain a single political system to encompass its diversity or permit its varied neighborhoods to go their own way, with different local governments for different social and economic groupings. Sam B. Warner, Jr., has described the debate in Boston during the late nineteenth century:

> Annexationists appealed to the idea of one great city where work and home, social and cultural activities, industry and commerce would be joined in a single political union. Boston, they said, would share the fate of Rome if the middle class, which heretofore had provided the governance of the city and the force of its reforms, abandoned the city for the suburbs.
>
> Opponents of annexation countered with the ideal of small town life: the simple informal community, the town meeting, the maintenance of the traditions of rural New England. They held out to their audience the idea of the suburban town as a refuge from the pressures of the new industrial metropolis. Nor were the opponents of annexation slow to point out that the high level of city services maintained by Boston meant higher taxes, and further, they frankly stated the independent suburban towns could maintain native American life free from Boston's waves of incoming poor immigrants.
>
> . . . It was already apparent in the 1880's that to join Boston was to assume all the burdens and conflicts of a modern industrial metropolis. To remain apart was to escape, at least for a time, some of these problems. In the face of this choice the metropolitan middle class abandoned their central city. [39]

Almost everywhere, the advocates of suburban separation from the city prevailed. Boston was the first major city to stop growing, adding no new territory after 1873. Over the next half century, every major city in the Northeast, Midwest, and Far West was encircled by independent suburbs. Some cities stopped expanding because of natural barriers or the impediments imposed by state or county boundaries. A few city governments refused to annex new territory because of an unwillingness to underwrite costly capital improvements and service extensions in developing areas. In some instances, cities controlled by machines were willing to let middle-class areas go in order to dilute the electoral strength of the municipal reform movement. But the underlying cause of the end of annexation and the political containment of the city was the universal desire of the periphery for political autonomy from the core. This objective was rooted in class and ethnic conflict and the desire of middle-class areas for local control over their relatively homogeneous communities.

The division of the urban turf between city and suburb, of course, varied from metropolitan area to metropolitan area. A city's share of the newer residential, commercial, and industrial development—as well as of the middle- and upper-income families of the metropolis—depends primarily on its age and when it ceased annexing territory. Most of the older centers of the Northeast and Midwest stopped growing before the widespread introduction of the automobile. As a result, they encompass little low-density development and have relatively high proportions of lower-income and black residents, as well as stable or declining populations. The newer cities of the South and West, on the other hand, grew primarily during the automobile era. As a result, cities such as Alburquerque, El Paso, Orlando, Phoenix, Tampa, and Tucson are more "suburban" than "citylike" in terms of settlement patterns, residential densities, and commercial and industrial development. Neither foreign immigration nor the political machine was a significant factor in the development of most of these newer cities. As a result, differences between the center and the periphery tend to be less pronounced than in older metropolitan areas. Because differences are muted, there has been less reason to create independent suburbs, less need to use small-scale suburban political systems for exclusionary purposes, and a greater willingness on the part of the new areas to be annexed to the central city.

In separating themselves politically from the city, the residents of the newer neighborhoods superimposed a fragmented political system on the spatially differentiated population of the metropolis. The proliferation of suburban jurisdictions, each with independent control over access to residential, educational, and recreational opportunities within its borders, greatly reinforced the social, economic, ethnic, and racial differences among urban neighborhoods. Because of the local political boundaries which balkanize metropolitan areas into more than 20,000 units of government, no local jurisdiction encompasses the diversity of the typical metropolis. Given the spatial differentiation of residences and jobs in the metropolis, neither the need for services nor the ability to pay for them is evenly distributed among local governments whose activities are financed primarily by property and other locally based taxes. As a result, the metropolitan political economy is characterized by great variations in the costs and benefits of public services to residents of different communities. In the words of the Advisory Commission on Intergovernmental Relations, "political splintering along income and racial lines is akin to giving each rich, middle class, and poor neighborhood the power to tax, spend, and zone. Such decentralization of power can and does play hob with the goal of social justice." [40]

Political separation of the city and suburbs has left central cities with twice as many poor residents as suburbia, four blacks for every one living in the suburbs, little room for growth, and a declining share of the metropolis's population and economic base. By cutting most cities off from the benefits of urban growth, and concentrating the most serious urban problems within city limits, the organization of autonomous suburbs has played a key role in the worsening plight of older cities. Independence from the city shields residents of suburbs from much of the public burden of providing for poor families who live in the city. Local autonomy also enhances the ability of suburbanites to exclude lower-income and minority groups, thus intensifying the concentration of the poor and blacks within the city limits. These developments, in turn, increase the attraction of independent suburbs which insulate their residents and businesses from the people and problems of older cities.

As a consequence of the political fragmentation of the metropolis, city taxpayers bear a substantially larger share of the public costs associated with lower income populations than residents of the suburbs, even though the ability of city dwellers to underwrite these expenditures usually is less than that of suburbanites. Higher taxes alone do not explain the flight of middle-income families and businesses to the suburbs, but they combine with poor schools, racial tensions, rising crime rates, and other problems in the older cities to accelerate the process. As the mayor of Camden, an aging industrial city across the Delaware River from Philadelphia, emphasized in explaining why his city lost one-fifth of its population during the 1950s and 1960s: "Business says it can't afford to locate here, and a homeowner with a $20,000 house is taxed over $1,500, about twice as much as if he owned a similar house in the suburbs." [41]

Fiscal disparities between city and suburbs are only one result of the concentration of the poor and minority groups in the urban core. Mounting dependency has overwhelmed the public-welfare arrangements of most cities. Deteriorating city schools impel more and more middle-class families with school-age children to abandon the city for more attractive suburban school systems, while lower-income and minority families moving into neighborhoods abandoned by the middle class have found local schools ineffective and unresponsive to their needs. The concentration of blacks in the urban core means that most racial confrontation in the metropolis occurs in the central city. Competition for housing between blacks and whites takes place primarily within cities, with rapid racial neighborhood transition resulting far more often in cities than suburbs. As a result, "many central-city neighborhoods and housing markets have been in a state of frequent or continuous ferment for much of the past twenty-five years. This instability is an important qualitative difference between life in these central-city neighborhoods and in most suburban neighborhoods." [42]

Racial concentration also makes central cities the scene of most struggles over school desegregation. Almost three-quarters of all black pupils in metropolitan areas live in the central city. Since areawide school districts are rare, almost all of these black youngsters are enrolled in central-city school systems, where they accounted for 31 per cent of all pupils in 1971. By contrast, less than seven percent of the public-school population of the suburbs was black. Acceptance by federal courts of the boundaries of existing school districts in most metropolitan areas has made central cities the locus of almost all efforts to desegregate urban school districts. [43] Confining integration to central cities has meant that the brunt of the busing issue—the most emotional and explosive political conflict of recent years—has been borne largely by city dwellers. School integration limited by the boundaries of the central city also is counterproductive, since whites with the means to move can escape integration by leaving the city for the sanctuary of the suburbs. In Boston, as a member of the school board points out, "no one wants to stay in the city . . . and risk busing their children to an integrated school, when they can move five miles outside of the city and send their kids to a nice, all-white neighborhood school." [44]

Whites who leave the city to avoid integrated schools illustrate how the combination of changing conditions in the city and the existence of the political boundary between city and suburbs push city dwellers in the direction of the suburbs. Once there, what the city has become in the bifurcated metropolis strongly reinforces the suburban desire to maintain the political separation of city and suburb. The independent suburb and local school district are widely perceived as the essential defense of the suburbanite's values which must be protected at all costs from the threat posed by the city and its dwellers. As a state legislator in the Atlanta area notes, "the suburbanite says to himself, 'The reason I worked for so many years was to get away from pollution, bad schools, and crime, and I'll be damned if I'll see it all follow me.' " [45] In Cleveland, as in most metropolitan areas, the more recent arrivals in the suburbs often are the most hostile to those who remain in the city:

> Between 1950 and 1965 some 235,000 whites left Cleveland . . . for its suburbs. They left and continue to leave Cleveland, half with the feeling that they are being pushed out, half with the impression that they are refugees escaping to what they believe to be a liberated zone. They are not likely to be overly concerned about the plight of the city; rather they seem disposed to blame city people for their problems. . . . A large part of the hatred of the city stems from the characterization of its inhabitants as black, poor, and lawless—and thus, to most suburbanites, deserving of their plight. [46]

Heightening suburban indifference and hostility to the city is the growing decentralization of the metropolis, which steadily reduces the number of suburbanites who come into direct contact with the city, its residents, and their problems. At the same time, the growth of crime, racial conflict, drug abuse, neighborhood decay, and other "city" problems in suburbia have not noticeably stimulated suburban concern with urban interdependence or the need for cooperative ventures with the central city. Quite the opposite has occurred in many instances. As social problems become more serious in the suburbs, suburban determination is reinforced to build the walls of political and social separation even higher in order to keep out a plague whose source is seen as the city and its lower-income and black residents.

As a result of these considerations, few in the suburbs believe that their local political jurisdiction has any obligation to contribute to the solution of the urban maladies which are concentrated in the inner city.

"Responsibility?" asks a businessman in the St. Louis area, "I don't see why. What did the city ever do for us?" [47] Similar thoughts are expressed by a suburban city manager in California: "Social problems in the city. People here would say, 'Sympathy, yes. But willingness to help? That's their tough luck. That's their problem.' " [48] Even when the interdependence of city and suburb is perceived, it rarely leads to suburban recognition of the need for sharing of burdens. A member of the St. Louis County Council articulates a common suburban perspective: "St. Louis has become just another neighborhood in the whole community. They're the poor cousin and we're the rich cousin and they have to accept that." [49]

Suburbs are separated politically from each other as well as from the central city. In most metropolitan areas, suburbia is subdivided into a number of local jurisdictions, which vary in size, age, tax resources, major land uses, and, most important, the socio-economic composition of the population. Differentiation among suburbs results primarily from superimposing the small scale of the typical suburban jurisdiction on the spatial specialization of land uses and population in metropolitan areas. Differences among suburbs commonly are reinforced by the policies of local governments. Land-use controls which permit only the construction of single-family houses on large lots, or severely restrict the size and location of multiple-unit dwellings, or prohibit mobile homes affect the socio-economic composition and community character of suburban jurisdictions. So does local unwillingness to participate in subsidized housing programs, or zoning for major commercial or industrial developments.

Because neither affluent residents nor industry and commerce are equally distributed among suburban jurisdictions, wide variations exist in the tax resources available to individual units. These disparities in taxable wealth produce considerable differences in suburban tax rates and local governmental services. It is not uncommon for affluent residential suburbs, such as Weston and Dover in the Boston area, to have five times as much taxable property per capita as the poorest suburbs. Wealthy Great Neck in suburban Nassau County in the New York area can afford to spend almost three times as much per pupil as the school district which encompasses the modest homes of Levittown. In the suburbs of the Cleveland area, North Royalton can muster only half as much revenue for each of its students as Bratenahl. Inkster, a black working-class suburb in the Detroit area with almost no commercial or industrial development, has one of the highest school property-tax rates in Michigan, yet could raise only $171 per pupil in 1969. Nearby Dearborn, with a predominantly white, middle-class population and a large industrial base, had a tax rate two-thirds that of Inksters, but raised five times as much per pupil. Even greater disparities exist between industrial enclaves and low-income bedroom suburbs. In Los Angeles County, Vernon had almost $13,000 in local revenue available for each of its 228 residents in 1965, compared with the less than $35 Baldwin Park could muster for each of its 45,000 inhabitants.

Differences in local resources, tax rates, and service levels increase the attractions of political independence and exclusionary policies in the suburbs. Jurisdictions which are well off seek to isolate themselves from the rest of the metropolis. A local official in a wealthy suburb in Southern California explains his constituents' parochialism in the following terms: "Newport Beach people don't want to identify with anything else. They came here because they don't like any other places. They like Newport Beach the way it is and they don't want it changed." [50] Unwanted change can come from other suburbs as well as the central city, especially as the suburban population and economy diversify, so the walls of suburban exclusion in affluent jurisdictions are directed at outsiders from both city and suburbs. At the other end of the suburban spectrum, poor suburbs employ land-use controls to protect themselves from more lower-income residents.

As a result, lower-income and minority groups tend to be concentrated in the older and poorer suburban jurisdictions. These aging suburbs usually are adjacent to the central city, and, in the larger metropolitan areas, increasingly distant from the suburban periphery where more and more of the nation's economic growth occurs. By contrast, the expanding outer portions of the metropolis are populated primarily by middle- and upper-income families. Thus, within suburbia as in the metropolis as a whole, political fragmentation and suburban exclusion reinforce and institutionalize the spatial separation of groups along economic and social lines, and lengthen the distance between economic opportunities and the location of lower-income and black households.

The Significance of Suburban Exclusion

Income differences and housing costs, as well as racial, ethnic, and other social considerations, would produce spatial differentiation in the American metropolis even if local governmental policies had a negligible effect on where people live. This is certainly the case in other societies where local governments play a minor role in regulating land use and housing. In these societies, however, spatial separation along social and economic lines is far less pervasive than in the United States. While communities are differentiated from each other, lower-income families tend to be spread throughout the metropolis, including the developing areas on the rim. As Anthony Downs notes:

> Where there are no constraints on the quality of new housing, new-growth areas around the urban periphery . . . [add] accommodations for all income groups. The poorest households build their own new housing—usually shacks—on land they have expropriated. Wealthy and middle-income groups build much higher quality housing on land they have bought. Wealthier households deliberately exclude the poorest people from their neighborhoods. . . . But either there are no area-wide prohibitions against the creation of new low-quality housing, or such prohibitions are largely ignored by local authorities.[51]

In addition, substantial amounts of subsidized housing have been constructed on the outskirts of many metropolitan areas outside the United States, further increasing the housing opportunities in the growing sectors of the metropolis for families with modest incomes. As a result, Downs points out, "both wealthy and poor live in the new growth areas, and no such drastic spatial separation of the rich and poor occurs as in the U.S. (although they usually occupy different suburban neighborhoods)."[52]

By contrast, local governments in the United States mandate high standards for housing construction almost everywhere in the developing portions of the metropolis. Zoning regulations, building codes, and other local policies prevent construction of inexpensive housing, increase the cost of the houses which are built, and otherwise severely restrict access to the metropolitan rim by lower-income families. Local governments in most of the newer areas also have been able to limit the construction of subsidized housing within their boundaries. As a result, the exclusionary policies of local governments, particularly in the newer suburbs, produce far more spatial separation than would be the case if only economic and social factors influenced the distribution of people in the spreading metropolis.

By greatly increasing the barriers to the outward movement of lower-income groups, the exclusionary policies of suburban governments have

played a major role in the growing separation of the poor and blacks
from jobs in the decentralizing economy of the metropolis. Especially in
the larger metropolitan areas, the dispersal of jobs to the suburbs combines with restrictions which limit the supply of inexpensive housing to
break the historical connection between urban growth and economic opportunity for the disadvantaged. Before the exodus of employment from
the central city, housing available to the urban poor was close to the bulk
of industrial and service jobs, and the unskilled worker usually could
reach his job relatively quickly and cheaply by walking or riding on
public transportation. In the decentralized metropolis, jobs increasingly
are located far from the residences of the poor. More and more employment is situated in areas which lack moderately priced housing. Public
transportation between the central city and these dispersed suburban job
locations often is nonexistent. As a result, suburban job seekers and commuters from inner-city residences to employment in the suburbs must
depend heavily on the private automobile. Many of the suburban jobs
available to the lower-income groups denied access to housing in the
suburbs, however, do not pay enough to make the long and expensive
trip from inner city to suburb worthwhile. And the travel burdens for
those isolated from economic opportunity are bound to grow in an era of
rising fuel costs.

Blacks tend to be more adversely affected by these developments
than whites. They are more concentrated than other groups in the older
neighborhoods of the central city which are farthest from expanding job
opportunities in the suburbs. Labor-market studies indicate that "the farther one moves from the concentrated minority population, the smaller
the percentage of minority workers in each occupation." [53] Illustrative of
the obstacles faced by blacks in securing employment in the developing
suburbs of larger metropolitan areas is the situation of a resident of
Chicago's Cabrini public housing project who finds a factory or service
job in suburban Weston, thirty-three miles away. In 1971, he would
have had to travel 80 minutes each by subway and commuter railroad at
a monthly cost of $59, and then face a substantial walk from the train
station to the typical job located along a highway. If he were one of the
less than 20 percent of blacks in Chicago who owned an automobile, its
use would have cut one-way travel time to an hour, while tripling
monthly costs to $174.[54]

For many working-class whites, the key to economic opportunity in
the decentralizing metropolis has been their ability to move near jobs in

industrial suburbs. Residence in suburbia has also made suburban factory, retail, and service jobs accessible to spouses and other working members of the white families who live in these blue-collar and lower-middle-class communities. Such opportunities have been far less available to blacks. Many more whites than blacks with modest incomes were able to move outward to inexpensive new housing before rapidly rising housing costs and the spread of restrictive suburban land-use and housing policies began to limit severely the availability of moderately priced dwellings in suburbia. Once in the suburbs, working-class whites have strenuously resisted the movement of blacks into their communities, which usually contain most of the suburban housing within the means of black families. In the aging suburb of Clifton in northeast New Jersey, over 99 percent of 82,000 inhabitants were white in 1970, despite the availability of substantial amounts of inexpensive housing and the proximity of Paterson, an industrial city with a large minority population. Blacks constituted 30 percent of the work force of the industries located in Warren in the Detroit area, but the blue-collar suburb had only 132 black residents in a population of 175,000 in 1970.

As suburbia grows and diversifies, the impact of suburban exclusion widens. The increasing heterogeneity of suburbia means that more and more suburbanites as well as city dwellers are affected by local policies which limit access to the growth of the metropolis. For example, local prohibitions on apartments are more important at a time when half or more of all new suburban housing units are apartments than was the case two decades ago when the overwhelming majority of suburban residential construction was single-family dwellings. Further increasing the significance of local land-use and housing restrictions has been the rapid rise in the price of land, construction materials, labor, and mortgages. These higher costs combine with restrictive suburban policies to narrow the housing options of millions of suburbanites, particularly in the developing sectors of the metropolis which offer newer housing, more spacious surroundings, and easy access to expanding employment opportunities. Many lifelong suburban residents, particularly among the young and the old, are being squeezed out of their communities by rising prices and the unwillingness of their neighbors to permit the construction of inexpensive housing. Teachers and other local civil servants cannot afford to live in many of the jurisdictions they serve. Blue-collar and service jobs in many suburbs become increasingly difficult to fill because of the lack of moderately-priced housing in the vicinity of the new employment centers on the metropolitan rim. Local governmental limitations on the supply of moderate-cost dwellings also reduce the housing prospects of those moving from smaller cities, towns, and rural areas to the metropolis. Increasingly, this group bypasses the central city to take advantage of the expanding employment opportunities found in suburbia. In twenty-seven of twenty-eight of the largest metropolitan areas, more suburban newcomers during the 1960s were from outside metropolitan areas than were from the area's center city.[55]

Thus, the popular image of middle- and upper-class white suburbanites resisting the influx of poor and black city dwellers is only part of the picture of suburban exclusion. Working-class residents of the suburbs usually are the most vociferous defenders of the integrity of their neighborhoods, particularly when newcomers are black. Whites as well as blacks are the targets of the politics of exclusion in the suburbs. Moreover, suburbanites seek to exclude from their communities other residents of the suburbs, as well as limit the access of new arrivals from outside the metropolis. As a result, suburban exclusion affects the ability of a large and growing number of Americans to live and work in those parts of the spreading metropolis where the most land is available for housing and where most of the nation's economic growth is occurring.

Chapter Two

Suburban Autonomy

Suburbia is essentially a political phenomenon. Political independence is the one thing the increasingly diversified settlements beyond the city limits have in common. Local autonomy means that suburban communities seek to control their own destiny largely free from the need to adjust their interests to those of other local jurisdictions and residents of the metropolis. Since local governments in the United States bear the primary responsibility for the provision of basic public services such as education, police and fire protection, as well as the regulation of housing and land use, independence provides suburbs with considerable control over the vital parameters of community life, including the power to exclude unwanted neighbors. In the differentiated and fragmented metropolis, these powers are exercised by suburban governments which are usually responsive to the interests of their relatively homogeneous constituencies. The result, as Robert C. Wood notes, is the division of the metropolitan population into "clusters homogeneous in their skills and outlook which have achieved municipal status and erected social and political barriers against invasion." [1]

With few exceptions, political autonomy affords suburbanites a potential for exclusion which exceeds that usually available to the resident of the central city. Through zoning, building codes, and other planning powers, suburban communities to a far greater degree than city neighborhoods are able to protect the local turf from undesirable housing and residents. Independence also means that the formal consent of local government must be obtained before most state or federal housing programs for the poor can be initiated, a power rarely delegated by city hall to its neighborhoods. In addition, exclusionary policies are more easily pursued in small and relatively cohesive political systems than in large ones with diverse constituency interests. To protect itself from unwanted developments, a city neighborhood must keep an eye on a variety of agencies and possess substantial clout in complex political arenas.

By living in a smaller, more homogeneous, and less complex polity, the resident of an autonomous suburb tends to be insulated from unwanted change. Local actions are far less likely to threaten him with lower-income neighbors or other disturbing developments in a jurisdiction where both fellow citizens and public officials share his frame of reference. As a consequence, political independence reduces the chances that suburban dwellers will face the sorts of issues concerning race, status, property values, and community character that frequently confront blue-collar and middle-class neighborhoods in the central city. When suburbanites cannot avoid such challenges, they are more likely to enlist the support of a local government that is closely tuned to their interests and values than is commonly the case in the large and heterogeneous central city.

Because of these considerations, the use of local powers over land, housing, and urban development to promote local social values and protect community character are widely viewed as the most important functions of local governments in suburbia. Residents of upper- and middle-class suburbs in the Philadelphia area ranked maintenance of their community's social characteristics—defined in terms of keeping out "undesirables" and maintaining the "quality" of residents—as a more important objective for local government than either the provision of public services or maintenance of low tax rates. In suburbs of lower social rank, maintenance of social characteristics was considered more important than

Table 2.1. Attitudes of Residents of 16 Suburbs in the Philadelphia Area Toward the Importance of Various Objectives of Local Government

Attitude	Social Rank Grouping of Municipalities (percent judging objective very important)		
	Upper	Middle	Lower
Keep undesirables out	62.0	79.5	75.0
Maintain "quality" of residents	69.0	47.0	43.0
Maintain improved public services	44.8	41.2	35.7
Provide aesthetic amenities	50.0	38.2	32.1
Acquire business and industry	8.6	23.5	50.0
Keep tax rate down	56.9	79.5	82.0

Source: Oliver P. Williams, et al., Suburban Differences and Metropolitan Policies: A Philadelphia Story (Philadelphia: Univ. of Pa. Press, 1965), pp. 217–19.

the provision of local services and amenities, and almost as important as keeping down local tax rates.[2]

Exclusionary considerations, of course, are neither the sole nor the most important factor underlying the exodus to the suburbs. Most urban Americans have moved outward in search of better housing, nicer surroundings, social status, and separation from the inner city and its inhabitants. Increasingly, however, political separation has come to be an essential element of the appeal of the suburbs. In the words of a local leader in a blue-collar suburb in the Detroit area, "the most important thing to many people in Warren is just the simple fact that it isn't Detroit." [3] Speaking of the blacks who flocked to East Cleveland during the 1960s, the suburb's black city manager notes that "they feel that at least they are not living in the inner city." [4] Regardless of their reasons for moving outward, most suburbanites quickly discover the utility of local autonomy as a means of protecting their neighborhood, their social standing, their property values, and the racial integrity of the local schools from outside threats. As Daniel J. Elazar notes: "People sought *suburbanization* for essentially private purposes, revolving around better living conditions. The same people sought *suburbs* with independent local governments of their own for essentially public ones, namely the ability to maintain these conditions by joining with like-minded neighbors to preserve those life styles which they sought in suburbanization." [5] In the process, local autonomy and exclusion have become closely intertwined. Political independence greatly strengthens the suburban community's ability to exclude, while the desire to exclude both enhances the attractions of local autonomy and reinforces the suburban commitment to the preservation of local control over the vital parameters of community life.

The Scope of Local Autonomy

In its simplest form, suburban autonomy involves a ring of unincorporated communities lying beyond the city limits, with local governmental services provided by town or county governments. The largest of these "doughnut" types of metropolitan political systems is found in the Baltimore area. Baltimore County, whose 610 square miles and 616,000 inhabitants surround the city of Baltimore and its 895,000 residents, has no incorporated municipalities or elected local officials except for a county executive and a seven-member council.[6] While approximately half of all suburbanites in the United States live in unincorporated areas, arrangements typically are more complex than those in Baltimore County. Rarely does the entire suburban portion of a metropolitan area consist of unincorporated territory. Instead, municipalities are usually scattered amidst the unincorporated neighborhoods. Public services for unincorporated areas tend to be provided by a melange of authorities, school districts, county governments, and state agencies. Regulatory and planning activities affecting land use and housing normally are the responsibility of county governments in unincorporated areas.

Greater control over land, housing, and other key local functions is exercised by suburban communities which have incorporated as municipalities under state law. Municipal governments have more extensive authority than local governments in unincorporated areas to tax, to borrow, to provide services, and to regulate urban development. Another attraction of incorporation is the protection it provides a suburb against absorption into other local jurisdictions. In most states, incorporation guarantees the political independence of a community, since territory in a municipality cannot be annexed by another local government. On the other hand, incorporation usually means more extensive and expensive local services. As a result, many suburbanites prefer unincorporated status, particularly when essential public services are available from other public agencies and when state law protects unincorporated areas from the territorial ambitions of adjacent municipalities.

Incorporation also provides suburbanites with a local government more responsive to community desires than is the case with unincorporated areas. Responsiveness results primarily from size and spatial differentiation. Most suburban municipalities are quite small. In 1967, two-thirds of all incorporated local jurisdictions in metropolitan areas had fewer than 5,000 inhabitants. And half of all suburban municipalities encompassed less than a square mile of land area.[7] Superimposing these small governmental units on the spatially differentiated population of the metropolis commonly results in relatively homogeneous local constituencies. Within these jurisdictions, local government tends to be highly responsive to the wishes of residents, particularly on sensitive issues such as housing and community development. By contrast, constituencies are larger and more diverse in most unincorporated areas in suburbia. In these larger local units, governments generally are less concerned about particular neighborhoods than is the typical small-scale incorporated suburban government.

The desire to secure local control over land use, housing, and urban development has been a common motivation for the incorporation of suburban municipalities. Local land owners, builders, and developers have employed incorporation to secure control over planning and zoning in order to advance or protect their economic interests. On the other hand, residents, particularly in newly suburbanizing areas, have frequently sought to incorporate their communities in order to transfer planning responsibilities and land-use controls from the hands of county and township officials to those of local residents, elected to office by their neighbors. Often with good reason, these larger units of suburban local government are considered to be too sympathetic to development interests and insufficiently concerned with the interests of individual communities. As the leader of a homeowner's group seeking to incorporate a suburban neighborhood in the Chicago area explains: "Our main goal in trying to incorporate is to protect our residents from improper zoning. Present restrictions by the county, which . . . controls zoning within our boundaries, is rather loose." [8]

Another common but usually unvoiced concern which has stimulated incorporation efforts is the desire to exclude blacks and subsidized housing. In the San Francisco area, John H. Denton believes "that one of the principal purposes (if not the entire purpose) of suburban incorporations is to give their populations control of the racial composition of their communities." [9] Municipal status substantially enhances the capability of a suburban community to exclude subsidized housing, and the blacks who might live in such units. Incorporation permits local officials to decide whether the community will participate in subsidized housing programs. It also provides local residents with control over zoning and other powers which can prevent the construction of subsidized housing.

An illustration of the creation of a suburban municipality to foreclose the construction of subsidized housing is provided by the incorporation of Black Jack, a community of 2,900 in the St. Louis area. [10] Late in 1969, a nonprofit group organized by church organizations in the St. Louis area took an option on a twelve-acre site in an unincorporated section of St. Louis County known as Black Jack. The land in question was part of 67 acres which had been zoned by the county government for multiple-family dwellings; and over 300 apartments already had been constructed by private developers on fifteen of the acres. The church group planned to construct 210 apartments for rental to families earning between $5,700 and $10,200 under the federal government's Section 236 program for moderate-income housing. The site was chosen by the church groups because they "wanted to determine the feasibility of providing subsidized housing for people—black and white—just beginning to climb above the poverty line but still too poor to move to the suburbs." [11]

For residents of the area, almost all of whom were white, middle-income, and living in single-family homes costing between $25,000 and $45,000, the notion of subsidized and integrated housing for lower-income families in their community was not at all feasible. Their reaction was vehement and their actions swift. With local neighborhood associations leading the opposition, circulars were distributed, mass meetings held, and public officials contacted. In addition, a delegation was dispatched to Washington to present petitions to top officials of the Department of Housing and Urban Development. In opposing the project, residents emphasized the lack of public services, overcrowded local schools, poor transportation links with the rest of the metropolis, and the absence of jobs in Black Jack's portion of St. Louis County. Concern also was expressed over the impact on property values and community character if lower-income families, and particularly poor blacks, were to live in Black Jack.

Dissatisfaction with county housing and land-use policies in the Black Jack area had stirred thoughts of incorporation before the subsidized housing project materialized. With the announcement of the project, local residents moved quickly to seek incorporation in order to deny the development of the site for apartments. Two weeks after the federal government agreed to finance the project, over 1,400 residents of the area petitioned the St. Louis County Council for incorporation of 2.65 square miles encompassing the proposed housing. At the request of the county council, the incorporation proposal was evaluated by the county planning department, which opposed the creation of a new municipality "on fiscal, planning, and legal grounds." [12] Far more influential with the county council, however, was the strong local support for incorporation. Black Jack's advocates successfully linked opposition to incorporation with support for subsidized housing. Suburbanites throughout the northern portion of the county were warned by the Black Jack Improvement Association that approval of the project "could open the door to similar projects being located almost anywhere in the North County area. By stopping this project, you would lessen the chance of one perhaps appearing in your neighborhood." [13] Obviously, the way to stop the project was to permit incorporation. Framing the issue in these terms, as one observer notes, rendered the council members "powerless. The housing issue which precipitated the incorporation was too politically sensitive to allow the council to turn down the petition, and thus indirectly sanction" the construction of subsidized housing.[14]

The result was approval by the county council of the creation of the city of Black Jack, the first new municipality in St. Louis County in over a decade. With incorporation, control over land use within Black Jack was transferred from the county to the new municipality. Less than three months after incorporation, Black Jack's City Council enacted a zoning ordinance which prohibited the construction of apartments within the municipality, thus blocking the proposed subsidized housing.[15]

While the powers available to independent local governments provide suburban communities such as Black Jack with the capability to exclude, local autonomy is relative rather than absolute. Local control over land use, housing, and related matters, like all local powers in the United States, is derived from state governments. Autonomy of suburban governments is limited by municipal charters which are granted by the state and by delegation of responsibilities to other units of local government, such as townships and counties by the state constitution or legislature. The states oversee a wide range of local activities and provide local governments with substantial financial assistance, particularly for public education. They also construct most of the major roads and regulate sewer development, a pair of activities which greatly influence the accessibility of land for development. State actions may constrain suburban autonomy, as in the establishment of public agencies empowered to supersede local land-use controls, such as New Jersey's Hackensack Meadowlands Development Commission or New York's Urban Development Corporation.[16] On the other hand, the state may expand the powers of residents of independent suburbs, as have those states which require that public housing proposals be approved by local voters in a referendum.

Local autonomy in the suburbs also is affected by activities of metropolitan and federal agencies, as well as by intervention from the courts. A wide variety of metropolitan agencies exercise responsibility for areawide planning, major public works, and other activities which affect housing and development patterns within local jurisdictions in the metropolis. The federal government supports housing, highway, water, sewer, planning, and other programs which influence the ability of suburban governments to shape the nature and timing of development within their boundaries. The federal government also has substantial powers to prevent local governments from discriminating against minorities in the development, sale, and rental of housing. In addition, all local authority is subject to review in state courts, and the exercise of many local powers raise issues which fall within the jurisdiction of federal courts.

In the policy areas of greatest importance for exclusion, however, local autonomy tends to be particularly broad. As Richard F. Babcock notes: "Local control over use of private land has withstood with incredible resilience the centripetal political forces of the last generation." [17] State governments typically have delegated virtually all responsibility for planning, zoning, building codes, and related activities to local governments. Few states even maintain an administrative machinery to oversee local land-use and housing controls. Only in response to environmental problems and pressures have states begun to develop plans and regulatory mechanisms which seek to guide or supercede the land-use activities of local governments. Almost all of these state efforts, however, are limited to areas of critical ecological concern, such as coastal zones and floodplains. [18]

Most states also have done little to enlarge the scale of land-use control in suburbia. County governments usually are limited to regulating unincorporated areas, with few states providing counties with a significant land-use role within suburban municipalities. When states provide for county agencies or regional bodies to review local zoning actions, the review power typically, as Coke and Gargan note, "is advisory only; the reviewing agency has no authority unilaterally to overrun the zoning action." [19] Nor have states necessarily permitted metropolitan governments, in the few areas where they have been created, to exercise land-use controls throughout their jurisdiction. In Miami, as the National Commission on Urban Problems pointed out, "the metropolitan government has zoning authority only in unincorporated territory. In Nashville-Davidson County, several small suburban municipalities continued in existence after the creation of the metropolitan government and retained their zoning powers." [20] The state law creating Unigov in the Indianapolis area also permitted suburban municipalities to continue to control land use.

Local autonomy over housing and land use is bolstered further by the absence of a direct federal role in zoning and other development controls. Moreover, local rather than federal officials determine the location of housing units supported by national subsidy programs.[21] A final factor enhancing the ability of suburban governments to use their autonomy to foster exclusion has been the reluctance of most courts to impose significant constraints on the exercise of local land-use powers.[22]

As a result of these developments, suburban governments have been able to use their autonomy to influence housing opportunities with relatively little outside interference. And because land-use patterns strongly affect local taxes and public services, community character, and the quality of local schools, zoning has become the essence of local autonomy for most suburbanites.

Using Local Autonomy

Local autonomy, of course, does not guarantee success to suburbanites in their efforts to control development. Great variations exist in the use of local controls. A few suburbs permit almost any kind of development, others seek to exclude practically everything. Most, however, pursue more selective policies which result from the concerns and values of local residents, fiscal realities, environmental constraints, and the pressures for growth and change which constantly test the effectiveness of local controls. Some suburbs are highly skilled in their use of the means available to influence settlement patterns, employing sophisticated planning techniques and acting in a timely fashion to shape the forces of change. Others are far less skillful, and their tardy and piecemeal efforts tend to be overwhelmed by private developers.

Size is a major barrier to the acquisition of planning and zoning expertise in many suburbs. In his analysis of suburban land development in three northeastern metropolitan areas, Marion Clawson emphasizes that:

> Most of these local governments are . . . too small in most instances to engage any full-time employees for any of these functions. Those which do hire usually pay low wages. Only the largest of the local governments have top-ranking jobs that pay enough to attract and hold well-trained professional or technical people. Staffing levels in planning and land-use-related activities are low in relation to numbers of persons engaged in the construction activities affected by their work.[23]

Many suburbs, however, have overcome the handicaps posed by small size and limited resources. Mounting suburban concern over the implications of unregulated development during the 1960s increased local willingness to invest in the acquisition of sophisticated planning capabilities. The financial burdens imposed by these activities were eased by assistance from federal and state planning programs. And the shortage of skilled local employees was offset by the availability of advice from private planning consultants.

Acquisition of planning skills, however, cannot insure that local efforts will strongly influence development. Accessibility, topography, land values, and other physical and market factors play a major role in shaping settlement patterns in suburbs. So do the decisions of metropolitan, state, and federal agencies concerning roads, water supply, sewers, and other major public facilities. Control over land use, the primary power available to local government, is essentially negative. Zoning, subdivision regulations, building codes, and other planning devices may prevent undesirable development, but by themselves cannot induce desired change. Zoning vacant land in a working-class suburb for two-acre estates may foreclose the construction of more tract houses on small lots. In the absence of excellent schools, attractive surroundings, and separation from lower-status neighbors, however, such local action is unlikely to result in construction of expensive housing for an upper-income clientele. Similarly, creation of a commercial or industrial district within a suburb will not attract developers unless the site is desirable in terms of the availability of an adequate tract of land at a competitive price, its proximity to highways and other transportation facilities, and its accessibility to markets, suppliers, and labor force.

The ability of suburban governments to shape urban development is frequently undermined by the very factors which afford growing suburbs an opportunity to influence settlement patterns. Having vacant land and being in the path of development in the decentralizing metropolis often means that growth overwhelms the capacity of small and amateur local governments to cope with the complexities of suburbanization. For some fiscally hard-pressed suburban jurisdictions, the perceived tax benefits of growth outweigh the advantages of effective controls, at least during the crucial initial phases of the development process. Local planning controls often fail to check the private sector because of the dominant influence in newly developing areas of large land owners, real-estate operators, bankers, and related interests. Local officials frequently are closely tied to those who are profiting from suburbanization. In Santa Clara County in California, as in many rapidly developing areas, local "officials and the greedy land speculators and developers . . . were never really opposing interests. With few exceptions the local officials were also involved in real estate speculation, had other vested interests in the rapid development of the valley, or . . . simply were unable to make a strong stand against the powerful development interests and their allies in local government." [24]

Outright corruption also subverts suburban plans and zoning regulations. The high financial stakes of land development combines with the importance of local land-use controls to produce offers which some suburban officials cannot resist. Illustrative is the experience of Hoffman Estates, a suburb in the Chicago area where three officials were convicted of bribery, conspiracy, and tax evasion in 1973 after taking bribes from Kaufman & Broad Homes, one of the nation's largest homebuilding firms. As Ed McCahill has pointed out, the rewards in this instance were high for both local officials and the developer:

> For about $90,000 in bribes, Kaufman & Broad nearly were able to plop an entire town of 25,000 residents right in the middle of a community which had no hospital or industry to speak of, an inadequate transportation system, and schools filled to capacity. The rezoning proposal allowed 33 housing units per acre when Hoffman Estates had no zoning specifications other than "residential." The $90,000 in bribes paid during the 1960s, when the village had only recently been incorporated and was unaccustomed to planning for subdivisions. One of the incidents that tipped off Hoffman Estates homeowners that something was amiss was when their showers went dry in 1970, as 2,500 new neighbors started tapping into the inadequate water system. [25]

As more and more people move to suburbs residential interests are less likely to be compromised by local governments in contests involving developers. With growth constantly augmenting the ranks of those who seek to use local autonomy to preserve and protect their local community from unwanted change, residents have become increasingly active participants in the politics of suburban development. Doubts, often well founded, concerning the ability or desire of local officials to withstand the pressures and other blandishments of developers has stimulated a great deal of political activity at the grass roots. Neighborhood organizations have been created or politicized to bring pressure to bear on local governments, and to fight adverse land-use actions in the courts. [26] An official of a neighborhood civic organization opposed to more apartment construction in East Brunswick, New Jersey, explains the evolution of his group's political activities as follows: "We were a loose social organization that met for July 4 neighborhood picnics before this zoning dilemma blew up. That action pulled us into legal action, with each of the families contributing money to legally fight the variance before the Zoning Board." [27] To check the discretionary power of local officials, suburbanites in some jurisdictions have sought direct public participation in land-use questions. Voters in Eastlake, a suburb in the Cleveland area, approved an amendment to the local charter in 1971 which required approval of all rezoning actions by 55 percent of those voting in a public referendum. Residential interests supporting the provision "wanted to get the power back to the people" by making it necessary for "a developer to convince the voters he's bringing something good into the city." [28]

Local officials who fail to respond to these residential pressures increasingly face retribution at the polls. In many suburbs, a new generation of office holders is emerging dedicated to using local autonomy to protect residential interests rather than to facilitate developers and land owners. As Fred P. Bosselman notes:

> The most important manifestation of the new mood is the changing character of suburban political leaders. Traditionally suburban governments have been dominated by the local businessmen, especially real estate brokers, many of whom owned substantial tracts of vacant land. They naturally saw growth as good for business—as long as it didn't attract "undesirables," of course.
>   This is changing. . . . [In] many parts of the country in the past few years . . . voters have ousted the incumbents and replaced them with a new type of local official. They are housewives, junior executives, engineers, mechanics, truck drivers—in short, typical suburban homeowners who's only contact with the community is to live in it, not to make money off it. This might be characterized . . . as "suburbia for the suburbanites." [29]

As a consequence of these developments, more and more public officials in suburbia reflect the values of the relatively homogeneous constituencies which elect them or hire them. Zoning and planning boards increasingly are composed of members sympathetic to the interests of local residents. In Greenwich, Connecticut, as in thousands of suburbs, "no one can get elected unless he swears on the Bible, under the tree at midnight, and with a blood oath to uphold zoning." [30] Suburban city managers, planning directors, and the consultants who provide much of the technical and planning advice in many suburbs commonly adjust their attitudes, proposals, and actions to the limited horizons of the suburban jurisdiction which hires them. As a former suburban mayor emphasizes, "the officials they elect understand that their responsibility is to keep the community the way the people here want it." [31]

Of course, the growing influence of residents in suburban politics does not mean that local controls over housing and land use always are employed to advance residential interests. Residents are not cohesive on every development issue, especially in the larger and more heterogeneous suburban jurisdiction. Moreover, landowners and developers retain considerable influence, particularly in areas in the path of suburbanization where residents often are outnumbered by those who seek to profit from development. Nor does local autonomy protect residents of suburbs from losing battles with state highway departments and other outside agencies which are able to alter the pattern of suburban development without the consent of the affected localities.

Despite these limitations, local autonomy constitutes an effective shield against social change in many suburban jurisdictions. As residential influence mounts, autonomy offers most suburbanites local governmental institutions responsive to their interests. Equally important, political independence provides the legal means to pursue these objectives through the exercise of local planning, land-use, and housing controls. In the typical community, the purposes of local autonomy tend to be defined by the widespread suburban preoccupation with home and school, class and status concerns, racial separation, and the desire to be insulated from the problems of the inner city. Internal consensus on the uses of local autonomy, particularly in smaller and relatively homogeneous suburban jurisdictions, is likely to be high when property values, educational quality, community character, or the influx of blacks or lower-income residents are at issue. The result, in the words of one suburban political leader, is "the politics of the territorial imperative . . . [which] means opposing new housing and new people, anything that might change the status quo." [32]

Maximizing Internal Benefits

Local autonomy combines with limited size, a fairly homogeneous population, and the mobilization of residential interests to provide most suburbanites with a highly parochial perspective on the metropolis. The community tends to be perceived solely in terms of the interests of its current residents, who claim "a right to decide how their town develops." [33] Residents of the suburbs and their local governments rarely take the interests of nonresidents into account. Nor do they consider housing, land use, and other issues in an areawide perspective. Within this narrow frame of reference, the overriding purpose of government in suburbia becomes the protection and promotion of local interests. In defense of "the fact that the poor and middle income people cannot afford to move into Mount Laurel" because of local land use controls, a suburban attorney contends that "the Mount Laurel fathers are trying to do their best for the people of Mount Laurel." [34] Doing their best for constituents usually means that local officials ignore broader issues. For example, when deciding whether to permit the construction of apartment units, suburbanites rarely consider metropolitan housing needs or the growing demand of a diversifying suburban population for multiple-family dwellings. Instead, local debate centers on the costs and benefits of apartments to the community and its residents, and construction commonly is permitted only when the local jurisdiction is convinced that the development will make a net contribution to local revenues. "We must be selective as possible—approving only those applications which are sound in all respects" argues a local committeeman in Mount Laurel. "We can approve only those development plans which will provide direct and substantial benefits to our taxpayers." [35]

Suburban indifference to broader needs, including those created by their own land-use policies, is illustrated by the frequent refusal of jurisdictions which have been successful in attracting industry and commerce to permit the construction of housing within the means of local workers. The presence of the Grumman Corporation with 30,000 workers and the arrival of forty-five new industries during the late 1960s produced no changes in zoning and housing policies in Oyster Bay. This Long Island suburb prohibited apartments except by special exception, required one- and two-acre lots for single-family homes, and had less than 350 units of subsidized housing, most of which had been reserved for the elderly. In New Jersey, Mahwah steadfastly refused to alter its zoning codes to permit the United Automobile Workers Housing Corporation to build subsidized housing within the price range of workers at a Ford Motor Company plant which employed 5,200 in Mahwah. The presence of the automobile factory and other industries gives Mahwah a substantially lower tax rate than neighboring suburbs. Yet the town has been no more willing to open its doors to Ford workers—40 percent of whom are black—than are adjacent suburbs with less industry and higher tax rates. In Mahwah, as in nearby Franklin Lakes, which welcomed a large IBM installation but not garden apartments, the local beneficiaries of nonresidential development see no obligation to provide housing for workers: "There is lots of empty land and cheap housing further out—there's no reason why people should feel that they have to live in Franklin Lakes just because they work here." [36] A member of the planning commission in Oak Brook, an affluent suburb of 4,000 in the Chicago area which attracted $350 million in offices, hotels, research facilities, and shopping centers without providing any low-cost housing, insists that "we are sympathetic to the achievers and the underprivileged," but adds: "We have provided for the achievers, however." [37]

Cooperation among neighboring suburbs to secure adequate housing for the local work force also is rare. In 1970, the zoning ordinances of twenty suburbs in central New Jersey set aside sufficient land for industrial and research purposes to support 1.17 million jobs, but would allow residential development to house only 144,000 families, for an imbalance between new jobs and residences of eight to one. [38] Less than one in five mayors surveyed in a New Jersey study indicated that their communities were willing to cooperate with neighboring jurisdictions on zoning. Even fewer suburbs actually consulted adjacent muncipalities in setting land-use policies, leading the study to conclude that "cooperation is almost non-existent" in planning and zoning matters in New Jersey. [39]

Exclusion is a natural concomitant to suburban insularity. Since the community's resources are perceived as belonging to its residents, outsiders cannot share in these resources without local consent. Suburbs commonly employ the local police power to exclude nonresidents from parks, beaches, and other public recreational facilities. In suburban Westchester and Nassau Counties in New York, local governments ban nonresidents from parking lots adjacent to commuter railroad stations, or set parking fees for nonresidents many times higher than those for residents. These policies are justified on the grounds that community facilities belong to local taxpayers, that restrictions are essential to insure enjoyment of public facilities by local residents, and that the locality must be able to protect itself from the crowds, traffic, and other burdens that large numbers of nonresident swimmers, picnickers, or parkers would impose on the limited capabilities of the typical suburb. As a suburban official on Long Island explains, "our town has grown so large there is barely enough beach room for our own people." [40] The same rationale is commonly applied to other facilities by suburbanites. River Hills, an affluent suburb in the Milwaukee area, sought to block the construction of a church, arguing that no need existed because only three members of the congregation were residents of the community. "We are not trying to keep outsiders out," explained the suburb's planning commissioner, "but it is not feasible to have people come in here with things which [serve] no residents from the village." [41] In northern New Jersey, Saddle River sought to block construction of a college because the community was "not the type of town for any large school." According to the suburb's mayor: "This is a residential community, there are no public transportation facilities, and we have no sewage disposal system. We haven't even got a full-time police department and 90 per cent of our roads are private." [42]

Local considerations are of paramount importance in the case of housing and land-use policies which determine who "our own people" are in a particular suburb. Exclusion of those who threaten to change a community's character, lower the status of its residents, jeopardize local property values, or burden public services is widely perceived by suburbanites as an inherent aspect of local autonomy. As Anthony Downs notes, "defenders of residential exclusion argue that any group of citizens ought to be able to establish a physical enclave where certain standards of environmental quality and behavior are required for all residents. The resulting exclusion of those too poor to meet the standards is considered essential to protect the rights of those who established the standards." [43] The more homogeneous a suburb, the more easily it can seek to maximize internal benefits through exclusionary housing policies. And the more successful these policies, the less likely becomes the presence of dissenting voices within the local constituency.

Efforts to maximize internal benefits often go beyond using local autonomy to exclude outsiders. Suburban jurisdictions also have sought, with considerable success, to get rid of residents deemed undesirable by the local community. Zoning changes, code enforcement, urban renewal, road building, and other governmental actions have eliminated substandard and lower-income housing in many communities. Rarely is adequate housing provided for the displaced. The urban renewal plans of thirteen suburbs in Westchester County in the New York region called for the demolition of over 4200 housing units in 1967, most of which were occupied by lower-income and minority families, and their replacement by less than 700 subsidized units.[44] Displacement without replacement, as in one New Jersey suburb, often reflects the widespread local desire "to clear out substandard housing . . . and thereby get better citizens."[45] Facilitating these efforts in most suburban jurisdictions is the meager political influence of lower-income residents, who usually are outnumbered and almost always lack political resources in contrast with their more affluent neighbors.[46]

Black suburbanites are the most common targets of suburban efforts to displace "undesirables." A study conducted for the U.S. Commission on Civil Rights concluded that "development control activities in Baltimore County over the past ten years have functioned to substantially reduce housing opportunities in the county for low-income, predominantly (but not exclusively) black households."[47] One black residential area was eliminated by rezoning for commercial purposes, another was destroyed by zoning the area for industrial uses. In the St. Louis area, federal urban-renewal funds were used by suburban Olivette to redevelop a black neighborhood for industrial purposes. In the process, all but six of the thirty black families in the community of 10,000 were forced to move away.[48]

Reinforcing suburbia's exclusionary tendencies is the dependence of most local governments on tax sources located within their boundaries. Defending his community's ban on nonresident commuter parking, a suburban mayor in the New York area contends that "there is no way I can morally justify spending the tax revenue of my little village on nonresidents."[49] Speaking of restrictions on the use of Nassau County's recreational facilities, County Executive Ralph G. Caso emphasizes that "it is our residents who pay for them and maintain them through taxes."[50]

Local property taxes, and their relationship to public-school costs and land-use patterns, have an especially important influence on suburban policies affecting housing and urban development. Over 80 percent of all local revenues in the suburbs are derived from property taxes, while 60 percent or more of all public expenditures are for education. Yields from the property tax depend primarily on the extent and value of development within a jurisdiction. School costs are directly related to the density of residential settlement. The logic of these relationships leads suburbs to judge development increasingly in fiscal terms. Speaking of Westchester County, New York's Regional Plan Association notes that in "municipality after municipality, planning to achieve a satisfying local

environment has been replaced by planning to meet the school tax
bills." [51]

From the perspective of the individual suburb, desirable development
generates a profit for the local government and its residents, hopefully at
not too high a cost to other things valued by the community, while undesirable development creates a net deficit of tax revenues to local costs.
As a result of tax considerations, suburbs both compete for desirable development and are attracted to exclusionary policies designed to foreclose
undesirable development. In the words of the U.S. Advisory Commission on Intergovernmental Relations, "the name of the game is cutthroat
intergovernmental competition, and the object of the game is to 'zone in'
urban resources and to 'zone out' urban problems." [52]

The desire to "zone in" tax resources and "zone out" problems for fiscal reasons influences land-use and housing policies to some degree in
most suburban jurisdictions. Few suburbs, and particularly bedroom
communities whose tax base is wholly or largely residential, can afford
to ignore the fact that most residential development costs local government more than it contributes in taxes. As indicated in Table 2.2, a typi-

Table 2.2. Residential School Cost-Revenue Comparisons for Single-Family
Homes, Barrington, Illinois—1968

Number of Bedrooms	Total Students	Total School Costs *	Total School Taxes	Net Tax Benefit or Deficit
Three	.50	$ 400	$ 962	$+562
Four	2.02	1,616	1,218	−398
Five	2.28	1,824	1,334	−490
Six	2.60	2,080	1,396	−684
All Units	2.10	$1,680	$1,254	$−426

* Based upon $800 per student.
Source: Darwin G. Stuart and Robert B. Teska, "Who Pays for What: A Cost Revenue
Analysis of Suburban Land Use Alternatives," Urban Land 30 (Mar., 1971), p. 5.

cal four-bedroom house in a Chicago suburb generated approximately
$1,200 in school taxes in 1968, but the costs of educating the two school-
age children likely to live in the house exceeded $1,600. With more
school-age children in the family, or in the case of a cheaper house which
would generate less tax revenues, the local deficit would be even greater.
In general, the gap between local costs and revenues is greater for subsidized housing occupied by families with children. Such housing typically involves higher residential densities than is the case with conven-

tional single-family housing, as well as lower per capita property tax receipts and greater demands on local public services. Local taxes on subsidized housing financed by the New Jersey Housing Finance Agency, for example, cover 20 percent or less of the public service costs imposed on local governments and school districts by the residents of the projects.

In New Jersey, where local property taxes provide a particularly large share of all local revenues, a state planner believes that most local land-use controls are "designed for the . . . purpose of trying to avoid the costs implied in residential growth and its effect on public school growth." [53] Even in New Jersey, however, relatively few suburbs base their housing and land-use policies solely on tax calculations. Instead, concern over the implications of housing development for local taxes tends to reinforce, and to be reinforced by, exclusionary behavior rooted in community, property-value, class, and racial considerations. Equally important, the workings of the property tax provide suburbanites with a respectable rationale to justify the exclusion of lower-income groups, subsidized housing, and blacks, regardless of the actual mix of motives which underlie a particular local policy.

The same fiscal considerations which lead suburban governments to exclude lower-income families and higher-density residential development induce them to seek commercial and industrial tax ratables as a means of easing the burdens of financing local services. Some affluent suburbs prefer to remain exclusively residential, although their ranks have been thinned in recent years with rapid rises in the costs of local services. Others can afford to be selective, accepting only research or office activities in campus-like settings. Many suburban jurisdictions, however, are sufficiently hardpressed financially that they are willing to take any nonresidential tax ratable they can get, even at considerable cost to local amenities and community character.

Suburbs frequently attempt to reduce the impact of these developments on local residents by restricting large-scale commercial and industrial facilities to areas that are separated from residential neighborhoods within the community by highways or natural features. In the process, costs often are displaced to adjacent communities, which receive no tax benefits from the development. A study by the League of Women Voters in Bergen County, New Jersey, indicated that one "community proposed to zone for heavy industry in an area adjacent to one of the most expensive residential areas of a neighboring town." In another instance, access roads "to a new plant were placed so that the traffic moved along roads in an adjacent community." [54] The principle of beggar-thy-neighbor embodied in the common suburban conception of local autonomy and maximization of internal benefits was succinctly expressed by the former mayor of Wayne in northern New Jersey in explaining the impact of Willowbrook shopping center on residents of his community. "Willowbrook doesn't bother anyone here because it's way on the south border, next to Little Falls Township. It bothers them; they get all the traffic and harassment. We get all the taxes." [55]

Residents of both rich and poor suburbs frequently rue the necessity for local efforts to bolster the tax base with nonresidential development. "Our town is slipping away from us," complains a resident of affluent Greenwich, where 150 companies located during the 1960s. [56] The spread of such feelings, along with the rising influence of residential interests in suburban politics, has increased resistance to the location of commercial and industrial facilities in suburbs across the nation. For example, Greenwich's Planning and Zoning Commission responded to widespread local opposition late in 1973 by rejecting the application of Xerox for a zoning change needed to construct a $20 million corporate headquarters on a 104-acre site in an area reserved for single-family homes. Reinforcing these concerns over community character and status is the fear that offices and factories will lead to requirements that housing be provided locally for employees and other lower-income families. As an official in New Canaan, another Connecticut suburb, explains, "we would welcome RCA's contribution to the tax base, but not if we have to take the caboose of low income housing as well." [57]

Businessmen too seek to maximize internal advantages in the suburbs. From the perspective of many, the most attractive suburban location is within a jurisdiction with as few residents as possible. As a result, people have been zoned out of a number of municipalities in order to create a favorable tax situation for commerce and industry. With fewer than a dozen residents, Teterboro in northern New Jersey offers its fifty industries an extremely low tax rate, with almost all local revenues devoted to public services needed by industry. Similar considerations led to the incorporation of Emeryville, Vernon, Union City, Industry and Commerce, all in southern California. In 1960, Vernon had fewer than 300 residents, but over 70,000 worked in industries located there, insuring highly attractive tax rates. [58] Low rates give these enclaves substantial competitive advantages over other suburbs and the central city in the quest for desirable tax ratables. Moreover, by separating the taxable wealth of commercial and industrial development from the needs of employees and the metropolitan community more generally, these single-purpose suburbs intensify disparities among local governments in the politically fragmented metropolis, and thus enhance competition and exclusion.

Environmental considerations also reinforce the suburban desire to maximize internal benefits through exclusionary local policies. Rapid and usually unplanned growth has exacted a heavy environmental price in many suburban areas. In the scramble for private profit and desirable tax ratables, environmental costs commonly have been ignored by developers and local officials. As a result, suburban growth has left in its wake bulldozed hills, treeless and tasteless subdivisions and apartment complexes, garish highway strip development, acres and acres of parking lots, overtaxed sewerage and water systems, polluted and silted streams, and a general lack of the open space that was the original attraction of suburbia to so many of its inhabitants. Political fragmentation has exacerbated these problems. In most metropolitan areas, the mosaic of small and independent suburban jurisdictions has foreclosed comprehensive planning, areawide controls on development, and regional instrumentalities empowered to regulate and conserve land, water, and other natural resources. The ability of developmental interests to dominate many of the local governments in newer areas has negated the role of local land-use controls in guiding growth and protecting the environment along the metropolitan rim. Further contributing to haphazard and shortsighted development is competition for attractive tax ratables among suburban governments heavily dependent on local property taxes.

With the movement of ecological concerns to the forefront of the American political consciousness in the late 1960s, most suburbanites responded in typically parochial fashion. Relatively few recognized the role of the decentralized suburban political system in fostering the erosion of environmental amenities in their communities and surrouding areas. Instead, residents of the suburbs commonly emphasized the need to employ local autonomy to preserve and protect their local turf. To maintain the quality of life for residents of the particular suburban community, the powers of local governments over land use and housing have been widely employed to prevent outsiders from sharing the local environment with those who already live there. As in the case of the local property tax, ecological concerns tend to be mixed with other exclusionary motivations as the typical suburb seeks to maximize internal benefits. For example, the desire to exclude "unprofitable" residential development bolsters the case for "no growth" policies and other environmental controls on housing. And, as Ernest Erber of the National Committee Against Discrimination in Housing emphasizes: " 'No Growth's' pervasive spread provides an insidious rationale . . . to perpetuate racial and economic segregation. It serves to remove the stigma of local, selfish motivations from exclusionary acts and cloaks them with broad national purposes." [59]

The Changing Suburbs

Growing suburban concern with environmental issues is one manifestation of the physical, economic, social, and political changes which constantly increase the scale and complexity of life in the suburbs, and in the process alter the nature and autonomy of local governments in suburbia. With growth and diversification of the suburban population and economy have come expanding pressures on local governments to provide services, deal with a widening range of problems, and resolve conflicts which multiply in suburban jurisdictions with increasingly diverse constituencies. In response, the tasks, budgets, and staffs of local governments have steadily expanded. Independent functional agencies have proliferated to provide water, sewerage, and a host of other local services. And perhaps most significant, "big" government, with its professional politicians and specialized bureaucracies, has become increasingly common in the land of small scale, amateur, neighborhood government. A growing proportion of the suburban population lives in larger local jurisdictions such as Oyster Bay in the New York area which had 330,000 residents in 1970, Warren in the Detroit area with 179,000, Woodbridge in New Jersey with 99,000, and Bloomington in the Twin Cities area with 82,000. County governments also have expanded significantly in many metropolitan areas, both to serve burgeoning unincorporated areas and to provide a variety of services for the residents of suburban municipalities located within county boundaries. As a result of these changes, a declining proportion of suburbanites live in the prototypical small and homogeneous local jurisdiction.

Despite this general increase in the scale of local government in the suburbs, political fragmentation and spatial differentiation mean that few suburban jurisdictions reflect the increasing heterogeneity of suburbia. Even the larger suburban units tend to encompass considerably less diverse socio-economic development than the central cities of most metropolitan areas. And the smaller local units, which continue to be the most common type of suburban government, typically retain both their relatively homogeneous constituency and their extremely narrow perspective on issues such as housing and land use.

With respect to local governmental efforts to influence settlement patterns, growth and heterogeneity have produced changes in the tone and style of suburban politics rather than its basic exclusionary aims. Increasing scale and diversity have made many suburban units less responsive to particular neighborhood interests. Consensus on particular development policies is also more difficult to reach in larger suburban jurisdictions which encompass a variety of interests on such issues as construction of apartment houses, large-scale industrial or commercial development, or local participation in subsidized housing programs.

At the same time, apartment houses, shopping centers, industrial and research parks, office clusters, sports complexes, and other harbingers of change in the suburbs reinforce the desire of suburbanites to maintain local autonomy and to use the powers of local government to control the local turf. Growth and change in the suburbs also bolster the fears of the inner city, of lower-income and minority groups, of crime and drugs, of housing projects and integrated schools. As a result, in suburbs of every size and type, the common response to diversification and heterogeneity are efforts to protect and preserve the local community, its residents, and their environment from external threats. Increasingly, suburban officials are confronted by aroused constituents who want their local government to find a means of shielding them from change. In DeKalb County outside Atlanta, as in suburbs across the nation, activists "raise hell twenty-four hours a day." In the words of a suburban state legislator: "It's enough to drive a normal person insane." [60]

Chapter Three

Zoning for Fewer People

Land is the most valuable resource in the suburbs. Its control by local government is the key to suburban exclusion. Suburbs attempt to influence land use through a variety of means. Roads, sewers, water lines, schools, and other public facilities and services can be utilized to foster or preclude various types of residential, commercial, and industrial development. Tax policies may be manipulated to attract business, or to stimulate the construction of particular kinds of housing. In addition, federal and state funds can be sought or eschewed for sewerage systems, urban redevelopment, or housing for lower-income families. Direct land-use controls, however, are the principal instruments available to suburban governments seeking to shape development and control population within their boundaries.

Of the various land-use controls, the most important is zoning, which involves the specification of land uses for designated areas within a local jurisdiction. In 1968, zoning powers were exercised by nearly all suburban municipalities with more than 5,000 residents, and by more than half of the smaller ones. Most of the local governments using zoning ordinances employ subdivision regulations, which govern the provision of utilities and other improvements, dedication of land for public purposes, architectural design, siting of houses, landscaping, and other aspects of residential development not covered by zoning ordinances.[1] Most suburbs also enforce building codes which specify minimum construction standards for methods and materials.

Zoning and building codes are inherently exclusionary. Their aim is to exclude land uses deemed inappropriate by a local jurisdiction. Regardless of the intent of local restrictions, they inevitably limit housing opportunities. As Lawrence G. Sager has emphasized: "Almost all zon-

Table 3.1. Proportion of Municipalities in Metropolitan Areas Employing
Land-Use Controls–1968

Size	Number of Municipalities	Percent of Municipalities with:		
		Zoning Ordinances	Subdivision Regulations	Building Codes
50,000 or more	314	98.7	92.7	98.7
5,000 to 49,000	1,303	97.0	90.0	91.8
Under 5,000	3,360	54.0	47.7	57.4
Total	5,007	63.0	45.0	60.9

Source: U.S. National Commission on Urban Problems, *Building the American City*, Report to the Congress and President of the United States, 91st Cong., 1st sess., House Doc. No. 91-34 (Washington: U.S. Government Printing Office, 1968), p. 209.

ing restrictions are 'exclusionary' in the sense that they raise the price of residential access to the area which is regulated." [2] While a suburban official in Connecticut contends that the purpose of local zoning "was to preserve the rural character of this small town, to prevent the leveling of the countryside, to keep intact our open fields, winding roads, brooks, and old stone walls," she admits that "these restrictions have had the economic effect of making residency in New Canaan difficult for all low-to-moderate income groups." [3]

Zoning is based on the police power. As such, its specific aim is to protect public health and safety. More generally, zoning is supposed to promote the general welfare and foster rational patterns of development. In language similar to that found in most state enabling legislation, Massachusetts provides that:

> Zoning regulations and restrictions shall be designed among other purposes to lessen congestion in the streets; to conserve health; to secure safety from fire, panic, and other dangers; to provide adequate light and air; to prevent overcrowding of land; to avoid undue concentration of population; to facilitate the adequate provision of transportation, water, sewerage, schools, parks, and other public requirements; to conserve the value of land and buildings; to encourage the most appropriate use of land throughout the city or town; and to provide and increase its amenities. [4]

Since most states provide little guidance to their local subdivisions in the area of land-use control, these general objectives tend to be interpreted in the light of local interests. In the typical suburb, the power to zone becomes a mandate to exclude land uses which threaten community character, property values, or the fiscal well-being of the locality.

The common result is suburban zoning which far exceeds the standards required to protect public health and safety. As Anthony Downs has pointed out:

> No household "must have" a one-acre lot for healthful living, since millions of healthy Americans live on far smaller lots. In fact, there is no known, well-documented minimum lot size per household for healthful living. Thus, nearly all suburban minimum lot size requirements lack any relation whatever to health or safety needs. The same thing is true of minimum set-back and building placement requirements.
>
> Prevailing structure type and minimum size requirements are also unsupported by any real data related to health needs. In fact, they are contradicted by a great deal of evidence. For example, most residential zoning regulations prohibit mobile homes. Yet there is absolutely no evidence that it is more healthful to live in a conventionally built home than in a mobile home.[5]

Most suburbanites, however, consider mobile homes undesirable, as they do apartments. And they attempt, with considerable success, to enforce these values by means of local land-use controls. "In effect," as a study of suburban housing policies in New Jersey emphasizes, "local officialdom acts as a gatekeeper: picking and choosing among the various alternatives offered [by housing developers] on the basis of such criteria as interest them." [6]

Table 3.2. Acceptability of Various Housing Types to
Suburban Leaders in New Jersey

Housing Type	Considered Desirable	Considered Undesirable
	(percent of total sample)	
Single family, large lot	79	20
Single family, small lot	49	48
Garden apartment	46	52
High-rise apartment	27	70
Mobile home	9	91

Source: State of New Jersey, County and Municipal Government Study Commission, *Housing & Suburbs: Fiscal & Social Impact of Multifamily Development*, Ninth Report, Oct., 1974 (Trenton, 1974), p. 78.

Restrictions on Apartments

Of the various zoning controls employed by suburbs which directly affect population distribution, the most effective is prohibition of multiple dwellings. Large numbers of suburbs ban apartments completely. In the

New York metropolitan area, where exclusionary zoning is particularly widespread, over 99 percent of all undeveloped land zoned for residential uses is restricted to single-family housing. For example, in suburban Bergen County in northern New Jersey, only 131 acres of developable land was zoned for apartments in 1970, compared with more than 27,000 acres for single-family homes.[7] When apartments are permitted, their location, size, and other features are constrained by local governments in a variety of ways. Almost all zoning ordinances consider apartments an inferior and therefore more restricted land use than single-family residences. This distinction was accepted in the first zoning case to reach the U.S. Supreme Court. In upholding the constitutionality of the zoning ordinance enacted by the Village of Euclid, a suburb of Cleveland, the Court agreed that

> the development of detached house sections is greatly retarded by the coming of apartment houses, which has sometimes resulted in destroying the entire section for private house purposes; that in such sections very often the apartment house is a mere parasite, constructed in order to take advantage of the open spaces and attractive surroundings created by the residential character of the district.[8]

Prohibitions on apartments result from a variety of considerations. Preserving the "suburban" character of a community is commonly perceived by its residents as mandating the maintenance of the single-family status quo. Daniel R. Mandelker concludes that "much of the zoning attention to apartment development . . . has been motivated by a desire to exclude apartment development from those suburban and single family residential preserves in which the apartment is considered a violation of the environment." [9] Apartments are seen by many suburbanites as harbingers of undesirable population changes which will increase the number of transient residents with no interest in the local community. A suburban critic of apartments in northern New Jersey "came from a community of apartments, where people don't have the vital interests as taxpayers of [owners of] homes." [10] With apartments, suburbanites believe, will come traffic problems, intensified demands on local schools and public services, increased taxes, and other unwanted changes.

At the heart of suburban opposition to apartments is fear of the city. As one study emphasizes:

> The apartment in general, and the high-rise apartment in particular, are seen as harbingers of urbanization, and their visibly higher densities appear

to undermine the rationale for the development of the suburbs, which includes a reaction against the city and everything for which it stands. This is particularly significant, since the association is strong in suburbia between the visual characteristics of the city and what are perceived to be its social characteristics.[11]

"I moved out here . . . to escape the city," explains an opponent of apartments in Huntington on Long Island, "I don't want the city following me here."[12] In a similar vein, a former New York City official argues against a zoning change that would permit multifamily housing to be built in Westport, a Connecticut suburb of 30,000, because apartments "would simply turn Westport into a city—the beginning of the urbanization of our town. Those of us who moved here to try and shape a well-rounded community object to this."[13]

For many suburbanites, apartments mean higher residential densities which are automatically equated with slums and the kinds of people who live in slums. "Multifamily dwellings are not considered as housing for people" by suburban foes of apartments in the St. Louis area, "but as some kind of blight."[14] "We don't want this kind of trash in our neighborhood," shouts an opponent of luxury apartments in Suffolk County on Long Island, pointing to newspaper stories of crime and welfare in New York City.[15] "With this notion of potential slum character," notes the Rockland County (N.Y.) Planning Board, "there often goes the fear that the apartments will be occupied by members of a minority group."[16] Reinforcing these concerns is the possibility that the construction of apartments in a suburban community will open the door to subsidized housing. By zoning all vacant land for single-family housing, as was done in Black Jack after incorporation, most types of subsidized housing are automatically eliminated from a suburb.

Fear of apartments has carried over to cluster and planned-unit developments which seek to minimize construction, site, and utility costs through the clustering of dwellings and the preservation of open space for community use. Even if these innovations result in no higher residential densities than traditional subdivisions, they look like apartments to many suburbanites and thus raise the same hackles. In many instances, developers have confused the issue by attempting to mask plans for conventional garden apartments by calling them cluster or planned-unit developments, townhouses, or some other euphemism designed to assuage the suburban fear of apartments.

Opposition to multiple-family dwellings also has been fueled by the experience of some suburbs which have permitted the construction of townhouses, garden units, and other kinds of apartments. The prevalence of badly designed units, shoddy construction, and poor maintenance has contributed to the negative suburban image of apartments. So has inadequate or nonexistent local planning with respect to the impact of apartments on schools, police and fire protection, sewerage, and other local services. Parking problems, traffic congestion, and safety problems have been common results of haphazard siting of apartment units. In some instances, unrestrained apartment construction has overwhelmed suburban governments with rapid growth, spiraling service costs, and rising tax bills. Widespread opposition to more apartments commonly results, leading to the adoption of local moratoriums on multiple-unit dwellings and enactment of other restrictive measures. As one study notes a "classic case" of such "boom-bust cycles in local development" is provided by "the Northern New Jersey community of Parsippany–Troy Hills, in which nearly 5,000 units of garden apartments, poorly planned and often poorly constructed, were built between 1962 and 1967. Since that time, a near total ban on apartments has been enforced in that community." [17] "Horror" stories concerning the adverse effects of apartments in jurisdictions such as Parsippany–Troy Hills, in turn, spur opposition elsewhere in the suburbs.

At the same time that local opposition grows, the diversification of the suburban economy increases the demand for apartments. Growing numbers of unmarried and divorced suburbanites, more couples without

Table 3.3. Single and Multiple Family Housing in Metropolitan Areas, 1960–1970

	1960 (000)	1970 (000)	Total Increase (000)	Percent Increase
Cities				
Single family	11,002	11,471	469	4.3
Multiple family	9,335	10,919	1,584	17.0
Suburbs				
Single family	15,180	17,793	2,613	17.2
Multiple family	2,674	5,244	2,570	96.1
Metropolitan Areas				
Single family	26,182	29,264	3,082	11.8
Multiple family	12,009	16,163	4,154	34.6

Source: U.S. Department of Commerce, Bureau of the Census, *Census of Population and Housing: 1970; General Demographic Trends for Metropolitan Areas, 1960 to 1970,* Final Report PHC(2)-1, United States (Washington: U.S. Government Printing Office, 1971), p. 82.

children, and the trend toward smaller families underlie the shift to apartments. Rapid rises in the costs of single-family housing also have made apartment construction increasingly important in suburban areas across the nation.[18] Four out of every seven dwelling units added to the metropolitan housing stock during the 1960s were apartments; and over 60 percent of these multiple-family units were built in the suburbs. During the decade, almost as many apartment units were constructed as single-family units in the suburbs, resulting in 1970 in a ratio of one apartment for every 3.4 single-family homes, compared to a ratio of one to 5.7 in 1960.

As the demand for apartments grows in the suburbs, more and more communities are subject to pressures from developers and landowners for the construction of multi-family dwellings. The increase in the number of localities involved multiplies the number of suburbanites concerned with the threat posed by apartments. As a result, in the words of a Long Island apartment developer:

> Public opposition is unbelievable. There's a desperate need for this kind of housing, but people just go crazy when you talk about building in their town. Four out of five projects I've started have been stopped—people scream that they'll increase traffic, put more kids in the schools, change the neighborhood. They're afraid of any kind of change out here.[19]

Local officials often have been caught in the middle in such struggles. Most are sensitive to constituency concerns about the adverse impact of apartments on the local community, concerns that are easily translated into intense political pressures aimed at supporters of multi-family developments. At the same time, suburban officials are more likely than their constituents to perceive the financial attractions of apartments. With limitations on the number of bedrooms, apartments generate more local tax revenues than expenditures. "We're concerned primarily with [tax] ratables," explains an official in a New Jersey suburb, "and apartments are the best source." [20] Residents, particularly of the neighborhood involved, rarely share the same perspective. "The politicians think in terms of tax dollars, but we think in terms of a better life," explains a spokesman for a homeowners' group in a Westchester suburb.[21] In the wake of these cross pressures comes growing conflict in suburbia, with officials who favor apartments increasingly challenged at the polls or in court by local opponents.

Successful efforts to restrict apartments take a number of forms. The most absolute, effective, and widespread curb is the lack of a provision in the local zoning code for apartments. Prohibitions of limited duration (or moratoriums, as they are commonly called) also have become increasingly popular, particularly in communities inundated by apartments or faced with strong pressures for the construction of multiple-family units. Such pauses permit the local government to determine the impact of existing apartments on public services and their cost, to assess the implications of future construction, and to develop appropriate policies. Until these determinations are made, building permits for apartments are not issued, regardless of the provisions of the local zoning ordinance. Communities which have sanctioned apartments in the past can prevent future construction by limiting multiple-family housing to a fixed percentage of the total dwelling units in the local jurisdiction. Once the quota is established, no further apartment development is permitted, even though vacant land may be zoned for apartments.

Another means of precluding apartment development is to prescribe regulations which increase costs sufficiently to make construction economically impractical. Garden apartments may be limited to commercial areas where land costs make their construction uneconomical. As a suburban official explains, "one way to kill apartments is to mandate that they go in impossible places. A commercial acre is going for about $300,000, and how can any middle-income apartments be built on land that expensive?" [22] Land zoned for apartments also may be unsuitable for development of multiple-family housing. In 1968, only 29 of 513 acres zoned for apartments by Concord in the Boston area were in parcels sufficiently large to make actual construction financially feasible. [23] Restrictions may be imposed which prevent the development of apartments priced for anything but upper-income tenants. Regulations dealing with the maximum acreage which may be covered by buildings, minimum room size, parking and internal circulation facilities, and the provision of public utilities all tend to increase costs, thus reducing the likelihood that families with modest incomes will be able to live in the community.

Many suburban jurisdictions which permit apartments restrict access on the basis of family size and age, as well as on the basis of income. For most suburbanites, the only persuasive argument for allowing apartments is their potential profitability to the local jurisdiction and its residents. A number of studies have shown that apartments can make a net contribution to the local exchequer if they cater to a clientele which makes few demands on the local school system.[24] To insure that school costs do not escalate, children can be explicitly banned from apartments. Local policies also may permit only those multiple-unit developments which are restricted to retired couples without children, or to singles. For apartment developments where children are not directly restricted, the key to minimizing school costs is limitations on the number of bedrooms. In a study which inspired a number of restrictive zoning ordinances in New Jersey, George Sternlieb demonstrated that "three-bedroom units, perhaps excepting very costly ones, will create far more education costs than tax revenues," with two-bedroom apartments roughly breaking even, and one bedroom and efficiency units resulting in a surplus of school taxes over educational outlays.[25]

Table 3.4. Restrictions on Apartments in Middlesex County, New Jersey

Nature of Restriction	Number of Municipalities
Apartments Excluded	7
90% one-bedroom, 10% two-bedrooms	2
85% one-bedroom, 15% two-bedrooms	1
80% one-bedroom, 20% two-bedrooms	6
80% one-bedroom, 15% two-bedrooms, 5% two-plus bedrooms	1
75% one-bedroom, 25% two-bedrooms	1
75% one-bedroom, 20% two-bedrooms, 5% two-plus bedrooms	1
70% one-bedroom, 30% two-bedrooms	1
50% one-bedroom, 30% two-bedrooms, 20% two-plus bedrooms	1
No restrictions	4

Source: Marshall R. Burack, "Apartment Zoning in Suburbia" (Senior Thesis, Princeton University, 1971), p. 84.

On the basis of these calculations, many suburbanites have been persuaded to accept apartment developments which are planned to be unsuitable for families with school-age children. For example, over half of the municipalities which permitted apartments in Middlesex County, a middle-income suburban area in New Jersey, required in 1970 that more than 80 percent of the units have one bedroom. Some jurisdictions further restricted the number of people who were permitted to live in an apartment. In Woodbridge and East Brunswick, no more than three people could live in a one-bedroom apartment, and at most four in a two-bedroom unit. Only four of Middlesex's twenty-five local jurisdictions imposed no significant restrictions on apartments.

Apartments built in accordance with bedroom restrictions have proved to be extremely profitable tax ratables. During the 1970 school year, Madison, a Middlesex County suburb which limited two-bedroom units to 20 percent of the total, collected 13.5 percent of its school taxes from apartment buildings, while only 5.8 percent of its school population lived in multiple dwellings. As a result of this favorable balance, apartments contributed $326 per unit in school taxes, but generated school costs of only $135 per unit. By contrast, single-family homes in Madison paid an average of $675 in school taxes, $280 less than the educational outlay necessitated by the typical single-family dwelling.[26] For New Jersey as a whole, a 1974 study concluded that apartments constructed with bedroom limitations "are almost assured of generating fiscal benefits for the communities in which they are built. Only when one finds certain combinations of relatively low rent, and relatively high bedroom counts, does a development begin to move into the deficit category."[27]

Limitations on Single-Family Homes

Access to the vast suburban realm reserved for single-family homes is limited by local governments in a variety of ways. Across the nation, suburban zoning ordinances have steadily reduced the amount of land available for single-family development and increased the minimum size of lots and houses. Subdivision regulations and building codes have further added to the costs of new single-family housing through a lengthening list of site requirements and construction restrictions imposed on home builders.

Large-lot zoning is probably the most popular means of limiting inexpensive single-family residential development in the suburbs. Almost 80 percent of a sample of suburbanites in Delaware County in the Philadelphia area in 1961 favored "using zoning laws to keep out of your community the type of people who usually build cheaper houses on smaller lots."[28] As James G. Coke and Charles S. Liebman have pointed out: "By the simple device of large lot zoning, suburbanites believe that a municipality can achieve its developmental goals in a single stroke. The community will be beautiful, its taxes will be low, and 'undesirables' will be kept out."[29]

Suburbanites typically rest the case for large-lot zoning heavily on economic considerations. In the words of a defender of four-acre zoning in wealthy Greenwich, Connecticut, in the greater New York area, his community's zoning policies have "nothing to do with racial or religious factors. It's just economics. It's like going into Tiffany and demanding a ring for $12.50. Tiffany doesn't have rings for $12.50. Well, Greenwich is like Tiffany." [30] Large-lot zoning is defended by a New Jersey legislator as a means of making sure "that you can't buy a Cadillac at Chevrolet prices." [31] An official of St. Louis County, where 90,000 acres were zoned for three-acre lots in 1965, indicates that his suburban county welcomes anyone "who has the economic capacity [to enjoy] the quality of life that we think our county represents . . . be they black or white." [32]

Large lots are defended on a variety of economic grounds. They are seen as reducing local educational outlays, since lower residential densities mean fewer school children, requiring fewer streets, and generating less demand for police and fire protection. In addition, low-density development permits many suburbs to forego sewers, water supply, sidewalks, street lights, and other public infrastructure investments. Suburbanites also commonly view large lots as an essential means of protecting property values by insuring that new residential development will not undermine the market for existing single-family housing. Economic considerations are closely linked with social concerns in the minds of most suburban residents. "In a development of low-priced, cheap homes," contends a local leader in a suburb in the New York area, "one gets a certain type of people who are not capable of organizing and just don't know how to manage the community. With more expensive homes, you get a more intelligent group, more capable, and taking greater pride in the area." [33]

Large lots are closely associated in many suburban minds with space and privacy. A study of zoning in Connecticut concluded that "a primary reason for higher minimum lot-size requirements is to fulfill the individual home owner's desire for space and privacy, which he finds in the open and uncongested character of low-density residential development." [34] Suburbanites also defend large lots on aesthetic and environmental grounds. They are seen as necessary for the preservation of open space and natural beauty, as well as dictated by topographic and soil conditions. Encompassing all of these rationales is the desire to maintain community character through the preservation of low-density settlement patterns. "We are going to make sure that the type of township we have now will be preserved in the future," explains a suburban mayor in New Jersey in defense of rezoning three large tracts from one-half-acre to two-acre minimum residential plots. [35]

The attractions of large-lot zoning led to a doubling of the average lot size in the major suburban counties of the New York area during the 1950s. Because of more restrictive zoning, the residential capacity of Westchester County in New York dropped from 3.2 million in the early 1950s to 1.8 million in the late 1960s. Between 1960 and 1967, over 150 municipalities in New Jersey increased minimum lot sizes, while none reduced their requirements. As a result of these changes in suburban zoning policies, the supply of lots of a quarter acre or smaller—which is the size used by most single-family homes built before 1960—steadily declined. In the sixteen counties which encompass most of New Jersey's suburbanizing area, less than five percent of the vacant residential land was zoned for lots of 10,000 square feet—which is approximately a quarter acre—or smaller in 1966. On the other hand, more than half of the land zoned for residential development in the same counties required minimum lots of more than one acre; and three of the major suburban counties, and two more in the path of suburbanization, had zoned two-thirds or more of their available residential land for one or more acres.[36] A similar situation prevailed in Connecticut's suburbs, where more than half of all land zoned for residential uses had minimum lot requirements of one to two acres. While restrictions on lot size tend to be most extensive in the Northeast, these practices are important in other metropolitan areas. In the Cleveland area, for example, suburban governments in Cuyahoga County zoned 67 percent of their available residential land for half acre or larger lots during the 1960s, while in Geauga County 85 percent of all the residentially zoned land was reserved for lots of one acre or larger.[37]

Generally, minimum building-size regulations have a more direct impact on the cost of single-family housing than requirements for large lots, a circumstance which explains their growing popularity in the suburbs. Over 75 percent of the land in northeast New Jersey in 1966 was zoned for dwellings with a mimimum floor space of 1200 square feet, which was one-third more space than the minimum required by the federal government for a single-family dwelling to be eligible for federal mortgage insurance. Individual suburbs employ even larger minimum space standards in their efforts to exclude less affluent residents. Bloomington, in the Minneapolis–St. Paul area, mandated 1,700 square feet in 1968. Frontage requirements offer another means of discouraging moderately-priced residential development, as well as a device to preserve the semi-rural setting desired by so many residents of the suburbs. Minimum lot widths of 150 feet were required in 1966 for 82 percent of the land in Somerset County in New Jersey, while 87 percent of the residential land was similarly zoned in Monmouth County, another rapidly suburbanizing area in New Jersey.

Construction of moderately-priced single-family housing is also checked by building code prohibitions on various materials and techniques, and by requirements that more expensive ones be used. Restrictions are common against the use of plastic in place of copper in plumbing systems, less expensive foundation and framing materials, and the installation of prefabricated electrical and plumbing components. Another constraint is imposed by architectural controls which preclude standardization, mass production, and low-cost single-family housing designs of the type employed in large-scale developments such as the early Levittowns. Subdivision regulations increase costs further by requiring that the home builder provide streets, sewer facilities, schools, parks, and other public facilities whose cost is borne by the purchaser of a new home rather than by all of the taxpayers in the community.

Reinforcing the impact of these techniques for limiting the construction of single-family housing and increasing its cost is the common use of a variety of restrictions by a single suburb. A local government is likely to zone land for large lots with substantial frontage, on which a good-sized house must be built with expensive materials. The house cannot resemble other dwellings on the block; and the developer is required to provide streets, sewers, and perhaps even school buildings. Costs are further increased by variations among local governments which preclude standardization within a metropolitan area. In the case of building codes, for example:

> Variations within a single region add time-consuming and expensive "customizing" costs to an area builder's overhead. In one new house, straddling a city-county line, a builder had to install one brand of wiring for the city half of the house and a second type for the county side of the house. Then, no less than eight inspectors were necessary to approve the house for sale.[38]

Excluding Prefabricated Housing

Suburban land-use, building, and design controls also effectively bar factory-built housing and mobile homes from the developing portions of most metropolitan areas. Spurred in large part by the rapid rise in the cost of conventional housing, a variety of mass-production methods has been developed which substitute factory assembly for on-site construction, thus reducing labor costs. Over 54,000 units of modular housing were produced in 1972, at a somewhat lower average cost than conventional housing. Factory-built housing, however, cannot be assembled economically unless there is considerable standardization of local requirements at the various sites where the units will be erected.[39] While suburban codes rarely prohibit modular construction and other forms of prefabrication, the specifications of local codes and their variations from suburb to suburb pose insuperable obstacles to the use of industrialized housing in many areas. In Los Angeles County, for example, 34 of 77 municipalities employ building codes which are inconsistent with those of other local jurisdictions in the county.[40] Factory-built housing also usually faces the same kind of local opposition which commonly is aroused by apartments and other housing perceived by suburbanites as attractive to lower-income and minority families.

An even more universal and usually direct, target of suburban land-use controls is mobile homes. Eight million Americans lived in mobile homes in 1973. Almost 576,000 mobile homes were produced in 1972. The most popular units sold for around $8,000, or about 40 percent of the cost of the least expensive single-family house. Incomes of mobile-home owners tend to be low, with the typical resident a blue-collar worker who earned less than $7,000 a year in 1970.[41] The very attractions of mobile homes to lower-income families makes them anathema to more established communities in metropolitan areas. Only nine of 101 suburbs in the Boston area permitted mobile homes in 1972.[42] Of the 1.34 million acres of land available for residential development in sixteen New Jersey counties in 1966, only 1700 acres, or less than one-tenth of one percent was zoned for mobile homes. All local governments in eleven of the counties banned mobile homes entirely.[43] As a result of these restrictions, 54 percent of all mobile homes were located outside metropolitan areas in 1970, although only 32 percent of all housing units were so situated.

When mobile homes can be located in the suburbs, they are usually permitted only in unattractive commercial and industrial zones, or restricted by local regulations similar to those imposed on apartment developers. One of the few mobile-home parks authorized within the New York region in recent memory was limited to residents without children, with relatively expensive mobile homes with large lots, underground utility lines, off-street parking, and other features designed to exclude lower-income families. "One of the reasons we were allowed in here," the developer emphasized, was "that we agreed to certain conditions imposed by the municipality." [44]

"The exclusion of mobile homes," the National Commission on Urban Problems notes, "in large part reflects a stereotyping of their appearance and of their occupants. Many see mobile homes as unattractive and occupied by people who do not take care of their homes or neighborhood." [45] The fact that many mobile homes are poorly built reinforces these stereotypes. So does the kind of locations forced on mobile home owners by local regulations. As one planner points out: "It's a circular problem. Mobile homes are relegated to the fringe areas and the poorest land. They often don't have adequate sewage and water services. This has all resulted in poor planning and bad developments because of unnecessary restrictions on developers." [46] Another negative factor is the exemption of mobile homes from local property taxes in many states, which means that densely-settled trailer parks can place a heavy burden on the local treasury.

Stopping Growth

Increasingly, suburbanites have responded to the impact of rapid population growth and new development with measures designed to stop all growth in the interests of preserving community character, protecting the local environment, and reducing pressures on local public services, facilities, and finances. Interest in "no growth" and "contained growth" policies has been heightened by mushrooming public concern with the environment. In communities across the nation, increasingly vocal and influential local groups with acronyms such as PURE and SAVE insist that local government check growth and safeguard the local environment from outside threats. [47] Grass-roots support for efforts to limit growth is substantial. In suburban San Mateo County in the San Francisco area, for example, 83 percent of the respondents in a 1973 survey opposed any additional population growth. [48] Among the supporters of "no growth" are conservationists, opponents of higher local taxes, and suburbanites seeking to exclude lower-income and minority groups from their communities. As William L. Wheaton notes, "the ratio of [the] mix differs from one community to another, but it is the coalition of these three elements that provides the political clout." [49]

As growth and its consequences become increasingly important political issues at the local level, suburban politicians ignore the rising political influence of the no-growth movement at considerable peril. In the Washington area:

A candidate for chairman of the Fairfax County, Va., Board of Supervisors took out newspaper ads headlined, "I simply won't allow big developers to go on getting rich at taxpayers' expense." The ad blamed increased property taxes on too-rapid development and said, "It's about time we controlled growth in Fairfax County." She was the only Democrat to win in that county. In neighboring Arlington, Va., the independent candidate for the county board characterized his Republican opponent as a tool of the real estate developers. The independent's campaign stressed, "We must control growth before it controls us." He won.[50]

Environmental considerations have become particularly potent in local politics in California. Over 70 percent of 500-odd elected local officials, most from suburban jurisdictions, attending a 1973 meeting of the League of California Cities indicated that environmental issues were the primary factor in their success at the polls. Conservation issues and campaigns against growth also played a major role in county elections in California in the early 1970s. Environmentalists won control in 20 of the 58 counties between 1971 and 1973. And newcomers to the county electoral scene, most of whom campaigned against growth, won almost half of all the county supervisor elections. Typical of the victors was a classics professor who was elected to the Santa Barbara County Supervisors on a platform which promised "not one more house in Santa Barbara." [51]

Concern over growth has stimulated widespread interest in the use of traditional land-use controls as a means of restricting development, as well as prompting the invention of some new approaches to the old problem of exclusion. Bans or restrictions on apartments, larger lot sizes and coverage requirements for single-family housing, and more stringent and costly subdivision and building regulations have found new advocates and justifications based on environmental grounds. In suburban areas across the nation, environmental groups such as the Suffolk County Defenders of the Environment on Long Island seek the development of new zoning laws "based on the physiographic, hydrologic, geologic, meteorologic, and ecological characteristics of the Regional Ecological System." [52] Zoning land for nonresidential purposes, the establishment of protected agricultural districts to preserve open space, and the public purchase of land for parks or conservation areas in order to prevent development are increasingly used by local governments to control residential development. After a cost-benefit analysis indicated that any kind of development of Palo Alto's largely vacant foothills would involve a net deficit to the suburb in the San Francisco area, the affluent community rezoned the area from one unit per acre to one per ten acres and set aside more than $4 million to acquire land to foreclose development. Palo Alto and conservation interests also campaigned successfully for the creation of the Midpeninsula Regional Park District, which was empowered to acquire and preserve open space in the upper foothills of the Santa Cruz range.[53]

In a growing number of instances, local governments have used their land-use powers to block large-scale residential developments. Loudoun County in Virginia, which is in the path of development spreading westward from the Washington area, rejected a major proposal prepared by Levitt and Sons, the largest residential builder in the nation. The county government and local residents concluded that the burdens 13,000 new residents would place on services and amenities would outweigh the tax benefits to be derived from development. "It just seems to be the time for somebody to say 'whoa,' " explained a county official.[54]

Moratoriums of various kinds and duration have become one of the most popular means of checking growth in the suburbs. In Orange County in the northern part of the New York area, moratoriums were in force in six towns in mid-1973, had recently expired in another, and were under consideration by an eighth local government. Fairfax County in northern Virginia imposed moratoriums on apartments in 1955 and 1964, and halted all construction in 1972 and again in 1974. Moratoriums typically last from thirty days to two years, although longer construction bans have been considered by some suburbs. In 1974, Prince Georges County in the Maryland portion of the Washington area was studying a proposal which would forbid development in its eastern half for ten years. Refusal to issue building permits and denial of permission for sewer connections are the most common means of enforcing moratoriums in the suburbs. Inadequate sewerage facilities have been the major rationale for moratoriums. Typically, moratoriums are designed to permit a community to catch up with the growth process by developing or updating its plans, devising new zoning controls to regulate development, or installing sewerage and other facilities needed if further growth is to occur.

Some localities have sought to limit growth more directly. Boca Raton, an affluent community in southeast Florida which grew sixfold between 1960 and 1972, has set an absolute limit within its boundaries of

40,000 dwelling units. While an effort by environmental groups to limit to 100,000 the population of Boulder, Colorado, which grew from 20,000 in 1950 to almost 67,000 in 1970, failed at the polls in 1971, over 70 percent of those voting approved a resolution sponsored by the local administration which provided that local government "shall take all steps necessary to hold the rate of growth in the Boulder Valley to a level substantially below that experienced in the 1960s and shall insure that the growth that does take place shall provide living qualities in keeping with the policies found in the Boulder Valley Comprehensive Plan." [55] Elsewhere, public-works proposals of various kinds have been defeated because of the widespread desire by residents of the suburbs to foreclose development. Voters in suburban Marin County in the San Francisco area blocked construction of a new water-supply system because of fears that developers would be attracted. In Rockland County in the New York area, environmental groups persuaded the county legislature to delete two interceptor lines from a $30-million sewer plan in order to preclude development in a local river valley. "It sounds odd to get impassioned about sewer lines," explained one conservationist, "but sewer lines—more than zoning maps—are what dictates land use today.[56]

Measures designed to control the timing of development are another innovation inspired by the concern over growth which promises to become an important limitation on housing. In an effort to influence the staging and quality of residential development, voters in Petaluma, a rapidly expanding suburb in Sonoma County to the north of San Francisco, overwhelmingly approved in 1973 a local ordinance which restricted to 500 the number of building permits to be issued annually. Within this overall quota, limitations were established on the number of building permits for different kinds of housing, as well as for construction in various sections of the community. Allocation of permits under these quotas were based on the availability of public services, conformance of a proposed development with Petaluma's planning objectives, and the quality of the design.[57]

Other localities have sought to condition residential construction directly on the availability of local services. In 1972, voters in Livermore, a fast growing suburb in the eastern portion of the San Francisco Bay Area, approved a measure promoted by a local environmental group which provided that:

> no further residential building permits are to be issued by the . . . city until
> satisfactory solutions, as determined by the standards set forth, exist to all
> the following problems:

1. EDUCATIONAL FACILITIES—no double sessions in the schools nor overcrowded classrooms as determined by the California Educational Code.
2. SEWAGE—the sewage treatment facilities and capacities meet the standards set by the Regional Water Quality Control Board.
3. WATER SUPPLY—no rationing of water with respect to human consumption or irrigation and adequate water reserves for fire protection exist.[58]

Probably the most sophisticated attempt to control growth is the development timing technique adopted in 1969 by Ramapo, a burgeoning suburb of 82,000 in the northern portion of the New York area. Under Ramapo's approach, residential development is regulated according to the availability of local public services. Each housing proposal is evaluated in terms of the availability of sewage facilities, adequate drainage, roads, parks, and firehouses. Only developments that secure fifteen of a maximum of twenty-six "points" can be approved. To restrict the number of developments that qualify under these standards, Ramapo proposed to stage the construction of these various public facilities over an eighteen-year period. The Ramapo scheme survived a court challenge, thus providing a model for many developing suburbs eager to gear residential development to the provision of public facilities.[59] For Ramapo, the court victory vindicated "the right of a community to control its own destiny and to develop itself according to a rational plan for growth controlled by the community in the community interest, not by speculative developers."[60] Critics were far less enthusiastic, noting the prevalence of large-lot zoning in Ramapo, the lack of housing for low-income families, and the fact that the controlled-growth ordinance "substantially reduced the number of housing units being constructed in the town and increased their cost."[61]

Similar policies were adopted by the Fairfax County Board of Supervisors in 1973, six months after overloaded sewage treatment facilities had forced the suburban county to impose a moratorium on the issuance of building permits in the portion of the county encompassing most new residential construction. As in Ramapo, Fairfax's aim was to employ comprehensive planning and development controls to insure that future residential growth was closely related to the provision of public facilities. Points would be awarded to developers based on the availability of public services. For instance, a project would receive five points if public sewers were installed, but only three if septic systems were to be used. Only when twenty-two points were accumulated could development proceed. "What we're trying to do is orchestrate growth," explains a Fairfax official. "We want to balance such things as transportation, housing, schools with the quality of life." [62] The result of seeking such "balance," however, is bound to be less housing at higher cost. In the words of another Fairfax official troubled by the implications of the county's new development controls, "I can't help but think that new houses are just going to cost too much for the ordinary citizen to buy." [63]

The Spread of Exclusionary Controls

In recent years, the impact of local controls on housing opportunities has steadily increased as the use of zoning and planning techniques has become more widespread. During the early years of the postwar suburban boom, relatively few local governments were aware of the more sophisticated techniques being developed to control development. Only a handful possessed the expertise to employ planning methods aimed at restricting population growth. This was particularly the case in rural areas in the path of suburbanization. Nor were the local fiscal implications of unrestrained residential growth widely perceived; and environmental concerns were of little consequence in most jurisdictions. Instead, growth was considered to be synonymous with prosperity, especially by the rural land owners, speculators, and developers who reaped enormous benefits from suburban land development.

As a result, developers were able to secure large amounts of land for residential construction in most suburbs. After studying suburban land conversion during the 1950s and early 1960s, Marion Clawson concluded:

> Zoning, as it has operated to date, is a tool of social control over land use that is too weak to be effective in the growing suburbs.
> There are likely to be landowners, developers, and others who see gains they could make from land uses different from those planned and zoned. Those who would lose as a result of their actions are not yet resident in the area, or do not realize their probable losses, or are not adequately organized politically. [64]

Even if zoning measures restricted residential developers in some jurisdictions, the political fragmentation of the suburbs permitted them to find fertile ground in other localities. The spotty success of suburban controls on residential and other development in the New York area during the 1950's was emphasized by Robert C. Wood in his study of the political economy of the nation's largest and most complex metropolis:

> An industry barred from one locality can in all probability find a hospitable reception in another with equivalent economic advantages. High-income families take refuge in Westchester, southern Putnam, and Fairfield, while mass developers make breakthroughs in Nassau or Monmouth or Rockland to provide middle class housing.[65]

In the 1960s, however, developers began to encounter increasingly effective obstacles in both suburban jurisdictions and rural areas which lay in the path of suburbanization. A growing proportion of the residents of these areas became aware of the costs of growth and diversification, as well as of the potential of local controls to exclude unwanted development. "People," notes a suburban official in northern Virginia, "realized the cost of growth. It wasn't providing us with anything. It was costing us. The taxes keep going up and the schools and roads keep getting more crowded—things that everyone sees every day." [66] Analyses of the fiscal implications of various kinds of development are widely available, and are used in sophisticated fashion by local officials, candidates for public office, environmentalists, civic groups, and others who contest development interests along the suburban frontier. Even more influential in arousing resistance to further development is the ubiquitous evidence of the consequences of bad planning and unrestrained growth in the suburbs. Inadequate sewer systems, overcrowded schools, highway strip development, and the general loss of open space and visual amenity all build support at the grass roots for stricter controls on development.

With growing awareness and concern over development has come a steady increase in political activity by residents of both suburbs and rural areas beyond the metropolitan rim. As pointed out in chapter 2, the political mobilization of these interests has made local governments more responsive to and representative of their residential constituencies, and thus more likely to impose effective controls on developers. Facilitating these efforts is the spread of knowledge concerning land-use controls, as well as the technical expertise needed to apply controls to particular circumstances. The availability of knowledge and expertise has received a powerful assist from the federal government through its program of local planning assistance. Federal aid has helped suburbs acquire local professional staff and the services of private planning consultants, activities which have flourished in the wake of heightened concern over preserving community character, maximizing internal benefits, controlling growth, and safeguarding the local environment.

Another factor influencing the spread of restrictive land-use controls is the political fragmentation of suburbia. Fragmentation poses serious risks for the jurisdiction that fails to maintain its competitive position. As David S. Schoenbrod points out: "The suburb that falls behind in the zoning race may quickly become a target for mass developers catering to the less wealthy spectrum of the homebuying market, thus burdening it with unusually fast development and a loss of relative prestige." [67] Such communities are likely to experience serious financial and service problems, which in turn undermine their ability to attract more desirable development. All of these problems have been particularly severe in recent years for suburbs which have permitted indiscriminate apartment construction. Their experiences have spurred other communities to safeguard themselves by employing measures aimed at limiting the size of apartments, restricting school-age children, or raising the cost of housing.

With the spread of efforts designed to restrict residential development, "snob" zoning has become a misnomer for exclusionary land-use controls. Suburbs of all kinds, as well as rural areas beyond the metropolitan fringe, now employ large lots, minimum building size, frontage requirements, costly building codes, apartment-house restrictions, development timing, and other sophisticated techniques. As a consequence, local zoning has become a far more significant factor in restricting housing opportunities than was the case in an earlier era when exclusionary zoning was used primarily by affluent bedroom communities. As Paul N. Ylvisaker, former Commissioner of Community Affairs in New Jersey, explains:

> It isn't snob zoning that produces the problem in New Jersey. The snob zoning of three acres or more happens to be in the northern, less buildable areas, the "horse country" of Morris and Somerset Counties. . . . The really devilish arrangements that are freezing the market and blocking the movement out of overcrowded areas are one-acre zoning, 1,200 square feet building minimums, and 200 front feet on a highway. Put those three together—as most of our suburban towns are doing—and you have ruled out practically all of the land for housing within the economic reach of 80% of New Jersey's population. [68]

Growing awareness of the consequences of growth and the availability of techniques that promise to regulate the growth process increase the probability that controls will be used by local governments in advance of development. As a result, local controls are likely to be more effective than in the past, since, as Wood notes, "the real effectiveness of land use policies hinges on their timing." [69] Rural areas that once were highly vulnerable to subdividers now confront developers with a variety of land-use controls, as well as a populace far more dubious about the benefits of growth than was the case a decade ago. In Hunterdon County in New Jersey, a sparsely populated area on the verge of suburban development, 97 percent of the residential land is zoned by municipal governments for lots of one acre or larger, and 78 percent of the residential land carries 200 foot minimum frontage requirements. Increasing growth pressures led the governing body of rural Fauquier County in the rolling Virginia countryside forty miles west of Washington to declare a moratorium on building in 1973 in order to give the local government time to implement development controls keyed to the provision of capital improvements. Southampton, located 80 miles from Manhattan in the path of the suburban development that moves inexorably eastward on Long Island, has developed a sophisticated master plan that keys future development closely to environmental constraints. "We studied the climate, the flood plain, the elevation, the topography, the soil, the fish and game, the natural vegetation, and the scenic features," explains a local planner. [70] The result was a plan that seeks to limit Southampton's population, maintain low residential densities, and protect the area's recreational, farming, and fishing industries.

The spread of land-use controls has also increased the ability of local governments to influence informally the plans, prices, and clientele of developers. Just who is to be permitted to live in a community cannot be made explicit in a zoning ordinance or subdivision regulation. But it can often be determined in negotiations between the local government and the developer. A common technique is to zone vacant land for very low densities, thus requiring developers to seek a specific zoning change. Complex procedures usually compel builders to negotiate, often with a variety of local officials. Increasingly, suburban growth controls explicitly call for negotiations. For example, one community in the path of suburban development in the Boston area has adopted "negotiated landscape impact zoning," which has been described as involving "some good old-fashioned horse trading. The town allows the developer to build at higher densities, to cluster his units, or to build multifamily housing; in return the developer agrees to take the town's ecology into account, to mix his housing types in a way that would have a favorable impact on the school budget and to set aside permanent open space." [71] Negotiations also result from the ability of local governments to delay or harass developers, thus increasing their costs and risks. "Intentional delays," as the National Commission on Urban Problems noted in 1968, "are not uncommon in communities which would, in fact, prefer no development at all." [72]

Another important development is the growing tendency of suburbs to handle development requests through petitions for rezoning or special exemptions, a procedure which mandates negotiation and greatly enhances the discretion of local government. Apartments in particular are likely to be regulated through special permit. In New Jersey, for example, almost all suburban apartments have been authorized by use variances, special exceptions, or zoning amendments. Between 1965 and 1972, over 17,000 multifamily units were constructed in Middlesex County despite the fact that only 317 acres were zoned for apartments. And in Monmouth County, where no land was zoned for multifamily dwellings, more than 22 percent of the building permits issued during the 1960s were for apartments.

Employing these discretionary devices, local officials can withhold permission for developers to proceed until satisfied with the size and costs of the proposed housing, rents or selling prices, and the sort of market the developer has in mind. A common goal of suburban governments in these negotiations is "to bid up the price or cost . . . in order to limit the number of people who can come in at lower cost." [73] For one suburban planner, "the thing to focus on" in negotiations with apartment developers was "the rent schedule. If the rent schedule is high enough . . . I don't think you have to be apprehensive about being flooded by a slew of public school children." [74] With considerable justification, a New Jersey study commission termed the use of these discretionary devices "the essence of the gatekeeper role" in the suburbs:

> Were appropriate amounts of land to be zoned for apartments, with appropriate criteria (setbacks, parking requirements, etc.) written into the zoning ordinance, builders could purchase land, submit plans meeting these criteria, and construct multi family housing without regard to the various unwritten goals of the community, be they fiscal, social, or visual. Such goals, of course, can rarely be written into a local ordinance without immediate

challenge in the courts. By the use of the variance process, with quiet word passed to appropriate developers that variances will be considered in certain areas, the community can enforce many of its preferences through an informal process of negotiation between the developer and the planning board or council.[75]

As Herbert M. Franklin has emphasized, the widespread use of these discretionary practices in the suburbs makes it increasingly difficult "to discern a community's exclusionary motives simply from an examination of its formal zoning ordinances or subdivision regulations. The *pattern* of exclusion emerges from the exercise of local governmental discretion in permitting or forbidding certain uses." [76]

Suburban Zoning and Housing Opportunities

Whether formal or informal, suburban controls on residential development contribute to the rising cost of housing, and consequently reduce housing opportunities. The cost of housing, of course, results from a variety of factors. The rising price of land, money, materials, and labor all contributed to the increase of the median price of a new home from $18,000 in 1963 to $32,800 in 1973.[77] Between 1946 and 1975, land costs as a component of the selling price of single-family homes doubled to approximately 25 percent, and land in the mid-1970s consumed as much as 30 cents of the new housing dollar in many suburban areas. With mortgage rates reaching new highs in the 1970s, the proportion of the costs of single-family housing represented by financing charges has doubled over the past two decades. Increased labor and material costs have also contributed significantly to mounting housing costs. Salary increases in the building trades have outstripped most other occupations, with hourly construction wages averaging 60 percent higher than those other major industries. During the winter of 1972–73 alone, increased lumber prices added $1,200 to the cost of the average single-family home, and the prices of other construction materials have not been far behind.

Local policies have an important effect on housing costs because they directly influence the costs of land and construction, and because they indirectly contribute to mortgage costs, as do other factors which raise the base price of the dwelling unit. Zoning controls affect land prices in a variety of ways. Their most important role is to reduce the availability of land for residential purposes. Large lots limit the supply of land which can be used for more intensive housing development, thereby contributing to higher prices for the remaining land available for single-family housing on smaller lots and multiple-unit dwellings. Local restrictions further reduce the land which can be used for apartments; and this governmentally-induced scarcity increases the value of land zoned for multiple-family dwellings. Bans on mobile homes induce an artificial scarcity of land for trailer parks, which inevitably increases the housing costs of mobile-home owners. "With zoning as tight as it is," a trailer-park owner on Long Island explains, "the operator runs out of sites. He can't sell any new homes . . . so he starts to raise rents." [78] Moratoriums, ecological zoning, population limits, and other measures which contribute to the scarcity of land for development have the same general effect on land costs. For example, prices of vacant lots zoned for residential use rose more than 25 percent in the first three months following the decision of Boca Raton to limit its population to 100,000.

Large lots themselves increase the price of land, since they tend to cost more than smaller ones. As indicated in Table 3.5, however, the

Table 3.5. Price of Vacant Lots by Residential Zoning Category, Montgomery County, Md., 1967

Minimum Lot Size	Median Sales Price
2 acres	$18,000
.92 acres	11,800
.46 acres	7,650
.34 acres	5,400
.21 acres	4,000
.14 acres	3,600

Source: U.S. National Commission on Urban Problems, *Building the American City*, p. 214.

relation between the size of lots and their cost is not direct since the unit value of land increases when it is zoned for more intensive use. Large lots and the low-density settlement patterns produced by restrictive zoning also raise the costs of utility connections, streets, sidewalks, and other expenses normally borne by the purchaser. The cost of these improvements is further increased by the scattered or leapfrog development that is encouraged by the variations among suburban governments in making land available for different types of residential development in a metropolitan area.

Higher construction costs result from minimum building requirements, building codes, apartment-house ordinances, and subdivision regulations. Restrictions on the minimum area of a single-family house or an apartment unit have a direct impact on construction costs. In effect, they are minimum-cost requirements since each additional square foot of area adds a constant to the overall price of the unit. For example, if residential construction costs $22 per square foot, a 1,200 square foot minimum means that houses will be priced at no less than $24,000 plus the cost of land and improvements, which are likely to add at least $6,000 to the final selling price. The impact of building codes and subdivision regulations on housing costs varies considerably from jurisdiction to jurisdiction, but rarely is insignificant. In 1972, the New Jersey Builders Association estimated that replacement of municipal building regulations with a statewide code would save an average of $1,500 per dwelling unit in construction costs.[79] The National Commission on Urban Problems calculated that the net effect of the most common local code requirements which exceeded national building standards was to add 15 percent to the cost of a prefabricated housing unit.[80]

Clearly, less expensive housing would be built if builders were not confronted by local restrictions which reduce the supply of land available for housing, increase its cost, and prevent the most economical construction methods and materials from being used. Just as obvious is the fact that changes in other elements in the cost of housing would reduce prices, most notably with respect to mortgage and labor costs. None of these elements by itself, however, is likely to produce a dramatic breakthrough in the price of housing. Instead, as the President's Committee on Urban Housing emphasized, efforts to reduce the cost of housing "must work on all the bits and pieces which make up the initial costs of a housing unit." [81] The importance of these "bits and pieces" is underscored by the estimate that "every $2,500 increment in housing costs eliminates another one-half million families from the housing market." [82] In the view of many knowledgeable observers, restrictive local policies are the most important of these bits and pieces. Anthony Downs terms "the quality standards that newly built suburban (and other) housing units are required to meet . . . a more fundamental cause of high housing costs" than the costs of construction and operation.[83] According to Levitt and Sons, the nation's largest homebuilding firm, "a breakthrough in housing costs in the near future will be accomplished not by new technologies and methods, but by the adoption of uniform building codes and a breakthrough in land utilization practices." [84]

Breakthroughs on zoning, building codes, and other local regulatory measures would open housing opportunities for families now unable to afford new suburban housing. In some of the larger metropolitan areas, four out of five households have been priced out of the market for new housing. Assuming that 25 percent of income is available for housing, the Metropolitan Council of the Twin Cities estimated in 1971 that 84 percent of the households in the Minneapolis–St. Paul area could not afford the average new single-family home, then selling for $38,500. Nor could half of the households pay the $211 needed to rent the average new apartment without using more than a quarter of their income for housing.[85] In the New York area, the Regional Plan Association found that over 80 percent of all households whose heads are 30 to 34 years old—the period during which families are most likely to buy their first home—were priced out of the market for new housing in a six-county suburban area in 1969.

Table 3.6. Housing Prices in the New York Suburbs, 1969

Area	Dominant Ranges in Housing Prices	Income Needed *	Percent of Young Households Able to Afford New Housing
Nassau and the western two towns of Suffolk	$35,000–50,000	$17,000	11%
Westchester	45,000–65,000	22,000	8%
Putnam, Rockland, Orange	30,000–45,000	15,000	17%

* Assumes that households can afford only two and one-half times income to buy a new house.
Source: "Housing Opportunities," *Regional Plan News*, No. 91 (Sept., 1969), p. 7.

Eased local restrictions would permit the construction of inexpensive single-family tract housing on small lots, such as that built by Levitt and other developers from the late 1940s to the early 1960s, development which played a key role in permitting lower-middle- and working-class families to move to the suburbs. As Lynne B. Sagalyn and George Sternlieb conclude in their study of the impact of zoning on housing costs in New Jersey, "changes in the major zoning *practices* would appear to enlarge the effective housing market considerably provided that builders made concomitant reductions in the size and amenities of the housing offered." [86] In 1972, the president of the New Jersey Builders Association claimed that small suburban houses could be built profitably for $16,500 if local zoning were to permit the use of 50 by 100 foot lots.[87] Relaxation of local controls also would result in larger and less expensive apartments in the suburbs, the need for which steadily grows as land costs and single-family housing prices mount. Standardization of building codes would facilitate the construction of prefabricated dwellings, a potentially significant means of reducing housing costs for families with modest incomes. And less restrictive zoning would greatly increase the use of mobile homes in metropolitan areas, the only new housing currently being produced in large quantities which is within reach of lower-income families. Finally, an increase in the supply of new suburban housing would increase the flow of used housing which filters down to poorer families still unable to afford new housing.

Blacks would benefit more than whites from these developments. Because of lower average incomes, 89 percent of the black population was priced out of the new housing market in 1972, compared to 76 percent of the white population.[88] Blacks also benefited less from lower suburban housing prices in the past. As the U.S. Commission on Civil Rights has emphasized, many "white suburbanites bought their houses at a time when prices were significantly lower. Today the supply of inexpensive suburban housing is insufficient for even those black purchasers or renters whose income is comparable to that of whites." [89]

As a consequence of the lower average income of blacks, suburbs do not have to pursue overtly racist policies to exclude blacks, since "a successful policy of economic segregation will automatically bring about a very high degree of racial and ethnic segregation." [90] For example, a study of housing in the St. Louis area concluded that "the prohibition of multi-unit housing in a jurisdiction . . . has a proportionately greater effect on housing opportunities in that jurisdiction for black households than for white households. The proportion of black households affected by such a prohibition is about twice as high as the proportion of white households affected." [91] Commenting on the claim of a suburban zoning and planning commission that "discrimination does not exist in Greenwich in schools, in recreation areas, in housing, or in any other areas which are not controlled by individual choice," an official of the Anti-Defamation League underscored in testimony before the National Commission on Urban Problems "the fact [that] zoning restrictions make it unnecessary for such discrimination to develop since they have kept members of the minorities in question, who are concentrated in the lower economic levels, from living in the town." [92]

Chapter Four

Excluding Subsidized Housing

Despite the key role of land-use controls in increasing costs and reducing housing opportunities, zoning reform alone cannot make suburban housing available to large numbers of lower-income families. Even if all local land-use controls were swept away, new private housing in the suburbs would be far too expensive for most of those earning less than the median family income, which was $12,840 in 1974, especially if 25 percent of a family's income is considered the desirable maximum for housing expenditures. As a result of these economic realities, governmental assistance of some sort is needed if housing conditions for most lower-income families are to be improved, and particularly if newer housing in the suburbs is to be available to the less affluent.

Suburbanites, however, have employed local political autonomy with considerable success to keep subsidized housing out of their communities. Suburban jurisdictions have refused to participate in subsidized housing programs which require active involvement by local government. Zoning and other land-use controls have been employed to block the construction of subsidized units under a variety of housing programs which rely on private developers to acquire project sites. As a consequence of local opposition, as well as the traditional emphasis of subsidized housing programs on the needs of poorer families living in slum areas, relatively little housing for lower-income Americans has been built in the suburbs.

During the 1960s, however, suburban locations became increasingly attractive for developers of low-cost subsidized housing, primarily as a result of the enactment of a series of new federal housing programs.

Rental housing under the Section 221(d)3 and Section 236 programs, as well as units available through the Section 235 homeownership program were aimed at families with higher incomes than the clients of traditional public housing, thus increasing the market for subsidized housing in the suburbs.[1] Income limits in both the Section 221(d)3 and Section 236 programs were set 35 percent higher than those prevailing in public housing, resulting in an income range of approximately $4,000 to $9,000 for a family of four.

The federal programs developed during the 1960s also relied heavily on nongovernmental organizations and private developers rather than local public agencies as in public housing. In 221(d)3 and 236 housing, projects eligible for assistance could be sponsored by nonprofit developers, cooperatives, and private entrepreneurs who agreed to limit their profits to six percent. Basic responsibility for the provision of housing in the Section 235 homeownership program rested with private developers. In broadening the base of sponsorship, the new federal programs made it possible to develop subsidized housing in suburbs which had not established local housing authorities as required by the public-housing program. Widening the range of sponsors also provided nonprofit organizations and private developers with an incentive to participate in subsidized housing activities, a stimulus which was absent when public housing was the only means of constructing low-income housing in most communities.

Table 4.1. Major Federal Housing Programs for Lower-Income Families, 1971

Program	Enacted	Total Units	Tenure	Sponsor
Public Housing	1937	1,160,700	Rental, some ownership	Local housing authority
Section 221(d)3	1961	190,800	Rental or cooperative	Nonprofit, cooperative, or limited profit private developer
Rent Supplement	1965	75,000	Rental or cooperative	Nonprofit, cooperative, or limited profit private developer
Section 235	1968	266,120	Ownership	Private developer
Section 236	1968	201,900	Rental or cooperative	Nonprofit, cooperative, or limited profit private developer

Another key factor affecting the suburbs was the rapid increase in the production of subsidized housing that resulted from implementation of

Sections 235 and 236 of the Housing and Urban Development Act of 1968. Between 1950 and 1965, approximately 42,000 units of subsidized housing were constructed annually, with practically all of the units developed under the public-housing program. By 1970, production had increased tenfold, largely as a result of the 235 and 236 programs which together accounted for two-thirds of the 431,000 subsidized units begun that year.

Inevitably, this vast increase in the production of subsidized housing turned developers toward the suburbs, which contain most of the vacant land available for housing development in metropolitan areas. As Secretary of Housing and Urban Development George Romney pointed out in 1970, "you can't move housing production for low- and moderate-income families to the extent we have without being confronted with the

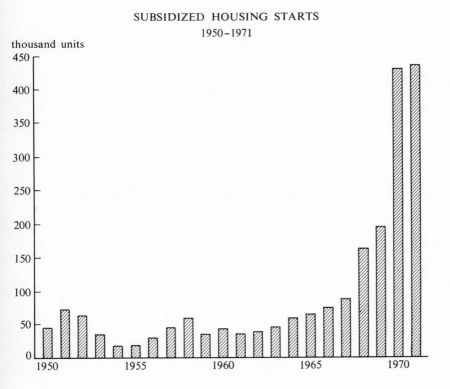

SUBSIDIZED HOUSING STARTS
1950–1971

Figure 4.1. Subsidized Housing Starts, 1950–1971

Source: U.S. Department of Housing and Urban Development

need for new locations . . . and this has made it necessary to locate a lot more land . . . outside the central core cities." [2]

The pressure on the suburbs to provide sites for low-cost housing mounted for two additional reasons. First, the need to locate subsidized housing near the proliferating industrial and commercial developments in the suburbs was becoming increasingly apparent in the late 1960s. Second, opposition was rising to the continued concentration of housing projects in black neighborhoods in the urban core. Law suits in Chicago, Philadelphia, and Cleveland led to federal court rulings which severely limited the amount of subsidized housing that could be constructed in areas with large concentrations of blacks and public-housing projects. [3] In response to these court actions, the federal government sought to encourage the location of subsidized housing in attractive environments which were outside minority areas, away from existing concentrations of low-income housing, and likely to enhance employment opportunities for minorities.

All of these developments combined to increase the amount of subsidized housing constructed in the suburbs in the years immediately following passage of the Housing and Urban Development Act of 1968. As indicated in Table 4.2, 2,790 units of Section 235 and 236 housing were located in the suburbs of the Denver area through 1971, in contrast with 410 units of public housing constructed in suburban communities be-

Table 4.2. Federally Subsidized Housing in the Suburbs of Four Metropolitan Areas, 1972

Metropolitan Area	Total Units	Public Housing (1937)	Section 202 * (1959)	Section 221(d)3 (1961)	Rent Supp. (1965)	Section 235 (1968)	Section 236 (1968)
Denver	3,678	410	298	0	180	2,167	623
Detroit	31,969	6,046	1,249	7,849	—	8,492	8,333
Minneapolis– St. Paul	2,878	340	551	†	—	1,826	551
Philadelphia	15,839	5,901	0	†	—	454	8,831

* Housing for the elderly, similar to Section 221(d)3 program.
† Combined with Section 236 totals.
Source: Denver Regional Council of Governments, *Housing in the Denver Region* (Denver, 1972), p. 24; Southeast Michigan Council of Governments, "Housing Plan and Program for Southeast Michigan" (draft), Feb., 1973, p. A-30; Metropolitan Council of the Twin Cities Area, *Distribution and Types of Subsidized Housing in the Twin Cities Metropolitan Area*, Housing Report One (St. Paul, 1971); and Delaware Valley Regional Planning Commission, "Subsidized Housing in the Delaware Valley," Technical Record No. 8 (draft), May, 1973, p. 16.

tween 1937 and 1972. By mid-1972, the 235 and 236 programs accounted for more than half of the total stock of subsidized housing in the suburbs of the Detroit area. Almost 58 percent of all subsidized housing built in the suburbs of the Philadelphia area through 1972 was financed under the Section 236 program. Testifying before a subcommittee of the House of Representatives in late 1971, Secretary Romney documented the shift in the locus of federally subsidized housing projects in other areas. Twenty-two of twenty-four major projects started before 1970 in the Baltimore region were in the central city, twenty of twenty-nine during the first half of 1970, but only four of sixteen during the latter part of the year. Through mid-1970, forty-nine of fifty projects in the San Antonio area were located within the city limits, while twelve of twenty-three started in the second half of 1970 were on suburban sites. Similar patterns were indicated in the Jacksonville, Pittsburgh, San Diego, and Washington areas.[4]

With more subsidized housing came increased concern, conflict, and opposition in suburban jurisdictions across the nation. As a consequence of the Housing and Urban Development Act of 1968, far more suburbanites than in the past were confronted with the prospect of subsidized housing in their communities. Most reacted, as suburban dwellers always have, with hostility and emotional opposition to any form of subsidized housing.

The Roots of Suburban Hostility

For large numbers of suburbanites, subsidized housing is a threat, the incarnation of everything in urban society they have sought to insulate themselves from in politically autonomous communities. In a survey of residents of suburban Westchester County in the New York area, those opposed to subsidized housing identified its advent with undesirable changes in community character, higher taxes, overcrowding in the schools, unwanted neighbors, slums, and increased crime and drug problems.[5] A survey in four suburban communities in the Dayton area indicated widespread association of lower-income households with falling property values, neighborhood instability, deteriorating housing conditions, rising property taxes, more crime, unsuitable neighbors, and a loss of social status for existing residents.[6]

In the view of an official of a Long Island suburb, "additional public housing in Hempstead will trigger a renewed exodus of disenchanted souls from neighboring New York City." He was ready to "resist all efforts which will result in our community becoming so overpopulated that we lose the suburban nature of our town and become the jungle of high-rise apartments that most of our residents came to Hempstead to escape." [7] For an opponent of Section 236 housing in Black Jack, Missouri, the essence of the campaign was "fighting against the establishment of another Pruitt-Igoe in the suburbs." [8] It mattered little to residents of Black Jack that the garden apartments planned for their community bore little resemblance to Pruitt-Igoe, a notorious high-rise public-housing project in the black ghetto of St. Louis. Suburbanites commonly lump all subsidized housing together and "transfer the substantial stigma of public housing to any other subsidized project." [9] As a result of this widespread suburban perception, any kind of subsidized housing is seen as undermining the local community and the interests of its residents. In explaining why 240 homeowners in Blue Springs, a suburb in the Kansas City area, signed a petition in 1970 opposing a Section 236 townhouse project, an attorney for the local residents insisted that "regardless of how well built and how beautifully designed the units might be, they will still be federally subsidized housing and thus devalue the surrounding property." [10] Or, as a resident of Bedford in New York's Westchester County puts it: "Nearly everyone's against anything that smacks of a project. A project is a project is a project." [11]

The belief that subsidized housing will downgrade a suburban community rests heavily on the assumption that lower-income residents will bring with them crime, drugs, delinquency, and other problems of the inner city. "By . . . making it easier for low-income residents to get out of the city, you're actually moving city problems to a new location," argues a resident of Brecksville in the Cleveland area.[12] This viewpoint is echoed constantly in discussions of subsidized housing in the suburbs. According to an official in suburban St. Louis County, "if we scatter the poor, . . . we would only spread the blight." [13] In defending a New Jersey suburb's exclusionary zoning, a spokesman claimed that revising local land-use regulations to meet the housing needs of lower-income families "just moves the ghetto around." [14]

Suburbanites also argue that their communities are unsuitable for lower-income families. They point to the absence of social services, special educational programs, public-health clinics, public transportation, and other services frequently available to the poor in the central city. Also emphasized is the high cost of living in affluent suburbs. In opposing a proposal for subsidized housing in a Connecticut suburb, a local official emphasized that "it is difficult for anybody making less than $11,000 a year to live here." [15] Many residents of the suburbs see class and income differences generating envy and frustration on the part of the occupants of subsidized housing, which will produce tension, crime, and violence. "We're afraid that if they build the project," explained an opponent of subsidized housing in Black Jack, "they'll fill it with a bunch of have-nots who, once they see what we've got, will be walking up the street to take it." [16]

Concern with overcrowded schools, traffic congestion, overloaded sewerage facilities, increased local tax burdens, and other standard suburban arguments against higher densities and multiple-family dwellings are commonly advanced by opponents of subsidized housing. In addition, suburbanites worry that low-income housing will increase local welfare and social-service burdens. Fiscal objections are particularly persuasive to residents of the suburbs because subsidized housing typically involves higher net costs than most other forms of residential development. Low-income units built under the public-housing program pay 10 percent of their gross rentals in lieu of local taxes, a contribution which rarely equals the tax liability of private housing of equal value. Other types of subsidized housing are generally taxed in the normal manner by suburban governments, but tend to generate less revenue per occupant than privately-financed residences because their tax base per resident is relatively low.

The small scale of most suburban jurisdictions heightens local fiscal concerns. Because most suburbs are small, individual housing projects have a larger impact on local taxes and public services than is typically the case in the center city. As a result, the entire community rather than a particular neighborhood is likely to react negatively to the fiscal and service implications of subsidized housing. Suburban sensitivity to local fiscal considerations was underscored in the survey of attitudes toward subsidized housing in Westchester County referred to earlier. Although 53 percent of those questioned were not opposed to subsidized housing in principle, 71 percent were against "a subsidized housing development within [their] community" which would increase local "property taxes . . . even slightly." [17] In the light of these fiscal realities and local attitudes, as a housing official points out, "very few suburban leaders are willing to make a political decision which calls for an influx of low-income families, a reduction in potential taxes from real estate, an increase in the volume of public services, and therefore the possibility of a tax increase." [18]

Fear that local governments would be obligated to assume additional burdens in the event of the financial failure of low-income projects has reinforced suburban fiscal concerns about subsidized housing. These fears have been fueled by the deepening fiscal crisis of the public-housing program and the financial difficulties encountered in the newer federal housing programs. By 1972, income deficiencies had driven scores of local public-housing agencies into deficit operations. The fiscal woes of public housing were rooted in the steady increase in the proportion of tenants on welfare, whose rents were limited by Congress in 1969; and by the concomitant failure of the federal government to provide sufficient subsidies to compensate the local agencies for diminished rent revenues and rapidly rising operating costs. Sizable numbers of welfare tenants and inadequate revenues also were a major problem in the Section 236 rental program, with 26 percent of the projects falling into default by mid-1972.

Shoddy construction, widespread corruption, poor maintenance, abandonment of newly built units, and other well-publicized problems, particularly in the Section 235 homeownership program, further enhanced suburban opposition to subsidized housing in the early 1970s. Speaking of the problems encountered by the Department of Housing and Urban Development in implementing the 1968 housing legislation, Secretary Romney admitted in early 1972 that "shady get-rich-quick schemes abound, involving some realtors, some builders, some developers, and even some housing authorities, who line their pockets with the [money] of the uninformed, unsuspecting home buyer or renter." The result, in Romney's words, was "housing with leaky roofs, leaky plumbing, leaky basements, slipshod carpentry work, loose stair treads, paper-thin walls, inoperative furnaces and appliances, inadequate insulation, inferior wiring, and a whole host of complaints." [19]

Although the most serious scandals involved units in the central cities, the shortcomings of the 235 and 236 programs were particularly damaging to the cause of subsidized housing in the suburbs. By stimulating private involvement in the production of subsidized housing and making low-cost units indistinguishable from other dwellings, both programs were designed to remove the stigma of public housing and increase local acceptance of subsidized developments in the outlying areas. Instead, suburban resistance to subsidized housing was augmented, especially in metropolitan areas such as Chicago and Detroit where scandalous practices were widespread. "We want new housing," contended the mayor of a working-class suburb in the Detroit area, "but we want the best housing available for all our citizens, and not cheap, prefab, subsidized shacks on a slab." [20]

Low standards and shoddy construction intensified concern about the impact of subsidized units on local property values, and reinforced the determination of suburban governments to use local zoning and building codes to safeguard their constituents' interests. As a suburban major in the Milwaukee area explained in connection with his community's opposition to subsidized housing:

> Because we required . . . people who built when these subdivisions were laid out to certain standards, we implied to them that we were going to require the vacant lots that remain to have structures of comparable quality on them. . . . I think we have an obligation to enforce our building codes and our zoning codes, because actually, we are enforcing promises. We are carrying out promises we made to people who built five years ago and ten years ago. [21]

Intensifying the resistance of many communities to subsidized housing, and especially to single-family homes built under the 235 program, was the limited capability of small suburban governments to insure that developers complied with local building codes and other regulations. This lack of competence usually is offset in the case of local builders by market considerations and the desire of the builder to build more houses in or near the community in the future. Large-scale 235 developers, on the other hand, were operating in a sellers' market with inexperienced customers, often on a one-shot basis in a particular suburb. As a result, many of these firms were under little pressure to maintain a good reputation within particular communities by conforming to local standards.

Shabby construction, poor site planning, and inadequate sewerage and drainage in many 235 and 236 units also bolstered environmental opposition to subsidized housing in the suburbs, already stirred in most areas by the increased pressures on suburban land unleashed by the new housing assistance programs. Environmental groups and local officials who employ ecological rationales commonly contend that they are not opposed to subsidized housing in their suburbs *per se*, but to measures that will consume more land, stimulate growth, and downgrade the local environment. For example, after indicating its general willingness to ac-

cept subsidized housing, the village council of Maplewood in the Minneapolis–St. Paul area balked on specific proposals. The suburb's
planner was concerned because of "the local responsibility [to maintain] a
quality environment," while a councilman feared that "if we bunch up
low-income people, they'll change our environment." [22] Environmentalists in Boulder in the Denver area "agree that there should be construction of 'living units for all income groups,' but hope that the bulk of
this effort can be done by replacement and renovation of existing dwellings rather than by extension of an already over-extended community." [23] Which, of course, means keeping lower-income groups where
they are.

Another suburban concern heightened by the rapid expansion of federal support for subsidized housing was fear that large numbers of lower-
income units will be attracted to a community that lowers its zoning barriers. Let in a few, opponents argued, and there will be no way to keep
out more subsidized housing. Land-use lawyers concede that "zoning
law tends to accelerate the concentration of low-cost housing in the community that takes any. It is easier legally to exclude all subsidized housing than to hold it to a managed program—just as it is safer to keep out
the first gas station at the intersection than to try to keep out the second
or the third." [24] Once the door is opened, contend the advocates of the
status quo, poor families will inundate the community, overwhelming its
local services, raising its taxes, undermining property values, and driving
out those residents who can afford to leave. For documentation, they
pointed to suburbs such as Beecher in the Flint area or Prince Georges
County to the east of the District of Columbia. In Beecher, the construction of a large number of 235 units resulted in an influx of lower-income
blacks with large families, net deficits of $800 per pupil for the local
school district, racial transformation of the student body, and white
flight from the community. [25] Prince Georges experience was similar:

> Because it was one of the few Washington area suburbs to allow FHA-sub-
> sidized apartments, it has wound up with nearly all of them—several thou-
> sand apartments in all. Thus, rather than being integrated into the suburbs
> generally, the lower-income families moving into these projects have . . .
> been concentrated in a few areas, where . . . community services for them
> are inadequate and social problems have festered. The county, moreover,
> did not provide new schools or recreational facilities in adequate proportion
> to the large numbers of children moving into these projects, and school
> overcrowding, delinquency, and vandalism resulted. [26]

Difficulties with the new subsidized housing programs were far from universal in the suburbs. Many of the units built under Sections 235 and 236 blended into their surroundings, had little adverse impact on local services and taxes, and raised few suburban hackles. Concentration of units did not occur in many of the suburban jurisdictions which authorized lower-income housing. The bad experiences with subsidized housing, however, tended to outweigh the success stories in their influence on suburban attitudes. Tales of depressed property values, shabby housing, unscrupulous developers, overbuilding in particular communities, crowded schools, and local tax increases found a receptive audience among the large numbers of suburbanites who were strongly predisposed to oppose subsidized housing on social and economic grounds.

Race and Subsidized Housing in the Suburbs

Many proponents of subsidized housing question the sincerity of suburbanites who express concern about the impact of lower-income housing on local property values, public services, taxes, and the environment. Civil-rights groups tend to see racial discrimination as the underlying motive in suburban policies which limit housing opportunities, with considerations such as property values, community character, local taxes and services, and environmental protection providing a respectable rationale for racially-inspired practices. For an official of the National Committee Against Discrimination in Housing, there is no question "that the overriding concern in every suburban community is the fear that minority citizens will move into their communities and change the complexion of their lily-white situation." [27] From the perspective of a developer of subsidized housing in the Kansas City area, "the issue in Johnson County is . . . racial and economic exclusion, pure and simple." [28] Human motivations, however, are rarely pure or simple. That class, status, and racial considerations underlie much of the suburban opposition to subsidized housing is beyond question. Racial motivations, however, are difficult to isolate from other factors which prompt exclusionary policies. Certainly the fact that many middle-class black suburbanites resist subsidized housing indicates that racial prejudice is not the only element in the exclusion of lower-income blacks from the suburbs.

If civil-rights interests commonly overstate the importance of race in suburban exclusion, suburbanites almost universally underestimate its role in local determinations affecting subsidized housing. Opponents of

236 housing in Black Jack insisted that their fight had "nothing to do with race. It's simply a matter of economics—everything from land and housing values to overcrowded schools and cluttered streets." [29] In fact, racial concerns are never far from the surface in most suburban discussions of subsidized housing. As noted above, suburbanites tend to equate all forms of subsidized housing with public housing, which in turn is closely identified with blacks. In 1970, blacks accounted for more than 50 percent of the residents of public housing, and more than 90 percent of all occupants of public housing in many larger cities. In the common suburban shorthand, subsidized housing means lower-income blacks on welfare who will bring crime, racial tensions, and, inevitably, more blacks, lower property values, and the end of their community. "We all know what the mores in the ghetto are," confides a spokesman for a local civic association in a suburb outside Washington, D.C., "if you want something, just take it. This has nothing to do with the racial question. I personally know some very fine black people I'd like living next door to me. But I wouldn't want blacks on welfare living next to me." [30]

Given these common suburban perceptions, racial euphemisms abound in suburban debates over subsidized housing. "They'll put the low-class umemployed, these noisy welfare cases, in my backyard," complains a postal worker in Stanford, Connecticut. [31] Protesting plans for subsidized townhouses in Fairfax County in the Washington area, a suburbanite complained that the development would turn into a ghetto because its density of almost seven units per acre would lead its "boxed-in" residents to "bust out some hot summer night." [32] In Black Jack, the shorthand for blacks was "Pruitt-Igoe," the public-housing project in St. Louis's black ghetto. One of the sponsors of the project noted, "the most common statement we heard at the meetings out there was 'we don't want those people, we don't want another Pruitt-Igoe.' If that's not racial discrimination, I don't know what is." [33] Among those that agreed that racial discrimination was a primary motivating factor behind the incorporation of Black Jack and the subsequent rezoning to prevent the construction of subsidized housing were some of the twenty black families living in the community. One black felt that incorporation "was a blatant attempt to exclude people from living here because of their race." [34] Another called the local actions "about 90 percent racist." [35] The U.S. Department of Justice agreed that race was a prime consideration, bringing suit against Black Jack on the grounds that the zoning action was racially inspired, and was another chapter in "a long and melancholy history of deliberate discrimination in housing by both public and private bodies" in the Black Jack area.[36]

Suburban scrutiny of subsidized housing proposals tends to be more detailed and local obstacles more numerous when blacks are thought to be potential residents. In the San Francisco Bay Area, according to a study prepared for the National Committee Against Discrimination in Housing,

> whenever any minority occupancy is expected in a proposed project, the opponents lie in wait for every step in the approval process and try to force planning commissions and city councils to hold endless hearings as pressure against the projects. If hearings are refused . . . then the opponents use this refusal as justification for lawsuits and threats of lawsuits.[37]

Racially motivated opposition to subsidized housing tends to be greatest among less affluent suburbanites. In the Westchester survey, 60 percent of the lower- and moderate-income respondents were "against subsidized housing because it forces racial integration on people," while only 36 percent of upper- and middle-income suburbanites shared this view.[38] In part, these attitudinal differences reflect the fact that lower-income suburbs are likely to attract subsidized housing and blacks. Affluent suburbanites are shielded from subsidized housing by high land costs in their towns. They also tend to live in communities which have little or no industry, and which often lack local public transportation, sewers, and other public facilities usually considered necessary for lower-income developments. Moreover, should subsidized housing or other changes bring poor blacks into their neighborhood, affluent suburbanites have the means to move to another community. Just the opposite is the case in lower- and moderate-income suburbs where land prices usually are within reach of the developer of subsidized housing, employment opportunities tend to be closer, and residents are less able to move if unwanted change comes to their community.

Undesirable change is closely identified with the arrival of blacks by the residents of less affluent suburbs. And for most, subsidized housing is equated with blacks. Many working-class and lower-middle-class suburbanites already have fled once or twice from city neighborhoods in the wake of the arrival of blacks, and they do not intend to move again. As one suburban mayor puts it, "sixty-five percent of our people moved out from Cleveland and they consider this the last place for them. They are determined to stay here and keep their houses as they are now." [39] Maintaining the racial status quo for most of these suburbs means keeping out subsidized housing. In recent years, residents of blue-collar Warren in the Detroit area rejected 100 units of public housing, jeered the Secretary of Housing and Urban Development after learning that Warren was to be a target of federal efforts to promote racial integration in the suburbs, and voted not to participate in the urban-renewal program because of fears that blacks would accompany the federal dollars.

Racial prejudice is an important factor in the resistance of these communities to subsidized housing. But residents of suburbs such as Warren also "are acting on the most real evidence they have—the evidence of conditions in Detroit where property loses value and schools decline because, they believe, the blacks have moved in." [40] Suburban determination to keep out subsidized housing is reinforced by the fact that a few blacks in a community frequently means more, as well as the possibility of panic selling, block busting and other unscrupulous real-estate tactics, and the rapid flight of whites. As a state legislator from a suburban district in New Jersey warns: "No white community is going to let down its gates if it thinks it's going to be inundated." [41]

To the degree that these attitudes toward subsidized housing limit the access of blacks to suburban housing they can afford, pressure increases on communities where racial barriers have already been breached. These pressures, in turn, heighten both suburban resistance to subsidized housing and the likelihood of white flight if blacks succeed in establishing a foothold in a community. The viciousness of this circle is intensified in suburbs with substantial amounts of lower-income housing and large black populations. In Kirkwood, a suburb in the path of the black advance outward from Atlanta, "crime rates are up and physical decline is evident. That picture is not encouraging to neighborhoods nearby, where whites still tend to associate the coming of blacks with—see what happened in Kirkwood?—a lowering of values and community standards." [42]

Exclusion Through Action and Inaction

Almost everywhere local autonomy provides suburbanites with the means to exclude subsidized housing. Except for experimental activities and housing on military and other federal installations, the national government does not build or locate subsidized housing. Instead, as Secretary Romney explained to a Senate committee in 1970:

> Housing production and site selection decisions and actions are taken by local organizations, public and private—builders, developers, local housing authorities, and the like. HUD reserves the right to approve or reject a site proposed by a local sponsor, but the initiative in site selection and the decision to build is local. To be eligible for Federal assistance, any proposed new housing must conform to local zoning and building code requirements.[43]

As a consequence of these federal policies, zoning ordinances, building codes, and other local regulations preclude the construction of subsidized housing in many suburban jurisdictions. Even when land and building controls pose no direct barrier, other local actions are commonly needed before subsidized housing can be constructed in suburbs, such as creation of a local housing authority, preparation of a housing plan, formal agreement to participate in the federal rent-supplement program, or approval of local utility connections.

Prior to passage of the Housing and Urban Development Act of 1968, the most widely employed and effective suburban defense against subsidized housing was nonparticipation in federal programs which required formal local governmental initiative or consent. Under the Public Housing Act of 1937, projects could not be built unless the local jurisdiction created a housing authority or agreed to the construction of units within its boundaries by another housing authority. In addition, federal public-housing assistance was conditioned after 1954 on local preparation of an acceptable "workable program" for housing improvement, urban renewal, and community development. The major innovations in public housing developed during the 1960s also required active local involvement. Under the "turnkey" program, public housing could be developed or operated by private entrepreneurs, but only in agreement with a local housing authority. And the Section 23 program, which permitted private housing to be leased for use by families eligible for public housing, was predicated on the existence of a local housing authority.

Most suburbs never created local housing authorities to construct or lease public housing. In Middlesex County, N.J., for example, eighteen of twenty-three suburbs never established housing authorities. Nor does the existence of a housing authority guarantee the construction of public housing in the suburbs. Three of the five suburbs in Middlesex which had organized a housing authority built no units for over two decades. Members can be appointed, Herbert Franklin points out, "who will see that it takes no action on local or regional housing problems. Two of the five members usually suffice to see that nothing happens, even in the unusual case where the authority staff wishes to act imaginatively and constructively." [44] In the Chicago area, the DuPage County Housing Authority was established in 1942, but had yet to construct a single unit thirty years later. Suburban St. Louis County created a housing authority with jurisdiction in unincorporated areas in 1956. Fourteen years later, the agency had built no public housing.

Some inactive suburban housing agencies result from the failure of local governments to cooperate in the development of public housing. Unless the locality approves a "cooperation agreement" which covers the provision of local services to the project, as well as other local action essential to the construction of the housing, federal funds cannot be obtained by the housing agency. Local governments also can prevent the development of public housing by failing to adopt a workable program as required by federal law. In 1971, "not one of the five county governments of the [Atlanta] area [had] a 'workable program,' so that none may receive funds for public housing or urban renewal. This may be assumed to be a calculated policy." [45]

In some instances, suburban housing authorities have been organized for defensive reasons. Creation of a housing agency for defensive purposes is most likely to occur in states where city housing agencies are permitted to acquire sites beyond the city limits providing no local housing authority has jurisdiction. In the Atlanta area, the Fulton County Housing Authority was created to prevent the Atlanta Housing Authority from developing units in unincorporated portions of the county. [46] Agencies organized to preclude the location of subsidized housing in the suburbs rarely undertake programs of their own.

Local autonomy provides suburbs with other defenses against the extraterritorial powers of city housing agencies. Baltimore's housing authority is empowered to develop projects on land owned by the city beyond its limits. But no public housing can be built because suburban Baltimore County has zoned the city's land for one-acre single-family dwellings. [47] Other states permit city or county housing authorities to operate within incorporated suburbs which are agreeable to the arrangement. As in the case of Baltimore County, however, such consent usually is not forthcoming from suburban jurisdictions.

Illustrative of suburban resistance to joint endeavors with the city is the experience of the Cleveland Metropolitan Housing Authority, which is authorized to develop public housing in all but one of Cuyahoga County's suburban jurisdictions, provided the local government enters a cooperation agreement with the city agency.[48] The Cleveland authority began a campaign for suburban sites in 1969, claiming that over 20,000 units were needed outside the city. All but three of the fifty-eight suburban municipalities in the county rebuffed the authority's overtures. Most of the suburbs also ignored a subsequent report by the Cleveland planning commission which recommended that each community in the county agree to the construction of public housing units equivalent to two percent of its population. Nor were many suburban attitudes affected by the changing of the housing authority's name to the Cuyahoga Metropolitan Housing Authority in 1971, since a city housing agency by any other name means the same thing to most suburbanites. Two years later, suburban political leaders reacted vehemently to the release of a plan by the housing authority calling for the construction of 9,800 units in the suburbs.[49] One mayor denounced the plan as "concocted by well-intentioned dreamers" who were seeking to "take large portions of Cleveland's poverty-stricken population and move them to other more delightful localities, thus eliminating the problem in Cleveland and passing the problem of poverty on to the suburbs."[50] The mayor of suburban Parma insisted that "Parma people have to take care of themselves and leave Cleveland problems for Mayor Ralph J. Perk to solve," adding that if his suburb needed public housing, "we want to provide it for our people ourselves. We don't want anybody over which we have no jurisdiction doing anything in our city."[51]

The Chicago metropolitan area provides another example of suburban resistance to involvement with outside public-housing agencies. Responding to a federal court order urging voluntary cooperation with the suburbs, the Chicago Housing Authority negotiated an agreement with the Housing Authority of Cook County in 1971 under which the county agency agreed to

use its best efforts to locate sites suitable for development for low-income family housing in areas outside the municipal boundaries of the City of

Chicago, with the intent and purpose of providing thereon some units of housing to house low-income families who are residents of Chicago and who are certified by [the Chicago Housing Authority] to be eligible for housing.[52]

Since the county agency was unable to construct or lease public housing outside unincorporated areas without local consent, the two authorities sought to develop suburban support for the program, which was limited to 500 units for the three-year life of the agreement. Over 100 suburban municipalities were queried, with only thirteen responding and eleven of these indicating that they were not interested in public housing.

Nonparticipation by suburban governments also proved to be an effective constraint in the Section 221(d)3 and rent supplement programs, despite the absence of a federal requirement for the involvement of a local housing agency. Like federal funds for public housing, however, federal approval of mortgage subsidies for developers of 221(d)3 housing was conditioned on the existence of a local workable program for community improvement. In the typical metropolitan area, few suburbs adopted workable programs. For example, in the mid-1960s, "only 15 communities besides Boston within the Boston Standard Metropolitan Statistical Area, most of them part of the inner ring of the 76 communities comprising the Boston SMSA, had certified Workable Programs, and . . . none of these communities had a superabundance of worthwhile land for development.[53] As a result of the workable-program requirement, "no matter how interested a residential construction company or community group might have been in building" under the 221(d)3 program, "its hands were tied if the local government had no workable program and refused to adopt one, as was the case in more than a few suburban areas that did not want [this] housing."[54] In similar fashion, local governments were given a veto over rent supplement funds, which were available only within communities which had workable programs or had formally consented to the use of rent supplements within their boundaries.

With the advent of the Section 235 and 236 programs in 1968, which required neither the participation of local housing authorities nor the existence of workable programs, land-use controls became the key suburban weapon to check the construction of subsidized housing. "No 235 housing goes into a community unless that community is zoned for it," Secretary Romney told a congressional committee in 1972. "If the communities do not want it, they have ample authority to prevent it. . . . If they have provisions for it, then builders and others can make application for the programs and it can go in, but it is entirely up to the local communities." [55]

Within some suburban jurisdictions where zoning controls were relatively weak, a substantial amount of 235 and 236 housing was constructed, at least in comparison with previous subsidy programs. More often, however, zoning changes were required since subsidized units under the 235 and 236 programs could not be built under existing local land-use regulations. In DuPage County in the Chicago area, for example, "zoning and building ordinances make it virtually impossible for anyone to build housing units for persons with low or moderate incomes without first obtaining a special use, variance, or variation from the County." [56] In response to an inquiry by a nonprofit group seeking to build subsidized apartments, a suburb in New Jersey concurred on the need for moderate-income housing but specified "that such housing must be constructed subject to all zoning, planning, building, and other applicable ordinances and codes. This meant single-family dwellings on 20,000-square-foot lots." [57]

Efforts to secure the rezoning of land for subsidized housing are fraught with risk. As Rubinowitz points out, the necessity to seek a zoning change "gives local officials the opportunity to determine the precise nature of the development before approving its construction. Questions concerning the income groups to be served and the numbers of bedrooms must be answered by the developer in a way that is acceptable to the community." [58] Acceptable answers usually are hard to come by in the case of subsidized projects in the suburbs. "It is not zoning so much that is a restraint within our area," a Dayton planner emphasizes, "as it is the [in]consistent or inaccurate or arbitrary administration thereof. . . . We find that many, many times a rezoning application will be treated different if it is for a luxury apartment than if it is for a 236 project." [59] Requests for rezoning or special exceptions also alert local residents to the developer's plans before approval has been secured. In the wake of disclosure that subsidized housing is planned for a site, opponents usually turn out in force, dominating hearings and other public proceedings of local planning, zoning, and governing bodies. In the emotional climate that often results, rezoning for subsidized housing usually is rejected by suburban officials responsive to the interests of their local constituents.

Because of these hazards, "the wary developer of low-cost housing will take an option on land already zoned for the density needed for his project, rather than attempt to seek a zoning change." [60] The failure of developers in New Jersey to utilize the new federal housing programs has been attributed in large part to the fact that "it was virtually impossible to obtain a variance for a multifamily development that was to be subsidized for low or moderate income families." [61] Further inhibiting developers has been the refusal of the federal government to accept an application for subsidized housing unless the site in question is appropriately zoned. Reluctance to seek zoning changes obviously limits the number of suburban sites available for subsidized projects, especially for apartments, since relatively little suburban land can be used for multiple-family dwellings without some kind of local governmental action.

Acquisition of a site zoned for the intended use, however, does not guarantee success to the developer. Many suburban ordinances that permit the construction of lower-cost and higher-density housing provide local government with a variety of means to discourage the development of subsidized housing, and these means are frequently exploited by opponents. Variances or special permits may be required before construction can proceed. Discretionary planning and design controls can be exercised, as in the case of the refusal of a suburb in the San Francisco area to approve a subsidized project on the grounds that the plans called for too many bedrooms, even though the local zoning ordinance made no reference to restrictions on the number of bedrooms permitted in multiple-family dwellings. [62] Building permits may be denied, or other necessary local actions withheld. "Wave a flag, shoot a gun, ring a bell, and do everything to make all of our people aware of the situation," advised one official of suburban Fulton County in the Atlanta area after discovering that subsidized housing rather than "nice apartments" were to be built on land rezoned for multi-family dwellings. [63] Once alerted, the Fulton County Commissioners refused to issue a building permit for the project which threatened their suburban domain with lower-income black tenants. The developer of subsidized housing, as Mary E. Brooks points out, also "is probably at the mercy of the fire department, water and sewer authorities or a public works department, the engineering department, the school board, the traffic department or state highway department, the park and recreational department or park authority, the redevelopment and housing authority, and so on." [64] Even if all the formal consents are finally forthcoming, the developer of subsidized housing who seeks to build in a hostile suburban environment usually encounters delaying tactics, red tape, and a generally uncooperative local government, a fact of life which tends to discourage potential developers of subsidized housing from even trying in most suburban jurisdictions.

The instruments of local control provide suburbs with a variety of other means to check the development of subsidized housing. Local zoning may be changed to prohibit multiple-family dwellings, as was done in Black Jack in order to foreclose the construction of Section 236 housing. Prince Georges County in Maryland imposed a 10 percent limit on the number of apartments with more than two bedrooms "immediately after [a] Section 236 housing development was built in the county and the commissioners discovered that they could do nothing to prevent its construction." [65] In the Milwaukee area, Wauwatosa raised its requirements for minimum house size sufficiently to prevent the construction of Section 235 units, which were limited to a total cost of approximately $24,000 by the federal government. Vehement opposition to the location in a white area of Lackawanna, a working-class suburb in the Buffalo area, of a 236 project sponsored by the Colored People's Civic and Political Organization led the local government to enact a moratorium on all new subdivisions, to rezone the land in question for use as open space and parks, and to refuse permission for the project to connect with the local sewer system. [66] Moratoriums also have been used by suburbs in southern California to block housing projects. La Puente declared a moratorium on all subsidized housing in order to determine whether low-cost units were needed in the community, while Torrance banned all building in an effort to foreclose the construction of a 236 project. A third suburb, Pomona, enacted a local resolution in 1970 declaring that Section 236 housing was unacceptable to the community. [67] Another potent suburban weapon is eminent domain. In the Boston area, construction of a 236 project was prevented in Framingham when the local government acquired the site through condemnation for public use.

Local voters also can directly block subsidized housing in some jurisdictions. The constitution of California, for example, provides that no low-rent housing project may be developed, constructed, or acquired by any public body unless such projects are approved by the voters in an election. Seven other states had similar provisions in 1973. [68] Typically, the requirement for public approval applies to public housing built or acquired by local agencies, but not to subsidized units constructed by nonprofit sponsors and private developers under programs such as

221(d)3, 235, and 236. Between 1950 and 1970, about half of all the public-housing proposals in California were rejected by local voters.

The use of local referendums poses a particularly formidable obstacle to subsidized housing in the suburbs. In some cases, public votes have been forced by opponents seeking to overturn actions of local government favorable to proposals for subsidized housing. After local officials approved zoning changes needed for the construction of a Section 236 project sponsored by the Southern Alameda Spanish Speaking Organization, 22 percent of the 4,000 registered voters in Union City, a suburb on the eastern side of San Francisco Bay, petitioned for a public vote on the issue. Of those who participated in the election which followed, 60 percent voted to overturn the rezoning and thus kill the project. In the Boston area, over 1,100 residents of Lexington signed a petition in 1971 calling for a referendum on a housing project for 106 units which had been approved by the town meeting. In the ensuing election, the proposal was rejected by a vote of 5,175 to 2,718.

Following the enactment of the 235 and 236 programs in 1968, many suburban opponents of subsidized housing advocated local referendums on all proposals involving lower-income projects. Underlying the demands for direct public participation in local decision-making has been the fear of many suburbanites that their local governments would be unable to resist pressures from private developers of subsidized housing. Efforts to provide local residents with a veto over subsidized housing were bolstered in April 1971 when the U.S. Supreme Court rejected the contention that California's requirement for a referendum on public-housing proposals denied lower-income groups equal protection under the federal constitution. "Provisions for referendums," according to the majority opinion, "demonstrate devotion to democracy, not to bias, discrimination or prejudice." [69]

A number of suburbs wasted little time in demonstrating their "devotion to democracy." Following efforts of a developer to build a high-rise Section 236 project in Parma, a suburb in the Cleveland area, voters in November 1971 overwhelmingly endorsed a proposal requiring public approval for all subsidized housing projects. [70] Over the next eighteen months, similar provisions were enacted by a number of Cleveland's suburbs, including Eastlake, Middleburg Heights, Moreland Hills, Strongville, and Independence. [71] Racial fears were prominent in the controversy which led to enactment of the mandatory referendum requirement in Parma, which in 1970 had fifty black residents out of a population of 100,216. During consideration of the 236 proposal, one official announced that he did "not want Negroes in the City of Parma," while the mayor opposed opening Parma to poor families from the East Side of Cleveland, the city's sprawling black ghetto.[72] Two years later, in April 1973, the U.S. Department of Justice filed suit against Parma, alleging that the suburb's referendum requirement had "the purpose and effect of preventing the construction of racially integrated housing for persons of low and moderate income, and of discouraging prospective sponsors of such housing from attempting to build it in Parma."[73]

SPECIAL MESSAGE

YOUR ENTIRE ENDORSED DEMOCRATIC SLATE IS PLEDGED TO DEFEND THE RIGHTS OF THE RESIDENTS OF PARMA TO ESTABLISH BUILDING STANDARDS BY REFERENDUM BALLOT AND WILL FIGHT IN THE FEDERAL COURTS ANY PRESSURE FROM OUTSIDE AGENCIES OR ORGANIZATIONS.

Figure 4.2. Excerpt from a political advertisement, *Parma* (Ohio) *Sun Post*, May 3, 1973.

Subsidized Housing in the Suburbs

In the face of local inaction, zoning constraints, and other barriers, not much subsidized housing gets built in the suburbs. Even with the surge in construction following the enactment of the 235 and 236 programs,

Anthony Downs estimates that no more than a quarter of the record 433,480 subsidized units produced in 1971 were located in the suburbs.[74] Because the 1968 programs account for most of the subsidized housing built in the suburbs, almost no housing was built in suburbia for families with annual incomes below those required for 235 and 236 housing. In rapidly suburbanizing Suffolk County on the eastern end of Long Island, a total of 60 units of public housing was available in 1970 to serve a population of over one million. Suburban Baltimore County, which grew from 492,000 to 621,000 during the 1960s, opened its first 250 units of public housing in 1972. The resistance of most suburban governments to public housing has meant that almost all subsidized housing for the poor in the metropolis is located within the central cities. In 1970, St. Louis had 10,000 units of public housing for its 622,000 residents, while suburban St. Louis County had 50 units for a population of 956,000. One of the consequences of concentrating public housing in the urban core, of course, has been the reinforcement of the negative image of low-income housing held by most suburbanites, which in turn bolsters suburban determination to keep out projects which might serve city dwellers.

Much of the public housing that is built in the suburbs is reserved for the elderly. In the Boston area, where suburbs have constructed substantially more public housing than elsewhere in the nation, 65 percent of all units produced by suburban housing authorities through 1972 were for the elderly. By contrast, only 14 percent of the units in Boston's public-housing projects were designed for the elderly, although Boston, like most central cities, has a higher proportion of aged residents than most of the surrounding communities. The fears raised by public housing for families—blacks, crime, welfare, delinquency, overcrowded and downgraded schools—are muted in the case of housing for what a federal official calls "the socially safe elderly." [75] As a result, improved housing for Westport's "1,000 elderly is a cause without opponents" in the affluent suburb in southwestern Connecticut where residents bitterly oppose other proposals for apartments or subsidized housing.[76] In Ramapo, to the north of New York City, suburbanites were willing to accept the construction of 200 units of public housing only if 75 percent of the apartments were reserved for the elderly. And suburban housing agencies such as the Housing Authority of Cook County find that housing for the elderly is their only entrée to most suburbs.

Public housing for families outside the central cities tends to be located in older suburbs with substantial numbers of poor and minority residents. Suburbs with serious housing problems are more likely than communities with little blight to create local housing authorities or consent to the construction of family units by housing agencies with broader jurisdictions. For example, almost all of the 800 units of family housing produced by the Housing Authority of Cook County has been located in low-income, largely black, suburbs such as Chicago Heights and East Chicago Heights. In the latter community, where 300 units were built by the county agency, one of five of the municipality's 5,000 residents lived in public housing in 1972.

Lower-income areas also account for a good deal of the subsidized housing produced in the suburbs under the newer federal programs.

Table 4.3. Public Housing in Three Metropolitan Areas, 1972

Area	Total Region	Total Suburbs	Percent Suburbs	Total Suburbs for Elderly	Percent Elderly in Suburbs
Boston	39,261 *	17,375 †	.44	11,223	.65
Denver	5,376	410	.08	178	.43
Philadelphia	36,432	5,901 ‡	.16	1,913	.32

* Excludes leased public-housing units.
† All municipalities in the region except Boston, Brookline, Cambridge, Chelsea, Everett, and Somerville.
‡ All municipalities in the region except Philadelphia, Camden, and Trenton.
Sources: Metropolitan Area Planning Council, Subsidized Housing in the Boston Region as of December 31, 1972, Planning Information Series: Housing (Boston, 1973), p. 14; Denver Regional Council of Governments, Housing in the Denver Region, p. 24; and Delaware Valley Regional Planning Commission, "Subsidized Housing in the Delaware Valley," p. 16.

Land is cheaper in such communities, and its use less likely to be severely constrained by restrictive zoning regulations. A private builder located 400 units of 235 housing (all of which were sold to blacks) in Harvey, a suburb of 34,000 in the Chicago area whose black population increased from under 2,000 in 1960 to almost 11,000 in 1970. Large numbers of 235 units, as well as 500 apartments financed under the 236 program, were concentrated in a lower-income section of Montgomery County in the Washington area. High land costs in settled areas and resistance to subsidized housing in suburban municipalities in the Chicago area forced 235 and 236 developers to seek sites in isolated unincorporated areas, where county zoning controls have been minimal. Such areas have been termed "no man's land—a sort of Gaza Strip," by one federal official in Chicago.[77] Lacking public transportation, community and commercial facilities, and other amenities, the only thing these areas tend to attract is more subsidized housing.

High costs and zoning restrictions in the suburbs also have had a strong influence on the distribution of 235 and 236 housing across the nation. By and large, subsidized housing under the new programs has been located in metropolitan areas where land and construction costs have been low, zoning constraints minimal, and local resistance manageable. As a result, the South and the West proved far more hospitable to the new federal programs than the Northeast and Midwest. As indicated in Table 4.4, 43 percent of all the new and rehabilitated 235 and 236 units

Table 4.4. 235 and 236 Housing by Region, 1971

Area	1970 Pop. (000,000)	Percent of 1970 Pop.	Total 235 and 236	Percent of 235 and 236	235 and 236 per million
Northeast	49	.24	28,051	.11	572
North Central	56	.28	62,483	.25	1,116
South	62	.31	107,194	.43	1,729
West	34	.17	49,583	.20	1,458

Source: George Sternlieb, "Housing Subsidies Falling . . . Where the Housing Shortage Isn't," *New York Times*, Dec. 24, 1972.

developed in 1971 were in the South, almost four times as many as were located in the Northeast. The combination in the heavily urbanized Northeast of high costs, "suburbs . . . terrified of newcomers," and "central cities [which] frequently provide a hostile environment for new investment" has produced, in the view of one housing expert, "federally subsidized housing—where the consumers ain't." [78]

Reliance on private developers in the 235 and 236 programs also had an important effect on the availability of subsidized housing in the suburbs, particularly for blacks and other minoroties. After studying the home-ownership program in the Denver, Little Rock, Philadelphia, and St. Louis areas, the U.S. Commission on Civil Rights concluded in 1971 that "the traditional pattern of separate and unequal housing markets for majority and minority families is being repeated in the operation of Section 235." [79] According to the Commission:

> Most brokers and builders participating in the program marketed their houses to separate racial and ethnic groups. Operating on the assumption that minority buyers did not want to live outside areas of minority concentrations, both white and minority real estate brokers only showed minority

235 applicants houses in minority areas or "changing" neighborhoods. In some cases, brokers used discriminatory advertising to reach their chosen racial or ethnic market. . . .

Most builders also acted on the assumption that minority buyers would not want to live in white areas. The new 235 houses were constructed in predominantly white suburban areas and builders used newspaper ads designed to appeal to white buyers only, or limited their advertising to "open house" signs at the construction sites.[80]

As a result of these practices, most new suburban housing in the four metropolitan areas was purchased by whites, while minority buyers were largely limited to segregated subdivisions. Racial separation also has been the rule in Section 236 apartments built by private developers. Of 389 projects surveyed by the Department of Housing and Urban Development in 1971, 21 percent were all-white, 37 percent less than 15 percent black, and 24 percent more than half black.[81]

Few suburban governments objected to these racial practices in the 235 and 236 programs, just as officials in suburbia rarely challenge the policies of the private sector which more generally limit housing opportunities for blacks within their borders. In the typical suburb, most residents and officials tacitly endorse private housing practices which exclude blacks and depend upon the private sector to play a key role in the exclusion of minority groups. As a result, public support for fair housing is meager and positive commitment on the part of local officials rare. When subsidized housing is the issue, with all the fears it raises in the suburbs of blacks and other unwanted neighbors, suburbanites are most likely to challenge developers who deviate from the racially exclusionary practices which characterize the normal operations of the private housing sector in suburbia.

The paucity of public housing in the suburbs, the emphasis on housing for the elderly, the concentration of low-income units in poor and black suburbs, and racial barriers in the newer federal programs—all these combine to produce relatively little housing in suburbia that fits the suburban stereotype of subsidized housing attracting hordes of poor blacks on welfare from the central cities. Further reducing the likelihood of "outsiders" is the priority most suburbs give local residents in the subsidized housing they permit to be constructed. For example, in a 100-unit project underwritten by the New Jersey Housing Finance Agency in suburban Lawrence Township in which tenants were eligible for federal rent supplements, first priority was given to local residents living in substandard housing, second priority to former Lawrence residents forced to leave the community because of the lack of housing priced within their means, third to people working but not living in Lawrence, fourth to any resident of the township, and lowest priority to all others.

Because of these developments, white suburbanites rather than black city dwellers account for most of those who live in subsidized housing in the suburbs. A substantial portion are elderly. Most of the rest, particularly in 235 and 236 housing, are suburban families with moderate incomes—teachers, policemen, blue-collar workers, and others who have been priced out of conventional housing in the suburbs. The reality of subsidized housing in the suburbs, however, has done little to lessen suburban apprehension and opposition. As a result of this continuing hostility, few in the suburbs protested when the Nixon Administration—seeking to extricate itself from embarrassing scandals, rapidly mounting costs, and rising political conflict in city and suburb—declared a moratorium on federal subsidized housing programs at the end of 1972.[82]

On the other hand, for the minority of suburbanites who sought to expand housing opportunities in their communities, the federal moratorium constituted a fatal blow at the end of a long and perilous gauntlet. Promoters of subsidized housing who had survived local opposition, zoning restrictions, suburban moratoriums on new construction, rising costs, the reluctance of private developers to become involved in controversy, and the mind-boggling complexity of federal housing programs often found their plans dashed by the refusal of the Department of Housing and Urban Development to undertake new commitments for subsidized housing after January 1973. Suburban supporters of subsidized housing who were at an earlier stage of the arduous process often capitulated in the face of the loss of federal funds and encouragement. The result was a sharp drop in subsidized housing starts in 1973 and 1974, as well as the loss of momentum for many of those who struggled against unequal odds to lower suburban housing barriers.

Chapter Five

Unequal Odds

With growing awareness of the impact of suburban policies on metropolitan settlement patterns in the late 1960s came increasing criticism of local land-use and housing practices. One major civil-rights group, the National Committee Against Discrimination in Housing, concluded that "there can be no effective progress in halting the trend toward predominantly black cities surrounded by almost entirely white suburbs . . . until local governments have been deprived of the power to exclude subsidized housing and to manipulate zoning and other controls to screen out families on the basis of income and, implicitly, of race." [1] At the same time, the National Association for the Advancement of Colored People called the suburbs "the new civil rights battleground" and urged blacks "to do battle out in the townships and villages to lower zoning barriers and thereby create new opportunities for Negroes seeking housing closer to today's jobs at prices they can afford to pay." [2]

Similar views were being expressed by a wide variety of urban interests. Central-city officials castigated the suburbs and their business allies, warning that "if business and communities continue in the present mindlessly selfish way, we will Los Angelize our Land, Balkanize our Region's Finances, and South Africanize our Economy." [3] Residential developers attacked "selfish and exlusionary zoning barriers" and urged that a way "be found to get away from the constrictive home-rule aspects of the legislation that supports and protects these restrictions." [4] Editorials in metropolitan newspapers warned "the entrenched, well-to-do suburbanites" that they must recognize "that one-half of the nation cannot afford to build barriers of any sort against the other half—whether it be the barrier of racial discrimination or the practical barrier of long and time-consuming commuting." [5] And housing experts like Anthony

Downs condemned an "arrangement that benefits the wealthy and the middle class at the expense of loading large costs onto the very poor" as "a gross injustice that cries out for correction." [6]

To most of this clamor, the average suburbanite and the typical suburban office holder turn a deaf ear. Few of those who demand changes in local policies live within particular suburban jurisdictions in sufficient numbers to have a significant impact on local opinion or the actions of local officials. Lower-income and minority families which would benefit from relaxed suburban barriers are kept out of most communities by the high cost of housing and exclusionary policies motivated by racial prejudice, the fear of crime, fiscal and environmental considerations, and the desire to preserve community character. As a result, neither victims of exclusion nor local supporters of open housing usually can aggregate sufficient political strength to secure much influence or representation on local councils and planning boards, particularly in smaller and more homogeneous suburban jurisdictions.

The negative response of local political systems to calls for change also reflects the satisfaction of most suburbanites with the existing system of housing and land-use control. Relatively few residents of the suburbs see housing for less affluent groups as a major problem. Only 10 percent of those questioned in a survey in New York's Westchester

Table 5.1. Perceptions of State and Local Governmental Priorities by Residents of Westchester County, N.Y.

	All Residents	Upper & Middle Income Residents	Moderate & Lower Income Residents
		(Percent listing problem as important)	
Drugs	47	44	51
Property Taxes	46	48	43
Crime	31	30	31
Education	27	28	27
Air and Water Pollution	25	25	24
Help for Senior Citizens	25	20	34
Mass Transportation	21	24	15
Low & Mod. Income Housing	14	13	16
Middle Income Housing	10	8	14
Race Relations	8	9	7
New Jobs	8	9	7
Roads and Highways	7	8	6
Planning and Zoning	7	8	7
Recreation	7	9	4

Source: Oliver Quayle and Company, *A Survey of Attitudes Toward Government Assisted Moderate and Low Income Housing in Westchester County, New York*, Study #1546 (Bronxville, N.Y., 1972), p. 21.

County in 1972 expressed concern over housing problems. Drugs, property taxes, crime, education, pollution, the problems of the elderly, and mass transportation were all considered more important than broadened housing opportunities.[7]

In addition, few suburbanites are willing to acknowledge the role of suburban exclusion in fostering and maintaining an economically and racially separated society. Instead, most emphatically reject the notion that the "suburban sanctuary of the middle class has been created at the expense of the urban poor by compelling them to live in areas of concentrated poverty."[8] Nor are many suburban dwellers prepared to accept any responsibility for city residents and their housing problems. A suburban mayor in the Cleveland area believes "the public housing people are just looking for a lot of land for Cleveland's problems which Cleveland isn't willing to take care of,"[9] while in the St. Louis area an influential official rejects suburban involvement in "the problems of the unfortunate people in the city."[10]

Given local autonomy, the nature and attitudes of suburban constituencies, the benefits that residents of the suburbs derive from exclusionary policies, and the dependence of local governments on property taxes, the suburban political system provides few incentives for its components to act in anything but their self-interest. Speaking of the costs associated with subsidized housing, a suburban mayor emphasizes that "appeals to the good nature and selflessness of the suburban official or the suburban voter will be pointless if the economic cards are stacked the wrong way."[11] As a result of these political realities, most suburbs successfully resist pressures at the local level for major changes in their housing and zoning policies, particularly when the aim is the expansion of housing opportunities for lower-income and minority groups.

Variations Among Suburbs

Resistance, however, is not a universal suburban reaction to demands that local housing barriers be lowered. Large suburban jurisdictions with heterogeneous populations tend to be more responsive to pressures for change than smaller scale and relatively homogeneous suburbs. Opinion is less monolithic in these suburbs, and political leaders are less constrained by dominant constituency interests. In addition, minorities are more visible, their collective voices louder, and their interests more easily aggregated in larger jurisdictions. Big suburbs, particularly suburban county governments in major metropolitan areas, also are more likely to employ planning and housing professionals. These officials examine housing needs and development trends on a community-wide and metropolitan basis; and their professional training and personal values prompt concern with the problems of lower-income and minority groups.[12] All of these factors lead to greater recognition of housing problems by political leaders in suburban jurisdictions such as Nassau County in New York, which had 1.4 million residents in 1970. "There is no excuse for a generally affluent suburban community, where 90 percent of the people enjoy good housing," Nassau's elected executive told the county legislature in 1969, "to permit the other 10 percent to live in conditions which rival some of the worst slums in the nation." [13] Two large suburban counties in the Washington area, Fairfax and Montgomery, have been among the most active suburban governments in seeking to broaden housing opportunities for their diversifying populations. On the other hand, many large suburbs such as Oyster Bay in New York and Baltimore County steadfastly resist efforts to ease local housing restrictions.

Here and there, affluent suburbs with troubled social consciences seek to diversify their populations. In Princeton, a university community amidst the suburbs of central New Jersey with a penchant for both liberal causes and exclusionary zoning, the planning board warned in 1973 that "Princeton will become a one-class, upper-income community [unless] positive steps are taken to halt the trend." Arguing that "the health and vitality of the community depend on a diversity of people of different cultural backgrounds, ages, incomes, and interests," the local planners recommended that almost half of all new housing construction during the 1970s and 1980s be earmarked for families presently priced out of the local housing market.[14] Concern in Summit, an upper-income suburb of 25,000 in northern New Jersey, over housing conditions for local blacks led to community sponsorship of 90 units of low-rent garden apartments in 1968. Across the continent in Palo Alto, similar constituency concerns spurred the local government in 1972 to approve the construction of 740 units of mixed-income housing.

Local officials with strongly held views about the social responsibilities of their communities also can make a difference. A successful campaign for a limited number of units of subsidized housing in Ramapo in New York's Rockland County was led by the community's mayor, a self-styled "believe[r] in public housing from way back" who was "willing to absorb 500 units to make the point that public housing isn't the horrible thing that most of the recent expatriates from New York City think it is." [15] One of the few suburbs to react positively to efforts to disperse subsidized housing in the Milwaukee area was Brown Deer, whose manager argued that "the community . . . can afford to take care of a number of people that are disadvantaged." [16] Relatively few suburban officials, however, get very far in front of their constituents on an issue as sensitive as housing for lower-income families. A survey of attitudes toward subsidized housing in the Dayton area found that "the majority of the public officials, whether elected or appointed, are knowledgeable concerning the attitudes and preferences of their constituents—and the majority are willing to incorporate these desires into their policy and program formulations.[17] Similar findings emerged from a study of suburban officials in New Jersey.[18] Reinforcing these cautious tendencies is the fact that local opponents are almost always more vociferous than supporters of expanded housing opportunities.

Fear of losing local autonomy also has motivated some suburban leaders to advocate eased zoning barriers. In the view of a council member in an exclusive Connecticut suburb, "local zoning restrictions must be eased not only for social reasons, but because if this does happen, then sooner or later our local autonomy or choice will be taken away by the State Legislature." [19] While unmoved by arguments concerning the social responsibility of suburbanites, a business leader in another affluent Connecticut suburb endorses opening the door a bit because "if we don't get 50 units in the next five years, we'll get 500 units in ten years, probably built by Big Brother." [20]

For most suburbanites, however, perhaps the only persuasive argument for relaxing exclusionary barriers is the housing needs of local residents. In the Westchester County survey, 78 percent agreed with the statement: "I tend to favor more moderate and low income housing in Westchester so that public servants such as teachers, firemen, and policemen can live in the communities they serve"; while 70 percent supported "more subsidized low and moderate income housing in Westchester to enable our young people to stay here instead of being forced to live elsewhere." [21] Support for subsidized housing was heavily conditioned on its availability to members of the local community. While 83 percent were favorable if first priority was given to "people now living in this town . . . and second priority to people now working here," 76 percent were opposed if no priorities were assigned on the basis of where the occupants lived or worked. [22]

Concern over the housing needs of local public employees was the principal factor underlying the enactment of legislation in Fairfax and Montgomery Counties designed to spur the construction of lower-cost housing by private developers. The Fairfax Board of Supervisors approved a series of ordinances in 1971 requiring that six percent of the housing in most developments of fifty or more units be priced below $20,000, and that nine percent be priced between $20,000 and $25,000, provided that federal subsidies were available. A somewhat similar plan was adopted by the Montgomery County Council in 1973.[23] A group of ministers organized as the Coalition for Housing Action led the campaign in Fairfax, and placed heavy emphasis on the needs of county employees, 90 percent of whom earned less than $12,000 a year in 1971. Supporters of the new law in Montgomery also stressed the needs of employees, pointing to the requirement that county police officers making $12,000 a year were required to live within a jurisdiction where an annual income of $25,000 was needed to purchase a new home in 1973. In both counties, backing for the housing plans came from public employees. Typical was the view of the Fairfax County Police Association which emphasized that "most of our police officers, in order to buy a home, must go out into Prince William and Loudon Counties. We feel they should be able to buy housing here." [24]

In most suburbs, however, concern over local housing needs is not automatically translated into broadened housing opportunities. The fact that "our own cops, firemen, and teachers can't buy houses in Westport" [25] led the Planning and Zoning Commission of the affluent Connecticut suburb to approve a change in local zoning in 1973 to permit the construction of 400 apartments in scattered sites, with sixty of the units priced within the range of town employees and others with moderate incomes. Within a month, vehement opposition to apartments from residents prompted the forty-member representative town meeting to overturn unanimously the proposed apartment ordinance. In Bergen County in northern New Jersey, 1,600 residents of a community signed petitions that helped kill a garden-apartment proposal despite concerns such as those expressed by one local resident: "My daughter will be getting married in a few years and I'd like to see her remain here. A nice little development wouldn't hurt anyone. Give our kids a chance. It's unfair. We had our chance to move out here." [26]

Opposition to improving housing opportunities for local residents stems from many of the basic considerations that fuel the politics of exclusion—dislike of apartments, the bad image of subsidized housing, fear of community change, worries about property values, and concern over local services and taxes. Another important factor is the suspicion of suburbanites that priority for local residents cannot be maintained if the barriers to the construction of lower-cost housing are lowered. As the mayor of one of New Jersey's largest suburbs notes: "We'd welcome lower-cost housing for our youth and elderly. But there's no guarantee we could keep it for them. And given the choice, we just won't do it." [27] Or as an opponent of liberalized zoning in another suburb in New Jersey puts it: "You can't provide housing for your sons and daughters and still keep people from Paterson from moving in." [28]

Variations among suburbs also reflect the inherent difficulty of achieving general policy changes in a decentralized polity through political action at the grass roots. Extraordinary political resources, a highly decentralized base of support, or a widely perceived need for action resulting from a crisis are required to produce similar policy changes in large numbers of local governments. When the units are small and numerous, as is the case with suburbs in most of the larger metropolitan areas, the prospects for securing general policy changes through grass-roots efforts are further reduced. At best, such efforts are likely to result in occasional victories and piecemeal change in local policies.

Local Arenas and Local Interests

Because of the obstacles to broad-based action at the grass roots, the suburban political arena primarily attracts those with local interests and narrow objectives. Groups whose concerns transcend a particular locality tend to focus their energies on the states, the national government, or the courts, where successful efforts frequently result in policy changes which affect large numbers of local jurisdictions rather than only a single unit as is the case with victories at the grass roots.

Efforts to change suburban housing and land-use policies have followed this general pattern quite closely. Among open housing groups, challenges at the grass roots have come primarily from locally oriented interests, such as fair-housing committees, neighborhood stabilization groups, civic and civil-rights organizations, and community-based developers of low-cost housing. Typically, these interests have limited objectives and capabilities. They tend to focus on housing conditions in their particular community and the needs of local residents. More often than not, their activities are confined to a single jurisdiction. Thus, a suburban fair-housing committee seeks to expand housing opportunities for middle-income blacks within its community, while a local civil-rights group campaigns for municipal approval of a housing project for lower-income families.

As suburban housing restrictions attracted increasing attention in the late 1960s, national civil-rights and religious groups, labor unions, foundations, and public-interest organizations were drawn to the issue. Unlike local groups, these broader interests devoted little of their energy to persuading individual suburban governments to change their housing and land-use policies. Few had the capability, experience, or desire to take on the suburbs directly. Moreover, their objective was policy changes which would improve the access of lower-income and minority groups to housing in large numbers of suburban jurisdictions rather than in a particular community. Thus, even when dealing "with local cases or problems," as Sheilds and Spector emphasize, the national open-housing interests "seek situations which will have importance nationally." [29]

These objectives led the American Civil Liberties Union, the Lawyers' Committee for Civil Rights Under Law, the NAACP Legal Defense and Education Fund, and the National Housing and Economic Development Law Project to focus almost exclusively on court actions designed to overturn restrictive suburban housing and land-use policies. Other national groups, such as the Leadership Conference on Civil Rights, the Center for National Policy Review, and the Housing Opportunities Council of Metropolitan Washington, concentrated on lobbying for changes in federal policies. Coordination, and the collection and dissemination of information concerning suburban housing problems were the primary activities of another set of groups, including the National Urban Coalition, the Exclusionary Land-Uses Practices Clearing House, and the National Job-Linked Housing Center.[30]

Not all national open-housing interests, however, eschew involvement at the local level. Much of the energy of the National Committee Against Discrimination in Housing since its creation in 1950 has been devoted to the organization of fair-housing groups at the grass roots and efforts to secure local fair-housing legislation. Other national organizations with local affiliates have been active at the suburban grass roots. A number of the NAACP's 1,700 local branches sought to broaden housing opportunities in particular suburbs. Local affiliates of the American Jewish Committee and the Urban League also have been engaged in grass-roots activities designed to broaden housing opportunities in the suburbs.

Among the national organizations interested in opening the suburbs, probably the most active at the local level has been the League of Women Voters. The League is more decentralized than the other major open-housing groups as well as being the only one with a substantial political base in suburbia. A federation of 1,250 chapters with a largely white, upper-income suburban membership of 170,000, the League places considerable emphasis on local autonomy and grass-roots action. In the early 1970s, over 100 of its chapters were engaged in efforts "to educate their communities to the goal of a free choice of a decent home in a decent environment for every family." [31] In the process, LWV chapters pressed for the creation of local housing authorities, supported the construction of low-income housing, participated in the organization of nonprofit development corporations to sponsor subsidized housing, fought local discriminatory practices, endorsed zoning reform, and backed metropolitan "fair-share" plans for the allocation of subsidized housing among suburban jurisdictions.

Despite the importance of local activities for groups such as the NAACP, NCDH, and LWV, none concentrated all of its efforts on grass-roots activities. The national headquarters of the NAACP challenged suburban zoning in the courts, lobbied for open housing in Washington, and conducted educational efforts aimed at reducing suburban hostility to residential integration. During the 1970s, NCDH became increasingly committed to suburban housing activities that transcend particular localities, including litigation, lobbying in Congress and administrative agencies, and research and technical assistance. Even the highly decentralized League of Women Voters entered the judicial arena through its national litigation office.

Given the orientation of the broader-based open-housing interests, the primary burden for action at the suburban grass roots falls on local groups, be they purely local or affiliated with national organizations. Among these organizations, substantial differences exist in size, resources, and constituency base. Their objectives, programs, priorities, vitality, visibility, and effectiveness also vary considerably. In general, diversity reduces the incidence of cooperation and cohesion among open-housing interests within a particular community or suburban area. Collective action also is impeded by the fragmentation of local government in suburbia, since supporters of open housing typically are scattered among a variety of local jurisdictions. And the combination of group diversity and dispersed constituency support handicaps efforts to change local housing policies in the hostile political climate of the typical suburban jurisdiction.

Among the various open-housing interests in the suburbs, fair-housing groups are the most common. A substantial majority of the more than 2,000 local fair-housing committees in the United States have been organized in suburban areas. Their goal is the elimination of racial discrimination in the sale and rental of housing, and they have taken the lead in pressing for the enactment of fair-housing ordinances and local human-relations commissions in the suburbs. Most suburban fair-housing groups lack professional staff, have a membership composed largely of upper-income whites, and devote much of their energy to finding housing for blacks who can afford to live in the suburbs.

Exceptions to this general pattern are the handful of fair-housing groups which have full-time staff, a substantial membership base, and other resources which enable them to pursue more ambitious and systematic programs. For example, the Mid-Peninsula Citizens for Fair Housing in the San Francisco area tests compliance with local fair-housing laws, investigates complaints of racial discrimination, undertakes legal actions against discriminatory housing practices, seeks to educate local officials and the suburban housing industry about their legal obligations to insure equal housing opportunities, and campaigns more generally for open housing. Elsewhere, larger and more sophisticated fair-housing groups operate housing information centers and comprehensive housing listing services, provide counseling services for families seeking homes in the suburbs, and undertake "carefully planned and conducted testing operations for the purpose of filing complaints with state human rights agencies and with HUD and the Department of Justice." [32]

Despite the increasing sophistication and capability of some fair-housing groups, most continue to focus their resources on discriminatory practices affecting the access of blacks to the existing housing stock in suburbia. Relatively few local groups have followed in the footsteps of the national fair-housing organization, NCDH, which in the 1970s placed more and more emphasis on increasing the supply of lower-cost housing in the suburbs and removing zoning and other local barriers which reinforce segregated residential patterns. Typical of the attitude of local groups is that of the Fair Housing Congress of Southern California, which sees so much illegal discrimination in the existing housing market that its leaders are reluctant to divert their scarce resources to other activities.

Another local open-housing interest with a limited perspective on the suburban housing problem is the neighborhood stabilization movement. Neighborhood stabilization groups were organized in the 1960s in a number of city and suburban areas undergoing racial transformation. Their primary concern was existing housing conditions, and the creation of stable racially-integrated neighborhoods. Most of these groups and their umbrella organization, the National Neighbors, "have recognized that to stabilize any one neighborhood, it is essential to assure an open housing market and general mobility." [33] These groups, however, tend to be preoccupied with neighborhood problems; and few have the time or resources to get very involved in broader issues such as production of suburban housing or removal of local barriers to the outward movement of lower-income and minority families. Moreover, most of the stabilization groups are active in communities undergoing racial transformation, which typically are the result rather than the cause of suburban exclusion.

Direct challenges of suburban zoning and housing policies usually come from more amorphous local groupings. Campaigns for subsidized housing and zoning reform have been launched by local coalitions of civil-rights, civic, and religious groups. Similar groupings have organized nonprofit housing corporations in suburbs. In Princeton, New Jersey, for example, the local chapter of the League of Women Voters and other community groups formed Princeton Community Housing to build subsidized housing. Nonprofit housing corporations which have sought to build in the suburbs also have been created by labor unions as in the case of the Region Nine United Automobile Workers Housing Corporation in Mahwah, New Jersey, religious groups like the Park View Heights Corporation in Black Jack in the St. Louis area and the Interfaith Housing Corporation in the Boston region, and minority-group organizations such as the Colored People's Civic and Political Organization in Lackawanna outside Buffalo and the Southern Alameda Spanish Speaking Organization in suburban Union City in the San Francisco Bay area.

More often than not, these efforts are limited to a single local jurisdiction. When the groups involved also are locally based, there tends to be a heavy emphasis on community needs. Local groups and coalitions seeking eased zoning, the creation of a local housing authority, or permission for a nonprofit housing corporation to build suburban housing typically stress the community's responsibilities to its own residents rather than its obligations to lower-income and minority families in general. Suburban open-housing interests are especially likely to ignore or downplay the housing needs of inner-city blacks.

Even when suburban open-housing groups have a broader perspective, political realities often narrow their focus. The ministers who launched the campaign for zoning reform in Fairfax County initially were drawn to the issue by concern over the plight of blacks unable to find housing outside the District of Columbia. As the campaign developed, however, the search for support led the Coalition for Housing Action to an increasing emphasis on local housing needs, and especially the housing problems of teachers, policemen, and other local-government employees, most of whom were white. The leaders of the campaign justified the shift on pragmatic grounds. They also argued that increasing the stock of lower-cost housing in Fairfax would inevitably benefit inner-city blacks. "When you open up a community economically," insisted the Rev. Gerald Hopkins, "you open it up racially." [34] But this objective of zoning reform was rarely voiced during the drive for political support among the overwhelmingly white population of Fairfax County.

Opening the Suburbs Through Confrontation

Concern for local sensibilities, priorities, and political feasibility has not been a conspicuous feature of the activities of the Suburban Action Institute, a public-interest organization founded in 1969 by Paul Davidoff, a planner and attorney, and Neil Gold, a former staff member of NCDH. Based in Westchester County, Suburban Action directly challenged local zoning in a variety of communities in the New York area. Unlike most local open-housing groups in the suburbs, SAI emphasized the need "to open the suburbs for all, in particular for the non-affluent and non-white." [35] Suburban Action's stress on bringing blacks and the poor to affluent suburbs, its insistence on far-reaching changes in local housing and land-use policies, and the abrasive and publicity-oriented style of its founders made SAI the most controversial of all the open-housing interests active at the suburban grass roots. The organization's approach is reflected in the rhetoric of Paul Davidoff, its chief spokesman:

> Suburban populations . . . have employed the power of the state to protect their own very selfish desire to create a community that is amenable to

themselves, but to prohibit the large mass of the population from sharing in those amenities. They have not bought the land, but instead have done the cheap and nasty thing of employing the police power to protect their own interest in the land and to exclude the largest part of the population. . . . We think this is terribly abusive, terribly inappropriate for a group which is politically not inclined to argue the case for increased government control.[36]

Suburban Action's perspective on housing in the suburbs has been broader than that of most local open-housing groups. SAI stressed the linkages between the plight of the older cities and suburban policies which restrict access to housing and jobs. For Davidoff, "decent housing means reasonable access to employment, good education, recreation and environment, and . . . the key to these is locational choice." [37] In broadening locational choices, and in particular in creating "new opportunities for linking suburban jobs to unemployed and underemployed residents of slums and ghettos," SAI saw the contemporary problem in the suburbs "as larger and more complex than the fair housing issue of the fifties and sixties . . . [when] no changes were necessary in the allocation of land resources." [38] Solution of this problem, in SAI's view, required fundamental changes in the suburban land-use control system, heavy emphasis on the production of housing for lower-income and minority groups in the suburbs, and public policies which insured that low-cost housing was dispersed throughout the metropolis.

To accomplish these objectives, Suburban Action engaged in a wide range of activities. Research was undertaken on a variety of suburban housing and land-use issues. Efforts were made to educate and raise the consciousness of suburbanites, large suburban employers, and opinion leaders. Local zoning ordinances and housing policies were criticized in a variety of local forums and the media, with the "focus on rich people's communities, especially those with rich liberals as residents." [39] Information and advice was provided to governmental units concerned with suburban exclusion, including the Pennsylvania Department of Community Affairs and the city of Hartford, Connecticut. Corporate decisions to locate offices and plants in suburban areas which excluded moderately-priced housing developments also came under fire, with SAI filing complaints with the Equal Employment Opportunities Commission and other federal agencies in an effort to check corporate moves to exclusionary suburbs. Litigation was another important element of Suburban Action's program. By early 1974, it had brought suit against dozens of suburbs in the New York area. SAI also went to court to block the federal government from making sewer and recreation grants to an exclusionary suburb in Westchester County, to prevent construction of an Internal Revenue Service processing center in a community on Long Island with strict housing controls, and to force construction of low-cost housing on the site of a former military base in Nassau County.[40]

Of most importance to local government, and certainly the most controversial of Suburban Action's activities, were its efforts to build housing in suburbs with restrictive land-use controls. Typically, SAI quietly secured options on land, often in conjunction with private developers. Then plans were prepared for a major housing development which could not be implemented without changes in local zoning. Finally, a well-publicized announcement of the plan was accompanied by a threat to seek judicial relief if local approval is not forthcoming. In 1973, for example, SAI declared that it was ready to develop housing for 8,000 people on 253 acres adjacent to Candlewood Lake in New Fairfield, Connecticut, in the northeastern corner of the New York area. In explaining how the plan would be implemented in the face of local hostility, Neil Gold indicated that Suburban Action probably would have to go to court, and expressed confidence "that the courts will sustain our right to build a mixed-income, racially integrated community on Candlewood Lake." [41]

Suburban Action unveiled similar plans for a number of other suburbs in the early 1970s. Most ambitious was a scheme for a $150-million planned community on 720 acres in Mahwah in northern New Jersey. If built, the project would almost triple Mahwah's 1970 population of 10,000. Of the 6,000 housing units in the proposed new community, 2,400 were to be priced for families with annual incomes under $10,000, with the remainder within reach of those with incomes of less than $20,000 a year. In this instance, litigation preceded the housing proposal, as SAI challenged restrictive zoning in Mahwah and three neighboring suburbs in the courts a few months before its plans for "Ramapo Mountain" were announced.[42] For Readington, a rural area strategically located in the path of suburbanization in New Jersey's Hunterdon County, SAI sought to have 230 acres rezoned from single-family homes on large lots to permit the construction of 2,000 apartments. In Western Suffolk County on Long Island, Suburban Action wanted to build as many as 6,000 housing units on 400 or more acres. And an 850-unit complex was designed for a site in Fairfax County in Virginia.

The coupling of local development plans with court action reflected SAI's conviction that litigation alone would do little to broaden housing opportunities for lower-income families in the suburbs. Unless open-housing groups were prepared to construct housing when suburban land became available, private builders and affluent families would be the prime beneficiaries of successful litigation against zoning. To provide home-building capability, SAI created Garden Cities Development Corporation to handle the preparation of development plans, land acquisition, and construction. Although Garden Cities was "geared up [and] ready to move" in 1974,[43] the development corporation had yet to construct a single unit of housing in any of its proposed new communities.

In fact, except for stimulating a flock of lawsuits, nowhere had the politics of confrontation borne fruit for SAI. Instead, the proposals of Suburban Action and Garden Cities encountered fierce local resistance. Three-fourths of the adults in New Fairfield, a community of 8,000, signed petitions against the SAI plan for Candlewood Lake; and the local zoning board unanimously rejected the project. In another Connecticut suburb where SAI took an option on eleven acres for the purpose of building 160 units of Section 236 housing, the mayor told the press that "everyone I've spoken to is wholeheartedly opposed to the project"; [44] and the local planning board refused to rezone the land in question. A local official in Suffolk County insisted that "they are going to have to abide by our zoning ordinances" and predicted "an uphill fight all the way" if SAI persisted with its planned 6,000 housing units on Long Island.[45] Nor was local support forthcoming in Mahwah, whose mayor indicated that "the town and the country are fed up with loudmouths and radicals seeking to divide us and destroy everything we love and have worked for." [46] The planning board in Mahwah refused to consider SAI's request for rezoning, citing a moratorium it had imposed on rezoning pending revision of the local master plan, a revision prompted in part by the fact that the existing master plan permitted planned-unit development in the area selected by Suburban Action for "Ramapo Mountain."

In all of these suburbs, SAI's motives in seeking changes in local housing and land-use policies were attacked. "What are they going to get out of it?" was constantly asked by suburbanites in communities confronted by SAI.[47] Fueling these questions was the involvement of Suburban Action and Garden Cities with private developers and landowners. SAI was accused by a prominent resident of Candlewood Lake of playing "the part of a destroyer" by paving the way for "big land speculators" who are "cheering every time Suburban Action Institute brings another suit in another court." [48] Suspicions about SAI's arrange-

ments with private developers, as well as complaints about its efforts to
influence local legislation, prompted suburban foes to seek a federal investigation of the organization's tax-exempt status. Suburban Action also
was called "a racist organization" which "uses black Americans as pawns
and patsies in its effort to upset the zoning laws." According to this
critic, SAI had no real concern with the housing problems of inner-city
blacks and Puerto Ricans, most of whom could not afford to live in the
developments proposed by Suburban Action and Garden Cities. Instead,
the plight of lower-income blacks was "a means by which Suburban Action Institute can wheedle money from foundations and instill a feeling
of guilt in middle-class white liberals." [49]

To counter local opposition, Suburban Action's founders hoped to
build "a local base of support" among "the suburban church; builders
and housing developers; some groups within the fair housing movement;
and suburban employers of low and moderately skilled workers." [50] Little backing for SAI, however, came from any of these groups. Other
open-housing interests in the suburbs found Suburban Action's aggressive style counter-productive. They feared that their efforts would be
jeopardized by the backlash from local confrontations with SAI. In addition, Suburban Action had, in the view of its founders, "run up against
strong opposition" because of its insistence "that local housing groups
begin to demand housing not only to meet the needs of local residents,
but also to meet the needs of the region's population." [51]

Relations between Suburban Action and broader-based housing interests also were turbulent. SAI was criticized by other groups for its
emphasis on publicity and conflict, its lack of results, and its limited capability to follow through on a multiplying set of projects. Publicity em-
anating from Suburban Action rarely gave attention to other groups
allied with SAI in litigation, even when Suburban Action was not the
principal party in the suit. The ability of SAI to attract media and public
attention also led to considerable jealousy among other open-housing organizations.

While winning Suburban Action few allies in the suburbs or within
the open-housing fraternity, public attention helped SAI secure funds
from the handful of social-action oriented foundations which succor all of
the major open-housing groups. Suburban Action received support from
the Field Foundation, the Ford Foundation, the Dr. and Mrs. Martin
Peretz Foundation, the Florence and John Schumann Foundation, the
Stern Foundation, the Taconic Foundation, and the Fund for New Jer-

sey. In fact, most of the major victories of Suburban Action's politics of confrontation were won in the board rooms of foundations during its first six years rather than in suburban town halls. While these successes enabled Suburban Action to make some headway with two of its prime aims—"to document social and economic discrimination [and] focus public attention on it"—the unequal odds posed by the local political arena to the advocates of open housing in the suburbs thwarted SAI's professed central purpose of developing "strategies that can lever significant change." [52] Unable to make any progress with its ambitious plans in the face of local opposition, and thus increasingly unable to attract foundation funds, Suburban Action was moribund by the end of 1975.

The Lack of a Suburban Constituency for Open Housing

Regardless of their approach, open-housing groups in the suburbs have failed to mobilize significant constituency support. This failure results primarily from the desire of most suburbanites to maintain existing local housing and land-use policies rather than from the organizational, strategic, and tactical weakness of open-housing interests in the suburbs. To be sure, an approach such as Suburban Action's which emphasized large-scale change and suburban responsibilities for the urban poor is much less likely to appeal to residents of the suburbs than efforts which seek small additions to the local housing stock to meet the needs of those who live and work in a particular community. Even when campaigns are focused on local needs, however, widespread support rarely is forthcoming.

Among the various components of the suburban population, lower-income suburbanites clearly have the most to gain from an expansion of the supply of moderately-priced housing. Joseph Kraft has identified three groups of "suburban malcontents" who he sees as providing support for those who would dismantle "fortress suburbia"—blue-collar workers, older people, and younger suburbanites. [53]

These residents, however, are hardly a cohesive force in suburban politics. Large numbers of suburbanites with modest incomes have little stake in increasing housing opportunities. Many are homeowners who perceive a substantial interest in the suburban status quo. Others are satisfied with their existing housing. Even more are fearful that relaxed housing and land-use controls will bring blacks into their neighborhoods. These racial fears are played on with considerable success by opponents of open housing in the suburbs. Awareness of these fears also leads advocates of change to deemphasize or ignore the needs of blacks in their efforts to mobilize support from lower-income whites in suburbia.

Those lower-income suburbanites who are dissatisfied with existing housing conditions commonly lack influence in most suburban political arenas. The spatial differentiation of the suburban population leaves many jurisdictions with few lower-income residents. In the communities where poorer suburbanites live, those with modest incomes typically participate less than the more affluent. They tend to be poorly informed, to fail to perceive their stake in local public policies, and to lack the time, resources, skills, and organizational capabilities to promote and defend their interests effectively. Further limiting the influence of lower-income groups is the small scale of most suburbs, which makes it difficult for minority interests to overcome their political weaknesses by the strength of numbers, as is possible in larger jurisdictions.

Because they often possess an organizational base which others with modest incomes lack, public employees have been more active on housing issues than other lower-income suburbanites. Local public employees played an important part in the campaigns for zoning reform in Fairfax and Montgomery Counties. Teachers, firemen, nurses, and other local civil servants were mobilized in Greenwich, Connecticut, during the mid-1960s to support rezoning so that they could realize the "dream of owning a moderately priced house in their hometown." [54] Such efforts have been limited, however. Socio-economic differentiation and the small scale of most suburbs means that many local employees do not live in the same jurisdiction in which they work. As a result, local employees and other less-affluent residents of the suburbs neither have flocked to the banners of the open-housing movement nor otherwise organized effectively to press for changes in local housing policies in most of suburbia.

Black residents of the suburbs also have provided little support for the open-housing movement at the grass roots. Since many suburban blacks have relatively modest incomes, the same factors which limit involvement of lower-income whites in local politics restrict black participation. Further constraining the political capabilities of suburban blacks on the housing issue is their concentration in a handful of jurisdictions and their almost complete exclusion from many suburbs. In addition, blacks who have made the move to attractive suburban areas often are as hostile to open-housing policies as whites. Frequently with good reason, middle-class blacks fear that their neighborhoods will be the prime targets for subsidized housing should suburban housing barriers be lowered. Opposition from homeowners caused local officials in North Hempstead on Long Island to drop plans for the construction of public-housing units in a black neighborhood. In Manhasset, also on Long Island, middle-class blacks organized as the Great Neck Civic Association fought the location of a $10-million public-housing project adjacent to their homes, contending that it would concentrate minority housing.

Because of these constraints, blacks have not been conspicuous in most open-housing groups. While the NAACP has had some success in mobilizing black suburbanites, the prime thrust of NAACP activity in the suburbs has come from the organization's national headquarters rather than from blacks at the grass roots. And when blacks become involved in housing controversies in the suburbs, their outrage at suburban exclusion often is counterproductive to the building of support for open housing among whites. A case in point is the statement of the chairman of the NAACP chapter in Plainfield, an aging New Jersey suburb with a sizable black population, to the planning board of wealthy and exclusive Bedminster. Arguing against Western Electric's proposal to locate its corporate headquarters in a community with five-acre zoning and no provision for apartments, Frank Allen warned that "the black folk from Newark and other towns around you will soon be here to destroy you. You will get the same thing here as they did in ancient Rome when the barbarians came down. May God bless you in your hypocritical way for trying to zone out the black people in this county and township." [55]

Among other groups in suburbia, support for open housing comes primarily from backers of liberal causes at the upper end of the income and education scales. Affluent suburbanites troubled by the socio-economic separation of the metropolis provide most of the backing for the efforts of fair-housing organizations, chapters of the League of Women Voters, affiliates of the American Jewish Committee, and other groups promoting open housing. They also constitute most of the audience for educational efforts in the suburbs. Most of the 2,000 suburbanites who discussed housing issues at "town meetings" sponsored by the Regional Plan Association in the New York area were "people with college educations and substantial incomes." [56]

Inevitably, much of the effort of local open-housing interests is focused on affluent suburbanites. The League of Women Voters boasts that "our constituency is best able to handle breaking down zoning barriers in terms of eliminating prejudice and fears" because its members are "right next door to the people they're trying to persuade." [57] League members, however, usually live next door to other well-educated, upper-income suburbanites. Such individuals are less likely to be hostile to lowering local housing barriers than residents of white-collar Black Jack, blue-collar Warren, or hundreds of other less-affluent suburbs which rarely are strongholds of the League of Women Voters.

While building support among upper-income suburbanites is hardly a waste of time (witness the fierce opposition in New Fairfield to Suburban Action's plan for Candlewood Lake), affluent liberals in the suburbs do not provide a sufficient constituency base for open-housing action in most communities. In the typical metropolitan area, such individuals constitute a significant proportion of the population in only a handful of suburbs. Where concerned suburbanites are concentrated, local governments often are more willing to seek to diversify their populations than is generally the case. Even when successful, however, the impact of these efforts is inherently limited by the small number of jurisdictions involved. Also restricting the amount of lower-cost housing that is feasible within these suburbs is local concern about higher taxes, fears of change in community character, and the high price of land in wealthier suburban areas. Whatever housing results, it usually falls short of the needs of local residents, to say nothing of a particular suburb's "fair share" of the housing needs in the metropolis as a whole. It is probably true that "communities with the attitude of Summit are in a ratio of one to several hundred," as NCDH noted in praising the New Jersey suburb for its plans to provide low-cost housing for local blacks.[58] But the ninety planned units would accommodate less than a quarter of Summit's families with housing problems. And four years after the plan was announced, only forty of the units had been constructed, with progress on the remainder stalled by siting controversies.

Moreover, within this "natural" constituency of better-educated and affluent suburbanites, open-housing groups have faced increasingly severe competition for support from the environmental movement. Throughout suburbia, upper-income activists have been diverted from housing problems by the rising concern with ecological issues. In the competition for constituency support in the suburbs in the early 1970s, environmental protection enjoyed a considerable advantage over open housing. Preserving the local environment is an inherently less conten-

tious issue in affluent suburbs than lowering housing barriers, since almost all suburbanites have a direct interest in protecting the local environment. Safeguarding the environment attracts both those who favor
expanding suburban housing opportunities and those who want to maintain exclusionary housing and land-use policies in their communities.
Greater concern for the environment appeals to the former because of
their interest in more effective planning, more rational development patterns, and more control of urban sprawl. For the latter, the environmental movement provides a respectable rationale for opposition to the
lowering of local housing barriers. Ecological concerns also benefitted in
the suburbs by being a new issue—an important consideration for any
issue in terms of its public appeal, particularly among those participants
in politics whose involvement often is motivated by more than self-interest.

Because of the overlapping constituency and broad popular appeal of
environmental concerns in the suburbs, housing advocates have been understandably reluctant to risk direct confrontation between the two interests. Instead, groups such as NCDH and Suburban Action have emphasized the compatibility of opening the suburbs and safeguarding the
environment, and have worked to bring housing and environmental interests together in order to reconcile differences and emphasize common
concerns. Support for the notion of compatibility has come from a
number of socially oriented environmentalists. At a conference on "The
Environment of the Open Society" sponsored by Suburban Action Institute in 1973, Ian McHarg, an ecological planner, insisted that "proper
ecological study cannot be used for exclusionary purposes." [59]

Emphasizing "proper ecological study" and the misuse of legitimate
ecological concerns, however, oversimplifies the inherent conflict between the goals of the environmental and open-housing movements.
Preserving the environment through the regulation of growth cannot be
fully compatible with expanding housing opportunities. Environmentalists seek to redress the balance between nature and man. Housing
advocates, on the other hand, argue that "people have got to come
first." [60] Protectors of the environment stress the need to conserve land,
while housing activists insist that "we are filthy rich with land in
America's metropolitan areas." [61] Even when exclusionary motives are
absent, environmentally inspired land-use controls limit the land available for development, thus increasing its cost and reducing its use for
lower-cost housing. An ordinance in Contra Costra County in the San

Francisco Bay area sponsored by local environmental groups required 500 square feet of green space for each new housing unit, a provision which an NCDH official believed would "substantially increase the cost of multiple unit housing and virtually foreclose the possibility of low to moderate cost construction." [62] Goal conflict, rather than the use of ecological arguments to bolster exclusion, creates most of the cross-pressures on the affluent suburban constituency shared by the housing and environmental movements.

A pair of court actions on suburban Long Island illustrate the inherent conflict between environmental groups opposed to growth and advocates of opening the suburbs for lower-income groups. Concern over the spread of higher density development led the Suffolk County Defenders of the Environment in 1970 to sue the county and forty local governments in an effort to halt all construction pending the development and implementation of land-use controls based on ecological considerations. A few months later, the NAACP filed a suit against Oyster Bay in adjoining Nassau County which sought to remove zoning and other local barriers to the construction of subsidized housing. As Richard F. Babcock and David L. Callies point out, "the NAACP is suing to compel the dismantling of barriers to the construction of precisely the same sort of housing, in virtually the same area, as the Suffolk County Defenders of the Environment are suing to prevent." [63]

Looking Elsewhere

At best, grass-roots advocates of opening the suburbs face unequal odds in their efforts to persuade local governments to alter housing and land-use policies. Local autonomy gives a community's residents the upper hand in most contests with open-housing interests; and in the typical suburb, an overwhelming majority of local residents are likely to favor maintenance of the status quo. Reinforcing this resistance, particularly in less affluent communities, is widespread suburban identification of open housing with inundation by blacks from the inner city. Further weakening the position of challengers of local policies is the lack of common concerns and cohesiveness among the various open housing interests, the low levels of political involvement on the part of those suburbanites most disadvantaged by existing policies, and the cross-cutting influence of the environmental movement on the upper-income issue-oriented constituency which provides most of the support for open housing in the suburbs. Given these circumstances, it is not surprising that local open-housing efforts either fail or are too limited to have much impact on metropolitan housing patterns.

Local resistance to change, the obstacles to aggregating influence within a particular community, and the marginal impact of success in a single jurisdiction inevitably led open-housing advocates to look elsewhere for support in their efforts to open the suburbs. Most of the broader-based groups interested in open housing concentrated on the courts and higher levels of government, approaches that reflect both their limited capabilities for action at the suburban grass roots and their desire to secure policy changes that would affect suburbs in general rather than individual local jurisdictions.

Opponents of exclusionary zoning also have sought to enlist a wider range of interests in efforts to change suburban housing policies. Large employers in the suburbs and home-building interests have been particularly attractive targets because of their presumed ability to influence suburban governments. A planner, noting that "the church groups, Leagues of Women Voters, and the like have been vigorous in their pleas for balance, but with little potent political effect," welcomed the apparent interest of suburban employers and developers in liberalized housing policies: "Now some other quarters are being heard from, quarters that may conceivably have more influence on suburban power structure. For they include elements of the power structure itself." [64] Others who sought to open the suburbs thought that blacks, the poor, and other central-city interests could be mobilized in the struggle against suburban exclusion. In the next chapter, the capabilities of these interests to induce changes in suburban housing and land-use policies are appraised.

Chapter Six

Latent Interests
with Limited Clout

During the early 1970s, advocates of opening the suburbs emphasized the need for housing groups to forge alliances with other interests in order to overcome the formidable power of suburbanites armed with local autonomy to maintain the walls of exclusion. An analysis of the open-housing movement prepared in 1972 concluded that lowering the walls of exclusion would require "a large and powerful political coalition" formed from

> the poor who wish to have access to suburban living; the central city well-to-do who want to shift the burden of supporting services for the poor to the suburbs; the liberal politicians and liberal public opinion leaders; the profit motivated high-density home builders who wish to develop the suburbs; and the suburbanites motivated by philosophical beliefs who wish to share the amenities of the suburbs with the poor.[1]

The following year, Anthony Downs identified a wide range of interests in the metropolis as "potential sources of political support" for policies designed to disperse the poor throughout the suburbs.[2] Ignoring the traditional constituency base of the open-housing movement in the suburbs, Downs focused on those groups with an economic interest in opening the suburbs—suburban businessmen and their employees, homebuilders and construction workers, lower-income residents of the suburbs, and public officials, businessmen, homeowners, and the poor in the older cities. In his analysis, Downs emphasized the community of interests among these parties. While conceding that "all of these groups combined do not comprise a majority in most metropolitan areas," he insisted that "they could muster great political strength if they organized effectively behind key dispersal policies." [3]

The obstacles to such collective action, however, are enormous. Among these groups, there is less community than diversity of interest, and objectives are as often in conflict as in harmony. Lower-income whites in the suburbs, for instance, vociferously oppose opening their communities to central-city blacks. Substantial differences also exist in the awareness of various parties of their stake in suburban housing restrictions. Many who are unable to live in the suburbs fail to perceive the role of suburban governments in the limitation of housing opportunities. Those who recognize their interest in suburban exclusion usually lack influence in local political arenas which determine housing and land-use policies. Nor are changes in suburban housing policies equally important to all of these interests. Large corporations are not as likely to assign the same priority to lowering suburban housing barriers as developers and land owners. Differences in perspective, priorities, and objectives also exist within these various groupings. Major home-building firms, for example, tend to be less concerned about their relations with particular suburban governments than small developers whose livelihood depends on maintaining effective relations with local jurisdictions.

Further limiting involvement are considerations which conflict with support for opening the suburbs. Black leaders worry whether dispersing the poor will erode their power base in older cities. Major suburban employers must appraise increasing housing opportunities for workers in the light of their desire to maintain local good will. The latent interest of a central-city businessman in dispersing the poor may be neutralized because the individual lives in the suburbs. All of these factors limit the ability of the home-building industry, suburban employers, central-city leaders, inner-city blacks, and other potential opponents of suburban exclusion to translate their latent interests into effective political action.

The Housing Industry

Developers, home builders, and land owners have a direct and continuous interest in suburban land-use and housing policies. Over the years, the housing industry has been the most successful challenger of local land-use controls. Development interests often have had a dominant influence on local zoning, particularly in rapidly developing areas along the metropolitan rim. Builders and land owners usually have limited objectives in their efforts to alter suburban restrictions. Typically, they seek to remove constraints on particular parcels of land, rather than overturn the general zoning and housing policies of a local jurisdiction. Although the housing industry increasingly cloaks its self-interest in social rhetoric (as in the case of the suburban developer who asks: "How long can the cities stay in misery while everybody out here sits, enjoying the American dream?" [4]) its primary aim is economic rather than social. Private developers challenge local restrictions because they seek higher profits through more intensive land use and higher residential densities. As an official of the National Association of Home Builders readily concedes: "Our motivation is pretty straightforward: If a guy can build all types of housing, he can make more dollars." [5]

Assuming that land can be secured for development, home builders prefer cooperation to confrontation with local governments. In the process of cooperating, developers typically adapt to local values and become willing partners with suburban jurisdictions in exclusionary arrangements. To secure permission to build retirement communities, for example, builders readily accept the responsibility for insuring that school-age children do not become residents. In a common arrangement, the developer of Holiday City in Dover Township in New Jersey created a private association, the Holiday City Organization, which all purchasers of homes had to join and which forbid any member household from having permanent residents under eighteen. In return for needed zoning changes, home builders also have agreed not to accept black customers or tenants, or to set rents at a sufficiently high level to discourage lower-income families from settling in the community.

The housing industry also has been willing to enforce privately the values and social prejudices of the local community, particularly with respect to racial segregation. As noted in chapter 1, discriminatory practices are pervasive in the entire process by which dwellings are sold and rented in suburbs. Even self-styled "liberal and progressive" organizations such as Levitt and Sons, the nation's largest home-builder, refused for years to sell to blacks. [6] The firm argued that it would be committing economic suicide if its Levittowns were open to blacks while other developers sold only to whites. From William Levitt's perspective, "most whites prefer not to live in mixed communities. . . . The responsibility [for this] is society's. . . . It is not reasonable to expect that any one builder could or should undertake to absorb the entire risk and burden of conducting such a vast social experiment." [7] Only after an eight-year struggle led by the National Committee Against Discrimination in Housing did Levitt agree to accept black buyers in its 5,000-home Levittown in suburban Bucks County in the Philadelphia area. On the other side of the Delaware River, an adverse ruling by the New Jersey Supreme Court was required before Levitt opened its massive development in Burlington County to minority families.

With the spread of more sophisticated land-use controls, as well as the increasing awareness of the fiscal implications of residential development and the growth of environmental concerns, home builders have encountered more and more resistance from suburban governments and their constituents. Even in sparsely settled areas along the metropolitan frontier where developers once enjoyed a free hand, they increasingly find it necessary to negotiate with local governments whose residents are unwilling to let the actions of homebuilders and land owners alone determine the pattern of future settlement. To secure permission to develop land at higher densities than specified in local ordinances, builders "may make design modifications, provide community facilities, or build more expensive homes." [8] As pointed out in chapter 3, water and sewer moratoriums, staged development schemes, and no-growth provisions further constrain developers.

As suburban restrictions on residential construction have proliferated, the process of securing local consent has become increasingly time-consuming, uncertain, and costly. Speaking of local restrictions in Westchester County, a builders' representative complains: "Take a county of 430 square miles. If you start not being able to build on 380 square miles because of zoning, [you] are left with the exhaustive, highly selective process of trying to change land use in isolated areas." [9] The prospect of delay often is enough to forestall development, since most builders cannot afford to tie up their limited assets in proposals that may result in protracted study, negotiation, and litigation.

Faced with far more effective controls backed by vocal residents opposed to further growth, the housing industry has become increasingly critical of suburban governments and their housing policies. Building moratoriums and other efforts to restrict or prohibit growth have been prime targets of developers. In the Washington area, the Northern Virginia Builders Association raised a $56,000 "survival" fund to finance a series of newspaper advertisements and other public-relations activities aimed at restrictive local policies. According to one spokesman, the builders were being blamed for the failures of local government, since "the problems we now have are not the fault of growth, but rather because no one planned for it." [10] On the West Coast, home builders, the building trades, real-estate brokers, land owners, and banking interests joined together to fight restrictions on development under the banner of the California Council for Environmental and Economic Balance.

Slowly but surely, the housing industry has begun to question local control of land use, a concept it had vigorously defended as long as local autonomy facilitated the interests of developers and land owners, and foreclosed more effective regulation by the states or the federal government. A representative of builders in New Jersey insists that a "way has got to be found to get away from the constrictive home-rule . . . that supports and protects these restrictions." [11] In New York's Westchester County, a large developer complains that "I've got 500 to 600 acres I can't do anything with because of zoning . . . We just can't run with local little hometown rule. Every idiot can come down to the town hall and have his say and the guys up front tremble because they're afraid they won't be reelected." [12]

Leading the criticism of the fragmentation of zoning and housing controls has been the National Association of Home Builders. In 1971, NAHB's president told the U.S. Commission on Civil Rights that "in far too many cases, zoning is being used to protect the narrow self-interest of a particular community without regard to the health, safety, and welfare of a community, and the Nation as a whole." [13] Once an avid proponent of local autonomy over land use and housing, NAHB increasingly called for greater state and federal involvement to insure that local governments determined "land use in accord with overall needs, encouraging housing for people of all incomes, race, and creeds." [14] The association pledged in 1973 "to fight no growth policies in all their manifestations including exclusionary and discriminatory zoning, limitations on approval to develop land or to build; needless delay in providing essential community services and facilities; and any and all other forms of limiting the attainment of housing goals or excluding economic, racial, or ethnic groups." [15]

To further these ends, NAHB has provided its members with information and technical assistance on ways of easing local zoning restrictions. It has sought to stimulate litigation by local builders aimed at overturning restrictive suburban zoning, as well as to maintain "contact with and cooperate with such organizations as the National Committee Against Discrimination in Housing and Suburban Action Institute in attempting to ease restrictive local zoning." [16] NAHB spent $200,000 in litigation in 1973, primarily in court actions aimed at growth restrictions. The national association supported new approaches to suburban land-use control and provided active backing for the local ordinances adopted by Fairfax County in 1971 which required new apartment and town-house developments to include some subsidized housing.

Another factor affecting the perspective of the housing industry on local zoning was its new-found interest in subsidized housing. During the 1960s, NAHB moved away from its previous opposition to publicly-supported housing to become a staunch advocate of federal subsidies for privately-developed low-cost housing. The organization played a major role in the development and enactment of the Section 235 home owner-ship program in the Housing and Urban Development Act of 1968. Once the new law was in operation, NAHB strongly encouraged its members to participate in the Section 235 and 236 programs. Many builders, however, needed little encouragement to join the rush to take advantage of the new federal programs. During 1970, when a credit squeeze limited the financing of conventional housing, the motto of the Tennessee Homebuilders Association was "Stay alive with 235." [17]

Much of the support for reducing local control over land use has come from larger home-building firms. One of the most vocal critics of suburban zoning and building restrictions has been the Council of Housing Producers, which represents the fourteen largest home builders. A number of major building firms endorsed state, federal, and judicial action to eliminate local zoning barriers to the production of lower-cost housing. Larger builders tend to be less inhibited by ties to particular local jurisdictions than smaller developers. Major builders have a greater interest in large-scale and higher-density housing than local contractors who typically construct single-family units in small tracts. Big firms also are more likely to employ industrialized building systems and other construction techniques which run afoul of building codes and other local restrictions.

In addition, major firms built most of the 235 and 236 housing, and thus had a much larger stake in the removal of suburban barriers to sub-sidized housing than the average contractor. Small suburban builders tend to eschew involvement in subsidized housing. Some are deterred by personal attitudes. Others are reluctant to antagonize local governments by proposing subsidized projects, fearing that local officials will retaliate against their plans for conventional housing. Another constraint on the average builder is lack of experience with government housing programs. "The trouble with subsidized housing," explains a New Jersey builder, "is that the paper work and red tape at any level of government is tremendous. Only the big contractors can handle it." [18] Major home builders involved in 235 and 236 housing were instrumental in making the National Association of Home Builders a vocal opponent of exclusionary zoning. One of the most outspoken foes of suburban restrictions was Leon N. Weiner, a former president of NAHB and the leading builder of subsidized housing in the nation. "When I build out in the suburbs," Weiner angrily asserts, "I don't need any local participation. They don't want me out there, they don't want any more people out there, they don't want low- and moderate-income people there." [19]

Clearly, this growing opposition to suburban control of land use from influential elements of the housing industry has important consequences for the politics of exclusion. Yet the views of the larger firms and national leaders provide a distorted picture of the concerns of the housing industry as a whole. Housing is hardly a monolithic enterprise in which a few spokesmen accurately reflect the views of the rest. Instead, it is a highly decentralized array of contractors, developers, land owners, realtors, and financing institutions, most of whose components are small. In home building alone, over 50,000 concerns were engaged in the production of residential housing in 1970, with an average output of only thirty units. Most of these local builders are not interested in subsidized housing. Nor do they spend much time worrying about their social responsibilities at conferences with housing activists from NAACP, NCDH, Suburban Action, and other groups seeking to open the suburbs. Moreover, many have reaped substantial benefits from the existing system in suburbia, and are suspicious of the motives of the larger regional and national firms in advocating a dilution of local control over land use.

A good example of the divergence between national and local perspectives is provided by the opposition of local builders to zoning reform in Fairfax County, Virginia. Strong support came from the National Association of Home Builders for the proposal to require the provision of subsidized housing in multifamily projects in return for allowing developers to build at higher densities than otherwise would be permissible. But the influence of NAHB's Washington headquarters on its local members on the other side of the Potomac River was negligible. An NAHB staff member "worked hard to convince the home builders in Fairfax County," but "was unable to overcome their opposition to the law." [20] Local builders, while insisting that they were "not opposed to more low- and moderate-income housing in Fairfax County," found the new zoning provisions "unlawful, cumbersome, and . . . crippling to our industry." [21] After the zoning amendments were enacted by the Fairfax Board of Supervisors in 1971, six members of the Virginia Builders Association carried the fight into the courts, where they succeeded in overturning the new zoning regulations. [22] A similar law approved in nearby Montgomery County in 1973 was denounced by the Suburban Maryland Homebuilders as "unfair to builders" and "inverse condemnation." [23]

Defense of the status quo by local builders reflects their vested interest in the exercise of zoning authority by suburban governments. The fragmentation of public control over land use and housing has played an important role in sustaining small developers in an era of rapid increases in the scale of most enterprises. The local contractor's comparative advantage is his ability to develop intimate knowledge of local regulations and close relations with local officials. Builders in the suburbs are understandably reluctant to see changes in the present system which would jeopardize their privileged status or encourage competition from outsiders who lack their access to local officials and familiarity with local zoning, building, and subdivision codes. In Fairfax, local builders saw the provisions for subsidized housing and higher densities as threatening "their luxury home market and [offering] the apartment and tract developers from Washington, D.C., and other nearby counties an entering wedge into the Fairfax County home building market." [24] Local developers certainly would like greater freedom of action than more and more suburbs allow, but not at the cost of their favored local position. As a result of these considerations, suburban contractors tend to be wary of any shift in the locus of control over land use and housing which threatens their "home court" advantage. Instead, they prefer to use their influence to secure local housing and land-use policies which advance their interests and protect them from the competition of outsiders.

Given this perspective, successful builders in the suburbs often join local officials and residents in defending the existing system of land-use control, as well as criticizing "outsiders" who do not play the game according to the local rules. Suburban Action's efforts to develop mixed-income housing in Mahwah in northern New Jersey were attacked by George Lethbridge, a major local builder, as "unfair and a scare tactic. These groups should not try to intimidate borough officials by using tac-

tics which are not cricket." [25] At the same time that SAI was unsuccessfully attempting to force changes in Mahwah's zoning to permit higher-
density development and the construction of moderately priced housing,
Lethbridge was seeking local approval of a 385-acre office-park project.
The builder emphasized that he had "filed for the zoning change through
the proper channels" and that he could not "conceive of the planning
board not approving it because it's for the good of Mahwah." [26] Local
opponents of both Lethbridge and Suburban Action asked: "How can
you change our Master Plan for a man like Lethbridge so he can make a
profit when we're telling the low-income housing people we don't want
them because we don't want to change our Master Plan?" [27] Officials in
Mahwah brushed aside these concerns and rewarded Lethbridge's faith
in working within the system by rezoning his land from single-family
housing on one-acre plots to an office and luxury-apartment zone.

Other components of the housing industry at the grass roots echo the
support of suburban builders for local control over land use. Suburban
lawyers active in zoning matters, for example, perceive their interests in
the same terms as the contractors, developers, and land owners they represent. The same is true for architects, engineers, and other professionals
engaged in housing and land development. In the fight over zoning reform in Fairfax County, "no Fairfax lawyer could be obtained to defend
the ordinance when it was challenged—nor could a local architect or en-
gineer be obtained as an expert witness." [28]

Perhaps the staunchest advocates of local control have been the real-
estate industry. Realtors have a long-standing antipathy to increased
state or federal control over access to housing opportunities, primarily
because of their bitter opposition to measures aimed at discriminatory
practices in the sale and rental of housing. According to the National Association of Real Estate Boards, local zoning is "an important measure
for achieving local aspirations in environmental quality that our cities
and towns must retain." [29] Realtors have opposed measures which would
dilute local control over land use and prevent localities from exercising a
veto over the location of subsidized housing within their boundaries,
such as legislation aimed at zoning restrictions on subsidized housing
proposed by the Department of Housing and Urban Development in
1970. For NAREB, the proposal represented "a misguided attack upon
zoning" which sought "to impose a high density of use upon land that
has been planned for a relatively open type of environment." [30] By contrast, the National Association of Home Builders endorsed federal re-

straints on exclusionary zoning, but questioned whether HUD's proposal, which dealt only with the suburban fringe, went "far enough" since more developed suburban areas "frequently do all under their power to keep out federally assisted housing for low- and moderate-income families." [31]

Because of these grass-roots perspectives, advocates of opening the suburbs received little help from most suburban components of the housing industry. A top federal official argued in 1971 that "local builders are perfectly situated to help get community acceptance of low- and moderate-income housing. They know the community, they know the local politicians and they did the developing." [32] What was overlooked in this optimistic appraisal was the fact that local developers generally live in the suburbs. Most closely identify with the dominant values and attitudes of suburbia. They value local autonomy and are wary of "big" government, "outsiders," and federal "handouts." Their attachments to local governments are strong, and their personal economic stakes in the existing housing and land-use system substantial. As long as land continues to be available for traditional suburban development, which seems assured, few local developers or realtors are likely to turn against the hand that feeds them. Even fewer of these prototypical suburbanites can be expected to ally themselves with housing activists, inner-city blacks, and others who seek to rewrite the rules of the housing game in suburbia.

While major changes in local policies are not in the interest of most suburban builders and land owners, they are probably unattainable for the smaller number of developers who have become disenchanted with local autonomy. Large home-building firms face the same problems as other interests in seeking general policy changes through local action in a decentralized political system. They lack the resources to mount political action in thousands of suburban jurisdictions. NAHB, for example, is unable to mobilize most of its 60,000-odd members at the grass roots to liberalize zoning, much less have a significant impact on suburban governments and their constituents. When subsidized housing is the goal, developers have even less chance of persuading suburbs to ease local restrictions. Even the extra-legal inducements employed by some builders are unlikely to persuade local officials to permit housing for poor blacks. No developer, an official of a major housing firm points out, "is going to bribe his way past the specter of racial and economic integration. . . . The building industry doesn't have the money to bribe community sentiment on any change in the community's social composition." [33]

For all of these reasons, the major firms, like the broadly-based open-housing interests, seek to shift the locus of control over housing and land use to the higher levels of government. In the growing dissatisfaction of major developers with local control, Fred P. Bosselman notes a parallel with the situation faced by public utilities in the early years of the twentieth century:

> The utilities were beginning to feel the wrath of a public annoyed at various abuses that had taken place. This wrath was expressed in the form of a wide variety of controls which made operations difficult. The utilities responded by seeking a single statewide system of regulation which would preempt the regulatory powers of local governments.
>   The development industry is just beginning to realize that it is in a similar predicament. . . . The stop-growth movement is destroying the formerly harmonious relationship between developers and local governments. The development industry is beginning to wish for "one-stop shopping" laws to consolidate permitting programs in a single state agency, avoiding the need to deal with a whole host of boards, commissions, and local governments.[34]

Inevitably, these policy goals lead the major development firms to take their case to the broader political arenas of the state and the nation, as well as into the courts. Of course, the larger firms are not the only elements of the housing industry which can mobilize for action in the courts or at the higher levels of government; witness the successful litigation of the Fairfax developers and the strong opposition to proposals for a federal role in land-use regulation voiced by realtors and other locally oriented housing interests in the early 1970s. Given the lack of cohesiveness of the housing industry on these issues, as well as the responsiveness of federal and state officials to the interests of expanding suburban constituencies, large developers have sought allies among advocates of opening the suburbs to the disadvantaged. Identifying one's economic interests with the needs of the poor and blacks often is an effective political strategy, particularly in Washington. Certainly, the approach is familiar to the home builders who pressed for the 235 and 236 programs, and then reaped substantial profits in the process of helping the poor.

Alliances with big developers are difficult for open-housing groups to resist, given their lack of constituency support and other resources. On the basis of builders' track records, however, joining with developers is a risky endeavor for housing activists. As Sheilds and Spector note, the big builders "are willing, at least for the present, to ally themselves with civil rights groups in order to pry open the pot of gold which waits for high-density developers in the suburbs." [35] Whether the alliance will survive once developers get their hands on the gold is far more problematical. Moreover, fears that builders will be the main beneficiaries of zoning reforms reinforces suburban suspicions of housing schemes offered in the name of the poor. "The only thing we can see coming out of making smaller lots," argues a suburban skeptic, "is a bigger profit for the developer." [36] Pointing out that "the speculative builder is not running a charitable operation," a suburban official in New York insists that his community "will relax its zoning ordinance to admit various types of apartments only if a social purpose beyond the enrichment of the builders is achieved." [37]

Businessmen and Suburban Exclusion

"Self-interest, a force that has long proved a powerful instrument for social change in American society," is bound, in the view of Malcom D. Rivkin, to involve business and industry in efforts to open the suburbs. Rivkin believes that "the simple fact that . . . entrepreneurs cannot get or retain a labor force for their activities" will lead major employers in the suburbs to press for a relaxation of local housing restrictions.[38] Since businessmen are not without political influence, the expectation is that their involvement will induce suburban governments to alter housing and land-use policies. Without question, the inability of many employees to live near their jobs is costly to suburban employers. Labor shortages are encountered by many firms in the suburbs, particularly when they seek to fill lower-paid jobs in large metropolitan areas where the new suburban plants, offices, and shopping centers are considerable distances from lower-income residential neighborhoods in the central city. Long journeys to work increase absentee rates, especially during bad weather and among lower-paid workers who are most dependent on car pooling and public transportation. In 1972, the National Job-Linked Housing Center estimated the "cost to industry of lack of housing . . . in the hundreds of millions of dollars." [39]

Whether these costs are sufficiently high to induce national corporations and other major suburban employers to bring substantial pressures to bear against local governments, however, is more problematical. A survey of major corporations concerning housing for blue-collar workers conducted in the fall of 1972 indicated that a majority of the firms did not believe that the distance between home and job was a cause of absenteeism. Only 32 percent of the 210 respondents were certain that local zoning policies were a cause of labor shortages.[40]

Moreover, there is little evidence of much concern on the part of business with housing conditions for their employees in the suburbs. Since the end of World War II, large corporations and other businessmen have made thousands of locational decisions which have resulted in the vast growth of suburban jobs. Few of these determinations have been influenced by the availability of housing for employees in the vicinity of their jobs. Nor have corporate locational choices been much affected by the existence of local policies which restricted the construction of apartments or inexpensive single-family housing suitable for production workers, secretaries, and other employees with modest incomes. In addition, little attention has been paid to the accessibility of new suburban facilities to the poor, blacks, and others with severely limited housing options. And in seeking locations for corporate headquarters, research laboratories, and other operations which require large numbers of executives and professionals, major corporations and their top leadership have been attracted to upper-income suburban areas where exclusionary local policies and high housing costs bar all but top-level employees from living near their work.

Business has been particularly oblivious to housing and accessibility considerations when locating industrial facilities with large blue-collar work forces in suburbs. In the 1950s, the Ford Motor Company decided to build an automobile assembly plant in Mahwah in northern New Jersey. Mahwah and most of the surrounding communities had little inexpensive housing available, were zoned for large lots and few apartments, and were hostile to blacks and Puerto Ricans who soon constituted close to half of the hourly workers at the plant. Less than 32 percent of the plant's 4,000-odd production workers lived in Bergen or neighboring Rockland County in 1962, while over 34 percent commuted to Mahwah from New York, Newark, Jersey City, and other older cities twenty or more miles distant.[41] In 1963, General Motors moved an automobile assembly plant from Oakland to suburban Fremont, where little low-cost housing was available, particularly for the blacks and Chicanos who made up 40 percent of the work force. Six years after the move, less than one percent of Fremont's population of over 100,000 was black, and only three percent was Mexican-American; while one in five of the 5,800 workers at the factory continued to commute from Oakland twenty miles to the north.[42]

Corporations moving to suburbia usually are more solicitous of the housing needs of management and white-collar workers. Industrial firms commonly pay moving expenses and provide other assistance for supervisory personnel when opening a new factory in the suburbs. When office or research activities move outward, corporations often become deeply involved in the problems of relocation. In the course of moving its headquarters from New York City to Purchase, an exclusive suburb in Westchester County, Pepsico surveyed local real-estate dealers in order to identify housing opportunities for its employees, and helped secure mortgages for employees purchasing homes near the new offices. To facilitate the move of 1,800 employees as a result of a shift of corporate headquarters from New York City to affluent Greenwich in southwestern Connecticut, The American Can Company counseled employees on local housing conditions, ran seminars dealing with housing and schools in the area, provided free bus tours of surrounding communities, arranged meetings with realtors, and assisted with mortgages. In addition, moving expenses were paid for those who were relocating to reduce commuting time; and bonuses of up to $1,500 were offered to employees making less than $15,000 who agreed to continue working for the firm after the move to the suburbs.[43]

Despite growing corporate awareness of suburban housing problems, IBM professed to be surprised at the difficulties encountered by many of its employees in finding housing in the wake of the corporation's move of its Office Products Division from mid-Manhattan to Franklin Lakes. Almost no single-family housing in Franklin Lakes or surrounding suburbs in Bergen and Rockland Counties was available for less than $50,000; and zoning restrictions foreclosed the construction of moderately priced homes or apartments throughout the area.[44] In evaluating a planned move from New York City to Westchester in 1973, Texaco made no studies of the housing or transportation needs of 1,000 employees it intended to move into a suburban area with severe housing shortages.[45]

Corporate moves from central locations to the suburbs are particularly difficult for blacks whose housing choices are highly constrained by discriminatory practices. In the case of IBM's move to Franklin Lakes, the 100-odd black and Puerto Rican employees involved faced the choice of finding housing in an overwhelmingly white area or commuting long distances by car. Rarely are as many blacks as whites able to follow their jobs to the suburbs. When State Farm Mutual moved an office employing 900 in the inner portion of the San Francisco Bay area to Santa Rosa, which is more than an hour from black neighborhoods in the urban core, only six of 75 black employees made the move. On the other hand, "the vast majority of the white employees stayed with the company and moved" to Santa Rosa, where only two percent of the population was black.[46]

With the growth in awareness of the dimensions of metropolitan separation during the 1960s, business came under increasingly sharp criticism for its failure to insure that housing opportunities were available in the vicinity of new suburban plants, offices, and other facilities. In 1971, the chairman of the National Urban Coalition charged that "every time business decides to move or build a plant or other facility out in the hinterland without insisting upon housing, schools, and other services for its workers—present and prospective—it is helping to exacerbate the problems of an already deeply divided country." [47] After the American Telephone and Telegraph Company announced plans in 1971 to move some of its offices from Manhattan to Bernards Township, an affluent New Jersey suburb which banned apartments and had nineteen blacks among its 13,500 residents, AT&T was attacked by Suburban Action Institute for "social viciousness" and "building a segregated society in America." [48] Suburban Action asked both the Federal Communications Commission and the U.S. Equal Employment Opportunities Commission to prevent AT&T from making the move to "a region of New Jersey where zoning controls preclude the development of housing for potential non-white and Spanish-speaking employees." [49] Earlier, the chairman of the Equal Opportunities Commission had indicated that "the physical removal of jobs beyond the reach of minority workers [may be] a violation of . . . Title VII of the 1964 Civil Rights Act." [50]

Criticisms, legal challenges, and growing labor-force problems have all contributed to increasing concern with local housing on the part of major suburban employers. Almost two out of three of the corporations which responded to the survey cited earlier agreed that "companies have a role to play in securing increased housing for their employees so that they can live within reasonable proximity to their place of work." [51] Businessmen have cosponsored conferences on subsidized housing in a number of suburban areas. Some corporations, such as the American Can Company, have turned to open-housing organizations like NCDH for assistance in improving housing opportunities for their employees. A few firms have considered changing their criteria for selecting suburban sites in order to increase the weight attached to accessibility of the location to workers. Occasionally, corporate spokesmen have even publicly attacked suburban housing policies. After years of bad publicity and labor-force difficulties at its Mahwah assembly plant, the Ford Motor Company in 1972 criticized "zoning that precludes local housing opportunities for large numbers of our workforce" and endorsed efforts such as those of Suburban Action Institute to meet "the need for additional moderate-income housing in the Mahwah area." [52] The following year, the Grumman Corporation scored opponents of a subsidized housing project in the Wyandanch section of Babylon in Suffolk County, New York. In a statement that emphasized Grumman's economic role as the largest employer and taxpayer on Long Island, the corporation disagreed "very strongly with what it believes to be vacuous arguments clothed in specious rhetoric that seek to deny a fair shake for the citizens of Wyandanch." [53]

In the view of some critics, large suburban employers can do much more to influence local housing policies. Sol M. Linowitz, who once headed the Xerox Corporation, contends that

business and businessmen can exercise great power within their local communities in this as in other significant issues. Although an industry's clout in any community is probably greatest before it locates there, its influence remains considerable after it becomes part of that community. It brings a payroll as well as people who can contribute to community life; it pays taxes; it makes bank loans and deposits; it does business with local merchants. Its presence and its policies have a powerful impact upon the economic and social life of that community. It can, if it is willing, do a great deal to break down the barriers to the construction of low and moderate income homes and the maintenance of good schools and other public services, near plants and factories. It can get land rezoned for small lots and multifamily dwellings. It can help set up nonprofit corporations to develop residential land banks and take advantage of low interest government housing programs. It can encourage the creation of county-wide public agencies to use the federal rent supplement program. [54]

Few major employers embraced the activist roles outlined by Linowitz. In the Dayton and Rochester areas, support from major suburban employers played an important role in the development of metropolitan housing plans in the early 1970s. [55] Occasionally, a firm has used its influence more directly to produce changes in local housing policies. Quaker Oats conditioned the location of a plant in Danville, Illinois, on enactment of a local open-housing ordinance. Pressure from IBM, directed through the bank that was handling the financing of a new plant in Lexington, Kentucky, forced local real-estate brokers to treat IBM's black employees in a non-discriminatory fashion. Later, a major realtor indicated "that IBM carried more weight than either the Kentucky open housing law or the Supreme Court decision banning housing discrimination." [56]

Not many companies, however, are willing to go as far as Quaker Oats or IBM. Moreover, both Danville and Lexington are cities of less than 65,000. Their business communities are relatively cohesive; and a single local jurisdiction encompasses most of their urbanized area. Business influence is more difficult to employ effectively in the fragmented and differentiated political and economic arenas of the major metropolitan areas. In these contexts, which are where most of the nation's new jobs are being located, few major employers have been willing to bring their potential influence to bear directly in efforts aimed at easing local housing restrictions.

A typical corporate attitude was expressed by a spokesman for Western Electric in response to suggestions that the company had an obligation to help secure housing for its employees if its headquarters were to be moved from New York City to suburban Bedminster in New Jersey. "Western Electric is not against low- or middle-income housing for anyone. But we do think that this is a matter that local zoning officials have to decide for themselves. . . . [We] don't think this is something that we as a company can properly go to a community and say that we want changed." [57] When asked by an official of the U.S. Commission on Civil Rights whether "the McDonnell Company has a responsibility to do more in the way of providing housing for its employees . . . in the neighborhood of the plant," a McDonnell executive replied that "we have our hands pretty full trying to run our plant and build airplanes." [58] Another McDonnell official added that "we know how to make jobs. . . . We don't know anything about housing." [59]

Criticism of its plans to move to New Canaan, which Suburban Action characterized as "a virtually all white, upper-income, exclusionary community" prompted the following reply from RCA: "If they don't like New Canaan's zoning, their quarrel is with the town, not with us." [60] In Franklin Lakes and surrounding suburbs, IBM deliberately eschewed using its "muscle" to force changes in zoning laws, preferring instead to rely on "employees, as citizens, [to] express their opinions in their communities regarding rezoning." [61] IBM's reliance on local democracy must have smacked of "Catch-22" for those employees who could not afford to live in the communities which excluded them, and thus lacked an opportunity to express their opinions where it counted. Increasing the irony of IBM's position, of course, was the fact that IBM executives who can afford to live in suburbs like Franklin Lakes are no more likely to press for lowering zoning and housing barriers than their affluent neighbors who work for American Can, Ford, or Quaker Oats.

The reluctance of major suburban employers to become directly involved in expanding the supply of suburban housing results from a number of considerations. The American experience with company housing and company towns has left bitter memories. Nor are many firms interested in either direct landlord-tenant or seller-buyer relationships with their employees. With respect to local governments and their policies, most companies are eager to maintain a low profile, to be a "good neighbor," to avoid controversy, and especially not to antagonize the locals when permission is being sought to develop a new facility. Far from using their influence to drive hard bargains on social concerns, corporate spokesmen constantly emphasize the minimal impact of their facilities and employees on the local community, as well as their dedication to maintaining the "character" of the surrounding neighborhoods. The aim is to counter local opposition to the coming of business to the suburbs, not to increase the opposition by making "unrealistic" demands on the local community.

A good example of the typical corporate approach to the suburbs is provided by Western Electric's unsuccessful campaign to persuade Bedminster to approve zoning changes needed to permit the construction of a large headquarters facility. Company officials emphasized that only twenty-five of the 1,500 employees expected to work in Bedminster would actually live in the community. Corporate reluctance to press on the housing issue also is illustrated by IBM's negotiations with Franklin Lakes, where "there was some mention of moderate-income housing in early discussions with the Mayor, but the overtures were rebuffed and no further efforts were made." [62]

Further constraining businessmen in the suburbs is the rise of suburban fears that acceptance of industry will force a community to provide housing for workers. Certainly such fears were an important consideration in the refusal of Bedminster to grant Western Electric's request for the zoning changes needed to build its new headquarters. In some instances, companies have agreed to ignore housing in return for local permission to build a plant in a desired location. To obtain industrial zoning, one Massachusetts company has "pledge[d] to the communities . . . that we will not . . . deal in housing." [63]

Business behavior on the housing issue also is strongly influenced by the values and interests of the affluent suburbanites who predominate in executive suites. Most corporate decision-makers live in the suburbs, usually in exclusive communities with highly restrictive zoning. Because of their personal stake in local autonomy and exclusionary policies, they approach the issue of opening the suburbs to lower-income groups with mixed emotions. Paul Davidoff of Suburban Action Institute thinks the perspective of the typical businessman has been a major factor underlying the lack of "strong support in the business community for what we seek to do. Many of the executives of suburban enterprises reside within local suburban communities and comprise a part of that majority which wishes to keep conditions as they are." [64]

That the suburban orientations of businessmen influence their thinking about using corporate influence in the suburbs is not surprising. After all, many corporate decisions to move to the suburbs have been strongly motivated by the desire of executives to get their jobs as well as their residences out of the older cities. In considering corporate moves to affluent communities, top executives tend to be more concerned with their own convenience than with the accessibility of their facilities to lower-paid employees, city residents, and blacks. As one observer of the suburban housing scene notes, "no matter how high a price the suburban housing shortage may exact in the future, the executives who made the decision to move are not themselves much affected by the cost of housing." [65] For an executive of Western Electric, the essential reason for the company's plan to move its headquarters to the suburbs was "that we're missing the human amenities by living and doing business in the city." [66] For the vast majority of suburbanites, including both business executives and corporations that have moved to greener pastures, restrictive housing and land-use policies are an essential means of maintaining the amenities which initially attracted them to the suburbs. And this reality neutralizes much of the potential influence which major employers might bring to bear against the walls of exclusion in suburbia.

Ambiguity in the Central City

Almost everyone in the older cities would appear to have a clear interest in altering suburban policies which limit housing opportunities. Central cities contain most of those who are disadvantaged by suburban housing and land-use restrictions. Moreover, by contributing to the concentration of lower-income and minority groups in older cities, suburban exclusion adds to the burdens that poverty and dependency impose on more affluent city dwellers, businesses, and city governments. By distributing the costs of poverty throughout the metropolis, opening the suburbs would reduce the pressures on the city's public services and taxpayers. Dispersing the poor and minority groups also would benefit cities by lessening the attractions of flight to the suburbs, particularly on the part of those who seek to escape blacks, integrated schools, and scattered-site public housing. At the same time, cities would have a better chance of attracting business and the middle class, and thus of reviving their lagging economies, revitalizing their decaying neighborhoods, replenishing their depleted exchequers, and refurbishing their overburdened public services.

Despite these considerations, relatively few in the older cities have echoed Cleveland councilmen who demand: "Let the suburbs take their share." [67] Mayor Richard J. Daley of Chicago has spoken of the need to "include the resources of the suburban areas in sharing responsibility for housing." [68] Mayor John V. Lindsay of New York insisted that as "jobs move to the suburbs, the suburbs must make room for workers." [69] Support for dispersing the poor also has been voiced by the mayors of Atlanta, Cleveland, Newark, Trenton, and a few other cities. In 1970, the National League of Cities and the U.S. Conference of Mayors called for every community in the metropolis to "accept its responsibility to provide a full range of housing opportunities for all income and racial groups. [70]

Many in the central cities, however, remain dubious about any urban strategy that emphasizes suburbs. Housing officials, community leaders, and other city interests insist that federal and state funds be concentrated in older cities where housing needs are the greatest, rather than in suburbs where most people already have adequate shelter. Older cities were fearful that a suburban focus for federal housing efforts would, in the words of one mayor, result "in a net loss of housing dollars to the central city." [71] In return for diminished federal aid, cities had no guarantee that suburbs would provide housing for lower-income and minority families from the urban core.

Critics of dispersing the poor also have questioned whether more decentralization will help older cities. In their view the outward movement of people and jobs had caused the problems of the central cities. The major beneficiaries of eased housing restrictions in the suburbs, they argued, would be lower-middle-income and blue-collar whites, as well as upward mobile blacks, who remained in the city only because they could not afford to move to the suburbs. Substantial numbers of these city residents could be expected to leave if less expensive housing became available in suburbia. Thus, by facilitating the exodus of these city residents, opening the suburbs would make things worse rather than better in the urban core. A higher proportion of the city's population would be poor and black or Spanish-speaking. Financial problems would become more severe, public services would continue to deteriorate, the local economy would decline even more rapidly, and the city's ability to attract new residents and jobs would decrease. Considering these prospects, George Sternlieb contends that "the only thing holding our central cities together is the suburban housing shortage." [72] From this perspective, the solution to the problems of older cities lies in reversing the outward flow to the suburbs, not in further augmenting the decentralization of the metropolis by increasing housing opportunities beyond city limits.

Advocates of opening the suburbs found these views dangerously shortsighted. "No city is an island," warned an NCDH official, "and cities that ignore this truth will discover unmistakably that the bell tolls for them." [73] Most of the growth in the metropolis, insisted spokesmen for organizations such as NAACP, NCDH, and Suburban Action, was bound to occur in the suburbs. Those seeking to open the suburbs also argued that cities could not expect to make much headway with their housing problems unilaterally. Land within most older cities was too scarce, too expensive, and too difficult to assemble to expect the housing needs of lower-income city dwellers to be met solely by programs within the cities. Nor, in the view of those favoring suburban strategies, could business and the middle class be attracted to older cities unless there was a concomitant easing of suburban housing constraints. Because of the concentration of the poor and minority groups in the urban core, Anthony Downs believed that "recapturing the middle class" would remain "a largely rhetorical strategy [until] combined with deliberate dispersal of low- and moderate-income housing throughout the metropolitan area." [74]

Opening the suburbs, its supporters conceded, "might accelerate the withdrawal of whites from central cities." [75] But they saw the long-range benefits of dispersal for older cities outweighing the short-run costs in terms of the departure of working- and middle-class families to the suburbs. Moreover, argued Downs, a deliberate choice to maintain suburban housing barriers in order to prevent these groups from leaving the cities would be "penalizing them for being ambitious and stable." [76]

Regardless of which of these assessments is closer to the mark, the debate over the costs and benefits of dispersing the poor to suburbia tends to be too abstract to attract much public attention in the older cities. Far more relevant in terms of political support for opening the suburbs is the strong resistance of a substantial portion of the central-city electorate to dispersing lower-income and minority groups within the city. In most white city neighborhoods, opening up anything to blacks is not a very popular cause. Both blacks and whites in working- and middle-class areas strongly resist proposals for scattering low-cost housing. Attitudes toward dispersing the poor and blacks are much the same in outer city neighborhoods as in the suburbs beyond. For a white middle-class resident of Woodland Hills in Los Angeles protesting an attempt to rezone his neighborhood to permit Section 236 housing, "low-income housing represents all the problems I moved here to the San Fernando Valley to get away from." [77] In explaining the fierce resistance of residents of Forest Hills to a plan to locate public housing in the middle-class Queens neighborhood as part of New York City's scattered-site program, a local leader insisted that "we're not racists or bigots, but we do believe that low-income housing leads to crime and you can't expect people to go along with more crime just because the city wants to help the poor." [78]

City politicians and officials have been responsive to these concerns from the earliest days of the public-housing program. Local resistance, expressed through councilmen, ward leaders, and other channels of political influence, has kept public housing out of all but the poorest neighborhoods in most cities. Councilmen frequently possess an informal veto over the location of subsidized housing within their districts. Neighborhood influence is particularly significant in cities which require formal approval of public-housing sites by the city council, as in Chicago. [79] In New York City, the exclusionary interests of working- and middle-class neighborhoods have been protected by the informal veto over public-housing sites possessed by the borough presidents, who are members of the Board of Estimate which approves all housing projects.[80]

With the intensification of city problems and racial strife in the 1960s, greater local control over housing became a key goal in city neighborhoods seeking to protect their turf against subsidized housing, lower-income families, and blacks. Particularly as pressures to scatter subsidized housing intensified, residents in many cities insisted on playing a formal role in the housing and planning determinations which affected their neighborhoods. Efforts by blacks to secure community control over schools, housing, and other activities reinforced the demands of white neighborhoods for effective citizen participation. Mayors with strong ties to ethnic, blue-collar, and lower-middle-class constituencies, such as Ralph Perk in Cleveland and Frank Rizzo in Philadelphia, were particularly sympathetic to these demands. Council members from outlying areas in a number of cities have sought charter changes which would permit neighborhoods to veto housing projects. In an effort to "bring government closer to the people" because "the public would like to make the determination," an alderman from a white ward in St. Louis introduced amendments to the city charter in 1971 which provided for a city-wide referendum on public housing, with future projects to be banned in any ward in which a majority was against public housing.[81]

In the atmosphere that prevails in most of these city neighborhoods, little headway had been made with the argument that opening the suburbs would reduce the pressures for scattering subsidized housing within the city. For many city dwellers and their political representatives, the linkages between fewer local constraints on housing in the suburbs and reduced demands for public housing in their neighborhoods is too subtle to have much impact on political behavior. Instead, city residents outside the ghetto typically perceive a common interest with white suburbanites in keeping the poor and blacks out of their neighborhoods. As a result, they are far more interested in making their part of the city more like the suburbs by increasing community control than in making the suburbs more like the city by reducing suburban autonomy. The situation in housing closely resembles that in school integration. Very few white neighborhoods in the cities have supported metropolitan-wide school integration as a means of sharing the burden of integration with the suburbs. Quite the contrary, white areas in cities and their representatives in state legislatures and Congress have joined forces with suburbanites to form powerful coalitions which seek to ban all busing designed to foster racial integration.

Although inner-city blacks probably have more latent interest in lowering the walls of suburban exclusion than any other group in the metropolis, few blacks in older cities have become involved in efforts to open the suburbs. In the view of one black open-housing activist, "most blacks and black leaders do not yet consider exclusionary zoning a gut issue. They do not feel it every day like they do job discrimination, and did de jure segregated schools and segregated public facilities." [82] For most lower-income blacks in the central cities, the relationship between suburban zoning and housing, employment, and educational opportunities is at best obscure. Lacking information about the suburbs and having strong ties to existing black communities, many blacks are not eager to leave the central city for the *terra incognita* of suburbia. Reinforcing this strong tendency to confine residential choices to black areas within older cities is fear of white hostility in both the outer city neighborhoods and the suburbs.

Even if more blacks were interested in moving outward, many black spokesmen doubt that efforts to open the suburbs can benefit enough blacks to matter. The movement of large numbers of blacks to the suburbs, they contend, is unrealistic in the face of overwhelming suburban opposition to subsidized housing for inner-city blacks. Given this resistance, pressing for the dispersal of low-cost housing for blacks in the suburbs threatens to undermine political support for subsidized housing programs in general. Skeptics in the black community also question whether poor blacks who were relocated in the suburbs would benefit economically, since most could not afford automobiles, and thus would be unable to travel from home to job.

Under these circumstances, whites rather than blacks are seen as the prime beneficiaries of housing programs that focus on suburbia. Advocates of opening the suburbs concede that "only a small fraction of suburban housing initially made available to low- and moderate-income households would be occupied by blacks." [83] Further bolstering the arguments of blacks who are dubious about the benefits to be obtained from opening the suburbs was the experience of the Section 235 and 236 programs. Black access to subsidized housing in the suburbs under the new federal programs, as pointed out in chapter 4, was sharply limited by suburban preferences for local residents, the suburban emphasis on housing for the elderly, and marketing practices which ignored blacks, as well as by black reluctance to move to unfamiliar and potentially hostile areas. In addition, as noted in chapter 5, open-housing advocates find it necessary to emphasize the needs of local residents and ignore inner-city blacks in order to win support for subsidized housing in the suburbs, an emphasis which makes it highly unlikely that much housing will be available to blacks from the cities in whatever projects are approved in the suburbs.

Because of these meager benefits, blacks argue, the principal effect of emphasizing the improvement of housing opportunities in suburbs would be to shift resources away from the inner city where most blacks live, where housing needs are the greatest, and where blacks, because of their strength in numbers, have some potential to influence public policy. Black contractors and workers also would be less likely to be employed on subsidized housing constructed in suburbs than on projects in central cities. In this light, the campaign to open the suburbs appears to be another sophisticated cop-out on the part of whites for abandoning the black ghetto. Blacks in cities across the nation bitterly protested the new federal emphasis in the early 1970s on locating subsidized housing outside lower-income black areas. In Kansas City, for example, the Department of Housing and Urban Development in 1972 refused to approve a 280-unit project in a black model-cities area because it would perpetuate residential segregation. HUD's action was attacked by blacks as "negat[ing] its own Model Cities program and all of its fine purposes. HUD's treatment of the Kansas City Model Cities community's efforts to demonstrate innovative solutions to neighborhood development is a travesty, a slap in the face of the principle and fact of self-determination through citizen participation activities." [84]

As in Kansas City, black concerns are reinforced by the widespread black demand for community control over public institutions and programs which affect the lives of blacks. Building housing in the suburbs rather than the cities moves decision-making to political arenas in which blacks usually are heavily outnumbered, and thus able to exercise little influence. In the older cities, on the other hand, the concentration of blacks steadily enhances their political power. Efforts to move blacks to the suburbs are opposed because they threaten to erode this growing black power base. For a new generation of black leaders in the inner city the geographic concentration of blacks is a strength rather than a weakness, since it provides blacks with the means to control the local political system. From this perspective, the underlying problem of blacks is no segregation, but the lack of social, economic, and particularly political power. Black nationalists, as Charles S. Hamilton has emphasized, "firmly believe that blacks can begin to consolidate their political power only if they remain geographically consolidated." [85] As a result, blacks of this persuasion strongly resist efforts to dilute their constituency, either through metropolitan governmental arrangements which would submerge black voters in a largely white metropolis, or through the dispersal of blacks throughout the metropolitan area. For these reasons, opening the suburbs has been rejected by groups with largely black inner-city constituencies such as the National Tenants Organization and the National Welfare Rights Organization. For Anthony R. Henry of the National Tenants Organization: "Dispersal would . . . dilute pockets of low-income people in center cities which are coming to control the political life there. Regardless of what people say, center cities are the heart of U.S. economic life, and now there is an effort to disperse those centers at exactly the time when the black and the poor are coming to power there." [86]

Black strategists who would let white America have the suburbs while they build black power in the cities have come under sharp attack from other blacks. The NAACP has insisted that "the urban and ghetto problem cannot be successfully attacked until those confined in the inner city have the opportunity to go where the jobs and housing are." [87] For Bayard Rustin, concentrating black political energies exclusively on the cities means "surrender of the suburbs to white domination. Blacks . . . will have the ghetto with its drug addiction, soaring crime rate, high unemployment, and deplorable housing. Whites will keep the suburbs, where job opportunities are expanding, the air is unpolluted, housing is decent, and schools provide superior education." [88]

Black and white advocates of opening the suburbs argue that suburban whites will gain far more than inner-city blacks from further institutionalization and politicization of the racial befurcation of the metropolis. Accepting the walls of exclusion, they insist, will permit more and more whites to insulate themselves in the suburbs from the problems of lower-income blacks. From this perspective, black power in the city is at best a partial solution to the problems of the black community. With decentralization and suburban growth rapidly eroding the economic resources and political significance of the older cities blacks are likely to control, an increasing proportion of the resources needed by impoverished cities such as Cleveland, Detroit, Gary, and Newark must come from outside the city—from the suburbs and from the states and the federal government where suburban interests are increasingly influential. "What good does it do," asks Nathaniel Jones of the NAACP, "to have political power over a decayed corpse?" [89]

Because of these economic and financial realities, a more practical approach, in the view of supporters of dispersion, would be for blacks to sacrifice some potential power in the central city in exchange for more black influence in the suburbs. While agreeing that "scattered black suburbanites could not amass as much direct elective power as they might if concentrated together as part of a larger central-city voting bloc," Anthony Downs argues:

> Yet the presence of at least some black residents in most suburban areas would greatly reduce the probability that white suburbanites would define suburban interests in ways that are antiblack as well as anti-central-city. Black suburbanites would be able to exercise at least some beneficial influence that would not arise if nearly all urban blacks remained in central cities. Their presence would also keep open a much broader set of residential and employment choices to future black citizens. In my opinion, those goals are worth the sacrifice of marginal increases in black central-city power required to achieve meaningful racial integration in the suburbs. [90]

Percy Sutton, the black borough president of Manhattan in New York City, concurs, arguing that "black people must seek power in the suburbs as well [as in the cities]. They must seek . . . to influence the conduct of elected officials in the suburbs for if we are ever to change our zoning . . . we must be able to exercise some influence in the suburbs." [91]

Even if these disagreements did not exist among black and other city interests, efforts by older cities to lower suburban housing barriers would be severely handicapped by their lack of influence in the government arenas of suburbia. The fragmented political system of the typical metropolitan area denies city officials and their constituents formal means of influencing suburban governments. Informal opportunities are limited because few suburbs welcome outside interference in their affairs, particularly when the outsiders are from the central city and want to talk about housing blacks and the poor. City officials for their part, preoccupied with their own responsibilities and problems within the city, usually lack time or resources to monitor the activities of the scores of suburban agencies which make decisions affecting housing opportunities for city residents.

The constraints which limit involvement in the suburbs are particularly severe in the case of housing agencies in older cities. Fighting for financial and political survival, most of these agencies grapple increasingly with militant tenant organizations, rent strikes, project abandonment, controversies over scattered sites, complex federal policies, fiscal crises, and intervention by the courts in their operations. Like its counterparts in other cities, the Chicago Housing Authority in the early 1970s found itself in a crossfire between court orders to locate public housing throughout the city and adamant opposition from white neighborhoods and their city councilmen. In seeking a way out of this dilemma, CHA officials advocated "a metropolitan solution to what is truly a metropolitan problem." [92] The efforts of CHA to find a metropolitan solution, however, bore little fruit because of the agency's preoccupation with its mounting fiscal, legal, and political problems, its limited jurisdiction, and the need for suburban consent for projects located beyond the city's boundaries.

Exceptions to the general lack of direct intervention by city officials are few and far between. Late in 1970, the Development Administrator of New York City journeyed across the Hudson to urge Bedminster Township to reject Western Electric's request for a zoning change unless the exclusive suburb was prepared to make housing available for workers at the planned corporate headquarters. [93] At the same time, Mayor Richard Daley sought to use some of his fabled clout to relieve court pressures on the Chicago Housing Authority by getting public housing built for poor Chicagoans in the suburbs. Daley was able to persuade his Democratic confreres among the officialdom of Cook County to agree to the joint development of 500 units of public housing in the suburbs by CHA and the Housing Authority of Cook County, with some units available to residents of Chicago. As noted in chapter 4, even this token program was stalled by the unwillingness of individual suburban municipalities, in which Daley's influence was minimal, to accept public housing, as well as by financing and other difficulties.

Of all the parties examined in this chapter, nowhere is the gap between latent interests and actual influence on suburban housing policies more striking than in the case of older cities. Despite the stake of many city interests in lessening suburban exclusion, involvement for most is foreclosed by ignorance, indifference, doubts, opposition, cross-cutting pressures, and preoccupation with other problems. For the handful in central cities who actively seek to open the suburbs, lack of access largely precludes effective participation in the suburban political arenas which determine local housing policies. As a consequence of weak constituency support, lack of internal cohesion, and limited influence, city advocates of opening the suburbs, like other open-housing interests, turn to higher levels of government and courts in search of more sympathetic decisional arenas. Thus, Simeon Golar, chairman of the New York City Housing Authority, calls on Congress to create a federal housing agency empowered to override local controls in order to scatter subsidized housing throughout the metropolis.[94] And Baltimore's housing commissioner talks of asking the Maryland legislature or the courts to ban all residential construction in the metropolis until suburbs assume their share of the burden of housing lower-income families.[95] The prospects and perils of enlisting the courts in efforts to open the suburbs are analyzed in the next chapter, while the ensuing three chapters examine the politics of exclusion in federal, metropolitan, and state arenas.

Chapter Seven

Exclusion and the Courts

Litigation is the most common recourse for those who are unable to persuade suburban governments to change their land-use and housing policies. That those who fail to prevail in the political arenas of suburbia turn to the courts is hardly surprising. The availability of the courts to groups which lose—or fear that they will lose—in other political arenas is a key feature of politics in the United States. Recourse to the courts is facilitated by the concepts of judicial review, due process, and equal protection. These features of the constitutional system, along with the brevity of the national constitution, enumerated powers, and federalism, have made judges central actors in most of the major political dramas of American history. Furthermore, dependence of local governments on the states for their legal powers and fiscal resources brings the courts into many of the conflicts which enliven a highly decentralized political system.

For minority interests of all kinds, the fundamental attraction of courts is their insulation from many of the pressures which bear on other components of the political system. Life tenure for federal judges, and long terms for most members of state courts, make the judiciary less responsive to constituency pressures and public opinion than legislative and executive bodies. The nature of the judicial process reinforces this insulation. Courts are controlled settings with formal and complex rules. Issues come before judges only when they are framed in the context of specific cases. Direct participation is limited to those with an interest recognized by the courts. As a result of these features, courts are less accessible to the general public than most legislative and executive arenas. Another important factor is the widespread perception of the legitimacy of an independent and authoritative judicial branch of government. The norms of an autonomous court system, judicial fairness, and judges free from outside pressures are widely supported in the society as a whole. So is the obligation to comply with judicial rulings. In this context, courts are able to make unpopular decisions, to invalidate laws and other official actions, and to compel government to act. In the process, courts have advanced the interests and rights of individuals and groups which lack political support, advocate unpopular causes, or challenge accepted practices at the local, state, or national level.

Judicial insulation from political considerations, however, is relative rather than absolute. Few judges are political eunuchs. Instead, the typical judge has been active in public affairs before securing a place on the bench. Most have run for public office, served in legislative or executive positions, been involved in party politics, or otherwise been exposed to controversy and the pressures of public life. Inevitably, these experiences shape policy preferences, political philosophies, and personal values, as well as the political sensitivities of jurists. Rare indeed is the judge who is totally immune to constituency considerations or public opinion. Those elected to the bench, especially if they must stand for reelection, frequently are mindful of the concerns of the electorate on controversial legal issues such as school desegregation, abortion, and church-state relations. Appointed judges, particularly if they have aspirations for advancement to a higher court, sometimes are attentive to the interests of those who hold the power of appointment. More generally, concern for public opinion often leads courts to avoid controversy and unpopular decisions, particularly in policy areas such as housing and zoning where judicial rulings are not easily enforced.

Enhancing the reluctance of the courts to tackle controversial issues are the constraints over judicial power exercised by other components of the political system. On complex questions of public policy, judicial rulings cannot be enforced without active involvement by other public officials. Insuring official compliance with court orders is greatly complicated by the decentralization of the American federal system. Another constraint is the ability of other political actors to alter over time the composition of various courts through the appointment or election of judges with different positions on key issues. Certainly judicial outcomes on controversial issues such as school desegregation, school finance, and housing during the 1970s were strongly influenced by the appointment of four "strict constructionists" to the U.S. Supreme Court by Richard Nixon.[1]

Unpopular rulings also may provoke legislative efforts to restrict the jurisdiction of courts, or stimulate laws or constitutional amendments aimed at overturning controversial decisions. Illustrative is the political storm stirred by a federal court ruling in 1971 which ordered the merger of suburban school districts with the Detroit school system.[2] Forty suburbs immediately appealed the ruling, as suburbanites vowed to keep their children out of the public schools rather than have them bused to ghetto neighborhoods in Detroit. Suburban outrage stirred an emotional campaign against court-ordered busing to achieve school integration, led by President Nixon and most of the members of the Michigan congressional delegation. In overturning the lower-court ruling in 1974, the Supreme Court, with the four Nixon appointees voting together to provide the five-to-four majority, emphasized "the logistical and other serious problems attending large-scale transportation of students" in denying the need for metropolitan-wide remedies for segregated schools.[3]

Involvement of the courts in zoning and housing controversies in the suburbs provokes similar responses from political leaders. Efforts by a federal judge to disperse public housing in the Atlanta area led to angry calls for congressional action by two local representatives. "We are headed for the same catastrophe in court-ordered housing that we have now with court-ordered busing," argued one, while the other saw "Middle America . . . losing control of its own country. We are seeing things done to schools and now communities by . . . court decree that wouldn't have been done by a legislature. Congress just has to face up to its responsibility to deal with the courts." [4] The action of a state court in New Jersey in setting aside part of a local zoning ordinance to permit the development of apartments was condemned by one gubernatorial candidate in 1973 as "outrageous and unconstitutional." To check usurpation by the courts, he urged local residents to "rise up every time someone challenges their right to govern themselves and their right to zone their own towns." [5]

The Attractions of the Courts

Traditionally, legal action has been a last resort in zoning and housing disputes in the suburbs. Developers and land owners generally prefer negotiation to litigation; and they rarely go to court unless their proposals have been rejected or shelved by local government. Among open-housing advocates, local groups primarily interested in building housing typically follow the same path. Before suing suburban DuPage County and a number of its municipalities, an organization seeking to develop subsidized housing in the Chicago area "tried every other way. We tried providing housing ourselves. We tried working with municipalities and the county. As a last resort, we turned toward the courts." [6]

Litigation has been viewed in a different light by open-housing interests with broad general objectives. Rather than being a last resort, the courts were a preferred arena for organizations such as NAACP, NCDH, Suburban Action, the Lawyers Committee for Civil Rights Under Law, and the American Civil Liberties Union, who hoped to secure sweeping policy change through favorable decisions on a few cases. Successful litigation held the promise "of establishing new rights for the whole class of inner city residents and of prohibiting entire ranges of conduct by local zoners." [7]

Legal action also was better suited to the capabilities of the national open-housing movement than activities aimed directly at suburban governments. Staffed by a handful of middle-class professionals, supported primarily by foundation grants, and lacking a grass-roots constituency of any significance, these groups could not help but view the courts as an appealing alternative to direct action in suburban political arenas in which the odds against outside challengers of local zoning were formidable. [8] Rarely is the absence of constituency support an important constraint on contesting issues in the courts. Moreover, shifting the locus of decision to the courts promised to neutralize much of the inherent political advantage possessed by local interests within the suburban boards and councils which determine housing and land-use policies. Reliance on litigation also permits battlegrounds to be chosen with care. Decisions as to where to file suits, and whether to sue in state or federal court, rest with those who initiate litigation, who can seek test cases which appear to have wide impact and high potential for success.

Another political attraction of legal action is the opportunity afforded weakly articulated interests to build political support. Litigation generates publicity for a cause, drawing attention to both the substance of an issue and the groups pressing for change. Suburban Action Institute was particularly effective in using lawsuits to draw media and public attention to the organization's goals and activities. Favorable decisions, of course, further enhance the visibility of successful litigants and the issues they raise. Equally important, "court victories help demonstrate the legitimacy of the movement, elevating activists' calls for housing change from the status of impudent demands on behalf of a bunch of down-and-outers to firm insistence on the enforcement of constitutional and statutory rights." [9]

By publicizing an issue, legitimating demands for reform, and raising the prospect of drastic change, court action can amplify the political influence of the challengers of the status quo. In effect, litigation can enlist the courts with their formidable powers on the side of advocates of change. Open-housing groups in New Jersey had little direct influence on Governor William T. Cahill, a suburban Republican, but successes in court stimulated Cahill to seek changes in the state's system of land-use control which could pass judicial muster. The "message" from the courts, Cahill told the state legislature in 1970, "should be loud and clear! We must undertake corrective measures now if we are to insure the maintenance of controls in the hands of the local officials." [10] President Nixon sounded a similar theme the following year, arguing that local zoning policies "no doubt will end up in the courts if they are not satisfactorily dealt with outside the courts through timely and enlightened local action." [11] Federal court rulings growing out of open-housing litigation also stimulated the Nixon Administration to file suits against allegedly racially discriminatory practices by suburbs in the St. Louis and Cleveland areas. And decisions in federal courts limiting the location of public housing in black neighborhoods forced the Department of Housing and Urban Development to seek to disperse low-cost housing beyond the inner city.

For groups interested in building housing in the suburbs, litigation also offers a means of bringing pressure to bear on local government. Developers and landowners have long used the threat of court action to bolster their bargaining position in negotiations with local officials. As Shields and Spector point out, the same tactics are available to open-housing interests:

> Civil rights and housing groups can use the threat of a lawsuit against local officials to enhance their bargaining position in negotiations for zoning change; they can file suit to increase the pressure, and then drop it if a settlement is hammered out; in some cases they can get preliminary injunctions which hamstring local officials for an extended period until the main case is tried. Litigation puts the initiative in the hands of the open suburbs activist, and where his case is strong, gives him considerable clout in the bargaining situation. [12]

The Risks of Litigation

Going to court, of course, does not insure success for any group. The courts are an arcane political arena, full of pitfalls for the inexperienced litigant and occasional surprises even for the experienced. Particularly when the goal is new law in a complex area of public policy such as housing and land use, successful litigation requires substantial technical expertise, staying power, and financial and organizational resources. Considerable skill is required in selecting cases from among the scores of possibilities, as well as in determining whether to file in federal or state court. The intricacies of local zoning policies and practices must be mastered so that a detailed record can be developed for clear and persuasive presentation to a busy judge whose knowledge of such matters is necessarily limited. Data need to be accumulated and analyzed on housing and employment patterns in the particular suburban area and its metropolitan surroundings. Choices must be made from among a variety of constitutional approaches of the legal principles on which a case will rest. Open-housing litigants also have to consider the kinds of remedies they want the courts to apply in a particular case should the challenge be successful. In the process of litigating, briefs must be filed or contested, oral arguments prepared, witnesses arranged, appeals filed, and a variety of other costly and time-consuming chores performed, all of which sorely test the limited resources of most open-housing litigants.

Another important constraint is the fact that litigation does not occur in a vacuum. When suburban zoning and housing policies are challenged in court, the typical response is not conciliatory. Legal action by the New York Civil Liberties Union and Suburban Action aimed at zoning practices on Long Island led one local official to promise to "vigorously oppose this [suit] with all that I have in me." [13] After suits were filed against housing procedures in Parma, Ohio, the mayor of the suburb in the Cleveland area pledged to fight "as far as necessary." [14] When faced with legal action, most suburbs have not hesitated to tap the local exchequer in order to hire expensive legal talent to prepare their defense in court. Oyster Bay on Long Island retained a large Wall Street firm to defend home rule and local control in a zoning suit brought by the NAACP, while a major New Haven firm was hired to contest a challenge to New Canaan's zoning by Suburban Action.[15] In Mahwah in northern New Jersey, Suburban Action's adversaries in court were established law firms from Newark and the suburbs.[16]

Local governments also bring substantial staying power to zoning and housing contests in court, which provides them with a considerable advantage over adversaries who rarely can afford protracted delays. Crowded calendars, postponements, appeals, and other factors mean that courts seldom settle issues with dispatch. In New Jersey, the landmark zoning case involving Mount Laurel Township was in the state courts for almost five years before the Supreme Court finally ruled in 1975.[17] Since time is a particularly important constraint in the production of housing, the delays in the legal process make most developers reluctant to go into court. As a builders' representative in New Jersey explains: "It's no secret that many developers operate on borrowed money. With interest rates rising and construction costs rising all the time, delays of any kind can mean the difference between a fair profit and no profit at all." [18] Fear of tying up their assets in a disputed parcel of land, as well as concern over the costs of litigation, lead most developers to seek sites elsewhere or to compromise with local government rather than bring actions in court. In the northwestern portion of the New York region, home builders have been unwilling to contest local moratoriums on new construction in court because, in the words of a zoning lawyer, delays inherent in the process mean "the victory would be Pyrrhic." [19]

Illustrative of such Pyrrhic victories is the suit brought by a developer against Nether Providence Township, a suburb in the Philadelphia area, which refused to permit the construction of apartments. After almost six years in the courts, Joseph Girsh won a ruling from the Pennsylvania Supreme Court in 1970 that Nether Providence had to make some land available for multiple-family dwellings.[20] In response, the suburb zoned land in a quarry for apartment development rather than rezone Girsh's property. The developer returned to the Court, which eventually ordered township officials to issue a building permit for the apartment project. By this time, however, Girsh had died.

Suburbs also can switch from one exclusionary device to another in an effort to frustrate challengers of local zoning who seek relief in the courts. If the courts rule four-acre zoning unconstitutional, "a town can preserve large lots by requiring long setbacks from lot lines or large minimum yard widths. If these provisions are invalidated the town may then require a minimum house size and a maximum lot coverage, which would also preserve large lots. And so on, if not ad infinitum at least ad nauseum as far as the frustrated plaintiff is concerned." [21]

Nor do victories in court assure that suburbs will readily alter their zoning in accordance with judicial mandates. In 1975, the New Jersey Supreme Court invalidated exclusionary zoning in suburban Mount Laurel in a ruling which indicated that all developing suburbs in the state must zone in an inclusionary rather than exclusionary basis.[22] A representative of the New Jersey Builder's Association, however, cautioned that "we are assuming too much if we thought voluntary compliance with this decision would be the major result." Instead, "many municipalities will sit pat . . . so as not to appear to be inviting development of [subsidized] housing. That's not what the court wants to see, but it is a fact of life. They will tell developers of low- and moderate-income housing to 'sue us,' and the developer will have to use [the court's] opinion as a club." [23]

Delays in court, foot-dragging by local officials, and changes in local restrictions designed to frustrate the courts pose even more serious problems for organizations which seek to build subsidized housing in the suburbs. Non-profit developers of low-cost housing typically have fewer financial resources and less staying power than private builders. Opponents of subsidized housing in Newton in the Boston area "realized that the best chance of stopping the housing plan was to stall the developers in court until land options expired or [the Newton Community Development Fund] was out of money." [24] Legal costs also are a substantial deterrent for most open-housing groups seeking to build subsidized units in the suburbs. In Chicago, a federal court ordered a hearing on the merits of a case brought by a non-profit developer which charged that Evanston's refusal to permit construction of low-cost apartments was motivated by racial discrimination.[25] The plaintiffs, however, were unable to press the action because of inadequate funds. After emerging victorious from a five-year struggle in the courts to build subsidized housing in Union City in the San Francisco Bay Area, the Southern Alameda Spanish Speaking Organization had to sell part of the site in order to meet the financial burdens imposed by the lengthy legal wrangle.

Compared with private developers, organizations seeking to construct subsidized housing have few alternatives to the courts when they face local hostility. Compromise with local government is difficult since there is little to negotiate when the community is opposed to all low-cost housing. Once the open-housing group goes to court, its staying power is bound to be tested in a contest in which most of the advantages lie with the local government. Speaking of the Black Jack litigation, one observer noted that "the eventual outcome may rest on the plaintiffs' financial ability to withstand Black Jack's delaying tactics." [26] With costs for the project rising $300 a day, the case did not go to trial for almost two years, and another three years passed before the issue was settled in the federal courts. Such delays can force open-housing organizations to surrender their options on the site in question, mooting the litigation. Lengthy court battles also can cost developers of subsidized housing the federal funds needed to finance their projects, since typically these funds are not committed until the developer secures all local consents. By the time the sponsors of the Black Jack project won their case in federal court, the Section 236 program was defunct, and no other federal funds were available for constructing moderate-income housing in the suburbs.

Access to the courts is another important obstacle to the use of litigation to open the suburbs. To secure access, or standing,

first, . . . the individual bringing a case has to show that he is suffering or is immediately threatened with injury; mere possibility of injury is not sufficient. Second, the right must be a legally protected one, not merely a "moral" or "natural" right. Third, the right must be a personal one of the plaintiff, not the right of another person; a general claim that a law is unjust, unfair, or unconstitutional does not fill the standing requirements. Fourth, the two parties to the suit must be truly adversaries. Their interests have to be in conflict; they cannot be friends who merely want the court to settle a difference of opinion. Fifth, if the contested action is that of a government agency, that action must be final to be "ripe" for review. Unless there are exceptional circumstances, a potential litigant has to demonstrate that he has used all available administrative procedures to secure redress. Sixth, the decision sought must be one that is within the province of the judiciary to give, not a dispute on which a judge may merely tender advice or one whose solution the Constitution entrusts to other organs of government. [27]

These criteria are important for judges, who are both busy and human. Limiting access to the courts prevents judges from being overwhelmed by litigation. Standing also permits judges to duck controversial issues, or to decide them on technical points rather than on their substantive merits.

In zoning matters, the courts traditionally have accorded standing only to those whose rights have been directly affected by the local ordinance in question, typically property owners in the area covered by the particular zoning provision. Given this narrow formulation of access, open-housing lawyers must convince a court that plaintiffs such as a

non-profit housing developer, or residents of the community who need
subsidized housing, or nonresidents who are prevented from living in
a suburb by zoning restrictions, have a legitimate stake in the validity of
a suburban zoning ordinance. In some jurisdictions, these efforts have
borne fruit, as judges willing to examine the exclusionary implications of
suburban housing and zoning policies have opened their courts to those
who claim to be disadvantaged by local restrictions.[28] Legislatures also
can prod judges by broadening the criteria for standing, as occurred in
New Jersey with the enactment of a 1969 law which permitted any resident of the state to challenge local zoning ordinances in court.[29]

Broadening of standing in housing and land-use litigation, however,
has been far from universal. Despite the willingness of many federal
judges to widen access in zoning cases, the U.S. Supreme Court in 1975
denied standing to poor blacks and Puerto Ricans to challenge land-use
restrictions in Penfield, a suburb in the Rochester area. The Supreme
Court found no evidence that the plaintiffs, all of whom lived in Rochester, had "personally . . . been injured" by Penfield's housing policies.[30]
"None of these petitioners," the majority opinion emphasized, "has a
present interest in any Penfield property; none is himself subject to the
ordinance's strictures; and none has ever been denied a variance or permit by [Penfield] officials." [31] In the wake of this decision, open-housing
litigants were forced to revise their legal strategies in a variety of cases in
the federal courts. One lawyer thought the ruling "requires plaintiffs virtually to prove in advance the very issue they are bringing to court." [32]
One of the first casualties of the Supreme Court's ruling was a suit
against Oyster Bay on Long Island, which was dropped because
NAACP lawyers doubted they "could ever reach a substantial issue on
exclusionary zoning" in light of the high court's restrictive interpretation
of standing.[33]

Even if open-housing litigants can establish standing, there is of
course no guarantee that the courts will accept their arguments that
suburban zoning and housing policies which restrict access of lower-
income and minority groups are unconstitutional. Just the opposite, in
fact. Courts traditionally have been reluctant to become involved in zoning issues, a judicial posture which has enabled local governments to
turn back most legal challenges over the years. The prevailing tone of
judicial restraint and deference to local determinations was set by the
U.S. Supreme Court when it upheld the constitutionality of zoning in
1926. "If the validity of the legislative classification for zoning purposes

be fairly debatable," the Court ruled, "the legislative judgment must be allowed to control." [34] One of the consequences of this ruling was to limit greatly the involvement of federal courts in zoning cases. The Supreme Court's presumption of the validity of local regulations also strongly influenced state courts, which hear most zoning cases. A typical perspective was expressed by the New Jersey Supreme Court in 1970: "the judicial role in reviewing a zoning ordinance is tightly circumscribed. There is a strong presumption in favor of its validity, and the court cannot invalidate it, or any provision thereof, unless this presumption is overcome by a clear showing that it is arbitrary or unreasonable." [35]

Defeats in the courts, like victories, can have repercussions far beyond the particular case or issue at hand, particularly if a case reaches the highest state courts or the U.S. Supreme Court. In deciding *James* v. *Valtierra* in 1971, the Supreme Court ostensibly was determining whether California's requirement for a local referendum on public-housing proposals constituted a denial of the constitutional right of equal protection under the law. But in upholding mandatory referenda for public housing, the Court dampened hopes of open-housing litigators across the nation, while encouraging defenders of suburban autonomy. Equally important, the Court advanced a narrow view of racial discrimination and the scope of equal protection in housing cases which impeded litigation aimed at a variety of other exclusionary practices in the suburbs. [36]

A final risk in relying on the courts to open the suburbs is the likelihood that most victories in zoning cases will have limited impact on housing opportunities across the nation. By its nature, suburban zoning does not lend itself to the kind of sweeping judicial pronouncements which began the desegregation of southern schools and the reapportionment of state legislatures. The sheer number of local governments involved, and the variety of their policies and practices, make it extremely difficult to secure court rulings that will have an effect on local policies in every suburb. As Richard F. Babcock has emphasized, "the almost unlimited variations in fact from one zoning case to another make a school desegregation case appear like simple arithmetic." Nor, Babcock continues, "should the advocates of judicial relief from exclusionary local regulations overlook what bruised zoning lawyers have lived with: a decree involving Golden Bough, Ill., or Grunt, Neb., usually settles only a dispute involving one parcel in one municipality." [37]

Approaches to the Courts

Disputes over particular parcels in Golden Bough, Grunt, and thousands of other local jurisdictions give rise to most court actions concerning land use. The typical legal challenge of local zoning involves an individual landowner seeking to free his property from the specific provisions of an ordinance which restricts its use, and thus its value. These suits rest on the claim that the owner's constitutional property rights have been violated by the zoning restriction in question. In the standard scenario, the property owner contends that the local ordinance bears no relation to the needs of public health, safety, or welfare, the considerations which form the basis for the regulation of land use. The owner then argues that the proposed use is consistent with the health, safety, and general welfare of the public. Given these circumstances, the plaintiff contends that the zoning restriction is not valid. Since the local government is unwilling to compensate the owner for the difference between the value of the property as zoned and its worth on the open market, the provision in question deprives the owner of his property without due process of law. Usually embellishing these basic arguments are allegations concerning denial of procedural due process resulting from failure of local officials to hold hearings, provide adequate notice, or maintain a record of their proceedings.[38]

Open-housing litigation often resembles traditional legal disputes between property owners and local governments over zoning, with a nonprofit developer seeking to free a specific parcel of land from restrictions which prevent the construction of subsidized housing. A case in point was an effort by HOPE, an open-housing group in the Chicago area, to have the courts set aside floor-space requirements which prevented the construction of moderately-priced housing in suburban Lombard. HOPE was denied a building permit for two-story homes with 750 square feet because Lombard required a minimum of 1,000 square feet on the ground floor of such homes. HOPE charged that the rule "bears no relation to health, safety, or the general welfare. It's merely an exclusionary device [which] sets a minimum cost for a home. If we built our home with 1,000 square feet . . . on the ground floor, it would be impossible to sell it to a low- or moderate-income family." [39]

With the rapid growth of open-housing litigation in the years since 1969, however, have come efforts to broaden the basis of legal action against zoning. Particularly within organizations such as NAACP,

NCDH, and Suburban Action, lawyers have been eager to move beyond the case-by-case approach of traditional zoning litigation, with its focus on the rights of property owners, a single parcel of land, and specific provisions of the zoning code of a particular municipality. Increasingly, open-housing groups have sought to widen the scope of litigation to include all land-use controls in a suburban jurisdiction, or in a group of suburbs, or throughout a metropolitan area or even a state. On Long Island, the NAACP and NCDH challenged Oyster Bay's entire zoning code rather than a specific provision, charging that the huge suburb's zoning made it financially impossible for lower-income families, and especially blacks, to live in the community.[40] In New Jersey, Suburban Action used a single lawsuit to try to set aside exclusionary zoning in a group of neighboring municipalities in Bergen County.[41] SAI also launched a more general class action against five New Jersey suburbs in 1972 aimed at invalidating all forms of restrictive zoning throughout the state.[42] Two years later, the New Jersey American Civil Liberties Union and NCDH filed a class-action suit against twenty-three suburbs in Middlesex County, charging that "the policies and practices of all defendant municipalities taken together bar plaintiffs from securing housing and employment opportunities throughout a major and expanding market area."[43]

A primary motivating factor in the development of these broader-based suits is the desire to escape the limited consequences of traditional litigation. Suburban Action justified its general class action in New Jersey on the grounds that zoning suits brought against a single suburb had no impact on other communities:

> Various lawsuits have been brought in New Jersey to challenge the legality of the exclusionary zoning ordinances of one or another community. But as succeeding lower courts strike down such ordinances, no other communities manifest an intention to voluntarily remove their own illegal exclusionary provisions. In fact, their positions appear to be hardening. The situation is grave because it gives every indication of requiring the same kind of legal attack on a community-by-community basis that was necessary to eliminate segregated school systems in the Deep South. Such an effort will exhaust the resources of plaintiffs and their lawyers, will require an exhausting investment of time of the judiciary, and will commit an entire generation of people to becoming permanent victims of exclusion.[44]

SAI sought an injunction which prohibited all municipalities in New Jersey from enforcing or enacting zoning laws which prohibited mobile homes or apartments, limited the number of apartments that could be constructed in the community, restricted the number of rooms or bedrooms permitted in apartments, or established minimum floor sizes for single family homes.

Concomitant with efforts to broaden the target of litigation, open-housing groups have sought to persuade judges to consider a wider range of interests than those associated with traditional zoning litigation. Open-housing suits often attempt to link local restrictions to the housing needs of lower-income and minority families who do not live in the community. In making their case, civil-rights groups document the general need for lower-cost housing in the area surrounding the suburb or suburbs whose zoning is being challenged. Then they argue that these housing deficiencies result at least in part from local housing and land-use restrictions. Efforts often are made to bolster the case with data on metropolitan employment patterns which demonstrate the decentralization of jobs, the dearth of moderately-priced housing adjacent to suburban employment centers, the high incidence of unemployment and dependency in the older cities, and the difficulties encountered by poor city dwellers in finding and commuting to jobs in the suburbs. The utility of this general approach, at least in the federal courts, was seriously damaged by the U.S. Supreme Court's refusal to accord standing to low-income plaintiffs who were unable to demonstrate that they had been directly injured by local zoning restrictions.[45]

Groups seeking to open the suburbs also have tried to expand the legal basis of litigation beyond the traditional emphasis on due process and property rights. Of greatest attraction among the legal weapons available has been the equal protection clause of the Fourteenth Amendment to the Constitution, which provides that no state shall "deny to any person within its jurisdiction the equal protection of the laws." This constitutional guarantee has been the cutting edge of the civil-rights movement in the federal courts in recent decades, underlying the historic rulings of the Supreme Court on issues such as school desegregation and voting rights. Since most of the organizations which have sought to use judicial power to pry open the suburbs have been civil-rights groups primarily interested in ending racial discrimination, it is hardly surprising that they have embraced equal-protection arguments in the fight against suburban exclusion.

Central to the use of equal protection in challenging suburban exclusion in the courts is the claim that suburban housing and zoning policies discriminate against certain classes of the population.[46] Some suits have focused on charges of explicitly discriminatory behavior, seeking to invalidate local ordinances or actions on the grounds that suburban officials or voters were motivated by the desire to exclude blacks or other minorities. Other litigation has been based on the claim that suburban zoning inherently discriminates against the poor by creating a classification of people on the basis of wealth who are not afforded the same treatment under the law as other citizens. Suits grounded on the argument that suburban zoning denies equal protection to the poor have grown in favor, even among groups primarily interested in the housing problems of blacks. Overt racial discrimination tends to be difficult to prove in housing matters, and there is almost infinite variety in the kinds of discriminatory acts that can be employed by suburbs. Economic discrimination, on the other hand, can be demonstrated in almost any suburb by documenting the impact of local housing and land-use policies on the cost of housing within the community, and then showing the effect of these cost limitations on the ability of lower-income groups to reside in the community. Discrimination against the poor, moreover, automatically excludes large numbers of blacks and other minorities, a consequence strongly emphasized in most open-housing briefs based on equal protection.

Despite the appeal of these arguments to many open-housing groups, equal protection did not become the central legal strategy in the struggle against suburban exclusion in the courts, as it had in school integration, voting rights, and a number of other civil-rights issues. Among the other available approaches to the courts is the claim that restrictive housing and land-use policies infringe on the constitutional right to travel since "exclusionary zoning ordinances deny a specific class of citizens the right to enter a community with the hope of bettering their lives in terms of housing and education." [47] Open-housing litigators also have argued that suburban zoning constitutes a denial of voting rights, since nonresidents are excluded from participating in local public decisions which affect where they can live.[48] Due process grounds which have been the stock in trade of zoning lawyers also provide the legal basis for some civil-rights suits. Open-housing interests have challenged the use of local zoning power to prohibit subsidized housing, mobile homes, and apartments as unreasonable exercises of local power, bearing no relationship to public health, safety, or the general welfare. Due process also provides a legal rationale to attack suburban zoning on the grounds that it promotes "illegitimate public objectives such as racial segregation." [49]

Civil-rights groups also have sought to attack exclusionary zoning through litigation aimed at federal agencies rather than local governments. Suburban Action challenged federal sewer and recreational grants to a Westchester suburb on the grounds that the affluent community "denie[d] minority citizens Federal benefits by using its zoning regulations and land-use practices to exclude blacks and other minorities and persons of low and moderate income." [50] In 1971, NCDH sought in federal court to block the location of a large office for the Internal Revenue Service in Brookhaven on Long Island, contending that the suburb excluded housing for lower-income and minority families.

Nor has zoning *per se* been the sole target of open-housing litigation. Suburban unwillingness to participate in subsidized housing programs has been attacked in a number of suits, most of which have challenged the constitutionality of the federal requirement for local cooperation agreements in public-housing programs. Use of the initiative and referendum to bar lower-cost housing also has been contested in a number of court actions, including the unsuccessful effort aimed at public-housing referenda in California which reached the U.S. Supreme Court in 1971. [51]

In part, this variety of legal approaches reflects the complexity of housing and land-use issues, as well as the diversity of local policies and procedures in the highly decentralized political world of suburbia. It also results from the pluralism of the efforts to open the suburbs through the courts. In the early 1970s, scores of organizations across the nation were involved in open-housing litigation, ranging from local groups pursuing very specific objectives in a single court action to national civil-rights groups seeking sweeping changes in a variety of cases. None of the latter groups, however, was able to provide central coordination and intellectual leadership for open-housing litigators, in contrast with the role of the NAACP Legal Defense and Education Fund in the campaign against segregated schools in the South.

Reinforcing this plurality of approaches has been the existence of fifty-one court systems in the United States. Equal protection arguments have been used primarily in the federal courts. Cases brought in the states, on the other hand, tend to build on the due-process foundation of zoning law which has been erected by individual state courts over the years. As long as federal judges were expanding the scope of the equal-protection clause, open-housing litigators were strongly attracted to this line of reasoning in the hope of securing a far-reaching ruling by the U.S. Supreme Court invalidating exclusionary zoning. Once the Supreme Court began to retreat from extending equal protection in areas such as housing, school finance, and metropolitan school desegregation, civil-rights groups interested in suburban exclusion turned to other legal arguments. They also exhibited greater willingness to bring cases on due-process grounds in the state courts. As a consequence of these circumstances and developments, most open-housing groups employ a variety of legal approaches—often in the same case—in the hope that one of the many keys available would open the doors of the suburbs to lower-income and minority groups.

Judicial Breaches in the Walls of Exclusion

By the middle of the 1970s, open-housing interests had yet to find the legal key that would open the door to suburbia in general. Their efforts, however, had won victories in courts that narrowed the legal base of exclusion in a number of jurisdictions. Large lots had been invalidated by state courts "as unrelated to the general welfare, health, or safety of the community and as an unreasonable use of the police power in violation of the due process and equal protection clauses of the Fourteenth Amendment." [52] Requirements for minimum floor areas and minimum building sizes have been overturned in various states, together with restrictions on the number of apartments that might be constructed in a community, limitations on the number of bedrooms in apartments, exclusion of mobile homes, and the zoning of large amounts of land for industrial development in order to foreclose residential construction. Age limitations and general population ceilings have been rejected by judges, as have limits on the number of dwelling units that might be built in a community.

Fiscal rationales for exclusion also received short shrift in some state courts. In a 1971 decision invalidating a highly restrictive apartment ordinance enacted by Glassboro in the Philadelphia area, a New Jersey judge ruled that "the attempt to equate the cost of education to the number of children allowed in a project or a community has no relation to zoning. The governmental cost must be an official concern but not to an extent that it determines who shall live in the municipality." [53] Four

years later, the New Jersey Supreme Court, while recognizing that a developing suburb "may properly zone for and seek industrial ratables to
create a better economic balance for the community vis-a-vis educational
and governmental costs engendered by residential development," denied
"the validity of municipal exclusion by zoning of types of housing and
kinds of people for the same local financial end." [54] Minimum lot
requirements of four acres were set aside by the Pennsylvania Supreme
Court in 1965 in a decision which rejected the use of local land-use controls "to prevent the entrance of newcomers in order to avoid future burdens, economic and otherwise, upon the administration of public services and facilities." [55]

In the process of making these decisions, judges in a number of states
moved away from presuming the validity of local land-use regulations.
More and more judges began to question the value judgements expressed
in local ordinances, the motives of officials in administering them, and
their effects on interests beyond those of the affected property owners.
An appeals court in California ruled in 1970 that the trial court in a zoning case "was not limited to the face of the ordinance, but could receive
evidence of its immediate purpose, its ultimate objective, and of the circumstances attending its adoption." [56] In Pennsylvania, the courts have
placed the burden of proving that mobile homes or apartments are "det-
rimental to the public health, welfare, safety, and morals of the community" on the municipality whenever such uses are excluded.[57] Courts in
Michigan also shifted the burden of proof to local governments when
they exclude mobile homes or apartments, insisting that "the massive nationwide housing shortage . . . necessitates a redefining of the term
'general welfare' as applied to justify residential zoning." [58]

In line with the conclusion of the Michigan courts, judges have steadily broadened the definition of the general welfare in connection with
local zoning and housing. Federal courts in California and New York
have held that a community cannot ignore needs of local residents, and
particularly lower-income and minority residents, in developing and implementing housing plans and policies. The California case grew out of
efforts by residents of Union City, a suburb on the eastern side of San
Francisco Bay, to block the construction of subsidized housing sponsored
by a Chicano group. In ordering a hearing on the substantive merits of
the issue, the U.S. Court of Appeals for the Ninth Circuit concluded
that "given the recognized importance of equal opportunities in housing,
it may well be . . . the responsibility of a city and its planning officials

to see that the city's plan as initiated or as it develops accommodates the needs of its low-income families, who usually—if not always—are members of minority groups." [59] After rehearing, the district court ordered Union City to make provision for its lower-income residents; and eleven acres eventually were rezoned by Union City for the project. In the New York case, Lackawanna in the Buffalo area was sued after the local government blocked construction of an integrated housing project in a white neighborhood. A federal district court struck down the obstacles erected by the blue-collar suburb, ruling that the "city officials of Lackawanna have the obligation to consider and plan for all the citizens in the community." [60]

An even broader view of the general welfare in zoning and housing cases has been adopted by some state courts, which have considered housing needs in a regional or metropolitan context. In setting aside a prohibition on apartments in Nether Providence Township in 1970, the Pennsylvania Supreme Court noted that "it is intolerable to allow one municipality (or many municipalities) to close its doors at the expense of surrounding communities and the central city." [61] At the same time, the Pennsylvania court struck down two-acre zoning in Concord Township, ruling that "it is not for any given township to say who may or may not live within its confines, while disregarding the interests of the entire area." [62] The following year, a suit against Madison Township by two developers and Suburban Action led a New Jersey court to invalidate large lots, minimum house sizes, and apartment restrictions in a decision which rested heavily on the conclusion that the "general welfare does not stop at each municipal boundary." In the judge's view, "large areas of vacant and developable land should not be zoned, as Madison Township has into such minimum lot sizes and with such other restrictions that regional as well as local housing needs are shunted aside." [63]

Judicial broadening of the definition of the general welfare involved in local housing and land-use determinations inevitably has led courts to consider whether those whose housing needs are not satisfied by local policies are being denied equal protection. In dealing with equal protection issues, several federal courts have been willing to examine the housing patterns produced by local policies as evidence of racial discrimination, rather than require plaintiffs to demonstrate that the allegedly discriminatory actions were motivated by racial prejudice. For example, in ruling favorably on a suit designed to force five suburbs in the Cleveland area to accept subsidized housing, a federal district court accepted as *prima facie* evidence of racial discrimination the paucity of blacks in the five communities, the general need for lower-cost housing in the suburbs, and the refusal of the five municipalities to cooperate with the Cuyahoga Metropolitan Housing Authority.[64]

As illustrated by the Cleveland case, the growing concern of the federal courts with local policies which produce racial segregation in the metropolis also has jeopardized the ability of suburbs to use local autonomy to exclude subsidized housing. In cases dealing with public housing in Philadelphia, Chicago, and other cities, federal judges ruled that the placement of subsidized housing in black areas constituted a denial of equal protection, and that projects must be dispersed throughout the city.[65] These principles were first extended to the suburbs in 1972 as a result of litigation arising from the refusal of officials in Fulton County to permit the Atlanta Housing Authority to construct low-income housing in Fulton County. After finding that "the only objection the County authorities have . . . is that the apartments would be occupied by low-income, black tenants," the court ordered Fulton County to work with Atlanta in devising a plan for dispersing public housing throughout the metropolitan area.[66] In Cleveland, the federal district court instructed suburban officials to negotiate agreements with the metropolitan housing authority for the location of subsidized units within their boundaries. And in 1976 the Supreme Court indicated that metropolitan remedies might be appropriate in the public-housing case in Chicago because the two agencies which had engaged in racial discrimination in locating projects, the Chicago Housing Authority and HUD, had authority to operate beyond the city limits.[67]

State judges have gone even further in extending the coverage of equal protection to those disadvantaged by suburban zoning. While the federal courts have limited themselves to racial discrimination in dealing with equal protection in housing cases, state courts, particularly in New Jersey, have dealt with economic separation as well. In one New Jersey case, apartment restrictions which increased the cost of housing beyond the means of most residents of suburban Glassboro, "a community where Mr. Average Man lives with his family," were judged to constitute "discrimination based on economic status [which] offend[s] the equal protection mandate of the Constitution."[68] As in federal cases dealing with racial discrimination, state courts have considered the effect as well as the intent of suburban zoning regulations in determining whether the less affluent have been discriminated against. A New Jersey court invalidated zoning in Mount Laurel Township, which prohibited apartments and mobile homes, because local "patterns and practice clearly indicate that [the] municipality through its zoning ordinances has exhibited economic discrimination in that the poor have been deprived of adequate housing and the opportunity to secure the construction of subsidized housing." [69]

In March 1975, the New Jersey Supreme Court affirmed the trial court in the Mount Laurel case in a major judicial attack on exclusionary zoning. For the state's highest court, the basic issue was whether a developing suburb could employ zoning to "make it physically and economically impossible to provide low and moderate income housing in the municipality for the various categories of persons who need and want it and thereby, as Mount Laurel has, exclude such people from living within its confines because of the limited extent of their income and resources." [70] In unanimously ruling that Mount Laurel could not zone out the poor, the court insisted that local zoning must promote the general welfare by providing "for adequate housing of all categories of people." [71] In considering the general welfare, the court went on, developing suburbs like Mount Laurel had to take regional as well as local housing needs into account. Following this line of reason led the court to a sweeping conclusion:

> Broadly speaking, the presumptive obligation arises for each such municipality affirmatively to plan and provide, by its land use regulations, the reasonable opportunity for an appropriate variety and choice of housing, including, of course, low- and moderate-cost housing, to meet the needs, desires and resources of all categories of people who may desire to live within its boundaries. Negatively, it may not adopt regulations or policies which thwart or preclude that opportunity. [72]

In other words, the burden was on growing suburbs to demonstrate that they were promoting a variety of housing within their boundaries, not on those excluded to prove that they were being kept out by local zoning. To fulfill its housing obligations, communities like Mount Laurel "must permit multifamily housing, without bedroom or similar restrictions, as well as small dwellings on very small lots, low cost housing of other types and, in general, high density zoning, without artificial or unjustifiable minimum requirements as to lot size, building size and the like." [73]

Limiting the Scope of Equal Protection

For the public-interest lawyer who argued the case, Mount Laurel was "the decision which will open the suburbs to the poor." [74] Earlier decisions had prompted many interested parties to predict the inevitability of a judicial revolution that would force suburbia to lower its barriers to the poor. Few of the rulings expanding housing opportunities, however, represent the law of the land. State judges and lower federal courts rather than the U.S. Supreme Court produced all of the opinions which opened cracks in the walls of exclusion through 1975. Rulings by state courts, of course, directly affect housing and zoning in only a single state. Decisions by lower federal courts can be reversed on appeal, a not uncommon fate for expansive interpretations of the equal protection clause in the early 1970s. During these years, an increasingly conservative Supreme Court overturned lower court rulings in a set of decisions which clouded the prospects for sweeping judicial action against suburban exclusion in the federal courts.

James v. *Valtierra*, the first of these rulings, involved the requirement of the California constitution that local voters approve all public-housing proposals. In reversing a federal district court which found that the provision for a mandatory referendum denied blacks and the poor equal protection, the Court majority in a 5-3 decision concluded that "it cannot be said that California's Article XXXIV rests on 'distinctions based on race.' " [75] The majority opinion, written by Justice Hugo Black, emphasized that the California constitution required "referendum approval for any low-rent housing project, not only for projects which will be occupied by a racial minority." Black went on to note that the record in the case "would not support any claim that a law seemingly neutral on its face is in fact aimed at a racial minority." [76]

Justice Thurgood Marshall's dissent echoed the arguments of the plaintiffs and the lower court that the California constitution treated the poor differently with respect to subsidized housing than other groups. "The article explicitly singles out low-income persons to bear its burden. Publicly assisted housing developments designed to accommodate the aged, veterans, state employees, persons of moderate income, or any class of citizens other than the poor, need not be approved by prior referenda." Marshall also rejected a narrow formulation of equal protection based on explicit racial discrimination, as set forth in the majority opinion. "It is far too late in the day," wrote the first black to serve on the Supreme Court, "to contend that the Fourteenth Amendment prohibits only racial discrimination; and to me, singling out the poor to bear a burden not placed on any other class of citizens tramples the values that the Fourteenth Amendment was designed to protect." [77]

These contentions were rejected by the majority, which insisted that "a lawmaking procedure that 'disadvantages' a particular group does not always deny equal protection." Instead, the Court found much to be said for California's use of local referenda on matters such as public housing, terming it a "procedure for democratic decision-making" that "ensures that all the people of a community will have a voice in a decision which may lead to large expenditures of local governmental funds for increased public services and to lower tax revenues. It gives them a voice in decisions that will affect the future development of their own community." [78]

In terms of its direct impact on housing in the suburbs, the *Valtierra* decision was limited by the relatively narrow issue before the Court. The case did not deal with housing in general, or even all forms of subsidized housing. Instead, the issue was the constitutionality of mandatory referenda for low-income housing built by local governments under the public-housing program. As a consequence, the Court's ruling did not apply to subsidized housing in which local governments lack a direct role, such as the 235 and 236 programs where units were constructed by private developers or nonprofit organizations. Nor, given the emphasis in the majority opinion on California's long tradition of employing the referendum for a wide variety of public questions, did *Valtierra* provide any assurance that the Court would look with favor on provisions for voter approval of low-cost housing which might be enacted in the future by governments lacking California's tradition of direct democracy.

Despite these limitations, the *Valtierra* ruling had a significant impact on efforts to open the suburbs, both in and out of the courts. Inevitably, the decision disheartened advocates of open housing, particularly those who had pinned their hopes in the fight against suburban exclusion on a favorable ruling by the Supreme Court on *Valtierra*. Opponents of subsidized housing, on the other hand, were encouraged, as were suburbanites eager to employ local autonomy to strengthen the barriers against the poor and minority groups. As noted in chapter 4, a number of suburbs enacted housing and zoning referenda in the wake of *Valtierra*. And wherever local referenda were in force, whether directly sanctioned by *Valtierra* or not, proponents of subsidized housing were more likely than ever to be deterred from seeking local approval of their proposals. In California, for example, *Valtierra* "triggered the shelving of a number of 236 projects . . . thus dulling much of the salutary impact that a number of successful civil rights zoning cases were having." [79]

Valtierra's greatest significance, however, lay in the impact of its narrow conception of equal protection on federal judges in the lower courts. In the wake of the Court's ruling, a number of open-housing suits based on equal-protection arguments were rejected by federal judges who read *Valtierra* to require that "there must be some showing that a policy or activity which has a racially discriminatory effect results from a prior pattern of discrimination or that such policies affect only racial minorities." [80]

Early in 1974, a federal court in New York rejected a suit filed by Suburban Action which sought to force Nassau County to build low-income housing at Mitchel Field, a surplus military installation acquired by the county from the federal government. There was no doubt in the judge's mind that "community opposition to this form of housing had been racially motivated" in suburban Nassau County. But the court found "no proof of official conduct which has as its purpose the containment of Blacks or which has the effect of denying Blacks rights and opportunities available to whites." [81] Across the continent, a federal judge agreed that the effect of zoning in Los Altos Hills, in the San Francisco area, was to keep low-income housing out of the suburban community. Nonetheless, he ruled against the developer who brought suit, concluding that there was no denial of equal protection because the plaintiffs did not demonstrate that any non-residents suffered "as a direct, proximate and unavoidable consequence of the Los Altos Hills ordinance." [82]

Citing *Valtierra*, a three-judge court in Cleveland upheld the federal requirement that local public-housing agencies must enter into a cooperation agreement with the government of the community in which units are to be located. "On its face," the court concluded, "this requirement does not discriminate on the basis of race. Moreover, it does not establish an invidious discrimination based upon wealth." [83] In another aspect of the same litigation, the U.S. Court of Appeals for the Sixth Circuit used *Valtierra* in overturning a district court ruling that five suburbs in the Cleveland area were guilty of racial discrimination because of their failure to enter into cooperation agreements with the Cuyahoga Metropolitan Housing Authority. [84] According to the appeals court, "the plain language" of the Housing Act of 1937 means "exactly what it says, namely, that it is for the municipalities to decide whether they need low-rent housing and whether they desire to sign cooperation agreements. There is no basis to infer discrimination on the part of a municipality for doing what it has a lawful right to do under the express provisions of the Housing Act." [85]

While the lower federal courts were applying *Valtierra* to restrict legal challenges against suburban exclusion, the Supreme Court in April 1974 strongly endorsed local zoning in a case arising from the refusal of a suburban community to permit six college students to rent a house. Zoning in Belle Terre, a village of 700 upper-income residents located near the Stony Brook campus of the State University of New York, restricted land use to one-family dwellings occupied by families or unmarried couples, thus effectively excluding all apartments, boarding houses, fraternity houses, and the sharing of a house by more than two unrelated individuals. Writing for the majority in a 7-2 decision, Justice William O. Douglas warmly endorsed local zoning ordinances which restrict land uses in order to preserve community character:

> The regimes of boarding houses, fraternity houses, and the like present urban problems. More people occupy a given space; more cars are parked; noise travels with crowds.
>
> A quiet place where yards are wide, people few, and motor vehicles restricted are legitimate guidelines in a land use project addressed to family needs. . . . The police power is not confined to elimination of filth, stench, and unhealthy places. It is ample to lay out zones where family values, youth values, and the blessings of quiet seclusion, and clean air make the area a sanctuary for people. [86]

For those seeking to use the courts to open the suburbs, *Belle Terre* was more damaging than *Valtierra*. Unlike *Valtierra*, it dealt specifically with restrictive zoning in the suburbs. Moreover, *Belle Terre* was the first suburban zoning case to reach the Supreme Court in more than forty-five years, a circumstance which inevitably increased its significance. Most important, in upholding Belle Terre's housing restrictions, the Court seemed to endorse a wide range of exclusionary devices—such as apartment house prohibitions, large lots, minimum house sizes, and moratoriums on development—which could be justified by suburbs on the grounds that they were essential to provide "a quiet place where yards are wide" and "people few." Certainly this was the interpretation of Belle Terre's mayor, who claimed "that in pursuing the matter to the

Supreme Court we did a service to the nation as a whole because the issue of a community's right to privacy was truly crystalized and resolved." [87] And the following year, the U.S. Court of Appeals for the Ninth Circuit drew heavily on *Belle Terre* in upholding stringent growth controls in Petaluma, a rapidly growing suburb in Sonoma County to the north of San Francisco. "Under *Belle Terre*," the appeals court concluded, "the concept of the public welfare is sufficiently broad to uphold Petaluma's desire to preserve its small town character, its open spaces and low density of population, and to grow at an orderly and deliberate pace." [88]

Another problem in *Belle Terre* for open-housing litigators was the Court's exclusive concern with the desires of the local community. No mention was made of the interests of nonresidents in local zoning restrictions, or of the relationship between local zoning and regional housing needs. The court also strongly reaffirmed the presumption of validity of local zoning, arguing that "exercise of discretion . . . is a legislative not a judicial function." [89] A final negative aspect of *Belle Terre* for advocates of opening the suburbs was the Court's view that zoning involved "no 'fundamental' right guaranteed by the Constitution." [90] By adopting a narrow conception of the extent of equal protection afforded by the constitution on housing and zoning matters, the Court reinforced the presumption of validity of local actions. This perspective also enhanced the Court's unwillingness to substitute judicial for legislative judgment in local zoning. Obviously, these were not encouraging developments for those seeking to involve the courts in the lowering of the walls of suburban exclusion.

Open-housing litigators, however, cautioned against reading too much into either *Valtierra* or *Belle Terre*. The implications of both rulings, they emphasized, were limited by the specifics of the cases. Another cause for guarded optimism was the fact that not all federal judges received the same message from the Supreme Court. Illustrative of the different readings of *Valtierra* was the treatment of the issue of racial discrimination by federal judges in the Justice Department's suit against Black Jack in the St. Louis area. In light of *Valtierra*, the district court insisted that "racial considerations must be shown as part of the legislation or as a significant reason for the legislation." Opponents of the 236 project in Black Jack, the judge noted, had cited a variety of reasons for blocking the housing, including "the character of the community, road congestion, school impaction, property devaluation, and opposition to transient apartment dwellers." All of these, the district court concluded, "are valid state reasons to pass such an ordinance and supply a rational basis for the actions of the City of Black Jack." [91] The U.S. Court of Appeals for the Eighth Circuit disagreed, holding that the district court had "failed to take into account either the 'ultimate effect' or the 'historical context' of [Black Jack's] action." [92] On the basis of these considerations, the appeals court found that Black Jack's zoning discriminated against blacks in violation of the Civil Rights Act of 1968.

Another encouraging development for civil-rights groups was the refusal of the Supreme Court, two weeks before the *Valtierra* ruling, to review affirmative lower-court rulings in the housing case involving Lackawanna in the Buffalo area. [93] The *Lackawanna* rulings, however, did not test the limits of equal protection soon to be suggested by *Valtierra*. Instead, the *Lackawanna* decision rested heavily on commission of overt acts of discrimination against blacks by local officials, actions which the U.S. Court of Appeals for the Second Circuit characterized as "amounting to specific authorization and continuous encouragement of racial discrimination, if not almost complete racial segregation." [94] Both the mayor and the president of the city council of Lackawanna had signed petitions protesting the location of the black-sponsored housing project in a white neighborhood. The city council rezoned the property in question for park and recreational use in order to prevent the construction of low-cost housing for blacks. It also declared a moratorium on new subdivisions in the area. And the mayor refused to authorize a sewer extension to the property.

Overt racial discrimination was also a key factor in the case involving public housing in the Atlanta suburbs. Officials in Fulton County initially rezoned the land in question for apartments because they believed that the developer was going to build expensive "executive" units. Instead, the developer sought to construct public housing for the Atlanta Housing Authority under the "turn-key" program. Protesting that they wanted "nice, luxury apartments" rather than public housing, the county commissioners refused to issue the building permit, were sued, and lost the case, with the judge admonishing local officials that having "already zoned these sites for apartments, it should be obvious that the county may not restrict the class of Americans to be housed therein." [95]

Most suburbs, however, are more sophisticated than Lackawanna or Fulton County in devising means to exclude lower-cost housing and blacks. Talented lawyers can be hired, court rulings studied, and environmental rationales elaborated in the development of local ordinances which are likely to pass muster with the equal-protection standards suggested by *Valtierra*. Moreover, even when explicit acts of racial discrimination appear to have occurred, judges may not unravel them from other rationales, as illustrated by the ruling of the federal district court in the Black Jack case. In a complex area of public policy such as housing and land-use control, as Donald Foley has emphasized, "it is difficult to disentangle deliberate discriminatory practices from a larger fabric of practices and purported reasons why decisions are made." [96] These realities lead many involved in efforts to open the suburbs through the courts to conclude that "the burden of proof in cases alleging racial purpose or effect . . . will become virtually insurmountable" if the restrictive post-*Valtierra* rulings "stand the test of time." [97]

Alternatives to Equal Protection

Federal constraints on use of equal protection in housing and land-use cases inevitably led to more actions in state courts. As an open-housing lawyer explained, with "the Supreme Court backing off on equal protection cases, becoming more conservative . . . we are going into the state courts more." [98] Greater reliance on the state courts, with thir broad experience in zoning and housing issues, was welcomed by some legal strategists. Even before *Valtierra*, Richard F. Babcock was counseling: "Don't place all your bets on the equal protection clause of the 14th Amendment and, above all, do not overlook the possibility of using the state courts as a forum in which to change the rules. The state courts know what is going on at the local level. They understand how planning jargon can be used as a cover for prejudice." [99]

As indicated earlier, zoning litigation in state courts produced important victories for those seeking to open the suburbs. State judges have struck down a variety of exclusionary devices, rejected fiscal rationales for housing restrictions, and invalidated suburban zoning which ignored the needs of nonresidents and banned the less affluent. These triumphs, however, have been limited to a handful of states. Judges in most states have moved neither in the same direction, nor with the same dispatch, as those in New Jersey and Pennsylvania in questioning the validity of exclusionary land-use controls. Nor are the courts in one state under any compulsion to accept rulings developed in another state, even if the issues are similar.

At the same time that judges in New Jersey were striking down exclusionary zoning, New York's highest court upheld a set of sophisticated housing restrictions devised by suburban Ramapo in Rockland County. Under Ramapo's timing controls, all development was regulated through special permits, which were granted only when roads, sewers, and other public facilities were available, with delays of up to eighteen years contemplated in the provision of services to some parts of the town. New York's Court of Appeals found "something inherently suspect in a scheme which, apart from its professed purposes, effects a restriction upon the free mobility of a people until sometime in the future when projected facilities are available to meet increased demands." [100] The court also insisted that local controls of any kind that were exclusionary or sought to immunize a community from growth were unacceptable. Five of the seven members of the court concluded, however, that Ramapo's timing controls, "far from being exclusionary . . . merely seek, by the implementation of sequential development and timed growth, to provide a balanced cohesive community dedicated to the efficient utilization of land." [101] Advocates of opening the suburbs strongly disagreed with the New York court. For one, "giving tools like this to suburban governments is somewhat akin to giving the atom bomb to Libya." [102]

Rulings like Ramapo underscore the problem of standards, an issue which vexes any court attempting to deal with housing restrictions on substantive grounds. Given the complexity of urban settlement patterns, the variety of ways in which communities have developed, and the absence of consensus on what "exclusion" or "opening the suburbs" mean, judges encounter great difficulty in establishing general criteria which can be applied to specific situations. How diverse must a community be in order to be considered non-exclusionary? Do "all municipalities" have an obligation to "provide the opportunity for every individual to obtain housing within his means," as an attorney in one zoning case argued? [103] Or is the responsibility of each community to take its "fair share" of regional housing needs? If the latter, how are these general needs to be translated into obligations for particular suburbs? In making this calculation, how much weight should be given to the present socio-economic composition of communities, the presence or absence of subsidized housing, the availability of employment opportunities in a suburb, and the local resource and service base? With respect to these last two issues, Richard F. Babcock asks: "Does the absence of industry mean a community can have a pass on providing moderate-income housing? . . . Do overstretched municipal services, overcrowded schools, a history of defeated bond issues, inadequate fire and police, provide a defense against low-income housing?" [104]

None of these questions is easily answered by the courts, or anyone else for that matter, as the discussion in chapter 9 of efforts by metropolitan agencies to allocate housing responsibilities among suburbs illustrates. In New Jersey, Madison Township's zoning was judged "invalid because it failed to provide for the township's fair share of housing to meet the housing shortage . . . [in] the area from which, in view of available employment and transportation, the population of the township would be drawn, absent invalidly exclusionary zoning." [105] In attempting to determine Madison's fair share of housing needs in this region, however, the judge considered demographic data for Madison rather than some broader area, holding that "Madison Township's obligation to provide its fair share of the housing needs of its region is not met unless its zoning ordinance approximates in additional housing unit capacity the same proportion of low-income housing as its present low-income population, about 12%, and the same proportion of moderate-income housing as its present moderate-income population, about 19%." [106]

Endorsement of the fair-share concept also came from the New Jersey Supreme Court in the case involving suburban Mount Laurel. Developing suburbs like Mount Laurel, the court ruled, had an affirmative obligation to provide low and moderate income housing "at least to the extent of the municipality's fair share of the present and prospective regional need therefor." [107] Going beyond the trial court in the Madison case, the state's highest court defined the relevant region for determining Mount Laurel's fair share as those sections of Camden, Burlington, and Gloucester County within twenty miles of the center of Camden. The court, however, did not indicate how fair shares within this area were to be determined, nor did it specify who was to make the allocations. Instead, the judges suggested that "a reasonable figure for Mount Laurel can be determined . . . through the expertise of the municipal planning adviser, the county planning boards and the state planning agency." [108]

The problems faced by the courts in devising standards tend to be discounted by open-housing attorneys. The lawyer who won the *Mount Laurel* ruling insists that "fair share" and "region" are "planning concepts and planners can easily define and establish them. There is no problem. The state can do it one, two, three." [109] Planners, however, are less certain that these are simple tasks. For one with experience in assisting a judge to devise housing standards, "fair share" and "region" are "indeterminate and ambiguous concepts" requiring computations based "upon underlying premises and theories of extrapolation about which competent and honest professional planners may differ." [110] Another attorney active in open-housing litigation concedes that the problems of definition and application can be complicated, but he argues that the problem is manageable in the context of existing suburban restrictions:

> The complexity of the measurement of the constitutional responsibility here designated the "fair share" is ameliorated by the fact that the vast majority of suburban communities fall radically short of satisfying this requirement. While it may be difficult, as a community approaches the "fair share" threshold, to measure the precise point at which its burdens are met, it will not be difficult to establish flagrant violations of the fair share norm. [111]

Unfortunately, this approach begs the question of how judges are to determine the "fair share norm."

Compounding judges' problems of the courts in developing standards is the fact that they grapple with these complex issues on a case-by-case basis in a decentralized system of adjudication. Thus, courts in New Jersey and Pennsylvania invalidate local zoning which fails to take regional housing needs into consideration, while judges in other states such as New York continue to give primacy to the interests of the local community in land-use regulation. Judges also may reject measures designed to increase the supply of lower-cost housing on the grounds that inclusionary as well as exclusionary housing policies constitute invalid "socioeconomic zoning," as the Supreme Court of Virginia did in overturning the zoning reforms adopted by Fairfax County in 1971. [112] As Norman Williams pointed out some years ago, the absence of clearly defined and widely-accepted standards to guide courts in zoning cases "practically leaves it up to the judge's preferences to choose his presumptions and to decide on the validity of public regulation." [113]

Opening the Suburbs for Whom?

Even when victories are won in court, open-housing interests face the substantial problem of insuring that the intended and actual beneficiaries of successful litigation are the same. Arguments based on housing needs of lower-income and minority groups have carried great weight with most judges who have struck down restrictive housing and zoning measures. As one civil-rights lawyer notes: "You won't get a federal court to buy [a challenge to the zoning laws] without the appeal of poor or minority plaintiffs." [114] There is little assurance, however, that lower-income families will benefit from rulings designed to open the suburbs to blacks and the poor. Even in cases which deal specifically with subsidized housing, the lowest-income groups whose plight figures so prominently in open-housing briefs rarely occupy whatever housing eventually is built in the suburbs. "We are helping moderate-income families, not the poor, but must phrase causes of action [in the courts] as if we were helping the poor," admits the attorney who represented the unsuccessful 236 developers in the Black Jack suit filed by the American Civil Liberties Union. [115]

Benefits for the poor are even more problematical in suits which attack restrictive zoning in general rather than deal specifically with proposals for subsidized housing. The fact that a court was influenced by housing problems of the poor in deciding to invalidate a local zoning ordinance provides no guarantee that inexpensive housing will be built in the affected community. Pennsylvania's Supreme Court has cited regional housing needs in striking down large-lot and apartment restrictions. But, as Norman Williams and Thomas Norman point out, the Pennsylvania decisions "mistakenly assume an identity of interest between developers and those who are excluded from access to good housing." [116] As a result, the zoning rulings of the Pennsylvania court have resulted in no significant expansion in the range of suburban housing opportunities. Instead, these decisions have facilitated the construction of middle-class and luxury housing, which was the only goal of the builders and land owners who brought the suits.

Even when successful legal attacks on suburban zoning originate with public-interest groups, private developers often are in a better position to benefit than the poor in whose name open-housing suits are brought. For example, in competition for land made available for apartments as a result of invalidation of a local ban on multifamily dwellings, builders of high-rent apartments are likely to enjoy a substantial advantage over sponsors of subsidized housing. The private developer also has more freedom of action than the builder of subsidized housing, who is constantly constrained by the complex regulations that accompany almost all housing subsidies.

Of course, these fortuitous outcomes for private interests make legal attacks on suburban housing restrictions more attractive than ever to developers and land owners. The growing receptivity of some judges to attacks on zoning which fails to consider the housing needs of the poor has led developers to echo the arguments of open-housing litigators in court. In northern New Jersey, for example, Centex Homes Corporation contended in 1974 that a restriction against apartments in Tenafly was "contrary to the general welfare, in that excessive land is being diverted from development in the face of the shortage of housing in this [area] in particular and in Bergen County in general.[117] Similar themes were sounded in the *Petaluma* litigation, which was brought by the Construction Industry Association of Sonoma County. Some of the funds for the *Petaluma* suit, as well as for court actions brought by the Northern Virginia Builders Association and the Maryland Homebuilders Association, came from the National Association of Home Builders, which in the early 1970s was eager to support broad-based litigation aimed at suburban exclusion which would become the "*Brown* v. *Board of Education* of the zoning field."[118]

Development interests also have sought to join forces with open-housing groups in attacking exclusionary housing and land-use policies in the courts. Both the National Association of Home Builders and the National Association of Building Manufacturers, along with a number of civil-rights and open-housing groups, sought to file a brief with the U.S. Supreme Court in support of the plaintiffs in the *Valtierra* case. At the grass roots, Suburban Action Institute in particular cooperated with private developers in attacking restrictive zoning in the courts. Madison's zoning, for example, was challenged by SAI and Nathan Kaplan, a developer whose inability to secure local permission to build over 2,300 units of garden apartments provided the grounds for the litigation. The plaintiffs' attorney claimed that "the interests of the poor coincided exactly with the interests of a major developer" in Madison.[119] Perhaps, but there is little to suggest that the developer in Madison intended to build housing for the poor. In Madison and elsewhere, the primary aim of builders and landowners has been to open the suburbs for their own benefit by securing court rulings which maximize their freedom to use land in the most profitable fashion.

A suit brought by a large-scale developer against Bedminster Township in northern New Jersey in 1971 nicely illustrates the problem of who will benefit from opening the suburbs. All of the rhetoric of the open-housing movement was employed by the Allan-Deane Corporation, which charged that zoning in the affluent suburb "constitutes economic segregation" as well as discriminating "on account of age and marital status in that it does not permit zoning for adequate housing for either the young or the old, the unmarried and the widowed." The developer also claimed that five-acre zoning and prohibitions on apartments have "the effect of excluding others from the utilization of [its] property because of religious principles, race, color, ancestry, or national origin." [120] Allan-Deane, however, was not exactly proposing that Bedminster emulate the Statue of Liberty and open its gates to the poor and downtrodden. Instead, the company wanted the court to invalidate local zoning restrictions so that it could develop ninety-two acres for office and research facilities, six acres for a conference center, twenty-one acres for a golf course, sixty-four acres for fifty-four single-family homes, and thirty-three acres for town houses. Suburban Action, the sometime ally of private developers, and the New Jersey Civil Liberties Union intervened in the suit the following year, agreeing with the developer that Bedminster's housing restrictions were unconstitutional, but contending that Allan-Deane should not be permitted to build housing on the site unless provision were made for lower-income families. [121]

The Limits of Judicial Activism

Concern over the beneficiaries of legal victories in zoning cases has led more and more open-housing litigators to seek the active involvement of the courts in the provision of housing in the suburbs. With growing frequency, judges have been asked to go beyond the usual judicial remedies in zoning cases, which typically involve a court order setting aside the local ordinance or action with respect to the parcel of property in question. In place of traditional reliance on injunctive relief, advocates of opening the suburbs have petitioned the courts to impose affirmative obligations on local governments to meet the housing needs of lower-income and minority groups. For example, in a suit filed against a suburb on Long Island, the NAACP and NCDH sought a court order:

> Directing the Defendant Town . . . to formulate and implement forthwith a comprehensive plan which will eliminate the racially segregated housing enclaves within the Town and which will provide for and assure land-use opportunities for the construction of low- and moderate-income dwelling units within the Town to meet the needs of the Plaintiffs and the members of the classes they represent, and will end existing racial segregating in housing therein. [122]

In seeking affirmative solutions from the courts, open-housing interests have followed in the footsteps of other groups which have sought to apply the authority of the judiciary in order to compel meaningful action by recalcitrant public officials on complex issues. Despite the desire of most judges to eschew involvement in matters more appropriately left to other branches of government, the concern of the courts with problems such as school segregation and legislative apportionment has drawn judges inexorably into "political thickets" which necessitate direct and continuing judicial intervention in arenas traditionally handled by legislative or executive action.[123] In the two decades following the *Brown* decision in 1954, litigation on school desegregation led the federal courts to order affirmative action to compensate for past discrimination, to rezone local school districts, and to develop plans for busing to promote racial balance. And the quest to implement the Supreme Court's standard of "one person, one vote" has required judges to develop and implement reapportionment schemes in a number of states, often with the assistance of academic specialists, computer experts, and court-appointed masters.

In the case of suburban housing and zoning, both federal and state judges have sought to devise affirmative remedies. The Union City case came to a close when the federal district court in effect ordered the suburb in the San Francisco Bay area to zone an appropriate site to permit construction of a 236 project by the Southern Alameda Spanish-Speaking Organization.[124] In the Atlanta litigation, the federal judge directed Fulton County and the Atlanta Housing Authority to develop jointly a plan designed to scatter subsidized housing throughout the metropolitan area, including the unincorporated portions of the suburban county. Officials of Fulton County also were ordered to "meet with representatives of the Atlanta Housing Authority for the purpose of implementing the recommendations" of the plan within thirty days after its completion, with the "results of that meeting . . . reported to this court." [125]

Substantial judicial involvement in the development and implementation of housing plans in the suburbs also resulted from the challenge of zoning in Mount Laurel by a local chapter of the NAACP. The community was ordered to determine the number of low-cost housing units needed to meet the needs of its residents, local employees, and those expected to be employed within the township in the future. On the basis of this analysis, Mount Laurel was to "develop a plan of implementation, that is, an affirmative program, to enable and encourage the satisfaction" of its present and projected housing needs. The judge cautioned local officials to "set forth in explicit detail" every factor which might interfere with implementation of the plan. Finally, Mount Laurel was to return to court within ninety days of the judgment "for a determination of whether defendants have complied with the order of this court and whether further action is necessary." [126]

A year after Mount Laurel, another judge in New Jersey retained planning consultants to develop apartment regulations for a suburb in Bergen County which refused to zone a tract of land for garden apartments. After being ordered by the court to end its ban on apartments, Washington Township rezoned land other than that owned by the developer who had challenged the restriction. In response, the judge turned to planning experts for assistance in devising appropriate relief. [127] After analyzing the local and regional need for apartments, and considering the constraints imposed by environmental considerations and the existing pattern of development in the low-density and almost exclusively single-family community, the consultants recommended changes in Washington Township's zoning designed to permit "a modest amount of middle income apartment development without suffering damage to the community's social fabric and its amenities." [128] Also appraised were potential sites for apartments, which led the consultants to conclude that the thirty-acre tract at issue was suitable for apartments, although only at substantially lower densities than desired by the developer. On the basis of the consultants' report, Washington Township was ordered to issue a building permit for apartments on the contested site, as well as to remove a variety of other restrictions which served to increase the cost of apartments. [129]

For most open-housing groups, increased involvement by judges in local planning and housing determinations is a hopeful development in the often discouraging struggle to open the suburbs. For Paul Davidoff of Suburban Action, the court order in the Mount Laurel case "demonstrated a sophisticated understanding of the problems of exclusionary zoning by requiring the community to provide adequate remedies to overcome past discrimination." [130] Even innovations and remedies such as those in Washington Township which have little impact on housing opportunities for lower-income families are welcomed because of the precedents which can be employed in other legal actions to convince judges of the need for wide-ranging remedies. "The judge had no choice but to bring in planners," insists Richard F. Bellman of Suburban Action in speaking approvingly of the court's activities. "If the towns are going to continue to refuse to change, the judges will have to call in planners to determine what should be done logically." [131]

Attempting to plan for suburbs with or without expert assistance, however, threatens to transform courts into *de facto* planning boards, a specter which has deterred most judges from intervention in land-use disputes ever since zoning was invented. Even if experts were widely available, the sheer volume of cases, the complexity of housing and land-use issues, and the myriad variations among suburbs surely would overwhelm the courts. Supervising the preparation of scores of local plans would be a monumental undertaking, particularly if the courts, as the trial judge in the Mount Laurel case suggests, "can only meet each specific situation as it is presented." [132] Time and resources clearly beyond the ken of most courts also would be needed to oversee the implementation of plans, given the delicate interactions which are requisite to the production of housing and the skill of most suburban governments at stifling unwanted change through delay and evasion.

When subsidized housing is an essential component of court-ordered remedies in the suburbs, the problems inherent in judicial activism are multiplied. Most subsidy programs assume willing local participation, or at least formal approval by the jurisdiction in which the housing will be built. Local hostility or inaction would require judges to become involved in creating local housing agencies, negotiating intergovernmental agreements, insuring compliance with complex federal or state procedures, and providing the local consents needed to locate and construct the housing units. Further hindering the role of the courts is their lack of control over the public funds which finance subsidized housing. Without presidential budgetary requests, congressional appropriations, administrative allocations, and other steps in the funding process, court orders dealing with federally-subsidized housing are meaningless. "You can do all the mandating you want," notes an official of the New Jersey League of Municipalities, "but if there's no money available, nothing will be built." [133]

Some indication of the difficulties judges are likely to encounter with subsidized housing in the suburbs is provided by the futile efforts of a federal district court in Chicago to force local officials to scatter public housing throughout the city. Ruling in favor of black public housing tenants in a suit brought by the American Civil Liberties Union, Judge Richard B. Austin invalidated Chicago's site-selection procedures in 1969 because they reflected "a deliberate policy to separate the races." [134] To "undo the effects of past discrimination," the Chicago Housing Authority was ordered to build three new units of public housing in white areas for every one located in black neighborhoods. In attempting to secure compliance with this and subsequent orders, Judge Austin encountered what he termed "every known method of procrastination" from the housing authority. [135] Year after year, court orders were issued and ignored, appeals won and lost on various issues, deadlines set and reset, stays granted and refused, and mountains of reports filed with the court. When sites in white areas were reluctantly selected by CHA, they were rejected by the city council, leading Judge Austin to enjoin federal officials from funding the model cities program in Chicago and then to order CHA to ignore the state law requiring local governing bodies to approve public-housing sites. Six years after the initial order was issued, the only tangible result of the complex, costly, and time-consuming litigation was the cessation of construction of all public housing in Chicago, in both black and white neighborhoods.

In moving from the city to the suburbs, the task of the judge who wants to disperse low-cost housing becomes even more arduous. Beyond the city limits, judges must deal with a large number of local governments rather than a single jurisdiction. Problems of allocation are more troublesome in the politically fragmented suburbs, with their diverse fiscal and economic bases. At the same time, the multiplicity of local units dilutes the ability of the courts to monitor official action to insure compliance with court orders. Moreover, in the suburbs as in the city, judicial activism is severely constrained by the limited powers and resources available to the courts to deal with housing problems. As Alexander Polikoff (the attorney who launched the Chicago litigation in 1966 and continually pressed Judge Austin for affirmative remedies) readily acknowledges, "ultimately the courts cannot build houses." [136] Awareness of the limitations on the ability of the courts to secure construction of housing helped persuade Judge Austin to rule against Polikoff's motion that an appropriate remedy in the *Gautreaux* case encompass the entire metropolitan area rather than merely the central city. [137]

Certainly among judges who have grappled directly with suburban exclusion, awareness of the inherent limitations on the role of the judiciary in devising effective remedies is widespread. In striking down two- and three-acre zoning in Concord Township, the Pennsylvania Supreme Court indicated that "we fully realize that the overall solution to these problems lies with greater regional planning, but until the time comes that we have such a system we must confront the situation as it is." [138] Even judges who have pioneered with affirmative remedies in the suburbs readily admit that they are ill-equipped to oversee development and implementation of housing plans. The trial judge in the Mount Laurel case emphasized that the "judiciary cannot be expected to alleviate a condition that definitely calls for legislative action from either the national or state governments." [139] In the same case, the state Supreme Court acknowledged that: "Courts do not build housing." "Nor," the court added in an opinion which showed far more understanding of the housing process than most judicial rulings, "do municipalities. That function is performed by private builders, various kinds of associations, or, for public housing, by special agencies created for that purpose by various levels of government." [140] Judicial frustration at the impediments posed by the complex processes by which subsidized housing is financed, located, and constructed was expressed by the federal judge in Atlanta who sought to disperse public housing. "There's nothing I can do," conceded Judge Newell Edenfield. "The court, by the nature of the institution, cannot go out and execute the laws. I can't build public housing or have it built. I can't appropriate the funds." [141]

In the face of these obstacles, many judges have shied away from involvement in housing and zoning matters. Concern over the lack of judicial capability to devise appropriate remedies helped persuade a lower court in Pennsylvania to dismiss an open-housing suit brought against county agencies and fifty-four municipalities in Bucks County. The court was unwilling to "assume the awesome task of becoming a super planning agency with no expertise in the field; and . . . to make immediate and basic initial policy determinations of a kind clearly for nonjudicial discretion, and to carry out this tremendous responsibility with an entire lack of judicially discoverable and manageable standards for resolving it." [142] In rejecting a suit filed by developers challenging a local ban on all housing construction, a New Jersey court insisted in 1974 that the issue was "more appropriate for legislative action than the slow development that necessarily must accompany definition on a case by case basis." [143] And the U.S. Court of Appeals for the Sixth Circuit, in overruling the federal district judge who ordered five suburbs in the Cleveland area to participate in the public-housing program of the Cuyahoga Metropolitan Housing Authority, noted "that the remedy for social change lies with Congress rather than with the courts." [144]

Many open-housing litigators acknowledge the limitations on the ability of judges to broaden suburban housing opportunities. Richard F. Bellman, who has sought affirmative remedies in a variety of legal actions launched by NCDH and Suburban Action, admits that "litigation itself will not solve the issue. It is one arm of a broad based attack. You never get really major social changes in litigation. At best, you get a legal precedent that will allow legislators so inclined to proceed in that area." [145] Similar views are expressed by Richard F. Babcock, who sees "the limited, if essential role of the courts . . . to act as a predicate to legislative reform." [146]

Awareness of these limitations, however, has not lessened the heavy dependence of the open-housing movement on legal action. Nor have the numerous delays and defeats suffered in the courts by the foes of suburban exclusion. Despite its shortcomings, litigation remains well suited to the talents and resources available to the major organizations seeking to open the suburbs. Given the lack of a substantial constituency for open-housing efforts, lawsuits and court rulings provide these groups with their most significant weapons in the struggle against suburban housing restrictions. Judicial determinations can force action that open-housing interests could never accomplish on their own. For example, three days after the New Jersey Supreme Court ruled against exclusionary zoning in Mount Laurel, the Delaware Valley Regional Planning Commission voted to withhold endorsing applications from Burlington County for more than $2 million in federal community-development grants until the county began to develop an allocation plan for subsidized housing. According to one member of the regional planning agency, the court ruling had "everything" to do with its decision: "That was the point of reference. Until Mount Laurel came down, there was no pressure." [147]

As the next three chapters illustrate, however, these judicial pressures are countered by strong opposing forces in federal, metropolitan, and state political arenas which are increasingly dominated by suburban politicians, voters, and interests.

Chapter Eight

Opening the Suburbs from Washington

In light of the limited role of the courts and the dismal prospects for local reform in most jurisdictions, opening the suburbs necessitates major policy changes at the higher levels of government. While any strategy to open the suburbs ultimately must involve both national and state government, Washington has attracted more opponents of suburban exclusion than the state capitals. Like most organized interests in American society, advocates of opening the suburbs have been drawn to the nation's capital by the vast expansion in the scope of the activities of the federal government, a development which has significantly enhanced the ability of federal agencies to influence public and private behavior.

Economy of effort is another benefit of the national political arena, and is particularly appealing to minority interests which are unable to aggregate substantial strength at the local or state level. Compared with efforts aimed at producing change in fifty diverse states, political activity in Washington requires fewer resources. Moreover, success at the federal level can generate great pressure on all the states to alter their policies, while a victory in one state usually has little impact beyond its borders.

Past performance by the national government also led opponents of suburban exclusion to concentrate their efforts on Congress and federal agencies. Over the previous quarter century, the federal government had been much more responsive on civil-rights issues than all but a few of the states. Washington also played a far larger role than the states in the financing of housing, both public and private. In 1970, when suburban exclusion was beginning to attract public attention, over eighty-two percent of all the public resources devoted to housing in the United States was provided by the national government.

Another consideration was Washington's relative distance from the passions of the local scene. Federal officials, both elected and appointed, tend to be more insulated from intense community pressures on issues such as housing and land use than their counterparts at the local or state level. Districts in the House of Representatives are much larger than in state legislatures, providing congressmen with substantially more diverse constituencies than those of state legislators. Senators typically enjoy even more freedom of action from local pressures than representatives, thanks to their larger and more heterogeneous state-wide electoral bases and a six-year term of office. Within executive departments, federal officials tend to be more responsive to clientele groups, professional criteria and other specialized concerns than to geographically defined constituency interests.

All of these considerations led most reformers to conclude that federal involvement was essential to opening the suburbs. Testifying before a Senate committee in 1970, an official of NCDH insisted that lower-income blacks could not escape the ghetto unless "the Federal Government itself demand[ed] that zoning practices, land-use controls, building and construction codes be changed." [1] Simeon Golar, a housing official in New York City, called in 1972 for the creation of a federal agency empowered to override local zoning if necessary in order to build housing, arguing that a federal instrumentality would find it easier than a local or state agency to ignore local opposition. [2]

Going to Washington, however, does not free those who would open the suburbs from the political constraints that make liberalization of housing policies so difficult within suburbia. The insulation of federal officials from local pressures is relative rather than absolute; and few can afford to ignore local opposition which is widespread and vocal. By making grass-roots support essential for nomination and election, the decentralized American party system insures the sensitivity of elected officials in the nation's capital to local concerns. Reinforcing responsiveness to local perspectives is the fact that most congressmen, as well as many top officials in the executive branch, have held local and state offices before coming to Washington. Members of Congress and administrative officials also can count. When those who oppose federal intervention are far more numerous than their adversaries, as in the case of reforming housing and land-use policies, federal officials are likely to proceed with considerable caution. They are even more likely to be cautious in instances where the majority is able to associate its interests with such traditional virtues as grass-roots democracy, local autonomy, and the protection of property values.

Also of enormous importance on issues such as exclusionary zoning and scattered-site housing has been the growth of suburban political power. The burgeoning of suburbia has greatly enhanced the influence of suburban voters and politicians in state and national politics. By 1973, more members of the House of Representatives were from suburban than either city or rural districts, reflecting the fact that more Americans

Table 8.1. Demographic Characteristics of House Districts,
1966–1973

	1966	1973	Change 1966–1973
City	106	102	−4
Suburban	92	131	+39
Rural	181	130	−51
Mixed	56	72	+16

Source: Congressional Quarterly Weekly Report 39 (Apr. 6, 1974), p. 878.

in 1970 lived in the suburbs than in either the central cities or outside metropolitan areas, and the same trend was at work in the state legislatures. The influence of suburban voters also has been steadily growing in presidential and gubernatorial elections. Candidates who succeed in these increasingly suburban constituencies tend to be recruited from suburbia where their political perspectives have been shaped by the localistic and exclusionary preoccupations of their constituents. The result, as one influential suburban politician has written, is a steady shift in "the balance of political power and influence . . . to those political leaders who articulate and strive to maintain the suburban way of life." [3]

The Federal Government and the Separated Society

Fostering the suburban way of life was hardly a new concern for the federal government in the early 1970s. Long before the emergence of the suburban plurality, federal policy had been encouraging decentralized settlement patterns, political fragmentation, spatial differentiation, and racial segregation in the metropolis. Suburbanization was greatly facilitated by massive federal highway investments which opened vast areas along the metropolitan periphery for development. Water and sewer grants, school aid, and other federal programs provided hard-pressed suburban governments with financial help in coping with the problems of rapid growth.. Federal planning assistance enabled thousands of suburbs to develop sophisticated zoning ordinances and other exclusionary devices. And by accepting political fragmentation and independent suburbs as the norm, all sorts of federal programs have played a key role in sustaining autonomous and small-scale local governments in suburbia.

In its role as the nation's largest employer, the federal government also fueled the exodus to the suburbs. Like business, federal agencies have been moving outward in search of space, easier commutation for an increasingly suburban work force, and the greener grass and other amenities of suburbia. Beginning with the departure in 1958 of the Atomic Energy Commission for Germantown, Maryland, a steady stream of federal agencies have deserted the District of Columbia for the pleasanter surroundings of the Maryland and Virginia suburbs.[4] Over 17,000 federal jobs moved outward between 1963 and 1968 alone. In relocating to the suburbs, most federal agencies paid little attention to the availability of housing opportunities for black and lower-income employees. Over four million square feet of space was leased by federal agencies in Arlington County, where local voters and officials steadfastly rejected low-cost housing.[5] Blacks have been particularly disadvantaged by the dispersal of federal jobs in the Washington area because "black migration to the suburbs is going east" while "the Federal migration of jobs is going west along with the white population."[6] When the National Bureau of Standards moved to suburban Gaithersburg, its employment increased by 125, but the number of black employees dropped by 75 because of the lack of housing opportunities in surrounding areas and the difficulties and expense of commuting twenty or more miles to Gaithersburg.[7] Moreover, like their counterparts in the private sector, federal officials generally have not used the location of major installations as a means of applying leverage on local governments to liberalize their housing policies. For example, neither the Atomic Energy Commission nor the General Services Administration made an effort to couple the location of a large research facility in the Chicago suburbs with eased housing restrictions in surrounding communities. After examining the housing implications of the location of federal facilities, the U.S. Commission on Civil Rights concluded in early 1970 that "the Federal Government has failed to comprehend the full equal opportunity implications of its site selection policies."[8]

Since their inception in the 1930s, federal housing programs favored suburbs and suburbanites over older cities and their lower-income and minority residents. Between 1934 and 1970, federal mortgage guarantees permitted over eighteen million families to purchase homes with long-term, low down-payment mortgages. During the same period, less than 1.5 million housing units were constructed for low-income families with public support. From its beginning, the Federal Housing Administration focused its mortgage activities on new housing in "outlying residential areas . . . developed as a result of the decentralization movement." [9] As a result, almost all federal mortgage subsidies have gone to families seeking new housing in the suburbs. As the National Commission on Urban Problems pointed out in 1968: "The poor and those on fringes of poverty have been almost completely excluded. . . . Even middle-class residential districts in the central cities were suspect, since there was always the prospect that they, too, might turn as Negroes and poor whites continued to pour into the cities, and as middle- and upper-middle-income whites continued to move out." [10]

In addition, suburbanites have been the principal beneficiaries of the tax benefits associated with home ownership, which constitute the largest single federal subsidy affecting housing. Deductions for mortgage interest and local property taxes provided 24 million families with tax savings of $6.2 billion in 1972. In the same year, approximately one-third of this amount was expended by the national government for all other housing subsidies. Almost 65 percent of these tax savings went to households with incomes over $10,000. [11] Given the high incidence of home ownership in the suburbs, a substantial portion of the recipients were suburbanites.

Federal housing policies also have played a major role in maintaining segregated residential patterns and insuring the racial bifurcation of the metropolis. Throughout the 1930s and 1940s, FHA and other federal lending institutions explicitly promoted racial separation as a means of protecting the properties it insured from "adverse influences." Officials in the field were instructed by FHA to investigate

areas surrounding the location to determine whether or not incompatible racial and social groups are present, to the end that an intelligent prediction may be made regarding the possibility or probability of the location being invaded by such groups. If a neighborhood is to retain stability it is necessary that properties shall continue to be occupied by the same social and racial classes. A change in social or racial occupancy generally leads to instability and a reduction in values. [12]

To safeguard its investments from threats posed by such "adverse influences," FHA recommended use of deed restrictions designed to prohibit "the occupancy of properties except by the race for which they are intended"; and a model restrictive covenant was included in its underwriters manual.[13] Although direct references to race were dropped in the late 1940s, FHA failed to abandon its racial practices for almost two more decades. The Veterans Administration, the other major source of federal mortgage assistance, "never openly advocated segregated housing;" instead, the VA "struck a neutral pose, allowing builders or lenders to discriminate if they wished." [14] Almost all did, further narrowing housing opportunities for blacks in the moderately-priced subdivisions that spread across suburbia in the years following the Second World War.

Even after these discriminatory policies were altered in the late 1960s, federal mortgage programs continued to reinforce racial separation in the metropolis. George Romney, the Secretary of Housing and Urban Development, admitted in 1970 that "changes in FHA policies have thus far had little practical effect on the pattern of residential segregation which has come to characterize our great metropolitan areas." [15] A few months later, an examination of housing practices in the Atlanta area concluded that "even in the time since the passage of the 1968 Fair Housing Act, the Atlanta and Washington administrators of federal programs have helped produce large new areas of segregated housing in Atlanta's suburbs." In Atlanta, as elsewhere, the FHA remained "the principal culprit . . . largely by failing to undo the segregation it helped create over a period of decades, and by failing to deal forcefully with all the real estate firms that perpetuate the patterns." [16]

As pointed out in chapter 4, FHA's heavy reliance on private builders and financial institutions kept blacks out of almost all of the housing built in the suburbs under the housing programs initiated in 1968. In a review of Section 235 housing released in 1971, the U.S. Commission on Civil Rights found that FHA, "traditionally attuned to serving the housing needs of white, middle class families, has been poorly prepared to serve a different racial and ethnic group of home seekers and has done little to develop affirmative procedures and mechanisms to assure that lower income 235 buyers are treated fairly." The Commission concluded that "this pattern is unlikely to change [until] FHA abandons its current passive role and becomes a vigorous champion of the rights of minorities and of lower-income families generally." [17]

Racial and economic separation in the metropolis also has been fostered by the public housing and urban renewal programs. Washington's acceptance of municipal boundaries as the jurisdiction of local housing authorities helped concentrate lower-income and minority groups in the older cities. Within the cities, federal requirements that local governing bodies approve projects insured that most public housing was built in black areas. In the suburbs, as seen in chapter 4, federal insistence on the creation of local housing authorities, the negotiation of cooperation agreements for the construction of public housing, and the development of workable programs enabled most jurisdictions to exclude subsidized housing merely by inaction. For over two decades, the urban renewal program dislocated large numbers of low-income families, two-thirds of them black, while causing a net reduction of 51,000 housing units, almost all of which were occupied by the poor. In older cities, urban renewal typically reinforced the concentration of blacks and other minority groups, while in the suburbs, urban-renewal funds often underwrote plans which drove lower-income and minority households out of the community entirely.

Majority Values and Local Interests

As important as the nature of these national policies in considering the prospects for federal leadership in opening the suburbs are the reasons why Washington has consistently promoted exclusion, segregation, and spatial differentiation. Certainly this pattern of action was not imposed on an unwilling public by a national government whose conscious goal was the creation of an urban society stratified along racial and economic lines. Instead, what the federal government has done results largely from the responsiveness of Congress and the federal executive to the interests and values of a substantial majority of the American people. At almost every step in the development of the federal policies which have shaped metropolitan settlement patterns, Washington has passively followed rather than actively shaped the dictates of personal preferences and the private sector.

Speaking of the origins of federal housing policies, George Romney has emphasized that "the dominant majority supported or condoned social and institutional separation of the races. This attitude became fixed in public law and public policy . . . at every level of government and every branch of government, and thus it was adopted as a matter of course by the Federal Government when it entered the housing field in the 1930s." [18] Middle-class Americans have been the primary beneficiaries of federal housing subsidies because they are far more numerous than the poor, and because the housing industry traditionally has had little interest in building subsidized housing for lower-income families. Housing for the poor has gotten the short end of the stick for the same reason. The Housing Act of 1949 established a six-year goal of constructing 810,000 units of public housing. Twenty years later, the nation was still almost 40,000 units short of the target.

The dominance of middle-class and homeowner interests also provides the answer to Herbert M. Franklin's question: "Why should Federal housing subsidies for the moderate income or middle income family be freely transmitted to every locality through basically private mechanisms while subsidies are available for the poor only through the sufferances of a local public action?" [19] Most Americans are neither poor nor black, and they do not want to live in the same neighborhood with those who are. Responsiveness to these desires, particularly on the part of Congress, has strongly shaped the development of subsidized housing programs, beginning with the public-housing program in 1937 with its reliance on community initiative and local control over the selection of sites. More generally, these concerns have led Congress to limit the federal role in housing and land use. Washington cannot command local governments to change zoning, build housing, or participate in federal programs. Except for the Department of Defense, the federal government constructs no housing itself, depending instead for the implementation of its housing programs on local governments and developers who are subject to local regulations.

Illustrative of congressional sensitivity to local fears of low-cost housing in middle-income neighborhoods was the emasculation of the rent-supplement program by the House of Representatives in 1966. Rent supplements were the Johnson Administration's principal response to racial and economic separation in the metropolis. Under the program, the outer neighborhoods of cities and suburbs would be opened to the poor through federal subsidization of rents in housing built with FHA mortgages by non-profit organizations, cooperatives, and limited dividend corporations. Since the scheme involved only the federal government and the private sponsor of the housing, no provision initially was made for formal participation by local government. Builders of rent-supplement units, however, had to conform to local zoning ordinances, building codes, and other regulations. As one supporter of the rent-supplement program has noted, the Administration's intent in not requiring formal local approval "was to help penetrate the wall of exclusion erected by many suburban communities against the introduction of housing for low- and moderate-income families." [20]

Despite massive Democratic majorities, President Johnson's popular mandate in the 1964 election, and the President's legendary mastery of Congress, rent supplements barely squeaked through the House of Representatives by a vote of 208 to 202, and only carried the Senate by seven votes. Among the more outspoken critics was Representative Paul A. Fino, a Republican from a middle-class district in New York City, who attacked rent supplements as a "social planner's dream [which] would give the Housing Administration a blank check to federalize American residential patterns and subsidize forced economic integration." [21]

Another opponent was James D. Martin, an Alabama Republican who concluded that with rent supplements, "private homeownership in America is doomed because a man cannot protect the value of his property nor the desirability of his neighborhood. Every neighborhood in America will be opened up to public housing." For Martin, home-ownership was

> the keystone of the American system. It is the dream, the desired goal of practically all Americans to own your own home in a neighborhood you have carefully chosen among the kind of people you want to raise your family. Now the American people are going to have that basic right taken away from them and the Federal Housing Administration is going to decide the makeup of a neighborhood. A Washington bureaucrat is going to pick your neighbor, and if his choice is too poor to be able to afford to live in your neighborhood, or too indolent to want to strive to better his economic condition, then the Federal Government will take your tax money to pay his rent so he can live next door to you. [22]

As often occurs in Congress, opponents who failed to defeat the enabling legislation were able to cripple the program during the appropriations process. No funds were appropriated for rent supplements in 1965; and the Administration's request was halved the following year. In addition, the House Appropriations Committee attached a provision to the funding measure in 1966 which required local approval of all rent-supplement contracts. When the appropriations bill reached the House floor, the local veto was attacked by William Fitts Ryan, an outspoken liberal from Manhattan, as having "been written into the bill to block the possible exodus of low-income families into communities outside the central core of our cities." [23] Rising to the defense of local involvement was George H. Mahon of Texas, the chairman of the Appropriations Committee, who expressed the views of most congressmen when he insisted that no federal housing program could work without active local support. "The committee believes," Mahon told his colleagues before they approved the measure, "that if the program is to be successful it will have to have acceptance by the local communities. They will have to participate. If they do not want it, they do not have to have it. After all, the local people know their problems and needs better than anyone else." [24]

Rejection of the local veto was urged in the Senate by a group of urban liberals. In their view, the provision attached by the House "would render the program unworkable and effectively destroy it." They reminded the Senate that "a major objective of the rent supplement program, as adopted by the Congress in the Housing Act of 1965, was to permit the dispersal of decent low-income housing throughout an entire community through the free choice of individual developers and non-profit and limited-profit associations." They argued that "the problems of our cities will never be resolved if we establish walls or immovable curtains beyond which the poor and elderly cannot go to find decent housing." [25] Despite this plea, the Senate went along with the House. As Senator John O. Pastore of Rhode Island explained during a hearing on the rent-supplement program, "local participation . . . is very zealously guarded around here." [26]

In agreeing with the House that some kind of local role was required, Senator Pastore ingenuously argued that the local veto would have little adverse affect on the program. Who, asked the Rhode Island Democrat, "is going to shoot Santa Claus coming down the chimney? . . . Can you imagine a case where a municipality will say we don't want to help these people if the Government is going to subsidize part of the rent with new construction?" [27] Far more realistic was the appraisal of Representative Ryan who predicted that "local officials in these lily-white bedroom suburbs can be expected to exercise this veto power to prevent the have-nots from coming into the community and mixing with the haves." [28] And they did. During the program's first four years, less than ten percent of all rent supplement units were built in the suburbs. [29] Over the same period, construction was begun on only one-seventh of the 375,000 apartments originally projected for the years 1966 to 1969. As a result of these developments, the Great Society's major effort to disperse the poor had almost no effect on suburbia and the separated society, except to demonstrate the political perils of any federal effort which bypassed "the local people" who "know the problems and needs better than anyone else."

Pressures for Change

On August 11, 1965, the day before the Senate approved the Housing and Urban Development Act of 1965, an altercation between a white highway patrolman and a black motorist touched off six days of violence in the Watts section of Los Angeles which left thirty-four dead and almost nine hundred injured, and caused close to $200 million in property damage. Over the next three years, riots in black ghettos across the nation underscored the crisis of the older cities and the racial bifurcation of the American metropolis. With this turbulence came heightened racial hostility, increased black militancy, accelerated white flight to the suburbs, and reinforced resistance in suburbia to the dispersal of blacks and subsidized housing. At the same time, the racial disorders and the festering problems of the black ghettos spurred a great deal of soul-searching in Washington over metropolitan segregation and the role of the federal government in creating a separated society.

Suburban exclusion was identified by the National Advisory Commission on Civil Disorders, appointed in the wake of the 1967 riots in Newark and Detroit, as one of the principal causes of the movement of the United States "toward two societies, one black, one white—separate and unequal." [30] To unite "a white society principally located in suburbs, in smaller central cities, and in the peripheral parts of large central cities . . . [with] a Negro society largely concentrated within large central cities," the commission urged a massive increase in the production of low-cost housing to permit construction of six million units in five years, combined with a "reorientation of Federal housing programs to place more low and moderate-income housing units outside of ghetto areas." [31]

Similar conclusions emerged from other appraisals of federal urban policies completed during the last days of the Johnson Administration. The National Commission on Urban Problems, headed by former Senator Paul Douglas, recommended "programs which would build low-rent housing in the suburbs as well as in the cities, provided sites in outlying areas, give States incentives to act where localities do not, lease houses for the poor in middle class neighborhoods, and tie a locality's eligibility for Federal grants such as for highways, sewers, and water to that community's effort to house its share of the poor." [32] President Johnson's Task Force on Suburban Problems also concluded that "there is no justification for federal assistance or encouragement of any kind that would make the suburbs separated, segregated pockets of privilege. That would be to encourage and perpetuate injustice and discrimination." [33] Impediments to the production of housing rather than metropolitan segregation were the principal concern of the President's Committee on Urban Housing, whose chairman was industrialist Edgar F. Kaiser. Nonetheless, Kaiser's committee strongly supported dispersing the poor from older cities, recommending that subsidized housing be constructed wherever economically feasible. The Kaiser report also called for elimination of workable program requirements in order to reduce local control over location of subsidized housing. To facilitate the acquisition of sites in the face of local opposition, the Kaiser Committee suggested that the federal government be empowered to secure land, through purchase or condemnation, for lease to developers of subsidized housing, and that "power be granted to the Secretary of HUD to pre-empt local zoning codes . . . [and] any state codes or other local ordinances—such as subdivision regulations—which are exclusionary in purpose or effect . . . from application to Federally subsidized low- or moderate-income housing projects." [34]

While these proposals were being developed, HUD and the White House were designing Lyndon Johnson's "Magna Carta of housing," the Housing and Urban Development Act of 1968. Beginning with a reaffirmation of the goal of "a decent home and suitable living environment for every American family," the legislation sought to give "the highest priority and emphasis . . . to meeting the housing needs of those families for whom the national goal has not become a reality." [35] In seeking to fulfill these goals, the housing programs created by the 1968 legislation unleashed powerful pressures for federal measures aimed at suburban exclusion. Opening the suburbs, however, was not an explicit goal in 1968, although dispersal certainly was an important objective of architects of the housing provisions in the bill. Mindful of the hornet's nest stirred in Congress by identification of the rent-supplement program with racial and economic integration, supporters of the 1968 bill focused on increasing production of lower-cost housing, homeownership for the poor, and expanding the role of private enterprise in supplying subsidized housing.

One of the few witnesses at the congressional hearings on the 1968 legislation to discuss dispersal was the chairman of the National Commission on Urban Problems, and even Paul Douglas downplayed the suburban aspects of the new subsidy programs. Instead, Douglas stressed the availability of sizable amounts of land for subsidized housing in most of the older cities, and underscored his expectation "that the majority of the poor and the majority of the Negroes, even perhaps many of the middle class, would elect to stay in the cities." [36] Among liberal supporters of the 1968 legislation in Congress, a common theme was sounded by Senator Robert F. Kennedy of New York, one of the opponents of the local veto over rent supplements, who did not think "that it is a practical possibility" to disperse blacks to the suburbs "on a large scale immediately." [37]

Certainly it was not a practical possibility politically. And the muting of the racial and dispersal implications of the massive new subsidy programs established by the 1968 legislation greatly eased the bill's path through Congress. Disputes over local control of the kind which plagued the rent-supplement program were absent from the debates on the Housing and Urban Development Act of 1968. Republicans, who provided most of the opposition to rent supplements, were supportive because of the Johnson Administration's endorsement of homeownership for poor families, an approach to housing problems developed by Senator Charles H. Percy, a Republican from Illinois, and subsequently backed by a substantial number of Republicans in Congress. With bipartisan support and nothing said about dispersing the poor, the new programs sailed through the 90th Congress with no attempts made to provide for specific local approval as in rent supplements and public housing.

Once the Section 235 and 236 programs were implemented, however, their suburban implications quickly became apparent. As pointed out in chapter 4, building 600,000 units of subsidized housing annually in relatively low-density projects, as the 1968 legislation proposed, inexorably pushed developers toward the suburbs in search of open land. As builders sought sites in the outlying portions of the metropolis, they encountered growing local resistance to 235 and 236 projects. In response, developers turned to Washington, seeking federal intervention to prevent localities from using zoning and other housing controls to block low-income projects.

Another mounting set of pressures on Washington to open the suburbs was generated by the courts and the rising volume of open-housing litigation, which was stimulated in part by the increased opportunities to develop subsidized housing provided by the new federal programs. Most troubling to federal housing officials were a pair of decisions handed down in 1969 and 1970 which affected the location of subsidized housing in the black city neighborhoods. The first was Judge Richard B. Austin's ruling against the Chicago Housing Authority and HUD in the *Gautreaux* case, which forced HUD to reconsider its role in the site-selection process for public housing.[38] The following year, the U.S. Court of Appeals for the Third Circuit upheld a challenge of federal approval of a project in Philadelphia on the grounds that the housing would increase the concentration of low-income blacks in the area. In the court's view, HUD had ignored the intent of federal law in approving the project:

> Read together, the Housing Act of 1949 and the Civil Rights Act of 1964 and 1968 show a progression in the thinking of Congress as to what factors significantly contributed to urban blight and what steps must be taken to reverse the trend or to prevent the recurrence of such blight. In 1949 the Secretary . . . possibly could act neutrally on the issue of racial segregation. By 1964 he was directed . . . to look at the effects of local planning action and to prevent discrimination in housing resulting from such action. In 1968 he was directed to act affirmatively to achieve fair housing.[39]

Paralleling these developments were steadily rising pressures on the federal government growing out of the mounting concern of civil-rights groups with suburban exclusion. During the late 1960s, HUD and other federal agencies with responsibility for housing came under close scrutiny from organizations such as the National Committee Against Discrimination in Housing, the Center for National Policy Review, and the Housing Opportunities Council of Metropolitan Washington, which wanted federal laws rigidly enforced in order to broaden housing opportunities for minorities and the poor. NCDH's opening salvo in 1967 was particularly harsh, charging the federal government with being "the prime carrier of galloping segregation [in] American cities and suburbs. . . . First it built the ghettos; then it locked the gates; now it appears to be fumbling for the key." [40]

For most of these groups, the key to opening the suburbs was federal use of grant programs as a lever to force suburbs to accept subsidized housing and lower-income residents. Open-housing interests argued that existing laws provided HUD and other agencies with authority to withhold federal funds for roads, sewers, water supply, schools, hospitals, law enforcement, planning, and other programs from those communities that failed to provide housing for blacks and the poor.[41] In particular, they pointed to the Civil Rights Act of 1964 which forbids discrimination "under any program or activity receiving Federal financial assistance," [42] and to the Civil Rights Act of 1968, which directed "all executive departments and agencies [to] administer their programs and activities relating to housing and urban development in a manner affirmatively to further" that statute's fair-housing policies and to "cooperate with the Secretary [of Housing and Urban Development] to further such purposes." [43]

A sweeping endorsement of this approach came from the U.S. Commission on Civil Rights in 1970. The Commission recommended that all federal assistance, direct and indirect, be denied any community which refused to undertake affirmative action to encourage racial desegregation in the metropolis. At a hearing on exclusionary practices in suburban Baltimore County, the commission's chairman, Theodore M. Hesburgh, pungently expressed its viewpoint:

> This commission has had it up to here with communities that have to be dragged kicking and screaming to the Constitution. If this country really believes in the Declaration of Independence and the Bill of Rights . . . it ought to spend its Federal dollars in a way that benefits all the people. If a state or a locality is not willing to do that, then we ought to say, "O.K., if you don't want to be part of the federal system we won't help you." It's as simple as that.
>
> And we're not doing it. We're spending millions and millions of Federal dollars on things to which people do not have equal access.[44]

Choices for the Nixon Administration

All of these pressures came to bear on Washington during Richard M. Nixon's first two years in office. The new Republican Administration, however, was not a very promising instrument for opening the suburbs. During more than two decades in public life, Nixon had hardly been a prominent supporter of civil rights or open housing. Fair housing and school desegregation received short shrift from Nixon during the 1968 campaign as he sought to secure traditional Republican strongholds in suburbia, as well as attract voters away from Hubert Humphrey and George Wallace in the South and the white ethnic neighborhoods of the older cities. Elected with only 43 percent of the popular vote in 1968,

Nixon was eager to transform what his aides saw as "an emerging Republican majority" based in suburbia and the South into a solid foundation of support that would ensure his reelection in 1972 and Republican majorities in Congress.[45] Out of these calculations came the Administration's "Southern strategy," sensitivity toward suburbia and its interests, and a strong distaste for federal policies which jeopardized this political base, such as school busing or "forced integration" in the suburbs.

Nixon and his top aides also were eager to reduce rather than expand the federal role in areas such as housing. Under the banner of the "New Federalism," Nixon proposed to return power and resources to state and local governments through revenue sharing and block grants as a means of reducing federal "interference" in state and local decision-making.[46] Providing state and local officials with more control over funds from Washington also would reduce the power of the federal bureaucracy, which was perceived by the White House as staffed by Democrats hostile to the goals and priorities of the Administration.[47] Criticizing federal bureaucrats was a favorite presidential pastime for Nixon, who found the "idea that a bureaucratic elite in Washington knows what is best for people everywhere and that you cannot trust local government . . . completely foreign to the American experience."[48] So was extolling the virtues of local government, which the President saw as "the government closest to the *people*, it is most responsive to the individual *person*; it is people's government in a far more intimate way than the Government in Washington can ever be."[49] This responsiveness, of course, was what had produced suburban exclusion; and it was what compelled advocates of open housing to seek federal "interference."

Despite its desire to keep Washington out of the suburbs, the Nixon Administration could not ignore the rising pressures for federal actions to lower the barriers to low-cost housing in the suburbs. By themselves, the civil-rights groups that clamored for change had too little clout or constituency support to carry much weight with the White House. Less avoidable, however, were pressures from the courts resulting from open-housing litigation, since judicial rulings affecting the location of subsidized housing required federal action. Also troublesome was the sympathetic response of many officials in HUD, the Justice Department, the Equal Employment Opportunities Commission, and other agencies to demands for active federal leadership to open the suburbs. Such behavior both underscored the pluralism of the executive branch and reinforced the White House's distrust of the bureaucrats responsible for housing and civil-rights programs. And hardly unimportant for a Republican Administration with a strong penchant for relying on the private sector were the pressures from home builders for help in freeing land for the construction of 235 and 236 housing. With the new programs in full swing, production of subsidized housing rose to 431,000 units during the Nixon Administration's first year in office, more than double the output in 1968. Paralleling this sharp increase in construction was mounting concern among home builders over local housing and land-use regulation; and these worries were bound to intensify with HUD predicting over 700,000 subsidized-housing starts for 1972.

Bolstering these pressures from the private sector was the strong commitment to increased housing production on the part of George W. Romney, the new Secretary of Housing and Urban Development. Romney came to Washington convinced that the fragmented housing in-

Figure 8.1. HUD Secretary Romney seeks way to better housing

Source: Detroit Free Press

dustry had to be transformed into an instrument capable of producing far more housing at costs "within reach of almost all Americans." [50] To bring these changes about, Romney spent most of 1969 launching Operation Breakthrough, which was designed to facilitate the large-scale production of factory-built housing by large corporations. In pursuit of this objective, the program sought ways around labor practices, local zoning and building codes, and other obstacles to lower construction costs, technological change, and volume production. If successful, Romney saw Breakthrough resulting in the annual assembly of as many as 300,000 industrialized units by 1972.

Opening the suburbs was not an explicit objective of Operation Breakthrough. The program was not aimed primarily at lower-income families, although some subsidized units financed under 235 and 236 were to be included in Breakthrough projects. Nor was moving blacks into the suburbs articulated as a major aim of the program. Far from it, as Romney and other HUD officials studiously avoided mentioning race in their tireless efforts to build political support for the program. Breakthrough developers, however, were required by HUD to employ affirmative fair-marketing practices in order to maximize housing opportunities for minority groups. [51]

Despite its emphasis on production rather than social goals, Operation Breakthrough inevitably brought Romney face-to-face with suburban exclusion. Local land-use and housing restrictions prevented the construction of the sort of housing planned under Breakthrough in most suburbs. To overcome these obstacles, HUD counted on Romney's salesmanship, the housing shortage, market and corporate pressures, and the attractiveness of the eleven demonstration projects planned for the initial phase of the plan. The HUD official in charge of the program was certain that "these Breakthrough systems will bring so much housing in looks, costs and safety that they will make present codes and zoning for land use outdated. We will just show a better way of designing, especially for land use." [52] In addition, HUD was ready to sweeten the pot for participating communities by guaranteeing that water, sewer, and other housing and urban development grants administered by the Department would be available for public facilities needed for a Breakthrough project. Initial reaction from the grass roots seemed to justify HUD's optimism, as over 200 communities waived local zoning and building codes in order to compete for designation as a demonstration site.

Once the sites were chosen, however, substantial local opposition materialized to some of the projects when it became known that Breakthrough would involve subsidized housing and blacks. Instead of providing showcases that would give HUD a "good housing seal of approval," [53] Breakthrough suddenly was being identified locally with public housing and poor blacks. HUD hastened to reassure troubled officials facing community opposition by deemphasizing the role of subsidized housing in Breakthrough projects. The "message we're trying to get across," explained one official, "is that Breakthrough is a demonstration program to lower the cost of housing rather than a demonstration program for low-cost housing. Options for low-income housing will be only a part of the program and there will be no public housing projects involved." [54] Suburban officials in the Houston and Wilmington areas were more impressed with the messages received from their constituents than with the soothing words from HUD. Residents' fears of low-income blacks, depressed property values, and neighborhood change led to withdrawal from the program. In the end, only one suburban site was developed under Operation Breakthrough.

Local opposition to Operation Breakthrough, despite the program's attractions to participating communities, provided Secretary Romney with a graphic lesson in both the sensitivity of suburbanites to housing proposals which threatened social change and the responsiveness of local officials to their constituent's concerns. The problems encountered by Operation Breakthrough at the grass roots also underscored the close interrelationship between the fears which fuel the politics of exclusion and the barriers to change in housing production in the suburbs. By concentrating on the technological and economic aspects of the problem, the program failed to come to grips with the more fundamental obstacles to a "breakthrough" for housing in the suburbs—obstacles rooted in social attitudes and their expression in highly responsive local political systems.

By the time the lessons of Breakthrough were being learned in 1970, HUD was deeply involved in a more general effort to open the suburbs. In deciding to marshal his department's resources for an attack on suburban exclusion, Secretary Romney was pushed by the pressures from home builders, civil-rights groups, and the courts. He also was pulled by his desire to increase housing production, a strong personal commitment to social justice and racial equality, and the arguments of top aides eager to use HUD's influence to increase housing opportunities in the suburbs. [55] Although not close to President Nixon or the inner circle in the

White House, Romney was well aware of the Administration's fears about federal actions which might threaten its suburban and Southern constituencies. He also recognized that efforts to open the suburbs would run against the grain of Nixon's emphasis on a larger role for state and local governments and fewer federal controls. Nor was the new Secretary of HUD unaware of the risks to his cherished goal of increasing housing production posed by moving low-cost housing out of the inner city. As the Chicago public-housing case was soon to indicate, efforts to disperse subsidized housing into hostile neighborhoods and communities were more likely to produce stalemate than housing.

Weighted against these considerations was Romney's deep concern over the crisis of the older cities and the role of his Department in creating and reinforcing the separated society. The former Governor of Michigan was profoundly troubled by the racially-segregated metropolis, the separation of the poor from jobs in the suburbs, and the hostility of suburbanites towards the city and its disadvantaged residents. For Romney, the division of urban society along racial and economic lines was the fundamental issue facing the United States:

> I believe the greatest threat to the future of this nation—physically, socially, and politically—is the confrontation in our states and cities between the poor and the minority groups, who are concentrated in great numbers in the central core of our cities, and the middle income and affluent families who live in the surrounding and separate communities.
> This confrontation is divisive. It is explosive. It must be resolved.[56]

Resolutions to this confrontation, in Romney's view, were not likely to be found in federal programs which concentrated on the inner city. Instead, the Secretary and his key aides were convinced that HUD "must now put greatly increased resources where the solutions are, not where the problems are." [57] Strong support for this view came from Daniel P. Moynihan, the White House's resident urban expert during 1969 and 1970.[58] Moynihan was an outspoken advocate of dispersal, insisting that "efforts to improve the conditions of life in the present caste-created slums must never take precedence over efforts to enable the slum population to disperse throughout the metropolitan areas." [59] More surprising was the endorsement of dispersal by the Nixon Administration's chief link with suburbia, Vice President Spiro T. Agnew. Early in 1970, Agnew rejected the notion that "because the primary problems of race and poverty are found in the ghettos of America, the solutions to these problems must also be found there." Solutions, argued the one-time county executive of suburban Baltimore County, had to be found in the suburbs which had the "resources needed to solve the urban poverty problem—land, money, and jobs." [60]

HUD's movement toward the suburbs also was bolstered by the findings of two study groups commissioned by the Nixon Administration to examine federal housing policies. In reports filed in January of 1970, both panels strongly endorsed federal action to disperse subsidized housing, including the denial of grants to exclusionary communities. The President's Task Force on Low-Income Housing wanted "the federal government to use the full extent of its influence to overcome racial and economic discrimination as an obstacle to the development of its housing programs, and to use eligibility to participate in federal housing assistance and community assistance programs to this end." [61] Suburban exclusion was treated more explicitly in the report of the Task Force on Urban Renewal, which "strongly" believed "that greater efforts should be made to break the suburban barrier around the central cities so that people of all income levels can find housing within their means at a reasonable distance from their places of work." The urban-renewal panel went further than the low-income housing study group in urging Washington to withhold "federal aids *of all sorts* . . . from communities unless they undertake a program to expand the supply of low- and moderate-income housing within their boundaries." [62]

Devising a Strategy

Grants were also the preferred instrument of those within HUD who sought leverage on local communities. During the heady days when Operation Breakthrough was being formulated, leaders of the department spoke confidently of using HUD programs to punish localities which refused to make sites available for industrialized housing. "If the carrot is not enough," insisted one of Romney's aides, "then we are prepared to go to the stick . . . by withdrawing HUD grants from those communities with restrictive practices." [63] Top officials eager to attack suburban exclusion wanted to apply the same approach more generally to local restrictions on subsidized housing. Like other advocates of levering open the suburbs with federal grants, they rested their case heavily on the Civil Rights Act of 1964 which prohibited discrimination in fed-

eral aid programs, and the Civil Rights Act of 1968 which required affirmative action by federal agencies to further fair housing.

Employing federal grants to open the suburbs, however, was not as
simple as many opponents of suburban exclusion made it sound. HUD's
efforts, of course, were limited to those programs administered by the
agency—subsidized housing, urban renewal, model cities, new communities, planning, water and sewer, and local public facilities. Of these
programs, aid for subsidized housing, urban renewal, and model cities
provided HUD with no leverage on most exclusionary suburbs. Denying
federal aid for what a community did not want was unlikely to produce
changes in local policies. In suburban Baltimore County, for example,
fears of blacks moving into federally-funded projects in white neighborhoods led to the abolition of the local urban-renewal agency in a 1965
referendum. HUD responded by cutting off funds for urban renewal
and subsidized housing, a move which was welcomed by those who
wanted the county to have nothing to do with low-cost housing.

Other grant programs offered more inducements for change in suburbia, but not everyone in HUD agreed that the Civil Rights Acts of 1964
and 1968 provided legal authority to withhold assistance from exclusionary communities. The civil-rights statutes, it was pointed out, dealt only
with discrimination based on race, color, religion, and national origin.
Nowhere did these laws mention economic discrimination or the exclusion of subsidized housing. As a result, some HUD officials argued that
grants could be withheld only in the case of explicit racial discrimination, a circumstance which, as open-housing litigants were learning in
the federal courts, was much more difficult to prove than economic discrimination which *de facto* excluded large numbers of lower-income
blacks.

Even using HUD programs as carrots rather than sticks was a problematical means of opening the suburbs. Legally, there were no major
obstacles to rewarding suburbs which were receptive to low-cost housing. Most HUD programs involved competitive rather than formula grants, which meant that localities were not entitled to a fixed portion of
federal funds. Moreover, the existence of more applicants than funds for
programs such as water and sewer facilities made it reasonable for the
agency to develop criteria to guide the allocation of grants among potential recipients, including standards which enhanced the prospects of
communities with liberal housing policies and reduced those of localities
which excluded subsidized housing. But for such actions to be effective,

federal assistance had to be sufficiently valuable to the local community to induce changes in housing policies. HUD's open space and planning programs clearly were not. And in the case of water and sewer grants, HUD's most prized program in the suburbs, only one out of ten suburban communities had indicated an interest in federal money.[64] As a result, withholding federal aid was not a credible threat for most suburbs. A survey in the San Francisco area concluded that "suburban communities may actively seek a sewer or open space grant when they know it is available, but they will not undertake an ongoing program of housing development or maintain a workable program certification on the chance that they may someday get a federal grant, nor would they be anxious to accept a grant with 'strings' attached to it." [65]

Moreover, when grants were highly valued in suburbia, formidable political obstacles stood in the way of using the leverage provided by federal funds to secure changes in housing policies. State and local governments usually complain when they fail to get what they want from Washington. When complaints are made, the decentralized base of the American political system insures a response from elected federal officials that cannot be ignored by administrative agencies. Thus, the more influence provided HUD by an aid program, the louder were local protests likely to be about "irrelevant" criteria, and the greater the probability that congressmen would take notice of and echo local complaints that "refusal of assistance in the provision of sewerage facilities seems a poor way to promote [subsidized] housing." [66] And the more likely that Nixon's White House, nervous about its suburban constituency, would blow the whistle on HUD. While this grass-roots counterweight to the power of the federal government was blissfully ignored by civil-rights groups clamoring for a hard line on federal grants to the suburbs, it was a key consideration for those in HUD seeking a policy that was both effective and politically viable. As one HUD official noted: "We talk a lot about carrots and sticks, but looked at closely all we have are carrots." [67]

The Open Communities program that finally emerged from HUD was strongly conditioned by both the policy levers available to the Department and the constraints which limited their use. Grants would be used to bring pressures to bear on communities that excluded subsidized housing, but on a selective rather than general basis. Particular attention was to be given to blatant instances of racial discrimination by local governments, both in administering grant programs and in bringing actions by the federal government in court. New standards were developed to govern the awarding of water, sewer, and other grants, which assigned substantial weight to local provision of subsidized housing. Site selection criteria for subsidized housing also were overhauled, with a heavy emphasis placed on avoiding racial concentration. In addition, developers of subsidized housing would be required to market their units affirmatively to all racial groups in an effort to insure that minorities were aware of subsidized housing opportunities throughout the metropolis.

Only one element of the Open Communities program dealt directly with local land-use controls. It was also the sole aspect of Romney's plan which required congressional action. The proposed legislation prohibited local governments from using "planning, zoning, subdivision controls, building codes or permits, or other matters affecting land use" to prevent the "reasonable" provision of federally-subsidized housing.[68] In presenting the proposal to a congressional committee, Romney termed it "a necessary first step in ending the ominous trend toward stratification of our society by race and by income." [69] Certainly, the bill was a cautious first step, reflecting HUD's awareness of the political perils awaiting any measure that aroused suburbia's spokesmen in Congress and the White House. Built-up communities were not covered by the ban, which applied only to undeveloped areas in the path of urbanization.[70] In addition, local zoning could only be questioned if it were inconsistent with a comprehensive plan for the area, an unlikely circumstance considering the lack of areawide plans calling for the racial and economic integration of the suburbs. Finally, enforcement provisions were cumbersome, requiring the filing of civil actions in federal court by the Attorney General or an aggrieved private party, a process bound to involve delay and all the other problems encountered contesting suburban exclusion on a case by case basis in court.

The Political Education of George Romney

Implementation of the Open Communities program began without fanfare in 1969. Local governments in a number of areas were told that they would have to accept subsidized housing in order to qualify for water or sewer assistance. Initial results of these low-key pressures were encouraging. In the Boston area, Stoughton approved a housing project over local opposition after HUD held up the suburb's application for a water grant on the grounds that "all public improvements supported by federal funds . . . should work toward the common goal of establishing housing throughout the nation." [71] The following year, over $15 million in HUD funds earmarked for Toledo was cut off after the city council had killed three scattered-site projects in response to opposition from white neighborhoods. HUD also withheld a $1.4 million sewer grant from Baltimore County because of the suburban jurisdiction's refusal to accept subsidized housing. And in a fateful step, Warren in the Detroit area was threatened with the loss of urban-renewal assistance unless its housing policies were altered.

At first glance, Warren appeared to be a perfect target for the new HUD program. The large, rapidly-growing industrial suburb had thousands of blue-collar jobs, almost no black residents, and a long history of racial exclusion. Warren had doubled its population during the 1950s, and again during the 1960s. By 1970, 180,000 people lived in Warren, most of whom were working-class ethnic Americans. Industrial growth was just as striking, with over 80,000 employed in the community in 1970. Approximately 30 percent of the labor force was black, but only twenty-eight minority families lived in Warren, and most of these were housed on a military reservation. Blacks clearly were not welcome; and violence resulted when a racially-mixed couple moved to Warren in 1967.

Compared with most suburbs, Warren was more vulnerable to pressure from HUD because it was receiving urban-renewal funds under the Neighborhood Development Program. In return for an initial federal grant of $1.3 million to rehabilitate an aging section of the community, Warren agreed to accept 100 units of low-income housing. When Warren officials returned for a second installment of $2.8 million in 1970, they found that HUD had raised the price sharply. Unless Warren altered housing policies which discriminated against blacks, funding for the urban-renewal project would be terminated. During the complex negotiations which followed, some local officials dug in their heels, contending that racial integration was political suicide in Warren. For one member of the Warren council, what HUD was "asking us to do is give up our jobs." [72] Secretary Romney was unsympathetic. "You can try to hermetically seal Warren off from the surrounding areas if you want to" he told a delegation of officials from Warren, "but you won't do it with federal money." [73]

Two months after the meeting with Romney, the dispute between HUD and Warren burst into public view, producing a flood of controversy which undermined Romney's Open Communities program.

Late in July, the *Detroit News* broke the Warren story in sensational fashion. Under a banner headline which read "U.S. Picks Warren as Prime Target in Move to Integrate All Suburbs," the newspaper reported that the "federal government intends to use its vast power to force integration of America's white suburbs—and is using the Detroit suburbs as a key starting point." [74] Featured in the initial story, and those that followed over the next week, were quotations from memoranda prepared in HUD's Chicago office which claimed that "Detroit suburbs present an unparalleled opportunity for the application of a fair housing strategy" and identified Warren as one of the most "blatant offenders . . . using federal money to perpetuate 'segregated housing.' " [75]

Hard on the heels of these revelations came angry denunciations of Romney, HUD, and Washington by suburban spokesmen in the Detroit area. "I don't want HUD shoving stuff down our throats," protested one suburban mayor. [76] Another suburban official flexed suburbia's growing political muscle. "We are much stronger than they think. We have congressmen and lobbyist groups. Local units, especially in the Detroit area, are the kind that rear back and speak up. HUD is not so powerful that it can render the [suburbs] powerless." [77] And when suburbia reared back and spoke up, distress was immediate in the White House and Congress.

A week after the furor began, Romney rushed to Warren in an effort "to clear the air." Meeting with officials from Warren and forty other suburbs, he found the air in the high-school auditorium full of hostility. Romney denied that HUD was promoting forced integration, or would impose racial quotas on suburbia. "There is not now, nor will there be, a HUD policy mandating forced racial integration in the suburbs," Romney told his skeptical audience. "The department does encourage integration through voluntary action. And we have a statutory mandate to enforce a national policy of fair housing. But our role is not to prescribe quotas or numerical standards which a community must meet." [78] Gone was all trace of the tough position adopted by Romney at his previous meeting with Warren's officialdom. Far from cutting off grants, HUD would rely on local "good faith" to broaden housing opportunities in the suburbs for lower-income families and blacks. [79]

As Romney left the meeting, he caught a glimpse of the furies that the threat of subsidized housing had unleashed in suburbia. His car was set upon by hundreds of angry protestors, and a police escort was necessary to extricate the embattled Secretary from a shouting mob, some of whom pounded the car while others waved placards suggesting that

Romney take HUD's open-housing efforts to exclusive Bloomfield Hills, the nearby suburb where the Secretary lived. In the months that followed, these emotions overwhelmed urban renewal in Warren. Although a bare majority of the local council voted to continue the program on the basis of Romney's assurances, grass-roots sentiment was strongly in favor of withdrawal. Over 14,800 signatures were collected in eight days on petitions calling for a referendum on urban renewal. At the polls in November, urban renewal was overwhelmed as 57 percent of those voting supported repeal.

Back in Washington, George Romney soon made it clear that HUD's efforts to open the suburbs had been substantially affected by his exposure to the raw emotions of suburban exclusion and the political storms stirred by these passions. Testifying before a Senate committee one month after Warren, Romney dwelt on the dangers of "setting things back as a result of pushing too hard too fast." [80] He strongly endorsed local control over land use, insisting that "the Federal Government should not . . . require a community to accept a housing development which does not conform to code or zoning requirements imposed for the benefit of the community as a whole and which are uniformly enforced." [81] With this formulation, Romney tacitly endorsed most restrictive devices in suburbia, since, as Joseph P. Fried has pointed out, "most exclusionary suburban zoning requirements are 'imposed for the benefit of the community as a whole,' at least as far as the imposers are concerned, and often are 'uniformly enforced.' " [82] As in Warren, Romney disavowed the use of federal power to assure economic and racial integration. In addition, he specifically rejected the argument that existing civil-rights statutes provided his department with authority to cut off assistance from suburbs that excluded low-cost housing. While HUD would continue to give priority in making grants to communities that were seeking to expand housing opportunities, funds would not be withheld.

Romney's refinement of his policies was welcomed in the White House, which had been greatly distressed by the debacle in Warren. Despite misgivings, Nixon and his top aides had gone along with Romney prior to Warren, paying relatively little attention to the details of HUD's efforts in the suburbs. Romney, however, was expected to emphasize neutral themes such as "broadening freedom of choice" rather than provocative ones like "forcing integration." [83] And most of all, he was to avoid controversy that would endanger the Administration's standing with its suburban constituency. Headlines proclaiming that the

Nixon Administration planned to promote forced integration in the suburbs were a mark of Romney's disastrous failure. Warren and its aftermath confirmed the direst predictions in the White House concerning the political risks inherent in tampering with suburban housing. The Warren incident also reinforced the Administration's substantial doubts about the competence, reliability, and loyalty of Romney and his inner circle at HUD.[84] Even those with a marginal political stake in the Nixon Administration, such as Democrat Daniel P. Moynihan, were distressed by Romney's approach to dispersal in Warren. For Moynihan, the essential ingredient of a successful suburban policy was to avoid confrontations and coercion: "Any kind of threat situation will fail; the community will find some way either to evade or repudiate the threat. Government should not be in the business of failing; therefore it should not try threatening." [85]

To prevent more failures, the White House asserted its authority, assuming direct control over the formulation and implementation of federal policies affecting the location of subsidized housing. John D. Ehrlichman, Assistant to the President for Domestic Affairs, instructed all federal agencies to hold off on policies designed to promote residential integration until the White House had settled on a uniform policy. The components of the Open Communities program were carefully reviewed by Administration working groups; and each was rewritten to place less emphasis on opening the suburbs and more on narrow programmatic goals. As a result, public-health considerations became much more important in the revised version of the water and sewer regulations, while the weight assigned to low-income housing in evaluating applications for these grants was halved.

Despite Warren, Romney's reservations, and the intervention of the White House, advocates of opening the suburbs within HUD insisted that the Open Communities program was alive and well. "We've been doing our thing quietly," noted one, "but we really plan to fly after the November elections." [86] What seemed far more likely to fly after the 1970 election, however, was George Romney, as signs mounted that he was about to be booted out of the Cabinet. For weeks, Romney and his suburban policies had been strongly criticized by columnist Kevin P. Phillips, a former aide to Attorney General John N. Mitchell and author of *The Emerging Republican Majority* who maintained close ties with his former boss and other key conservatives in the Nixon Administration. Early in November, Phillips charged that HUD's "blueprint and objectives stand in basic conflict with the Nixon Administration's announced 'support' of neighborhood schools and its opposition to the idea that desegregation requires ethnic or racial balance." [87] Later in the month, the threat to Romney materialized in the formidable person of the attorney general, who advised Romney to resign unless he was willing to stop pressing the suburbs and prepared to follow the Administration's housing policies. Romney's response reportedly was: "What the hell is the Administration policy? It changes from day to day and hour to hour." [88]

Saving the Suburbs from "Forced Integration"

A few weeks later, President Nixon sought to end Secretary Romney's confusion by clarifying the Administration's policies on opening the suburbs. At a press conference in December, Nixon was asked: "concerning Governor Romney's plan, to what extent should the Federal Government use its leverage to promote racial integration in suburban housing?" Obviously prepared for the question, the President answered: "Only to the extent that the law requires—in two cases, as a result of acts passed by the Congress that the Federal Government not provide aid to housing, or to urban renewal where a community has a policy of discrimination and has taken no steps to remove it." [89] After restricting efforts to open the suburbs to housing assistance, and placing the burden for that federal responsibility on Congress, the President went on to make his major point, assuring the suburbs "that it is not the policy of this Government to use the power of the Federal Government or Federal funds in any other way, in ways not required by the law for forced integration of the suburbs. I believe that forced integration of the suburbs is not in the national interest." [90]

In emphasizing his opposition to "forced integration," the bogeyman that had materialized in Warren, Nixon sought to convince suburbanites that they had nothing to fear from his Administration. Framing the issue of suburban housing in terms of "forced integration," however, was bound to reinforce suburbia's identification of subsidized housing with low-income blacks, a connection which Romney was strenuously trying to deemphasize. "The President hurt us badly," one of Romney's aides told a reporter. [91] Moreover, Nixon's preoccupation with forced integration could not help but legitimize racially-based suburban animosities toward lower-cost housing. As one reporter commented, "the President, his eye fixed on the suburban vote for 1972, draped the dreaded race-mixing shroud over the entire Romney effort to move subsidized housing beyond city limits." [92]

Over the next two months, Nixon continued to play to his suburban constituency. In a television interview in January, he termed federal action "to force integration on the suburbs . . . unrealistic. I think it will be counterproductive and not in the interest of better race relations." [93] At a press conference in February, the President differentiated federal action to overcome overt racial discrimination from federal intervention to lessen economic exclusion:

> First, this Administration will enforce the law of the land which provides for open housing. Open cities, open suburbs, open neighborhoods are now a right for every American.
> Second, however, this Administration will not go beyond the law or in violation of the law by going beyond it by using Federal power, Federal coercion, or Federal money to force economic integration of neighborhoods. [94]

The following month, he told a national television audience that "forced integration" through the use of federal power to "break up [a] community . . . from the economic standpoint, because homes are too expensive for some people to move into," was unconstitutional." [95]

In June, the President elaborated these themes in an 8,000-word "Statement of Equal Housing Opportunity," which represented the definitive articulation of the Nixon Administration's policies on opening the suburbs. Publication of the policy paper also marked the completion of George Romney's painful conversion to the narrow and legalistic approach to suburban exclusion favored by the White House. Romney had fallen in line after a climactic meeting with Nixon and Mitchell late in December. Soon afterward, he indicated that he was in complete agreement with the President on the evils of forced integration, on the distinctions between racial and economic integration, and on the limitations on federal power to apply leverage on the suburbs. [96] And Romney's good soldiers at HUD dutifully drafted the presidential statement which repudiated much of what the Department had fought for over the previous eighteen months.

As in his previous statements, Nixon drew a sharp distinction between racial discrimination and economic integration. The former would not be tolerated by Washington; the latter would not be imposed on any locality by the federal government. Equal housing opportunity was proclaimed as the Administration's goal, but in Nixon's definition it was a right severely limited by what an individual could afford: "By 'equal housing opportunity,' " the President explained, "I mean the achievement of a condition in which individuals of similar income levels in the same housing market area have a like range of housing choices available to them regardless of their race, color, religion, or national origin." [97] Also narrowly interpreted was the affirmative action mandate of the Civil Rights Act of 1968, with the President again insisting that the requirement that federal agencies promote fair housing applied only to housing programs and could not be used to justify withholding other kinds of federal aid.

Permeating the policy paper was a strong endorsement of local control over housing and land use, the desirability of a limited role for the federal government, and the necessity to rely on voluntary local efforts. "This administration," the President emphasized, "will not attempt to impose federally assisted housing upon any community." [98] While the federal government would "encourage communities to discharge their responsibility for helping to provide decent housing opportunities" to lower income families "who live or work within their boundaries," the President urged all concerned with suburban housing to

recognize that the kind of land use questions involved in housing site selection are essentially local in nature: They represent the kind of basic choices about the future shape of a community, or of a metropolitan area, that should be chiefly for the people of that community or that area to determine. The challenge of how to provide fair, open, and adequate housing is one that they must meet; and they must live with their success or failure. [99]

That many suburbs would rise to the President's challenge "to provide fair, open, and adequate housing" on a voluntary basis was a forlorn hope indeed. The failure of most suburbs to open their doors in the absence of strong outside pressures was what had brought open-housing advocates to Washington. Typical of what could be expected from appeals to suburbia's good will was the cool response to Vice President Agnew's suggestion in early 1970 that suburbs open their doors to the poor. Suburban leaders quickly reminded their former colleague of suburbia's problems and insisted that their obligation was to serve the needs and interests of their constituents. [100] Moreover, Nixon's comments about the local community living with "the success or failure" of its efforts "to provide fair, open, and adequate housing" was pure sophistry. Most suburbs were happy to live with the consequences of this kind of "failure," since for the exclusionary community it was in fact a "success." On the other hand, those that paid the heaviest price for such failures were the lower-income and minority families that were excluded, and thus were unable to participate in making "basic choices about the future shape" of a particular local community. With Nixon's statement, the Catch-22 of suburban exclusion became the official policy of the national government.

"Look At What We Do Rather Than What We Say"

Not everyone received the same message from the President's statement. A knowledgeable commentator with close ties to HUD interpreted the message as endorsing Romney's efforts to open the suburbs, and thus constituted "an enormous political triumph" for the secretary and his top aides.[101] Other journalists, however, emphasized the negative aspects of the message, and headlines such as the *Phoenix Gazette*'s "Nixon Won't Push Poor on Suburbs" were common.[102] For a law professor associated with the development of the open-housing program at HUD, headlines such as those in Phoenix were "an incredible interpretation. . . . A more accurate headline would have read," he contended, "Nixon Urges Suburbs Accept Blacks and Poor—Pledges Federal Support."[103] Even the august *New York Times* encountered difficulty in determining the main thrust of the Administration's policy. The initial story on the President's message was capped "Nixon To Enforce Rights Measure for U.S. Housing."[104] But an article appearing the following day in the Sunday "News of the Week in Review" was entitled "A Bit of Help for the Pure White Suburbs."[105]

Part of the confusion arose from Nixon's strong endorsement of federal action against racial discrimination. Optimists pointed to the statement that "we will not countenance any use of economic measures as a subterfuge for racial discrimination."[106] Also encouraging was the suggestion that effect as well as intent would be taken into account by the federal government in determining whether an action involved racial discrimination: "If the effect of the action is to exclude Americans from equal housing opportunity on the basis of their race, religion, or ethnic background, we will vigorously oppose it by whatever means are most appropriate—regardless of the rationale which may have cloaked the discriminatory act."[107] Another cause for a favorable interpretation was the President's indication that the federal government was prepared to sue suburbs in which racial considerations had led to rezoning designed to block subsidized housing, a course of action which HUD had urged on the White House and Justice Department for months in the case of Black Jack.

Civil-rights and housing groups, however, generally were not impressed with the President's words, and doubted that effective action would follow. Bayard Rustin of the Leadership Conference on Civil Rights spoke for most when he termed the Administration's housing policies a "disaster" and indicated that he did "not believe there is a will and a commitment by the Administration to deal with the housing problems of poor blacks and Puerto Ricans and other minorities." [108] Nixon's distinction between racial and economic discrimination was attacked as artificial. Suburban Action, in expressing its "keen disappointment" with the message, emphasized that "racial discrimination in the suburbs is the direct and calculated result of economic discrimination." [109] NCDH, which had answered Nixon's earlier remarks on "forced integration" with an advertised plea that the President "enforce the law," attacked the June statement as nothing less than an open endorsement of apartheid in the United States." [110]

During the ensuing months, the pessimists were proved correct as the remodeled Open Communities program soon floundered and then perished in the general collapse of subsidized housing programs engineered by the Nixon Administration early in 1973. A very different outcome seemed possible, however, when the new effort was launched with a flurry of action three days after the President's message; it was the same day, not coincidentally, when the Civil Rights Commission opened hearings on suburban exclusion. Attorney General Mitchell announced that the federal government was suing Black Jack under the provision of the Civil Rights Act of 1968 which authorized the Department of Justice to bring civil actions against "any person or group of persons engaged in a pattern or practice" that discriminated on the basis of race, color, religion, or national origin. [111] Half an hour earlier, the proposed federal guidelines for water, sewer, and other community-development grants were issued by Secretary Romney. At the same time, HUD and the General Services Administration signed an agreement designed to insure the availability of low-cost housing for federal employees in the vicinity of proposed new federal installations. [112] And ten days later, HUD proposed new site-selection criteria for subsidized housing.

None of these ventures, however, was to leave much of a mark on the

Mr. President: We call on you to enforce the laws of the land.

All citizens of the United States shall have the same right, in every State and Territory, as is enjoyed by white citizens thereof to inherit, purchase, lease, sell, hold and convey real and personal property.

U. S. Congress
Civil Rights Act
April 9, 1866

...the general welfare and security of the Nation and the health and living standards of its people require...realization as soon as feasible of the goal of a decent home and a suitable living environment for every American family....

U. S. Congress
Housing Act
July 15, 1949

...the granting of Federal assistance for the provision, rehabilitation, or operation of housing and related facilities from which Americans are excluded because of their race, color, creed or national origin is unfair, unjust, and inconsistent with the public policy of the United States as manifested in its Constitution and laws....

Presidential Executive Order 11063
Equal Opportunity in Housing
November 20, 1962

No person in the United States shall, on the ground of race, color, or national origin, be excluded from participation in, be denied the benefits of, or be subjected to discrimination under any program or activity receiving Federal financial assistance.

U. S. Congress
Civil Rights Act
July 2, 1964

Sec. 804...it shall be unlawful — (a) To refuse to sell or rent after the making of a bona fide offer, or to refuse to negotiate

for the sale or rental of, or otherwise make unavailable or deny, a dwelling to any person because of race, color, religion, or national origin.

(b) To discriminate against any person in the terms, conditions, or privileges of sale or rental of a dwelling, or in the provision of services or facilities in connection therewith, because of race, color, religion, or national origin.

Sec. 813 (a) Whenever the Attorney General has reasonable cause to believe that any person or group of persons is engaged in a pattern or practice of resistance to the full enjoyment of any of the rights granted by this title...he may bring a civil action in any appropriate United States District court....

U. S. Congress
Fair Housing Act
April 11, 1968

...when racial discrimination herds men into ghettos and makes their ability to buy property turn on the color of their skin, then it too is a relic of slavery....At the very least, the freedom that Congress is empowered to secure under the Thirteenth Amendment includes the freedom to buy whatever a white man can buy, the right to live wherever a white man can live. If Congress cannot say that being a free man means at least this much, then the Thirteenth Amendment made a promise the Nation cannot keep.

Supreme Court of the United States
Jones v. Mayer Co.
June 17, 1968

No Administration, if it is to maintain respect for law, can be selective in the enforcement of the law. For that reason, we urge that you personally declare this Administration's commitment to immediate, nationwide enforcement and implementation by all departments, and agencies of the Executive of the requirements of affirmative action for open housing and open communities in all Federal programs and activities concerned with housing and urban development.

NCDH Recommendations
to the President
December 7, 1970

Q. Mr. President, concerning [Secretary] Romney's plan, to what extent does the Federal Government use its leverage to promote racial integration in suburban housing?

A. Only to the extent that the law requires. In two cases, as a result of acts passed by the Congress, that the Federal Government not provide aid to housing or to urban renewal where a community has a policy of discrimination and has taken no steps to remove it.

On the other hand, I can assure that it is not the policy of this Government to use the power of the Federal Government or Federal funds in any other way, in ways not required by the law, for forced integration of the suburbs. I believe that forced integration in the suburbs is not in the national interest.

President Richard M. Nixon
News Conference
December 10, 1970

Mr. President: We think you missed the point. We don't ask that you "force integration." We only ask that you enforce the law.

National Committee Against Discrimination in Housing, Inc. (NCDH)
1865 Broadway — New York, N.Y. 10023
Robert L. Carter, President
D. John Heyman, Chairman of the Board
Dr. Frank S. Horne, Chairman, Executive Committee
William H. Oliver, Vice-Chairman, Executive Committee
Edward Rutledge and Jack E. Wood, Jr.
Chief Executive Officers

Figure 8.2.

segregated residential patterns of the American metropolis. The significance of the Black Jack suit was primarily symbolic, demonstrating the willingness of the federal government to move against what Secretary Romney called a "blatant violation of the Constitution and the law." [113] Federal use of the courts to contest discriminatory local policies by exclusionary suburbs was an inherently limited approach. Before a suit could be brought, the Justice Department demanded evidence of an "actual display" of discrimination by local government.[114] Such "displays" were not easily documented; and racial motivation, as pointed out in chapter 7, was even more difficult to prove in court. Moreover, for the federal government as for private parties, litigation was a process fraught with delay, high risks of failure, and uncertain prospects for achieving significant changes even if a particular suit resulted in a favorable outcome.

In mid-1971, Secretary Romney was still hopeful that water and sewer grants could be used to persuade suburbs to accept subsidized housing. Asked when the new guidelines were made public whether a community which refused to approve subsidized housing would have to forego federal help with its sewers, Romney answered "Sure, they don't have to do it. That's leverage, but it's not force." [115] Nor was it much leverage. Availability of low-cost housing accounted for only 10 of the 100 points that could be awarded to an applicant for a water or sewer grant.[116] With subsidized housing so lightly weighted, as the Commission on the Cities in the '70s pointed out, the "new water and sewer guidelines . . . could still reward Black Jack with a federal grant to support its exclusionary urban growth." [117] Even more significant in reducing HUD's leverage was the lack of interest on the part of most suburbs in the department's programs, particularly when the grants carried unattractive conditions. As Romney later conceded: "The fact is the HUD programs are of marginal interest to most well-established suburbs, and it is therefore sheer illusion to think that HUD can bring about overnight changes in the entire existing suburban physical and social landscape by turning Federal money on or off." [118] Romney, of course, was delivering his own epitaph, since the illusions were his as much as anyone's in Washington.

Almost as illusory in their impact on suburban exclusion were the site selection criteria for subsidized housing which finally went into effect in early 1972. Designed, according to Secretary Romney, to discourage "minority concentration of housing and to obey the orders of federal courts which have ruled on these questions," the Project Selection Criteria favored applications for housing assistance that proposed to build outside black neighborhoods and to build in areas with few subsidized units.[119] Nothing in the new standards, however, changed the basic relationship between the federal government and the recipients of housing subsidies. HUD remained totally dependent on applications from local governments and developers, who continued to bear the responsibility for locating sites.[120] As Secretary Romney emphasized to a congressional committee in 1971, "the decision to propose a housing project in a particular place is made by somebody outside the Department. . . . The Department doesn't locate land or sites, it doesn't initiate housing projects, it receives proposals . . . from public bodies or private organizations."[121] Consequently, the Project Selection Criteria had little impact on suburbs which were unwilling to take the official actions necessary for participation in the public-housing or rent-supplement programs, or which refused to zone land to permit the construction of 235 or 236 housing by private developers. "Local communities," as Romney told a House committee in 1972, "have the control over the type of housing that is going to be built within the communities through zoning, building codes and other means."[122]

While the Project Selection Criteria had little effect on most suburbs, they caused great concern in the older cities where their rigorous application threatened to eliminate federal funding for most subsidized housing. Pointing to the impasse in Chicago that resulted from Judge Austin's efforts to disperse public housing, city leaders argued that the new policies were counterproductive, since HUD would be keeping projects out of the areas where they were needed while being unable to insure that the housing would be built in the suburbs. And with the realization that cities would lose assistance as a result of efforts to disperse low-cost housing, most mayors lost interest in federal action to open the suburbs.

So did George Romney. Meager results, along with suburban resistance, disinterest and distrust in the White House, and constant criticism from advocates of opening the suburbs took their toll on the Secretary of Housing and Urban Development. By 1972, Romney was talking more and more about voluntary action and the moral obligations of suburbanites to their less fortunate neighbors, an approach which is the last resort of those who are unable or unwilling to apply more effective leverage on suburban housing and land-use policies. Expanding housing opportunities for the poor, argued Romney, would not result from approaches "where you are trying to ram [low-cost housing] down the throats of people in every suburb in this country," but had to be achieved through cooperative efforts between city and suburbs to solve housing and development problems on a metropolitan-wide basis. [123] Romney now saw the federal role as limited "primarily [to] providing financial assistance to local communities and states with minimal redtape and controls." [124]

Whatever remained of Romney's flagging efforts to open the suburbs was swept away by the political and financial crisis which engulfed subsidized housing in 1972. Criticism of the 235 and 236 programs mounted rapidly in the wake of revelations of shoddy construction, profiteering, fraud, and abandonment of housing. Controversies over racial segregation, site selection, and HUD's efforts to open the suburbs also eroded political support for subsidized housing programs. Soaring costs became a major concern to federal budget makers, as rapid increases in the production of subsidized housing led to a five-fold increase in outlays during Nixon's first term, with almost $2 billion allocated for housing subsidies in fiscal 1973. Adding to these costs were mortgage failures and abandonments which threatened to saddle the federal government with an enormous financial burden as Washington found itself the owner of thousands of worthless properties.

Secretary Romney—whose stress on production had exacerbated the situation—concluded that the problems were beyond solution, and in January 1973 he announced a moratorium on all new subsidized housing construction. [125] Prior to adopting this Draconian solution to a serious but hardly universal set of problems, HUD made no effort to remedy the defects in the 235 and 236 programs. Nor was the decision based on any systematic analysis of either the problem or the available alternatives. Instead, formal justification for Romney's decision was hastily developed after the freeze was announced, and HUD's rationales for the action were later criticized within the Department as "paper-thin, highly subjective, and totally unsupported by any back-up data." [126]

President Nixon eventually justified the termination of housing subsidies on the grounds that the programs were ineffective, wasteful, and inequitable. Considerable emphasis was placed on the question of equity. "Rather than treating those in equal circumstances equally," Nixon argued, "our present approach . . . arbitrarily selects only a few low-income families to live in Federally supported housing, while ignoring others. Moreover, the few often get a *new* home, while many other

families—including those who pay the taxes to support these programs—
must make do with inferior older housing." [127] For Nixon, the answer to
these problems lay not in reforming existing subsidy programs, but in
shifting the emphasis of federal policy toward housing allowances and
better utilization of existing housing by lower-income families.[128] The
Administration's new goal, according to one official, was "maximization
of existing housing stock." [129]

Concentrating on existing rather than new housing obviously had
great political appeal for the Nixon Administration. Using existing units
to house the poor posed little threat to most suburban communities
where homes were priced far beyond the reach of lower-income families,
even in the unlikely event of generous housing allowances becoming
widely available. At least in the suburbs, Nixon's fundamental problem
with the housing programs enacted in 1968 was their success. Subsidized
housing was being built in record numbers, and in the process proving
increasingly threatening to Nixon's suburban constituency, as builders,
civil-rights groups, and the courts pressed for liberalized local housing
policies. "The easy way out," as Leonard S. Rubinowitz emphasizes,
"was to stop the programs." [130]

Congress and the Suburbs

With the concomitant collapse of Romney's efforts to open the suburbs
and cessation of subsidized housing programs, the burden for developing
new federal housing policies shifted to Congress. During the first two
years of the Nixon Administration, Congress was not a central partici-
pant in efforts to use federal influence to lessen suburban exclusion.
Pressures from open-housing groups for changes in federal policies were
directed primarily at HUD and other executive agencies. Moreover,
most of the elements of the Open Communities Program did not require
new legislative authority. When HUD's pressures began to have an impact in suburbia, however, congressional awareness of the implications
of these activities mounted rapidly, demonstrating both the responsiveness of most congressmen to grass-roots concerns and the rising political influence of the suburbs in Congress. As one congressional supporter
of HUD's efforts indicated in 1970: "There is a large measure of un-
awareness in Congress about the department's direction; when that
changes, there will be the danger of HUD running [into] a backlash." [131]

Congressional backlash surfaced in the aftermath of Warren, and its first victim was Romney's 1970 zoning bill. As already indicated, HUD's proposal hardly constituted a serious threat to most suburban communities, applying only to newly developing areas, requiring the existence of comprehensive plans which called for dispersion, and relying on the courts for enforcement. Almost all those who advocated opening the suburbs found the proposal too weak. Typical was the view of the Urban League, which termed the bill "totally ineffective." [132] Even this exceedingly modest measure, however, was unacceptable to suburban congressmen like Representative Benjamin B. Blackburn, from the Atlanta area, who called Romney's proposal an "infringement by the Federal Government on the . . . power of State and local governments to provide for the welfare of their citizens through zoning and subdivision controls." [133] Opposition from suburban spokesmen like Blackburn killed the proposal in the Housing Subcommittee of the House Banking and Currency Committee. Four of the six votes against the bill were cast by Republicans from suburban districts—Blackburn, Florence P. Dwyer from suburban Essex and Union Counties in New Jersey, J. William Stanton from Keuka and Lake Counties in the Cleveland area, and William B. Widnall from Bergen County in northern New Jersey. [134]

Suburban congressmen also reacted negatively to HUD's efforts to use water and sewer grants as leverage for low-cost housing. Representative Fletcher Thompson, a Republican from Georgia whose district encompassed suburban Fulton County, was a particularly outspoken foe of "the use of federal dollars for water and sewer purposes to force social change . . . which the local people do not think is in their best interest." [135] Protests from suburban congressmen stimulated by local reactions to HUD's new water and sewer policies played an important role in convincing the White House to take a direct role in revising the policies late in 1970. Of particular significance were the complaints of Representative Widnall, the ranking minority member of the House Banking and Currency Committee, and one of the original sponsors of the water and sewer program. Widnall insisted that local need for water and sewers rather than housing considerations "should be primary" in allocating federal funds. [136] In December, these concerns led the House to accept without debate an amendment to the proposed Housing and Urban Development Act of 1970 offered by Representative Blackburn which prohibited HUD from withholding water and sewer grants from communities that failed to provide subsidized housing.

Blackburn's amendment eventually was dropped by the conference committee which resolved the differences between the House and Senate versions of the 1970 legislation. Acceptance of the amendment by the House, however, signalled growing congressional awareness of the political sensitivity of the suburban housing issue. No longer was Congress likely to overlook the implications of major housing legislation for suburbia, as it did in 1968. Nor were federal agencies going to find it easy to bypass Congress in moving administratively against suburban exclusion, as HUD was able to do during the first two years of the Nixon Administration. Instead, by the end of 1970 Congress was on guard against legislative proposals or administrative actions which threatened "forced integration" in the suburbs.

Among the victims of heightened congressional responsiveness to suburbia on housing issues was a proposal by Senator Abraham Ribicoff designed to insure the availability of housing for lower-income workers at new government and corporate facilities. Ribicoff's bill applied to new federal and state installations, as well as those built by corporations holding federal contracts. It also provided federal funds for local public services needed by the lower-income families which would be added to local populations.[137] The measure died in committee, as did legislation sponsored by Senator Jacob A. Javits of New York, which provided special federal assistance to communities agreeing to accept subsidized housing. Also coming to naught were the efforts of Senator Walter F. Mondale and his Select Committee on Equal Educational Opportunity to "encourage development of low- and moderate-income housing opportunities outside areas of present concentration, and to assure that communities which accept low- and moderate-income housing are not overburdened."[138] Nor was Senator Henry M. Jackson able to deliver on his promise to include a provision in his national land-use bill requiring that "new major suburban developments provide a minimum percentage of housing opportunities for low-income housing families—or lose eligibility for Federal Housing Administration and Veterans Administration mortgage insurance and other federal-aid programs."[139]

The major casualty of congressional fears about "forced integration" was a plan developed in the House which proposed to distribute federal housing subsidies primarily through metropolitan agencies. With opponents arguing that local communities would lose their control over subsidized housing, the proposal was rejected by the Housing Subcommittee of the House Banking and Currency Committee in 1972.[140] Instead of diluting the local role in site selection, the bill that emerged from the House committee enhanced suburban autonomy. All 235 and 236 projects in the future would have to be approved by local government through specific resolutions. Providing "local officials a voice in the location of subsidized projects" was needed, according to the Banking and Currency Committee, to prevent "the sudden influx of large-scale developments of subsidized housing in small communities [from] overloading . . . school systems, water and sewerage systems, and other community facilities." [141] A top HUD official termed the "local approval provision . . . dynamite" and predicted that it would "reinforce the wall already surrounding the suburbs." [142] The House bill also prohibited HUD from using housing for the elderly as a means of forcing communities to accept housing for lower-income families. Nor could the granting of assistance to local communities for water and sewer facilities be conditioned in any way on local participation in subsidized housing programs.

All of these restrictions reflected rising constituency pressures from the suburbs, as well as the concomitant desire of congressmen to avoid being tarred with the "forced integration" brush. The limitation on the use of housing for the elderly was the work of Representative Norman F. Lent, a Republican from suburban Nassau County in New York, an area where HUD had come under fire for allegedly holding projects for the elderly hostage in return for local commitments on subsidized family housing.[143] Lent saw low-income housing as "a mecca for the people from the city . . . young families, more children in the schools, narcotics, and high crime rates. This is what has been brought into community after community by these low-income housing projects and my constituents out in Nassau County know about this." [144] Other representatives from suburban districts objected to federal measures which "would deprive the majority of a voice" in local commmunities, or prevent local officials from being "responsible to their constituencies." [145]

Even strong supporters of dispersed housing found themselves, like Representative Thomas L. Ashley of Ohio, between "the rock and the hard place." [146] An influential member of the Housing Subcommittee, Ashley was the principal architect of the metropolitan housing legislation which was rejected in 1972. He also had supported HUD's action in cutting off aid to Toledo in his district in an effort to secure local approval for scattered-site housing. "Unhappily," as Ashley explained, "my convictions and actions on this issue are an unpleasant surprise to the local Democrats and other people to whom I look for support, especially middle-class working whites . . . who have earned the money to buy their houses." [147]

In 1972, neither the metropolitan approach favored by Ashley nor the pro-suburban measures adopted by the House committee survived the legislative gauntlet, as differences between the House and the Senate prevented the enactment of any housing legislation. When an omnibus housing bill finally was passed in 1974, congressional sensitivity to suburban interests resulted in legislation that respected local autonomy. As one influential congressman emphasized: "Unless the bill carries a broad appeal for governments other than [central] cities, we don't have a chance of winning on the floor." Legislation acceptable to the suburbs was needed, he went on to note, because "more and more congressmen find themselves representing suburban constituents." [148]

For suburbs, as well as cities, the basic appeal of the Housing and Community Development Act of 1974 was its emphasis on local discretion in the use of federal funds. Local governments, not metropolitan agencies, were the prime recipients of federal funds under the new law.[149] Local discretion was enhanced because federal funds were to be distributed in the form of block grants which could be used for almost any kind of community-development project rather than for specific purposes as in categorical programs for urban renewal, model cities, and water and sewer facilities.[150] Under the new approach, localities could allocate federal funds according to local priorities, with far less federal oversight than had been the case with categorical programs.

At the same time that local discretion was broadened, Congress emphasized that its primary objective in the new legislation was "development of viable urban communities by providing decent housing and a suitable environment and expanding economic opportunities, principally for persons of low and moderate income." To advance these national social objectives, local jurisdictions were directed to promote economic integration by their community-development grants to reduce "the isolation of income groups within communities and geographical areas" and promote "an increase in the diversity and vitality of neighborhoods through the spatial deconcentration of housing opportunities for persons of lower income and the revitalization of deteriorating or deteriorated neighborhoods to attract persons of higher income." [151]

To qualify for community-development grants, local jurisdictions had to develop housing plans which dealt with the housing needs of both existing residents and new residents anticipated as a result of economic development in the community. Locations designated for subsidized housing in the plan were supposed to advance community revitalization, enhance residential choice among lower-income families and avoid their undue concentration, and assure the availability of public facilities and services. In addition to insuring that community-development projects were coordinated with housing development and would benefit lower-income families, the housing plans were to provide the basis for the allocation of federal housing subsidies.

Despite these objectives, the Housing and Community Development Act of 1974 was not designed to have a significant impact on suburban exclusion. Most suburban jurisdictions were not directly covered by the new law, which allocated community-development funds only to suburban cities of over 50,000 and suburban counties of over 200,000.[152] Even these larger suburban jurisdictions were under no obligation to participate in the program, as long as they were willing to do without federal aid for community development. As for the rest of suburbia, it was up to local jurisdictions to decide whether they would apply for funds available under the new legislation. Failure to apply relieved the community of any obligation to prepare a housing assistance plan, much less accept subsidized housing. Moreover, as Herbert M. Franklin has pointed out, for those suburbs that did participate, the "bill imposed no affirmative action requirement, only an affirmative planning requirement." [153]

Equally important, housing subsidies under the new legislation did not assign a high priority to opening the suburbs. Allocation heavily favored existing jurisdictions with existing needs, "as reflected in data [on] population, poverty, housing overcrowding, housing vacancies, amount of substandard housing, or other objectively measured conditions." [154] No new funds were authorized under Section 235, and only limited new funding for Section 236, the two federal programs that had by far produced the most subsidized housing in the suburbs. Moreover, heavy emphasis was placed by HUD on existing rather than new housing in implementing the Section 8 leased-housing program created by the new law. HUD's regulations also made it difficult for recipients of subsidies under the new program to seek housing across local jurisdictional lines.[155] As a result, relatively few subsidized units were likely to be located in the suburbs under the Housing and Community Development Act of 1974. Moreover, low-cost housing proposed for the suburbs faced an additional hurdle as Congress increased local control over the location of subsidized housing in 1974. Jurisdictions participating in the community development program could veto subsidized proposals inconsistent with their housing-assistance plans. Communities without a housing plan also were given a veto, thanks to an amendment offered by Representative John H. Rousselot, a suburban Republican from Southern California.[156] In addition, all federally-subsidized units had to conform with local zoning. An effort by Representative Herman Badillo, a Democrat from New York City, to prohibit suburbs from using zoning laws to prevent the construction of subsidized housing was shouted down on the House floor.

Nor was there much likelihood that HUD would interpret the new legislation expansively in order to open the suburbs. Just the opposite, in fact, since HUD had learned the same political lessons in the suburbs as had Congress. Greater local control and reduced federal oversight were the watchwords of HUD under Romney's successors, James T. Lynn and Carla A. Hills. Under Lynn, HUD had promoted community-development legislation which would have involved no application process, no restrictions on local use of federal funds, and minimal federal oversight. Although the Administration bill was rejected by Congress in favor of the approach embodied in the Housing and Community Development Act of 1974, HUD made no secret of its intention "to distribute funds under the 1974 Act in the spirit of the Nixon Administration's proposed . . . bill." [157]

Even before the 1974 legislation was passed, HUD officials were indicating that local applications for community-development grants would be automatically approved unless "some community gets blatantly out of line." [158] Once the bill was enacted, HUD severely limited its role in reviewing applications for block grants. As a result, suburban housing plans submitted during the first round of community development grants were approved by HUD "routinely and almost without exception," despite the use of "grossly inadequate data to describe lower income needs" in some jurisdictions, widespread emphasis on housing for the elderly rather than families, and failure on the part of some suburbs to make any provision for subsidized housing.[159] In the field, HUD officials sought to reassure suburbs that were fearful about the housing implications of accepting block grants. Illustrative was the reaction of the HUD's Chicago office after suburban Berwyn refused to apply for its community-development grant and officials in neighboring Cicero expressed doubts about proceeding with an application. John L. Waner, HUD's director in Chicago, emphasized that "the housing provision was meant to help poor people already living in the communities as much as it was to provide new housing for people wishing to leave the city for the suburbs." [160]

Chapter Nine

Fair Shares
for the Metropolis

Metropolitan approaches are the preferred solution of almost every critic of suburban housing and land-use policies. Anthony Downs insists that "the entire subject of controlling future urban development should be viewed from a metropolitan-area-wide perspective that takes the interests of *all* the area's residents into account." [1] An advisory panel of the National Academy of Sciences concluded in 1972 that "ultimate responsibility for the supply of housing [should] be located at the metropolitan level." [2] Lawyers seeking to open the suburbs argue that "it is impossible to assess whether a community is doing its fair share or whether a community through the use of its land use controls is preventing a region's poor and moderate-income population from obtaining minimally adequate housing until you understand what the sum total of the region's housing needs are." [3]

Similar conclusions were being reached by judges, congressmen, and other officials in the early 1970s. In Atlanta and Chicago, as noted in chapter 7, federal judges ordered the development of areawide plans to insure the dispersal of subsidized housing, while state courts in New Jersey and Pennsylvania struck down suburban zoning ordinances which ignored regional housing needs. During 1971, metropolitan approaches were embraced by many members of Congress with responsibility for formulating housing policy. Strong endorsement also came from the U.S. Commission on Civil Rights, which argued that "the chaos and irrationality that characterizes the racial residential patterns we now have in metropolitan areas" would be perpetuated unless "the location of subsidized housing is determined on the basis of a metropolitan-wide analysis of the various social and economic factors involved." [4] And George Romney was convinced that housing and other major urban problems could "only be resolved on a metropolitan-wide basis," in terms of what Romney was fond of calling "the real city basis." [5]

Few governmental institutions, however, exist in metropolitan America empowered to deal with housing and land use on the basis of Romney's "real city." Only a handful of areas possessed metropolitan governments in the early 1970s. Special-purpose metropolitan agencies were more common, but very few had been created to deal with housing and land use. In the vast majority of urban areas, as detailed in chapter 2, control over housing and zoning is fragmented among local governments which jealously guard their land-use powers. Within the typical metropolis, dedication to local control has prevented areawide agencies from acquiring direct influence over suburban housing and land-use policies. As a result, metropolitan institutions concerned with land-use and settlement patterns tend to be weak organizations which cannot compel local compliance with their plans or policies.

During the 1960s, the federal government sought to encourage metropolitan approaches by using federal aid to stimulate the development of institutions which could plan comprehensively for metropolitan areas. Such agencies were nourished by planning grants under Section 701 of the Housing Act of 1954, particularly after 1959 when increasing priority was given to comprehensive planning. Another boost for metropolitan planning came with the enactment of the Federal-Aid Highway Act of 1962, which conditioned highway assistance in metropolitan areas on the existence of "a continuing comprehensive transportation planning process carried on cooperatively by States and local communities." [6] In 1964, federal aid for mass transportation was also tied to areawide planning, and similar provisions were written into other federal grant programs in subsequent years.

Even more significant for the development of metropolitan institutions was the Demonstration Cities and Metropolitan Development Act of 1966, which in Section 204 provided for review, by an areawide agency, of applications for federal aid to insure that the project was "consistent with comprehensive planning developed or in the process of development for the metropolitan area." [7] Initially, the programs subject to review were highways, airports, other transportation facilities, water supply, sewerage systems, open space, conservation, hospitals, libraries, and law enforcement. By early 1974, however, over 140 grants came under the A-95 process, so called because the procedures for implementing Section 204 were spelled out by the Office of Management and Budget in Circular A-95.[8]

Following passage of the 1966 legislation, metropolitan areas scurried to create planning and review agencies with areawide jurisdictions in order to insure the uninterrupted flow of federal aid. In some areas, the responsibility for developing comprehensive plans and reviewing applications for federal aid was assigned to metropolitan planning agencies. More often, these functions were assumed by councils of governments, which proliferated at a rapid rate. Prior to 1966, only thirty-five councils of government had been organized by local elected officials. Six years later, their ranks had increased tenfold.

All of this organizational activity, however, failed to produce very influential institutions in most metropolitan areas. Few of the agencies were delegated authority by the state legislatures to implement their plans. In many instances, COGs were voluntary organizations of local officials with no statutory base or governmental powers. Local governments usually assumed no obligations by joining COGs, and were free to withdraw if dissatisfied with the actions of a council. Whatever influence they exercised derived from their ability to persuade governmental units to act, which in turn depended heavily on their role in reviewing applications for federal aid. Washington, however, was unwilling to assign its metropolitan protégés an authoritative role in the grant-making process. "The A-95 process is not an approval process," Secretary Romney told a congressional committee in 1972. "It is a process by which the Federal agencies get the benefit of the counsel and advice of the A-95 review body." [9]

Local officials, for their part, rarely sought to create strong metropolitan institutions. Instead, most preferred to satisfy Washington's planning and review requirements without disturbing local autonomy. Here and there, to be sure, the new federal policies stimulated significant institutional, political, and policy change. But far more common was the accommodation of the new regional arrangements to the political realities of the fragmented and differentiated metropolis. As Melvin B. Mogulof has noted, council members "do not seem to want the COG to emerge as a force different and distinct from the sum of its governmental parts. Member governments do not generally see the COG structure as an independent source of regional influence but rather as a service giver, a coordinator, a communications forum, and an insurance device for the continued flow of federal funds to local governments." [10]

Suburban Exclusion in the Metropolitan Arena

Most areawide councils and planning agencies were not eager to tackle controversial issues such as suburban housing and zoning. For these fledgling institutions, maintenance of the fragile consensus that brought their constituent units together required the avoidance of conflict whenever possible. As a federal official emphasized in 1971, metropolitan agencies "demonstrated relatively little capability or taste for coping with social issues. Thus, such organizations have been more receptive to applying the review procedures to areas where there is a known community of interest among member governments, rather than to potentially controversial matters." [11]

Reinforcing the common reluctance to deal with divisive social issues such as suburban zoning and metropolitan school desegregation was the localistic perspective of most members of the boards of areawide agencies. COGs were composed almost entirely of local elected officials, and local officials usually were well-represented on regional planning agencies. Given their constituencies, responsibilities, and frame of reference, local officials naturally tended to define their role on regional agencies in terms of protecting local interests and prerogatives. Few members viewed sensitive issues such as housing and zoning in a metropolitan context, particularly if their local constituency was suburban. "I'll be damned," observed a suburban official serving on the Northeastern Illinois Planning Commission, "if I know how I can faithfully serve both the region as commissioner and my local constituents as their mayor." [12]

Further reducing the likelihood of efforts by regional agencies to expand housing opportunities was the predominance of suburban officials on these organizations. In part, of course, the prevalence of suburban representatives reflected the fact that suburbanites constituted a growing majority of the population in almost every metropolitan area. Suburbia's population advantage, however, usually was magnified by institutional arrangements which overrepresented smaller units of government and under-represented larger ones. Councils of government typically were organized on the basis of governmental units rather than population. Cleveland, for example, had only three of forty-nine seats on the Northeast Ohio Coordinating Agency despite having twenty-five percent of the area's population. When Cleveland's tiny delegation called on governments throughout the seven-county region in 1970 to provide housing for city residents displaced by highway and other projects approved by the metropolitan council, suburban representatives promised: "We will bury your housing resolution." [13] And they did overwhelmingly.

As a result of these political realities, most metropolitan planning and review agencies, in the words of a HUD official, were "scared to death of the housing issue." [14] For its part, Washington was neither indifferent to these fears, nor insensitive to the political considerations which caused them. Instead, as Randall W. Scott has pointed out, federal officials were reluctant to insist that the A-95 process be used as a "major anti-exclusionary vehicle" because of their "unwillingness to live with the political consequences of intensified housing and planning requirements." [15] Thus, Washington required A-95 agencies to comment on whether a project contributed to appropriate land uses, conservation of natural resources, balanced transportation, adequate open space, protection of scenic areas, well-planned community facilities, and the preservation of the environment. But there was no federal requirement for evaluation of a project's contribution to expanding housing opportunities for lower-income and minority groups. Only in 1972 were the civil rights implications of projects added to the A-95 list, but as an optional rather than mandatory element in the review process. Moreover, applications for housing assistance were not subject to regional review until 1971.

In the absence of federal requirements dealing with housing and related issues, most metropolitan planning and review agencies ignored exclusionary zoning, the availability of low-cost housing, and the accessibility of jobs to lower-income workers in evaluating applications for federal aid which would be spent in the suburbs. When someone sought to relate applications for federal aid to local housing restrictions, suburbanites quickly claimed foul play. After city officials in New Britain recommended that the Central Connecticut Regional Planning Agency withhold endorsement of Berlin's application for a $760,000 sewer grant because of its exclusionary zoning policies, the affluent suburb protested that its housing policies were none of the city's business. "Since when does one town become subservient to another?" asked Berlin's community development coordinator. "Why should the town of Berlin have to give any assurance to New Britain? Are they the big brothers?" [16]

Housing also was given little attention in the comprehensive plans that were supposed to guide the A-95 review process. Prior to 1968, HUD did not require specific treatment of housing in metropolitan plans financed with federal 701 funds. On their own initiative, few planning agencies were willing to risk alienating suburbs by tackling areawide housing needs, suburban exclusion, and dispersal of subsidized housing. For example, the Association of Bay Area Governments, founded in 1961 and one of the first COGs to develop a comprehensive metropolitan plan, ignored housing in its initial regional planning efforts. Like most regional agencies, ABAG concentrated its planning resources on population projections, general land-use patterns, and transportation development. With respect to housing, as Victor Jones has noted: "ABAG realized that some day it would have to face the division among its members over the proper regional distribution of low- and moderate-cost housing, but was not willing to do so before it had to." [17]

As a consequence of these political inhibitions, areawide planning for housing was "so new and so little used" in 1968 that the American Society of Planning Officials found it "virtually impossible to give a status report on it." [18] Few regional planning agencies had assembled data or developed expertise on housing needs, zoning restrictions, and the complexities of subsidized housing. With the passage of the Housing and Urban Development Act of 1968, however, metropolitan agencies receiving federal planning assistance could no longer avoid housing issues. As part of its reaffirmation of the national goal of "a decent home and suitable living environment for every American family," Congress required comprehensive land-use plans financed with federal funds to include a "housing element" dealing with "the housing needs of both the region and local communities . . . in terms of existing and prospective inmigrant population growth." [19]

Initially, HUD did not assign a high priority to compliance with the new planning requirements. Both federal officials and metropolitan planners tended to view the new housing standards as "perfunctory requirements to be administered uncritically" rather than something that "was supposed to make a difference in getting housing to families of low and moderate income." [20] In 1970, however, George Romney's search for federal leverage on the suburbs placed the requirements for metropolitan housing plans in a new light. As a result, HUD escalated its demands on regional agencies, insisting that action-oriented housing plans be developed that dealt explicitly with the dispersal of subsidized housing throughout the metropolis. Almost half of the first batch of preliminary housing plans reviewed by HUD were deemed unacceptable. Failure on the part of metropolitan agencies to develop more viable housing schemes, warned HUD, would jeopardize future federal support for planning.

In complying with the new federal standards, metropolitan agencies sought to accommodate HUD's demands to the political realities which had led them to steer clear of controversial housing issues prior to 1968. COGs and areawide planning commissions typically initiated their housing efforts with considerable deliberation, emphasizing the need to develop a substantial data base in order to understand the complexities of housing problems and programs. In discussions of their housing activities, areawide agencies frequently downplayed both the needs of the poor and exclusionary suburban practices. To protect their suburban flank further, regional agencies often stressed HUD's role in pressing for action on housing, as well as the areawide body's lack of authority to enforce a regional housing plan on local governments.

Illustrative of the reluctant response of most metropolitan agencies were the efforts of the Southeastern Wisconsin Regional Planning Commission, whose jurisdiction encompassed Milwaukee, suburban Milwaukee County, and six surrounding counties. At the outset, SEWPRC proposed a three-year study of housing in the region, designed to determine whether the Milwaukee area had a housing problem. In deference to its suburban and rural constituency—all of SEWPRC's twenty-one board memebers were appointed by the county governments and the city of Milwaukee was not directly represented—the commission's housing prospectus made little mention of the needs of poor and black families. The prospect was equally circumspect on the issue of dispersing subsidized housing. SEWPRC officials defended their deliberate approach as the proper way for professional planners to proceed, particularly if suburban support was to be developed for a regional housing program.

Central-city and open-housing interests disagreed. SEWPRC's effort was termed "obvious procrastination" by Milwaukee's mayor, who was eager to deflect outward the open-housing pressures arising from the civil-rights activities within the city.[21] Housing activists also called for action rather than study by the regional planners. The region's housing problems were obvious, they claimed, pointing to the lack of subsidized housing in the suburbs, the widespread use of exclusionary zoning, and the concentration of the poor, the elderly, and blacks in Milwaukee's run-down neighborhoods. The leader of one open-housing group wanted SEWRPC to "come . . . in with quotas," and to enforce them with "the Housing and Urban Development Club." [22]

Early in 1971, HUD also concluded that SEWRPC's approach was too passive. Urging the commission to play a more active and timely role, HUD suspended $309,000 in 701 planning funds until SEWRPC agreed to develop a short-range action plan designed to disperse 8,000 units of low-cost housing throughout the region. SEWRPC's commissioners strongly resented HUD's action. One protested, "HUD's holding a knife in our back and making us do this study." [23] Another threatened that his county would "drop out and pay our own way" if federal aid was affected by local housing policies.[24] In the end, SEWPRC reluctantly agreed to develop an interim housing plan for 2,000 units rather than the 8,000 sought by HUD. The interim plan, however, was undertaken only to fulfill the federal requirement, with little commitment to dispersing subsidized housing on the part of the regional agency. SEWPRC's chairman didn't "view it particularly as a must." [25] No effort was made by the commission to promote the plan with local officials, groups, and the general public. Instead, SEWPRC suggested that "citizens groups interested in the provision of low- and moderate-income housing should initiate educational programs through the various communications media to . . . assist in alleviating the unfortunate stigma of low quality that low- and moderate-income housing suggests to many people." [26] SEWPRC itself did not "have the funds or the time . . . to push" the unwanted housing plan.[27]

Dayton's Initiative

Not every metropolitan agency, however, undertook areawide housing planning reluctantly. During 1970, the Miami Valley Regional Planning Commission developed the nation's first "fair-share" plan designed to increase the supply of housing for lower-income families both numerically and geographically. Under the scheme, over 14,000 units of subsidized housing were allocated for construction in the five-county Dayton metropolitan area over a four-year period. Before the end of 1970, the housing plan had been adopted without a single dissenting vote by the regional planning commission, almost all of whose members were local elected officials.

At first glance, the nation's fortieth largest metropolitan area was not a particularly promising locale for regional innovation. In general political, economic, and demographic terms, little differentiated the heavily industrialized area in southwestern Ohio with its aging central city from scores of other urban complexes in the midwest and northeast. In analyzing voting patterns in the 1970s, Richard M. Scammon and Ben J. Wattenberg characterized the "typical voter in America" as a "forty-seven-year-old wife of a machinist living in suburban Dayton, Ohio." [28] Jim Fain, editor of the *Dayton Daily News,* termed the area "middle-sized, middle-West, middle-class, Middle-American [and] as representative as you could find." [29] In 1970, the city of Dayton was encircled by suburban jurisdictions, had been losing population for a decade, and held a steadily declining share of the region's jobs. Only twenty-nine percent of the metropolitan area's population of 850,000 lived in the central city in 1970. Of these 244,000 residents, over thirty percent were black, compared with less than three percent of the region's population outside the city. Almost all of the 3,350 units of subsidized housing in the five-county area was located in the central city.

Unlike many larger metropolitan areas, however, Dayton was relatively cohesive. Most residents of the area identified with the central city. A 1973 survey indicated that two-thirds of those living outside the central city considered their community to be part of the Dayton area. [30] The scale of the area also facilitated personal relationships, communication, and joint action among business, governmental, labor, civic, and community leaders. Modest size, for example, permitted every major local government in the area to be directly represented on the Miami Valley Regional Planning Commission, a situation that was impossible in larger and more complex areas such as New York, Chicago, and St. Louis, with their hundreds of local jurisdictions. As a result, every suburb in Dayton was directly rather than indirectly involved in the development of the regional housing plan. The size of the region also permitted almost every group with an interest in the fair-share plan to participate directly in the discussions, negotiations, and debates on the area's housing problems. Jim Fain summed up the advantages offered by the region's size and scale as follows: "We aren't so big, or so decayed, or so polarized that maybe we can't be saved." [31]

While important in creating a situation in which areawide cooperation was facilitated, size fails to explain the development of metropolitan consensus strong enough to produce agreement on dispersing lower-income families into the suburbs. The Providence, San Antonio, Louisville, Memphis, Sacramento, Birmingham, and Toledo areas all were approximately the same size as the Dayton region; and their local jurisdictional patterns were roughly similar, at least with respect to the number of local units. But none of these areas took the initiative in dealing with housing problems on a metropolitan basis.

Nor did Dayton's innovative role result from the existence of a metropolitan agency with exceptional powers or unique organizational arrangements. Under Ohio law, the Miami Valley Regional Planning Commission was limited to an advisory role. Whatever formal authority MVRPC wielded as the A-95 review agency for the Dayton area was not much different than that employed by the hundreds of other regional clearinghouses certified by the federal government. All forty-two of MVRPC's commissioners represented local governments; and all but five were elected local officials. Moreover, as on most regional agencies, suburban and rural interests predominated, since the city of Dayton had only one representative on MVRPC.

What was different about the Miami Valley Regional Planning Commission was its leadership. Dale F. Bertsch had been executive director of MVRPC from its inception in 1964. Unlike most of his counterparts in the front offices of metropolitan agencies, Bertsch was a politically sophisticated activist, committed to building a viable regional institution capable of tackling controversial issues. Little in his approach resembled the cautious style of the passive apolitical planners who studiously avoid conflict. One member of MVRPC characterized Bertsch as "a mover rather than a guy who sits back and does as little as possible so he can keep his job." [32] For Bertsch, the planner's responsibility was to "address ourselves to the kinds of issues that need action taken, to document them in such a way that action is the next logical step." [33] One such area clearly was housing, with Bertsch convinced that "it's up to local government and it's up to agencies like ours to guarantee" that poor people can live where they want. [34]

Bertsch's approach was not universally admired by the local officials on MVRPC. Some commissioners from suburban and rural areas strongly preferred more traditional metropolitan planning limited to data analysis, physical planning, and other advisory activities. To offset this internal opposition Bertsch and his staff assiduously cultivated political support. By working closely with commissioners, other local elected officials, and a wide variety of public agencies, MVRPC earned the respect of a substantial segment of local officialdom in the region. Backing also was developed among business, civic, and community interests, as well as from the two major Dayton newspapers. Unlike most areawide planning and review agencies, MVRPC sought public visibility and an independent political base of sorts. With this political base, the commission staff was able to employ the A-95 review process with considerable success to further its planning and development objectives.

Although more venturesome than most metropolitan planning agencies, MVRPC had done little about housing before 1969. Once its staff began pulling together data on housing conditions and needs, however, it became clear that a good deal more low-cost housing would have to be produced in the region. Equally obvious to Bertsch and his colleagues was the fact that "much greater production . . . alone would not suffice; MVRPC would have to take the responsibility of setting forth a Dispersal Plan for scattering the needed housing throughout" the metropolis.[35] Having reached this conclusion, the MVRPC staff found itself in largely uncharted waters. "There were no guidelines as to how to go about it, no examples to follow," explained Bertsch and Ann Shafor, MVRPC's housing director. "And on the question of how to numerically distribute the units to sub areas of the region, no one had touched that with a ten-foot pole."[36]

In grappling with these problems, MVRPC first determined the housing needs for each of the five counties in the region, arriving at a total of approximately 16,000 units, of which 14,125 were required for lower-income families. For the purposes of allocating the housing, the region was divided into fifty-three planning units based on existing patterns of development. Subsidized housing was distributed on the basis of a formula which took into account existing housing, the planning unit's share of both total and low-income households in the county, the assessed valuation of property per school child in the unit, and the degree of overcrowding in the unit's schools. To reduce the concentration of subsidized housing in neighborhoods with large numbers of lower-income families, the poverty factor was weighted both directly and inversely. Application of the formula produced a numerical "fair share" of subsidized housing for each of the planning units. Only 1,700 of the 14,000 units were to be located within Dayton. On the other hand, middle-class Kettering, the largest suburb in the area, with almost 70,000 residents and fewer than ten black families, was assigned 678 units. More affluent Oakwood was designated as the site of 634 units over the next four years.[37]

Local residents reacted to the allocation scheme in typical suburban fashion, screaming "never" and packing meetings to denounce the commission's plan. For many suburbanites, the "housing plan conjured up visions of hordes of Black and poor people . . . pouring across the boundaries of whatever the jurisdiction happened to be." [38] Opposition was particularly vehement in Miamisburg, whose large blue-collar population objected vociferously to the community's allocation of 740 units. Black suburbanites were no happier with the plan than whites. According to Bertsch, "the black suburban community didn't differ a whole lot from the white suburban community. There was a general feeling in some of the area immediately outside of the central city where the blacks have expanded . . . of disliking low- and moderate-income people as much as the white suburbs." [39] Along with the groundswell of grassroots opposition came denunciations of the allocation plan by local officials, who termed it unnecessary, unfair, and illegal. Joining this chorus were most of the school superintendents in the suburbs and outlying communities in the metropolitan area. As emotions rose, Bertsch became the target of threatening telephone calls, his family was harassed, and violence lurked just below the surface at some of the more turbulent local hearings on the plan.

Such reactions usually presage the end of efforts to open the suburbs, but a different scenario unfolded in Dayton. Before the allocation plan was unveiled, Bertsch and his staff had been building support for their approach. Early in 1970, MVRPC began publicizing the region's housing problems, and emphasizing the need for local action to broaden housing opportunities throughout the metropolis. A housing conference was held in January which brought together most of the groups and individuals in the area interested in improving housing opportunities. The meeting also focused public attention on the housing problem. Later in the month, Bertsch told the Montgomery County Mayors and Managers Association that "local governments must resolve first, to accept their share of lower-income housing within their boundaries, and second, they must not only strike down all of the real and hidden barricades (both legal and illegal) which hinder the building of such housing, but actively promote its construction." [40] During the same period, Bertsch indicated that quotas would be assigned to each community in the region; and that MVRPC was prepared to use its A-95 review powers to enforce a regional housing plan.

Support for the plan was developed among a broad spectrum of inter-

'Yep, Good Fences Make Good Neighbors.'

MIKE PETERS, DAYTON DAILY NEWS

Figure 9.1.

ests. Most public and private organizations interested in housing were directly involved with MVRPC as members of the commission's Housing Advisory Committee, including the Dayton Plan Board, the city's community development department, its model cities and community action agencies, the Homebuilders Association of Metropolitan Dayton, the Urban League, and the League of Women Voters. Members of the LWV were particularly active in promoting the plan locally, lobbying mayors and council members, and defending the fair-share scheme at community meetings. Dayton's black leaders lined up behind the plan, despite some opposition on the grounds that dispersal would dilute black power in the city and divert federal housing funds to the suburbs. Urban League and NAACP leaders countered these arguments by stressing that the plan was designed to increase housing options rather than force anyone to move outward. Major employers throughout the region endorsed MVRPC's approach; and the quiet efforts of top business leaders played an important role in the plan's eventual acceptance by local elected officials. Organized labor also was favorably inclined, largely because the projected construction promised to increase employment in the region. Both the *Dayton Daily News* and the *Dayton Journal Herald* enthusiastically backed MVRPC's efforts, and in the process provided extensive coverage of the commission's housing activities, encouragement to supporters of the fair-share plan, and public censure for outspoken opponents of dispersed housing. According to Bertsch, "without the support of the business community and the newspapers, we'd have published a technical dissertation that would not have been carried out in action." [41]

As important as all of this support was for MVRPC, it did not guarantee approval by members of the commission. Consequently, Bertsch and his staff gave the highest priority to convincing the commissioners and other local officials of the need for action. Briefings were held on the housing needs of lower-income families, the barriers to increasing housing opportunities, and the need for all local governments to assume responsibility for increasing the supply of housing. One of the more persuasive rationales for action stressed during these discussions in mid-1970 was the signals from Washington that federal aid would be conditioned on opening the suburbs. Bertsch also insisted that a fair-share plan was not as politically unattractive as might appear at first glance. Fair shares were a ceiling as well as a minimum, thus guaranteeing that individual communities would not be overwhelmed by subsidized housing. This was a compelling consideration for local officials in Trotwood, an older suburb of 30,000 in the path of blacks moving outward from Dayton. In the face of vociferous local opposition, the mayor and all of the councilmen supported the allocation scheme. "If we don't have this plan, this umbrella," argued Mayor Edward Rausch, "we'll be inundated long before other communities have any." [42]

Bertsch's willingness to compromise also made it easier for some local officials to support the plan. Part of the original scheme called for MVRPC to seek legislative authority to override local zoning if necessary to secure compliance with the plan. Opponents denounced this direct attack on zoning as fatal to local autonomy. By agreeing to drop the zoning provision, MVRPC demonstrated its "reasonableness." At the same time, supporters of the plan with unhappy constituents could argue that its most objectionable feature had been eliminated. A price was paid for these benefits, of course, since MVRPC's lack of any direct leverage on local zoning power increased the difficulties encountered in implementing the plan.

Before the problems of implementation could be faced, however, the plan had to be approved. In the end, not a single suburb voted against fair shares, and only six commissioners abstained. Among the twenty-six members who supported the plan was one who had been instructed to vote "no" by his local council. As is always the case when a legislative body takes a position on a controversial issue, different members were motivated by different factors. Dale Bertsch and Ann Shafor later identified three major considerations which influenced the local officials in the region:

> For some, it was a matter of pure conscience. They felt that the concept of the plan was right, that supporting it was the only moral thing to do. At the other end of the scale, some took affirmative action purely to save face, because negative action was going to publicly confirm their bigotries and 'tarnish' their images. The strength of this motivation was sometimes startling.
> For still others, the motivation was highly pragmatic. Moderate income housing construction was already beginning to occur in a few suburban areas, and the decision makers there viewed the Dispersal Plan as a safeguard against their areas being deluged with such housing. [43]

Although Dayton took the initiative in devising its fair-share plan, the next step depended heavily on federal backing. Without funds from HUD, the 14,000 units of subsidized housing could not be built. Even more important in the view of supporters of the plan was federal willingness to use its assistance programs to bring pressure on the suburbs, and thus put teeth in MVRPC's employment of the A-95 review process to enforce its plan. For Trotwood's mayor, "the key" was whether "the federal government will cooperate and deny assistance on everything we need if we don't measure up on housing." [44] Another local official was convinced that if "political pressures build up so that the suburbs can continue to flout low- and moderate-income housing and still get their money from Washington there is little we can do." [45] By the time MVRPC adopted its plan at the end of September, political pressures already had undermined HUD's commitment to deny federal aid to exclusionary communities, with Secretary Romney in full retreat in the wake of the Warren debacle two months earlier. As Dayton began implementing the plan during the winter of 1970–71, President Nixon was inveighing against forced integration, defending economic exclusion, and otherwise reassuring suburbia.

None the less, HUD sought to reassure Dayton with a strong endorsement of the fair-share approach and promises of support. In May

1971, Romney congratulated Dayton for facing the problem of housing lower-income families by having "the communities in the Miami Valley [agree] to take their proportion . . . during the next few years." [46] Later in the year, Romney told a congressional committee that HUD wanted "the Miami Valley plan [to] succeed . . . because we think it is a good example of what could be done." [47] To increase the prospects of success, HUD promised increased 701 funding for MVRPC, as well as priority attention to applications for housing subsidies to fulfill the Dayton plan. In addition, full backing was pledged for A-95 recommendations based on compliance with the plan, with HUD indicating its willingness to deny sewer and other grants to communities when MVRPC indicated that housing quotas had not been met. [48]

HUD also promoted Dayton's housing plan as a model for other metropolitan areas. Once the White House foreclosed the use of federal money to open the suburbs, Romney began to advocate voluntary cooperation among local governments as the only viable means of dispersing the poor. Dayton quickly became Romney's prime—and for some time only—example of what could be accomplished on housing through local initiative. In seeking to persuade other metropolitan areas to follow Dayton's lead, HUD emphasized that fair-share plans negotiated by local leaders were far more preferable than court-imposed dispersal plans. Another attraction stressed by Romney, as by fair-share proponents in Dayton, was that "every community knows that if it does its fair share and locates housing in relationship to jobs and other activities, and does it on a planned basis, it is not going to be inundated and go through the block busting and all of the other horrid experiences that are occurring in so many metropolitan areas." [49] Romney also promised to reward metropolitan areas that took the initiative and developed allocation plans. In October 1971, he told the Metropolitan Washington Council of Governments that if it devised "a fair share plan . . . our department will be happy to reward that by a bonus beyond what the Washington area, the real city area, would get in the form of housing funds." [50]

The Spread of Fair-Share Plans

A few months later, Washington became the second metropolitan area to adopt a fair-share plan. Washington's scheme was less ambitious than the plan adopted in Dayton, since it dealt not with the area's overall housing needs, but only with the 4,500 units of subsidized housing allocated to the region by HUD for the coming year. As the Metropolitan Washington Council of Governments admitted, "using this formula, the number of units distributed will meet only a small fraction of the identified needs" for subsidized housing in the region.[51] On the other hand, the small base employed in calculating quotas for the COG's fifteen members increased the political acceptability of the proposal since the size of individual suburban shares was limited. For example, Montgomery County with 156,000 households was allocated only 1,200 units of subsidized housing. Moreover, these proportionately small shares made it highly unlikely that units constructed in the suburbs would be occupied by low-income blacks from the District of Columbia. An official in suburban Fairfax County indicated that under the fair-share plan it would take twenty-five years to meet existing needs of county residents for subsidized housing.[52]

By 1972, metropolitan agencies across the nation were drafting and adopting regional housing plans in order to satisfy HUD's requirements. With fair-share plans becoming George Romney's latest cure for suburban exclusion, Dayton became an unlikely mecca for regional planners. A few came to see whether the MVRPC approach could be transplanted. Others were primarily interested in finding a means of satisfying HUD without antagonizing suburban constituents. In preparing housing plans, some agencies adopted with little change MVRPC's method of determining needs and allocating fair shares. Others developed more sophisticated techniques for determining housing needs than those employed in Dayton. Allocation formulas also were based on a wide variety of factors in addition to the population, poverty, fiscal-capacity, and classroom-space indices used by the MVRPC. Washington's fair-share plan, for example, distributed units to local governments based on fiscal capacity, developable land, local housing needs, and housing required by those employed in a local jurisdiction but unable to live there. Other allocation schemes included measures of population density, adequacy of local facilities and services, accessibility to jobs, availability of public transportation, proximity of existing subsidized housing, and environmental costs.[53]

In devising allocation schemes, metropolitan planners did not always accept the universalist conception of fair shares adopted by Dayton. Requiring that every suburban community be assigned some subsidized housing, it was argued, was less important than insuring that housing for lower-income families was constructed in appropriate locations. The housing plan developed by the Metropolitan Council of the Twin Cities

Area emphasized "opening up more housing opportunities in well-serviced locations," [54] and was designed to complement the council's general objective of minimizing urban sprawl. Priorities for the development of subsidized housing were based on the availability of public services in a locality, its accessibility to jobs and commercial facilities, and its fiscal capacity. Within this general framework, higher priorities were given to sectors without many poor residents in order to widen housing choices for lower-income families. To reduce concentration in Minneapolis and St. Paul, subsidized housing in the central cities was limited to urban-renewal areas and other replacement needs. Applying these criteria, highest priority for low-cost housing went to the inner ring of suburbs, while the lowest was assigned to communities along the periphery of the metropolitan area. [55]

Innovative and sophisticated allocation plans, however, did not guarantee more dispersal of lower-income families. In fact, few of the metropolitan housing plans which were drafted and adopted by regional agencies in the early 1970s promised to have much impact on suburban exclusion. Rarely did these housing plans result from a strong commitment to disperse lower-income families on the part of the metropolitan agency or many of its members. Instead, they usually were motivated by a desire to satisfy HUD's requirement for a housing plan without antagonizing constituency interests opposed to scattering the poor throughout the metropolis. As a result, most of the plans with their reams of data and complicated formulas were, as Richard F. Babcock and Fred P. Bosselman concluded in a study prepared for HUD in 1973, "little more than pious statements of good will." [56]

In developing housing plans, most COGs and regional planning commissions sought to reassure suburbanites by stressing the key role of local government in housing. Also underscored was the regional body's limited ability to enforce its housing plan. The preliminary housing plan for the St. Louis area stressed that "neither the East-West Gateway Coordinating Council nor the federal government has the power to force subsidized housing on any local community. Such authority is not proposed or contemplated in this proposal." [57] In the wake of negative reaction from the suburbs and outlying neighborhoods in St. Louis, the preliminary plan was revised to place more emphasis on the role of local governments and less on the need for dispersing lower-income families. The revised plan conceded that "residents and government leaders of each jurisdiction in the region have insight into their own neighborhoods, which an outsider often does not possess." [58] And a spokesman for the regional council indicated that "subsidized housing would be concentrated in the more deteriorated areas where there is the greatest need for it." [59]

Active support for dispersal plans on the part of metropolitan agencies was rare. As in the case of Dayton, an energetic response usually resulted from special circumstances. In the Washington area, suburban support for dispersal was enhanced by the political structure of the region. Because Washington is far less fragmented politically than most metropolitan areas, its suburbs tend to be large and relatively heterogeneous. Local officials in these jurisdictions, especially Fairfax and Montgomery Counties, were responsive to the housing needs of their lower-income constituents. As indicated in chapter 5, both counties developed zoning reforms in the early 1970s in an effort to induce private builders to include subsidized housing in larger-scale developments. Given their interest in increasing the supply of low-cost housing for county residents, officials in Fairfax and Montgomery were attracted to the fair-share concept since it promised to increase their share of the total number of subsidized units allocated to the metropolitan area by HUD. Under the plan adopted by Washington's COG, over half of all subsidized units targeted for the area were allotted to Fairfax and Montgomery, while the District of Columbia, where most of the region's low-cost housing had been located in the past, had its share cut to one-fifth of the metropolitan total.

Another regional agency committed to dispersing subsidized housing was the Metropolitan Council of the Twin Cities Area. Although the Minneapolis–St. Paul area was large and complex, with two million people spread among almost 140 municipalities, it spawned one of the nation's strongest metropolitan councils during the late 1960s. [60] The Twin Cities Council was empowered to review and coordinate all activities affecting regional development. Its charter also permitted the council to veto the actions of other areawide agencies, as well as suspend local actions pending review by the council. Unlike most metropolitan agencies, the Twin Cities Council was not dominated by local officials, since local governments were not directly represented and few of its members held local office. As a result, its policy board was much less preoccupied with local prerogatives and perspectives than was usually the case on COGs and regional planning commissions. An important factor in the development of this influential metropolitan institution was the relative socio-economic homogeneity of the Twin Cities area, where city-suburban differences were much less pronounced than in most areas. Of particular significance for the dispersal of subsidized housing was the fact that less than two percent of the region's population was black, by far the smallest proportion of any major metropolitan area.

At HUD, action-oriented allocation plans continued to draw official praise, as well as promises of support for implementation. But after Secretary Romney's ardor for levering open the suburbs had been cooled by the White House in 1971, timid metropolitan housing plans no longer provoked adverse reactions. While all regional agencies funded with 701 money were expected to prepare plans, standards were not developed to guide the formulation of allocation schemes. Instead, Romney emphasized that "it is really best left to the areas themselves to determine what percentage of low-cost housing they want." [61] Nor did HUD push for the adoption of any particular fair-share arrangement. In June 1971, a few days after President Nixon released his statement on housing policy, Romney told the U.S. Commission on Civil Rights:

> I do not believe that it will promote the cause that we are concerned about here by talking about trying to get every little general purpose government in a metropolitan area to accept low- and moderate-income housing. Now many will. The Dayton Plan is a great example. I'm all for it. . . . But to undertake to bring this about through coercive means in my opinion would be self-defeating. [62]

Having painfully learned about the limitations on federal influence the previous year, Romney clearly was not prepared to risk another Warren by insisting that other metropolitan areas follow in Dayton's footsteps.

The Politics of Metropolitan Housing Plans

In most metropolitan areas, the development of housing allocation plans attracted relatively little public attention or political activity. Rarely did a fair-share proposal emerge as a major issue with vigorous public debate, well-attended community gatherings, and substantial coverage in the local press. Nor did the staffs of many metropolitan planning agencies or COGs devote much time to building political support for housing plans among their commissioners or council members, other local officials, and community leaders. This pattern of activity reflected the lack of commitment on the part of many regional agencies to dispersing the poor, as well as their desire to minimize public controversy on a sensitive issue like opening the suburbs. Limited public involvement also resulted from the general lack of visibility of the typical COG or metropolitan planning commission.

The desire of regional agencies to avoid controversy and their low visibility, however, did not fully account for the low level of political activity on metropolitan housing plans in most areas. Also important was the lack of support for the fair-share approach from many interests with a stake in opening the suburbs. Although a few mayors such as Stokes in Cleveland and Maier in Milwaukee pressed for allocation plans, central cities generally were unenthusiastic about fair-share schemes that promised to reduce the city's share of the limited amount of housing funds available from the federal government. In addition, opposition to dispersal plans came from city leaders whose political strength was rooted in ethnic and outlying neighborhoods, such as Mayor Frank Rizzo of Philadelphia and Stokes's successor in Cleveland, Ralph J. Perk. For their part, many blacks viewed fair-share plans as little more than sophisticated quota systems whose principal purpose was to protect the white suburbs from inner-city blacks rather than broaden housing opportunities for lower-income families. In many areas, home builders were wary of arrangements that threatened to put yet another restriction on their ability to locate sites for subsidized housing.

Open-housing interests also provided little backing for fair-share plans. As pointed out in chapter 5, most of these groups were organized on a local basis; and they typically focused their energies on housing problems within individual communities and neighborhoods. As a result of these grass-roots preoccupations and the low profile of many regional agencies, local housing groups often were unaware of the housing activities of COGs and metropolitan planning commissions. Even when they were cognizant of the development of regional housing plans, their members normally did not rush to get involved. For most, local fair-housing efforts, community housing projects, and other immediate concerns had a higher claim on limited resources than development of metropolitan housing plans.

In addition, many housing activists were dubious, usually with good cause, about the dedication of metropolitan agencies to opening the suburbs. Why, they asked, should a lot of time be invested in a process which appeared to be a charade designed to insure the continued flow of federal planning funds. Other open-housing supporters were hostile to the entire fair-share concept, arguing that the small shares distributed under most plans were a sophisticated form of tokenism that was anything but fair to the poor. Skeptics also contended that fair-share schemes would serve primarily to protect suburbs from the poor by establishing quota systems which limited housing opportunities in those communities most accessible to lower-income and minority families moving outward from the city.

Supporters of metropolitan approaches within the open-housing movement conceded the validity of these criticisms. But they argued that inaction was not an effective means of dealing with the weaknesses of regional agencies and their distributional schemes. Instead of ignoring areawide planning, opponents of suburban exclusion were urged to press COGs and planning commissions to develop effective housing allocations. NCDH called for fair-share plans based on "the concept of equality of opportunity" which were fair "to minorities and the poor . . . based on the opportunity to choose that locality best suited to give the individual and his family the greatest possible opportunity to improve their income, their educational opportunities, and their environment." [63]

In advancing this fair-share goal, NCDH concentrated its efforts in the San Francisco area. The Association of Bay Area Governments was criticized for "skirting the issue of housing . . . because its membership opposes a regional plan for housing," and for producing "voluminous reports . . . [in] place of a viable plan." [64] In 1971, NCDH called on ABAG to establish an advisory committee on housing to insure that citizens and minority groups were involved in the development of an effective dispersal plan. ABAG ignored the request, leading NCDH to file a complaint with HUD charging the regional agency with violating the Civil Rights Act of 1964. HUD responded by conditioning funding for ABAG on "satisfactory progress toward completion of a regional housing plan." [65] Bowing to HUD's pressure, ABAG created a regional housing task force which included representatives of the poor and minority groups. NCDH saw these activities as playing a major "role in escalating the pressure on . . . ABAG to give housing a high priority." [66] In the Philadelphia area, legal-aid groups brought pressure to bear on the Delaware Valley Regional Planning Commission with charges that the agency was violating federal requirements by failing to develop a housing plan which devoted "particular attention to the housing problems and lack of opportunities for housing of low-income and minority groups" throughout the Philadelphia area. [67]

Elsewhere, some housing, planning, and civic groups took an interest in the development of metropolitan housing plans. Involvement was more common on the part of broadly-based organizations such as Milwaukee's Metropolitan Housing Center, which was highly critical of the deliberate and passive approach of the Southeastern Wisconsin Regional Planning Commission, than on the part of community or neighborhood housing groups. In the St. Louis area, the Greater St. Louis Committee for Freedom of Residence urged the East-West Gateway Coordinating Council to strengthen its housing plan by making specific allocations to localities. Support for dispersal also came from the Metropolitan Housing Corporation and the St. Louis section of the American Institute of Planners. In the New York area, the Regional Plan Association, a private planning group, invested considerable effort in educational activities designed to increase suburban acceptance of dispersed housing. And many chapters of the League of Women Voters pressed regional agencies to take effective steps to open the suburbs. Few of these efforts, however, generated substantial pressure on metropolitan planners or their policy boards.

An exception among open-housing groups in terms of investment in the development of a regional housing plan was the Leadership Council for Metropolitan Open Communities in the Chicago area. The Leadership Council had a broader base than most open-housing organizations. Created to monitor the agreements which grew out of Martin Luther King's 1966 campaign against residential segregation in Chicago, its membership included major business, civic, and civil-rights leaders. The council's activities were better financed than those of most open-housing organizations; and its frame of reference was metropolitan rather than local. Despite these capabilities and perspectives, the Leadership Council experienced considerable difficulty in coming to grips with the housing issue in the complex and highly segregated Chicago area. Little came of its efforts to oversee the agreements which ended King's demonstrations. Nor was much accomplished with fair-marketing activities, efforts to moderate the rapid racial transformation of neighborhoods in the path of blacks moving outward, and a public-relations campaign called "Operation Good Neighbor" which failed to produce many good neighbors interested in promoting interracial neighborhoods. More successful were the Leadership Council's legal-action program and its Metropolitan Housing Development Corporation. Neither of these activities, however, had a significant effect on housing opportunities in general. Relatively few blacks benefitted from the fair-housing lawsuits filed by the council's attorneys; and the potential of a single non-profit development corporation to affect the overall supply of housing in Chicago's suburbs was severely limited.

By 1970, the Leadership Council was seeking an approach to the region's housing problems which would have more impact and visibility than its litigation and home-building activities. After considering various alternatives, the Council concluded that development of a fair-share plan for the Chicago area was the most promising means of increasing low-cost housing in the suburbs. Initially, the Leadership Council planned to formulate its own fair-share plan rather than seek to influence the housing planning already underway in the Northeastern Illinois Planning Commission. In part, the council's approach was motivated by a desire to play a central rather than a supportive role. The council also had little confidence in the ability of the Northeastern Illinois Planning Commission to produce a plan that would actually influence housing development. NIPC was a weak agency with little public visibility or political influence among local governments in the area. Suburban interests dominated the agency, eleven of whose fifteen commissioners in 1971 held office in the suburbs. NIPC's commissioners and top staff were eager to avoid the housing issue, which had been ignored until HUD demanded the preparation of a housing element in the late 1960s. NIPC responded to HUD's housing requirements reluctantly, with suburban commissioners urging the staff to proceed with great caution in order to avoid controversy.

Despite its preference for an independent effort, the Leadership Council was compelled by financial considerations to join forces with NIPC. Substantial outside resources were required to develop an allocation plan, organize support in the suburbs, and secure acceptance of the plan by hundreds of suburban jurisdictions. One possible source of funds was HUD, which already was supporting the council's legal action program. Federal officials, however, were unwilling to provide funds for direct support of planning, since they already were financing NIPC's regional housing plan. Also pushing the Leadership Council in the direction of NIPC was the Ford Foundation. In agreeing to underwrite part of the council's metropolitan housing program, Ford insisted that there be official involvement to insure that the housing plan that resulted would have the endorsement of a public agency. As a result of these developments, the Leadership Council formed a reluctant partnership with

NIPC, with the commission to prepare technical studies and a housing plan, while the council assumed responsibility for mobilizing support in the suburbs. The arrangement was agreeable to NIPC, since it promised to help shield the agency from whatever controversy might be generated in the suburbs by the housing plan.

Once the Leadership Council turned to developing political support in the suburbs, it formed another partnership which further diluted the influence of open-housing interests in the housing allocation process. Within the Leadership Council, a grass-roots approach to dispersing subsidized housing was strongly advocated by Jack D. Pahl, a former mayor of suburban Elk Grove who also served on NIPC. Pahl was convinced that the only way to build subsidized housing in the suburbs was to concentrate on developing support among suburban governments, and particularly among suburban mayors. If the mayors could be convinced of the need for more subsidized housing, Pahl argued, they would be able to win the support of local councils, planning and zoning boards, and local influentials more generally. To this end, Pahl organized a dozen suburban mayors into a steering committee with himself as chairman. Pahl's approach was endorsed by the Leadership Council, and the Mayors' Steering Committee along with NIPC became part of the Council's Metropolitan Housing Coalition.

With the endorsement of Pahl's strategy of concentrating on suburban mayors, the principal focus of the Metropolitan Housing Coalition inevitably became the needs, problems, and concerns of suburbia. At a series of meetings which attracted scores of suburban officials, coalition representatives stressed the housing needs of suburban communities. Little was said about regional housing needs, and even less about dispersing poor black families from Chicago's ghettos, which were the housing problems that had spurred the organization of the Leadership Council. Instead, the discussions were devoted to calming suburban fears about inundation by blacks, high-rise ghettos, the concentration of subsidized housing in particular communities, and the unscrupulous practices of some private developers of 235 housing in the Chicago suburbs.

Local autonomy was a major concern of suburban officials who attended the meetings; and the Metropolitan Housing Coalition responded by emphasizing voluntary compliance with the fair-share plan. Underlying the case for voluntary suburban action was the threat of outside intervention by the courts or the federal government. "We're attempting to head off a court-imposed public housing plan for the suburban area that most likely would be insensitive to the municipalities' needs and wants," insisted Pahl, who underscored that the "only alternative" to a voluntary approach "is a court-ordered solution, and I don't think too many of us want to see that happen." [68] The same theme was echoed by the Leadership Council: "It's only a matter of a few years," suburban audiences were told, "before the courts decide that it's entirely up to them to determine need within communities." [69] Enhancing the credibility of the spectre of housing plans being imposed by the courts were the efforts of the plaintiffs in the *Gautreaux* case to secure a ruling involving the suburbs in the dispersal of public housing beyond Chicago's black ghettos. By beating the courts to the punch, the Metropolitan Housing Coalition told suburban officials, they could "make sure that any plan proposed for housing in Chicago suburban communities is one that we can all live with" [70]

Certainly the allocation plan that resulted was one that most Chicago suburbs could live with easily. The plan was heavily weighted toward existing housing needs of local communities. While a ten-year need of 230,000 units was established, the interim plan proposed to allocate only 10,000 units initially, which was the approximate number of units programmed for the area by HUD. Moreover, allocations were made to sectors of the metropolis rather than individual communities. Compliance was left to local governments, which were asked to endorse the general program, to determine their own housing needs, and to take steps to insure that housing was provided locally to meet these needs.

Compared with developments in other regional arenas, the forging of the Metropolitan Housing Coalition and the preparation of the Chicago allocation plan represented a significant political accomplishment for open-housing interests. A weak regional agency with little intention of pressing a housing plan on the suburbs was sidestepped, and relegated to a secondary and largely technical role. Large numbers of local political leaders were engaged in discussions of their housing problems, and a smaller group participated actively in the development of the allocation plan. A variety of groups on both the regional and community levels were mobilized by the leadership council in support of increasing the supply of subsidized housing in the suburbs.[71] Perhaps most important, as a result of the Leadership Council's initiative, housing surfaced in Chicago's suburbs as a visible and legitimate issue, requiring public debate and community action of some sort. As one member of the Mayors' Steering Committee told his local council: "I am convinced that our refusal to participate in organized dialogue directed to the housing problem can only isolate us from the problem solving." [72] Through the involvement of local officials, well-attended public meetings, sometimes heated discussions, and substantial local press coverage, a dialogue developed of the kind which rarely emerged from the typically half-hearted and barely visible efforts to allocate housing in other metropolitan areas.

Producing these achievements, however, required substantial compromise in the original housing objectives of the Leadership Council. Never was the Metropolitan Housing Coalition able to come to grips with suburban exclusion, the dispersal of lower-income families, and the housing needs of inner-city blacks, problems which were the primary concerns of the Leadership Council before it embarked on its suburban campaign. In effect, the Leadership Council was trapped by the political logic of its effort to build support for more low-cost housing in the suburbs. Only by being sympathetic to suburban concerns and responsive to suburban demands was there any chance of building the broad-based coalition essential to implementing a grass-roots strategy. But the very nature of a suburban coalition precluded framing housing issues in broad terms. As a result, the Leadership Council found itself constrained by the same political realities which neutralize almost every effort aimed at lowering the walls of suburban exclusion.

The Problem of Implementation

Fair-share plans do not insure that housing will be built in accordance with their allocations. For a regional housing plan to be implemented, private developers, housing agencies, HUD, and local governments must act and interact to produce the decisions which ultimately result in the construction of particular types of housing in specific locations. Generally, the adoption of a housing plan by a regional agency does not commit any of these parties, and most significantly local jurisdictions, to anything concrete with respect to implementation. In the Dayton area, for example, the Miami Valley Regional Planning Commission, not its constituent local governments, adopted the fair-share plan. As Dale Bertsch has noted, the willingness of some local officials serving on MVRPC to endorse the allocation scheme clearly was influenced by their "recognition that we really have no legislative power and that the ultimate decision would be left up to the local community anyway." [73] Even acceptance of an allocation by a local government does not guarantee that specific local actions necessary for the construction of housing will be forthcoming. Edward L. Holmgren and Ernest Erber of NCDH point out that "some communities doubtlessly accept fair share with the consoling reservation that after all is said and done, a plan is still only a plan. It does not convert vacant land into housing projects. A community that votes to accept its allocation might still renege when it [comes] to granting zoning changes, subdivision approval, or building permits." [74]

Given these circumstances, implementation of housing plans required leadership which only the regional agency was usually in a position to provide. "The planning agency," argues one advocate of opening the suburbs, "must stimulate the interest of existing housing sponsors and assist in the formation of new ones. The planners must also knock on HUD's door, seeking extra funds and accelerated processing. In short, the planners [must] take the political heat if the numbers in the plan are to become houses for people to live in." [75] Very few COGs or metropolitan planning bodies, however, were willing to run the political risks inherent in playing an activist role in the development of subsidized housing in the suburbs.

One exception was the Metropolitan Council of the Twin Cities, which employed the A-95 review process aggressively, both to penalize communities within its priority areas which were doing little about low-cost housing and to induce builders to locate subsidized projects in these priority areas. For example, an application for federal open-space assistance by Golden Valley was negatively reviewed by the council because of the absence of low-income housing in the affluent suburb, an action which stimulated the development of a Section 236 project in the community. [76] Following adoption of the plan by the council, over two-thirds of all proposals for subsidized housing in the region were for suburban locations, and the actual production of subsidized units in suburbia more than doubled between mid-1971 and mid-1973. [77] After the enactment of the Housing and Community Development Act of 1974, the Twin Cities council developed a plan which permitted lower-income families to use Section 8 subsidies on a regional rather than local basis, within an area encompassing eleven suburban communities, as well as Minneapolis and St. Paul. [78]

Another regional agency willing to assume an active role in implementing its housing plan was the Miami Valley Regional Planning Commission, which quickly discovered that devising a fair-share plan was far easier than fulfilling its allocations. One problem encountered in the Dayton area was the frequent mismatch between the preferences of builders for sites and the distribution of subsidized units as prescribed in the plan. More serious was the intensification of local opposition that usually resulted as soon as specific locations for low-cost housing were identified. Local outcries invariably reinforced the reluctance of suburban governments to fulfill their quotas.

Particularly troublesome for MVRPC were the obstacles erected by suburban communities to the south of Dayton, whose housing programs were characterized in 1973 as "shamefully laggard" by the *Dayton Daily News*. According to the newspaper, the "problem in Kettering, Oakwood, Centerville, Moraine, Miamisburg and West Carrollton [was] . . . antagonism—an antagonism that often has turned to subversion of the plan, to elaborate foot-dragging, devoted nit-picking and shell games with zoning and building codes that have magical now-you-see-it, now-you-don't properties." [79] In Moraine, an industrial suburb with a large tax base and fewer than 5,000 residents, the local council reversed the zoning recommendations of its planner on one proposed low-cost project and killed another when it "discovered" that a road was planned to traverse the site. After 500 residents turned out at a hearing to protest high-rise slums, crime, vice, and overburdened local schools, Miamisburg refused to approve rent supplements for a 166-unit project. Centerville had to be taken to court before its local government would issue a building permit for 232 subsidized units. Oakwood, the region's most affluent suburb, refused to authorize subsidized housing, ostensibly because it was "discriminatory to point out the poor, be they white or black." While acknowledging that "we have some poor in Oakwood," a local official indicated that the community did not "think pointing out who they are with such a dispersal plan is the thing to do. [80]

MVRPC worked as hard to overcome local objections and obstruction as it had to win initial approval of the housing plan. Scores of meetings were held around the region to explain the plan, listen to local complaints, and build support for individual housing projects. Bertsch and his staff also were in constant contact with local officials, providing information, answering questions, evaluating housing proposals from developers, and pressing for commitments on projects that were consistent with the allocation scheme. Complicating these efforts was the erosion of support for the plan at the local level. Backlash defeated some backers of dispersed housing when they stood for reelection. Others who had endorsed the allocation plan as members of MVRPC defected in the face of constituency pressure when subsidized projects came before local councils for approval.

Lacking any direct authority over housing and land use, MVRPC had to rely on the A-95 process to bring pressure to bear on local governments and developers of subsidized housing. A-95 reviews, of course, could not insure that reluctant local governments would approve subsidized housing. Nevertheless, MVRPC derived leverage in a number of instances from its ability to threaten a locality with a negative review of a request for federal aid for sewers or open space should the jurisdiction fail to work toward fulfilling its housing quota. A-95, however, had to be employed with considerable skill since local resentment over the commission's efforts to secure implementation of the housing plan was substantial. Criticism of MVRPC escalated once it began to implement the plan, and threats of withdrawal became common. In urging his community to pull out, the city manager of West Carrollton charged that the "planning and coordinating functions for which the MVRPC was originally created have been downgraded in favor of social action programs." [81] Altogether, a dozen jurisdictions threatened to withdraw from MVRPC in the months following adoption of the plan.

Another constraint on the use of A-95 reviews to secure compliance with the housing plan was the failure of COGs and regional planning commissions in other areas to follow MVRPC's lead. As Bertsch explained to the U.S. Commission on Civil Rights in 1971, "if we aggressively implement our strategy . . . we find ourselves in many cases merely facing the possibility of turning down Federal aid for our area which [the federal government] in turn might very well funnel . . . into a region which hasn't even faced its responsibility in the development of a [housing] strategy." [82] The result was a bizarre situation in which the metropolitan area that had gone the farthest in meeting HUD's housing objectives was more likely to lose federal grants than areas which had ignored Washington. For Bertsch, the way out of this dilemma was federal action to insure that all regional agencies employed A-95 to implement their housing plans. Then, "all regions would have to evaluate themselves in the manner that we did. All regions would have to evolve a strategy reflecting the problems within their region. And all regions would have to . . . compete for the limited categorical and other types of grants that are available . . . on the basis of how effective that strategy was." [83] Federal unwillingness to take such a step, however, meant that regional self-interest had to moderate MVRPC's use of A-95 to promote its housing plan.

Less troublesome to local governments was MVRPC's use of A-95 to influence developers of subsidized housing. In these instances, MVRPC usually was seeking to restrict rather than promote the construction of low-cost units. MVRPC's objective was to insure that builders did not locate projects in areas that were inappropriate under the fair-share plan. Once A-95 was broadened by the federal government in April 1971 to encompass subsidized housing, the commission's hand was strengthened in these endeavors. A proposal by private developers to build 456 subsidized units in Madison, a suburb in the path of the outward movement of blacks from Dayton, was negatively reviewed on the grounds that the community already had met its housing quota. On the basis of this recommendation, the Federal Housing Administration rejected the application. From this setback, builders learned, in Bertsch's words, that they "would have to take their units and play someplace else." [84] MVRPC was eager to help developers find "someplace else" as long as the locations were consistent with the plan. But when builders persisted with sites that were not, the commission resisted. Through 1973, over 2,000 units proposed for locations judged inappropriate by MVRPC were vetoed. Home builders reacted bitterly to these developments, charging MVRPC with "being successful in killing applications which otherwise might have gone forward, but demonstrating no success in assisting applications which have met with heavy citizen resistance." [85]

Despite these obstacles, MVRPC's efforts bore some fruit. Within eighteen months of the adoption of the plan, the number of subsidized units beyond Dayton's city limits was in the process of being increased more than sixfold to almost 1,000; and 75 percent of the 3,300 units in the HUD pipeline were targeted for suburban or other outlying locations in the Dayton area. Moreover, MVRPC survived the initial phase of implementation with both its membership and the fair-share principle largely intact. Only one local jurisdiction, rural Darke County, actually withdrew over the housing plan. And all but one member of the commission voted for a revision of the plan in 1973 which preserved the basic concept, despite a great deal of vocal dissatisfaction from local governments with the allocation formula, the size of the shares of particular communities, and MVRPC's role in implementing the plan.

Greatly enhancing the political acceptability of MVRPC's plan in the suburbs was the fact that few poor people were dispersed during the initial phases of implementation. The coming of subsidized housing failed to confirm the worst fears of suburbanites. Neighborhoods were not destroyed by high-rise projects. Hordes of blacks from Dayton's ghetto did not overrun suburban communities. "They seem amazed that their fears have not materialized," a manager of one of the suburban projects noted. "They thought the place would be running over with blacks, and people would not take care of the property, but that has not happened." [86] even if large numbers of poor blacks—or poor whites for that matter—had been prepared to move outward, they would have found few of the new subsidized units in the suburbs available at rents they could afford. Only fifty of the subsidized units built outside the city of Dayton during the first two years of the plan were low-cost public housing. All of the rest were moderately priced units, built largely under the 236 program with rents beyond the reach of poor families. And, as with similar housing built in suburbs across the nation, most of the tenants of the first suburban housing built under Dayton's pioneering fair-share plan were white suburbanites, and very few were blacks from the inner city.

The Fading Commitment to Metropolitan Approaches

For some advocates of opening the suburbs, Dayton's success in dispersing subsidized housing was convincing evidence of the potential of metropolitan institutions for reducing economic and racial segregation. After appraising MVRPC's efforts, Lois Craig of the National Urban Coalition's housing staff concluded that the "Dayton regional council has accomplished something remarkable, is trying for something even more remarkable." [87] On the other hand, those who questioned the ability of metropolitan approaches to reduce suburban exclusion emphasized the modest amount of subsidized housing being built in Dayton's suburbs the minimal impact of these units on segregated residential patterns, and the failure of most metropolitan areas to emulate Dayton. "The fact that the Miami Valley Regional Housing Plan . . . received so much attention and was so lionized by HUD" suggested to Richard F. Babcock "how little it takes to give an appearance of success." [88]

Defenders of metropolitan housing strategies readily conceded that Dayton was at best a first step. Lois Craig also found it "remarkable that there are 435 other regional councils in America with the same mandate the same federal funding, the same review power as MVRPC, and innumerable cities with the same problems and inequities—yet Dayton plan are not springing up all over the nation." [89] To make housing plans blos som across the land, fair-share proponents counted heavily on the federal government. HUD, it was hoped, would require regional agencies to implement as well as develop metropolitan housing plans. Washington, in turn, would bolster the ability of regional agencies to enforce fair-share plans by tying the A-95 review process closely to housing, and by withholding federal grants from communities that failed to make progress toward meeting their housing quotas. With growing interest in block grants, some open-housing supporters anticipated even stronger federal commitments to metropolitan approaches. Federal housing subsidies might be distributed through metropolitan institutions. Or all community development grants could be funnelled through regional agencies, with local eligibility for aid conditioned on participation in an areawide housing plan.

All of these hopes, however, were dashed by Washington's mounting sensitivity to suburban resistance to the dispersal of subsidized housing. Fear of another Warren kept HUD from insisting on metropolitan housing plans with teeth, or from strengthening the hand of A-95 review agencies. In Congress, suburban objections undermined efforts to provide metropolitan agencies with an authoritative housing role. Under Title V of the proposed Housing and Urban Development Act of 1972, housing funds were to be allocated by HUD through metropolitan or state agencies on the basis of areawide housing plans which specified the number and kind of units needed, the income groups to be served, and the general location of the proposed housing throughout the area.

Title V's authors sought to mollify congressmen who were wary of any legislation which smacked of "forced integration." Local control over housing and land use remained intact in the bill. Housing would not be built by metropolitan agencies. Nor would these bodies select individual project sites or use the power of eminent domain to acquire land for housing. Most important, the new housing agencies would not be empowered to override local zoning ordinances, subdivision regulations, or building codes. The sponsors emphasized that the metropolitan agency's "power would simply be that of allocating Federal housing subsidy funds to eligible developers to build housing in general locations designated in the plan," with "specific project sites [to] be obtained by the developer who must, of course, obtain all necessary zoning and building code approvals from the community in which the site is located." [90] Also emphatically rejected were fair-share approaches which included all local jurisdictions. Title V's author, Representative Thomas L. Ashley of Ohio, did "not think every suburban community should or would be forced to have subsidized housing." [91] Advocates of inclusive fair-share plans, Ashley argued, were "being foolhardy in the extreme," given the political realities of the situation both locally and in Congress.[92] "I think I speak for every member of the Housing Subcommittee," Ashley told Paul Davidoff of Suburban Action, "when I strongly question the practicality" of insisting that housing allocation plans include all suburbs.[93]

Ashely's efforts to assure suburban representatives that subsidized housing would not be forced on local jurisdictions disappointed proponents of strong metropolitan approaches. Particularly disturbing to these interests was the failure of the Ashley bill to provide metropolitan agencies with any authority to insure local compliance with their allocations. The National Urban Coalition criticized Title V for not requiring suburbs "to accept a particular project even though a metropolitan housing agency had worked out prior agreements for that locality." [94] The U.S. Commission on Civil Rights found "few sanctions" in the proposal "to overcome the opposition that many suburban jurisdictions have exhibited to permitting lower income families to reside within their borders." [95] Instead of federal sanctions to enforce the dispersal of housing, Title V offered incentive grants of up to $3,000 per unit to finance public services in communities which accepted subsidized housing. Given the nature and intensity of resistance to subsidized housing in most localities, the Civil Rights Commission thought it "doubtful that this financial incentive is sufficient to overcome suburban opposition." [96]

Certainly incentive grants and concessions to local autonomy were insufficient to overcome opposition from suburban and other congressmen. Metropolitan approaches to housing were seen by conservatives as stifling local control; and by many liberals as an issue too easily exploited by an opponent in the next election. Among the more vocal suburban opponents was Representative Ben Blackburn from the Atlanta area, who charged that "in Dayton the local community is not actually making the decision, but a central planning agency . . . is actually trying to override local zoning." For Blackburn, as for others, elimination of local control was "really what Title V seeks to do . . . and this is the reason there [is] so much objection to Title V: it does interfere with local communities having the voice we think local communities ought to have." [97] Another suburban Republican, Joel T. Broyhill from the Virginia portion of the Washington area, thought the fair-share plan adopted by the Metropolitan Washington Council of Governments "smacks of forced integration." Broyhill saw such efforts as part of the movement to "complete the destruction of the community concept now under attack by forced busing." [98]

Despite the hyperbole, such sentiments constituted a kiss of death in the Ninety-Second Congress. Few congressmen, particularly in the House where Title V was developed, wanted to be associated with forced integration of any kind. As a result, Title V was abandoned by numerous liberal Democrats from metropolitan districts. In the end, supporters of Title V were unable even to muster support for an experimental trial of the metropolitan concept in a few areas. And the measure approved by the House Banking and Currency Committee in place of Title V prohibited areawide agencies from developing subsidized housing without the express approval of affected local governments. [99]

Another setback for metropolitan approaches came eight months after the death of Title V when HUD instituted its freeze on all new commitments under the various subsidized housing programs. Implementation of regional housing plans in Dayton, the Twin Cities, and Washington was slowed by the freeze. In the Minneapolis–St. Paul area, only 917 subsidized units were approved by HUD between mid-1973 and mid-1974, less than half the total authorized in 1972, and less than one-quarter of the total for 1971. [100] The federal moratorium, along with local housing bans resulting from sewer problems, braked implementation of the Metropolitan Washington Council of Governments' housing plan during 1973 and 1974. Elsewhere, the termination of federal housing subsidies provided metropolitan agencies and suburban governments with one more reason for not taking areawide housing plans seriously, while undercutting the efforts of those who favored allocation schemes. "Just as we are gaining acceptance of the principle of establishing parity and sharing the problems of poverty," complained Milwaukee's mayor, "the President has struck down every program which would make it possible to build low- and moderate-income housing in the suburbs." [101]

When new housing legislation finally emerged from Congress in 1974, local initiative and local autonomy were emphasized rather than metropolitan housing plans, incentives, and instrumentalities. Federal controls, as pointed out in chapter 8, were reduced in the Housing and Community Development Act of 1974; and community development and housing funds were allocated directly to local governments and housing agencies rather than through metropolitan bodies. While A-95 review of applications for housing assistance and block grants was provided under the new arrangements, local rather than metropolitan housing plans were the key element in determining eligibility for federal funds. Further reducing the role of metropolitan agencies was the heavy emphasis on existing housing in the Section 8 leased-housing program created in the new legislation. Metropolitan allocations were meaningless in the absence of federal funds to subsidize new housing in the suburbs.

Underlying these setbacks was the lack of any substantial political support in Washington for regional approaches to housing, either in Washington or in the metropolitan areas. Suburbanites feared that metropolitan arrangements would jeopardize local housing and zoning controls. The most influential foes of suburban exclusion, on the other hand, did not want metropolitan agencies dominated by suburban interests controlling the flow of federal housing subsidies. Ashley's plan was attacked by the National Association of Home Builders, which contended that Title V would "place complete control of HUD subsidy programs into the hands of the very same officials who now use zoning, land-use controls, and other devices to defeat the production of low- and moderate-income housing." [102] City officials also vigorously opposed an authoritative role for metropolitan agencies in the distribution of federal housing aid. One mayor hated "to think what my city's chances of getting a fair break on housing allocation would be in the hands" of the regional agency in his area. "Even on a one-man, one-vote basis we would still be vastly outvoted, although most of the low- and moderate-income residents of the area live within the city." [103] Echoing these views were representatives from central-city districts who argued that Title V put the city "in a virtually impossible position. It is placed at the mercy of the suburbs, which made clear their disinterest in the city's problems and their unwillingness to participate in their solution." [104]

In the absence of support from any major interest, federal action to bolster metropolitan housing plans and programs was foreclosed. Without federal pressure and subsidies, metropolitan housing efforts lost what little momentum they had been able to generate. A few areawide agencies continued to press for implementation of regional housing plans, but most did not. Nor did COGs and regional planning bodies subject suburban applications for community development grants under the 1974 legislation to close scrutiny in most areas. [105] And, as in Dayton, almost all of the housing built in the suburbs under metropolitan plans served suburban needs, rather than fulfilling the forlorn hope of using fair shares to disperse blacks and the poor out of the older cities.

Chapter Ten

The Reluctant Partner

The weakness of metropolitan institutions has helped turn many critics of suburban exclusion toward the state capitals. Richard F. Babcock argues that "it doesn't require a revolution in our institutions to establish a framework for change in our regional policies. All that is required is to vest responsibility for regional planning and implementation in that most comfortable, if badly scuffed, pair of shoes, the state." [1] In sharp contrast to most metropolitan agencies, states possess power to tax, to regulate, to exercise eminent domain, and to engage in a wide range of activities. State governments directly influence urban development through highway, education, sewer, and housing programs. Of paramount importance in the case of land use, local governments derive all of their authority from states. As a result, local zoning, subdivision regulation, building codes, and housing policies can be modified or revoked by state government.

Respect for the powers and potential of state government led the National Commission on Urban Problems in 1968 to urge states to remove local barriers to the provision of housing for lower-income Americans. "By using powers they already possess, by assuming new authority when necessary, and providing funds," state governments, in the commission's view, were in "a unique position to help . . . release urban areas from the excesses of localism." [2] To prevent smaller suburban communities from excluding unwanted housing, the commission report called on the states to take land-use controls away from local governments in metropolitan areas which encompassed less than four square miles or had less than 25,000 residents. The commission also wanted states to assert more authority over local building codes in order to promote uniformity and to eliminate unduly restrictive practices. In ad-

dition, the report recommended that states use their power of condemnation to provide sites for subsidized projects "in those municipalities or
counties which have received Federal or State assistance for urban renewal, planning grants, or water and sewer projects but which have not
built housing for [lower] income groups." [3]

Calls for state action to overcome local housing restrictions have come
from other study groups, central-city interests, developers, and open-
housing advocates. The President's Committee on Urban Housing in
1968 endorsed uniform statewide subdivision regulations and state controls over local zoning in order to facilitate the construction of subsidized
housing. [4] Concern over the state role in broadening suburban housing
opportunities mounted as the federal commitment to opening the suburbs
waned in the early 1970s. A typical reaction came from the *Milwaukee
Journal*, which demanded "aggressive state entry into the metropolitan
housing muddle." [5] The *Journal* endorsed legislation permitting the state
to override restrictive local zoning, as well as Governor Patrick Lucey's
proposal for the creation of a community development corporation to assemble land and promote balanced settlement patterns. In addition, the
newspaper asked whether it might not make sense for the state to build
housing directly by creating a housing construction agency.

In urging greater involvement by states, open-housing interests have
stressed the need for positive action to insure that the "delegation of local
autonomy over the zoning of land . . . will not be employed so as to
defeat the needs of whole classes of the state's citizens." [6] To this end,
Suburban Action Institute urged state governments to amend planning
and zoning laws to require localities to adopt inclusionary housing policies. Under SAI's approach, states would force local governments to
include apartments and subsidized housing in all residential zones. State
law also would require local jurisdictions to provide housing for workers
if land were rezoned for industrial or commercial use, as well as prohibit
state agencies from locating their facilities in communities which lacked
an adequate housing supply for state workers. Moreover, minimum lot
and house sizes would be set by state officials on the basis of statewide
health and building standards. [7]

Without question, the states have the authority to implement any of
these recommendations. As David M. Trubek pointed out to the U.S.
Commission on Civil Rights in 1971: "State legislatures have ample powers to make significant changes which would undoubtedly materially affect the land use policies and patterns that create the 'exclusionary prob-

lem.' " [8] What is much less clear is whether states will use their authority over local government to lower suburban housing barriers. Across the nation, the potential of states to open the suburbs is counter-balanced by suburbia's growing influence on state government. States are no more immune to the mounting political power of suburbs than other components of the American federal system. Rare is the governor of an urban state who ignores suburban views on explosive issues such as home rule, local zoning, and subsidized housing, as Governor William G. Milliken of Michigan did in 1970 when he characterized exclusionary suburbs as "split-level facades hiding an apathetic, selfish, status-seeking society." [9] Regardless of what a governor says, most suburban legislators are certain to oppose measures which are perceived as threats to local control over housing and land use. The ranks of such legislators have been swelled by the growth of the suburban population and the reapportionment revolution which has insured equitable representation of suburbanites in every state capital. These political realities lead many observers, including Trubek, to doubt "that in the final analysis state legislatures, in which suburban representatives have substantial and increasing powers, will act on their own." [10]

Of course, state legislatures are more than calculating machines which faithfully register constituency sentiments on every issue. Legislative outcomes can be affected by crises, personal commitments, gubernatorial leadership, the efforts of individual legislators, well-organized group pressures, public opinion, and changing general circumstances. As the remainder of this chapter illustrates, such factors have played an important role in the consideration of housing and land-use issues in some states. Nonetheless, growing suburban political influence poses formidable barriers to enlisting state governments in the struggle against suburban exclusion. Reinforcing the influence of suburbanites on housing issues has been the absence of strong counter-pressures in most states. Consequently, in the state capital as at the local, metropolitan, and federal level, advocates of change in suburban housing policies have faced unequal political odds.

On the Sidelines

Indicative of the responsiveness of the states to suburban interests has been the meager involvement of almost all state governments in housing development and land-use regulation. In calling for state action, the

Douglas Commission admitted that "most states have played a minor and passive role in housing the American people, including those with low incomes." [11] Of the various state policies which affect housing and land use, the most significant has been delegation of zoning and related regulatory controls to local governments. Rarely has this delegation of authority been accompanied by state standards or substantive state policies concerning housing, land use, and other planning and development issues. Instead, as Daniel R. Mandelker has emphasized, "the statutes are entirely permissive. The content of local policy is not at all determined by the typical state enabling act, which usually does not even mandate the exercise of planning and zoning powers. Exercise of these powers is optional with the municipality, and the content of planning and zoning policy is for local determination." [12]

One consequence of wholesale delegation of regulatory authority has been the absence of significant direct involvement by states in the residential development of suburbia. After analyzing suburban land conversion in three areas in the northeast, Marion Clawson concluded that "the role of the states can be described as aloof, indifferent, or unconcerned. There was little or no effort to deal with the problems of suburban growth and development directly by state action or indirectly by providing local government with a full kit of tools." [13] State delegation of land-use control to local government also has foreclosed the development of state planning agencies which might provide Clawson's "kit of tools" or otherwise exercise significant influence on settlement patterns in suburbia. Most state planning agencies possess no direct controls over land use or housing development; and their plans seldom are binding on local governments. State departments of community affairs also typically lack authority to regulate land use or control housing development. To be sure, some of these agencies have become involved in housing planning. For example, California's Department of Housing and Community Affairs was authorized by the legislature in 1970 to prepare a statewide housing plan designed to provide "all economic segments of the state" with "a choice of housing opportunities." [14] In California as elsewhere, however, power to carry out such plans remains a local responsibility.

In delegating zoning controls to local governments, states have provided suburbs with the main instruments for implementing exclusionary housing policies. At the same time, the availability of local land-use controls greatly enhanced the attractions of local autonomy to suburbanites. So has the acceptance by most states of local boundaries as limiting the jurisdiction of public-housing authorities. Political fragmentation and suburban exclusion also have been promoted by other state actions. Almost every state fostered the emergence of autonomous suburban jurisdictions. Responding to suburban desires for separation from the city, state legislatures commonly erected barriers to annexation and facilitated the incorporation of suburban municipalities. In addition, states generally permitted the creation of special districts and other arrangements that enabled small suburban jurisdictions to secure water, sewer connections, and other needed services and facilities. State tax and assistance policies also tend to magnify fiscal disparities in the metropolis; and these differences have increased the appeal of local autonomy and exclusionary housing and land-use policies. In Wisconsin, state sharing of funds with local government in the 1960s was "upside down from the standpoint of equalization: The rich industrial communities get $314 per capita, the high income suburbs get $161, and Milwaukee is low man with $88. It would be hard to devise a more perverse effect on local government financing—and the direct result is interlocal balkanization and ferocious fiscal zoning." [15]

Suburban exclusion also has been widely underwritten by state assistance for schools, roads, sewers, and other local programs. As with most federal grants to localities, state aid rarely provides state officials with leverage for broadening housing opportunities. Nor have many state officials sought such leverage. An exception was an effort in the early 1970s by Pennsylvania's Department of Community Affairs to withhold recreation grants from exclusionary suburbs. William Wilcox, the state's Secretary of Community Affairs and an outspoken critic of suburban exclusion, engaged Suburban Acton Institute to examine exclusionary housing practices in a number of suburbs. On the basis of Suburban Action's findings, recreation grants were withheld from a few communities on the grounds that state funds would not serve a wide range of public needs because of restrictive local housing practices. One of the suburbs subsequently received its grant after approving some lower-cost housing. Another, Upper Saint Clair Township in the Pittsburgh area, successfully challenged the state in court, winning a ruling that the Department of Community Affairs lacked the authority to withhold park and recreation funds because of "the asserted failure of the Township to prove . . . that its land development policies, though lawful, did not exclude the poor and minorities." [16]

Most states have been far more active in providing suburbs with the

powers and funds to pursue exclusionary policies than in stimulating the
production of low-cost housing, particularly in the suburbs. In 1968, the
Douglas Commission reported that only four states had implemented
subsidy programs worthy of note.[17] Of the four, Illinois's involvement
was limited to less than 1,000 units constructed jointly with Chicago in
the 1940s. More significant were the efforts of Connecticut and Massachusetts, with the former having constructed 1,200 units for the elderly and 9,600 for middle-income families, while the latter's programs
produced 8,100 units for the aged and 15,300 for lower-income veterans.
Dwarfing all of these activities were the subsidy programs of New York,
which had resulted in the construction of over 100,000 units by 1968.
Roughly half of this housing was developed for middle-income families
under a program developed in the 1920s which limited the sponsor's return on investment, used the state's power of eminent domain to assemble land, and provided exemptions from local property taxes. Almost all
of this housing was built in New York City because "the state's other
municipalities had been unwilling to grant the tax abatement central to
the program." [18] The rest of New York's subsidized units were constructed in older cities under a state public-housing program, which was
killed by the voters in a series of referendums in the 1960s.

More important for suburbs have been the activities of state housing
finance agencies, which proliferated in the late 1960s and early 1970s.[19]
Prior to 1966 only Connecticut and New York had created state agencies
to provide low-interest loans to private developers through the issuance
of tax-exempt bonds. Over the next eight years, thirty more states established housing finance agencies. By early 1973, these agencies had
provided mortgage funds for approximately 120,000 units of housing.
Federal subsidies also were available for most of these projects. Between
January 1969 and March 1973, almost 80 percent of the 90,000 units developed under state programs received federal assistance, mostly from
the Section 236 rental-housing program.[20] State-financed housing built
without federal aid has been priced for middle-income families, since the
lower interest rates provided by state financing provides only a modest
reduction in rent. Thus, the ability of state housing finance agencies to
serve a lower-income clientele was heavily dependent on federal subsidies. With the phasing out of Section 236 and other federal programs
after 1973, the activities of housing finance agencies promised to "perpetuate metropolitan economic segregation . . . instead of providing access
to the suburbs for lower-income people." [21]

While a fair amount of state-financed housing has been located in the suburbs, most state housing finance agencies have not played a direct role in locating projects in suburban or other areas. Instead, private and other developers have borne the responsibility for selecting sites and securing local approval. None of the states authorized their financing agencies to override local land-use and building codes which stood in the way of the development of a housing project eligible for state assistance.[22] Moreover, many states required explicit local approval of state-financed housing in addition to conformance with zoning and building controls. New Jersey's Housing Finance Agency, for example, cannot proceed with a project unless the municipality formally recognizes a local need for subsidized housing.

Limited subsidies, local approval, and a passive role in site selection have combined to restrict the impact of state finance programs on expanding housing opportunities for the poor in suburbia. Only a few agencies have actively sought to provide lower-income housing in the suburbs. Most successful have been the efforts of the Massachusetts Housing Finance Agency, which is required by law to provide one-quarter of its units to low-income households. Between 1968 and 1972, the Massachusetts agency financed the construction of 20,000 units, 6,000 of which were located in the suburbs. About one-third of these apartments were rented to low-income households. Most of these suburban units, however, were occupied by lower-income families who "lived in the immediate area of the project site. Consequently, . . . MHFA has had little impact in dispersing low-income residents from central cities to the suburbs."[23]

During the 1960s, more and more states also passed fair-housing laws. These efforts, however, have had relatively little effect on broadening housing opportunities in the suburbs. Like local fair-housing agencies, most state commissions rely on individual complaints, with only a few engaging in systematic analysis of discriminatory practices. More important with respect to suburban exclusion, state fair-housing laws do not apply to local zoning. Efforts to extend their coverage to encompass housing restrictions imposed by local governments have not been successful. One example is the fate of the complaint filed with the New Jersey Division of Civil Rights in 1971. The National Committee Against Discrimination in Housing and the United Automobile Workers alleged that zoning in Mahwah violated the state's fair-housing law because lower-income and minority families were effectively excluded from the community. New Jersey's Attorney General disagreed, ruling that the law did not apply to local governments:

> The legislature did not contemplate in 1961 when it outlawed the then dominant discrimination by owners in the sale and rental of real property that at some future time discrimination in zoning would emerge as an important new civil rights dilemma. The Division [of Civil Rights] is a creature of the legislature and is restricted to those tasks statutorily assigned to it by the legislature.[24]

This ruling was upheld by the state courts. Subsequent efforts to amend the fair-housing law to include zoning were buried in a state legislature dominated by suburban interests and dedicated to the preservation of local control over land use and housing.[25]

Trees Not People

For those who see the states playing a major role in opening the suburbs, more significant than the expansion of finance and fair-housing programs have been state efforts to exercise greater control over land use and development. Beginning with Hawaii, which adopted statewide land regulation in 1961, a lengthening list of states have enacted land-use and development controls of one sort or another. Most common have been state controls for floodplains, wetlands, coastal zones, and mountainous regions. California, for example, regulates all development along a 1,000-yard wide strip of its 1,000 miles of coastline, while New Jersey exercises land-use controls over 14 percent of the state's area under the provisions of its Coastal Area Facility Review Act. A few states also have undertaken the regulation of large-scale development proposed anywhere in the state. In addition, statewide building codes have been adopted by many states, particularly for prefabricated housing.[26] California prohibited local governments from discriminating against federally subsidized housing. And New York and Massachusetts empowered state agencies to override local zoning and building codes in order to facilitate the construction of subsidized housing.[27]

Richard F. Babcock and Fred P. Bosselman view this "recent resurgence of the state governments' involvement in development policy" as "one of the most significant events shaping the growth of the United States since the homestead laws." As a consequence of these developments, they think it likely that "the neofeudal system of independent municipal duchies, each pursuing its own desires regardless of the world at large, will be asked to account for the social and environmental consequences of their actions." [28] Writing with David Callies, Bosselman envisages "a quiet revolution" overthrowing the *ancien regime*" under "which the entire pattern of land development has been controlled by thousands of individual local governments, each seeking to maximize its tax base and minimize its social problems, and caring less what happens to all the others." [29] Babcock and Bosselman emphasize that both social and environmental concerns underlie the expanding land-use role of the states, arguing that "throughout all the states there run two common concerns: the deterioration of the environment caused by our present pattern of urban sprawl, and the social implications of continuing to restrict access to a desirable environment to certain segments of our society." [30]

Unfortunately for those who want state power used to open suburbs, Babcock and Bosselman overestimate the importance of social considerations in prompting state initiatives on land use. In all but a few states, environmental protection has been the paramount concern in the design of state land-use controls. State standards typically deal with water pollution, sewage disposal, soil conditions, wildlife habitat, preservation of open space, and existing land uses rather than housing needs. Far from seeking to expand housing opportunities, almost all of the new laws aim to limit development. In so doing, state land-use and environmental controls which affect housing inevitably restrict housing opportunities, both by foreclosing development in some areas and increasing the costs of those residences that can be built under the state standards. Babcock and Bosselman themselves concede that "too often the legislation has considered only a narrow range of environmental factors, not including the ability to find a decent place to live at a reasonable price among them." [31]

In Florida, compliance with the state's Environmental Land and Water Management Act of 1972, which provided for state review of all proposed large-scale development, is estimated to have added $1,800 to the cost of a housing unit in those residential developments covered by the law. [32] According to a Vermont developer, expenses incurred in securing a permit under the state's land-use controls averaged $1,000 per dwelling in a 400-unit residential complex. [33] As Bosselman and Callies point out, the "cost imposed on developers by land-use regulations have a peculiarly regressive nature. . . . The cost of processing an application to build a mobile home park and a luxury apartment building may be approximately the same, but when considered as a percentage of the consumers' cost per unit the costs loom much larger to the mobile home buyer." [34] State land-use regulation also can increase housing costs by rationing the land available for development. In Hawaii, where state powers over land use are more extensive than anywhere in the nation, many observers believe that housing costs have been driven up appreciably by the state's efforts to preserve agricultural land and otherwise limit land for urban development. [35] Similar results can be expected wherever state controls significantly restrict land use for residential development in a metropolitan area.

Sewer moratoriums, which are one of the most influential land-use controls available to state government, underscore the inherent conflict between environmentally oriented regulation and housing development. During 1973 and 1974, the New Jersey Department of Environmental Protection froze the issuance of building permits in over seventy communities pending the availability of adequate sewage treatment facilities. All forms of construction were affected, except where private waste facilities could be provided. Among the projects blocked were subsidized housing developments in a number of suburbs. At the same time, Maryland imposed a sewer moratorium in Montgomery and Prince Georges Counties in the Washington area. Close to $1 billion in construction was halted, including a pair of low-income projects in Montgomery County, an affluent suburban area with a severe shortage of low-cost housing.

Even when state environmental officials acknowledge housing needs, they tend to consider ecological considerations as imperatives which take precedence over the expansion of housing opportunities. In an *amicus* brief filed in an exclusionary zoning suit, New Jersey's Commissioner of Environmental Protection emphasized that there was "an overwhelming need for decent housing, especially for low- and moderate-income families." [36] At the same time, the brief argued that "zoning must be firmly rooted in local and regional environmental considerations," such as water quality, water supply, air quality, topography, geology, soils, drainage, fish and wildlife, recreation, historic values, and existing community character. [37] In the absence of offsetting considerations with respect to housing needs, the effect of land-use regulation, based on these environmental imperatives, was bound to be an increase in the state's "overwhelming need for decent housing."

Public preferences underlie the imbalance between environmental and social considerations in state land-use activities. Controlling development is far more popular than expanding housing opportunities for the poor, especially in suburbs which are both the locus of most development and the target of housing reforms. As a result, a growing segment of the suburban population is willing to sacrifice some local autonomy in order to insure more effective environmental controls on development. Moreover, for some suburbanites, the attractions of state environmental controls are enhanced by the fact that checking growth and increasing the cost of housing reinforce local barriers to the outward movement of lower-income and minority groups. As the New Jersey County and Municipal Government Study Commission indicated in connection with sewer moratoriums imposed by the state government, "some municipalities . . . welcome building bans to stabilize service costs, halt rapid growth, and even serve as a guise for elitist land-use policies." [38]

Legislative Barriers to Opening the Suburbs

In sharp contrast to the widespread acceptance by state legislatures of environmentally oriented state controls has been the failure of most efforts to modify exclusionary zoning. During the early 1970s, a variety of zoning reform bills died in state legislatures. In Wisconsin, lawmakers rejected legislation which created a state appeals board empowered to override local barriers to subsidized housing. Also killed was an Illinois bill which authorized the state courts to supersede local controls in order to permit the construction of subsidized housing. [39] Sponsors of legislation in Connecticut which established local quotas for subsidized housing were unable to muster much support. Equally unsuccessful was a bill developed by the Department of Community Affairs in Pennsylvania proposing the creation of a state appeals board to override local zoning that blocked the construction of low-cost housing. In New York, efforts failed to enact legislation which prohibited discriminatory zoning, the exclusion of apartments, limitations on the number of bedrooms in a housing unit, acreage and floor-space requirements that were not consistent with standards established by the state, and the zoning of land for industry without the concomitant provision of housing for lower-income workers.

Zoning reform bills usually have been sponsored by legislators from city districts. The New York proposals, for example, resulted from the efforts of an Ad Hoc Legislative Committee on Exclusionary Suburban

Zoning composed of state legislators from New York City, whose aim was to "break the stranglehold on urban areas caught in the vise of suburban zoning." [40] Backing for the bill came from Percy Sutton, the black Borough President of Manhattan, and liberal interests such as the New Democratic Coalition. Open-housing groups and home-building interests also have provided support for zoning reform measures. These groups, however, typically have been no match for defenders of the status quo in the state capital. Concern for home rule, particularly in connection with an issue as sensitive as subsidized housing, has been the predominant legislative concern. Capitalizing on these fears, opponents invariably frame the issue in terms of local autonomy and community control. From the perspective of the Pennsylvania State Association of Boroughs, the zoning legislation proposed by the state's Department of Community Affairs "would have the effect of Big Brother looking over the shoulder of every city and borough council." [41] For Lowell P. Weicker, Jr., at the time a member of the Connecticut legislature representing affluent Greenwich, the question posed by a zoning reform bill in 1967 was "simply whether or not communities can continue to determine their own destinies." [42]

Lowell Weicker's defense of local autonomy was repeatedly echoed in New Jersey during the late 1960s and early 1970s as successive state administrations sought to persuade the legislature to modify local housing controls. New Jersey was a prime candidate for zoning reform. Restrictive land-use controls were employed by a sizable proportion of the state's 567 municipalities. During the 1960s, moderately priced housing disappeared in many suburban areas in New Jersey, at least in part as a result of the spread of exclusionary zoning techniques. At the same time, jobs were moving outward rapidly from Jersey City, Newark, Camden and other decaying cities. In seeking to remedy the growing mismatch between jobs and housing, however, zoning reformers faced enormous political obstacles. Most municipalities in New Jersey were small, relatively homogeneous, and highly localistic. Reinforcing parochialism was the heavy dependence of local governments on property taxes. Further reducing the prospects of change was the pervasive localism of most members of the state legislature. As one state official emphasized: "In most states, zoning is the law. In New Jersey, it's a religion." [43]

Into this unpromising situation stepped Paul N. Ylvisaker, New Jersey's first commissioner of community affairs. Ylvisaker came to Trenton from the Ford Foundation, where he had won a national reputation for developing innovative approaches to urban problems. Deeply concerned about the plight of the older cities and their residents, Ylvisaker was convinced of the need to lower suburban housing barriers which confined blacks and the poor to the urban core. Ylvisaker thought "a suburban entity with zoning powers in the hands of people who are going to maximize their economic position by the present ground rules is a dangerous thing." Suburbs, he argued, would "have to rejoin the American Union" if "we are going to keep a mobile society, if we are going to solve some of the problems of the central city, the dense housing patterns, and the fiscal situation." [44]

Before taking on local zoning in general, Ylvisaker and Governor Richard J. Hughes engineered a significant breach in local control over land use by securing passage of the Hackensack Meadowlands Reclamation and Development Act in 1968. Under the Meadowlands law, a state agency was empowered to oversee and guide development of an 18,000-acre tract straddling the marshes of the Hackensack River in Hudson and Bergen Counties. Included among the powers of the Meadowlands agency was the authority to supersede local zoning, subdivision controls, and building codes in those portions of fourteen municipalities lying within the Meadowlands district.

Success in the meadowlands, however, did not presage more general zoning reform. Instead, the strong and persistent objections of local officials and state legislators to the loss of local autonomy in the meadowlands were overcome only by the site's unique features. Most important was the need for a comprehensive approach to insure federal participation in expensive flood-control measures which were essential to more intensive development of the area. In addition, the singular nature of the meadowlands, a largely undeveloped tract lying a few miles from the heart of the New York region, generated substantial pressures for state action to insure that the opportunity for comprehensive development would not be squandered. For many legislators, the most convincing argument for the meadowlands approach was the repeated assurance that the law would not create precedents for diluting local control over land use and housing elsewhere in the state. [45]

None of these advantages were associated with Ylvisaker's "Land Use Planning and Development Law" introduced in the spring of 1969. Instead of applying to a special situation, the legislation affected land-use controls throughout the state. Unlike the meadowlands scheme, the new proposal clearly was designed to expand housing opportunities for lower-income and minority groups by restricting exclusionary local policies. One of the bill's goals was to "provide maximum choice among a wide variety and price range of adequate housing types for all economic and social groups throughout the State, with conveniently available opportunities for employment, education, and recreation." [46] Municipalities were prohibited from using land-use and planning powers delegated to them by the state "for the purpose of excluding any economic, racial, religious, or ethnic group from the enjoyment of residence, land ownership, or land uses anywhere in the State." [47] Local zoning ordinances were to take account of the "need for various types of housing for all economic and social groups in the municipality, and in the surrounding region." [48]

In essence, Ylvisaker's proposal placed the legal burden on local governments to demonstrate that their land-use and housing controls were not exclusionary. Enforcement, however, was left largely to the courts. To facilitate legal action against exclusionary zoning in the courts, the legislation gave standing to nonresidents in local proceedings and state courts, as well as authorizing the commissioner of community affairs to join suits alleging discriminatory zoning. Furthermore, to dilute the role of local residents in land-use determinations, the bill prohibited the use of referendums for adopting or amending local zoning ordinances. [49]

A storm of protest was stirred by Ylvisaker's plan. Most local officials and state legislators saw the bill as a dire threat to home rule and local control over land use and housing. For one suburban mayor, the proposal was "a definite encroachment on home rule" designed to "force the municipalities, especially the suburban areas, to allot by compulsion by the czar in Trenton . . . some of their land for low [cost] homes, low-income purposes." [50] Particularly objectionable were the provisions requiring local governments to provide housing for all economic and social groups, which were seen by many as giving "radicals" like Ylvisaker the means to force poor blacks on any community in the state. Few members of a legislature dominated by suburban Republicans did anything but denounce the zoning proposal. Even the bill's sponsors thought the bill too radical to have any chance of passage. [51] Proponents of zoning reform were immediately put on the defensive. "There is no reduction in local zoning power," Ylvisaker insisted; "no state planning czar or super-agency is created to oversee local zoning." [52] Local officials and legislators, however, paid little attention to such disclaimers. Moreover, in contrast with the Meadowlands' legislation, which was actively promoted by a broad coalition of interests, zoning reform failed to attract wide support. Without such backing to offset the vehement opposition of local officials and their legislative spokesmen, the zoning bill was doomed. Unmourned by most, it perished in 1969 without even emerging from committee.

The uproar over Ylvisaker's zoning proposals spilled over into the 1969 gubernatorial campaign. The commissioner and his plan were denounced by Representative William T. Cahill, the Republican candidate and easy winner over former Governor Robert B. Meyner, who tried to avoid any association with the zoning albatross. In legislative races, few friends of zoning reform were visible, while many Republican candidates gleefully denounced Ylvisaker and the Democrats for planning to undermine home rule. With Cahill's election the zoning issue appeared dead, particularly after Ylvisaker was replaced with Edmund T. Hume. A former mayor of suburban Maplewood and a staunch defender of home rule, Hume was highly critical of Ylvisaker's approach, which he claimed "made the Commissioner of Community Affairs a dictator." [53] Local governments, in the new commissioner's view, had the right to zone without state interference. Private builders operating under local zoning, insisted Hume, could produce sufficient housing, with lower-income families being served primarily by the trickle-down process.

Many home builders, however, were less confident than Commissioner Hume about their ability to function within the constraints imposed by local housing controls. Rising housing costs also generated pressure on the Cahill Administration to develop a housing program. By the middle of 1970, the governor was talking of the need for state initiatives to deal with rising costs, lagging production, and the shortage of moderately priced housing units. Trial balloons were floated about possible modifications of local housing policies by the state. At one press conference, the governor indicated that "local zoning" was "one of the great deterrents to housing in New Jersey." Zoning, in Cahill's view, created "a real problem, particularly in suburban areas where a half acre, and sometimes two and three acres are required to erect a home, which prices the house out of the pocketbook of the average man." [54]

Local and legislative reaction to Cahill's trial balloon was largely negative. In the face of strong opposition to state involvement in zoning, the governor sought to avoid direct confrontation with the suburbs. Instead, he concentrated on trying "to get housing built without arousing emotions." [55] Reflecting these political realities, Cahill's "Blueprint for Housing in New Jersey," which he delivered to the legislature late in 1970, emphasized the nature of the state's "crisis in housing" rather than measures to deal with the problem. Detailed data was provided on housing costs, lot sizes, and the paucity of sites for apartments and mobile homes. While assuring the legislature that he was devoted to home rule and local control, Cahill warned that the system was "failing because it is not meeting the needs of all our people." [56] Pointing to the Pennsylvania rulings on exclusionary zoning, and underscoring the possibility of similar decisions in cases pending before courts in New Jersey, Cahill urged corrective action to "insure the maintenance of controls in the hands of the local officials." [57] But no specifics were offered, except for a general endorsement of a state building code and a recommendation that "some way" be found for the state's Housing Finance Agency "to overcome abusive application of local zoning laws." [58]

Despite Cahill's talk of a housing crisis, fifteen months were to pass before detailed zoning proposals were ready for the legislature. Underlying the delay were political considerations, particularly the desire to keep zoning out of the 1971 legislative elections. While the Cahill Administration bided its time, however, pressures for change in local zoning were steadily mounting in the courts. During 1971, one judge struck down apartment restrictions in Glassboro designed to limit school expenditures. [59] Another invalidated Madison's zoning code because of its failure to take regional housing needs into account. [60] In addition, challenges of local zoning restrictions were before the state courts in cases involving Mount Laurel and other municipalities.

Five months after the election of a new legislature in November 1971, Cahill unveiled his proposals "to relieve the housing crisis, guide the municipalities in the elimination of abuses in the zoning and planning areas, and insure the continuation of control in the hands of our local officials." [61] To achieve these goals, the Cahill Administration offered four bills. The first proposed a uniform state building code applying to all municipalities with enforcement by local building inspectors certified by the state. [62] The second created a Community Development Corporation empowered to develop housing, new towns, and commercial and industrial facilities, as well as engage in urban renewal. [63] The third element in the package was a fair-share housing plan, under which the state would determine the need for lower-cost housing and allocate quotas among counties, with counties then distributing responsibilities to municipalities on the basis of local needs, tax resources, availability of land, local zoning, and other factors.[64] The final bill provided for standardization and simplification of state enabling legislation affecting local zoning, as well as creation of a State Planning Commission to regulate land in critical areas.[65]

Despite its scope, Cahill's program involved little direct confrontation with exclusionary local practices. At one time, the governor had spoken about resorting "to harsher measures if nothing else works." [66] But these remarks proved to be idle threats since his freedom of action on housing and zoning policies was severely constrained. Instead of resorting to harsher measures, Cahill was forced to water down his proposals in the face of adamant opposition from legislators and local officials. An early version of Cahill's zoning bill, in language reminiscent of the Ylvisaker legislation, had specified that the "powers of this act shall not be used for the purposes of excluding, or result in a pattern of exclusion of, any economic group from the use of land anywhere in the state." [67] This provision, however, disappeared as Cahill's housing advisers searched for a program that was acceptable to suburban interests. In the end, a land-use bill emerged which avoided the issue of exclusion entirely. Unlike the Ylvisaker proposal, Cahill's zoning bill contained no mandate to local governments to promote maximum choice for all economic groups, failed to prohibit the use of zoning for the purposes of exclusion, and said nothing about local responsibilities for regional housing needs.

Compromises resulting from the conclusion that mandatory housing measures had no chance of being approved by the legislature also weakened the impact of other elements of Cahill's program on exclusionary zoning and other restrictive suburban practices. In the case of the proposed Community Development Corporation, local governments were given a veto over the activities of the agency. And compliance with Cahill's scheme for allocating low-cost housing was left entirely to local government. The governor emphasized that "this is a purely voluntary plan; no municipality is mandated or forced to comply." [68]

Despite these weaknesses, Cahill's program attracted more public attention and support than the zoning reforms proposed by the Hughes Administration. One factor accounting for increased interest was the greater visibility of the zoning issue in 1972. Litigation and court rulings, controversies in Warren and other suburbs, statements by President Nixon and Secretary Romney, and the activities of open-housing interests all increased public awareness of exclusionary zoning between 1969 and 1972. Reinforcing this development had been the growing attention of the press and televison to suburban exclusion.

Open-housing interests generally supported the Cahill program, although most would have preferred stronger legislative proposals aimed directly at local restrictions. Groups involved in litigation, however, saw voluntary fair-share plans as an important weapon in court since the allocations would provide judges with a measure of local efforts to meet regional housing needs.

Within the legislature, Cahill's chief supporter was Assemblyman Albert W. Merck, a first-term Republican from suburban Morris County. Merck, who was chairman of the planning board in affluent Mendham, backed the proposals because he saw them offering local governments a viable alternative to court-imposed housing plans. He also was attracted to quotas as a means of protecting suburban communities from an influx of low-income residents. Using the same arguments employed in Dayton, Merck emphasized that allocation plans gave local residents "the assurance that even though sites will have to be provided for multi-family units, low and middle income, . . . the number of people in that income bracket that can come at any one time will be restricted.[69]

Merck worked hard to persuade suburbanites that Cahill's program was much less likely to erode home rule than adverse rulings on zoning from the state courts. So did Cahill and his top aides, who invested far more time and energy in zoning reform than had been the case with the Hughes Administration, which had viewed the Ylvisaker plan as a forlorn cause from the beginning. Early in 1973, meetings were held across the state at which Merck, Lawrence Kramer, Hume's successor as Commissioner of Community Affairs and a former mayor of Paterson, and other state officials promoted the housing and zoning bills. At these sessions, advocates of the program stressed the need for state action before judges forced less attractive alternatives on New Jersey's municipalities. "This bill," the state's top planner told an audience in Bergen County, "is probably the only hope we have of retaining a large municipal input into the land-use process. I don't mean the state will take it away; the courts are likely to see to that."[70]

None of these efforts, however, had much impact on the state legislature because the response from the grass roots was overwhelmingly negative. Resolutions were passed by suburban communities opposing any dilution of home rule. Letters, phone calls, and other negative messages poured into Trenton. Typical was the view of a suburban mayor in

Monmouth County who saw the bills as letting "Big Brother step on the little guy." [71] In many suburbs facing legal challenges of their zoning restrictions, the state was perceived as a bigger threat than the courts. United Citizens for Home Rule, an organization which came into existence in response to Suburban Action's litigation, attacked the proposals as a "Cahill power grab that ought to be resisted vigorously." [72] A similar organization in Bergen County called for an amendment to the state constitution to insure that planning and zoning would remain under local control.

For most members of the legislature, the message came through loud and clear, particularly in an election year in which few wanted to campaign with the burden of having opposed home rule and having favored low-income housing in the suburbs. Opposition within his suburban constituency led Richard DeKorte, the Republican floor leader in the Assembly house and normally a bulwark of the Cahill Administration, to emphasize that he did "not support the governor's zoning bills." [73] Another suburban legislator from Bergen County termed "the whole package destructive of home rule. Even the uniform state housing construction code is discriminatory because it would violate the right of a municipality to govern the character of the community in housing." [74]

Overwhelmed by local and legislative hostility, Cahill's modest proposals suffered the same ignominious fate as Ylvisaker's zoning reforms as none of the bills emerged from committee. Even if the package had reached the floor, a Republican leader indicated that: "You couldn't find more than 10 assemblymen who would vote for them." [75] For Cahill, zoning reform was not only a lost cause, but a factor in his loss of the governorship itself. Along with support of an income tax (which the legislature also rejected) and scandals involving key aides, Cahill's housing and zoning efforts contributed to his defeat in the 1973 Republican primary by Representative Charles W. Sandman, Jr., an outspoken advocate of home rule and local control over land use. Another loser in 1973 was Assemblyman Merck, whose identification with zoning reform and low-cost housing was a factor in an unsuccessful campaign for reelection in what had been a safe Republican district.

Democrats replaced Republicans in Trenton in the wake of the 1973 election, but the change did little to alter the stalemate over zoning reforms. Cahill's successor, Brendan T. Byrne, who had easily defeated Sandman in November, also recognized the need for state action on housing and zoning. A few months after Byrne took office, one of his top aides indicated that "the problems of breaking down exclusionary zoning barriers . . . would be the administration's foremost concern once it had dealt with tax reform and school financing." [76] Byrne, however, faced the same problem as his predecessors—legislative reluctance to dilute home rule, particularly on an issue as sensitive as housing and land use. A legislature controlled by Democrats offered little more hope for a successful zoning bill than the Republican majorities which had rebuffed the Hughes and Cahill Administrations. By and large, suburban Democrats had replaced suburban Republicans as a result of the 1973 election; and many of the victors had campaigned against Cahill's zoning proposals.

A new factor, however, was being added to the political equation. By 1974, the probability was very strong that the courts would force the state's hand on housing and land use. Two years earlier, Governor Cahill had warned the legislature that "unless we act together to help open the way for needed housing, the courts will do it for us and will continue to move strongly in the direction of bypassing home rule by judicial process." [77] But the courts never generated enough direct pressure during Cahill's tenure to make his warning creditable to the legislature. By the time Byrne was taking office, the threat of judicial intervention was more substantial. The Madison and Mount Laurel cases were being argued before the state Supreme Court, with one of the justices indicating that local officials "just may have to go along kicking and screaming" with zoning reform. [78]

Failure of the court to complete its work on the housing cases, as well as preoccupation with taxes and school finance, permitted the Byrne Administration to avoid the zoning issue during 1974. As the new year began, however, a ruling from the court was expected momentarily. In this context, Governor Byrne cautioned the lawmakers in January that "abuses of local zoning cannot be ignored by this Legislature." [79] Among the adverse consequences of restrictive zoning, "most troubling" to Byrne were "judicial solutions which burden the process of local government." [80] He called for state action that would "assist municipalities in responding to the judicial requirements to serve housing needs" while "giving maximum recognition to a municipality's right to its own personality and zoning objectives." [81]

With announcement of the sweeping Mount Laurel ruling in March came demands for state action. "The governor and legislators," insisted one editorial writer, "must help municipalities find a regional response to the new situation. . . . To reap the full harvest from the seed planted by the Mount Laurel decision, governments at all levels must fertilize the ground with housing subsidies, property tax reform, local housing authorities and other public services." [82] The *New York Times* saw the decision as forcing the "state to do what it ought to do in any case: execute a statewide plan for the best possible uses of its land. . . . that will take into account all the factors involved—environmental, economic, social and political." [83] A bar association committee called for "strong, affirmative action . . . by the New Jersey Legislature so that these vital matters can be settled . . . where they rightly belong, not in the courts by default." [84]

In responding to the Mount Laurel decision, the Byrne Administration focused on the court's mandate that each municipality "must bear its fair share of the regional burden." [85] Legislation was prepared which resembled the housing allocation bill developed three years earlier by the Cahill Administration. As with Merck's fair-share bill, compliance with the state housing quotas was voluntary rather than mandatory. "The state role ought to be to aid and assist," argued one of the governor's aides, "not to take over the local zoning process." [86]

For Byrne as for Cahill, the primary appeal of voluntary housing allocations was political. Mandatory approaches clearly had no chance of acceptance in the legislature, particularly since the ruling in Mount Laurel required no specific state action. Neither a state role in allocating housing nor in altering local zoning was mandated by the decision.[87] In the absence of direct court pressure for state involvement, however, even voluntary housing allocations had little political appeal. Local officials quickly registered their opposition to any legislation involving housing quotas, either voluntary or mandatory. The draft of zoning legislation supported by many local officials, which had been developed by the State League of Municipalities and dealt only with procedural reform, carried the following disclaimer on its cover: "This Draft Does Not Deal with Housing Quotas, either Mandatory Or Voluntary, and Should Not Be Confused with Previous or Pending Bills on that Subject." [88]

Without pressure from the courts, and in the face of widespread local opposition to housing quotas, legislators were in no hurry to wrestle with housing allocation. "I don't think there's any need to panic," cautioned an assemblyman from Bergen County. "This thing is going to take a little while to work itself out." [89] In the face of widespread opposition and apathy, the Byrne Administration wound up never introducing a housing allocation bill in 1975. Continuing legislative opposition led Byrne the following year to provide a state role in housing allocation by means of an executive order rather than legislation. Compliance with housing allocation under the plan would be voluntary, but state officials were to give priority in distributing some state aid to communities which sought to meet their housing quota. Legislators immediately threatened to block implementation of the order, with one legislative leader terming Byrne's action "another instance of kicking the middle class in the ass." [90]

An Aberration in Massachusetts

At the same time that Paul Ylvisaker was launching New Jersey's futile quest for zoning reform, Massachusetts was in the process of becoming the first state to enact legislation directly aimed at suburban exclusion. Massachusetts' Zoning Appeals Law, passed in 1969, was designed to remove local barriers to the construction of subsidized housing in the suburbs. Under the law, were an application for a low-cost project rejected or burdened with local conditions, the developer could seek redress from the state. A state Housing Appeals Committee was empowered to overrule local zoning actions found to be "unreasonable and not consistent with local needs" or local housing restrictions deemed "uneconomic." [91]

In assessing the validity of a local determination affecting subsidized housing, the legislation directed the state to consider whether the local restrictions on land use were "reasonable in view of the regional need for low- and moderate-income housing considered with the number of low income persons in the city or town affected." [92] Another consideration was whether local restrictions were necessary to protect the health and safety of either occupants of the proposed housing or local residents more generally. In addition, the Housing Appeals Committee was directed to evaluate whether local constraints were reasonable in terms of promoting "better site and building design in relation to the surroundings, or to preserve open space." [93] Local quotas for subsidized housing also were established, with restrictions on subsidized housing considered consistent with local needs in those communities which had met their quotas.

Massachusetts' Zoning Appeals Law was enacted in a heavily suburbanized state with strong home-rule traditions. Restrictive land-use controls were widely employed, particularly in the suburbs around Boston. Local opposition had negated efforts dating to the 1950s by the Home Builders Association of Massachusetts to persuade the legislature to restrict large lots and outlaw fiscal zoning. In 1955, a Special Commission on Planning, Zoning, and Subdivision Control established by the legislature had opposed as an "unnecessary interference in local government" the creation of a state zoning appeals board proposed by home builders.[94]

Worries about the housing problems of minorities, rather than the unhappiness of home builders with local restrictions, moved exclusionary zoning onto the legislative agenda in the late 1960s. Legislative concern over the possible use of suburban land-use controls to discriminate against minorities led to a detailed study of minimum lot sizes, open-space zoning, frontage and setback restrictions, height limitations, and other local housing constraints. While the study was unable to find any local restrictions explicitly aimed at blacks or other minorities, it underscored the role of local zoning in keeping subsidized housing and lower-income families out of suburban areas. "The interplay of these municipal regulations determines, in substantial degree," the 1968 report concluded, "the extent to which additional modest income housing is possible in relation to the local supply of 'buildable' land." [95]

Drawing on these findings, legislators introduced a number of bills in 1969 designed to provide state control over various aspects of local zoning. The Home Builders Association prepared legislation which set a maximum lot size of 15,000 square feet. Another bill required at least 15 percent of a city or town to be zoned for apartments. A third provided for the establishment of special housing districts within lower-density communities. Most sweeping was a bill which exempted subsidized housing from local restrictions, with appeals to the state in disputed cases. Out of this melange, the Committee on Urban Affairs developed the legislation which eventually was enacted. Emerging in June, the committee's bill was accompanied by a report which claimed that zoning-appeals legislation was essential to deal with the "acute shortage of decent, safe, low and moderate income housing throughout the commonwealth." [96]

The zoning bill quickly became the "hottest issue of the legislative session." [97] Opposition was widespread, with suburbanites sounding familiar themes. "Towns which establish two-acre zoning," wrote one defender of the status quo, "are simply trying to preserve the basic charac-

ter and social structure of the community." [98] Another saw the bill as
merely a means of shifting the problems of the older cities to suburbia:
"Unable to solve their housing problems in spite of the expenditure of
millions of dollars and the existence of scores of vacant lots and abandoned housing, the city now wishes to export this mess to the suburbs." [99] Local officials condemned the proposal, and their principal organization, the Massachusetts Selectmen's Association, lobbied against
passage. The Massachusetts Federation of Planning Boards argued that
the legislation "would deprive local communities of home rule on housing or ruin zoning and building codes which have been established and
proven over the years." [100]

Most suburban legislators opposed zoning reform, and they led efforts in both houses to kill the bill or cripple it by making local compliance voluntary. Typical were the objections of a suburban representative
who argued that the proposed law "will do away with local zoning" and
that it was "the first step to state controlled zoning." [101] Among the
suburban opponents were a number of liberals who had previously supported state legislation aimed at racial imbalance in the schools. As one
observer noted: "One of the most embarrassing sights of the current
legislative session was the spectacle of the so-called 'liberal' legislators,
who strongly advocated the racial imbalance law, casting their votes
against a bill which would really do something about the problem." [102]
In the end, eleven suburban and small-town representatives who had
supported the racial imbalance bill, whose principal impact was on
schools in Boston and other older cities, voted against the zoning proposal which threatened racial integration closer to home.

On the other side were groups like the Citizens Housing and Planning Association, the Massachusetts Federation for Fair Housing and
Equal Rights, Americans for Democratic Action, and the state council of
churches. Although the bill did not cover privately-developed housing,
backing came from the Home Builders Association, which viewed the
proposal as a "step in the right direction." [103] Boston's major newspapers
endorsed the bill, with a typical editorial arguing that no suburb "has the
right to impose such rigid zoning and building restrictions that persons
of moderate or low income are automatically priced out of its housing
market." [104]

Similar coalitions in New Jersey and other states, however, were unable to overcome suburban resistance to measures aimed at exclusionary
zoning. A key difference in Massachusetts was solid support from legis-

lators from the older cities. Some saw state involvement in suburban housing as a means of easing the burdens imposed on the older urban centers by lower-income families. A number also were eager to get even with suburbanites who had supported the school integration measure in 1965. As Robert Engler has noted, "Boston legislators . . . felt [the racial imbalance bill] was being shoved down their throats by liberal suburban legislators. Four years later they had not forgotten." [105] In the lower house, thirty-seven opponents of the school legislation, most from older cities, voted for the zoning bill in 1969. Support from urban legislators was essential for passage in both houses. A suburban move to make compliance voluntary was turned back in the lower house by a six-vote margin. And the measure squeaked through the state senate by only two votes.

Enactment of the Zoning Appeals Law also was made possible by its limited scope and impact. As one observer notes, "the most important factor contributing to the passage of the law was the political prudence of its architects." [106] Designed to be politically acceptable, the legislation hardly threatened to sweep away suburban housing barriers as feared by its adversaries. Control over land use remained in local hands. Throughout the legislative process, supporters of zoning reform emphasized that the bill preserved local zoning. Under the new legislation, the state was to play only an indirect role through an appeals procedure. Local governments were represented on the Housing Appeals Committee, with one of the five members being a town selectman and another a city councilman. [107] Moreover, no positive obligations were imposed on local governments to provide subsidized housing. Instead, the approach was passive, depending on developers to take the initiative to build moderate-cost housing within any particular community. Further efforts were made to reassure local communities by permitting them to insure that subsidized projects were compatible with local plans with respect to siting, the height of structures, and building materials.

Political considerations also led to the specification of modest quotas in the legislation. Localities were considered to have met local needs for subsidized housing if low-cost units constituted ten percent of all dwelling units, or occupied 1.5 percent of a community's land zoned for residential, commercial, and industrial development. Annual construction of subsidized housing covering .3 percent of the land area of a community—or ten acres for jurisdictions encompassing less than one-half square mile—also fulfilled the state standard. These quotas, moreover, were maximums rather than state minimums. They established absolute limits on the obligation of a locality to provide subsidized housing, not minimum requirements which every community was expected to meet. As in Dayton, New Jersey, and elsewhere, the argument that maximum quotas would protect suburbs from being overwhelmed by subsidized housing was stressed by supporters of the Massachusetts legislation.

Other limitations in the zoning-appeals bill further reduced its threat to local autonomy. Communities below the state quota were not obliged to approve subsidized housing projects found to be inconsistent with the public health and safety of local residents, or to accept proposals which threatened to downgrade the local environment. The law also dealt with subsidized housing in general terms, which meant "that a community could meet its legal obligation by granting rezonings for subsidized housing for the elderly that would occupy 1.5 percent of the jurisdiction's land. It would then have no responsibility to permit housing for lower-income families." [108] Another limiting feature was the legislation's failure to apply to all subsidized housing. Only developments proposed by public agencies, limited dividdend sponsors, and non-profit organizations were covered by its provisions. As a result, the appeals procedure was not available to private developers under programs such as Section 235 or turnkey public housing.

Moreover, in the case of developers covered by the law, the procedures were fraught with possibilities for costly delays. The legislation added another step to the approval process—state review—without eliminating either the local government or the courts. Developers bore the burden of appealing an adverse local action. Even if the state overturned a local determination, the community could always challenge the state's ruling in court. As indicated in chapter 7, long and costly proceedings usually provide an inherent advantage to local governments, which possess more staying power and financial resources than most developers of subsidized housing. The first two appeals under the procedures became moot when the developer encountered financial difficulties. Money problems also delayed implementation of both projects involved in the initial successful appeals and court cases arising from the zoning law. And, of the first twenty-two successful appeals under the law, only two projects actually resulted in the construction of housing by 1975. [109]

Some supporters of the Zoning Appeals Law were confident that developers could avoid the expense and delay involved in appeals and court cases. Local governments, they hoped, would alter their housing and zoning policies in the face of the threat of state action through the appeals procedure. Presumably, local officials would prefer to permit subsidized housing on their own terms rather than risk an adverse action by the state on a site selected by a developer. Or as a resident of Lexington (which responded to the state law by zoning for subsidized housing) put it more bluntly, the question was "whether we pick the blacks or take the ones the state throws at us." [110] Initially, however, most suburbs preferred to fight rather than switch as Lexington did. By standing fast, communities were able to tie up developers in costly and sometimes fatal delays. As one state official notes in 1972, "we've seen the most ingenious series of legal maneuvers to circumvent" the zoning law.[111] Two suburbs in the Boston area, Billerica and Winchester, successfully resisted the Burlington Development Corporation, which was unable to pursue its appeal because of financial difficulties. Suburban Hanover turned down an application from the Country Village Corporation to build 88 units for the elderly on a site not zoned for apartments. Another suburb, Concord, rejected 60 units of subsidized garden apartments in an area zoned for one and two-family homes. Chelmsford condemned a site sought for 450 units of subsidized housing, and added the land to its conservation reserve. After the actions of Hanover and Concord were overturned by the appeals committee in its first two rulings, both suburbs went to court, claiming that the state had no authority to override local zoning.

As long as the powers conferred by the Zoning Appeals Law were being challenged in the courts, relatively few developers were prepared to proceed under its provisions. For their part, suburbs were reluctant to accommodate unwanted subsidized housing as long as there was a chance that the courts might invalidate the appeals procedure. These hopes were dashed in 1973, when the Massachusetts Supreme Judicial Court unanimously upheld the zoning law in suits brought by Concord and Hanover. In affirming the legislature's right to expand the state's role in zoning, the justices concluded that:

> local restrictive zoning regulations have set up, in fact if not intentionally, a barrier against the introduction of low- and moderate-income housing in the suburbs. Moreover, this barrier exists at a time when our housing needs for the low- and moderate-income groups cannot be met by the "inner cities." This housing crisis demands a legislative and judicial approach that requires "the strictly local interests of the town" to yield to the regional need for the construction of low- and moderate-income housing. [The Zoning Appeals

Law] represents the Legislature's use of its own zoning powers to respond to the problem." [112]

With the favorable court ruling came a greater willingness on the part of developers to employ the law. During the next year, nine appeals were heard by the state, with eight decided in favor of developers. In the wake of these developments, some local governments began to respond more favorably to proposals for subsidized housing. At the same time, the failure of the worst fears of suburbanites to materialize increased local acceptance of state involvement in the zoning process. According to state officials, "the early hostility of municipal officials to the very existence of the zoning appeals law has subsided as they see that the procedures of the Committee are open and even-handed, do not represent any state effort to 'railroad' through new housing projects, and in the initial cases at least have involved projects that will benefit primarily low-income residents of the suburbs where they are to be built." [113]

Despite its flaws and politically-inspired limitations, the Massachusetts Zoning Appeals Law remained in the mid-1970s a rarity among state laws affecting land use. Unlike most state controls, which were making it more difficult to build housing, Massachusetts was stimulating construction of lower-cost housing in suburban areas where little had been built previously. In political terms, the Massachusetts law also represents an aberration. Certainly, there was nothing magical about the details of the Massachusetts approach which made it more acceptable politically than other schemes—witness the dismal failure of similar legislation to win support in the Connecticut legislature. Nor was the lineup of political forces in Massachusetts strikingly different from that found elsewhere. Instead, suburban opponents of zoning reform failed to prevail because of "a political quirk, a unique set of circumstances which produced a strange (and perhaps 'one-shot') coalition just strong enough to pass the bill." [114] Reinforcing this conclusion was the failure of subsequent efforts in Massachusetts to strengthen the appeals law. As one Massachusetts legislator explained his colleagues' reluctance to go beyond the Zoning Appeals Law: "We passed Chapter 774 in 1969 to get us off the hook on the housing issue, and still find it useful for that. But don't ask us to give you any more powers to make it work!" [115]

Suburban Power and New York's UDC

As Massachusetts' experience demonstrates, zoning reforms can facilitate the development of subsidized housing. Zoning changes alone, however do not guarantee that housing will be produced in the suburbs for lower-income families. Public agencies, nonprofit organizations, or private developers must be willing and able to locate subsidized units in the suburbs. Funds have to be available to subsidize projects which are feasible as a result of zoning reforms. "The plain fact," Paul Ylvisaker emphasized in discussing his ill-fated zoning proposals, "is that you could zone all of New Jersey for low-income housing and unless you had the money, manpower, technology, and a vast variety of other legal powers, you could not build one unit of low-cost housing." [116]

Last paragraph

A state agency with powers and resources of the sort Ylvisaker had in mind already was in existence during the initial round of the battle over exclusionary zoning in New Jersey. In the spring of 1968, New York had created a public corporation with sweeping authority to develop and finance housing of all sorts, including subsidized units. In addition to housing, the New York State Urban Development Corporation was empowered to engage in commercial, industrial, educational, cultural, recreational, and civic development and redevelopment. Unlike state housing finance agencies and local urban renewal authorities, UDC did not have to rely on outside developers for initiating projects, since it was authorized to select sites, acquire them, and develop housing and other facilities. To carry out this broad mandate, UDC was liberated from almost all local land-use and development constraints. Localities were prohibited from modifying UDC's plans and designs. The state agency also was exempted from local permits and certificates of occupancy. And most important, UDC was authorized to override local zoning ordinances, subdivision regulations, and building codes "when in the discretion of the corporation such compliance is not feasible or practicable." [117]

In addition to broad powers, the Urban Development Corporation was given substantial administrative and financial capabilities. To head UDC, Governor Nelson A. Rockefeller recruited Edward J. Logue, a skilled and outspoken public entrepreneur who had directed major urban redevelopment efforts in New Haven and Boston. In a sense, UDC's sweeping authority and Logue were a package deal. Conferring with Rockefeller before the legislation was developed, Logue insisted that the agency could not succeed without the ability to bypass local housing controls. Without the "power to override local zoning and codes," Logue argued later, "legislation will not amount to anything." [118] Once UDC was in business, Logue acquired a substantial staff of able and aggressive housing specialists, financing experts, lawyers, planners, and designers.

By 1972, UDC had 550 employees working in seventeen offices spread across the state. Ample funds also were provided by the state to launch the agency, including an initial $15 million appropriation, a $50 million loan, and $1 billion in borrowing capacity. UDC, however, was not given an independent source of funds for subsidizing housing. Instead, the new agency had to depend on existing state and federal housing programs to underwrite low-cost units in its projects.

All of these capabilities were enhanced by UDC's freedom of action as compared to most state agencies. Organized as a public corporation with an independent board of directors, UDC was able to operate outside normal budgetary, personnel, and other controls. Even more important was the strong personal commitment of a powerful, ambitious, and activist governor. This combination of legal power, financial and organizational capability, and political clout made UDC, in the view of the U.S. Commission on Civil Rights, "probably the most powerful instrumentality yet devised to locate and construct housing for low- and moderate-income families." [119] Logue agreed, terming UDC's enabling act "the most versatile and most all-inclusive development legislation on the books in any of the 50 states." [120]

Using these formidable powers to open the suburbs, however, was not Nelson Rockefeller's objective in ramming the Urban Development Corporation through the New York legislature in 1968. Instead, UDC was presidential candidate Rockefeller's "revolutionary" answer to the urban crisis, a crisis perceived by the governor almost exclusively in terms of the older cities.[121] Throughout the debate over the UDC proposal, Rockefeller and his supporters stressed the "urban" aspects of *Urban* Development Corporation. The legislation emphasized the ills of the urban centers, speaking of the need to eliminate blight, attract new industry to older cities, and provide more low-income housing within these jurisdictions. UDC's "drastic powers" to override local zoning and building controls were required, Rockefeller insisted, because of the manifest failure of the cities to conquer urban blight on their own.[122]

Aimed at the older cities, UDC drew criticism primarily from urban interests concerned about local control and responsiveness, with most of the outcry coming from New York City. One city councilman denounced the proposal as a "usurpation of the city's powers." [123] Mayor John V. Lindsay strongly opposed the superagency proposed by his political rival in Albany. "This encroachment on home rule rights of the localities cannot be tolerated," contended Lindsay. "Our cities cannot be renewed by state-operated bulldozers which move into local communities without their consent and without knowledge or concern about the increasing need for supportive services connected with all development." [124] Sharing these concerns was the *New York Times*, which supported the general concept of UDC but objected to the agency's "plenary powers to ride roughshod over local and regional plans and to ignore local sentiment." [125]

The Urban Development Corporation's sweeping power to override local land-use and housing controls also disturbed suburbanites, even though Rockefeller and his allies studiously avoided discussing possible UDC activities in the suburbs. Upstate rural interests grumbled both about home rule and pouring large amounts of state resources into the cities. Together the city, suburban, and rural critics of UDC composed a strange alliance that seemed likely to prevail despite the support for Rockefeller's plan from most of the legislative leadership, major developers, the construction industry, building trades' unions, and political leaders in upstate cities. UDC was saved, however, by a national tragedy and the formidable political influence of Nelson Rockefeller.

On April 4, 1968, while the UDC bill was awaiting legislative action, Martin Luther King was assassinated in Memphis. As grief, outrage, and riots swept across the nation, Governor Rockefeller called on the New York legislature to enact his urban program as a "memorial" to the fallen black leader.[126] Four days after King's murder, both chambers unanimously passed resolutions calling on each member to take "upon himself the responsibility to support appropriate legislation that will give every citizen the opportunity to achieve . . . the principles of justice and equality for which the Rev. Martin Luther King laid down his life." [127] The following day, the UDC bill breezed through the Republican-controlled Senate by a vote of 41 to 12. In the Assembly, however, UDC's critics questioned whether the superagency was an appropriate memorial to Dr. King. Democrats from New York City and upstate Republicans combined to reject the governor's bill, 69 to 63 on the critical vote, and then by a decisive 85 to 48 margin on the final tally.

At this point, Governor Rockefeller brought out the heavy artillery, resulting in what some Albany hands have called the biggest "arm-twisting day" in the history of the legislature.[128] Learning of the bill's defeat on the way back from King's funeral in Atlanta, "the governor was furious. He telephoned the Republican minority leader, and told him that he would refuse patronage and veto legislation in which the rebels were interested." [129] As Rockefeller later explained, "I [said] I would be unable to continue to do the personal favors. There was a long list, such as signing bills and appointments. Now I don't like to take this position, but I think that one has to use whatever authority one has when something of major importance to the people comes before you." [130] Seven hours after the Assembly had "defeated" the UDC bill, the legislation was reconsidered, and approved by a vote of 86 to 45 as almost forty assemblymen changed their votes in response to "whatever authority" Nelson Rockefeller was able to bring to bear.

After its tumultuous birth, the Urban Development Corporation assiduously sought to avoid additional political controversy wherever possible. Steering clear of UDC's suburban and rural adversaries, Logue concentrated his attention on older cities. An accommodation was quickly arranged with Mayor Lindsay, permitting UDC to commence a number of projects within New York City. Most of the rest of UDC's energies and resources initially were devoted to rescuing moribund urban renewal projects in other cities. As a result of these policies, over 85 percent of UDC's 31,000 housing starts through 1972 were in cities, with half of the total located in New York City. Moreover, to increase its political acceptability within the cities, the Urban Development Corporation emphasized middle-income rather than low-income housing. Most UDC projects were 70 percent middle- and moderate-income and only 20 percent low-income, with the remaining 10 percent for the elderly. Logue called the income mix "a pragmatic approach to the political realities." [131]

Political considerations also led Logue to avoid employing UDC's power to set aside local zoning and building codes except as a last resort. As Logue explained, "UDC's unique powers to override local building codes and zoning ordinances have been our principal source of controversy. We have used the powers . . . only rarely against the opposition of local government. And then only after consultation with local officials and when compliance was not feasible or practicable." [132] Through 1972, the agency used the override in only four of 101 projects. To be sure, the override provided UDC substantial leverage with local governments in its negotiations. Logue was certain that "if we didn't have the power to come in, the door would be shut before we started." [133] Under the circumstances, UDC clearly preferred to go into local jurisdictions which welcomed its involvement, rather than intrude in situations where its presence would stir political opposition. Following the course of least resistance meant building to meet local needs in older cities, an approach which had relatively little impact on settlement patterns in the state's metropolitan areas. As David Trubek emphasized in testimony before the U.S. Commission on Civil Rights in 1971, UDC "acted with extreme caution, placing projects where they will likely meet a high rate of local acceptability, rather than placing them where, if accepted, they would result in substantial economic integration. It would rather build than fight." [134]

Despite UDC's concentration on acceptable projects in older cities and its desire to let sleeping dogs lie in suburbia, Logue from the beginning acknowledged the need for his agency to build housing in outlying areas. "You can't get rid of urban blight," he told a reporter in 1969, "unless you can move some people residing in cities into the suburbs." [135] Logue also believed that construction of subsidized housing in suburbia was politically feasible. Soon after taking over UDC, he argued that it was "perfectly possible to develop a suburban-housing program for low-income families that will aid them while not threatening the character of the suburbs."

> The proposition is simple: build housing for low-income families, in groups of 40 to 50 houses, on the ample vacant land in suburban locations by providing exemptions from local zoning ordinances that perpetuate exclusiveness. . . .
>
> To make sure that there would not be an excessively large concentration in any one suburb, the number of such homes would be limited to five percent of the total local-housing supply. This would guarantee that no single community's character would be basically changed. . . .
>
> . . . Even with the five percent limitation, this program would have a very substantial impact. It would mean that anywhere from 20 percent to 50 percent of a city's low-income families could be rehoused within three years in such suburban colonies.
>
> This would be done without unbalancing suburban schools, without overcrowding suburban parks or unbalancing suburban tax rates. [136]

Logue, however, was not prepared to move into the suburbs with the boldness implied by his words. In the face of almost universal suburban resistance, his optimistic blueprint never got off the drawing board. Disclosure of possible UDC involvement in the development of subsidized housing provoked vehement and successful opposition in Rockland, Suffolk, and Westchester Counties. "Stop UDC" bumper stickers quickly appeared in Rockland, while the Islip Town Board on Long

Island sought to stop a proposed UDC housing project by having the land in question used for a county park. By 1972, Logue conceded that "the introduction, or threat of introduction of even modest numbers of attractively designed, low-rise dwelling units into areas previously restricted by local zoning has touched a sensitive local nerve which must raise serious questions about the feasibility of a metropolitan approach." [137]

Critics chided Logue for failing to use UDC's powers to override local zoning in order to force subsidized housing in recalcitrant suburbs. Suburban Action Institute complained that UDC was too concerned with local opposition and insufficiently troubled by suburban exclusion. "It is imperative" argued Paul Davidoff, "that housing be built now for low- and moderate-income families. But we know that no large number of houses can be built [without] great alteration of the present zoning regulations." [138] For his part, Logue insisted that UDC's desire to expand housing opportunities in the suburbs had to be weighed against the formidable political risks inherent in antagonizing suburbanites and their representatives in Albany. "If people want to say I'm too timid to go into the suburbs, I'll settle for that," Logue conceded in 1970. "But I feel that if I went into Scarsdale and started changing zoning laws, all my power would be stripped away." [139]

Logue's concerns about losing his powers were hardly imagined. Within a year of UDC's creation, suburban hostility was fueling efforts to check the new agency's ability to override local zoning and building controls. Legislation stripping UDC of its override was passed by the Assembly in 1969, 1970, and 1971. Each year, Governor Rockefeller was able to block these bills in the Senate. In 1972, as the Urban Development Corporation became more active and more controversial in the suburbs, ripper legislation passed both houses, forcing Rockefeller to employ his veto against a measure which, he asserted, "would weaken one of the most effective institutions available to meet the housing and economic needs of the State." [140]

In the face of these ominous portents, Logue sought to find suburban openings where the political risks could be minimized. Upstate metropolitan areas seemed to offer more promising terrain than the complex and highly differentiated suburban landscape of the New York region. Plans for new towns which included subsidized housing were developed for Amherst in the Buffalo area and Lysander on the outskirts of Syracuse. Following a local study which concluded that 45,000 units of low-cost housing were needed in the Rochester area, UDC and local interests jointly created UDC–Greater Rochester in mid-1970. The new organization quickly developed a five-year plan encompassing all eleven of Monroe County's suburban towns and calling for the construction of 5,500 subsidized units in the suburbs.

All of these activities stirred local opposition. In Amherst, for example, local officials vigorously protested the number of subsidized units planned by UDC, claiming that the community could not bear the fiscal burdens of housing which paid only ten percent of rental income in lieu of local taxes.[141] After Amherst brought pressure against UDC by filing a suit to block the project, the development corporation agreed to cut the number of subsidized units in half.[142] The loudest outcry against UDC came in the Rochester area where the scope and scale of the housing program developed by UDC–Greater Rochester directly affected far more suburbanites than was the case with the new towns proposed for Amherst and Lysander. Concern was expressed in the Rochester suburbs over the loss of local autonomy, changes in community character, and impact on local services and taxes. At meetings and public hearings, the familiar voices of suburbia were raised in opposition. One resident of Irondequoit served notice that: "We made the town what it is and will fight to keep it what it is," while another only wanted "to know how do we stop it? I don't want to know anything else about it." [143] A few miles away, a suburbanite didn't "want Penfield to become a low-cost development community. If I wanted that, I could move to the center city." [144] Racial animosity was muted in public, but lurked in the background in a metropolitan area which had experienced severe racial disorders during the 1960s. Speaking of the suburban opposition to UDC, an official of a local housing group noted that "people don't like to talk about it, but racism is responsible for a great deal of our trouble." [145]

Suburban officials were quick to capitalize on the issue. One mayor promised to seek "any legal means possible" to block UDC.[146] Another protested that the 250-unit project proposed for his town would cost local taxpayers $115,000: "All of us are well aware of the need for housing low and moderate income families, however, we do not feel that the citizens of any town, especially Irondequoit, where we have very little usable land left, should have to pay higher taxes to support this type of project." [147] In Greece, the largest suburb in the area, with a population of 75,000, the town board vehemently opposed a 550-unit project, both seeking state legislation to eliminate UDC's override and going to court in an unsuccessful effort to block UDC's actions with respect to the project.[148]

Despite local resistance, UDC–Greater Rochester prevailed in most suburbs. Two years after its inception, the housing plan was well on its way to being implemented, with approximately 3,000 of the 6,000 units under development in the suburbs by the end of 1972. In large part, UDC's success in Rochester resulted from the nature of the metropolis. Rochester was a medium-sized metropolitan area of less than a million residents in 1970. As in Dayton, the metropolitan community was relatively focused and cohesive. City-suburban differences were not as extreme as in many older and larger areas. One result of these characteristics was substantial suburban perception of metropolitan interdependence. At most public meetings on the housing plan, suburban voices were raised in support of UDC–Greater Rochester's proposals. "We must not allow Perinton to become a narrow, unrealistic slice of America," argued one suburbanite. "We must keep our doors open to those who have a little less. . . . The poor must have a chance. The young must have a better place to grow up than the ghetto." [149]

Another key factor was the existence of a cohesive business community which strongly supported the housing program. Unlike the situation in most metropolitan areas, Rochester's major employers were headquartered in the area and had strong local roots. In a metropolis the size of Rochester, giant international firms like Kodak and Xerox with a strong interest in local affairs have the potential to exercise substantial economic and political influence. UDC–Greater Rochester based its efforts on a blueprint developed by a committee chaired by a top executive from Xerox. Key business interests backed the creation of UDC–Greater Rochester, as did the area's major newspapers. Also important to the success of the housing program, particularly at the grass roots, was the cohesiveness of the area's group structure. Open-housing interests, civil-rights and church groups, the League of Women Voters, and other civic organizations were steadfast supporters of UDC–Greater Rochester's activities.

Last but certainly not least important in explaining UDC's success in Rochester was the agency's skill in developing its program. UDC–Greater Rochester assiduously built support among a wide range of officials, community groups, and local residents. During the winter of 1970–71, when the program was being shaped, meetings were held with state legislators, county officials, mayors, planning and zoning board members, municipal attorneys, educators, and other officials. Potential sites were discussed, as was project design. In some instances, adjustments were made on the basis of local concerns. Criticism from a local planning group in one community led to design changes, reduction in the number of bedrooms to lessen the impact on local schools, and increased parking spaces. Housing reserved for the elderly was doubled in another suburb. UDC–Greater Rochester officials also worked hard both to persuade suburban audiences of the need for moderately-priced housing in their communities and to quell local fears about an influx of lower-income outsiders. Suburbanites were assured that in such projects "nearly all of the new tenants come from the immediate area," and that there was "a definite need for such housing not only for minority groups . . . but for whites as well." As for the hordes of blacks at the back of most suburban minds, UDC–Greater Rochester expected "that about ten percent of each project" would be "inhabited by minority groups," but indicated "even that is being very optimistic." [150]

Reassurances and adjustments, however, were not sufficient to secure all of the targeted sites. Faced with unanimous opposition from the Irondequoit Town Board and school board, UDC–Greater Rochester dropped a 250-unit apartment project in an area zoned for single-family homes. UDC's override was not used, an official explained, because "the UDC local board is sensitive to local feelings. We have the powers (to go ahead), but we didn't want to use [it] because there was no local support." [151]

Despite the setback in Irondequoit, Rochester demonstrated that UDC's capabilities, skillful leadership tuned to local concerns, and a congenial setting could produce impressive results in the suburbs. At the same time that suburban housing barriers were falling in the Rochester area, however, UDC was embarking on a spectacularly unsuccessful effort to build subsidized housing in Westchester County. As in Irondequoit, UDC's ill-fated Nine Towns Program in Westchester underscored the dubious utility of the agency's override in the face of intense local opposition. Even more important, the Westchester campaign provoked legislative restrictions which substantially crippled any future activity by UDC in the suburbs, the outcome of suburban ventures always feared by Edward Logue.

From the beginning, the Urban Development Corporation was under no illusions concerning the political obstacles to building subsidized housing in Westchester County. Even the most tentative moves by the

agency stirred adverse local reactions. Early in 1970, Governor Rocke-
feller and Westchester's top elected official, County Executive Edwin G.
Michaelian, announced that the county and UDC would jointly develop
a comprehensive housing program. For inviting UDC into the county,
Michaelian was severely criticized by local officials and other spokesmen.
The following year, local opposition forced Manhattanville College to
withdraw a bid for UDC to help develop faculty housing in Harrison.
More than 500 local residents turned out to jeer Manhattanville and
UDC officials at a meeting which clearly indicated to one local official
that "U.D.C. doesn't belong in Harrison." [152] Resistance also was widespread to having UDC build 375 units of staff and student housing at the
Westchester campus of New York Medical College. As a result of these
reactions and pressures, UDC's initial activities in Westchester were confined to existing urban renewal projects in older communities such as
Yonkers and White Plains.

Neither Logue nor most of his staff, however, was satisfied with a
suburban program that dealt exclusively with salvaging urban-renewal
projects in a handful of urban jurisdictions. UDC was convinced that
housing opportunities needed to be developed in the newer portions of
the county. In these areas, open land was available, relocation and clear-
ance problems were minimal, job opportunities were multiplying, and
schools were better than in Westchester's older centers. Such considerations inevitably led UDC to focus on Westchester's sixteen towns, an
area which encompassed more than half of the county's land and a bit
less than thirty percent of its population. To succeed in these jurisdictions with their highly restrictive land-use controls, UDC needed an
approach that would attract sufficient political support to permit the use
of its override if necessary. In search of such backing, the agency developed a modest plan calling for the construction of only 100 units of subsidized housing in each of nine towns, with no more than one project per
school district.

By thinking small, UDC hoped to minimize the common suburban
perception of subsidized housing as a cause of massive community
change. UDC emphasized that the "Westchester Nine-Towns Program
is characterized by a smallness in scale rather than representing large
deviation from community values." [153] Conceding that the program's
"impact will be small in comparison to the need" which was estimated at
46,000 subsidized units by 1980, UDC was willing to settle for "a modest advance in the suburban housing supply." [154] UDC also promised

that local residents would have first priority in renting its housing, with local public employees, others employed locally, county residents, and nonresidents employed in Westchester receiving preferential treatment in that order. The final element in UDC's strategy was to propose projects simultaneously for nine of the towns. Through this "fair-share" approach, the agency hoped to avoid the political liabilities inherent in focusing on a particular community. As UDC assessed the situation, "no single town supervisor could allow himself to be in the position of accepting the UDC plan when all the other supervisors had managed to avoid it." [155] Thus, spreading the burden, and a very small burden at that, was seen as a means of enhancing the acceptability of subsidized housing in general.

Unfortunately for UDC, nothing worked as anticipated. Instead of spreading the burden, going into nine towns at once aggregated the opposition into a potent countywide political movement led by public officials that overwhelmed UDC. Three days after Logue revealed the targets of the Nine-Towns Program in June of 1972, United Towns for Home Rule was organized. Almost immediately, the organization raised over $20,000 to finance a crusade against the Urban Development Corporation. Angry opposition to UDC was voiced by congressmen, local officials, state legislators, and thousands of residents of the towns. Over 3,000 attended one emotional meeting; and opponents easily dominated the public hearings on UDC's proposed projects. As Logue later noted, the "intensity of the opposition was something to behold. . . . The clamor, the outrage, the anger—and, sadly—the hate displayed were disheartening." [156] Overwhelmed by its intensity were UDC's supporters in Westchester, whose ranks included Governor Rockefeller, County Executive Michaelian, the Builders Institute of Westchester and Putnam Counties, union leaders, newspapers in White Plains and a few other communities, the League of Women Voters and other civic groups, religious and civil-rights organizations, the Urban Coalition, the Regional Plan Association, and open-housing groups in most of the affected communities.

Nor did the modesty of UDC's proposal deflect much opposition. The Nine-Towns Program, suburban spokesmen insisted, was only an opening wedge. Once UDC had secured a foothold in Westchester with its small projects, opponents continued, thousands of subsidized dwellings would follow. Equally unconvincing to large numbers of suburbanites was UDC's contention that its priority system would minimize the influx of outsiders into the nine towns. Fear of inundation by city dwellers, welfare recipients, and blacks was rampant at public meetings. Like many of his neighbors, a resident of Bedford Hills wanted "to keep out those damn people . . . the scum from the cities." [157]

Compounding UDC's difficulties were the shortcomings of its own activities in Westchester. Some of the sites selected by the agency were extremely difficult to defend because of their isolation and lack of public facilities. Relatively little was done to educate the public about housing needs in the county. As one UDC official later confessed: "At the outset we failed adequately and persuasively to explain why this housing is needed. We did not make it clear enough who would occupy the housing." [158] Unlike its effort in Rochester, UDC's Westchester enterprise never developed a solid local base. To a degree this failure reflected the greater complexity of the New York area and Westchester County in comparison with Rochester and its suburbs. Westchester offered no equivalents to Kodak and Xerox to provide business support. UDC also failed to develop effective lines of communication with most local officials. Far less consultation took place than in Rochester, and little of what occurred was fruitful to either party. Underlying these difficulties was the hostility of many town officials toward UDC. A bad situation was made worse by UDC's insensitivity to the problems and perspectives of local elected officials. In the end, UDC failed to win the support or even the acquiescence of the key local officials in most of the nine towns.

For the opposition in Westchester, the issue was both subsidized housing and UDC's power to ignore local wishes by overriding land-use and building controls. With only one of UDC's sites in the nine towns zoned for apartments, Logue indicated that the agency would override local restrictions if necessary to build the projects. In response, UDC's foes rallied under the banner of local autonomy, organizing groups such as Harrison's Citizens for Local Control and the United Towns for Home Rule. They argued that the "Urban Development Corporation, with its unlimited power of real property condemnation and absolute capacity to ignore local authority, threatens an American heritage as old as our constitution itself—the right of every individual citizen to determine his or her community's destiny, growth, and future through locally elected and responsive officials." [159] By emphasizing local control, opponents sounded a powerful theme in suburbia, one that attracted both friends and foes of subsidized housing. Some indication of the appeal of local-control considerations to those favorably disposed to low-cost housing is provided by a survey conducted in Westchester for UDC in November 1972, when the campaign against the agency was at its peak. As shown in Table 10.1, 56 percent of the respondents in the nine towns favored locally developed projects, compared with only 44 percent who supported the UDC plan.

Table 10.1. Attitudes Toward the Development of 100 Units of Subsidized Housing by Local Government or UDC

	Residents of the Nine Towns			All Residents of Westchester		
	Favor	Oppose	Not Sure	Favor	Oppose	Not Sure
By Local Government	56	44	9	55	45	11
By UDC	44	51	5	45	43	12

Source: Oliver Quayle and Company, *A Study of Attitudes Toward Government Assisted Moderate and Low Income Housing in Westchester County,* Study #1546 (Brookville, N.Y., 1972), p. 111.

Local autonomy could be insured, insisted UDC's adversaries in Westchester, only by stripping the agency of its powers to override local zoning and building codes. To this end, the campaign against UDC centered on state legislators. With an election looming in November, incumbents and candidates rushed to get on the home-rule bandwagon with pledges to secure legislation limiting UDC. The public uproar over the Nine-Towns Plan also led the county's legislative delegation to seek immediate action in Albany. Fearful that Governor Rockefeller's strong support of his Urban Development Corporation would severely damage their party in November, Westchester's Republicans were eager to eliminate UDC as an election issue.

In response to these pressures, Logue first agreed to suspend UDC's activities in five of the towns where the opposition was most vociferous in order to permit consideration of alternative sites. Continued uproar at the grass roots led to a general postponement of the Nine-Towns Plan the following month. After meeting with Logue and Westchester legislators, Rockefeller announced a four-month moratorium. Ostensibly, the purpose of the delay was to permit individual communities to develop their own housing plans. According to the governor, "the Nine Towns should be given an opportunity to demonstrate their willingness to take [the] initiative . . . I would suggest to the supervisors that they, with the concurrence of their town boards, develop specific alternative housing proposals of their own to submit to UDC on or before January 15,

1973. During this period, UDC will hold in abeyance its Nine Towns program." [160]

In fact, the moratorium proved to be permanent even though six of the towns indicated a willingness to proceed with some form of subsidized housing. Bedford and Greenburgh accepted modified versions of UDC's original proposals, while Harrison, Lewisboro, North Castle, and Somers preferred to develop their own housing plans. The remaining communities, as well as large numbers of residents throughout the area, remained adamantly opposed. They were, in the words of New Castle's supervisor, prepared "to slug it out" with UDC.[161] For his part, Logue was ready to move ahead, including the use of UDC's override if necessary to secure the implementation of the plan in those communities which had not developed satisfactory alternatives. Logue, however, was whistling in the dark, since both the Nine-Towns Plan and UDC's suburban override were doomed once the legislature reconvened in Albany.

Faced with solid suburban support for limitations on UDC, most of which came from his own party, Governor Rockefeller bowed to the inevitable. As he later emphasized, "the strength of the opponents in support of the Westchester position was sufficient to make this an issue I had to deal with." [162] Failure to accommodate suburbia on the UDC issue threatened Rockefeller's political future, since he needed both his suburban political base and party support for another gubernatorial campaign or one last shot at the presidency. In the words of one supporter, the "Governor can't ride much longer with the UDC monkey on his back." [163] Nor could Rockefeller, despite his enormous resources and influence, afford open warfare with a substantial bloc of legislators, particularly when the votes in question were essential to Rockefeller's general program. For any political executive, as Logue pointed out, "there comes a time when such resistance distorts the legislative agenda." [164] Finally, Rockefeller and Logue were unwilling to jeopardize the entire UDC operation to preserve the agency's suburban override. Without limitations on UDC's powers, the legislature refused to authorize $500 million in additional bonding capacity needed to underwrite UDC's overall program. "We came to a situation where, in terms of the political realities," as Rockefeller conceded, "the votes were there to do much worse damage to U.D.C." [165]

With respect to UDC activities in the suburbs, the damage was substantial indeed. The legislation which Governor Rockefeller signed in

June 1973 gave suburbs more exclusionary authority than they had before the creation of UDC. Not only was the corporation's power to override zoning and building codes in towns and villages repealed, but these jurisdictions also were provided with a veto over UDC residential projects. Thus, UDC housing could be blocked even if in conformance with local zoning. UDC's powers in the cities were not changed by the new law, which one suburban legislator said was designed to bring UDC "back to . . . its original mission, aiding in the redevelopment of the state's inner cities." [166] Suburbanites hailed the legislation as a tremendous victory. For one newspaper on Long Island, the UDC bill was "without a doubt . . . the greatest accomplishment to come out of the State Legislature during this session" because "the individual citizen and the small municipality" no longer could be "stripped of their rights by big brother." [167] In Westchester, local governments swiftly used their new veto power to kill the Nine-Towns Plan.

Some UDC officials deemphasized the importance of the 1973 legislation, arguing that the local veto "will not essentially affect UDC operations since it has been normal practice in most cases to start with such assent." [168] Just how difficult such assent would be to obtain in the suburbs, however, was demonstrated on Long Island a few weeks after the local veto went into effect. UDC and a local community development corporation had proposed 182 units of subsidized housing for Wyandanch, a lower-income area with a substantial black population located within the Town of Babylon. The project was designed for local residents, with priority to be given to those displaced by public programs, Vietnam veterans, and residents of substandard dwellings in the community. Solid support existed for the project within Wyandanch, but it was strongly opposed elsewhere in Babylon. After almost 5,000 residents signed petitions against the project, the town board used its new power to veto the Wyandanch housing. Defeat in Babylon, along with recent events in Westchester and Albany, convinced Logue that UDC "will do less work in the suburbs than we expected." [169]

In fact, UDC was to do less work anywhere than either its supporters or detractors expected. During the months following the death of the Nine-Towns Program, financial problems mounted for the agency. Federal subsidies, which underwrote ninety percent of UDC's housing, were halted early in 1973 by the Nixon Administration. Rising interest rates sharply increased the cost of the money UDC borrowed to finance its projects. Delays in completing projects reduced the revenues available to meet the agency's financial obligations. UDC's financial difficulties reduced investor confidence in the corporation's "moral obligation" bonds, which were not backed by a clear-cut promise of state obligation in the case of default.[170] By the end of 1974, UDC was unable to generate sufficient income to support its debt service. UDC no longer could draw on the support of a powerful governor with substantial clout in the financial community, since Nelson A. Rockefeller had resigned as governor a year earlier.[171] With the major banks unwilling to advance additional funds, collapse came early in 1975 when UDC defaulted on $104.5 million in loan obligations. At the same time, Logue resigned under pressure from New York's new Democratic governor, Hugh L. Carey.

Complex negotiations produced a salvage operation designed to insure the completion of UDC's existing projects. Any new ventures in the cities or the suburbs by the nation's largest producer of subsidized housing, however, were highly problematical. As UDC's new chairman characterized the situation in 1975: "When a man is drowning, he doesn't worry where he'll take his next swim." [172] What did seem clear was that any phoenix arising from the ashes of UDC would be less venturesome, more politically constrained, and extremely unlikely to threaten suburbanites with unwanted subsidized housing.

Chapter Eleven

Whither an Open Society?

Of the many setbacks experienced by advocates of opening the suburbs, perhaps none was more sobering than the failure of New Yorks's Urban Development Corporation to overcome suburban opposition. UDC was a powerful and independent agency, with strong executive backing, substantial resources, and authority to override local zoning and building controls. Its enabling legislation was designed to provide "insulation from the occasional retributions that legislators might feel compelled, or be required by their constituents, to exact." [1] Despite capabilites greater than those of any other housing agency in the nation, UDC was unable to overcome suburban opposition. Suburban political influence is the fundamental reality of the politics of exclusion. The political clout of suburbia cannot easily be finessed by imaginative institutional engineering, at least not on an issue with the high stakes and emotional intensity of housing. As an official of UDC noted in the aftermath of the Nine Towns debacle: "We cannot hide from reality. UDC is a public, not a private agency. It cannot function effectively without being responsive to the will of the Governor and the Legislature that created it and to the attitudes of elected officials in the localities in which we work." [2]

Responsiveness to grass-roots interests is the central lesson of UDC's ill-fated encounter with suburbia, as well as of almost every effort to alter housing restrictions in the suburbs. These lessons, however, elude many foes of suburban exclusion who confidently insist that local recalcitrance can be overcome by the federal government, or the states, or metropolitan agencies. Those who look to Washington, the state capitals, or the metropolitan councils for support usually overlook the growing responsiveness of the higher levels of government to the expanding suburban plurality. The retreat of Congress and the federal executive from any substantial commitment to opening the suburbs, the failure of almost all of the states to restrict local land-use powers, and the reluctance of the most metropolitan councils to press for dispersed housing, all reflect sensitivity to suburban interests which severely limits the prospects of effective unilateral action from above.

For some who are optimistic about the prospects of opening the suburbs, the political significance of suburban growth is offset by the apparent convergence of cities and suburbs. Given the mushrooming of urban problems in suburbia, Nathaniel S. Keith believes that it is "unrealistic to assume that suburbs will remain large political enclaves by themselves, immune from the urban pressures which will generate demands for increased Federal aid, including housing and community development." In addition, he finds it "difficult to conceive how . . . exclusionary policies can long survive in the face of pressures from the central cities and of the suburbs' own demands for other Ferderal urban aids." [3] In fact, suburban exclusion has survived the diversification of suburbia quite well. Rather than diluting suburban insularity, continuing urbanization reinforces the desire of most suburbanites to employ local autonomy to protect themselves from the city, its people, and their problems. At the same time, mounting suburban political influence has secured larger shares of state and federal aid for suburbs without any substantial sacrifice of local control over land use and housing.

Inadequate attention to suburban political influence also leads many observers to characterize occasional breakthroughs in the suburbs as harbingers of more general changes which are bound to bring the walls of suburbia tumbling down. George Romney's policy initiatives, various court rulings, the creation of UDC, Dayton's fair-share plan, and the Massachusetts zoning appeals law have been seen as forerunners of sweeping alterations in suburban housing patterns. Illustrative of this tendency to overgeneralize from isolated events was an article entitled "The Coming Apart of Fortress Suburbia" written in early 1972 by Joseph Kraft, a knowledgeable political commentator. According to Kraft:

[Suburban] walls are beginning to crack. The crumbling process, which is going on all across the country, is perhaps the dominant feature of American political life today. And powerful outside agents speed the coming apart. For one thing, courts all over the country are upholding civil rights groups which challenge zoning and tax privileges. For another thing, Federal agencies, notably the Department of Housing and Urban Development, are pushing the suburbs to take on some of the burden of urban problems. [4]

As shown in the preceding chapters, developments which impressed Kraft in 1972 produced few significant changes in the suburbs. HUD's initiatives were checked by suburban political pressures, concern for suburban constituencies in the White House and Congress, and a lack of commitment to subsidized housing and social change in a conservative national administration. Courts, in fact, did not strike down local zoning "all over the country." Quite the contrary, the nation's top court strongly endorsed local zoning designed to preserve community character, upheld the use of local referendums for public housing, denied the existence of a fundamental right to housing, constrained the grounds for challenging local housing actions to explicit instances of racial discrimination, and severely limited access to federal courts by those excluded from suburbia. Few state courts have imposed significant restrictions on suburban land-use controls. Only New Jersey's supreme court has directly confronted suburban exclusion by mandating affirmative local action to insure the availability of land for a wide range of housing types. The court in New Jersey, however, also has emphasized the limited power of judges to insure the actual expansion of housing opportunities in the suburbs. And the hostility of the New Jersey legislature to zoning reform underscores the difficulties of translating judicial rulings into effective public policies in the face of suburban dedication to the preservation of the status quo.

Clearly, policy change on an issue as controversial as suburban exclusion requires substantial political support. Almost everywhere, such support has been lacking. Surveying the wreckage of his Westchester venture, Edward J. Logue bleakly concluded: "There is no constituency in the United States today of any consequence for opening up the suburbs." [5] Blacks or whites, the poor or affluent, city dwellers or suburbanites, none provide much backing for the handful of dedicated opponents of suburban exclusion. The excluded typically lack awareness of the complex processes which limit their housing opportunities. They also lack influence, particularly in the jurisdictions that exclude lower-income families. Many blacks question whether opening the suburbs is worth the effort, especially since dispersing the poor threatens to undermine their political base in the older cities. Leaders in the central cities, suburban employers, the housing industry, and others who might benefit from opening the suburbs tend to be internally divided on the issue, or to have more pressing concerns, or to lack influence in relevant political arenas. Support from affluent suburbanites with an interest in open housing is insufficient to produce change in most jurisdictions, and has been undercut by the growth of environmental concerns which affect suburban interests more directly than housing the disadvantaged.

Suburban exclusion also has failed to attract much attention from liberals and civil-rights supporters more generally. On issues such as voting rights and anti-discrimination measures, backing from national labor, religious, civil-rights, and allied interests often offsets local opposition, particularly in Washington. In part, the failure of suburban exclusion to mobilize widespread support from this quarter lies in the issue itself. As Geoffrey Sheilds and L. Sanford Spector point out, "the inherent nature of exclusionary zoning is less shocking or appalling than acts such as prison brutality or abuse of migrant workers which have formed the nucleus of many liberal causes." [6] Nor is suburban zoning as unambiguous an issue for defenders of civil rights as restrictions aimed directly at blacks. Instead, "restrictive land-use practices discriminate directly against the poor and 'only' indirectly against racial minorities. American society embraces the concept that distinctions based on wealth are normal and even desirable as incentives, while it generally disdains overt racial discrimination." [7]

Liberal support for opening the suburbs also was eroded by the deterioration of the civil-rights coalition during the late 1960s and early 1970s. Whites were alienated by the assertive quest of blacks for self-determination, as well as by the waning commitment of a new generation of black leaders to integration. White supporters were lost when the locus of civil-rights concerns shifted from the legally-segregated south to the spatially-separated north. Opening the suburbs, like desegregating schools in Denver or the Detroit area, comes uncomfortably close to home for many liberals. Finally, liberal confidence in social reform was shaken by the seemingly meager results of past victories, as well as by declining faith in centralized authority and presidential power in the wake of Vietnam and Watergate.

The absence of widespread political support has strongly influenced efforts to open the suburbs. The most active opponents of suburban exclusion lack a substantial constituency base, particularly among those elements of the population which would benefit from zoning and housing reforms. Civil-rights and fair-housing groups as Shields and Spector note, "are subject to review neither by their clientele—composed of discrete and unrelated local organizations—nor by their ultimate constituencies, the minority groups and the poor, with whom litigators rarely deal until their concerns have ripened into justiciable controversies." [8]

At least in part because of the weak articulation of political support, these groups have concentrated most of their energies on the courts, the policy arena most insulated from constituency pressures.

Is Opening the Suburbs Worth the Effort?

Considering the widespread opposition, lack of support from most of the excluded, and meager results from past efforts, one can reasonably ask whether opening suburbs is worth the trouble. Just listing "the range of strategies and tactics that would be necessary to implement a substantial level of movement of poor into the suburbs" leads Nathan Glazer to conclude that "the task is impossible." [9] In light of the formidable political and financial constraints encountered at every turn, perhaps those concerned with racial and economic disparities in the metropolis would be better advised to focus their political resources on aspects of public policy which promise more success and thus more benefits to the disadvantaged. Despite endorsing the use of housing programs "to break down income and racial discrimination," Robert Taggert believes that subsidized housing will have to be concentrated in the older cities in the future as in the past. "Subsidy programs," he argues, "should not be placed in the vanguard of the effort to break down housing discrimination, since they would undoubtedly be the first casualty." [10]

As indicated in chapter 6, some skeptics go further, questioning whether the urban poor would benefit even from successful efforts to open the suburbs. From this perspective, whites are seen as benefitting more than blacks from the easing of suburban exclusion. White city dwellers would be more likely than blacks to have the economic resources to take advantage of expanding housing opportunities in the suburbs. Unlike blacks, whites would not face racial barriers to moving outward. With whites predominating among those leaving the city, blacks would become more concentrated in the urban core. The higher proportion of blacks, and especially poor blacks, in the older cities would encourage even more whites and middle-class blacks to flee to the suburbs, as well as further reducing the attractions of central-city locations for industry and commerce. Thus, opening the suburbs is seen as accelerating rather than checking the process that has created the bifurcated metropolis. [11]

Instead of futile efforts to open the suburbs, many spokesmen for older cities want resources focused in the urban centers. Priority should be given, they argue, to housing in older neighborhoods and to attracting jobs back to the city. Another advantage of dealing with the poor within the confines of the city, in the view of some observers, is the availability of "excess housing, schools, hospitals, and transportation facilities [in] the declining cities," all of which would have to be built if large numbers of city dwellers were to be dispersed to the suburbs.[12] Advocates of concentrating resources in the cities invoke environmental and energy concerns to bolster their case, pointing to the profligate consumption of land and fuel inherent in the decentralized pattern of suburban development. "Urban conservation" became the dominant theme of the central cities in the mid-1970s, with leaders like Mayor Thomas Bradley of Los Angeles condemning "growth and unrestrained consumption" as "two deadly time bombs we have to deactivate if our cities are to survive."[13] Strong support for these views also came from Washington, with Secretary of Housing and Urban Development Carla A. Hills telling the nation's mayors in 1975 that "we can no longer tolerate policies which encourage the abandonment and waste of the central city" because "recycling cities is far less costly than suburban development in terms of capital, land, energy, and ecological costs."[14]

Proponents of urban conservation also contend that demographic and social trends no longer favor suburbanization. They see declining birth rates, smaller families, and more childless households increasing the proportion of Americans likely to be attracted to urban rather than suburban environments. Mayor Moon Landrieu of New Orleans believes "people are looking for reasons to come back to the cities, and we should encourage this interest."[15]

Environmental concerns, rising energy costs, and changing social patterns seem certain to stimulate more intensive settlement patterns, but not in the inner city. None of these developments are likely to offset the manifest disabilities of the older cities—an aging and deteriorating housing stock, large concentrations of minorities and the disadvantaged, poor schools and other public services, disproportionate tax burdens, and high crime rates. Anthony Downs thinks:

> It is unrealistic to expect that the energy shortage is going to have much effect upon poor ghetto neighborhoods. The millions of middle-class households—black and white—that have fled these areas are not going to move back to avoid higher commuting costs. Nor are white households who do not want to live in majority black neighborhoods likely to change because of gasoline troubles.[16]

Thus, apartments and town houses are likely to continue to be built in the suburbs and sections of the city which offer attractive sites insulated from lower-income areas.

Jobs as well as neighborhood considerations will draw most of these new multifamily units outward rather than inward—jobs in industrial parks, shopping centers, and office complexes. Surely no one expects energy and environmental considerations to lead to the abandonment of the massive investment made in new suburban factories, stores, and offices during the past quarter century. Nor are rising fuel and land costs likely to alter significantly the locational factors which have been pulling industry and commerce outward. To be sure, peripheral sites should become less attractive than closer-in suburban locations. But the overall trend of jobs will be outward rather than inward, and this continuing economic decentralization will draw population outward in the future as in the past.

Moreover, rising energy costs will enhance the attractiveness of suburban residential locations for those with jobs in suburbia. Minimization of the journey to work is a rational response to increasing gasoline prices. Relocation, however, is a viable strategy only for those able to afford housing in the suburbs. Suburban workers already locked in the inner city by low income or racial prejudice are bound to be further disadvantaged by mounting travel costs. And city dwellers seeking jobs in the suburbs will find their access to economic opportunity even more limited. Continued economic decentralization combined with rising travel costs clearly raises serious questions about the advisability of concentrating housing efforts in the older cities, particularly in larger metropolitan areas where the distances between inner-city residences and suburban jobs are substantial.

One way out of this dilemma, strongly adovcated by proponents of urban conservation, lies in developing more employment within cities for their lower-income residents. The trouble with this answer is that economic development efforts are not likely to generate much new employment, particularly for semiskilled and unskilled workers. Older cities do not command the resources to reverse the decentralization of the metropolitan economy. There is little most can do about the lack of suitable sites for industrial jobs, high local taxes, crime, and other disadvantages. Nor do city governments exercise much direct control over the location of jobs. And despite rhetoric about conserving the cities, federal or state government is highly unlikely to impose significant constraints on the location of private enterprise. At best, relatively modest gains can be expected from aggressive efforts to attract jobs to older cities. Much of this employment, moreover, will be in white-collar jobs more likely to be filled by suburbanites than by the urban poor.

Another possible solution to the problem of the separation of jobs and residences is public transportation. Unfortunately, existing transit systems rarely link inner-city residential areas with scattered job locations in the suburbs. Even the newest transit networks are poorly designed for this purpose. The rail lines of the Bay Area Rapid Transit District "do not provide stations which will serve a number of the low-income minority communities. The system rather serves suburban commuters very much like a suburban railroad system. Secondly, the system is not providing stations at those points of low-income jobs . . . so it serves neither the origins nor destinations adequately for low-income minority people." [17]

Little success has been encountered with special transit programs designed to improve bus service between ghetto residences and suburban jobs. Experiments in Boston, Los Angeles, New York, Oakland, Washington, and other areas attracted few riders. Common problems have been long trips, inconvenient service, inadequate connections of origins and destinations, and limited awareness on the part of potential users of the services. Such efforts also are politically vulnerable. In the Philadelphia area, a plan to bus inner-city blacks to suburban industrial parks developed by the Southeastern Pennsylvania Transportation Authority was killed by suburban representatives who "opposed the plan despite the interest of would-be employers. The political pressure against bringing in the poor black workers was too strong." [18]

Obviously, building more moderately priced housing in the suburbs will not solve the transportation problems inherent in linking residences and widely-dispersed job sites. Public transportation services within suburbia are limited at best. Most lower-income workers employed in the suburbs would continue to depend on automobiles for the journey to work. Trip lengths and fuel costs, however, would be shorter. In addition, locating lower-cost housing in the vicinity of suburban employment concentrations would enhance the prospects for developing public transport links between suburban residences and jobs. As Anthony Downs points out, "drastically reducing the basic commuting distance would surely simplify the problem" of public transportation in the suburbs, "making it possible to find solutions with less public investment." [19] An expansion of working-class housing in the suburbs combined with more extensive public transportation also would make suburban employment opportunities accessible to other members of lower-income families.

Perhaps the most serious flaw in emphasizing urban conservation is the relationship between revitalizing the city and dispersing the poor. As long as the poor and minority groups are forced to live in the urban core, most cities cannot easily attract a wider range of people and activities. "Housing mobility," argue Paul and Linda Davidoff, "must be increased in order to relieve the central cities of the impossible burden of providing adequate housing with the limited available resources." [20] "We must attract moderate- and upper-income people back because you can't survive with a town of poor people" argues an official of one impoverished city. "Poor people can't support poor people." [21] Unless housing opportunities in the suburbs are expanded, fiscal, economic, and racial disparities between older cities and newer suburbs will continue to increase. Rising taxes and increasing poverty burdens will compromise efforts to retain and attract economic development. Without some loosening of the suburban noose, seven million more blacks will be concentrated in central cities by 1985, while over ninety percent of all urban whites will be living in the suburbs. More than ninety percent of the children in the public schools of Baltimore, Chicago, Cleveland, Detroit, Newark, New Orleans, Philadelphia, St. Louis, and Washington will be black. The combination of these trends and the reluctance of most courts to transcend city limits in desegregating public schools largely confines the agonizing conflict over integration to central cities, further reducing the attractions of older cities to existing and prospective residents and employers.

In reality, neither urban conservation nor dispersal alone provides an adequate base for national housing policy. New housing certainly will have to be constructed in the core, since even the most ambitious suburban housing program could satisfy neither the needs nor the desires of inner-city residents. Sites for such housing in cities, however, are likely to be acquired more easily if moderate-cost housing is available in the suburbs, thus reducing the pressures on the city's limited supply of land. Moreover, any program involving substantial amounts of new construction must turn to the suburbs, as the Section 235 and 236 programs did. Most new housing will be built on vacant land, which is more available and less expensive in the suburbs and outer city neighborhoods. As President Johnson's Task Force on Suburban Problems emphasized, "Suburbia is where the land is: it is where the home building industry concentrates; it is where land is still available at prices lower than in the city and often in vast quantities. . . . Any national housing policy must rest in large measure on expanding the housing stock in the suburbs." [22] Last, but hardly least important, housing in the newer areas of the metropolis usually offers distinct locational advantages over similar units sited in ghettos. Housing is more than shelter. "The location of one's place of residence," the President's Committee on Urban Housing emphasized in 1968, "determines the accessibility and quality of many everyday advantages taken for granted by the mainstream of American society. Among these commonplace advantages are public educational facilities for a family's children, adequate police and fire protection, and a decent surrounding environment." [23]

What Might Be

Political constraints are the principal obstacle to increasing housing opportunities in the suburbs. In the view of one city housing official, "getting low-income housing up isn't a great trick or great mystery . . . it is a question of will. . . . We could house all the poor in Baltimore in the surrounding areas in three years without stretching our backs." [24] Were the political will available, the United States unquestionably has the resources, skills, and ingenuity to expand the supply of lower-cost housing in the newer portions of the metropolis.

Measures aimed at increasing income are the starting point for any effort to improve housing for the poor. Inadequate income is the principal barrier to exercising choice in housing. As a result, income differences are the most important factor underlying spatial separation in the metropolis. Income may be supplemented through general programs, such as a negative income tax or guaranteed employment, or through funds earmarked for housing in the form of rent subsidies or housing allowances. Increased income would permit poorer families to broaden choices in terms both of housing quality and location. Advocates of income approaches also contend that lower-income households would be freed from their dependence on subsidized housing. With more income available for housing, they foresee the private sector replacing subsidized producers. Reliance on the private housing market is seen as having the additional advantage of avoiding the problems inherent in securing local consent for the siting of subsidized projects. Since recipients of income supplements would be indistinguishable from others in the housing market, they presumably would filter into neighborhoods gradually rather than arrive *en masse* as is the case when housing is constructed specifically for the poor.

Despite the extravagant claims of some supporters of housing allowances, increased income is not likely to expand housing opportunities in the suburbs without a parallel effort aimed at increasing the production of lower-cost housing. "The housing allowance is only part of a good idea," argues Chester W. Hartman, because "it takes no steps to ensure that market conditions will be such that the low-income consumer can truly have free choice or satisfaction. Under the present realities of housing conditions and the housing market, freedom of choice can only be enhanced by more government intervention, not less." [25] None of the income-maintenance or housing-allowance plans developed during the early 1970s came close to providing recipients with sufficient income to afford newly-constructed private housing in the suburbs. Unless more lower-cost housing is produced in the suburbs and outlying sections of the central cities, income supplements have to be used primarily within the urban core. In an experiment funded by HUD in Kansas City, only a handful of more than two hundred recipients of housing allowances moved beyond the fringe of the ghetto, although almost all improved their housing.[26] Moreover, in tight metropolitan housing markets as are found in much of the northeast, housing allowances without increased production can only inflate the prices of existing housing in deteriorating areas. "The law of supply and demand makes the outcome very predictable" for an official in New York. "The rent levels of existing worn out housing will go up." [27]

Expanding the production of lower-cost housing in the suburbs involves both easing local zoning restrictions and allocating substantial construction subsidies to suburban areas. In the absence of zoning reforms in the suburbs, as Herbert M. Franklin points out, "local land use and building controls that inflate housing costs and otherwise frustrate the provision of an adequate supply will continue to exert the same negative influence with any likely housing allowance system." [28] Easing of zoning, building, and subdivision restrictions would permit private entrepreneurs to construct more small houses on small lots, a larger number of less expensive apartments and townhouses, multi-family dwellings with more bedrooms per unit, and mobile and factory-built homes. Changes in local land-use control also are necessary to facilitate the location of subsidized units in suburban areas.

Liberalization of local land-use and housing policies need not involve the destruction of local autonomy. The issue in zoning reform, as David M. Trubek has emphasized, "is to figure out how to make local autonomy compatible with the general welfare." [29] The answer lies in requiring local governments to take cognizance of a broader range of interests than those of the dominant majority within a particular community. The goal—to be achieved by local action, changes in state enabling legislation, federal requirements under the Housing and Community Development Act of 1974, or court orders—are local controls which are inclusionary rather than exclusionary. Herbert M. Franklin, David Falk, and Arthur J. Levin have defined an inclusionary land-use program as one which "includes the development of low- and moderate-income housing among many and often conflicting values to be served by local government." [30] Zoning and building regulations which do not inflate housing prices are an essential element in inclusionary policies. In addition, Franklin, Falk, and Levin believe an inclusionary program should include "procedures to assure that sufficient land is available at times and locations for the type of structures needed to fulfill housing objectives," as well as "a publicized official statement of community policy to signify to public and private developers and to the public in general that the community is receptive to a reasonable amount of housing development for low- and moderate-income families." [31]

Within such an inclusionary framework, localities should be able to zone for various kinds of development, plan for the future, determine their growth pattern, and otherwise use local authority to advance the values of their citizens. In a ruling which stressed the need both for inclusionary zoning and the maintenance of local autonomy, the New Jersey Supreme Court insisted:

> There is no reason why developing municipalities like Mount Laurel . . . may not become and remain attractive, viable communities providing good living and adequate services for all their residents in the kind of atmosphere which a democracy and free institutions demand. They can have industrial sections, commercial sections, and sections for every kind of housing from low cost and multifamily to lots of more than an acre with very expensive homes. Proper planning and governmental cooperation can prevent overintensive and too sudden development, insure against future subur-

ban sprawl and slums, and assure the preservation of open space and local beauty.[32]

Inclusionary zoning is only part of the answer to increasing the production of lower-cost housing in the suburbs. With eased zoning restrictions, private builders could serve a broader market than presently exists in most suburban areas. Rising construction costs and other factors, however, price most of this housing, with the possible exception of mobile homes, beyond the reach of a large majority of the families likely to qualify for general income supplements or housing allowances. Meeting these lower-income needs in units located in the suburbs necessitates federal subsidies to producers as well as consumers of housing. Fair-share plans, inclusionary zoning, state housing efforts, and implementation of court orders depend heavily on the availability of federal subsidies for new housing. All of these efforts faltered when federal aid was halted in 1973. None are likely to have any significant impact on suburban housing opportunities in the absence of housing programs similar to those established in 1968, which aimed at the annual production of 600,000 subsidized units and actually produced almost 450,000 new units in 1971.

Another important element in the production of subsidized housing is state programs. Funds from housing finance agencies played a key role in the development of Section 236 housing in some states. Action by the states also is needed to create public development agencies capable of capitalizing on the opportunities made available by eased zoning restrictions and increased federal funds. Such agencies should be empowered to develop as well as finance subsidized housing, through the selection and acquisition of sites, design and construction of housing, and the provision of community facilities. The most important lesson to be learned from New York's Urban Development Corporation is that UDC produced more subsidized housing than any other housing agency during its brief tenure. The need is for more effective financing arrangements, not less effective state housing and development agencies. "The real gut issue of UDC," the *New York Times* insisted, is "that it embraced a long-term social program in many ways not susceptible to conventional short-term financing." [33]

To insure that subsidized housing actually is built in the suburbs, allocation formulas for federal and state funds should be designed to promote dispersal. Relatively heavy weight should be placed on both

employment trends and the availability of sites. In assessing the suit-
ability of potential locations, schools, sewers, public transportation, and
other local facilities and services need to be taken into account. Political
reality, pressing human needs, and the objective of maximizing housing
choices necessitate that factors promoting the dispersal of subsidized
units be balanced against the housing needs of existing residents in order
to insure that older cities are guaranteed a substantial share of the available federal and state funds.

Political considerations also dictate that suburbs be provided some
protection against concentrations of subsidized housing, apartments, and
mobile homes. So do concerns for community character and the adequate provision of local facilities and services. Richard F. Babcock and
Fred P. Bosselman, strong foes of exclusionary zoning, insist that plans
for opening the suburbs "maintain a reasonable amount of types of housing in each community and not exceed a hypothetical tipping point.
Moreover, some assurance needs to be given to local communities that
the 'reasonable' number of apartments or mobile homes they might be
willing to accept is not the nose of the camel—the advance guard of an
inundation that will turn the community rapidly into a suburban
slum." [34] Quotas also have been supported as essential in fixing the
inclusionary obligations of the local community. Minimum and maximum housing allocations, argues David Trubek, provide a framework
for both local action and oversight by metropolitan, state, or federal
agencies. [35]

Anthony Downs pushes the case for quotas further, contending that
limitations on lower-income and minority families are required to insure
the continued dominance of white middle- and upper-income households
within individual suburban communities. Downs' strong support for
class and racial quotas results from his belief that affluent suburbanites
will accept inclusionary housing policies only under conditions that do
not threaten their life style, values, or vital interests:

> Most middle- and upper-income households want to live where they are
> personally safe, where their homes are safe and at least maintain initial eco-
> nomic values, and where their children are exposed to cultural value-rein-
> forcing experiences (mainly with children from other middle-income house-
> holds). These considerations create neighborhood viability for them. None
> would be seriously weakened by the presence of some low- and moderate-in-
> come households in the area. Hence middle- and upper-income households
> can attain their basic residential objectives through *dominance* of their neigh-

borhoods and do not require *total exclusion* of low- and moderate-income households.[36]

To guarantee the dominance of present residents, Downs favors small and scattered housing projects, low quotas for individual communities, and the screening of prospective tenants "to limit the percentage of multiproblem households among those entering middle-income areas." [37] Moreover, to secure "stable, racially integrated neighborhoods," he advocates "a workable mechanism [to insure] that whites will remain in a majority—such as some type of quota system—that is both legal and credible." [38]

Certainly Downs' concerns are far from trivial. As the preceding chapters amply illustrate, suburbanites strongly resist subsidized housing because they want to maintain their values and interests. Small and isolated housing projects undoubtedly are more acceptable in suburbia than large concentrations of lower-income and minority families, although no subsidized housing is even more preferable. Whites unfortunately do flee from the path of blacks, thus guaranteeing the perpetuation of segregated residential patterns. Nonetheless, opening the suburbs does not necessitate the degree of socio-economic integration postulated by Downs, especially since his approach threatens to reduce rather than expand housing opportunities in the suburbs, particularly for minority families. Racial quotas inevitably restrict housing opportunities for blacks because of white behavior. The purpose of opening the suburbs is to widen rather than limit the freedom of choice among locations for lower-income and minority families. Some surely will choose communities dominated by more affluent suburbanites, and opportunities to exercise such choices should be provided by housing allocation plans. Others, however, are likely to prefer working-class communities, or suburbs with substantial concentrations of one or another minority group. Such preferences also deserve respect. Within a general framework which opens suburban areas for lower-cost housing, some income, ethnic, and racial clustering is compatible with the overall objective of expanding housing and economic opportunities in the growing portions of the metropolis. Unlike the existing concentrations in the urban core, whatever suburban clusters emerged would be smaller and more dispersed, and most important, would provide better housing and improved access to jobs.

Blacks and other minorities will not be able to exercise housing choices throughout the metropolis on the same basis as whites, however, unless discrimination in housing is significantly reduced. Housing allowances cannot maximize freedom of choice as long as blacks are excluded from substantial portions of the metropolitan housing market. The importance of coupling effective fair-housing efforts with increased production of lower-cost housing was underscored by the limited access of blacks to housing built in the suburbs under the Section 235 and 236 programs. Extensive national commitments to open housing exist on paper, but have not been fulfilled in practice. Title VIII of the Civil Rights Act of 1968 barred discrimination in the sale and rental of approximately eighty percent of the nation's housing. During the same year, the Supreme Court interpreted an 1866 law as prohibiting racial discrimination in all housing.[39] Two-thirds of the states and hundreds of local jurisdictions have enacted fair-housing laws. Notwithstanding these expanding legal guarantees of equal treatment in the quest for shelter, "two housing markets" continue to exist as the U.S. Commission on Civil Rights concluded in 1974, "one for whites and another for blacks, Mexican Americans, Puerto Ricans, or whatever racial or ethnic group comprises a large and subordinated minority in the particular metropolitan area." [40]

Fair-housing laws cannot deliver on their promise of equal access to housing without more commitment to vigorous enforcement. Most fair-housing agencies have been inadequately financed and staffed. Enforcement powers often are narrowly prescribed. Under the 1968 civil-rights legislation, HUD cannot compel compliance with its regulations. Instead, open-housing officials rely on persuasion or lawsuits initiated by the Department of Justice. Almost everywhere, fair-housing laws are enforced primarily through the investigation of individual complaints, an approach which the Civil Rights Commission terms "the least effective way to enforce the law. Families that complain of housing discrimination cannot be assured of immediate relief." [41] Further reducing the probability of effective relief are the delays involved in processing cases, with HUD taking more than five months to handle the average complaint in 1973.[42] More attention must be given to positive approaches aimed at general patterns of discrimination. Some efforts along these lines have been made by local and state agencies, as well as by HUD with its communitywide patterns and practices reviews and affirmative marketing plans. Implementation of these innovations by HUD, however, has been plagued by hesitancy on the part of top officials, shortages of staff and funds, and inadequate monitoring and review of programs.[43]

Fair-housing programs also need to confront block-busting, red-lining, and other practices which accelerate white flight and foster the continued racial segregation of the metropolis. More generally, both the necessity and the feasibility of white flight should be reduced by the combined impact of the metropolitan housing program that has been outlined. Taken together, income supplementation, inclusionary zoning, greater production of lower-cost housing, allocation of housing subsidies across the metropolis, and strict enforcement of open-housing laws will broaden the housing choices available to blacks. At the same time, the dispersal of lower-income and minority households throughout suburbia will drastically reduce the number of white sanctuaries in the metropolis. As Dale Bertsch of the Miami Valley Regional Planning Commission has emphasized, one of the most important reasons for "opening the suburbs [is] to tell the . . . affluent that there *is* no place they can escape to." [44]

Large-scale development also can contribute to opening suburbia to lower-income families. Developers of large projects are more likely to engage in affirmative marketing than the typical small suburban builder. They also, as Downs emphasizes, "have more economic 'elbow room' for low- and moderate-income units that are less profitable than market-oriented units." [45] New towns and planned-unit developments usually have a mix of housing types, which more easily accommodates subsidized units than the traditional suburban subdivision or garden-apartment project. As one study notes, "harmonious blending of different price houses is far easier when a project is planned as a whole, free of inflexible rules that each house must satisfy." [46]

By itself, however, large-scale development does not guarantee the construction of housing for poor or minority families. In New Jersey, for example, planned-unit developments have resulted in no appreciable increase in the supply of lower-cost housing or the number of blacks in newer suburban communities.[47] Most of the privately developed new towns, such as Irvine in Southern California, include no low-cost housing.[48] Nor do good intentions insure the construction of lower-income units. The developers of Columbia, which lies between Baltimore and Washington, originally planned to provide ten percent of the new town's housing in subsidized units scattered throughout the community. Dwindling federal subsidies after 1973 combined with rapidly rising construction costs to cut the proportion of lower-income dwellings to under five percent by 1975.

To realize the potential of large-scale development for increasing housing opportunities in the suburbs, both housing subsidies and incentives for their use are required. One approach is to require developers to include a certain proportion of lower-income units in their projects. As noted in chapter 5, mandatory low-cost housing plans have been developed by Fairfax and Montgomery Counties in the Washington area. The Montgomery ordinance applied to all developments of fifty or more units; Fairfax's was limited to multifamily projects with at least fifty dwellings. Both suburban counties required developers to reserve at least fifteen percent of the homes for lower-income families. In return for including lower-cost housing, developers were permitted to increase residential densities by as much as twenty percent over that authorized. Through the end of 1975, the practicality of this promising approach remained untested, as court challenges, inadequate federal subsidies, and sewer moratoriums prevented implementation in either county.[49]

Another means of stimulating the construction of subsidized housing was provided in the early 1970s by federal efforts to spur the development of new towns. In return for federal loan guarantees and other assistance, developers of new communities agreed to include a significant number of subsidized housing units. The original plans for five federally-supported new towns on the outskirts of metropolitan areas called for the construction of 34,000 subsidized units, or 27 percent of the 126,000 dwellings planned for the communities.[50] Few of these new towns, however realized their potential for increasing housing opportunities. With their heavy initial outlays for land acquisition and infrastructure development, new towns proved particularly vulnerable to rapidly rising interest rates and construction costs. Mounting fuel prices added to the woes of the typical new town located on the outer metropolitan fringe. The developer of Jonathan, the first of fifteen new towns financed by HUD, defaulted on its federally guaranteed loan and no longer was building homes for lower-income families or anyone else. Only a few subsidized units were built at Jonathan, and they were "isolated from and distinctly inferior in design to the rest of the development."[51]

Complicating the difficulties of new-town developers has been the common problem of federal rhetoric outrunning commitment and resources. HUD provided little of the promised technical assistance and infrastructure aid, but supplied substantial amounts of red tape. Like other recipients of housing assistance, developers of new towns learned that federal decisions "are made, unmade, and obfuscated to a degree that makes the imperial Chinese bureaucracy appear decisive and swift-moving." [52] Early in 1975, HUD stopped accepting applications for new towns, thus ending another federal program which promised much but delivered little in the way of expanded housing choices for lower-income families.

In addition to programs designed to increase housing opportunities, opening the suburbs requires fiscal policies which reduce the local burdens associated with lower-income families. Federal assumption of the full costs of poverty-related programs would remove some of the fiscally-based objections to the dispersal of lower-income households into the suburbs. Equally important is state tax reform to weaken the connection between local wealth and the financing of public education, a link which constitutes one of the strongest fiscal rationales for excluding apartments, small houses, mobile homes, and subsidized projects. Pressures to reduce the disparities which result from relying heavily on local property taxes to finance public education have come primarily from the state courts. In 1971 the California Court ruled that dependence on local taxes to underwrite two-thirds of public-school costs "invidiously discriminated against the poor [by making] the quality of a child's education a function of the wealth of his parents and neighbors." [53] Courts in Michigan, New Jersey, and other states followed California's lead, calling for sweeping changes in the methods of financing public education. [54] Although the U.S. Supreme Court ruled in 1973 that local differences in tax resources to support education did not deny equal protection, [55] a growing list of states enacted programs which increased the state share of educational finance, and thus reduced the burdens associated with unprofitable residents and development.

Fiscal changes by themselves, however, are not likely to produce significant changes in suburban housing policies. Existing variations in the allocation of financial responsibilities between state and local governments have little apparent effect on the distribution of lower-income families in metropolitan areas. [56] Nor do local officials indicate much inclination to associate tax reform with eased housing restrictions. Only six percent of the respondents in a survey of suburban planning board officials in New Jersey indicated a willingness to lower minimum lot sizes in the event of a substantial reduction in local property taxes, and only eight percent were agreeable to more apartments in the wake of tax reform.[57] Short of full state and federal financing of all local services, certain kinds of housing and residents are bound to be more attractive fiscally than others. Moreover, as the preceding chapters illustrate again and again, financial considerations rarely are the sole or even the primary factors which lead suburbanites to develop and maintain exclusionary policies.

Nonetheless, school-tax and other fiscal reforms are essential to reduce the financial rationale for the maintenance of zoning and other housing barriers. Paul and Linda Davidoff argue that "one of the advantages of ridding the debate about land controls of the fiscal issue is that it would rob discrimination of a cloak to hide behind." [58] David Trubek agrees, noting that "until the 'fiscal smoke screen' is eliminated there is little hope that the real issues which underlie suburban exclusion can be brought to the surface." [59] More equitable arrangements for financing education and other local services, then, are both an essential complement and a political requisite to the development of policies directly aimed at broadening housing opportunities in the suburbs.

Also needed are direct federal and state financial incentives for communities which adopt and implement inclusionary housing policies. Such programs need not directly "punish" communities which fail to meet their housing obligations, as would be the case with proposals to withhold funds from exclusionary localities. Instead, federal and state policy should be weighted toward rewarding those communities which open their doors. Within categorical programs, localities which are meeting their housing obligations should be assigned priority in the allocation of funds for local roads, sewers, parks, and the like. Under revenue-sharing and block grants, bonuses could be awarded to qualifying jurisdictions. In addition, housing-impact programs should be developed by Washington and the states to assist local jurisdictions in providing additional local services and facilities necessitated by lower-income families.

What Will Be

Few of these policy changes are likely to be widely implemented. Most suburbanites have little reason to support broadened housing opportunities, particularly if the beneficiaries will be lower-income or black city dwellers. Residents of the suburbs generally identify the quality of life in their communities with policies that foster spatial separation. Diversity rarely is highly valued. Instead, poorer households and minority groups are seen as harbingers of diminished social status, lowered property values, poorer schools, more crime, and rapid racial transformation. In attacking the development of subsidized housing in the suburbs in 1971, Vice President Agnew expressed a common suburban viewpoint when he insisted that "if people are going to live together and be compatible with one another, they should have at least . . . a socio-economic identity with one another." [60] Like the *Wall Street Journal*, suburbanites argue that "we should be thankful for the sense of security and stability" provided by "those neighborhoods or communities with a commonality of interests" and should "seek to enhance rather then undermine them." [61]

As Chester W. Hartman has pointed out, "the notion of a right to decent housing conflicts with deeply rooted feelings about the meaning of housing. . . . Securing a good and satisfying place to live, in an area of one's choice, is generally regarded as something that must be 'earned,' and not without some struggle—particularly if it is a home the person owns." [62] Thus, for a suburban leader in New Jersey, building low-income housing in the suburbs was "contrary to our basic way of life" which involves living where "you can afford to live." While suburban "municipalities may have developed exclusivity . . . they have developed it by having people who could afford to live there." [63] Suburbanites naturally link these values to local autonomy, as in the case of a suburban congressman from Southern California who argues that a town "should not be denied the right to be a community of lovely homes that cater to people of extreme wealth, if that is what they wish. That is their wish. That is their right to govern themselves." [64]

Advocates of opening the suburbs have doggedly sought to counter these perceptions by attempting to persuade suburbanites that they have an interest in inclusionary housing policies. Babcock and Bosselman, for example, argue that residents of the suburbs will benefit from increased socioeconomic mixing because "higher density in suburbia could lead to a diversity of experience commonly associated with urban areas." [65] Unfortunately for this argument, the experiences commonly associated with urban areas—crime, inadequate schools, racial tension, and drugs—are just what suburbanites fear most. Babcock and Bosselman also point to economic development that would result from broadening housing opportunities, in the form of more business for local merchants and more jobs for local residents. Growth, however, is a mixed blessing at best for many suburbs. Most residents do not depend on the local economy for their livelihood since they work in other communities. Another reason for accepting lower-cost housing, suburbanites are told, is the comparative advantage such housing will provide their community in the competition for commercial and industrial development. This argument, too, is far from persuasive since jurisdictions that want attractive tax ratables can easily observe that inadequate housing for workers has not been a significant constraint on the location of firms in suburbia in the past.

The paucity of perceived advantages for suburbanites in lowered housing barriers inevitably leads to a search for incentives that would make inclusionary policies more attractive. Anthony Downs believes that opening the suburbs might be acceptable to local residents "if it were considered part of a longer-range urban development strategy likely to provide them with other outcomes they value highly" such as "reduced environmental pollution, lower urban crime rates, more control of suburban sprawl and future residential development, and less likelihood of future massive transition of neighborhoods from all middle-income to all low income or from all-white to all-black occupancy." [66] The trouble with this approach is that suburbanites usually view lower-income and minority families as causing environmental problems, increasing crime, intensifying pressures for sprawl, and producing neighborhood transformation. As a result, they seek to deal with these problems by keeping out the poor and blacks. Moreover, the growing political influence of the suburbs makes it unlikely that inclusionary housing policies will be closely linked with federal or state assistance for environmental, planning, or community-development problems.

Nor are the incentives very powerful for suburbanites to accept Downs' quota-based approach to dispersing lower-income and minority households. Presumably, localities will be attracted to this plan because limited numbers of lower-income families can be relocated "without significantly reducing the quality of life in middle-class neighborhoods." [67] Why, residents of the suburbs understandably might ask, should they accept even an insubstantial reduction in the quality of life, particularly when they cannot be certain that the costs will be marginal? For those who seek to maintain the local status quo, exclusionary policies clearly are preferable to inclusionary housing and land-use practices.

Given the plethora of costs and the paucity of benefits from the local perspective, advocates of opening the suburbs usually wind up emphasizing moral arguments. Some lecture suburbanites on the evils of their ways, insisting that "the suburbs must realize that segregation is wrong, socially damaging, and illegal." [68] Others seek to convince suburbanites of the moral benefits of alleviating segregation and poverty. Babcock and Bosselman write of the "spiritual pride" that can be felt only by a community "that commits itself to the broader society" and the satisfaction to be gained from easing "human suffering" by allowing "new homes in the suburbs for the urban poor." [69] Babcock and Bosselman also emphasize the corrosive effects of a spatially separated society on suburbia as well as on the city, arguing that when "large groups in society lose faith and respect in it, the major underpinning of the harmonious working of the society evaporates. Fear replaces trust. The result is, at best, difficulty in performing societal functions, and, at worst, violence." [70]

Unfortunately, moral appeals have little impact on suburban political behavior. After the Babylon Town Board rejected construction of housing in Wyandanch by the Urban Development Corporation, the *New York Times* felt that those "in Babylon who chose to reject the plan will, in conscience, have to take upon themselves the unwelcome burden of coming up with something better." [71] Given local autonomy and the strong pressures within the town against subsidized housing, Babylon's officials were able to ignore appeals to their conscience to deal with this "unwelcome burden" with impunity. Similarly, suburbs were under no compulsion to respond affirmatively to President Nixon's admonition in 1971 that local communities must "live with their success or failure" in providing "fair, open, and adequate housing." [72] As pointed out in chapter 8, most suburbs were quite happy to live with the consequences of their failure to provide housing for blacks and the poor.

With some justification, supporters of open housing contend that efforts to broaden suburban perspectives would be more successful if national leaders were to lend influential voices to the cause. Anthony Downs believes that

> most Americans are now opposed to opening the suburbs, partly because they do not realize the importance of doing so in order to help solve many of our key urban problems. Strong leadership by persons influential in shaping public opinion could therefore be extremely important in generating the political support needed to make this strategy feasible. The president, congressional leaders, governors, mayors, cabinet officers, and leading businessmen and labor union officials could be especially significant. Up to now, few of these officials have shown any inclination to exercise such leadership. [73]

Particularly lacking has been presidential leadership in the effort to expand suburban housing opportunities. Civil rights leaders argued that the president's "duty" was "to counter [suburban] prejudices and fears; to make clear that the remedies [do] not . . . impose a quarantine or . . . reinforce the ghetto conditions that bred them in the first place; to place before the American people the hard alternatives they face in the cities; to offer programs responsive to legitimate concerns." [74] Richard Nixon, however was unwilling to use the "bully pulpit" of the presidency to frame the housing issue in inclusionary terms. Nixon's conservative social views and desire to maintain his constituency base produced responsiveness to suburban rather than civil-rights concerns. Instead of appealing to suburban consciences or seeking to broaden localistic perspectives, Nixon negatively emphasized "forced integration," thus legitimizing suburban fears about racial and community change. At the same time, his insistence on local control and neighborhood sanctity reinforced the principal line of defence in suburbia against unwanted newcomers.

Other political leaders, however, have supported open housing in the suburbs without changing many attitudes at the grass roots. Governor William Cahill invested a great deal of time and political capital in a fruitless attempt to persuade New Jersey's suburban majority that local housing barriers had to be lowered. Congressional advocates of inclusionary housing such as Representative Thomas Ashley and Senators Walter Mondale and Abraham Ribicoff also made little headway in promoting an unpopular cause. Perhaps most sobering was the failure of George Romney to broaden suburban perspectives. A more promising champion of opening the suburbs than Romney would be hard to find. A Republican from the suburbs, the former corporate executive was clearly a doer rather than a "bleeding heart" or social experimenter. One housing specialist in Congress portrayed Romney's advantages as a promoter of dispersed housing in the following terms:

> When it comes to proselytizing, no one is better at it than George Romney. He's a super-salesman and he's the perfect kind of guy to be selling something as controversial as this—even if you disagree with what George Romney might be telling to you, you would never think that he was anything other than a solid all-America type. The message might strike some listener as radical but Romney himself never comes over as a radical. [75]

Yet Romney was unable to persuade suburbanites to accept blacks and lower-income families as neighbors, or to win support for his efforts from political leaders responsive to suburban interests.

Underlying the failure of Romney, Cahill, and other influential advocates of opening the suburbs was the entrenched political position of suburbanites on housing and land-use issues. Suburban strength in the struggle over exclusion is rooted in local control over zoning, housing design, and the location of subsidized projects. Because of local autonomy, opening the suburbs involves substantial alterations in the powers of local government rather than simply changes in housing policies. Such alterations are extremely difficult to achieve because of the dedication of Americans and their political leaders to local control over education, housing, and community character. "One need only attend a few public hearings on controversial zoning changes in suburban areas," observe Babcock and Bosselman, "to realize that people consider their right to pass judgment upon their future neighbors as sacred." [76]

Dedication to the doctrine of local control permeates the political system, influencing attitudes and actions on housing and land use at all levels of government. Grass roots fears that the application of a suburban county for federal community development funds would force localities to accept subsidized housing prompts officials to reassure their constituents that "it is absolutely essential for a community to consent to any activities before they are initiated within the borders of your community." [77] Throughout his campaign for zoning and housing reform, Governor Cahill insisted that his basic goal was to "insure the continuation of control in the hands of our local officials." [78] George Romney repeatedly expressed his opposition "to having the Federal Government step in the zone land throughout the country and all the localities of this Nation." [79] From the inception of federal housing programs, congressional action has been strongly influenced by the desire to have acceptance by the local communities" because "local people know their problems and needs better than anyone else." [80]

Local control and the maintenance of exclusionary housing policies is bolstered by the strength of suburbia's numbers. Within most suburban jurisdictions, substantial majorities support housing and land-use policies which block access by lower-income outsiders. Even in larger and more diverse suburban jurisdictions, such as Baltimore County, liberalization of housing restrictions attracts little support. In the larger arenas of the American political system, suburbia's growing numbers are augmented by other communities which staunchly oppose the "forced integration" of economic and racial groups. Residents of the outer neighborhoods of older cities, inhabitants of the sprawling newer cities of the south and west, and those who live in smaller cities and towns across the nation generally share suburban values and interests on housing issues. Suburbia also has more than numbers, important as numbers are in a democracy. The suburbs, as a key lobbyist for suburban interests in Washington emphasizes "are where it is at in contemporary America. They've got the thrust of economic development; they've got the young adults; they've got the professionals. Look at the cities and their political constituencies. They've got the Negroes; they've got the aged; they've got the poor. There isn't any comparison." [81] As a result of suburbs' manifest political advantages and growing influence, Daniel J. Elazar emphasizes, "they are now the embodiments of the normal and conventional in American society." [82]

To expect metropolitan planners, state legislators, or federal officials to ignore their expanding suburban constituencies is utterly unrealistic. Nor is understanding of the politics of exclusion advanced by mistaking responsiveness for stupidity or cowardice, as do some supporters of opening the suburbs. In urging political leaders to read Downs' *Opening Up the Suburbs* and "take up his cause," Robert Cassidy acidly notes that because "his proposal would make sense even to an idiot makes it even more doubtful that Downs' plan will be understood or implemented by our elected officials." [83] Cassidy apparently missed Downs' emphasis on the political realities of suburban exclusion:

> The legislative and administrative branches of government in a democracy are powerfully motivated to serve any desire strongly held by a majority of their constituents. Also, in the United States, a majority of citizens are in the middle class. They have enough money and political skills to evade policies they passionately oppose. Therefore, if public policies are to be effective, they should not usually seek to prevent a preponderant majority from achieving any of its strongly favored objectives. [84]

Clearly, Downs' proposals and those outlined earlier in this chapter run against the grain of "strongly favored objectives" of the "preponderant majority" which shares the suburban perspective on dispersing the poor.

Majorities, of course, cannot deprive minorities of their constitutional rights. Neither the federal courts nor most state courts, however, have established the right of anyone to live anywhere. Outside of New Jersey, judges have recognized no general right to decent housing, nor to reasonable access to a job, or better schools, or a more suitable environment. Even in New Jersey, where the courts have expanded housing rights significantly, formidable obstacles are posed to devising and implementing appropriate judicial remedies because of the political influence of suburbanites at all levels of government. The complexity and singularity of housing and land use issues also bedevil judicial intervention and the development of appropriate remedies, and in so doing strengthen the hand of local officials who make the ultimate public determinations about housing and land use. The manifold problems encountered by the courts support the conclusion of a court-appointed expert in one zoning case that the problem of exclusion "is one that is best resolved by the kinds of political negotiation and compromise upon which the democratic legislative process is based." [85] But legislative arenas, unlike the courts, are rarely disposed to support significant changes in suburban housing policies.

Opening the Suburbs for Suburbanites

Whatever changes occur in suburban housing and land-use policies will be shaped by these formidable political constraints, as well as by the financial barriers posed by rapidly increasing housing costs. Despite the handicaps faced by the courts, judicial intervention undoubtedly will alter housing restrictions in some communities. Most common, however, will be marginal adjustments designed to satisfy the courts at minimal cost to local interests. After the Mount Laurel decision, communities in New Jersey sought to head off the courts by zoning for a limited number of apartment units or subsidized dwellings. For example, East Windsor in Mercer County changed its zoning two months after Mount Laurel to require developers to include a fixed percentage of lower-income housing in one section of the community. A local official argued that the new provision "goes beyond what is asked for in the Mount Laurel decision." [86] But an attorney for a housing group that was challenging East Windsor's zoning in court did not believe "that under all the restrictions (for things such as lot size, open space, and frontage) low- and moderate-income housing would be economically possible" in the designated zone. [87] Housing for the elderly also is particularly attractive to suburbs seeking to preclude judicial intervention. As a suburban planner explains, "a lot of communities see this as the way to get themselves off the hook. Communities basically don't want any multifamily zoning. If they feel they have to take some they say, 'We'll take some old people. They don't mug anybody and they don't have any children that we have to educate.' " [88]

Local housing and land-use policies also can be expected to adjust to the dynamics of a changing suburbia. As in the past, some zoning restrictions will give way to population pressures as an expanding suburban economy increases the demand for a wider range of housing. Aided in some instances by court orders or the threat of judicial intervention, developers will succeed in building at higher densities in many suburban communities. Others, often with the assistance of new environmental standards, will withstand pressures for more intensive development. Particularly in those metropolitan areas or states where developers are able to build apartments without bedroom restrictions, modest homes on small lots, and mobile homes, housing opportunities will be expanded substantially by these changes. Except for housing for the elderly, however, demographic pressures by themselves seem unlikely to stimulate the development of much subsidized housing in most suburban jurisdictions.

Acceptance of subsidized housing can be expected primarily in response to political pressures. Louis H. Masotti and Jeffrey K. Hadden suggest that changes in "exclusionary practices . . . will come only through political pressure brought to bear on individual communities by civil rights and labor groups. . . , economic pressure exerted by corporations . . . , or a judicial breakthrough which overrides local zoning authority." [89] For the reasons examined in chapter 6, economic pressures do not figure to be an important consideration for most suburbs. Local civil-rights efforts to secure subsidized housing, as indicated in chapter 5, most frequently succeed in affluent suburbs such as Palo Alto or Princeton, and rarely produce enough units to meet local needs. Occasional victories in the courts, most notably the Mount Laurel ruling in New Jersey, are certain to stimulate more open-housing litigation, thus increasing the pressures on some suburban communities to provide subsidized housing on their own terms rather than on those imposed by judges.

Civil-rights activists also will continue to employ any other means available in their quest for leverage on suburban restrictions, although the effectiveness of these organizations usually depends heavily on the availability of funds from foundation or governmental sources. Illustrative of the adaptability of these groups were the efforts by a number of organizations to force local compliance with the housing standards established by the Housing and Community Development Act of 1974. A few months after President Ford signed the new legislation, the National

Committee Against Discrimination in Housing had prepared a handbook for open-housing groups interested in monitoring local applications for block grants.[90] NCDH also challenged the request of Parma for a $4.5 million grant under the new program, citing past efforts by the suburb in the Cleveland area to exclude blacks and low-cost housing.[91] An alliance between Hartford and Suburban Action Institute led the Connecticut city into federal court in a successful effort to enjoin HUD from granting $4.4 million in community development grants to seven suburbs because of their discriminatory housing and land-use policies.[92] In the Detroit area, the Coalition on Block Grant Compliance organized by open-housing, civil-rights, and religious groups filed a formal complaint against twenty-six suburbs, contending that almost all of the units proposed in the local housing plans were for the elderly, that most of the suburban plans did not conform to housing goals established by the Southeast Michigan Council of Government, and that many of the localities failed to propose construction of new subsidized units in the light of local needs.[93]

Other potential sources of pressure on suburban zoning restrictions are metropolitan, state, and federal agencies, as illustrated by the activities of the Miami Valley Regional Planning Commission, New York's Urban Development Corporation in Rochester, and the regional HUD offices which pressed for effective metropolitan housing plans in a few areas. For such pressures to produce results, however, a combination of factors is required. General federal or state policy is needed to provide an authoritative basis for the local endeavor. HUD's regulations for implementing the metropolitan housing provisions of the Housing and Urban Development Act of 1968 filled this bill in Dayton, while UDC's enabling legislation underwrote its effort in Rochester. In addition, leadership is required to develop allocation plans, build local support, and withstand the inevitable opposition from the grass roots. Dale Bertsch was a political rarity among metropolitan officials, while UDC's activities in Rochester exhibited far more political sensitivity than its abortive campaign in Westchester. Finally, resources must be available to permit implementation, as was the case in the initial stages in Dayton and Rochester. Without federal or state subsidies, pressures on local governments cannot be translated into actual housing for lower-income families.

Few of these conditions, however, seem likely to be fulfilled in most metropolitan areas, a circumstance produced in large part by widespread opposition to dispersing subsidized housing. To be sure, sections of the

Housing and Community Development Act of 1974 can be interpreted as providing an authoritative basis for inclusionary local housing policies, as they were by the federal district court in the Hartford case. Moreover, aggressive implementation of the law could generate strong federal pressures for local acceptance of subsidized housing, at least on the part of suburbs receiving block grants for community development. But forceful federal action was not forthcoming, at least during the administration of Gerald Ford, an outspoken foe of "forced integration" and fair-share plans while serving in the House of Representatives. As pointed out in chapter 8, HUD's initial approach to applying the housing standards in the community development program was extremely passive. In addition, most of the housing subsidies provided in the new law were allocated within older cities and for existing rather than new housing. Thus, neither commitment nor resources were available in Washington to bolster the efforts of the few hardy souls willing to press for subsidized housing in the suburbs. With UDC's demise, Massachusetts was the only state to provide encouragement for dispersing subsidized housing, and neither its commitment nor resources were sufficient to have a significant impact on the location of housing opportunities for poorer households.

At best, pressures from these various sources can produce piecemeal rather than general changes in suburban housing policies. If nothing else, an examination of the politics of exclusion underscores the tremendous diversity of urban politics in the United States. Cities, suburbs, and metropolitan areas are characterized by enormous differences in scale, wide variations in governmental arrangements and patterns of influence, and marked contrasts in demographic and developmental configurations. The implications of spatial separation are less troublesome in smaller than larger areas, since the distances involved are much less. Newer metropolises are less spatially differentiated than older ones, in part because they lack large concentrations of older housing in their centers. Hardly by accident, zoning restrictions tend to be most significant in the older, larger, and most spatially separated metropolitan areas. Moreover, metropolitan institutions tend to be weakest in areas where city-suburban differences are the greatest. In the absence of radical policy changes at the state or federal levels, liberalization of local housing policies is bound to be sporadic in the larger and more complex areas. General changes are more probable in some of the smaller and middle-sized metropolitan areas, particularly when leadership structures are reasonably cohesive, as in Dayton and Rochester. Even in these locales, however, development and implementation of areawide housing programs depend heavily on an elusive combination of commitment from the higher levels, skillful local leadership, and availability of substantial resources for construction of subsidized housing.

Piecemeal change also is inevitable as long as local governments retain significant control over housing and land-use determination. What will persuade one locality to alter its zoning may have little effect on another. Local supporters of subsidized housing may be particularly well organized in one community, and nonexistent in a neighboring suburb. Private developers and sponsors of subsidized housing are more likely to be attracted to communities which indicate an interest in broadening housing opportunities than to those which promise bitter resistance. As a consequence of the maintenance of local control, strong pressures often will be insufficient to produce changes in local housing and zoning policies. Even in failure, however, advocates of open housing sometimes are able to advance their cause by raising suburban consciousness about housing problems. Picking among the wreckage of its Nine Towns Plan, UDC was encouraged by the fact that "in Westchester County . . . there is a deeper, wider awareness than there was a year ago that low and moderate-income housing is critically needed." [94] Agreement with this assessment came from one of UDC's most outspoken foes in Westchester who conceded "that if it hadn't been for UDC we wouldn't have given housing the attention it deserves." [95]

What is likely to be given "the attention it deserves" in most suburbs, of course, is housing for people already living in suburbia, and preferably units reserved for elderly of the particular community. Suburbanites typically are more sympathetic to proposals aimed at local housing needs than to general housing programs. Discussing the housing plan his community would prepare in order to receive over $2 million in block grants under the Housing and Community Development Act of 1974, the mayor of an affluent suburb in the Chicago area expressed the common suburban view that "we have to concern ourselves with present residents, not those who might move in." [96] Metropolitan housing plans which depend on local action for implementation are almost certain to be skewed in the direction of local rather than regional needs. Illustrative is the heavy emphasis placed on local needs in the scheme developed by Chicago's Metropolitan Housing Coalition with the active involvement of suburban mayors.

Political pressures against opening suburbia to outsiders will be reinforced by limitations on production of subsidized housing. Far fewer new units will be constructed under the 1974 legislation than was the case under the subsidy programs established under Sections 235 and 236 of the Housing and Urban Development Act of 1968. In the competition for whatever units are built in suburbs, families already living in or near the community are in a more advantageous position than those from the urban core. Suburban households are more likely to be aware of the limited number of subsidized units available than are families in the inner city. And there is certain to be substantial demand for subsidized units from within suburbia given demographic changes and rising housing costs. With limited production, there simply will be no room in suburbia for outsiders, even if suburbanites were willing to accept them. "Only a vast increase of the supply," as Franklin, Falk, and Levin emphasize, "could in practice work effectively" to increase housing and employment opportunities in the suburbs for the urban poor.[97]

Concern over the prospects that liberalized housing policies in the suburbs will have little impact on inner-city families leads Anthony Downs to propose that "accessibility to a certain fraction of suburban subsidized housing (say, 20 to 25 percent) should be reserved for households moving out from central-city poverty areas."[98] Positive housing quotas for ghetto families, however, are anathema to most suburbanites. Why, they ask, should needy local families stand aside so that people with no connection with the community can occupy publicly-supported facilities? Far from supporting quotas which benefit poor city dwellers, suburban officials seek with considerable success to insure that local residents will obtain whatever subsidized housing is built within their jurisdictions. They insist that local residents receive priority, that subsidized units for the elderly rather than for families are constructed, and that middle- and moderate-income families be served rather than poor households.

Unlike opening the suburbs for the urban poor, opening the suburbs for suburbanites has the great virtue of wide political acceptability. The need among present residents for improved housing is increasingly recognized in suburbia. Local governments clearly are more willing to relax housing barriers to satisfy community needs. Courts are likely to accept limited suburban housing reforms as evidence of good faith, or at least as better than nothing. City interests are less threatened by suburban housing programs which concentrate on suburbia's needs. Such efforts generate less competition with the cities for scarce federal subsidies and pose no threat of dispersing existing constituencies in the older cities. Home-builders will be happy to settle for zoning reforms that permit higher-density development in the suburbs. And suburban employers undoubt-edly will welcome whatever lower-cost housing is permitted in their locales as gratifying evidence of community responsiveness and corporate statesmanship.

Limiting suburban responsibilities to the housing needs of subur-banites also greatly simplifies the issue of exclusion for the higher levels of government. State legislators, and congressmen obviously find solu-tions which are acceptable to their suburban constitutents much less troublesome than proposals which generate emotional responses from suburbanites fearful of being overrun by black hordes from the city. At the metropolitan level, most councils of government and regional plan-ning agencies entered the thicket of housing dispersal only because of federal pressures. Few metropolitan officials want anything to do with regional housing plans that are unacceptable to the suburban jurisdic-tions which dominate almost all areawide planning and review agencies.

Acceptability to suburbia also became the watchword of federal housing policy in the 1970s. As pointed out in chapter 8, HUD placed heavy emphasis on local housing needs in urging suburbs to participate in the community development program established in 1974. Explicit en-dorsement of opening the suburbs only for suburbanites came late in 1974 when the Ford Administration opposed metropolitan relief in the litigation involving site-selection policies in Chicago.[99] Areawide housing plans which sought to disperse the urban poor, argued the brief submit-ted to the U.S. Supreme Court on behalf of HUD, would "discourage participation by suburban jurisdictions in federally assisted programs." Metropolitan relief would have a "chilling effect" on suburban housing efforts because a locality approving new subsidized housing "risks an order directing that such units be made available, not only to the sub-urb's needy residents, but also to the plaintiff class in the center city suit—here, CHA's tenants and applicants."[100] After the Supreme Court rejected HUD's contention and opened the door to metropolitan rem-edies in the Chicago case,[101] Secretary of Housing and Urban De-velopment Carla A. Hills saw no need for increased federal efforts to open the suburbs. She was confident that "most communities do want to address [housing] needs" and insisted that HUD was not "going to find a lot of communities shirking their responsibility for subsidized housing."[102] Her optimism, however, could be justified only by a

definition of local responsibilities which focused on the housing needs of
local residents rather than those of city dwellers.

Given public attitudes, local autonomy, and responsiveness to majority interests, opening the suburbs for suburbanites is all that can be
reasonably expected from the American political system as presently
organized. Certainly, there is much to be said for improving housing for
lower-income, elderly, and other suburbanites who have been squeezed
by restrictive zoning, rising costs, and the exclusion of subsidized housing from their communities. Settling for locally-oriented housing reforms, of course, means accepting and perpetuating the spatially-
separated and racially-segregated metropolis. Those most isolated from
suburban employment will benefit the least from housing earmarked for
local residents or employees. And blacks, because they are the most
segregated, will pay the heaviest price in terms of both housing and economic opportunities for the maintenance of the suburban noose around
the older cities. These outcomes, however, are not very troubling to
most Americans, who are convinced that a decent home, nice neighborhood, and good schools depend heavily on the absence of lower-
income and minority groups. Nor will these developments cause much
concern among those who have convinced themselves that the urban
crisis has passed (if, indeed, it ever existed).[103]

Under the best of circumstances, housing patterns are not easily altered. Most units last forty or more years, leading to the replacement of
relatively little of the total housing stock each year. As a result, the location of various kinds of dwelling units shapes individual housing opportunities and general residential patterns for decades. "In housing," notes
the U.S. Commission on Civil Rights, "the legacy of the past has a much
stronger bearing on the present and future [than in employment and
education.] Patterns of residence have developed over a period of decades
in which government at all levels and private industry combined to establish a racially-dual housing market—separate and unequal." [104] Given
this legacy, the commission contends that the "problem facing us now is
not merely to end current discriminatory practices, but also to eliminate
the effects of past discrimination and reverse the residential segregation
that now exists." [105]

Far from reversing existing economic and racial segregation, concentrating on local housing needs in suburbia will intensify segregation and
broaden the gulf between older cities and developing suburbs. Moreover,
with the passage of time, the rectification of past trends becomes increas-

ingly difficult. In the words of a New Jersey judge, "even as we write, development proceeds apace. Once an area is developed, it becomes much more difficult to alter its social and economic character. There is a hazard that prolonged judicial inaction will permit exclusionary practices to continue to operate and will allow presently developing communities to acquire permanent exclusionary characteristics." [106] The same hazards accompany political inaction on the larger issues of exclusion, issues which are ignored by defining suburban housing responsibilities in terms of existing residents of the suburbs.

The fundamental issue "in terms of an open society," Richard Nixon once told the American people, "is mobility: the right and the ability of each person to decide for himself where and how he wants to live, whether as part of the ethnic enclave or as part of the larger society." [107] For lower-income and black Americans, that mobility has declined as urban development has spread across the landscape. Social and economic differences have been frozen into the spatial pattern of the metropolis. Political fragmentation and local control over housing and land use have enhanced the ability of millions of suburbanites to separate themselves from unwanted neighbors. A decade of urban unrest, racial turmoils, national soul searching, and earnest reform barely left a mark on the segregated metropolis, except to reinforce the lines of demarcation between the metropolitan haves and have-nots. Politically, these outcomes were predictable. National leaders, by and large, have echoed the general public on the desirability of maintaining a separated society. Asked about dispersing subsidized housing into the suburbs, one candidate for the presidency in 1976 saw "nothing wrong with ethnic purity being maintained" and promised that he "would not force . . . racial integration of a neighborhood by government action." [108] Much the same view was expressed by President Gerald Ford, who did not think that "federal action should be used to destroy [the] ethnic treasure" of existing neighborhoods. [109] Predictable outcomes, however, are not necessarily desirable, especially when they negate the fundamental tenets of an open society.

Notes

Preface

1. Michael N. Danielson, "Differentiation, Segregation, and Political Fragmentation in the American Metropolis," in Commission on Population Growth and the American Future, *Governance and Population: The Governmental Implications of Population Change*, edited by A. E. Kier Nash (Washington, D.C.: U.S. Government Printing Office, 1972), pp. 143–76. Adaptations of material from this paper appear in the chapters that follow, particularly in chapters 1 and 2.

2. See Michael N. Danielson, Alan M. Hershey, and John M. Bayne, *One Nation, So Many Governments* (New York: Third Press, 1976).

Chapter One: The Separated Society

1. Throughout this volume, the term "suburbs" refers to those portions of Standard Metropolitan Statistical Areas which lie outside central cities. The U.S. Census Bureau defines a Standard Metropolitan Statistical Area as a central city of 50,000 or more residents and those adjacent counties that are deemed to be "metropolitan in character" and "economically and socially integrated with the county of the central city." U.S. Department of Commerce, Social and Economic Statistics Administration, Bureau of the Census, *Statistical Abstract of the United States 1974* (Washington: U.S. Government Printing Office, 1974), p. 837.

2. These data understate suburban gains, since they classify as "central city" suburban areas which were annexed by central cities during the 1960s, and place all residents and housing lying within the jurisdiction of areawide local governments, such as those in Indianapolis and Nashville, in the central-city category.

3. *A Decent Home* (Washington: U.S. Government Printing Office, 1969), p. 140. See also Neil N. Gold and Paul Davidoff, "The Supply and Availability of Land for Housing for Low- and Moderate-Income Families," in U.S. President's Committee on Urban Housing, *Technical Studies*, Vol. 2, Housing Costs, Production Efficiency, Finance, Manpower, Land (Washington: U.S. Government Printing Office, 1968), pp. 287–409.

4. See Pierre de Vise, "The Wasting of Chicago," *Focus / Midwest*, No. 58, p. 7.

5. See Anthony Downs, *Opening Up the Suburbs: An Urban Strategy for America* (New Haven: Yale Univ. Press, 1973), pp. 19–20.

6. See Jack Rosenthal, "Nonurban Living Is Gaining Favor," *New York Times*, Dec. 17, 1972.

7. Downs, *Opening Up the Suburbs*, p. 19.

8. Sam Bass Warner, Jr., *The Private City: Philadelphia in Three Periods of Its Growth* (Philadelphia: Univ. of Pa. Press, 1968), p. 50.

9. National Academy of Sciences–National Academy of Engineering, *Freedom of Choice in Housing: Opportunities and Constraints*, Report of the Social Science Panel, Division of Behavioral Sciences, and the Recommendations of the Advisory Committee to the Department of Housing and Urban Development (Washington: National Academy of Sciences, 1972), p. 9.

10. "A Closer Look: Chicago," *City* 5 (Jan. / Feb., 1971), p. 38.

11. *Report of the National Advisory Commission on Civil Disorders*, Mar. 1, 1968 (Washington: U.S. Government Printing Office, 1968), p. 119.

12. See Karl E. Taeuber and Alma F. Taeuber, *Negroes in Cities: Residential Segregation and Neighborhood Change* (Chicago: Aldine Pub. Co., 1965).

13. See Harold X. Connolly, "Black Movement in the Suburbs," *Urban Affairs Quarterly* 9 (Sept., 1973), pp. 91–111.

14. See Peter C. Labovitz, "Racial Change Comes to the Suburbs," in American Society of Planning Officials, *Planning 1970*, Selected Papers from the ASPO National Planning Conference, New York, Apr. 4–5, 1970 (Chicago, 1970), p. 148.

15. Phoebe Cottingham, *Black Income and Residential Movement in the Philadelphia Metropolitan Area* (Philadelphia: Fels Center of Government, Univ. of Pa., 1973), p. 9.

16. See testimony of George H. Brown, director, Bureau of the Census, U.S. Commission on Civil Rights, *Hearing Held in Washington, D.C., June 14–17, 1971* (Washington: U.S. Government Printing Office, 1971), pp. 1060–72.

17. "Integration in the Suburbs—Who Needs It?" Highlights of an address before the Second Interfaith Conference on Suburban Housing Patterns on the North Shore, at Saints Faith, Hope and Charity Church, Winnetka, Ill., on Oct. 14, 1973, p. 1.

18. Suburbanizing blacks also have higher educations and better jobs than black city residents; see Eunice S. Grier, *Characteristics of Black Suburbanites*, Black Suburbanization in Metropolitan Washington, Report No. 1 (Washington: Washington Center for Metropolitan Studies, 1973).

19. "The Potential for Residential Integration in Cities and Suburbs: Implications for the Busing Controversy," *American Sociological Review* 38 (Oct., 1973), p. 602.

20. *Black Income and Residential Movement in the Philadelphia Metropolitan Area*, pp. 17–18; see also Phoebe H. Cottingham, "Black Income and Metropolitan Residential Dispersion," *Urban Affairs Quarterly* 10 (Mar., 1975), pp. 273–96.

21. See Nina Jaffe Gruen and Claude Gruen, *Low and Moderate Income Housing in the Suburbs: An Analysis for the Dayton, Ohio Region* (New York: Praeger Publishers, 1972), p. 26.

22. Sam H. Jones, executive director, Urban League, Indianapolis, quoted in Gordon Englehart, "A Closer Look: Indianapolis," *City* 5 (Jan. / Feb., 1971), p. 28.

23. National Academy of Sciences–National Academy of Engineering, *Freedom of Choice in Housing*, p. 13.

24. "Institutional and Contextual Factors Affecting the Residential Choices of Minority Residents," in Amos H. Hawley and Vincent P. Rock, eds., *Segregation in Residential Areas*, Papers on Racial and Socioeconomic Factors in Choice of Housing (Washington: National Academy of Sciences, 1973), p. 137.

25. John H. Denton, "Phase I Report" to the National Committee Against Discrimination in Housing, U.S. Department of Housing and Urban Development Project, No. Cal. D-8 (n.d.), pt. 2, p. Jb-6.

26. *Housing and Social Policy* (Englewood Cliffs, N.J.: Prentice-Hall, 1974), p. 13.

27. Stephen Horn, vice chairman; see U.S. Commission on Civil Rights, *Hearing Held in Washington, D.C., June 14–17, 1971*, p. 5.

28. See *Buchanan* v. *Warley*, 245 U.S. 60 (1917). In invalidating racial zoning, the Supreme Court was concerned with the property rights of whites rather than the civil rights of blacks, ruling that racial zoning restrictions unreasonably limited the right of whites to dispose of their private property.

29. See *Shelley* v. *Kraemer*, 334 U.S. 1 (1948). Prior to this ruling, judicial enforcement of restrictive racial covenants had been upheld by numerous courts, including the U.S. Supreme Court, on the grounds that such enforcement only involved insuring that the terms of a private contract were fulfilled; see *Corrigan* v. *Buckley*, 271 U.S. 323 (1926).

30. See, for example, Carol J. Cunningham and James M. Scott, *Land Development and Racism in Fairfax County* (Washington: Washington Suburban Inst., 1970).

31. Carl Holverstott, chairman, Human Relations Commission, Miamisburg, Ohio, quoted in Katie Krumm, "Human Relations Efforts Unaggressive in Suburbs," *Dayton Daily News*, Jan. 22, 1973.

32. Hedy Epstein, Greater St. Louis Committee for Freedom of Residence, quoted in Sally Thran, "Housing Codes Raise Question of Racial Bias," *St. Louis Post-Dispatch*, Oct. 3, 1972.

33. See Louis Harris, "Majority Sees Racial Bias in Housing," *Washington Post*, Jan. 15, 1973. Of the whites surveyed, 51 percent agreed that racial bias existed in housing, 44 percent that it existed in white collar and skilled labor jobs, 29 percent in quality education in the public schools, and 25 percent in treatment by the police.

34. See William Watts and Lloyd A. Free, eds., *State of the Nation* (New York: Universe Books, 1973), pp. 101–2.

35. *Ibid.*, p. 94.

36. "Integration in the Suburbs: Who Needs It?" p. 2.

37. *Neighborhood Government: The Local Foundations of Political Life* (Indianapolis: Bobbs-Merrill, 1969), p. 3.

38. Foreword to Zane L. Miller, *Boss Cox's Cincinnati: Urban Politics in the Progressive Era* (New York: Oxford, 1968), p. viii.

39. *Streetcar Suburbs: The Process of Growth in Boston* (Cambridge: Harvard Univ. Press and MIT Press, 1962), pp. 164–65.

40. *Urban America and the Federal System*, Commission Findings and Proposals, Oct., 1969 (Washington: U.S. Government Printing Office, 1969), p. 17.

41. Mayor Joseph M. Nardi, Jr., Camden, N.J., quoted in Donald Janson, "Camden, Like Newark, to Seek State Aid to Avert Bankruptcy," *New York Times*, Dec. 11, 1972.

42. Downs, *Opening Up the Suburbs*, p. 15.

43. Through 1975, desegregation across local school boundaries had been ordered by federal courts in the Richmond, Detroit, and Louisville metropolitan areas; see *Bradley* v. *School Board of the City of Richmond, Virginia*, 338 F.Supp. 67 (1972); *Bradley* v. *Milliken*, 338 F.Supp. 582 (1971); and *Newburg Area Council, Inc.* v. *Board of Education of Jefferson County, Kentucky*, 489 F.2d 925 (1973). Only in Louisville, however, was areawide desegregation upheld by higher courts. In Richmond, the district court was overruled by the U.S. Court of Appeals for the Fourth Circuit, a determination which was permitted to stand when the U.S. Supreme Court declined to review the case; see *In Re Bradley*, 456 F.2d 6 (1972). The ruling requiring areawide desegregation in Detroit was overturned by the U.S. Supreme Court in 1974, which found no evidence that suburban school districts bore responsibility for the development of segregated schools within Detroit; see *Milliken* v. *Bradley*, 418 U.S. 717 (1974). On the other hand, in Louisville, the Supreme Court refused to review the decision of the U.S. Court of Appeals for the Sixth Circuit, which found consolidation of city and suburban school districts an appropriate remedy because both school systems had once been segregated by law. In yet another case, involving Wilmington and suburban New Castle County in Delaware, the Supreme Court late in 1975 upheld a lower court ruling which opened the door to areawide school integration, with the district court decision resting on its finding that actions of the state government contributed to the racial imbalance in Wilmington's schools; see *Evans* v. *Buchanan*, 379 F.Supp. 1218 (1975).

44. John J. Kerrigan, Boston School Committee, quoted in Martin Waldron, "White Pupils' Rolls Drop as Families Flee the Cities," *New York Times*, Nov. 26, 1972.

45. See John Herbers, "The Outer City: Uneasiness Over Future," *New York Times*, June 2, 1971; reprinted as "A Deep Uneasiness About the Future," in Louis H. Masotti and Jeffrey K. Hadden, eds., *Suburbia in Transition* (New York: Franklin Watts, 1974), p. 284.

46. Roldo Bartimole, "A Closer Look: Cleveland," *City* 5 (Jan. / Feb., 1971), p. 43.

47. See Robert Adams, "Suburbs Feel No Debt to City," *St. Louis Post-Dispatch*, July 23, 1971.

48. See Jack Rosenthal, "The Outer City: U.S. in Suburban Turmoil," *New York Times*, May 20, 1971; reprinted as "Suburban Turmoil in the United States," in Masotti and Hadden, *Suburbia in Transition*, p. 271.

49. Councilman Gerald Rimmel, St. Louis County, Mo., quoted in Jack Rosenthal, "Urbanists Find Suburbs Hostile to Cities, Pinched for Money," *New York Times*, May 22, 1970.

50. Phillip Bettencourt, acting city manager, Newport Beach, Cal., quoted in Herbers, "A Deep Uneasiness About the Future," p. 286.

51. *Opening Up the Suburbs*, p. 2.

52. Anthony Downs, senior vice president, Real Estate Research Corporation; see U.S. Commission on Population Growth and the American Future, *Statements at Public Hearings of the Commission on Population Growth and the American Future*, Vol. 7 of Commission Publications (Washington: U.S. Government Printing Office, 1972), p. 168.

53. National Academy of Sciences–National Academy of Engineering, *Freedom of Choice in Housing*, p. 42.

54. See Chicago Urban League, *Linking Black Residence to Suburban Employment Through Mass Transportation*, Research Report (Chicago, n.d.).

55. Joseph Zikmund II, "Sources of the Suburban Population: 1955–1960 and 1965–1970," *Publius* 5 (Winter, 1975), p. 28.

Chapter Two: Suburban Autonomy

1. *Suburbia: Its People and Their Politics* (Boston: Houghton Mifflin, 1958), p. 128.

2. See Oliver P. Williams et al., *Suburban Differences and Metropolitan Policies: A Philadelphia Story* (Philadelphia: Univ. of Pa. Press, 1965), pp. 217–19.

3. See Walter S. Mossberg, "A Blue Collar Town Fears Urban Renewal Perils Its Way of Life," *Wall Street Journal*, Nov. 2, 1970.

4. Gladstone L. Chandler, Jr., city manager, East Cleveland, O., quoted in Paul Delaney, "The Outer City: Negroes Find Few Tangible Gains," *New York Times*, June 1, 1971; reprinted as "Negroes Find Few Tangible Gains," in Louis H. Masotti and Jeffrey K. Hadden, eds., *Suburbia in Transition* (New York: Franklin Watts, 1974), p. 278. East Cleveland had no black residents in the mid-1950s; by 1970, 60 percent of its population was black.

5. "Suburbanization: Reviving the Town on the Metropolitan Frontier," *Publius* 5 (Winter, 1975), p. 59.

6. The Baltimore standard metropolitan statistical area contains four additional counties—Anne Arundel, Carroll, Harford and Howard—which lie beyond Baltimore County.

7. See Allen D. Manvel, "Metropolitan Growth and Governmental Fragmentation," in A. E. Kier Nash, ed., *Governance and Population: The Governmental Implications of Population Change*, Vol. 4, Research Reports, U.S. Commission on Population Growth and the American Future (Washington: U.S. Government Printing Office, 1972), p. 181.

8. Robert Poltzer, Prospect Heights Improvement Association, quoted in

Dan Egler, "Prospect Heights Seeks to Incorporate," *Chicago Tribune*, Oct. 1, 1972.

9. "Phase I Report" to the National Committee Against Discrimination in Housing, U.S. Department of Housing and Urban Development Project, No. Cal. D-8 (n.d.), pt. 3, p. Jc-11.

10. For a summary of the events leading to the incorporation of Black Jack, see Ronald F. Kirby, Frank de Leeuw, and William Silverman, *Residential Zoning and Equal Housing Opportunities: A Case Study in Black Jack, Missouri* (Washington: Urban Inst., 1972), pp. 17–27.

11. See B. Drummond Ayres, "Bulldozers Turn Up Soil and Ill Will in a Suburb of St. Louis," *New York Times*, Jan. 18, 1971.

12. See *Park View Heights Corporation* v. *City of Black Jack*, 467 F.2d 1208 (1972) at 1211.

13. See William K. Reilly, ed., *The Use of Land: A Citizens' Policy Guide to Urban Growth*, A Task Force Report Sponsored by The Rockefeller Brothers Fund (New York: Thomas Y. Crowell Company, 1973), p. 90.

14. Jerome Pratter, "Dispersed Subsidized Housing and Suburbia: Confrontation in Black Jack," *Land-Use Controls Annual* (Chicago: American Society of Planning Officials, 1972), p. 152.

15. Black Jack's actions were challenged in court by the sponsors of the project, other organizations, and the federal government; see *United States* v. *City of Black Jack, Missouri*, 372 F.Supp. 319 (1974); *United States* v. *City of Black Jack, Missouri*, 508 F.2d 1179 (1974); *Park View Heights Corporation* v. *City of Black Jack*, 467 F.2d 1208; and the discussion of the Black Jack litigation in chapter 7.

16. Suburban opposition to this grant of power to the Urban Development Corporation led the New York legislature to rescind it in 1973; see chapter 10 for a discussion of the New York Urban Development Corporation's turbulent efforts to open the suburbs.

17. *The Zoning Game: Municipal Practices and Policies* (Madison: Univ. of Wis. Press, 1966), p. 19.

18. State land-use activities and their impact on suburban exclusion are discussed in detail in chapter 10.

19. James G. Coke and John J. Gargan, *Fragmentation in Land-Use Planning and Control*, Prepared for the consideration of the National Commission on Urban Problems, Research Report No. 18 (Washington: U.S. Government Printing Office, 1969), p. 6.

20. *Building the American City*, Report of the National Commission on Urban Problems to the Congress and President of the United States, 91st Cong., 1st sess., House Doc. No. 91-34 (Washington: U.S. Government Printing Office, 1968), p. 209.

21. The federal role in suburban exclusion is examined in chapter 8.

22. Judicial attitudes concerning exclusionary zoning and housing policies began to shift in the late 1960s; see chapter 7 for an analysis of the role of the courts in opening the suburbs.

23. *Suburban Land Conversion in the United States: An Economic and Governmental Process* (Baltimore: Johns Hopkins Univ. Press, 1971), pp. 65–66.

24. Leonard Downie, Jr., *Mortgage on America* (New York: Praeger Publishers, 1974), p. 111.

25. "Stealing: A Primer on Zoning Corruption," *Planning* 39 (Dec., 1973), p. 6.

26. For a discussion of suburban neighborhood associations, and their role in land-use politics, see R. Robert Linowes and Don T. Allensworth, *The Politics of Land Use: Planning, Zoning, and the Private Developer* (New York: Praeger Publishers, 1973), pp. 114–42.

27. George Post, vice president, Prides Wood Civic Association, East Brunswick, N.J., quoted in Ruth Ann Burns, "Apartment Proposal Stirs a Dispute in East Brunswick," *New York Times*, Oct. 8, 1972.

28. See "Eastlake Is Upheld on Requiring Vote in Rezoning Cases," *Cleveland Plain Dealer*, Oct. 31, 1972. Eastlake's ordinance was overturned four years later by the Supreme Court of Ohio; see *Forest City Enterprises, Inc.* v. *City of Eastlake*, 41 Ohio St.2d 187, 324 N.E.2d, 740 (1975).

29. "The Right to Move, the Need to Grow," *Planning* 39 (Sept., 1973), pp. 10–11.

30. See Ralph Blumenthal, "Pressures of Growth Stir Zoning Battles in Suburbs," *New York Times*, May 29, 1967.

31. Harry J. Butler, Wayne, N.J., quoted in Richard Reeves, "Land Is Prize in Battle for Control of Suburbs," *New York Times*, Aug. 17, 1971; reprinted as "The Battle Over Land," in Masotti and Hadden, *Suburbia in Transition*, p. 310.

32. John F. English, former chairman of the Democratic Party, Nassau County, N.Y., quoted in *ibid.*, p. 304.

33. James Walsh, chairman, Committee to Aid Lake Mohegan, Yorktown, N.Y., quoted in Paula R. Bernstein, "Suburbia Learning to Fight Town Hall," *New York Times*, July 15, 1973.

34. John W. Trimble, quoted in Walter H. Waggoner, "State High Court Weighs Attacks by Poor on Zoning," *New York Times*, Mar. 6, 1973. Mount Laurel is in Burlington County, N.J., and lies within the Philadelphia metropolitan area. The comment was made during oral arguments before the New Jersey Supreme Court in litigation which is discussed in chapter 7.

35. See *Southern Burlington County NAACP* v. *Township of Mt. Laurel*, 119 N.J.Super. 164, 290 A.2d 465 (1972) at 468.

36. See National Committee Against Discrimination in Housing, *Jobs and Housing: A Study of Employment and Housing Opportunities for Racial Minorities of the New York Metropolitan Region*, Interim Report, Mar., 1970 (New York, 1970), p. 116.

37. See Robert Cassidy, "Planning for Polo, not People," *Planning* 40 (Apr.–May, 1974), pp. 34–37.

38. See Middlesex-Mercer-Somerset Regional Study Council, *Housing and the Quality of Our Environment*, Research Report (Princeton, N.J., 1970), p. 1.

39. State of New Jersey, County and Municipal Government Study Commission, *Joint Services—A Local Response to Area-wide Problems*, Third Report, Sept., 1970 (Trenton: 1970), p. 26.

40. See John Darnton, "Suburbs Stiffening Beach Curbs," *New York Times*, July 10, 1972.

41. See "Next Thing You Know They'll Build a Church," *Planning* 37 (Aug., 1971), p. 126. The suburban effort to block construction of the church did not survive a challenge in the courts.

42. Mayor G. Tapley Taylor, Saddle River, N.J., quoted in Richard Johnston, "Act to Ban College," *Newark Evening News*, Mar. 23, 1961.

43. *Opening Up the Suburbs: An Urban Strategy for America* (New Haven: Yale Univ. Press, 1973), p. 65.

44. See Urban League of Westchester County, Housing Council, *Urban Renewal in Westchester County: Its Effect on the General Housing Supply and on the Housing Occupied by Negroes* (White Plains, N.Y., 1967), p. 3.

45. See *Southern Burlington County NAACP v. Township of Mt. Laurel*, 119 N.J.Super. 164, 290 A.2d 465 (1972) at 468.

46. The political weaknesses of lower-income and minority suburbanites are discussed in chapter 5.

47. Yale Rabin, "The Effects of Development Control on Housing Opportunities for Black Households in Baltimore County, Maryland," A Report to the U.S. Commission on Civil Rights, Aug. 1970, p. 2; reprinted in U.S. Commission on Civil Rights, *Hearing Held in Baltimore, Maryland, August 17–19, 1970* (Washington: U.S. Government Printing Office, 1970), p. 701.

48. See Simpson F. Lawson, *Above Property Rights*, U.S. Commission on Civil Rights, Clearinghouse publication #38, Dec., 1972 (Washington: U.S. Government Printing Office, 1972), pp. 21–22; and U.S. Commission on Civil Rights, *Hearing Held in St. Louis, Missouri, January 14–17, 1970* (Washington: U.S. Government Printing Office, 1970), pp. 384–410.

49. Mayor Kevin O'Neill, Irvington, N.Y., quoted in Linda Greenhouse, "Nonresident Autoists Seek Equal Parking Privileges," *New York Times*, Feb. 5, 1973.

50. Quoted in Darnton, "Suburbs Stiffening Beach Curbs."

51. *The Future of Westchester County*, A Supplement to the Second Regional Plan, Bulletin 117, Mar., 1971 (New York, 1971), p. 45.

52. *Urban America and the Federal System*, Commission Findings and Proposals, Oct., 1969 (Washington: U.S. Government Printing Office, 1969), p. 12.

53. Sidney Willis, director, Division of State and Regional Planning, N.J. Department of Community Affairs, quoted in Sharon Rosenhause and Edward J. Flynn, "The What, Why, How of Zoning," *Bergen Record*, Aug. 3, 1970.

54. League of Women Voters of Bergen County, *Where Can I Live in Bergen County? Factors Affecting Housing Supply* (Closter, N.J., 1972), p. 10.

55. Harry J. Butler, Wayne, N.J., quoted in Jack Rosenthal, "Suburbs Abandoning Dependence on City," *New York Times*, Aug. 16, 1971; reprinted as "Toward Suburban Independence," in Masotti and Hadden, *Suburbia in Transition*, p. 295.

56. See "The Battle of Greenwich," *Newsweek* 79 (June 5, 1972), p. 82.

57. See Marc Charney, "RCA's Move to New Canaan Raises Issue of Biased Zoning," *Hartford Times*, July 7, 1971.

58. See Samuel E. Wood and Alfred E. Heller, *The Phantom Cities of California* (Sacramento: California Tomorrow, 1963), pp. 47–48.

59. "Housing and Environment," Paper presented at the National Committee Against Discrimination in Housing Conference, Washington, D.C., Jan. 1973, p. 5.

60. Representative Howard Atherton, Marietta, Ga., quoted in John Herbers, "The Outer City: Uneasiness Over Future," *New York Times*, June 2, 1971; reprinted as "A Deep Uneasiness About the Future," in Masotti and Hadden, *Suburbia in Transition*, p. 283.

Chapter Three: Zoning for Fewer People

1. See U.S. National Commission on Urban Problems, *Building the American City*, Report to the Congress and President of the United States, 91st Cong., 1st sess., House Doc. No. 91-34 (Washington: U.S. Government Printing Office, 1968), pp. 208–9. See also Allen D. Manvel, *Local Land and Building Regulation: How Many Agencies? What Practices? How Much Personnel?* Prepared for the consideration of the National Commission on Urban Problems, Research Report No. 6 (Washington: U.S. Government Printing Office, 1968).

2. Lawrence G. Sager, " 'Exclusionary Zoning': Constitutional Limitations on the Power of Municipalities to Restrict the Use of Land," Paper prepared for the Biennial Conference of the American Civil Liberties Union, Boulder, Colo., June 8–11, 1972, p. 7. The term "exclusionary zoning" usually refers to local land-use controls which limit residential access by lower-income families. Paul and Linda Davidoff, for example, define exclusionary zoning "as the complex of zoning practices which results in closing suburban housing and land markets to low- and moderate-income families"; see "Opening the Suburbs: Toward Inclusionary Land Use Controls," *Syracuse Law Review* 22 (1971), p. 519. Throughout this volume, "exclusionary zoning" is employed in this more limited sense.

3. Town Selectman Henrietta Rogers, New Canaan, Conn., quoted in "New Canaan Aide Questions Zoning," *New York Times*, Mar. 7, 1971.

4. Mass., *Gen. Laws* (1968), Chap. 40A, sec. 3.

5. *Opening Up the Suburbs: An Urban Strategy for America* (New Haven: Yale Univ. Press, 1973), pp. 51–52. Charles M. Haar underscored the irrelevance of suburban zoning restrictions to health needs some years ago in commenting on the requirement that homes with attached garages in a New Jersey suburb have a minimum of 1,000 square feet, while those without attached garages had to be at least 1,200 square feet. "How," asked Haar, "can the presence of an attached garage favorably affect health or safety so as to warrant a reduction in the minimum living-floor area? Is it the 'health' of the automobile with which one is concerned? Where the garage is attached, thereby causing light and air to be cut off from one side of the dwelling, ought not the minimum floor area requirement be increased?" See "Zoning for Minimum standards: The Wayne Township Case," *Harvard Law Review* 66 (Apr., 1953), p. 1057.

6. State of New Jersey, County and Municipal Government Study Commission, *Housing & Suburbs: Fiscal & Social Impact of Multifamily Development*, Ninth Report, Oct. 1974 (Trenton, 1974), p. xiv.

7. See Report of Advisors to the Court, *Pascack Association Limited* v. *Mayor and Council of Township of Washington*, Bergen County, Superior Court of New Jersey, Law Div., Bergen Cy., Docket No. L-2756-70 P.W., Jan. 9, 1974, p. 10.

8. *Village of Euclid* v. *Ambler Realty Co.*, 272 U.S. 365 (1926) at 394.

9. *The Zoning Dilemma: A Legal Strategy for Urban Change* (Indianapolis: Bobbs-Merrill, 1971), p. 70.

10. See Max Rudmann, "Ridgewood Apartments Opposed," *Bergen Record*, Nov. 27, 1974.

11. N.J. County and Municipal Government Study Commission, *Housing & Suburbs*, p. xii.

12. See David A. Andelman, "Apartment Squeeze in the Suburbs Tightens," *New York Times*, Feb. 1, 1970.

13. Woody Klein, member of the Westport Town Meeting, quoted in Michael Knight, "Debate on Apartment Houses Roils Westport," *New York Times*, July 18, 1973. Klein had served in New York City as an assistant housing administrator, as well as press secretary to Mayor John V. Lindsay.

14. Dennis Schmickley, Park View Heights Corporation, quoted in "County Rights Panel Joining Fight Against Black Jack," *St. Louis Post-Dispatch*, Sept. 2, 1972. Park View Heights Corporation was the nonprofit developer of the subsidized project blocked by the incorporation of Black Jack.

15. See Jack Rosenthal, "Suburbs Abandoning Dependence on City," *New York Times*, Aug. 16, 1971; reprinted as "Toward Suburban Independence," in Louis H. Masotti and Jeffrey K. Hadden, eds., *Suburbia in Transition* (New York: Franklin Watts, 1974), p. 297.

16. Quoted in Lawrence O'Kane, "Rockland Favors Apartment Curbs," *New York Times*, Mar. 20, 1966.

17. N.J. County and Municipal Government Study Commission, *Housing & Suburbs*, p. xv. As a consequence of unrestrained apartment construction, the population of Parsippany-Troy Hills doubled between 1960 and 1970, from 25,000 to 50,000.

18. These developments are analyzed in detail in Robert Schafer, *The Suburbanization of Multifamily Housing* (Lexington, Mass.: Lexington Bks., 1974).

19. See Richard Reeves, "A Changing L.I. Is Opposed to Change," *New York Times*, June 3, 1971.

20. Mary E. Tappen, building inspector, Woodbridge, N.J., quoted in Campbell Allen, "Garden Apartments Set Trend in Middlesex," *Newark Sunday News*, May 2, 1965.

21. Richard Anderson, Wilmont Manor Community Association, Eastchester, N.Y., quoted in Paula R. Bernstein, "Suburbia Learning to Fight Town Hall," *New York Times*, July 15, 1973.

22. John Wassung, Planning and Zoning Commission, Westport, Conn., quoted in Knight, "Debate on Apartment Houses Roils Westport."

23. See Charles M. Haar and Demetrius S. Iatrides, *Housing the Poor in Suburbia: Public Policy at the Grass Roots* (Cambridge, Mass.: Ballinger Pub. Co., 1974), p. 142.

24. See, for example, George Sternlieb, *The Garden Apartment Development: A*

Municipal Cost-Revenue Analysis (New Brunswick, N.J.: Bureau of Economic Research, Rutgers Univ., 1964); Borough of Lincoln Park, Morris County, N.J., *Garden Apartment Study*, Prepared for Lincoln Park Planning Board by Passaic Valley Citizens Planning Association (Lincoln Park, 1964). City of Menlo Park, Cal., Planning Department, *The Apartment Community*, Planning Research Report No. 2 (Menlo Park, 1960): Nutley, N.J. Planning Board, *Apartments and Their Effect on Nutley*, A Report of the Apartment Committee of the Nutley Planning Board (Nutley, 1962); and N.J. County and Municipal Government Study Commission, *Housing & Suburbs*, pp. 30–47.

25. See *The Garden Apartment Development*, p. 15. Sternlieb's research indicated that no school-age children would live in efficiencies, .037 would dwell in one-bedroom units, .39 in two-bedroom units, and 1.03 in three-bedroom units.

26. See Marshall R. Burack, "Apartment Zoning in Suburbia" (Senior Thesis, Princeton University, 1971), pp. 112–14.

27. N.J. County and Municipal Government Study Commission, *Housing & Suburbs*, p. 35.

28. James G. Coke and Charles S. Liebman, "Political Values and Population Density Control," *Land Economics* 37 (Nov., 1961), p. 354.

29. *Ibid.*, p. 355.

30. See Ralph Blumenthal, "Pressures of Growth Stir Zoning Battles in the Suburbs," *New York Times*, May 27, 1967.

31. Assemblyman John H. Ewing, Bedminster, N.J., quoted in Ronald Sullivan, "U.A.W. Maintains a Jersey Suburb Keeps Out Poor," *New York Times*, Jan. 28, 1971.

32. Supervisor Lawrence K. Roos, St. Louis County, Mo., see U.S. Commission on Civil Rights, *Hearing Held in St. Louis, Missouri, January 14–17, 1970* (Washington: U.S. Government Printing Office, 1970), p. 367.

33. See Raymond May and Associates, *Zoning Controversies in the Suburbs: Three Case Studies*, Prepared for the consideration of the National Commission on Urban Problems, Research Report No. 11 (Washington: U.S. Government Printing Office, 1968), p. 65.

34. American Society of Planning Officials, *New Directions in Connecticut Planning Legislation—A Study of Connecticut Planning, Zoning, and Related Matters*, Prepared by Ross, Hardies, O'Keefe, Babcock, McDugald & Parsons (Chicago, 1967), p. 19.

35. Mayor Ralph F. Batch, Millburn, N.J., quoted in "Millburn OKs Zone Changes," *Newark Evening News*, Dec. 21, 1965.

36. See State of New Jersey, Department of Community Affairs, Division of State and Regional Planning, *Land Use Regulation: The Residential Land Supply* (Trenton: 1972), pp. 14–16. See also Norman Williams, Jr. and Thomas Norman, "Exclusionary Land Use Controls: The Case of North-Eastern New Jersey," *Syracuse Law Review* 22 (1971), pp. 475–507.

37. See National Commission on Urban Problems, *Building the American City*, p. 215.

38. National Association of Regional Councils, *Straight Talk About Housing Your Region* (Washington: National Association of Regional Councils, p. 11.

39. See John F. Collins, "Constraints," in Albert G. H. Dietz and Laurence S. Cutler, eds., *Industrialized Building Systems for Housing*, a compendium based on *Industrialized Building*, MIT Special Summer Session, Aug. 18–29, 1969, and *Systems Building and Industrialization for New Communities*, MIT Special Summer Session, June 16–20, 1970 (Cambridge: MIT Press, 1971), pp. 33–40.

40. See Joseph P. Fried, *Housing Crisis U.S.A.* (New York: Praeger Publishers, 1971), p. 153.

41. See Margaret J. Drury, *Mobile Homes: The Unrecognized Revolution in American Housing*, rev. 1972 ed. (New York: Praeger Publishers, 1972).

42. See Metropolitan Area Planning Council, *Residential Zoning in the MAPC Region*, Planning Information Series: Housing (Boston, 1972), p. 12.

43. See N.J. Department of Community Affairs, *Land Use Regulation*, pp. 10A, 12–13.

44. See Ania Savage, "Troubled Mobile-Home Market Detects Pick-Up," *New York Times*, July 6, 1975. The development was located in Spotswood in Middlesex County, N.J.

45. *Building the American City*, p. 216.

46. See Center for Auto Safety, *Mobile Homes: The Low-Cost Housing Hoax* (New York: Grossman, 1975), p. 56.

47. PURE is the abbreviation for People United to Reclaim the Environment, a group in Boulder, Colorado. SAVE stands for Save Our Valley Environment, an organization in the suburban Livermore-Amador Valley, which is located in the eastern portion of the San Francisco Bay Area.

48. See Fred P. Bosselman, "The Right to Move, the Need to Grow," *Planning* 39 (Sept., 1973), p. 9.

49. Quoted in Mary Ellen Leary, "California," *Atlantic Monthly* 232 (Nov.), 1973), p. 26.

50. Robert Cassidy, "Open Land or Open Housing," *New Republic* 167 (Nov. 25, 1972), p. 12.

51. See Leary, "California," p. 20.

52. Quoted in Richard F. Babcock and David L. Callies, "Ecology and Housing: Virtues in Conflict," in Marion Clawson, ed., *Modernizing Urban Land Policy*, Papers presented at an RFF Forum held in Washington, D.C., 13–14 April 1972 (Baltimore: Johns Hopkins Univ. Press, 1973), p. 207.

53. See Jay Thorwaldson, "The Palo Alto Experience," *Cry California* 8 (Spring, 1973), pp. 4–17.

54. James F. Brownell, Board of Supervisors, Loudoun County, Va., quoted in Leonard Downie, Jr., *Mortgage on America* (New York: Praeger Publishers, 1974), p. 84.

55. Quoted in Earl Finkler, *Nongrowth As a Planning Alternative: A Preliminary Examination of an Emerging Issue*, Planning Advisory Service Report No. 283 (Chicago: American Society of Planning Officials, 1972), p. 33. For a detailed discussion of no-growth activities in Boulder, see Earl Finkler and David L. Peterson, *Nongrowth Planning Strategies: The Developing Power of Towns, Cities, and Regions* (New York: Praeger Publishers, 1974), pp. 27–42.

56. Martus Granirer, West Branch Conservation Association, quoted in

"Rockland Rejects Sewer Plan; A Victory for Conservationists," *New York Times*, May 23, 1973.

57. Petaluma's growth limitations were invalidated by a federal district court in 1974, but upheld the following year by the U.S. Court of Appeals for the Ninth Circuit; see *Construction Ind. Assn., Sonoma Co.* v. *City of Petaluma*, 522 F.2d 897 (1975), and the discussion of the Petaluma litigation in chapter 7. For a useful examination of the issue from Petaluma's point of view, see John Hart, "The Petaluma Case," *Cry California* 9 (Spring, 1974), pp. 6–15.

58. City of Livermore, Cal., "Initiative Ordinance Re Building Permits," Apr. 11, 1972. A California court invalidated the ordinance for "being overbroad in scope and lacking in reasonably definable, or ascertainable, administrative standards and procedures"; see *Associated Home Builders of the Greater East Bay, Incorporated* v. *City of Livermore*, Superior Court of the State of California, Co. of Alameda, Dept. No. 14, Memorandum Decision No. 425754, Dec. 29, 1972, p. 2.

59. See *Golden* v. *Planning Board of Ramapo*, 30 N.Y.2d 359 (1972). The Ramapo decision is discussed in chapter 7.

60. Supervisor John F. McAlevey, Ramapo, N.Y., quoted in Herbert M. Franklin, *Controlling Urban Growth—But For Whom? The Social Implications of Development Timing Controls* (Washington: Potomac Inst., 1973), p. 19.

61. Bosselman, "The Right to Move, the Need to Grow," p. 10. Before the introduction of development timing, Ramapo issued an average of 620 building permits; after the new program was adopted, the annual average dropped to 350 permits.

62. Robert W. Wilson, acting county executive, Fairfax County, Va., quoted in Donnel Nunes, "Fairfax Board Backs Plan to Curb Growth," *Washington Post*, Apr. 9, 1973.

63. Audrey Moore, Board of Supervisors, Fairfax County, Va., quoted in *ibid.*

64. *Suburban Land Conversion in the United States: An Economic and Governmental Process* (Baltimore: Johns Hopkins Univ. Press, 1971), pp. 6–7, 176.

65. *1,400 Governments: The Political Economy of the New York Metropolitan Region* (Cambridge: Harvard Univ. Press, 1961), p. 112.

66. Jean R. Packard, chairman, Fairfax County Board of Supervisors, quoted in Kenneth Brademeier, "The Boom Fades as Area Weighs Value of Growth," *Washington Post*, Dec. 30, 1973.

67. "Large Lot Zoning," *Yale Law Journal* 78 (July, 1969), p. 1426.

68. "Density in the Urban Fringe Area," in Urban Land Institute, *Density: Five Perspectives* (Washington: Urban Land Institute, 1972), p. 3.

69. *1,400 Governments*, p. 111.

70. Thomas Thorsen, planning consultant, Southampton, N.Y., quoted in Barbara Delatiner, "A '21st Century' Master Plan Guides Southampton," *New York Times*, Oct. 21, 1973.

71. Natalie Gerardi, "The Town That Said No to No-Growth," *House & Home* 44 (Dec., 1973), p. 64.

72. *Building the American City*, p. 227.

73. Morton Lustig, U.S. National Commission on Urban Problems, *Hearings before the National Commission on Urban Problems*, Vol. 4, Sept. 1967: New York City, Philadelphia (Washington: U.S. Government Printing Office, 1968), p. 327.

74. See Brief of Plantiffs-Respondents, in *Southern Burlington County NAACP v. Township of Mt. Laurel*, Supreme Court of the State of New Jersey, Docket No. A-2846-71, Jan. 3, 1972, p. 21.

75. N.J. County and Municipal Government Study Commission, *Housing & Suburbs*, p. xiv.

76. *Controlling Urban Growth—But For Whom?*, p. 10.

77. See Daniel Lauber, *Recent Cases in Exclusionary Zoning*, Planning Advisory Service Report No. 292 (Chicago: American Society of Planning Officials, 1973), p. 3.

78. See George Vecsey, "Mobile-Home Owners Mobilizing into Suffolk's Newest Militant Minority," *New York Times*, Dec. 6, 1974.

79. See Earl Josephson, "State Building Code Seen Most Palatable Cahill Offering," *Trenton Evening Times*, Mar. 29, 1972.

80. *Building the American City*, p. 262.

81. *A Decent Home* (Washington: U.S. Government Printing Office, 1969), pp. 207–8.

82. National Association of Regional Councils, *Straight Talk About Housing Your Region*, p. 3.

83. *Opening Up the Suburbs*, p. 49.

84. "Levitt's Comments," Prepared for the President's Committee on Urban Housing by Levitt & Sons, in U.S. President's Committee on Urban Housing, *Technical Studies*, Vol. 2, Housing Costs, Production Efficiency, Finance, Manpower, Land (Washington: U.S. Government Printing Office, 1968), p. 70.

85. See Dan Wascoe, Jr., "Area Suburb Rents Called 2d Highest in Nation," *Minneapolis Tribune*, Sept. 15, 1972.

86. *Zoning and Housing Costs: The Impact of Land-Use Controls on Housing Price* (New Brunswick, N.J.: Center for Urban Policy Research, Rutgers Univ., 1973), p. 69.

87. Alfred S. Feibel, president, New Jersey Builders Association, quoted in G. G. Labelle, Wayne Beisert, and Sherry Conohan, "Everyone Wants To Be the Last Newcomer," *Trenton Evening Times*, Oct. 26, 1972.

88. See Lauber, *Recent Cases in Exclusionary Zoning*, p. 3.

89. *Equal Opportunity in Suburbia* (Washington: U.S. Government Printing Office, 1974), pp. 4, 7.

90. Norman Williams, Jr., "Planning Law and Democratic Living," *Law and Contemporary Problems* 20 (Spring, 1955), p. 330.

91. Ronald F. Kirby, Frank de Leeuw, and William Silverman, *Residential Zoning and Equal Housing Opportunities: A Case Study in Black Jack, Missouri* (Washington: Urban Inst., 1972), p. 16.

92. Sol Rabkin, counsel, Anti-Defamation League of B'nai B'rith, see U.S. National Commission on Urban Problems, *Hearings before the National Commission on Urban Problems*, Vol. 5, Oct. 1967: Detroit, East St. Louis, St. Louis, Washington, D.C. (Washington: U.S. Government Printing Office, 1968), p. 429.

Chapter Four: Excluding Subsidized Housing

1. Most federal housing programs are designated by the relevant parts of the national housing act. Section 221(d)3 was enacted in the Housing Act of 1961, Sections 235 and 236 in the Housing and Urban Development Act of 1968. From this point on, the term "subsidized housing" refers only to housing programs such as those described in Table 4.1 which are aimed at lower-income families. It does not refer to housing subsidies available to homeowners in general from federal mortgage guarantees and tax deductions for mortgage interest and property taxes.

2. Quoted in Monroe W. Karmin, "Romney's Departure Grows More Likely," *Wall Street Journal*, Dec. 16, 1970.

3. See *Gautreaux* v. *Chicago Housing Authority*, 206 F.Supp. 907, (1969); *Shannon* v. *United States Dept. of Housing & Urban Dev.*, 436 F.2d 809 (1970); and *Banks* v. *Perk*, 341 F.Supp. 1175 (1972).

4. See U.S. Congress, House of Representatives, Committee on the Judiciary, *Federal Government's Role in the Achievement of Equal Opportunity in Housing*, Hearings before the Civil Rights Oversight Subcommittee, 92d Cong., 1st and 2d sess. (Washington: U.S. Government Printing Office, 1972), pp. 381–83.

5. See Oliver Quayle and Company, *A Survey of Attitudes Toward Government Assisted Moderate and Low Income Housing in Westchester County, New York*, Study #1546 (Bronxville, N.Y., 1972), pp. 58–59.

6. See Nina Jaffe Gruen and Claude Gruen, *Low and Moderate Income Housing in the Suburbs: An Analysis for the Dayton, Ohio Region* (New York: Praeger Publishers, 1972), pp. 64, 89.

7. Francis Purcell, presiding supervisor, Township of Hempstead, Nassau County, N.Y., see U.S. Congress, House of Representatives, Committee on Banking and Currency, *Housing and Urban Development Act of 1972*, Hearings, 92d Cong., 2d sess. (Washington: U.S. Government Printing Office, 1972), p. 503.

8. See "U.S. Suit Over an Integrated Housing Project Distresses a Suburb of St. Louis," *New York Times*, June 20, 1971.

9. Ernest Salvas, regional director, Foundation for Cooperative Housing, Kansas City, Mo., quoted in Jeff Price and Mike Brush, "Low-Cost Housing Defies Stigma in Area Suburbs," *Kansas City Star*, Aug. 24, 1972.

10. *Ibid.*

11. See Martin F. Nolan, "The City Politic: Showdown Vote in Northern Westchester," *New York* 6 (June 4, 1973), p. 7.

12. See Marcus Gleisser, "Big Lots Battle Is Brewing," *Cleveland Plain Dealer*, July 23, 1972.

13. Supervisor Lawrence K. Roos, St. Louis County, Mo., quoted in Robert Adams, "Suburbs Feel No Debt to City," *St. Louis Post-Dispatch*, July 23, 1971.

14. Richard Plechner, attorney for Madison Township, N.J., quoted in Walter H. Waggoner, "State High Court Weighs Attacks by Poor on Zoning," *New York Times*, Mar. 6, 1973.

15. First Selectman Joseph L. McLinden, Ridgefield, Conn., quoted in Jonathan Kandell, "Ridgefield Faces a Housing Battle," *New York Times*, Aug. 6, 1972.

16. See "U.S. Suit Over an Integrated Housing Project Distresses a Suburb of St. Louis."

17. Oliver Quayle and Company, *A Survey of Attitudes Toward Government Assisted Moderate and Low Income Housing in Westchester County, New York*, p. 76.

18. See U.S. Congress, Senate, Select Committee on Equal Educational Opportunity, *Toward Equal Educational Opportunity*, Report 92-000, 92d Cong., 2d sess. (Washington: U.S. Government Printing Office, 1972), pp. 256–57.

19. "The Housing Challenge," Remarks prepared for delivery at the 28th Annual Convention and Exposition, National Association of Home Builders, Houston, Tex., Jan. 25, 1972, *HUD News*, p. 7.

20. Mayor Raymond Wojtowicz, Hamtramck, Michigan, quoted in "Housing Decision Irks Hamtramck," *New York Times*, Apr. 8, 1973.

21. Mayor Francis E. Kuckuck, Wauwatosa, Wis., see "Turning Points," transcript of broadcast, WMVS, Channel 10, Milwaukee, n.d., p. 10.

22. See "Subsidized Housing in Suburbia" (editorial), *Minneapolis Tribune*, Aug. 26, 1972.

23. See Richard F. Babcock and David L. Callies, "Ecology and Housing: Virtues in Conflict," in Marion Clawson, ed., *Modernizing Urban Land Policy*, Papers presented at an RFF Forum held in Washington, D.C., 13–14 April 1972 (Baltimore: Johns Hopkins Univ. Press, 1973), p. 210.

24. Richard F. Babcock and Clifford L. Weaver, "Exclusionary Suburban Zoning: One More Black Rebuff to the Latest Liberal Crusade," Fisk Univ., Nashville, Tenn., Apr. 7, 1972, p. 8.

25. See testimony of Martin E. Sloane, acting deputy staff director, U.S. Commission on Civil Rights, U.S. Congress, Senate, Select Committee on Equal Educational Opportunity, *Equal Educational Opportunity—1971*, Part 21: Metropolitan Aspects of Educational Inequality, Hearing, 92d Cong., 1st sess. (Washington: U.S. Government Printing Office, 1972), pp. 10457, 10462–63.

26. Leonard Downie, Jr., *Mortgage on America* (New York: Praeger Publishers, 1974), p. 133.

27. Richard Bellman, general counsel, National Committee Against Discrimination in Housing, see U.S. House of Representatives, *Federal Government's Role in the Achievement of Equal Opportunity in Housing*, p. 119.

28. See Price and Brush, "Low-Cost Housing Defies Stigma in Area Suburbs."

29. Mrs. Noah Epley, City Council, Black Jack, Mo., quoted in B. Drummond Ayres, "Bulldozers Turn Up Soil and Ill Will in a Suburb of St. Louis," *New York Times*, Jan. 18, 1971.

30. Robert Becker, vice president, North Springfield Civic Association, Fairfax County, Va., quoted in Monroe W. Karmin, "Forced Integration? Not in Fairfax," *Wall Street Journal*, Sept. 29, 1971.

31. See William Borders, "Controversy in Stamford," *New York Times*, Aug. 15, 1966.

32. Frances Marland and Jim Rice, "Citizens Boycott Housing Hearing," *Fairfax Globe*, July 26, 1973.

33. Jack L. Quigley, director, Inter-Religious Center for Urban Affairs,

quoted in "U.S. Suit Over an Integrated Housing Project Distresses a Suburb of St. Louis."

34. *Ibid.*

35. See Ayres, "Bulldozers Turn Up Soil and Ill Will in a Suburb of St. Louis."

36. Frank E. Schwelb, U.S. Department of Justice, quoted in "Housing and Race Stir Court Fight," *New York Times,* Apr. 1, 1973.

37. See John H. Denton, "Phase I Report" to the National Committee Against Discrimination in Housing, U.S. Department of Housing and Urban Development Project, No. Cal. D-8 (n.d.), pt. 3, p. Jc-29.

38. Oliver Quayle and Company, *A Survey of Attitudes Toward Government Assisted Moderate and Low Income Housing in Westchester County, New York,* p. 73.

39. Mayor Raymond A. Stachweicz, Garfield Heights, O., quoted in John Herbers, "The Outer City: Uneasiness Over Future," *New York Times,* June 2, 1971; reprinted as "A Deep Uneasiness About the Future," in Louis H. Masotti and Jeffrey K. Hadden, eds., *Suburbia in Transition* (New York: Franklin Watts, 1974), p. 287.

40. Ann Sheldon, Wayne State Univ., Detroit, quoted in Walter S. Mossberg, "A Blue Collar Town Fears Urban Renewal Perils Its Way of Life," *Wall Street Journal,* Nov. 2, 1970.

41. Assemblyman Albert W. Merck, Mendham, N.J., quoted in G. G. Labelle, Wayne Beissert, and Sherry Conohan, "Everyone Wants To Be the Last Newcomer," *Trenton Evening Times,* Oct. 26, 1972.

42. Reese Cleghorn, "A Closer Look: Atlanta," *City* 5 (Jan. / Feb., 1971), p. 36.

43. See U.S. Congress, Senate, Select Committee on Equal Educational Opportunity, *Equal Educational Opportunity,* Part 5: De Facto Segregation and Housing Discrimination, Hearings, 91st Cong., 1st sess. (Washington: U.S. Government Printing Office, 1971), pp. 2758–59.

44. "The Federal Government as 'Houser of Last Resort': A Policy for Democratic Urban Growth," *Urban Law Annual* (1972), p. 41.

45. Cleghorn, "A Closer Look: Atlanta," p. 37.

46. See Research Atlanta, "Atlanta's Public Housing Policy," (Atlanta: Research Atlanta, 1972), p. 25; and Leonard S. Rubinowitz, *Low-Income Housing: Suburban Strategies* (Cambridge, Mass.: Ballinger Pub. Co., 1974), p. 230.

47. See Peter H. Weiner, "Report: Third Conference on Exclusionary Land Use Policies," Taconic Foundation, Sept. 23, 1970, p. 12.

48. Chagrin Falls Township was outside the jurisdiction of the Cleveland Metropolitan Housing Authority. For a useful summary of CMHA's efforts to locate public-housing outside Cleveland in the suburbs, see Robert Beckham, "Detour Ahead: That's the Message Coming to Public Agencies Attempting to Move Down the Road to Suburbia to Build Low-Income Housing," *Journal of Housing* 30 (May, 1973), pp. 227–29.

49. See Cuyahoga Metropolitan Housing Authority, "Study by Cuyahoga Metropolitan Housing Authority Reflecting Need in Cuyahoga County Communities for Public Housing and Proposed Production Plan" (Cleveland, n.d.).

50. Mayor Robert M. Lawthur, Lakewood, O., quoted in "Lakewood Mayor Set to Fight Housing Plan," *Cleveland Plain Dealer*, June 28, 1973.

51. Mayor John Petruska, Parma, O., quoted in "Anger, Doubt Follow Housing Plan," *Cleveland Plain Dealer*, June 23, 1973.

52. Housing Authority of the County of Cook and the Chicago Housing Authority, "Agreement," Sept. 23, 1971, p. 1.

53. Interfaith Housing Corporation, *The Suburban Noose: A Story of Non-Profit Housing Development for the Modest-Income Family in Metropolitan Boston* (Boston, 1969), p. 26.

54. Joseph P. Fried, *Housing Crisis U.S.A.* (New York: Praeger Publishers, 1971), p. 98.

55. See U.S. House of Representatives, *Housing and Urban Development Act of 1972*, p. 644.

56. Second Amended Complaint of Plaintiffs, *Planning for People Coalition* v. *County of DuPage*, U.S. District Court, North. Dist. of Ill., East. Div., Civil Action No. 71 C 587, Sept. 8, 1972, p. 14.

57. See *Southern Burlington County N.A.A.C.P.* v. *Township of Mount Laurel*, 67 N.J. 151, 336 A.2d 713 (1975) at 722.

58. *Low-Income Housing: Suburban Strategies*, p. 39.

59. Dale F. Bertsch, executive director, Miami Valley Regional Planning Commission, see U.S. Commission on Civil Rights, *Hearing Held in Washington, D.C., June 14–17, 1971* (Washington: U.S. Government Printing Office, 1971) p. 35.

60. Denton, "Phase I Report," pt. 3, p. Jc-29.

61. State of New Jersey, County and Municipal Government Study Commission, *Housing & Suburbs: Fiscal & Social Impact of Multifamily Development*, Ninth Report, Oct., 1974 (Trenton, 1974), p. 119.

62. The community was Santa Venetia in Marin County, see Denton, "Phase I Report," pt. 3, pp. Jc-29–30.

63. See *Crow* v. *Brown*, 322 F.Supp. 382 (1971) at 392, 385.

64. *Lower-Income Housing: The Planners' Response* (Chicago: American Society of Planning Officials, 1972), p. 40.

65. James W. Dyke, Jr., "The Use of Zoning Laws to Prevent Poor People from Moving into Suburbia," *Howard Law Journal* 16 (Winter, 1971), p. 359.

66. See *Kennedy Park Homes Ass'n* v. *City of Lackawanna*, 318 F.Supp. 669 (1970), *Kennedy Park Homes Ass'n* v. *City of Lackawanna, N.Y.*, 436 F.2d 108 (1970), and Homer Bigart, "Upstate Steel Town Spawns Race Tensions," *New York Times*, Dec. 16, 1968. A challenge in federal court of Lackawanna's actions was successful; the case is discussed in chapter 7.

67. See testimony of Aileen Hernandez, western representative, National Committee Against Discrimination in Housing, in U.S. House of Representatives, *Federal Government's Role in the Achievement of Equal Opportunity in Housing*, p. 106.

68. Colorado, Mississippi, Montana, Oklahoma, Texas, Vermont, and Virginia. A requirement for local referenda on public-housing projects was repealed by the Iowa legislature in 1972.

69. *James* v. *Valtierra*, 402 U.S. 137 (1971) at 141. See chapter 7 for a discussion of the *Valtierra* ruling.

70. At the same time, a companion ordinance was ratified, setting a 35-foot height limit on all structures in Parma.

71. Eastlake's referendum requirement was invalidated in 1975 by the Ohio Supreme Court, see *Forest City Enterprises* v. *City of Eastlake*, 41 Ohio St.2d 187, 324 N.E.2d 740 (1975).

72. See "Cleveland Suburb Sued," *NCDH Trends in Housing* 17 (May / June, 1973), p. 2.

73. See Herbert M. Franklin, "Memorandum 73-5," Metropolitan Housing Program, Potomac Inst., Washington, May 14, 1973, p. 2. A separate suit was filed against Parma at the same time by the National Committee Against Discrimination in Housing.

74. See *Opening Up the Suburbs: An Urban Strategy for America* (New Haven: Yale Univ. Press, 1973), p. 156.

75. See William Lilley III and Timothy B. Clark, "Urban Report / Immense Costs, Scandals, Social Ills Plague Low-Income Housing Programs," *National Journal* 4 (July 1, 1972), p. 1081.

76. Michael Knight, "Westport Will Seek Special Apartments for Elderly," *New York Times*, July 19, 1973.

77. John L. Waner, director, Chicago Area Office, Department of Housing and Urban Development, quoted in John Herbers, "Federal Aid to Housing Has Produced Widespread Criticism and Condemnation," *New York Times*, Jan. 3, 1972.

78. George Sternlieb, "Housing Subsidies Falling . . . Where the Housing Shortage Isn't," *New York Times*, Dec. 24, 1972.

79. U.S. Commission on Civil Rights, *Home Ownership for Lower Income Families: A Report on the Racial and Ethnic Impact of the Section 235 Program* (Washington: U.S. Government Printing Office, 1971), p. viii.

80. *Ibid.*, pp. 60–61.

81. See Peter Braestrup, "New Housing Projects Called Segregationist," *Washington Post*, Oct. 15, 1972.

82. The housing policies of the Nixon Administration are discussed in detail in chapter 8.

Chapter Five: Unequal Odds

1. See Joseph P. Fried, *Housing Crisis U.S.A.* (New York: Praeger Publishers, 1971), pp. 50–51.

2. See Geoffrey Sheilds and L. Sanford Spector, "Opening Up the Suburbs: Notes on a Movement for Social Change," *Yale Review of Law and Social Action* 2 (Summer, 1972), p. 305.

3. City of New York, Economic Development Administration, "Statement by the Hon. D. K. Patton, Economic Development Administration, New York City, before the Bedminster, N.J., Planning Board Regarding Regional Economic Growth Patterns," Nov. 9, 1970, p. 4. See also David K. Shipler, "City Seeks Help of Jersey Town," *New York Times*, Nov. 10, 1970.

4. Steward M. Hutt, counsel, New Jersey Builders Association, quoted in Richard J. H. Johnston, "Low-Income Housing Exclusions in U.S. Assailed," *New York Times*, Nov. 7, 1969.

5. "People, Jobs, and Housing" (editorial), *Washington Post*, July 6, 1971.

6. *Opening Up the Suburbs: An Urban Strategy for America* (New Haven: Yale Univ. Press, 1973), p. 11.

7. Oliver Quayle and Company, *A Survey of Attitudes Toward Government Assisted Moderate and Low Income Housing in Westchester County, New York*, Study #1546 (Bronxville, N.Y., 1972), pp. 21, 26.

8. Downs, *Opening Up the Suburbs*, p. 166.

9. Mayor Robert Lawthur, Lakewood, O., quoted in Roldo Bartimole, "A Closer Look: Cleveland," *City* 5 (Jan. / Feb., 1971), p. 45.

10. Supervisor Lawrence K. Roos, St. Louis County, Mo., quoted in Robert Adams, "Suburbs Feel No Debt to City," *St. Louis Post-Dispatch*, July 23, 1971.

11. Supervisor John F. McAlevey, Ramapo, N.Y., quoted in Richard Reeves, "Counterattack by Cities," *New York Times*, Mar. 8, 1971; reprinted as "Counterattack by the Cities," in Louis H. Masotti and Jeffrey K. Hadden, eds., *Suburbia in Transition* (New York: Franklin Watts, 1974), p. 242.

12. For a similar line of argument, see Eric J. Branfman, Benjamin I. Cohen, and David M. Trubek, "Measuring the Invisible Wall: Land Use Controls and the Residential Patterns of the Poor," *Yale Law Journal* 82 (Jan., 1973), p. 503.

13. County Executive Eugene H. Nickerson, Nassau County, N.Y., quoted in Roy R. Silver, "Nickerson Urges Housing for Poor," *New York Times*, Jan. 12, 1969.

14. See Craig E. Polhemus, "Princeton Is Encouraging Low-Income Housing," *New York Times*, July 22, 1973.

15. Supervisor John F. McAlevey, Ramapo, N.Y., quoted in Alan S. Oser, "Innovator in Suburbs Under Fire," *New York Times*, Mar. 28, 1971.

16. Gerald Schwern, village manager, Brown Deer, Wis., see "Turning Points," transcript of broadcast, WMVS, Channel 10, Milwaukee, n.d., p. 15.

17. Nina Jaffe Gruen and Claude Gruen, *Low and Moderate Income Housing in the Suburbs: An Analysis for the Dayton, Ohio Region* (New York: Praeger Publishers, 1972), p. 80.

18. See State of New Jersey, County and Municipal Government Study Commission, *Housing & Suburbs: Fiscal & Social Impact of Multifamily Development*, Ninth Report, Oct., 1974 (Trenton, 1974), pp. 85–92.

19. Town Selectman Henrietta Rogers, New Canaan, Conn., quoted in "New Canaan Aide Questions Zoning," *New York Times*, Mar. 7, 1971.

20. See Franklin Whitehouse, "Westport Warms to Apartments," *New York Times*, May 24, 1970.

21. Oliver Quayle and Company, *A Survey of Attitudes Toward Government Assisted Moderate and Low Income Housing in Westchester County, New York*, p. 74.

22. *Ibid.*, p. 63.

23. For a discussion of the Fairfax and Montgomery ordinances, see Herbert M. Franklin, David Falk, and Arthur J. Levin, *In-Zoning: A Guide for Policy-Makers on Inclusionary Land Use Programs* (Washington: Potomac Inst., 1974), pp. 131–41.

24. Charles Boswell, president, Fairfax County Police Association, quoted in Monroe W. Karmin, "Forced Integration? Not in Fairfax," *Wall Street Journal*, Sept. 29, 1971.

25. See Whitehouse, "Westport Warms to Apartments."

26. See Richard Reeves, "Land Is Prize in Battle for Control of Suburbs," *New York Times*, Aug. 17, 1971; reprinted as "The Battle Over Land," in Masotti and Hadden, *Suburbia in Transition*, p. 308.

27. Mayor Newton Miller, Wayne, N.J., quoted in Jack Rosenthal, "Suburbs Abandoning Dependence on City," *New York Times*, Aug. 16, 1971.

28. Pano Constantine, Mahwah Taxpayers Association, Mahwah, N.J., quoted in Richard Zimmerman, "Town Bracing for Legal Defense," *Bergen Record*, Jan. 28, 1971.

29. "Opening Up the Suburbs," p. 305.

30. For a useful review of the activities of these and other national open-housing organizations, see *ibid.*, pp. 301–5.

31. League of Women Voters Education Fund, "Suburban Zoning, The New Frontier," (Washington, n.d.), p. 3.

32. George Schermer, "Strategy, Tactics, and Organization for the Fair Housing Movement," Jan. 16, 1973, p. 2. For a useful review of the activities of seven relatively broad-based fair-housing groups, see "Metro Center Activities," *NCDH Trends in Housing* XVIII (Sept. / Oct., 1974), pp. 1–2. A more general treatment of the open-housing movement is provided by Juliet Z. Saltman, *Open Housing as a Social Movement: Challenge, Conflict, and Change* (Lexington, Mass.: Lexington Bks., 1971).

33. Schermer, "Strategy, Tactics, and Organization for the Fair Housing Movement," p. 3. The concerns and activities of neighborhood stabilization groups are set forth in useful fashion in Musa Bish, Jean Bullock, and Jean Milgram, *Racial Steering: The Dual Housing Market and Multiracial Neighborhoods* (Philadelphia: National Neighbors, 1973).

34. Quoted in Karmin, "Forced Integration? Not in Fairfax."

35. Paul Davidoff, "A Lake Is Backdrop for Debate on Suburban Integration Plan: Pro," *New York Times*, Nov. 4, 1973. See also Paul Davidoff and Neil Newton Gold, Exclusionary Zoning," *Yale Review of Law and Social Action* 1 (Winter, 1970), pp. 57–63; and Linda Davidoff, Paul Davidoff, and Neil N. Gold, "The Suburbs Have to Open Their Gates," *New York Times Magazine*, Nov. 7, 1971, pp. 40–50, 55–60.

36. Quoted in Jerome Aumente, "Domestic Land Reform," *City* 5 (Jan. / Feb., 1971), p. 56.

37. "A Lake Is Backdrop for Debate on Suburban Integration Plan: Pro."

38. Suburban Action Institute, "Statement of Purpose," (Tarrytown, N.Y., Sept. 1973), pp. 2–3.

39. Neil Gold, Suburban Action Institute, see Peter H. Weiner, "Report: Seventh Conference on Exclusionary Land Use Policies," Clearinghouse on Exclusionary Land Use Problems, National Urban Coalition, Washington, June 24, 1971, p. 18.

40. For a general review of Suburban Action's activities, see Delroy Hayunga, *The Suburban Frontier* (New York: Suburban Action Institute and

Board of National Missions, United Presbyterian Church in the U.S.A., 1971), pp. 23–27.

41. Quoted in Michael Knight, "New Fairfield Zone Board Bars Candlewood Lake Development," New York Times, Oct. 12, 1973.

42. See "Unconstitutional Zoning Practices of Four Bergen County Towns Challenged in Law Suit," Suburban Action News, Feb. 17, 1972, and "Fully Integrated New Community Planned for Mahwah," Suburban Action News, Apr. 24, 1972.

43. Neil Gold, Garden Cities Development Corporation, quoted in Ernest Dickinson, "Activists in Suburbs Under Fire as Landlords," New York Times, Mar. 24, 1974.

44. First Selectman Joseph L. McLinden, Ridgefield, Conn., quoted in Jonathan Kandell, "Ridgefield Faces a Housing Battle," New York Times, Aug. 6, 1972.

45. Supervisor Charles W. Barraud, Jr., Brookhaven, N.Y., quoted in David A. Andelman, "Suffolk Is Facing Zone Challenge," New York Times, Feb. 28, 1973.

46. Mayor Lawrence Nyland, Mahwah, N.J., quoted in Jan Rubin, "Nyland Blasts Tactics of SAI," Ridgewood (N.J.) Herald News, May 4, 1972.

47. See Richard Zimmerman, "The Open Housing Activists: One Goal, Different Styles," Bergen Sunday Record, June 18, 1972.

48. Malcolm Cowley, "A Lake Is Backdrop for Debate on Suburban Integration Plan: Con," New York Times, Nov. 4, 1973.

49. Ibid.

50. Paul Davidoff, Linda Davidoff, and Neil Newton Gold, "Suburban Action: Advocate Planning for an Open Society," Journal of the American Institute of Planners 36 (Jan. 1970), p. 21.

51. Ibid., p. 17.

52. Suburban Action Institute, "Statement of Purpose," p. 1.

53. "The Coming Apart of Fortress Suburbia," New York 5 (Jan. 31, 1972), p. 26.

54. See William Farrell, "Greenwich Opens Zoning Hearings," New York Times, Mar. 2, 1966. The campaign was organized by Lewis S. Rosensteil, a large landowner, who offered to sell half-acre plots to local employees for under $1,000 if Greenwich would rezone his holdings to permit more intensive development. Nothing came of the effort, which was opposed by local officials and thirty-four neighborhood and civic organizations.

55. Quoted in John L. Cavnar, "Bedminster Committee Will Decide on Office Project," Newark Sunday News, Nov. 15, 1970.

56. C. McKim Norton, Regional Plan Association, see Peter H. Weiner, "Report: Sixth Conference on Exclusionary Land Use Policies," Clearinghouse on Exclusionary Land Use Problems, National Urban Coalition, New York, Apr. 15, 1971, p. 6.

57. Judy Morris, League of Women Voters, quoted in Sheilds and Spector, "Opening Up the Suburbs," p. 305.

58. National Committee Against Discriminations in Housing, Jobs and Hous-

ing: A Study of Employment and Housing Opportunities for Racial Minorities of the New York Metropolitan Region, Interim Report, Mar., 1970 (New York, 1970), p. 63.

59. Ian McHarg, remarks at "The Environment of the Open Society," Suburban Action Institute Annual Conference, New York, Jan. 17, 1973.

60. Richard Bellman, Suburban Action Institute, quoted in Nora Kerr, "Land-use Priority: People or Lawns?" *Bergen Record*, May 21, 1973.

61. Paul Davidoff, executive director, Suburban Action Institute, quoted in Aumente, "Domestic Land Reform," p. 56.

62. Aileen Hernandez, western representative, National Committee Against Discrimination in Housing, see U.S. Congress, House of Representatives, Committee on the Judiciary, *Federal Government's Role in the Achievement of Equal Opportunity in Housing*, Hearings before the Civil Rights Oversight Subcommittee, 92d Cong., 1st and 2d sess. (Washington: U.S. Government Printing Office, 1972), p. 108.

63. Richard F. Babcock and David L. Callies, "Ecology and Housing: Virtues in Conflict," in Marion Clawson, ed., *Modernizing Urban Land Use Policy*, Papers presented at an RFF Forum held in Washington, D.C., 13–14 April, 1972 (Baltimore: Johns Hopkins Univ. Press, 1973), p. 208.

64. Malcolm D. Rivkin, "Three Hopeful Augers of Suburban Change," *City* 5 (Jan. / Feb., 1971), p. 67.

Chapter Six: Latent Interests with Limited Clout

1. Geoffrey Sheilds and L. Sanford Spector, "Opening Up the Suburbs: Notes on a Movement for Social Change," *Yale Review of Law and Social Action* 2 (Summer, 1972), p. 323.

2. *Opening Up the Suburbs: An Urban Strategy for America* (New Haven: Yale Univ. Press, 1973), p. 177.

3. *Ibid.*, p. 178.

4. Robert Weinberg, Robert Martin Associates, Westchester County, N.Y., quoted in Richard Reeves, "Land Is Prize in Battle for Control of Suburbs," *New York Times*, Aug. 17, 1971; reprinted as "The Battle Over Land," in Louis H. Masotti and Jeffrey K. Hadden, eds., *Suburbia in Transition* (New York: Franklin Watts, 1974), p. 308.

5. See William Lilley III, "Housing Report / Romney Faces Political Perils With Plan to Integrate Suburbs," *National Journal* 2 (Oct. 17, 1970), p. 2252.

6. The phrase "liberal and progressive" is from an executive of Levitt and Sons, see Herbert J. Gans, *The Levittowners: Ways of Life and Politics in A New Suburban Community* (New York: Pantheon Bks., 1967) p. 372.

7. Quoted in Marvin Bressler, "The Myers' Case: An Instance of Successful Racial Invasion," *Social Problems* 8 (Fall, 1960), p. 127.

8. David S. Schoenbrod, "Large Lot Zoning," *Yale Law Journal* 78 (July 1, 1969), p. 1420.

9. George A. Frank, executive vice president, Builders Institute of Westchester and Putnam, Inc., quoted in "Building Drops in Westchester," *New York Times*, Sept. 5, 1971.

10. David H. Miller, Miller & Smith, Inc., McLean, Va., quoted in "Virginia Builders Open Fire," *Washington Star-News*, Sept. 21, 1973.

11. Steward M. Hutt, counsel, New Jersey Builders Association, quoted in Richard J. H. Johnston, "Low-Income Housing Exclusions in U.S. Assailed," *New York Times*, Nov. 10, 1969.

12. Robert Weinberg, Robert Martin Associates, Westchester, N.Y., quoted in Reeves, "The Battle Over Land," p. 305.

13. John Stastny, president, National Association of Home Builders of the United States, see U.S. Commission on Civil Rights, *Hearings Held in Washington, D.C., June 14–17, 1971* (Washington: U.S. Government Printing Office, 1971, p. 382.

14. National Association of Home Builders, "Statement of Policy: Land Use and the Environment," Sept., 1973, p. 1.

15. *Ibid.*, p. 4.

16. Letter from Marilyn R. Lowney, director, Urban Governmental Affairs, National Association of Home Builders, Oct. 18, 1973.

17. Quoted in William Lilley III, "Urban Report / Policy Makers Condemn Housing Programs; Seek Alternative to Builder-Subsidy Approach," *National Journal* 3 (July 24, 1971), p. 1541.

18. Alfred S. Feibel, president, New Jersey Builders Association, quoted in Lew Head, "Housing Remedy: Where It's Not," *Trenton Evening Times*, Feb. 14, 1973.

19. "A Private Developer Comments on 'Environmental Impact' Issues," *Journal of Housing* 30 (Nov., 1973), p. 483.

20. Sheilds and Spector, "Opening Up the Suburbs," p. 318.

21. Jefferson S. Smith, president, Virginia Builders Association, quoted in Monroe W. Karmin, "Forced Integration? Not in Fairfax," *Wall Street Journal*, Sept. 29, 1971.

22. See *Board of County Supervisors of Fairfax County* v. *DeGroff Enterprises, Inc.*, 214 Va. 235, 198 S.E.2d 600 (1973).

23. See LaBarbara Bowman, "Montgomery Votes Housing for Low-Income Families," *Washington Post*, Oct. 24, 1973; and "Montgomery Subdivisions Must Have Low-Income Housing," *Planning* 39 (Dec., 1973), p. 5.

24. Sheilds and Spector, "Opening Up the Suburbs," p. 317.

25. Quoted in Gausewell Vaughan, "Court Action Not the Right Road to Zoning Change, Builder Says," *Red Bank* (N.J.) *Register*, May 12, 1972.

26. *Ibid.*

27. See "Sparks Fly Over Zoning," *Paterson Evening News*, Aug. 10, 1972.

28. See Herbert M. Franklin and Lois Craig, "Report: Eighth Conference on Exclusionary Land Use Problems," National Urban Coalition, Washington, Oct. 5, 1971, p. 4.

29. See Joseph P. Fried, *Housing Crisis U.S.A.* (New York: Praeger Publishers, 1971), p. 151.

30. H. Harland Crowell, Jr., chairman, Realtors' Washington Committee of the National Association of Real Estate Boards, see U.S. Congress, House of

Representatives, Committee on Banking and Currency, *Housing and Urban Development Legislation—1970*, Hearings before the Subcommittee on Housing, 91st Cong., 2d sess. (Washington: U.S. Government Printing Office, 1970), p. 883.

31. Louis R. Barba, president, National Association of Home Builders of the United States, see *ibid.*, p. 766.

32. Richard C. Van Dusen, undersecretary, Department of Housing and Urban Development, quoted in William Lilley III, "Housing Report / Administration and Congress Follow the Courts in Promoting Residential Integration," *National Journal* 3 (Nov. 12, 1971), p. 2433.

33. Milton P. Semer, National Homes Corporation, quoted in Lilley, "Romney Faces Political Perils with Plan to Integrate Suburbs," p. 2255. Semer was a former general counsel of the Housing and Home Finance Agency, the predecessor agency to the Department of Housing and Urban Development.

34. "The Right to Move, the Need to Grow," *Planning* 39 (Sept., 1973) p. 11.

35. "Opening Up the Suburbs," p. 318.

36. Hans Sander, chairman, Princeton Township Planning Board, Princeton, N.J., quoted in Sharon M. Bertsch, "Princeton Twp. Master Plan Partial to Executive Living," *Trenton Sunday Times Advertiser*, Mar. 17, 1968.

37. John F. McAlevey, "A Method for Suburb to Aid Poor," *New York Times*, May 14, 1972. McAlevey was supervisor of the Town of Ramapo in Rockland County, New York.

38. "Three Hopeful Augers of Suburban Change," *City* 5 (Jan. / Feb., 1971), p. 67.

39. Raphael D. Silver, president, National Job-Linked Housing Center, quoted in John Henry, "The Key to Low-Income Housing: Corporate Pressure," *Newsday*, Dec. 14, 1972.

40. Questionnaires were sent to 1,250 corporations, with approximately one-sixth responding. To the question, "Do you feel that some of your employees live so far away from their work as to increase their absenteeism?" 35 percent of the respondents answered yes, 53 percent no, and 11 percent gave no answer. To the question, "Do you believe that these current zoning policies make it more difficult for industry to meet its labor needs?" 32 percent answered yes, 23 percent no, 33 percent did not know, and 12 percent did not answer. See Institute of Human Relations, *Questionnaire: Housing for the Semi-skilled and Unskilled Labor Market* (New York, 1972).

41. See Louis B. Schlivek, *Man in Metropolis* (Garden City, N.Y.: Doubleday & Co., 1965), p. 375.

42. See John H. Denton, "Phase I Report" to the National Committee Against Discrimination in Housing, U.S. Department of Housing and Urban Development Project, No. Cal. D-8 (n.d.), pt. 4, pp. Jd-16-18.

43. See Linda Greenhouse, "A Company Adjusts to the Suburbs," *New York Times*, Nov. 22, 1970; reprinted as "Painless Move to Suburbia," in *Planning* 37 (May, 1971), pp. 69–70.

44. See "I.B.M. Is Proving a Good Neighbor in Affluent Bergen Town,"

New York Times, May 20, 1973; and League of Women Voters of Bergen County, *Where Can I Live in Bergen County? Factors Affecting Housing Supply* (Closter, N.J., 1972), p. 2.

45. See James Feron, "Texaco Is Moving to Westchester," *New York Times*, July 19, 1973.

46. Denton, "Phase I Report," pt. 4, Jd-22.

47. Sol M. Linowitz, "We Must Have a New Definition of 'Business Success,'" *Washington Sunday Star*, May 16, 1971; text of a speech to the Rotary Club of New York, May 6, 1971.

48. See Ronald Sullivan, "A.T.&T. to Move Some Offices Out of City to Jersey Property," *New York Times*, June 3, 1971.

49. "FCC and EEOC Urged to Stop A.T.&T. Move to Discriminatory Suburb," *Suburban Action News*, June 2, 1971, p. 1. Suburban Action also filed complaints with federal agencies in connection with planned moves to the suburbs by RCA and General Electric. Nothing came of any of these requests for administrative action.

50. William H. Brown III, "Corporate Location and the Urban Crisis," in Suburban Action Institute, *Open or Closed Suburbs: Corporate Location and the Urban Crisis* (White Plains, N.Y., n.d.), pp. 14–15. During 1971, EEOC's legal staff concluded that "the proposition that a corporate relocation constitutes a *prima facie* violation of Title VII is consistent with Commission policy and Court precedent"; see U.S. Equal Employment Opportunity Commission, "Employment Discrimination by Relocation of Plant and Corporate Headquarters," memorandum from Stanley P. Hebert, general counsel, John de J. Pemberton, Jr., deputy general counsel, and Martin I. Slate, office of the general counsel, to William H. Brown III, chairman, July 7, 1971, p. 4. The commission, however, did not seek to apply this interpretation of its mandate to corporate moves to the suburbs. For a general discussion of these issues, see Alfred W. Blumrosen, "The Duty to Plan for Fair Employment: Plant Location in White Suburbia," *Rutgers Law Review* 25 (Spring, 1971), pp. 383–404.

51. See Institute of Human Relations, *Questionnaire: Housing for the Semiskilled and Unskilled Labor Market*, p. 4.

52. Ford Motor Co., "Statement by Charles H. Pillion, Regional Civic and Governmental Affairs Manager, Ford Motor Co., at Mahwah Township Planning Board Meeting, Monday, Dec. 11, 1972," Ford News Release, n.d. See also Linda Iceland, "Mahwah Skeptical about Planned Community," *Bergen Record*, Dec. 12, 1972. Ford's intervention had no appreciable impact on local officials and residents in Mahway, who were, as indicated in chapter 6, steadfast in their opposition to Suburban Action's housing proposals.

53. See New York State Urban Development Corporation, "In the Matter of Commonwealth Drive Housing Proposal for Wyandanch," transcript of hearing before Joseph A. Stabile, hearing officer, Wyandanch, N.Y., July 26, 1973, p. 62. Grumman's support, like that of a host of civil-rights, housing, and religious groups, was insufficient to overcome local opposition to the Wyandanch project, whose demise is examined in the discussion of New York's Urban Development Corporation in chapter 10.

54. "We Must Have a New Definition of 'Business Success.' "

55. The role of business and other groups in dispersing subsidized housing in the Dayton and Rochester areas is discussed in chapters 9 and 10 respectively.

56. Alexander Greendale, director, National Job Linked Housing Center, American Jewish Committee, "Statement at AFL-CIO Conference," Washington, Apr. 11–12, 1973.

57. See David K. Shipler, "Western Electric Rebuts City on Relocation to Jersey Town," *New York Times*, Nov. 11, 1970.

58. Howard A. Glickstein, staff director, U.S. Commission on Civil Rights, and Charles L. Windsor, director of personnel services, St. Louis area, McDonnell Douglas Corporation, see U.S. Commission on Civil Rights, *Hearing Held in St. Louis, Missouri, January 14–17, 1970* (Washington: U.S. Government Printing Office, 1970), p. 174.

59. G. S. Roudebush, McDonnell Douglas Corporation, see *ibid.*, p. 181. Although McDonnell Douglas was not ready to assume any direct responsibility for meeting the housing needs of its employees in the suburbs, it was willing to provide modest financial support for subsidized housing in suburban Black Jack, to the tune of a $35,000 loan to the sponsors of the project.

60. See Will Lissner, "Group Seeks to Bar RCA Shift of Executives to New Canaan," *New York Times*, Mar. 4, 1971.

61. Bart Stevens, president, Office Products Division, I.B.M., quoted in "I.B.M. Is Proving a Good Neighbor in Affluent Bergen Town," *New York Times*, May 20, 1973.

62. National Committee Against Discrimination in Housing, *Jobs and Housing: A Study of Employment and Housing Opportunities for Racial Minorities of the New York Metropolitan Region*, Interim Report, Mar. 1970 (New York, 1970), p. 114.

63. See U.S. Commission on Civil Rights, *Equal Opportunity in Suburbia* (Washington: U.S. Government Printing Office, 1974), p. 26.

64. Quoted in Jerome Aumente, "Domestic Land Reform," *City* 5 (Jan. / Feb., 1971), p. 57.

65. Linda Greenhouse, "Rise in Jobs Poses Problem in Suburbs," *New York Times*, Aug. 18, 1971; reprinted as "Jobs and Housing," in Masotti and Hadden, *Suburbia in Transition*, p. 318.

66. See "The Flight from the Cities," *Newsweek* 76 (Nov. 30, 1970), p. 61. For a variety of corporate views on moving to the suburbs, most of which are favorable, see The Conference Board, *Corporate Moves to the Suburbs: Problems and Opportunities* (New York, 1972).

67. See Donald Sabath, "Housing Crisis Shifting to the Suburbs," *Cleveland Plain Dealer*, July 29, 1971.

68. Quoted in Jane A. Silverman, "Chicago's 'Gautreaux' Cases," *Journal of Housing* 29 (June, 1972), p. 239.

69. Quoted in Steven R. Weisman, "Lindsay Urges Suburbs to Alter Laws to Provide Workers' Homes," *New York Times*, Dec. 18, 1970.

70. Mayor Carl B. Stokes, Cleveland, Ohio, see U.S. Commission on Civil Rights, *Hearing Held in Washington, D.C., June 14–17, 1971*, p. 717.

71. Mayor Lee Alexander, Syracuse, N.Y., see U.S. Congress, House of

Representatives, Committee on Banking and Currency, *Housing and Urban Development Legislation—1971*, Hearings before the Subcommittee on Housing, 92d Cong., 1st sess. (Washington: U.S. Government Printing Office, 1971) p. 504.

72. Quoted in Jack Rosenthal, "Suburbs Abandoning Dependence on City," *New York Times*, Aug. 16, 1971; reprinted as "Toward Suburban Independence," in Masotti and Hadden, *Suburbia in Transition*, p. 300.

73. Edward Holmgren, executive director, National Committee Against Discrimination in Housing, quoted in Brad Tillson, "Rate of Racial Change Called Key to Stability," *Dayton Daily News*, Nov. 29, 1972.

74. *Opening Up the Suburbs*, p. 123.

75. *Ibid.*, p. 141.

76. *Ibid.*, p. 80.

77. See "The Battle of the Suburbs," *Newsweek* 78 (Nov. 15, 1971), p. 61.

78. Jerry Birbach, Forest Hills Residents Association, quoted in Patrick W. Sullivan, "Opposition to Scatter Site Housing Grows Nationally," *Trenton Sunday Times Advertiser*, Apr. 16, 1972. See also Mario Cuomo, *Forest Hills Diary: The Crisis of Low-Income Housing* (New York: Random House, 1974).

79. See Martin Meyerson and Edward C. Banfield, *Politics, Planning, and the Public Interest: The Case of Public Housing in Chicago* (Glencoe, Ill.: Free Press, 1955), for a discussion of the politics of site selection in public housing in Chicago.

80. For a discussion of the role of the borough presidents in public-housing politics in New York, see Jewel Bellush, "Housing: The Scattered-Site Controversy," in Jewel Bellush and Stephen M. David, eds., *Race and Politics in New York City: Five Studies in Policy-Making* (New York: Praeger Publishers, 1971).

81. Alderman Doris Bass, Fifteenth Ward, St. Louis, quoted in "Mrs. Bass Proposes Housing Project Vote," *St. Louis Post-Dispatch*, Oct. 7, 1971.

82. James Harvey, Housing Opportunities Council, quoted in Sheilds and Spector, "Opening Up the Suburbs," p. 306.

83. Downs, *Opening Up the Suburbs*, p. 141.

84. Marvin Groves, president, East Attucks Community Housing, Inc., quoted in Charles Hammer, "Attucks Official Blasts HUD," *Kansas City Star*, May 11, 1972.

85. "The Nationalist vs. the Integrationist," *New York Times Magazine*, Oct. 1, 1972, p. 51.

86. Quoted in Lilley, "Romney Faces Political Perils With Plan to Integrate Suburbs," p. 2262.

87. Nathaniel Jones, general counsel, NAACP, quoted in William Lilley III, "Housing Report / Courts Lead Revolutionary Trend Toward Desegregation of Residential Areas," *National Journal* 3 (Nov. 27, 1971), p. 2347.

88. Quoted in Hamilton, "The Nationalist vs. The Integrationist," p. 38.

89. Quoted in Lilley, "Housing Report / Courts Lead Revolutionary Trend Toward Desegregation of Residential Areas," p. 2347.

90. *Opening Up the Suburbs*, pp. 82–83.

91. See U. S. Commission on Civil Rights, *Hearing Held in Washington D.C., June 14–17, 1971*, p. 279.

92. Kathryn Kula, general counsel, Chicago Housing Authority, "How Do We Solve the Problem of Low and Moderate Income Housing in Chicago," Speech to League of Women Voters, Chicago, Feb. 15, 1972, p. 1.

93. See City of New York, Economic Development Administration, "Statement by the Hon. D. K. Patten, Economic Development Administration, New York City, before the Bedminster, N.J., Planning Board Regarding Regional Economic Growth Patterns," Nov. 9, 1970; and David K. Shipler, "City Seeks Help of Jersey Town," *New York Times*, Nov. 10, 1970. Patton's journey to Bedminster was somewhat ironic, since before joining the Lindsay Administration he was a top official of the nation's largest corporate relocation service, and had played an important role in moving substantial numbers of jobs to the suburbs.

94. See Sullivan, "Opposition to Scatter Site Housing Grows Nationally."

95. See Antero Pietila, "City Hints Court Action to Stop New Housing," *Baltimore Sun*, Nov. 20, 1972.

Chapter Seven: Exclusion and the Courts

1. Chief Justice Warren E. Burger was appointed by President Nixon in 1969, Justice Harry A. Blackmun in 1970, and Justices Lewis F. Powell, Jr., and William H. Rehnquist in 1971.

2. See *Bradley* v. *Milliken*, 338 F.Supp. 582 (1971).

3. *Milliken* v. *Bradley*, 418 U.S. 717 (1974) at 743. Justice Potter Stewart joined the four Nixon appointees to form the majority.

4. Representatives Fletcher Thompson and Benjamin B. Blackburn, quoted in William Lilley III, "Housing Report / Courts Lead Revolutionary Trend toward Desegregation of Residential Areas," *National Journal* 3 (Nov. 27, 1971), p. 2342. Thompson and Blackburn, both Republicans, represented districts encompassing parts of Atlanta and substantial suburban areas. The court ruling in question was *Crow* v. *Brown*, 332 F.Supp. 382 (1971), which is discussed below.

5. Representative Charles W. Sandman, Jr., quoted in Joseph F. Sullivan, "Sandman Enters Dispute in Bergen," *New York Times*, Oct. 16, 1973. Sandman was the unsuccessful Republican candidate for governor in 1973. His opponent, Brendan T. Byrne, also questioned the constitutionality of this ruling.

6. Bernard J. Kleina, executive director, HOPE, Wheaton, Ill., quoted in Jerry DeMuth, "Fair-Housing Suits Challenge Zoning Rules," *Chicago Sun-Times*, Nov. 26, 1972.

7. Geoffrey Sheilds and L. Sanford Spector, "Opening Up the Suburbs: Notes on a Movement for Social Change," *Yale Review of Law and Social Action* 2 (Summer, 1972), p. 309. For an examination of the litigation goals of the open-housing groups, as well as a review of these efforts, see Mary Brooks, *Exclusionary Zoning* (Chicago: American Society of Planning Officials, 1970) and National Committee Against Discrimination in Housing and Urban Land Institute, *Fair Housing and Exclusionary Land Use*, ULI Research Report 23 (Washington, 1974).

8. Another consideration drawing open-housing groups to the courts was their legal status as tax-exempt organizations. As Leonard S. Rubinowitz notes, "many of these organizations must not engage in any substantial lobbying or they

will lose their tax-exempt status. . . . Loss of tax exemption would undoubtedly mean loss of foundation support. Consequently, they generally steer clear of lobbying." See *Low-Income Housing: Suburban Strategies* (Cambridge, Mass.: Ballinger Pub. Co., 1974), p. 202.

9. Sheilds and Spector, "Opening Up the Suburbs," p. 309.

10. State of New Jersey, Governor, *A Blueprint for Housing in New Jersey*, A Special Message to the Legislature by William T. Cahill, Governor of New Jersey (Dec. 7, 1970), p. 15. Cahill's unsuccessful efforts to ease local control over land use are discussed in chapter 10.

11. "Statement About Federal Policies Relative to Equal Housing Opportunity," June 11, 1971, *Public Papers of the Presidents of the United States: Richard Nixon, 1971* (Washington: U.S. Government Printing Office, 1972), p. 734.

12. "Opening Up the Suburbs," p. 309.

13. Supervisor Paul Fitzpatrick, Smithtown, N.Y., quoted in "2 Suffolk Towns Deny Zoning Bias," *Newsday*, July 16, 1973.

14. Mayor John Petruska, Parma, Ohio, quoted in Edward Watkins, "Bias Suits Pelt Parma," *Parma Sun Post*, May 3, 1973.

15. Counsel for Oyster Bay was Simpson, Thatcher, and Bartlett; New Canaan's lawyers were Tyler, Cooper, Grant, Bowerman & Keefe; see Sheilds and Spector, "Opening Up the Suburbs," p. 316.

16. Pitney, Hardin, and Kipp of Newark; Wittman, Anzalone, Bernstein, and Dunn of Hackensack; and Orbe and Nugent of Ridgewood. Mahwah and three neighboring communities also hired George Sternlieb, a housing economist and director of the Center for Urban Policy Research at Rutgers University, to assist in the preparation of the defense in a suit brought by Suburban Action.

17. See *Southern Burlington County NAACP* v. *Township of Mount Laurel*, 119 N.J.Super. 164, 290 A.2d 465 (1972) and *Southern Burlington County N.A.A.C.P.* v. *Township of Mount Laurel*, 67 N.J. 151, 336 A.2d 713 (1975).

18. Carl Buscher, executive director, North Jersey Builders Association, quoted in Richard Phalon, "More and More Suits Filed to Bar High-Rises in Bergen," *New York Times*, May 6, 1974.

19. Herbert J. Fabricant, Monroe, N.Y., quoted in "Moratoriums—Stalling the Inevitable?" *Middletown* (N.Y.) *Sunday Record*, Aug. 26, 1973.

20. See *Appeal of Girsh*, 437 Pa. 237, 263 A.2d 395 (1970).

21. Richard F. Babcock and Fred P. Bosselman, *Exclusionary Zoning: Land Use Regulation and Housing in the 1970s* (New York: Praeger Publishers, 1973), p. 7.

22. See *Southern Burlington County N.A.A.C.P.* v. *Township of Mount Laurel*, 67 N.J. 151, 336 A.2d 713 (1975).

23. John Bukovinsky, director of member services, New Jersey Builders Association, quoted in Leonard J. Fischer, "Trouble Expected for 'Open Zoning,' " *Newark Star Ledger*, Mar. 26, 1975.

24. Charles M. Haar and Demetrius S. Iatrides, *Housing the Poor in Suburbia: Public Policy at the Grass Roots* (Cambridge, Mass.: Ballinger Pub. Co., 1974), p. 124.

25. See *Sisters of Providence of St. Mary of the Woods* v. *City of Evanston*, 335 F.Supp. 396 (1971).

26. Daniel Lauber, *Recent Cases in Exclusionary Zoning*, Planning Advisory Service Report No. 292 (Chicago: American Society of Planning Officials, 1973), p. 13.

27. Walter F. Murphy and Joseph Tanenhaus, *The Study of Public Law* (New York: Random House, 1972), p. 70.

28. See David H. Moskowitz, "Standing of Future Residents in Exclusionary Zoning Cases," *University of Akron Law Review* 6 (Spring, 1973), pp. 189–214.

29. *Laws of New Jersey 1969*, Ch. 277.

30. *Warth* v. *Seldin*, 422 U.S. 490 (1975) at 502.

31. *Ibid.* at 504. Standing also was denied to an open-housing group, Metro-Act of Rochester, and to the Rochester Home Builders Association. The Supreme Court was closely divided on the issue, resulting in a 5-4 decision, and bitter dissenting opinions from Justices Brennan and Douglas. For Brennan, a ruling which "tosses out of court almost every conceivable kind of plaintiff who could be injured by the activity claimed to be unconstitutional . . . can be explained only by an indefensible hostility to the claim on the merits"; *ibid.* at 520. Douglas saw the majority opinion as a blow against the civil rights of minorities, and evidence that "standing has become a barrier to access to the federal courts for the disadvantaged"; *ibid.* at 519.

32. Randall Scott, quoted in Gladwin Hill, "Community Land Use," *New York Times*, July 4, 1975. See also Randall Scott, "Supreme Court Seen Missing Thrust of Case," *Washington Post*, July 12, 1975.

33. James Meyerson, quoted in Roy R. Silver, "N.A.A.C.P. Drops L.I. Zoning Suit," *New York Times*, Oct. 9, 1975.

34. *Village of Euclid* v. *Ambler Realty Co.*, 272 U.S. 365 (1926) at 388.

35. *Harvard Enterprises, Inc.* v. *Board of Adjustment, Township of Madison, County of Middlesex*, 56 N.J. 362, 266 A.2d 588 (1970) at 592.

36. See *James* v. *Valtierra*, 402 U.S. 137 (1971). The *Valtierra* case is discussed below in detail.

37. "The Courts Enter the Land Development Marketplace," *City* 5 (Jan. / Feb., 1971), p. 63.

38. For an irreverent general appraisal of traditional zoning litigation, see Richard F. Babcock, *The Zoning Game: Municipal Practices and Policies* (Madison: Univ. of Wis. Press, 1966).

39. Bernard J. Kleina, executive director, HOPE, Wheaton, Ill., quoted in DeMuth, "Fair-Housing Suits Challenge Zoning Rules."

40. As noted above, this suit eventually was dropped because of the U.S. Supreme Court's restrictive interpretation of the standing of non-resident plaintiffs in class-action suits aimed at exclusionary zoning.

41. The communities were Mahwah, Ramsey, Saddle River, and Upper Saddle River.

42. The suburbs named in the suit were East Brunswick in Middlesex County, Franklin Lakes in Bergen County, Holmdel in Monmouth County, Livingston in Essex County, and Wayne Township in Passaic County.

43. See "Suit to Expand Lower-Income Housing Filed by Civil Rights Unit in New Jersey," *Wall Street Journal*, July 25, 1974; see also "Area-Wide Zoning

Suit Filed," *NCDH Trends in Housing* 18 (July / Aug., 1974), pp. 1–2. The only municipalities in Middlesex County not named in the suit were the older cities of New Brunswick and Perth Amboy.

44. Quoted in Lauber, *Recent Cases in Exclusionary Zoning*, p. 22.

45. State courts also have rebuffed efforts by civil-rights groups to advance claims on behalf of those generally disadvantaged by local land-use restrictions. See, for instance, *Commonwealth* v. *County of Bucks*, 8 Pa.Cmwlth. 295, 302 A.2d 897 (1973).

46. For a general discussion of the application of equal-protection arguments to suburban exclusion, see Lawrence Gene Sager, "Tight Little Islands: Exclusionary Zoning, Equal Protection, and the Indigent," *Stanford Law Review* 21 (Apr., 1969), pp. 767–800.

47. Frank Aloi and Arthur Abba Goldberg, "Racial and Economic Exclusionary Zoning; The Beginning or the End?" *Urban Law Annual* (1971), p. 24. See also "The Rights to Travel and Its Application to Restrictive Housing Laws," *Northwestern University Law Review* 66 (Nov. / Dec., 1971), pp. 635–38.

48. See Peter Weiner, "The Constitutionality of Local Zoning," *Yale Law Journal* 79 (Apr., 1970), pp. 896–903.

49. Lauber, *Recent Cases in Exclusionary Zoning*, p. 7.

50. See James Feron, "Bias Suit Is Filed in Westchester," *New York Times*, Aug. 9, 1972. The suburb in question was New Castle, whose officials and residents were among the most vociferous opponents of the efforts of the New York Urban Development Corporation to locate subsidized housing in Westchester County, an issue which is discussed in detail in chapter 10. Suburban Action's suit initially was dismissed by a federal district judge on the grounds that low-income nonresidents of New Castle lacked standing to bring the action; see *Evans* v. *Lynn*, 376 F.Supp. 327 (1974). In 1975, the U.S. Court of Appeals for the Second Circuit reversed the district court on the standing issue, but did not rule on the substantive issues in the case; see *Evans* v. *Lynn*, U.S. Ct. of Appeals, 2d Cir. June 2, 1975.

51. See *James* v. *Valtierra*, 402 U.S. 137 (1971).

52. Lauber, *Recent Cases in Exclusionary Zoning*, p. 21.

53. *Molino* v. *Mayor and Council of Borough of Glassboro*, 116 N.J.Super. 195, 281 A.2d 401 (1971) at 405.

54. *Southern Burlington County N.A.A.C.P.* v. *Township of Mount Laurel* 67 N.J. 151, 336 A.2d 713 (1975) at 731.

55. *National Land and Investment Co.* v. *Kohn*, 419 Pa. 504, 215 A.2d 597 (1965) at 612.

56. *G & D Holland Construction Co.* v. *City of Marysville*, 12 Cal.App.3d 989, 91 Cal.Rptr. 227 (1970) at 231.

57. *Derry Borough* v. *Shomo*, 5 Pa.Cmwlth. 216, 289 A.2d 513 (1972) at 517.

58. *Bristow* v. *City of Woodhaven*, 35 Mich.App. 205, 192 N.W.2d 322 (1971) at 327. See also *Simmons* v. *City of Royal Oak*, 38 Mich.App. 496, 196 N.W.2d 811 (1972).

59. *Southern Alameda Spanish Speaking Organization* v. *City of Union City, Cal.*, 424 F.2d 291 (1970) at 295–96.

60. *Kennedy Park Homes Ass'n* v. *City of Lackawanna*, 318 F.Supp. 669 (1970) at 697.

61. *Appeal of Girsh*, 437 Pa. 237, 263 A.2d 395 (1970) at 399.

62. *Appeal of Kit-Mar Builders, Inc.*, 439 Pa. 466, 268 A.2d 765 (1970) at 768–69.

63. *Oakwood at Madison, Inc.* v. *Township of Madison*, 117 N.J.Super. 11, 283 A.2d 353 (1971) at 358.

64. The communities were Euclid, Garfield Heights, Parma, Solon, and Westlake. See *Mahaley* v. *Cuyahoga Metropolitan Housing Authority*, 355 F.Supp. 1257 (1973). This decision was overturned in 1974 by the U.S. Court of Appeals for the Sixth Circuit, see *Mahaley* v. *Cuyahoga Metropolitan Housing Authority* 500 F.2d 1087 (1974).

65. See *Shannon* v. *United States Dept. of Housing & Urban Dev.*, 436 F.2d 809 (1970); *Gautreaux* v. *Chicago Housing Authority*, 206 F.Supp. 907 (1969); and *Banks* v. *Perk*, 341 F.Supp. 1175 (1972).

66. *Crow* v. *Brown*, 332 F.Supp. 382 (1971) at 389.

67. See *Hills* v. *Gautreaux*, U.S. Sup. Ct. 74–1047 (Apr. 20, 1976).

68. *Molino* v. *Mayor and Council of Borough of Glassboro*, 116 N.J.Super. 195, 281 A.2d 401 (1971) at 405–6.

69. *Southern Burlington County N.A.A.C.P.* v. *Township of Mt. Laurel*, 119 N.J.Super. 164, 290 A.2d 465 (1972) at 473.

70. *Southern Burlington County N.A.A.C.P.* v. *Township of Mt. Laurel*, 67 N.J. 151, 336 A.2d 713 (1975) at 724.

71. *Ibid.* at 727.

72. *Ibid.* at 728. The ruling did not apply to all suburbs in the state, but to "developing municipalities" (like Mount Laurel, which had "sizable land area") which "have substantially shed rural characteristics and have undergone great population increase since World War II, or are now in the process of doing so, but still are not completely developed and remain in the path of inevitable future residential, commercial, and industrial demand and growth"; *ibid.* at 717. Lower courts in New Jersey tended to apply this limitation conservatively, exempting from its requirements suburbs which lacked substantial land area or the capacity for significant amounts of future development; see, for example, *Segal Construction Co.* v. *Zoning Board of Adjustment, Borough of Wenonah*, 134 N.J.Super. 421, 341 A.2d 667 (1975).

73. *Southern Burlington County N.A.A.C.P.* v. *Township of Mt. Laurel, N.J.* 67 N.J. 151, 336 A.2d 713 (1975) at 724.

74. Carl S. Bisgaier, Camden Regional Legal Services, Inc., quoted in Dan Eisenhurth, "Appeal Planned on Landmark Case," *Burlington County* (N.J.) *Times*, Mar. 25, 1975.

75. *James* v. *Valtierra*, 402 U.S. 137 (1971) at 141. In the majority were Chief Justice Burger, and Justices Black, Harlan, Stewart, and White, while Justices Blackmun, Brennan, and Marshall dissented. Justice Douglas did not participate in the decision.

76. *Ibid.*

77. *Ibid.* at 144–45.

78. *Ibid.* at 142–43.

79. George Lefcoe, "From Capitol Hill: The Impact of Civil Rights Litigation on HUD Policy," *Urban Lawyer* 4 (Winter, 1972) p. 118. See also George Lefcoe, "The Public Housing Referendum Case, Zoning and the Supreme Court," *California Law Review* 59 (Nov., 1971), pp. 1386–90 for a discussion of efforts in Torrance in the Los Angeles area to bar subsidized apartments in the wake of the *Valtierra* ruling.

80. *Citizens Committee for Faraday Wood v. Lindsay*, 362 F.Supp. 651 (1973) at 659.

81. *Acevedo v. Nassau County, New York*, 369 F.Supp. 1384 (1974) at 1389. The U.S. Court of Appeals for the Second Circuit affirmed the lower court's ruling; see *Acevedo v. Nassau County, New York*, 500 F.2d 1078 (1974).

82. *Ybarra v. Town of Los Altos Hills*, 370 F.Supp. 742 (1973) at 750.

83. *Mahaley v. Cuyahoga Metropolitan Housing Authority*, 355 F.Supp. 1245 (1973) at 1249.

84. For the decision of the lower court, see *Mahaley v. Cuyahoga Metropolitan Housing Authority*, 355 F.Supp. 1257 (1973).

85. *Mahaley v. Cuyahoga Metropolitan Housing Authority*, 500 F.2d (1974) at 1087. The Supreme Court declined to review the ruling of the appeals court.

86. *Village of Belle Terre v. Borass*, 416 U.S. 1 (1974) at 9. Joining Justice Douglas in the majority were Chief Justice Burger, and Justices Blackmun, Powell, Rehnquist, Stewart, and White. Justices Brennan and Marshall dissented.

87. Mayor James Philbin, Belle Terre, N.Y., quoted in Pranay Gupte, "Belle Terre Hails Ruling as Triumph for Privacy," *New York Times*, Apr. 2, 1974.

88. *Construction Ind. Ass'n., Sonoma Co. v. City of Petaluma*, 522 F.2d 897 (1975) at 908–9. The decision by the appeals court overturned a lower court ruling that Petaluma's growth controls, which limited annual housing construction to 500 units, violated the constitutional right to travel; see *Construction Ind. Assn. of Sonoma County v. City of Petaluma*, 375 F.Supp. 574 (1974). The U.S. Supreme Court declined to review the decision of the appeals court.

89. *Village of Belle Terre v. Borass*, 416 U.S. 1 (1974) at 8.

90. *Village of Belle Terre v. Borass*, 416 U.S. 1 (1974) at 7–8. Two years before *Belle Terre*, in a decision upholding the eviction of tenants who had failed to pay their rent, the Court had been unable to perceive . . . any constitution guarantee to access to dwellings of a particular quality"; see *Lindsey v. Normet*, 405 U.S. 56 (1972) at 74.

91. *United States v. City of Black Jack, Missouri*, 372 F.Supp. 319 (1974) at 329.

92. *United States v. City of Black Jack, Missouri*, 508 F.2d 1179 (1974) at 1186.

93. See *Kennedy Park Homes Ass'n v. City of Lackawanna*, 318 F.Supp. 669 (1970) and *Kennedy Park Homes Ass'n v. City of Lackawanna, N.Y.*, 436 F.2d 108 (1970).

94. *Kennedy Park Homes Ass'n v. City of Lackawanna, N.Y.*, 436 F.2d 108 (1970) at 114.

95. *Crow v. Brown*, 332 F.Supp. 382 (1971) at 390.

96. "Institutional and Contextual Factors Affecting the Residential Choices of Minority Residents," in Amos H. Hawley and Vincent P. Rock, eds., *Segregation in Residential Areas*, Papers on Racial and Socioeconomic Factors in Choice of Housing (Washington: National Academy of Sciences, 1973), p. 137.

97. Herbert M. Franklin, "Memorandum: Recent Developments," Metropolitan Housing Program, Potomac Inst., Washington, Mar. 29, 1974, p. 1.

98. Richard Bellman, quoted in George Kentera, "Attacks on Zoning Loom for Suburbs," North American Newspaper Alliance, *Milwaukee Journal*, Aug. 27, 1972.

99. "The Courts Enter the Land Development Marketplace," p. 64.

100. *Golden* v. *Planning Board of Ramapo*, 30 N.Y.2d. 359 (1972) at 375.

101. *Ibid.* at 378.

102. Fred P. Bosselman, "The Right to Move, the Need to Grow," *Planning* 39 (Sept. 1973), p. 10.

103. Frederick C. Mezey, Mezey and Mezey, New Brunswick, N.J., quoted in Carl Zeitz, "Low Income Housing Rules 'Just Move Ghetto,' Court Told," *Trenton Evening Times*, Mar. 6, 1973.

104. "The Courts Enter the Land Development Marketplace," p. 63.

105. *Oakwood at Madison, Inc.* v. *Township of Madison*, 128 N.J.Super. 438, 320 A.2d 223 (1974) at 224. This ruling, the Superior Court's second in the Madison litigation, dealt with amendments to Madison's zoning ordinance adopted after the initial judgement in the case.

106. *Ibid.* at 227.

107. *Southern Burlington County N.A.A.C.P.* v. *Township of Mt. Laurel*, 67 N.J. 151, 336 A.2d 713 (1975) at 724.

108. *Ibid.* at 733.

109. Carl S. Bisgaier, Camden Regional Legal Services, Inc., quoted in Mark Jaffe, "Suburbs to Battle Mt. Laurel Edict," *Trenton Evening Times*, June 16, 1975.

110. Jerome G. Rose, "The *Mount Laurel* Decision: Is It Based on Wishful Thinking?" *Real Estate Law Journal* 4 (Summer, 1975), p. 67. Rose was one of the consultants appointed by a New Jersey judge to appraise the need for apartments in Washington Township in Bergen County, a case which is discussed below.

111. Lawrence G. Sager, " 'Exclusionary Zoning': Constitutional Limitations on the Power of Municipalities to Restrict the Use of Land." Paper prepared for the Biennial Conference of the American Civil Liberties Union, Boulder, Colo., June 8–11, 1972, p. 42.

112. *Board of County Supervisors of Fairfax County* v. *DeGroff Enterprises, Inc.*, 214 Va. 235, 198 S.E.2d 600 (1973) at 602.

113. "Planning Law and the Supreme Court," *Zoning Digest* 13 (Mar. / Apr. 1961), p. 64.

114. Richard F. Bellman, Suburban Action Institute; see Peter H. Weiner, "Report: Third Conference on Exclusionary Land Use Policies," Taconic Foundation, Sept. 23, 1970, p. 11.

115. Lawrence G. Sager, see *ibid.*, p. 11. The ACLU suit against Black Jack was a separate action from that filed by the Department of Justice, and was heard

by a different federal judge; see *Park View Heights Corporation* v. *City of Black Jack*, 467 F.2d 1208 (1972).

116. "Exclusionary Land Use Controls: The Case of North-Eastern New Jersey," *Syracuse Law Review* 22 (1971), p. 499. See also Norman Williams, Jr., Tatyana Doughty, and R. William Potter, "The Strategy on Exclusionary Zoning: Towards What Rationale and What Remedy?" *Land Use Controls Annual 1972* (Chicago: American Society of Planning Officials, 1972), pp. 197–201.

117. See Phalon, "More and More Suits Filed to Bar High-Rises in Bergen."

118. John Couture, Department of State and Local Government Relations and Urban Government Affairs, National Association of Home Builders, quoted in Sheilds and Spector, "Opening Up the Suburbs," p. 318. See also "NAHB Policy in '74: Sue No-growthers," *House and Home* 45 (Mar., 1974), p. 8.

119. Frederick C. Mezey, Mezey and Mezey, New Brunswick, N.J., quoted in Sally Lane, "Zoning Forum Polarized?" *Trenton Evening Times*, Feb. 17, 1972.

120. See Carter B. Horsley, "Company Brings Suit to Fight 5-Acre Zoning in Jersey Area," *New York Times*, Sept. 2, 1971.

121. See *Allan-Deane Corporation* v. *Township of Bedminster*, Superior Court of New Jersey, Law Div., Somerset Co., Docket No. L 36896-70 P.W. & No. L 28061-71 P.W., Feb. 21, 1975.

122. Complaint of Plaintiff, *Fair Housing Development Fund* v. *Burke*, U.S. District Court for the Eastern Dist. of New York, Feb. 19, 1971, p. 16. The community in question was Oyster Bay, N.Y.; and the suit eventually was dropped by the NAACP after the U.S. Supreme Court restricted access to the courts by low-income non-residents in *Warth* v. *Seldin*.

123. Justice Felix Frankfurter cautioned the courts against entering the "political thicket" of legislative apportionment in a 1946 ruling by the U.S. Supreme Court dismissing a challenge of congressional districting; see *Colegrove* v. *Green*, 328 U.S. 549 (1946) at 556.

124. See *Southern Alameda Spanish-Speaking Organization* v. *City of Union City*, 397 F.Supp. 1188 (1970).

125. *Crow* v. *Brown*, 332 F.Supp. 382 (1971) at 396.

126. *Southern Burlington County N.A.A.C.P.* v. *Township of Mt. Laurel*, 119 N.J.Super. 164, 290 A.2d 465 (1972) at 474.

127. The consultants were Professor Melvin Levin, a planner, and Professor Jerome G. Rose, a lawyer, both of the Department of Urban Planning at Rutgers University.

128. Report of Advisors to the Court, *Pascack Association, Limited* v. *Mayor and Council of the Township of Washington, Bergen County*, Superior Court of New Jersey, Law Div., Bergen Co., Docket No. L-2756-70 P.W., Jan. 9, 1974, p. 38.

129. See *Pascack Association, Limited* v. *Mayor and Council of Township of Washington, Bergen County*, 131 N.J.Super. 195, 329 A.2d 89 (1974). This ruling was overturned on appeal on the grounds that Washington Township was a small and almost completely developed municipality which did not fall under the "developing municipality" rubric enunciated in the *Mount Laurel* decision; see *Pascack Association, Ltd.* v. *Township of Washington*, N.J. Superior Court, App. Div., June 25, 1975.

130. Quoted in Ronald Sullivan, "Jersey Town's Zoning Is Voided; Court Orders Housing for Poor," *New York Times*, Mar. 3, 1972.

131. Quoted in Martin Gansberg, "Action by Judge in Jersey Raises Issue of Court's Role in Zoning," *New York Times*, Mar. 31, 1974.

132. *Southern Burlington County N.A.A.C.P.* v. *Township of Mt. Laurel*, 119 N.J.Super. 164, 290 A.2d 465 (1972) at 472.

133. Robert Fust, executive director, New Jersey League of Municipalities, quoted in Lucy McCrary and Terry Bitman, "New Jersey Suburbs Must Have Low-Cost Housing Land," *Philadelphia Inquirer*, Mar. 25, 1975.

134. *Gautreaux* v. *Chicago Housing Authority*, 296 F.Supp. 907 (1969) at 914.

135. Quoted in Jane A. Silverman, "Chicago's 'Gautreaux' Cases," *Journal of Housing* 29 (June 1972), p. 237.

136. See Peter H. Weiner, "Report: Ninth Conference on Exclusionary Land Use Policies," Clearinghouse on Exclusionary Land Use Problems, National Urban Coalition, Washington, Feb. 8, 1972, p. 24.

137. See *Gautreaux* v. *Romney*, 363 F.Supp. 690 (1973). Judge Austin, however, was overruled by the U.S. Court of Appeals for the Seventh Circuit, which remanded the case to the lower court for further consideration of "a comprehensive metropolitan area plan"; see *Gautreaux* v. *Chicago Housing Authority*, 503 F.2d 930 (1974) at 939. Consideration of metropolitan remedies by Judge Austin was endorsed by the U.S. Supreme Court after HUD appealed; see *Hills* v. *Gautreaux*, U.S. Sup. Ct., 74-1047 (Apr. 20, 1976).

138. *Appeal of Kit-Mar Builders, Inc.*, 439 Pa. 466, 268 A.2d 765 (1970) at 769.

139. *Southern Burlington County N.A.A.C.P.* v. *Township of Mt. Laurel*, 119 N.J.Super. 164, 290 A.2d 465 (1972) at 472.

140. *Southern Burlington County N.A.A.C.P.* v. *Township of Mt. Laurel*, 67 N.J. 151, 336 A.2d 713 (1975) at 734.

141. Quoted in "Public Housing Sites Unused, Report Says," *Atlanta Journal*, May 3, 1973.

142. *Commonwealth of Pennsylvania* v. *County of Bucks*, 22 Bucks Co.L.Rep. 179 (1972). Quotations within quote omitted.

143. *New Jersey Shore Builders Association* v. *Township of Ocean*, 128 N.J.Super. 135, 319 A.2d 255 (1974) at 256.

144. *Mahaley* v. *Cuyahoga Metropolitan Housing Authority*, 500 F.2d 1087 (1974) at 1094.

145. Quoted in Kentera, "Attacks on Zoning Loom for Suburbs."

146. "The Courts Enter the Land Development Marketplace," p. 64.

147. Mayor Arthur J. Holland, Trenton, N.J., quoted in Jon Senderling, "Panel Backs Top Court on Zoning Ban," *Trenton Evening Times*, Mar. 28, 1975.

Chapter Eight: Opening the Suburbs from Washington

1. Edward Rutledge, executive co-director, National Committee Against Discrimination in Housing, see U.S. Congress, Senate, Select Committee on Equal Educational Opportunity, *Equal Educational Opportunity*, Part 5: De Facto

Segregation and Housing Discrimination, Hearings, 91st Cong., 2d sess. (Washington: U.S. Government Printing Office, 1971), p. 2668.

2. See Patrick W. Sullivan, "Opposition to Scatter Site Housing Grows Nationally," *Trenton Sunday Times Advertiser*, Apr. 16, 1972. Golar, a black, became chairman of the New York City Housing Authority in 1970, and was a key figure in the bitter struggle over the location of public housing in middle-class Forest Hills.

3. Ralph G. Caso, *Counties: New Suburban Power and Influence* (Mineola, N.Y.: Office of the Executive, Nassau County, 1971), pp. 11–12. Caso, a Republican, was elected County Executive in Nassau County, the nation's largest suburban county, in 1970. In 1974, he ran unsuccessfully for Lieutenant Governor of New York on a ticket headed by Malcolm Wilson of Westchester County, another suburban political leader.

4. See Robert Cassidy, "GSA Plays the Suburban Game on the Grand Scale," *City* 5 (Fall, 1971) pp. 12, 14, and 72, and U.S. Commission on Civil Rights, *Federal Installations and Equal Housing* (Washington: U.S. Government Printing Office, 1970).

5. See Leonard S. Rubinowitz, *Low-Income Housing: Suburban Strategies* (Cambridge, Mass.: Ballinger Pub. Co., 1974), p. 177.

6. James Gibson, president, Metropolitan Washington Planning and Housing Association, see U.S. Commission on Civil Rights, *Hearing Held in Washington, D.C., June 14–17, 1971* (Washington: U.S. Government Printing Office, 1971), p. 53.

7. See U.S. Commission on Civil Rights, *Federal Installations and Equal Housing Opportunity*, pp. 10–11.

8. *Ibid.*, p. 8. Beginning in the late 1960s, the federal government began to give more attention to the implications of the location of federal facilities on housing and employment opportunities; see *ibid.*, pp. 15–19; and Rubinowitz, *Low-Income Housing*, pp. 179–182.

9. U.S. Federal Housing Administration, *Underwriting Manual*, Underwriting and Valuation Procedure under Title II of the National Housing Act (Washington: U.S. Government Printing Office, 1936), Pt. II, para. 281.

10. *Building the American City*, Report of the National Commission on Urban Problems to the Congress and President of the United States, 91st Cong., 1st sess., House Doc. No. 91-34 (Washington: U.S. Government Printing Office, 1968), p. 100.

11. See U.S. Department of Housing and Urban Development, *Housing in the Seventies*, A Report of the National Housing Policy Review (Washington: U.S. Government Printing Office, 1974), p. 36. See also Henry Aaron, *Shelter and Subsidies: Who Benefits from Federal Housing Policies?* (Washington: Brookings Inst., 1972), pp. 53–66.

12. *Underwriting Manual*, Pt. II, para. 233.

13. *Ibid.*, Pt. II, para. 284(3).

14. *Bradley v. School Board of the City of Richmond, Virginia*, 338 F.Supp. 67 (1972) at 217.

15. See U.S. Senate, *Equal Educational Opportunity*, Pt. 5, p. 2756.

16. Reese Cleghorn, "A Closer Look: Atlanta," *City* 5 (Jan. / Feb., 1971), pp. 36–37.

17. *Home Ownership for Lower Income Families: A Report on the Racial and Ethnic Impact of the Section 235 Program* (Washington: U.S. Government Printing Office, 1971), p. x.

18. See U.S. Senate, *Equal Educational Opportunity*, Pt. 5, p. 2755.

19. "The Courts and Urban Growth Policy: The Quest for New Ground Rules," Paper delivered at the 1971 National Planning Conference, American Society of Planning Officials, New Orleans, Mar. 27–Apr. 1, 1971, p. 12.

20. Nathaniel S. Keith, *Politics and the Housing Crisis Since 1930* (New York: Universe Bks., 1973), p. 161. Keith was president of the National Housing Conference, a lobbying group which strongly supported the expansion of federal housing programs for lower-income groups.

21. *Congressional Record*, 89th Cong., 1st sess., III:20 (Oct. 14, 1965), p. 26988.

22. *Ibid.*, pp. 26979–80.

23. *Congressional Record*, 89th Cong., 2d sess., 112:6 (Mar. 29, 1966), p. 7116.

24. *Ibid.*, p. 7080.

25. See U.S. Congress, Senate, Committee on Appropriations, *Second Supplemental Appropriation Bill, Fiscal Year 1966*, Hearings on H.R. 14012, 89th Cong., 2d sess. (Washington: U.S.Government Printing Office, 1966), pp. 513–14. The statement was signed by Senators Clifford P. Case and Harrison A. Williams, Jr., of New Jersey, Joseph S. Clark of Pennsylvania, Paul Douglas of Illinois, Phillip A. Hart of Michigan, Jacob K. Javits and Robert F. Kennedy of New York, Edward M. Kennedy of Massachusetts, Walter F. Mondale of Minnesota, Wayne Morse and Maurine Neuberger of Oregon, Edmund S. Muskie of Maine, Gaylord A. Nelson of Wisconsin, and Joseph D. Tydings of Maryland.

26. *Ibid.*, p. 506.

27. *Ibid.*, pp. 506, 462.

28. *Congressional Record*, 89th Cong., 2d sess., 112:6 (Mar. 29, 1966), p. 7116.

29. See Robert Taggart III, *Low Income Housing: A Critique of Federal Aid* (Baltimore: Johns Hopkins Univ. Press, 1970), p. 59. Taggart identifies political resistance to low-income families as "the major reason" for the absence of rent supplements in the suburbs or outer city neighborhoods. Another factor, as he notes, was "the Spartan cost limitations which HUD . . . administratively imposed" on rent supplement housing under pressure from Congress.

30. *Report of the National Advisory Commission on Civil Disorders*, Mar. 1, 1968 (Washington: U.S. Government Printing Office, 1968), p. 1.

31. *Ibid.*, pp. 225, 260.

32. *Building the American City*, p. 26.

33. U.S. President's Task Force on Suburban Problems, *Final Report*, edited by Charles M. Haar (Cambridge, Mass.: Ballinger Pub. Co., 1974), p. 8.

34. *A Decent Home* (Washington: U.S. Government Printing Office, 1969), pp. 143–44.

35. 82 *U.S. Stat. at L.* (1968), 476; 12 *U.S. Code* (1969), sec. 1701t.

36. See U.S. Congress, Senate, Committee on Banking and Currency, *Hous-*

ing and Urban Development Legislation of 1968, Hearings before the Subcommittee on Housing and Urban Affairs, 90th Cong., 2d sess. (Washington: U.S. Government Printing Office, 1968), p. 759. Douglas went on to emphasize, however, that "the opportunity must be opened up for people to move if they want to and if they have the money with which to move." *Ibid.*

37. *Ibid.*, p. 633.

38. See *Gautreaux* v. *Chicago Housing Authority*, 206 F.Supp. 907 (1969).

39. *Shannon* v. *United States Dept. of Housing and Urban Dev.*, 436 F.2d 809 (1970) at 816.

40. National Committee Against Discrimination in Housing, *How the Federal Government Builds Ghettos* (New York, 1967), p. 15.

41. See, for example, the testimony of Robert L. Carter, president, National Committee Against Discrimination in Housing in U.S. Commission on Civil Rights, *Hearing Held in Washington, D.C., June 14–17, 1971*, pp. 693–99.

42. 78 *U.S. Stat. at L.* (1964), 252; 42 *U.S. Code* (1974), sec. 2000d.

43. 82 *U.S. Stat. at L.* (1968), 84–85; 42 *U.S. Code* (1973), sec. 3608c.

44. Quoted in Ben A. Franklin, "Rights Panel Expected to Urge Fund Curb on White Suburbs," *New York Times*, Aug. 29, 1970.

45. The term apparently was coined by Kevin P. Phillips, an aide to Attorney General John P. Mitchell, who elaborated the strategy in *The Emerging Republican Majority* (New Rochell, N.Y.: Arlington House, 1969).

46. See "Annual Message to the Congress on the State of the Union," Jan. 22, 1971, *Public Papers of the Presidents of the United States: Richard Nixon, 1971* (Washington: U.S. Government Printing Office, 1972), pp. 50–59.

47. For a thoughtful discussion of the Nixon Administration, the "New Federalism," and the federal bureaucracy, see Richard P. Nathan, *The Plot That Failed: Nixon and the Administrative Presidency* (New York: Wiley, 1975).

48. "Annual Message to the Congress on the State of the Union," Jan. 22, 1971, p. 55.

49. *Ibid.*

50. Quoted in William Lilley III, "CPR Report / Romney Lines Up HUD Money Programs to Back Operation Breakthrough Housing Push," *National Journal* 2 (Jan. 31, 1970), 239.

51. For a detailed discussion of Operation Breakthrough and racial integration, see Michael Stegman, "National Housing and Land Use Policy Conflicts," *Journal of Urban Law* 49 (May, 1972), pp. 649–63.

52. Harold B. Finger, assistant secretary of housing and urban development for research and technology, quoted in Lilley, "Romney Lines Up HUD Money Programs to Back Operation Breakthrough Housing Push," p. 236.

53. Harold B. Finger, quoted in *ibid.*, p. 234.

54. Alfred A. Perry, project director, Operation Breakthrough, quoted in William Lilley III "Housing Report / Romney Faces Political Perils With Plan to Integrate Suburbs," *National Journal Reports* 2 (Oct. 17, 1970), p. 2255.

55. The key advocates of opening the suburbs within HUD were Under Secretary Richard C. Van Dusen, a political associate of Romney's from Michigan, and two black assistant secretaries, Samuel C. Jackson, Assistant Secretary for

Metropolitan Planning, and Samuel J. Simmons, Assistant Secretary for Equal Opportunity.

56. "Toward a National Urban Policy," in National League of Cities, *Cities in the '70s*, Proceedings, 46th Annual Congress of Cities, San Diego, Cal., Dec. 1–5, 1969 (Washington, 1970), p. 8.

57. See Lilley, "Romney Faces Political Perils With Plan to Integrate Suburbs," p. 2251. Emphasis omitted.

58. Moynihan was executive secretary of the newly created Council on Urban Affairs during the first nine months of the Nixon Administration, and then served as counsellor to the President until Jan., 1971.

59. Quoted in Lilley, "Romney Faces Political Perils with Plan to Integrate Suburbs," p. 2253.

60. Quoted in Warren Weaver, Jr., "Agnew Advocates A Suburban Drive to Aid the Slums," *New York Times*, Mar. 8, 1970.

61. U.S. President's Task Force on Low Income Housing, *Toward Better Housing for Low Income Families* (Washington: U.S. Government Printing Office, 1970), p. 14.

62. U.S. President's Task Force on Urban Renewal, *Urban Renewal: One Tool Among Many* (Washington: U.S. Government Printing Office, 1970), p. 7.

63. Harold B. Finger, assistant secretary of housing and urban development for research and technology, quoted in Lilley, "Romney Lines Up HUD Money Programs to Back Operation Breakthrough Housing Push," p. 240.

64. See Secretary Romney's testimony before the U.S. Commission on Civil Rights, *Hearing Held in Washington, D.C., June 14–17, 1971*, p. 230.

65. William L. C. Wheaton, *et al.*, "Housing Needs and Urban Development," in U.S. Congress, House of Representatives, Committee on Banking and Currency, *Papers Submitted to Subcommittee on Housing Panels on Housing Production, Housing Demand, and Developing a Suitable Living Environment*, (Washington: U.S. Government Printing Office, 1971), pp. 614–15.

66. See Barbara Gill, "Readington May Seek U.S. Aid Again," *Trenton Sunday Times Advertiser*, Aug. 8, 1971.

67. Richard C. Van Dusen, undersecretary of housing and urban development, quoted in William Lilley III, "Housing Report / Administration and Congress Follow Courts in Promoting Residential Integration," *National Journal* 3 (Nov. 12, 1971), p. 2435.

68. See Mary E. Brooks, "HUD Proposes Legislation to Curb Exclusionary Controls," *Planning* 36 (July, 1970), p. 87.

69. See U.S. Congress, House of Representatives, Committee on Banking and Currency, *Housing and Urban Development Legislation—1970*, Hearings before the Subcommittee on Housing, 91st Cong., 2d sess. (Washington: U.S. Government Printing Office, 1970), pt. 1, p. 20.

70. One section of the legislation, dealing with the exclusion of subsidized housing solely on the grounds of its eligibility for federal assistance, applied to all local governments.

71. See Charles M. Haar and Demetrius S. Iatrides, *Housing the Poor in Suburbia: Public Policy at the Grass Roots* (Cambridge, Mass.: Ballinger Pub. Co.,

1974), p. 253; and Interfaith Housing Corporation, *The Suburban Noose: Housing Development for the Modest-Income Family in Metropolitan Boston* Boston, 1969), pp. 25–26, and Appendix F.

72. Lillian Klimecki Dannis, City Council, Warren, Mich., quoted in Hugh McDonald, "Warren Was Given Romney Ultimatum," *Detroit News*, July 24, 1970. Warren's mayor, Ted Bates, and some of the nine members of the city council were willing to go along with HUD in order to retain the federal grant, but other council members like Mrs. Dannis resisted; see Hugh McDonald, "Why Warren Sought Help of Romney," *Detroit News*, July 23, 1970.

73. Quoted in McDonald, "Warren Was Given Romney Ultimatum."

74. Hugh McDonald, "U.S. Picks Warren as Prime Target in Move to Integrate All Suburbs," *Detroit News*, July 21, 1970.

75. See *ibid.* and Hugh McDonald, "How Warren Became Integration Test City," *Detroit News*, July 22, 1970.

76. Mayor James Cline, Royal Oaks, Mich., quoted in Gary F. Schuster, "Suburbs Wary of HUD's Money Power," *Detroit News*, July 26, 1970.

77. City Administrator Peter Cristiano, Southfield, Mich., quoted in *ibid.*

78. Quoted in Martin V. B. Weston, "Tales of the Suburbs: 1. Warren Keeps Most of Its Castle Intact," *City* 5 (Jan. / Feb., 1971), p. 79.

79. See Jerry M. Flint, "Michiganites Jeer Romney Over Suburbs' Integration," *New York Times*, July 29, 1970; reprinted as "H.U.D.'s Failure in Warren, Michigan," in Louis H. Masotti, and Jeffrey K. Hadden, eds., *Suburbia in Transition* (New York: Franklin Watts, 1974), pp. 154–57.

80. See U.S. Senate, *Equal Educational Opportunity*, Pt. 5, p. 2786. The Select Committee, chaired by Sen. Walter F. Mondale of Minnesota, was exploring the links between school segregation and metropolitan settlement patterns.

81. *Ibid.*, p. 2759.

82. *Housing Crisis U.S.A.* (New York: Praeger Publishers, 1971), p. 53.

83. See Lilley, "Romney Faces Political Perils With Plan to Integrate Suburbs," p. 2262.

84. See William Safire, *Before the Fall: An Inside View of the Pre-Watergate White House* (Garden City, N.Y.: Doubleday & Co., 1975), p. 248; and Dan Rather and Gary Paul Gates, *The Palace Guard* (New York: Harper & Row, 1974), pp. 187–90.

85. Quoted in Lilley, "Romney Faces Political Perils With Plan to Integrate Suburbs," p. 2263.

86. *Ibid*, p. 2251.

87. See Kevin P. Phillips, "HUD Turns to Sewers," *Washington Post*, Nov. 6, 1970.

88. See John Herbers, "Mitchell is Said to Advise Romney to Take New Post," *New York Times*, Nov. 22, 1970.

89. "The President's News Conference of December 10, 1970," *Public Papers of the Presidents of the United States: Richard Nixon 1970*, (Washington: U.S. Government Printing Office, 1971), p. 1106.

90. *Ibid.*

91. See Monroe W. Karmin, "Romney's Departure Grows More Likely," *Wall Street Journal*, Dec. 16, 1970.

92. *Ibid.*

93. "A Conversation with the President," Interview with Four Representatives of the Television Networks, Jan. 4, 1971, *Public Papers of the Presidents of the United States: Richard Nixon 1971* (Washington: U.S. Government Printing Office, 1972), p. 12.

94. "The President's News Conference of February 17, 1971," *Public Papers of the Presidents of the United States: Richard Nixon 1971* (Washington: U.S. Government Printing Office, 1972), p. 164.

95. "A Conversation with the President," Interview with Howard K. Smith of the American Broadcasting Company, Mar. 22, 1971, *Public Papers of the Presidents of the United States: Richard Nixon, 1971* (Washington: U.S. Government Printing Office, 1972), p. 110.

96. See John Herbers, "How Do You Break the Ring around the City?" *New York Times*, Jan. 10, 1971. Romney also indicated that "forced integration" was an "unfortunate term" which he wished people would stop using, including, presumably, President Nixon, who more than anyone had popularized its use.

97. "Statement About Federal Policies Relative to Equal Housing Opportunity," June 11, 1971, *Public Papers of the Presidents of the United States: Richard Nixon 1971* (Washington: U.S. Government Printing Office, 1972), p. 730.

98. *Ibid.*, p. 731.

99. *Ibid.*, pp. 733–34.

100. See Wayne King, "Suburbia Is Cool to Agnew Advice," *New York Times*, Mar. 9, 1970.

101. Lilley, "Administration and Courts Follow Courts in Promoting Residential Integration," p. 2434.

102. June 11, 1971.

103. George Lefcoe, "From Capitol Hill: The Impact of Civil Rights Litigation on HUD Policy," *Urban Lawyer* 4 (Winter, 1972), pp. 121–22.

104. Robert B. Semple, Jr., "Nixon to Enforce Rights Measures for U.S. Housing," *New York Times*, June 12, 1971.

105. *New York Times*, June 13, 1971.

106. "Statement About Federal Policies Relative to Equal Housing Opportunity," June 11, 1971, p. 730.

107. *Ibid.*

108. Quoted in Paul Delaney, "Nixon Criticized on Housing Policy," *New York Times*, July 14, 1971. The Leadership Conference on Civil Rights prepared a detailed critique of Nixon's statement, which was issued jointly with a number of other civil rights and housing groups; see "Response by Public Interest Groups to Administration Pronouncement on Equal Housing Opportunity," in U.S. Congress, House of Representatives, Committee on the Judiciary, *Federal Government's Role in the Achievement of Equal Opportunity in Housing*, Hearings before the Civil Rights Oversight Subcommittee, 92d Cong., 1st and 2d sess. (Washington: U.S. Government Printing Office, 1972), pp. 165–73.

109. See Semple, "Nixon to Enforce Rights Measures for U.S. Housing."

110. Robert L. Carter, president, National Committee Against Discrimination in Housing, "Response to President Nixon's June 11 Statement on Housing / Civil Rights Policy," in U.S. Commission on Civil Rights, *Hearing Held in Washington, D.C., June 14–17, 1971*, p. 684.

111. 82 *U.S. Stat. at L.* (1968), 88; 42 *U.S. Code* (1973), sec. 3613.

112. The Memorandum of Understanding between HUD and GSA had been drafted more than a year earlier. It was designed to implement Executive Order 11512, issued by the President in February 1970, which instructed GSA to consider the adequacy of low-cost housing, along with approximately twenty other priorities, in evaluating sites for proposed federal facilities. See Cassidy, "GSA Plays the Suburban Game on the Grand Scale," p. 14.

113. Quoted in Philip W. McKinsey, "Zoning: New 'Rights' Target," *Christian Science Monitor*, Jan. 20, 1971.

114. Frank Schwelb, Housing Section, Civil Rights Division, Department of Justice, quoted in Geoffrey Sheilds and L. Sanford Spector, "Opening Up the Suburbs: Notes on a movement for Social Change," *Yale Review of Law and Social Action* 2 (Summer, 1972), p. 321.

115. Quoted in Jack Rosenthal, "U.S. Sues Suburb on Housing Bias," *New York Times*, June 15, 1971, reprinted as part of "The Justice Department vs. Blackjack, Missouri," in Masotti and Hadden, *Suburbia in Transition*, p. 162.

116. U.S. Department of Housing and Urban Development (Community Facilities), "Evaluation of Preliminary Applications for Basic Water and Sewer Facilities," *Federal Register* 36 (June 29, 1971), p. 12220.

117. *The State of the Cities* (New York: Praeger Publishers, 1972) p. 73.

118. See U.S. House of Representatives, *Federal Government's Role in the Achievement of Equal Opportunity in Housing*, p. 380.

119. Quoted in John Herbers, "U.S. Acts to Spread Subsidized Housing," *New York Times*, Sept. 30, 1971. The other criteria were need, accessibility to community facilities and job opportunities, consistency with local plans, environmental impact, ability of the applicant to carry out the project, potential for creating jobs for members of minority groups, and, for apartment projects, managerial capability. A "poor" rating on any of the eight criteria presumably would disqualify an applicant, while those proposals receiving an "excellent rating for each standard would be given the highest priority in the allocation of 235, 236, public housing, or rent supplement funds. For the final version of the selection criteria, see U.S. Department of Housing and Urban Development, Office of the Assistant Secretary for Housing Production and Mortgage Credit, "Project Selection Criteria," *Federal Register* 37 (Jan. 7, 1972), pp. 1–7.

120. See the critiques of HUD's various versions of the Project Selection Criteria by the U.S. Commission on Civil Rights, in letters to Secretary Romney which are reprinted in U.S. House of Representatives, *Federal Government's Role in the Achievement of Equal Opportunity in Housing*, pp. 7–15.

121. See U.S. Congress, House of Representatives, Committee on Banking and Currency, *Housing and Urban Development Legislation—1971*, Hearings before

the Subcommittee on Housing (Washington: U.S. Government Printing Office, 1971), Pt. 1, p. 278.

122. See U.S. Congress, House of Representatives, Committee on Banking and Currency, *Housing and Urban Development Act of 1972*, Hearings, 92d Cong., 2d sess. (Washington: U.S. Government Printing Office, 1972), p. 637.

123. See U.S. House of Representatives, *Federal Government's Role in the Achievement of Equal Opportunity in Housing*, p. 395.

124. See U.S. Congress, House of Representatives, Committee on Banking and Currency, *Real Estate Settlement Costs, FHA Mortgage Foreclosures, Housing Abandonment, and Site Selection Policies*, Hearings before the Subcommittee on Housing on H.R. 1337, 92d Cong., 2d sess. (Washington: U.S. Government Printing Office, 1972), Pt. 1, p. 49.

125. Romney departed HUD shortly after announcing the moratorium on subsidized housing. By then, most of the top HUD officials associated with the abortive efforts to open the suburbs also had been swept away in the general housecleaning that followed Nixon's reelection in 1972.

126. See Susanna McBee, "Subsidized Housing Frozen Before Justification by HUD," *Washington Post*, Dec. 3, 1973.

127. "Housing Policy: The President's Message to the Congress Recommending a Series of Legislative Proposals and Administrative Actions," Sept. 19, 1973, *Weekly Compilation of Presidential Documents* 9 (Sept. 24, 1973), p. 1147.

128. The implications of housing allowances for opening the suburbs are discussed in chapter 11.

129. Floyd H. Hyde, undersecretary, Department of Housing and Urban Development, quoted in James G. Phillips, "Housing Report / Standoff Likely Between Nixon and Hill, Democrats Hit Delay on Low-Income Programs," *National Journal Reports* 5 (Sept. 29, 1973), p. 1448.

130. *Low-Income Housing*, p. 146.

131. Representative Thomas L. Ashley, quoted in Lilley, "Romney Faces Political Perils with Plan to Integrate Suburbs," p. 2261.

132. See U.S. House of Representatives, *Housing and Urban Development Legislation—1970*, p. 860. At the same hearings, similar criticisms were voiced by spokesmen for the National League of Cities, U.S. Conference of Mayors, and National Association of Counties.

133. *Ibid.*, p. 170.

134. The other opponents of the bill on the subcommittee were Garry Brown, a Republican from Michigan, and Robert G. Stephens, a Democrat from Georgia. Five other Democrats on the subcommittee supported the bill.

135. Quoted in Lilley, "Romney Faces Political Perils With Plan to Integrate Suburbs," p. 2261.

136. Quoted in Gill, "Readington May Seek U.S. Aid Again."

137. See U.S. Congress, Senate, *Government Facilities Location Act of 1971*, 92d Cong., 1st sess., S.1282 (1971); and *Congressional Record*, 92d Cong., 1st sess., 117:5 (Mar. 16, 1971), pp. 6613–14, 6619–22.

138. U.S. Congress, Senate, Select Committee on Equal Educational Oppor-

tunity, *Toward Equal Educational Opportunity*, Report 92-000, 92d Cong., 2d sess. (Washington: U.S. Government Printing Office, 1972), p. 44.

139. Quoted in Lilley, "Administration and Congress Follow Courts in Promoting Residential Integration," p. 2438. The land use legislation developed by Senator Jackson and others that was approved by the Senate, only to be killed in the House of Representatives in 1974 and 1975, contained neither housing standards nor sanctions on federal aid that could be applied in suburbia or anywhere else.

140. See chapter 9 for a detailed discussion of the 1972 metropolitan housing proposal.

141. U.S. Congress, House of Representatives, *The Housing and Urban Development Act of 1972*, House Report 92-1429, 92d Cong., 2d sess. (Washington: U.S. Government Printing Office, 1972), pp. 38–39.

142. David O. Maxwell, general counsel, Department of Housing and Urban Development, quoted in William Lilley III and Timothy B. Clark, "Urban Report / Immense Costs, Scandals, Social Ills Plague Low-Income Housing Programs," *National Journal* 4 (July 1, 1972), p. 1083.

143. See testimony of Francis Purcell, presiding supervisor, Township of Hempstead, Nassau County, N.Y., in U.S. House of Representatives, *Housing and Urban Development Act of 1972*, pp. 501–32.

144. *Ibid.*, p. 699.

145. Representative Margaret M. Heckler, see U.S. House of Representatives, *Housing and Urban Development Legislation—1971*, p. 774. Heckler, a Republican from suburban Wellesley in the Boston area, represented a largely suburban district.

146. Quoted in Lilley, "Romney Faces Political Perils With Plan to Integrate Suburbs," p. 2257.

147. *Ibid.*, pp. 2257–58.

148. Representative William S. Moorhead, quoted in John L. Moore, "Outlook Improves for Passage of Community Development Bill," *National Journal Reports* 6 (Apr. 15, 1974), p. 561. Moorhead, a senior member of the Banking and Currency Committee, was intimately familiar with the impact of demographic change in congressional constituencies. For his first seven terms in the House, he represented a district lying wholly within Pittsburgh. Redistricting following the 1970 census, however, added approximately 150,000 suburbanites to Moorhead's constituency.

149. See chapter 9 for a discussion of the implications of the Housing and Community Development Act of 1974 for metropolitan housing programs.

150. The community-development grants replaced seven categorical programs previously administered by HUD: urban renewal, model cities, code enforcement and neighborhood development, water and sewer systems, open space, public facility loans, and neighborhood facilities and advanced land acquisition.

151. *Public Law* No. 93-383, 93d Cong., 2d sess. (Aug. 22, 1974), "Housing and Community Development Act of 1974," sec. 101c6.

152. Only those suburban counties empowered to deal with community development and housing were entitled to community development grants.

153. "Metropolitan Implications of House-Enacted Version of Housing and Community Development Act of 1974," Memorandum 74-6, Metropolitan Housing Program, Potomac Inst., Washington, June 28, 1974, p. 11.

154. *Public Law* No. 93-383, sec. 213d(2).

155. See Potomac Institute, Metropolitan Housing Program, *The Housing Assistance Plan: A Non-Working Program for Community Improvement?* A Preliminary Evaluation of HUD Implementation of the 1974 Housing and Community Development Act (Washington, 1975), pp. ii–iii.

156. Under the Housing and Community Development Act of 1974, developers of subsidized housing were not limited to sites within local jurisdictions participating in the community-development program.

157. "Citizens Mobilize for FH Advocacy: Focus on Use of Block Grant Funds," *NCDH Trends in Housing* 19 (Jan. / Feb., 1975), p. 3.

158. James C. Mitchell, general counsel, Department of Housing and Urban Development, quoted in Moore, "Outlook Improves for Passage of Community Development Bill," p. 557.

159. Potomac Institute, *The Housing Assistance Plan*, p. i. The Potomac Institute's conclusions were based on monitoring of the implementation of the Housing and Community Development Act of 1974 in six metropolitan areas— Atlanta, Boston, Chicago, Cleveland, Detroit, and San Francisco.

160. Tom Jones, "Eligible Suburbs Slow to Apply for New HUD Grants," *Chicago Sun-Times*, Dec. 8, 1974.

Chapter Nine: Fair Shares for the Metropolis

1. *Opening Up the Suburbs: An Urban Strategy for America* (New Haven: Yale Univ. Press, 1973), p. 170.

2. National Academy of Sciences-National Academy of Engineering, *Freedom of Choice in Housing: Opportunities and Constraints*, Report of the Social Science Panel, Division of Behavioral Sciences and the Recommendations of the Advisory Committee to the Department of Housing and Urban Development (Washington: National Academy of Sciences, 1972), p. 31.

3. Lawrence Sager, staff attorney, American Civil Liberties Union, see U.S. Congress, House of Representatives, Committee on the Judiciary, *Federal Government's Role in the Achievement of Equal Opportunity in Housing*, Hearings before the Civil Rights Oversight Subcommittee, 92d Cong., 1st and 2d sess. (Washington: U.S. Government Printing Office, 1972), p. 204.

4. *Ibid.*, p. 7.

5. *Ibid.*, p. 698.

6. 76 *U.S. Stat. at L.* (1962), 1148; 23 *U.S. Code* (1966), sec. 134.

7. 80 *U.S. Stat. at L.* (1966), 1262; 42 *U.S. Code* (1973), sec. 3334.

8. See U.S. Office of Management and Budget, *Circular No. A-95 Revised* (Washington: U.S. Government Printing Office, 1971).

9. See U.S. Congress, House of Representatives, Committee on Banking and Currency, *Housing and Urban Development Act of 1972*, Hearings, 92d Cong., 2d sess., (Washington: U.S. Government Printing Office, 1972), p. 685.

10. *Governing Metropolitan Areas: A Critical Review of Council of Governments and the Federal Role* (Washington: Urban Inst., 1971), p. 15.

11. Arnold R. Weber, associate director, Office of Management and Budget, see U.S. Commission on Civil Rights, *Hearing Held in Washington, D.C. June 14–17, 1971* (Washington: U.S. Government Printing Office, 1971), p. 353.

12. See Richard F. Babcock, "Let's Stop Romancing Regionalism," *Planning* 38 (July, 1972), p. 122.

13. See Norman Krumholz, "Cleveland's Fight for a Fair Share of the Region," *Planning* 38 (Nov., 1972), p. 276.

14. See Earl Finkler, "The Critics View SEWRPC," *Planning* 37 (July, 1971), p. 101.

15. "Exclusionary Land Use Practices, or the Rise and Fall of Exclusionary Zoning," submitted for presentation on Confer-In '72, Annual Conference, American Institute of Planners, Boston, Mass., Oct. 11, 1972; and "Exclusionary Land Use Practices," *HUD Challenge* 4 (Oct., 1973), p. 24.

16. Clifford A. Landry, Jr., community development coordinator, Berlin, Conn., quoted in Robert Cassidy, "The Battle of Berlin, Conn.," *City* 6 (Winter, 1972), p. 8. The metropolitan planning agency endorsed the application as consistent with the various A-95 criteria after Berlin agreed to consider zoning some land for apartments.

17. "Bay Area Regionalism: Institutions, Processes, and Programs," in U.S. Advisory Commission on Intergovernmental Relations, *Regional Governance: Promise and Performance*, Substate Regionalism and the Federal System, Vol. II, Case Studies (Washington: U.S. Government Printing Office, 1973), p. 100.

18. See Mary K. Nenno, *Housing in Metropolitan Areas: Roles and Responsibilities of Five Key Factors* (Washington: National Association of Housing and Redevelopment Officials, 1973), pp. 8–9.

19. 82 *U.S. Stat. at L.* (1968), 528; 40 *U.S. Code* (1969), sec. 461a.

20. Richard Spicer, "SEWRPC Tells Its Side," *Planning* 37 (July, 1971), p. 96.

21. Mayor Henry W. Maier, Milwaukee, Wis., quoted in Finkler, "The Critics View SEWRPC," p. 97.

22. Edward Seaver, coordinator, Metropolitan Housing Center, Milwaukee, Wis., quoted in "Rich Suburbs Told to Expect Housing for the Poor," *Milwaukee Journal*, May 24, 1971.

23. See Finkler, "The Critics View SEWRPC," p. 104.

24. Commissioner Eugene A. Hollister, Walworth County, Wis., quoted in Spicer, "SEWRPC Tells Its Side," p. 100.

25. George A. Berteau, chairman, Southeastern Wisconsin Regional Planning Commission, see "Turning Points," transcript of broadcast, WMVS, Channel 10, Milwaukee, n.d., p. 5.

26. Southeastern Wisconsin Regional Planning Commission, *A Short-Range*

Action Housing Program for Southeastern Wisconsin—1972 and 1973, Technical Report No. 12 (Waukesha, Wis., 1972), p. 33.

27. Harlan Clinkenbeard, assistant director, Southeastern Wisconsin Regional Planning Commission, see "Turning Points," p. 7.

28. *The Real Majority: An Extraordinary Examination of the American Electorate* (New York: Coward-McCann, 1970), p. 46.

29. "Dayton as Anytown, U.S.A.," *Dayton Daily News*, Apr. 20, 1971.

30. "Citizen Survey Yields Positive Response," Miami Valley Regional Planning Commission, *Planning Notes* 7 (Aug., 1973), p. 1.

31. "Dayton as Anytown, U.S.A."

32. See Jim Bland, "Planner Frets at Inaction," *Dayton Daily News*, Feb. 8, 1973.

33. Quoted in *ibid.*

34. See Peter H. Weiner, "Report: Sixth Conference on Exclusionary Land Use Policies," Clearinghouse on Exclusionary Land Use Problems, National Urban Coalition, New York, Apr. 15, 1971, p. 18.

35. Dale F. Bertsch and Ann M. Shafor, "A Regional Housing Plan: The Miami Valley Regional Planning Commission Experience," *Planners Notebook* 1 (Apr., 1971), p. 2.

36. *Ibid.*

37. See Miami Valley Regional Planning Commission, *A Housing Plan for the Miami Valley Region* (Dayton, O., 1970).

38. Bertsch and Shafor, "A Regional Housing Plan: The Miami Valley Regional Planning Commission Experience," p. 5.

39. See U.S. Commission on Civil Rights, *Hearing Held in Washington, D.C., June 14–17, 1971*, p. 12.

40. "The Housing Crisis: Responsibilities of Public Officials in Finding Solutions," Address before the Montgomery County Mayors and Managers Association, Jan. 28, 1970; see also Bertsch and Shafor, "A Regional Housing Plan: The Miami Valley Regional Planning Commission Experience," p. 4.

41. Quoted in Monroe W. Karmin, "How Dayton's Elite Opened Its Suburbs," *Wall Street Journal*, May 11, 1972.

42. Quoted in John Herbers, "Suburbs Accept Poor in Ohio Housing Plan," *New York Times*, Dec. 21, 1970; reprinted as "The Dayton Plan," in Louis H. Masotti and Jeffrey K. Hadden, eds., *Suburbia in Transition* (New York: Franklin Watts, 1974), p. 172.

43. "A Regional Housing Plan: The Miami Valley Regional Planning Commission Experience," pp. 5–6.

44. Edward Rausch, quoted in Lois Craig, "The Dayton Area's 'Fair Share' Housing Plan Enters the Implementation Phase," *City* 6 (Jan. / Feb., 1972), p. 54.

45. See Herbers, "The Dayton Plan," p. 169.

46. Quoted in John Thornes, "HUD Head Praises House Plan," *Dayton Daily News*, May 26, 1971.

47. See U.S. House of Representatives, *Federal Government's Role in the Achievement of Equal Opportunity in Housing*, p. 406.

48. See Peter H. Weiner, "Report: Sixth Conference on Exclusionary Land Use Policies," p. 14.

49. Quoted in William Lilley III, "Housing Report / Administration and Congress Follow Courts in Promoting Residential Integration," *National Journal* 3 (Nov. 12, 1971), p. 2436.

50. Quoted in *ibid.*, p. 2437. HUD fulfilled Romney's promise by allocating 1,800 additional units of subsidized units to the Washington area the following year.

51. Metropolitan Washington Council of Governments, *A Fair Share Housing Formula for Metropolitan Washington* (Washington, 1972), p. 4.

52. See Paul G. Edwards, "Fairfax Seeks to Keep Growth Controls," *Washington Post*, May 13, 1973.

53. See Ernest Erber and John P. Prior, *Housing Allocation Planning: An Annotated Bibliography*, Exchange Bibliography #547 (Monticello, Ill.: Council of Planning Librarians, 1974); Ernest Erber, "Metropolitan Housing Allocation Planning," *Urban Land* 33 (Apr., 1974), pp. 8–10; and David Listokin, "Fair-Share Housing Distribution: Will It Open the Suburbs to Apartment Development?" *Real Estate Law Journal* 2 (Spring, 1974), pp. 739–59.

54. Albert J. Hofstede, "Suburban Priorities in Housing," Delivered to the Housing Conference, St. Paul, Minn., Dec. 15, 1971, *Vital Speeches of the Day* 38 (Feb. 1, 1972), p. 247. Hofstede was chairman of the Metropolitan Council of the Twin Cities Area.

55. See Metropolitan Council of the Twin Cities Area, *Housing Review Manual* (St. Paul, Minn., 1975).

56. *Exclusionary Zoning: Land Use Regulation and Housing in the 1970s* (New York: Praeger Publishers, 1973), p. 139.

57. East-West Gateway Coordinating Council, "Initial Regional Housing Plan" (St. Louis, 1972).

58. East-West Gateway Coordinating Council, *Regional Housing Plan for St. Louis Metropolitan Area*, (St. Louis, 1973), p. 3.

59. Richard Hetlage, Citizens Task Force of the Regional Forum, East-West Gateway Coordinating Council, quoted in Charles Burgess, "South Side Residents Cool to Housing Plan, *St. Louis Globe-Democrat*, Mar. 27, 1973.

60. See Stanley Baldinger, *Planning and Governing the Metropolis: The Twin Cities Experience* (New York: Praeger Publishers, 1971).

61. Quoted in Lilley, "Administration and Congress Follow Courts in Promoting Residential Integration," p. 2437.

62. See *Hearing Held in Washington, D.C., June 14–17, 1971*, pp. 236–37.

63. Edward L. Holmgren, "The City and the Open Housing Movement," in National League of Cities, *Your City's Role in the Urban System*, Proceedings, 49th Annual Congress of Cities, Indianapolis, Ind., Nov. 28–30, 1972 (Washington, 1972), p. 12.

64. Aileen Hernandez, western representative, National Committee Against Discrimination in Housing, see U.S. House of Representatives, *Federal Government's Role in the Achievement of Equal Opportunity in Housing*, p. 111.

65. James H. Price, director, San Francisco Area Office, Department of

Housing and Urban Development, quoted in National Committee Against Discrimination in Housing, *Home Free? New Vistas in Regional Housing* (Washington, n.d.), p. 46.

66. *Ibid.*

67. See Leonard S. Rubinowitz, *Low-Income Housing: Suburban Strategies* (Cambridge, Mass.: Ballinger Pub. Co., 1974), p. 69.

68. Quoted in Stan Ziemba, "Suburb Mayors Seek Voluntary Housing Plan," *Chicago Sunday Tribune*, July 30, 1972.

69. Willis Caruso, general counsel, Leadership Council for Metropolitan Open Communities, quoted in Beth Christoffel, "Housing Panel Urges Local Action," *Evanston* (Ill.) *Review*, Nov. 15, 1972.

70. Metropolitan Housing Coalition, "Draft of Script for Mayors' Meeting," Chicago, Nov. 28, 1972, p. 8.

71. For a discussion of these activities, see Rubinowitz, *Low-Income Housing*, pp. 249–50.

72. Mayor Robert Teichert, Mount Prospect, Ill., see "Mayor Teichert Comments on Low-Income Housing," *Mount Prospect Herald*, Oct. 5, 1972.

73. See U.S. Commission on Civil Rights, *Hearing Held in Washington, D.C., June 14–17, 1971*, p. 13.

74. "Fair Share Formulas," *HUD Challenge* 4 (Apr. 1973), pp. 22–23.

75. Rubinowitz, *Low-Income Housing*, p. 84.

76. See Jane Silverman and Constance Whitaker, "Regional Government: To More and More People It's the Way to Define Urban America and Help Solve Its Problems," *Journal of Housing* 30 (Jan., 1973), p. 29.

77. See Metropolitan Council of the Twin Cities Area, *Subsidized Housing Activity: July, 1972–July, 1973*, Staff Report (St. Paul, Minn.: Metropolitan Council of the Twin Cities Area, 1974), p. 1.

78. See Ernest Holsendolph, "Minneapolis Area Begins Rent Plan," *New York Times*, Nov. 23, 1975.

79. "Magic Involved in Housing Plan" (editorial), *Dayton Daily News*, Mar. 25, 1973.

80. Vice Mayor Bonnie Macauley, Oakwood, Ohio, quoted in Clem Hamilton, "Housing Dispersal Foes to Get Hearing," *Dayton Daily News*, Apr. 27, 1973.

81. See Craig, "The Dayton Area's 'Fair Share' Housing Plan Enters the Implementation Phase," p. 56.

82. See *Hearing Held in Washington, D.C., June 14–17, 1971*, p. 28.

83. See *ibid.*, pp. 28–29.

84. Quoted in Craig, "The Dayton Area's 'Fair Share' Housing Plan Enters the Implementation Phase," p. 54. See also Bertsch's testimony in U.S. Congress, House of Representatives, Committee on Banking and Currency, *Housing and Urban Development Legislation—1971*, Hearings before the Subcommittee on Housing, 92nd Cong., 1st sess. (Washington: U.S. Government Printing Office, 1971), p. 770.

85. See statement submitted by John A. Stastny, president, National Association of Home Builders in *ibid.*, p. 1276.

86. Pamela Bolton, manager, Chevy Chase Park apartments, Centerville, O., quoted in Paul Delaney, "Dayton Suburbs Tackle Problems of 'Fair Share' Housing," *New York Times*, Nov. 17, 1974.

87. "The Dayton Area's 'Fair Share' Housing Plan Enters the Implementation Phase," p. 56.

88. "Let's Stop Romancing Regionalism," p. 122.

89. "The Dayton Area's 'Fair Share' Housing Plan Enters the Implementation Phase," p. 56.

90. U.S. Congress, House of Representatives, Committee on Banking and Currency, *Housing and the Urban Environment*, Report and recommendations of three study panels of the Subcommittee on Housing (Washington: U.S. Government Printing Office, 1971), p. 31.

91. Quoted in John Herbers, "New Housing Bill to Help Suburbs," *New York Times*, July 4, 1971.

92. See U.S. House of Representatives, *Housing and Urban Development Legislation—1971*, p. 477.

93. *Ibid.*, p. 682, and U.S. House of Representatives, *Housing and the Urban Environment*, p. 30.

94. M. Carl Holman, president, National Urban Coalition, see U.S. House of Representatives, *Housing and Urban Development Legislation—1971*, p. 902.

95. Theodore M. Hesburgh, chairman, U.S. Commission on Civil Rights, *ibid.*, p. 1104.

96. *Equal Opportunity in Suburbia* (Washington: U.S. Government Printing Office, 1974), p. 62.

97. See U.S. House of Representatives, *Housing and Urban Development Act of 1972*, p. 326.

98. Quoted in "Washington Panel Adopts Plan to Disperse Low-Cost Housing in Suburbs," *New York Times*, Jan. 16, 1972.

99. See John Herbers, "House Unit Backs Housing Measure," *New York Times*, Sept. 12, 1972.

100. See Metropolitan Council of the Twin Cities Area, *Subsidized Housing Activity; July, 1973–July, 1974*, A Supplementary Report (St. Paul, Minn., 1974), p. 2.

101. Mayor Henry W. Maier, Milwaukee, Wis., see "Turning Points," p. 3.

102. John A. Stastny, president, National Association of Home Builders, see U.S. House of Representatives, *Housing and Urban Development Legislation—1971*, p. 1244.

103. Mayor Lee Alexander, Syracuse, N.Y.; *ibid.*, p. 504.

104. Representative William F. Ryan, Democrat of New York City, N.Y.; *ibid.*, p. 1162.

105. See Potomac Institute, Metropolitan Housing Program, *The Housing Assistance Plan: A Non-Working Program for Community Improvement?* A Preliminary Evaluation of HUD Implementation of the 1974 Housing and Community Development Act (Washington, 1975), p. 24.

Chapter Ten: The Reluctant Partner

1. "Let's Stop Romancing Regionalism," *Planning* 38 (July, 1972), p. 122.

2. *Building the American City*, Report of the National Commission on Urban Problems to the Congress and President of the United States, 91st Cong., 1st sess., House Doc. No. 91–34 (Washington: U.S. Government Printing Office, 1968), p. 30.

3. *Ibid.*, p. 29.

4. See *A Decent Home* (Washington: U.S. Government Printing Office, 1969), p. 145.

5. "State Lags as Housing Drags" (editorial), Jan. 8, 1972.

6. Lawrence G. Sager, " 'Exclusionary Zoning': Constitutional Limitations on the Power of Municipalities to Restrict the Use of Land." Paper prepared for the Biennial Conference of the American Civil Liberties Union, Boulder, Colo., June 8–11, 1972, p. 43.

7. See Paul Davidoff and Linda Davidoff, "Opening the Suburbs," *Syracuse Law Review* 22 (1971), pp. 528–31.

8. See U.S. Commission on Civil Rights, *Hearing Held in Washington, D.C., June 14–17, 1971* (Washington: U.S. Government Printing Office, 1971), p. 882.

9. Quoted in Hugh McDonald, "Why Warren Sought Help of Romney," *Detroit News*, July 23, 1970. Milliken was addressing 175 suburbanites in affluent Birmingham in the Detroit area during the period when HUD was pressing blue-collar Warren to develop a local open-housing program.

10. See U.S. Commission on Civil Rights, *Hearing Held in Washington, D.C., June 14–17, 1971*, p. 883.

11. *Building the American City*, p. 191.

12. *The Zoning Dilemma: A Legal Strategy for Urban Change* (Indianapolis: Bobbs-Merrill, 1971, p. 3. See also R. Robert Linowes and Don T. Allensworth, *The States and Land-Use Control* (New York: Praeger Publishers, 1975), pp. 154–175.

13. *Suburban Land Conversion in the United States: An Economic and Governmental Process* (Baltimore: Johns Hopkins Univ. Press, 1971), p. 247.

14. See Richard F. Babcock and Fred P. Bosselman, *Exclusionary Zoning: Land Use Regulation and Housing in the 1970s* (New York: Praeger Publishers, 1973), p. 155.

15. U.S. Advisory Commission on Intergovernmental Relations, *Fiscal Balance in the American Federal System* (Washington: U.S. Government Printing Office, 1967), Vol. 2, p. 278.

16. *Upper St. Clair Township* v. *Commonwealth, Department of Community Affairs*, Pa. Cmwlth., 317 A.2d 906 (1973) at 910. For a fuller discussion of the activities of the Pennsylvanis Department of Community Affairs in seeking to tie recreation grants to local housing policies, see Leonard S. Rubinowitz, *Low-Income Housing: Suburban Strategies* (Cambridge, Mass.: Ballinger Pub. Co., 1974), pp. 120–30. For Suburban Action's findings, see Commonwealth of Pennsylvania, Department of Community Affairs, *A Study of Exclusion*, Prepared by Suburban Action Institute (Harrisburg, Pa., 1973).

17. See *Building the American City*, p. 112.

18. Joseph P. Fried, *Housing Crisis U.S.A.* (New York: Praeger Publishers, 1971), p. 140.

19. The development, powers, and activities of state housing finance agencies are treated in detail in Peter R. Morris, *State Housing Finance Agencies: An Entrepreneurial Approach to Subsidized Housing* (Lexington, Mass.: Lexington Bks., 1974). See also Robert C. Alexander, "Fifteen State Housing Finance Agencies in Review," *Journal of Housing* 29 (Jan., 1972), pp. 9–17; and Michael A. Stegman, "Housing Finance Agencies: Are They Critical Instruments of State Government?" *Journal of the American Institute of Planners* 40 (Sept., 1974), pp. 307–20.

20. See U.S. Department of Housing and Urban Development, *Housing in the Seventies*, A Report of the National Housing Policy Review (Washington: U.S. Government Printing Office, 1974), pp. 140, 143. From January 1, 1969 to March 1, 1973 state housing finance agencies undertook commitments to 90,587 units; of these, 71,399 (or 79 percent) received federal subsidies, with 65,994 of the units (or 73 percent of the total) assisted under the Section 236 program.

21. Rubinowitz, *Low-Income Housing*, p. 117.

22. New York's Urban Development Corporation, which was empowered to override local controls, is not considered a state housing finance agency for the purposes of this discussion, since it was organized as both a development and a finance agency. The Urban Development Corporation, its powers, and its activities in the suburbs are discussed in detail later in this chapter.

23. Melvin R. Levin, Jerome G. Rose, and Joseph S. Slavet, *New Approaches to State Land-Use Policies* (Lexington, Mass.: Lexington Bks., 1974), p. 104.

24. State of New Jersey, Department of Law and Public Safety, Letter from Attorney General George F. Kugler, Jr., to James H. Blair, director, Division of Civil Rights, Re: National Committee Against Discrimination in Housing, et al. vs. Township of Mahway, N.J., July 8, 1971, pp. 9–10; see also Earl Josephson, "Rights Group Lacks Authority on Zoning," *Trenton Evening Times*, July 9, 1971.

25. The legislation was sponsored by Assemblyman Ronald Owens, a black from Newark; see Richard Zimmerman, "Mahway Zoning Challenged Anew," *Bergen Record*, Oct. 12, 1972.

26. By mid-1974, thirty-six states, including all of the large urban states, had adopted statewide building codes for factory-built and modular housing.

27. Both of these developments are discussed in detail below.

28. *Exclusionary Zoning*, p. 151.

29. *The Quiet Revolution in Land Use Control*, Prepared for the Council on Environmental Quality (Washington: U.S. Government Printing Office, 1971), p. 1.

30. *Exclusionary Zoning*, p. 159.

31. *Ibid.*, p. 162.

32. See Ed McCahill, "Florida's Not-So-Quiet Revolution," *Planning* 40 (Mar., 1974), p. 12.

33. See Richard F. Babcock and David L. Callies, "Ecology and Housing: Virtues in Conflict," in Marion Clawson, ed., *Modernizing Urban Land Policy*,

Papers presented at an RFF Forum held in Washington, D.C., 13–14 April 1972 (Baltimore: Johns Hopkins Univ. Press, 1973), p. 213.

34. *The Quiet Revolution in Land Use Control*, p. 319.

35. *Ibid.*, pp. 25–28.

36. Brief of Richard J. Sullivan, Commission of Environmental Protection, *Amicus Curiae, Allan-Dean Corporation* v. *Township of Bedminster*, Superior Court of New Jersey, Law Div., Somerset Co., Doc. No. L 36896-70 P.W., p. 18.

37. *Ibid.*, p. 3.

38. *Water Quality Management: New Jersey's Vanishing Options*, Eighth Report, June, 1973 (Trenton: 1973), p. 46.

39. See Rubinowitz, *Low-Income Housing*, pp. 96–99.

40. Assemblyman Franz S. J. Leichter, Democrat of Manhattan, quoted in " 'Snob Zoning' Fought," *New York Times*, Mar. 6, 1971.

41. Gerald C. Godwin, deputy executive vice president, Pennsylvania State Association of Boroughs, quoted in "Suburbia Assailed on Housing Restrictions," *Trenton Sunday Times Advertiser*, Feb. 20, 1972.

42. Quoted in William Borders, "Suburban Zoning Is Again Attacked," *New York Times*, Mar. 26, 1967.

43. Edmund T. Hume, commissioner of community affairs, quoted in Ladley K. Pearson, "State Ponders Zoning Issue," *Newark Sunday News*, Apr. 25, 1971.

44. "Utter Chaos or Simple Complexity," in American Society of Planning Officials, *Planning 1970*, Selected Papers from the ASPO National Planning Conference, New York, Apr. 4–9, 1970 (Chicago, 1970), p. 13.

45. For an intensive analysis of the development of the meadowlands legislation, see Clifford Goldman, "The Hackensack Meadowlands: The Politics of Regional Planning and Development in the Metropolis" (Doctoral Thesis, Princeton University, 1975).

46. State of New Jersey, Legislature, Senate, *Land Use and Planning Development Law*, Senate No. 803 (May 12, 1969), p. 2.

47. *Ibid.*

48. *Ibid.*, p. 48.

49. Other provisions of the bill simplified and standardized zoning procedures throughout the state, clarified the roles and responsibilities of various participants in the zoning process, and authorized direct control over land in critical areas such as flood plains and adjacent to highways and airports by a State Planning Commission composed of cabinet officials.

50. Mayor F. Edward Biertumpfel, Union Township, N.J., quoted in Arthur G. Kent, "The Zoning Issue: A Study of Politics and Public Policy in New Jersey" (Senior Thesis, Princeton University, 1972), pp. 46–47.

51. See Sharon Rosenhause and Edward J. Flynn, "The What, Why, How of Zoning," *Bergen Record*, Aug. 3, 1970.

52. Quoted in Kent, "The Zoning Issue," p. 44.

53. Quoted in "The What, Why, How of Zoning."

54. Quoted in Earl Josephson, "Cahill Wants Zoning Solution: Sears," *Trenton Evening Times*, Aug. 13, 1970.

55. Quoted in Ronald Sullivan, "U.A.W. Maintains a Jersey Suburb Keeps Out Poor," *New York Times*, Jan. 28, 1971.

56. State of New Jersey, Governor, *A Blueprint for Housing in New Jersey*, A Special Message to the Legislature by William T. Cahill, Governor of New Jersey (Dec. 7, 1970), p. 13.

57. *Ibid.*, p. 15.

58. *Ibid.*, p. 17.

59. See *Molino* v. *Mayor and Council of Borough of Glassboro*, 116 N.J.Super. 195, 281 A.2d 401 (1971).

60. See *Oakwood at Madison, Inc.* v. *Township of Madison*, 117 N.J.Super. 11, 283 A.2d 353 (1971).

61. State of New Jersey, Governor, *New Horizons in Housing*, A Special Message to the Legislature by William T. Cahill, Governor of New Jersey (Mar. 27, 1972), p. 7.

62. See State of New Jersey, Legislature, General Assembly, *State Construction Code Act*, Assembly No. 1419 (Nov. 13, 1972).

63. See State of New Jersey, Legislature, General Assembly, *New Jersey Community Planning Corporation Act*, Assembly No. 1420 (Nov. 13, 1972).

64. See State of New Jersey, Legislature, General Assembly, *Voluntary Balanced Housing Plan Act*, Assembly No. 1421 (Nov. 13, 1972).

65. See State of New Jersey, Legislature, General Assembly, *Proposed Community Planning Law*, Assembly No. 1422 (Nov. 13, 1972).

66. Quoted in Sullivan, "U.A.W. Maintains a Jersey Suburb Keeps Out Poor."

67. See Vincent R. Zarate, "Proposed State Zoning Bill Would Bar Economic Exclusion," *Newark Sunday News*, Feb. 7, 1971.

68. *New Horizons in Housing*, p. 33.

69. Quoted in Michael Cleveland, "Merck Proposes Quota System on New Housing," *Passaic Herald-News*, Apr. 27, 1973.

70. Sidney L. Willis, assistant comissioner of community affairs, quoted in David Corcoran, "Zoning Power Tied to Legislation," *Bergen Record*, Apr. 9, 1973.

71. Mayor David Cohen, Holmdel, N.J., quoted in Dan Weissman, "Home Rule: Local Forces Line Up Against Statewide Planning Bills," *Newark Sunday Star-Ledger*, Apr. 24, 1973.

72. John Chappel, president, United Citizens for Home Rule, quoted in *ibid*.

73. Quoted in Gordon Murphy, "State Scene: Land-Use Bills Hurt Cahill," *Bergen Sunday News*, Apr. 1, 1973.

74. Assemblyman John Spirrizi, Wyckoff, N.J., quoted in Joe King, "Spizziri Talks on Home Rule," *Ridgewood* (N.J.) *Sunday News*, May 27, 1973.

75. Assemblyman Richard DeKorte, quoted in Weissman, "Home Rule: Local Forces Line Up Against Statewide Planning Bills."

76. See Ronald Sullivan, "Restrictive Zoning Facing Ban," *New York Times*, May 5, 1974.

77. *New Horizons in Housing*, p. 5.

78. Associate Justice Morris Pashman, quoted in Walter H. Wagoner, "Jus-

tices' Questions Hint at Zoning Curb Reversal," *New York Times*, Jan. 9, 1974.

79. State of New Jersey, Governor, *First Annual Message to the Legislature*, Brendan Byrne, Governor of New Jersey (Jan. 14, 1975), p. 11.

80. *Ibid.*

81. *Ibid.*, p. 12.

82. "Toward Fair Zoning" (editorial), *Trenton Evening Times*, Mar. 26, 1975.

83. "State Land Use Planning" (editorial), Apr. 1, 1975.

84. Robert S. Molnar, chairman, Committee on Housing and Urban Affairs, New Jersey Bar Association, quote in Mike Piserchia, "Housing Crisis: Bar Panel Faults Legislature for Inaction," *Newark Star-Ledger*, Apr. 4, 1975.

85. *Southern Burlington County N.A.A.C.P.* v. *Township of Mr. Laurel*, 67 N.J. 151, 336 A2d 713 (1975) at 733.

86. Lewis Kaden, special counsel to the governor, quoted in Dan Weissman, "Measure Drafted to Assign Goals for Fair Housing," *Newark Star-Ledger*, Apr. 3, 1975.

87. As pointed out in chapter 7, the court indicated that "the state planning agency" along with other planning bodies possessed the expertise to determine "a reasonable figure" for Mount Laurel's fair share of regional housing; see *Southern Burlington County N.A.A.C.P* v. *Township of Mt. Laurel*, 67 N.J. 151, 336 A2d 713 (1975) at 733.

88. See "State-Municipalities Battle Over Zoning Is Heading for Another Showdown," *New York Times*, Oct. 13, 1974.

89. Assemblyman Harold Martin, Cresskill, N.J., quoted in Fran Hawthorne, "Bergen Delegates Split on Zoning," *Bergen Record*, Mar. 26, 1975. Martin's district included Upper Saddle River and Washington Township, both of which were involved in exclusionary zoning litigation.

90. Senator Frank J. Dodd, quoted in Jim Goodman, "Mt. Laurel Invites Legal Fight," *Trenton Evening Times*, Apr. 15, 1976.

91. *Mass. Gen. Law*, (1975), Ch. 40B, sec. 23.

92. *Ibid.*, sec. 20.

93. *Ibid.*, sec. 20.

94. Commonwealth of Massachusetts, Special Commission on Planning, Zoning, and Subdivision Controls, *Reports*, House No. 2480 (Boston, 1955), p. 6.

95. Commonwealth of Massachusetts, General Court, Senate, *Report of the Legislative Research Council Relative to Restricting the Zoning Power to City and County Governments*, Senate No. 1133 (Boston, 1968), p. 91.

96. See *Board of Appeals of Hanover* v. *Housing Appeals Committee*, Mass., 294 N.E.2d 393 (1973) at 904.

97. Thomas Gallagher, "Risky Issue for the Governor," *Boston Herald*, Aug. 15, 1969.

98. Letter from Robert P. Clark, Belmont, Mass., *Boston Globe*, Aug. 9, 1969; the letter is quoted in Karen Jean Schneider, "Innovation in State Legislation: The Massachusetts Suburban Zoning Act," (Senior Thesis, Radcliffe College, 1970), p. 64.

99. Letter from Lucille Williams, Milton, Mass., *Boston Herald*, Aug. 8, 1969; the letter is quoted in Schneider, "Innovation in State Legislation," p. 65.

100. See Schneider, "Innovation in State Legislation," p. 44.

101. Representative Robert Aronson, Sharon, Mass., quoted in *Board of Appeals of Hanover* v. *Housing Appeals Committee*, Mass., 294 N.E. 2d 393 (1973) at 406.

102. Thomas Gallagher, "Suburbs Seek Sargent's Aid," *Boston Herald*, Aug. 22, 1969.

103. See Schneider, "Innovation in State Legislation," p. 45.

104. "Time to Unlock Suburbia" (editorial), *Boston Herald*, Aug. 12, 1969.

105. *Subsidized Housing in the Suburbs: Legislation or Litigation?* Issue Paper No. 1 (Boston: Department of Community Affairs, Commonwealth of Massachusetts, 1972), p. 72.

106. Schneider, "Innovation in State Legislatures," p. 115.

107. The two local officials were appointed by the governor; the other three members of the Housing Appeals Committee were appointed by the Commissioner of Community Affairs, one of whom was to be an official of the department.

108. Rubinowitz, *Low-Income Housing*, p. 91.

109. See James Austin, Shin Yoshida, and David O'Conner, "Beverly: Subsidized Housing and the Anti-Snob Zoning Act," in Lawrence Susskind, ed., *The Land Use Controversy in Massachusetts: Case Studies and Policy Options*, Prepared for the Special Commission on the Effects of Growth Patterns on the Quality of Life in the Commonwealth of Massachusetts (Cambridge: Massachusetts Institute of Technology, 1975), p. 123.

110. See Engler, *Subsidized Housing in the Suburbs*, p. 10.

111. Maurice Corman, chief counsel, Massachusetts Department of Community Affairs, and member of the Housing Appeals Committee, quoted in Liz Roman Gallese, "Housing for the Poor Blocked Despite Curb on 'Snob Zoning' Laws," *Wall Street Journal*, Oct. 17, 1972.

112. *Board of Appeals of Hanover* v.*Housing Appeals Committee*, Mass., 294 N.E.2d 393 (1973) at 423–24.

113. See McDonald Barr, "The Massachusetts Zoning Appeals Law: Lessons of the First Three Years," Submitted for Presentation at Confer-In 72 (Boston: Office of Planning and Program Development, Department of Community Affairs, Commonwealth of Massachusetts, 1972), p. 4.

114. Engler, *Subsidized Housing in the Suburbs*, pp. 96–97.

115. See Barr, "The Massachusetts Zoning Appeals Law," p. 17.

116. Quoted in the *Trenton Evening Times*, June 8, 1970.

117. *N.Y. Unconsolidated Laws*, Sec. 6266(3). Use of the power to override local zoning and other controls required a two-thirds majority on UDC's nine-member board of directors.

118. See U.S. Congress, House of Representatives, Committee on Banking and Currency, *Housing and Urban Development Legislation—1970*, Hearings before the Subcommittee on Housing, 91st Cong., 2d sess. (Washington: U.S. Government Printing Office, 1970), p. 687.

119. *Equal Opportunity in Suburbia* (Washington: U.S. Government Printing Office, 1974), p. 53.

120. Quoted in Richard Schickel, "New York's Mr. Urban Renewal," *New York Times Magazine*, Mar. 1, 1970, p. 30.

121. See Sydney H. Schanberg, "Governor Offers a $6 Billion Plan to Rebuild Slums," *New York Times*, Feb. 29, 1968.

122. *Ibid.*

123. Councilman Edward Koch of Manhattan, quoted in Richard E. Mooney, "Slum Plan Gets Mixed Reviews," *New York Times*, Feb. 29, 1968.

124. "Text of Statement by Mayor Lindsay on His Proposal for an Urban Bill of Rights," *New York Times*, Mar. 7, 1968; see also Charles G. Bennett, "Mayor Has a Plan, Rivaling State's, to Improve Cities," *New York Times*, Mar. 7, 1968.

125. "Governor's Noncompromise" (editorial), Apr. 3, 1968.

126. See Richard Witkin, "Governor Asks 'Memorial Laws,' " *New York Times*, Apr. 6, 1968.

127. See Sydney H. Schanberg, "Legislators Push State Slum Plan," *New York Times*, Apr. 9, 1968.

128. See Vic Ostrowidski, "State's Urban Development Corp., A Giant Not Yet Awake," *Albany Sunday Times Union*, Aug. 3, 1969.

129. Robert H. Connery, "Nelson A. Rockefeller as Governor," in Robert H. Connery and Gerald Benjamin, eds., *Governing New York State: The Rockefeller Years*, Proceedings of the Academy of Political Science, Vol. 31, May, 1974 (New York: The Academy of Political Science, 1974), p. 12.

130. Quoted in Sydney H. Schanberg, "How to Twist Arms: the Rockefeller Way," *New York Times*, Apr. 11, 1968.

131. "Housing and Community Development: How Then and How Now?" Lecture, Woodrow Wilson School of Public and International Affairs and School of Architecture and Urban Planning, Princeton University, Princeton, N.J., Apr. 23, 1975.

132. Quoted in William K. Reilly, ed., *The Use of Land: A Citizens' Policy Guide to Urban Growth*, A Task Force Report Sponsored by The Rockefeller Brothers Fund (New York: Crowell, 1973), p. 260.

133. See U.S. House of Representatives, *Housing and Urban Development Legislation—1970*, p. 698.

134. See U.S. Commission on Civil Rights, *Hearing Held in Washington, D.C., June 14–17, 1971*, pp. 877–78.

135. Quoted in Vic Ostrowidski, "Urban Development Chief Stresses Ties With Private Capital," *Albany Times Union*, Aug. 4, 1969.

136. "New York: Are Cities A Bust?" *Look* 33 (Apr. 1, 1969), p. 70.

137. New York State Urban Development Corporation, *UDC in '72*, Annual Report 1972 (New York, 1973), p. 8.

138. Quoted in Nancy Moran, "A Gingerly Step into Westchester Taken by Logue," *New York Times*, Feb. 22, 1970.

139. Quoted in *ibid.*

140. State of New York, Executive Chamber, Nelson A. Rockefeller, Governor, "Memorandum filed with Assembly Bill Number 650," Albany, May 22, 1972.

141. All UDC projects paid ten percent of rental income in lieu of local taxes, a formula which Logue admitted did "not cover the total increase in the school burden" in some of UDC's developments; see U.S. Congress, House of Representatives, Committee on Banking and Currency, *Housing and Urban Development Legislation—1971*, Hearings before the Subcommittee on Housing, 92d Cong., 1st sess. (Washington: U.S. Government Printing Office, 1971), p. 416.

142. See Rubinowitz, *Low-Income Housing*, pp. 109–10.

143. See Bob Beck, " 'How to Stop It?' They Ask," *Rochester Times-Union*, Apr. 20, 1972.

144. See Linda Van Kirk, "The Taxpayer: Housing Plan Opponent Says, 'I Can't Afford It!' " *Rochester Times-Union*, June 6, 1972.

145. John C. Mitchell, director, Housing Council in the Monroe County Area, quoted in "State Housing Agency Supported, Attacked," *Rochester Democrat and Chronicle*, Mar. 5, 1972.

146. Supervisor James J. Powers, Chili, N.Y., quoted in Jill Zelickson, "UDC Enters Greece; 2 More Due," *Rochester Times-Union*, Jan. 5, 1972.

147. Donald Deming, "Supervisor's Report: UDC Site Withdrawn," *Irondequoit* (N.Y.) *Press*, July 27, 1972. Deming was the Supervisor of Irondequoit, N.Y.

148. See *Town of Greece* v. *Urban Development Corporation–Greater Rochester, Inc.*, Supreme Court, New York County, Index No. 17437 / 1972, Nov. 30, 1972.

149. See "UDC Finds Friends in Suburbs" (editorial), *Rochester Times-Union*, Aug. 24, 1972.

150. Richard A. Miller, UDC-Rochester, Inc., quoted in Jim Castor, "Their Housing Won't Bring Suburban Ghettos: Official," *Rochester Democrat and Chronicle*, Feb. 26, 1972.

151. John H. Potter, chairman, UDC-Rochester, Inc., quoted in Christy Bulkeley, "UDC Drops Site for Irondequoit Housing Project," *Rochester Times-Union*, July 18, 1972.

152. Supervisor John A. Passidomo, Harrison, N.Y., quoted in Linda Greenhouse, "College's Plan Stirs Opposition," *New York Times*, Feb. 28, 1971.

153. New York State Urban Development Corporation, *Fair Share*, A Report on Westchester's Housing Shortage for Low- and Moderate-income Families and the Elderly (New York: Urban Development Corporation, 1972), p. 6.

154. *Ibid.*; see also the data on Westchester's housing on pp. 2–4. In addition, see Chris Kristensen, John Levy, and Tamar Savir, *The Suburban Lock-Out Effect*, Suburban Action Institute Research Report #1 (White Plains, N.Y., 1971).

155. See "9-Town Plan Set for Westchester," *New York Times*, Feb. 13, 1972.

156. *UDC in '72*, p. 11.

157. See Martin F. Nolan, "The City Politic: Showdown Vote in Northern Westchester," *New York* 6 (June 4, 1973), p. 7.

158. Daniel L. Miller, southern regional director, New York State Urban Development Corporation, "Remarks at the Westchester Municipal Planning Federation Annual Dinner," May 31, 1973, p. 2.

159. Home Rule Commission, "Society by Superagency (or the Public Be

Damned): A Comprehensive Study of New York's Urban Development Corporation" (Yorktown Heights, N.Y., n.d.), p. 1.

160. Quoted in Robert Beckham, "Detour Ahead: That's the Message Coming to Public Agencies Attempting to Move Down the Road to Suburbia to Build Low-Income Housing," *Journal of Housing* 30 (May, 1973), p. 232.

161. Supervisor George Oettinger, New Castle, N.Y., quoted in *ibid.*, p. 233.

162. Quoted in Nolan, "Showdown Vote in Northern Westchester," p. 8.

163. See Linda Greenhouse, "Accord Reached on Bill to Cut Urban Development Unit's Power," *New York Times*, May 20, 1973.

164. Quoted in Owen Moritz, "Logue Won't Quit Urban Corp. Post," *New York Daily News*, May 23, 1973.

165. Quoted in Nolan, "Showdown Vote in Northern Westchester," p. 8.

166. State Senator Bernard Gordon, Republican of Peekskill, N.Y., see Greenhouse, "Accord Reached on Bill to Cut Urban Development Unit's Power."

167. "UDC Harnassed" (editorial), *Suffolk Life* (Westhampton, N.Y.) May 28, 1973.

168. Frank S. Kristof, "Housing," in Connery and Benjamin, eds., *Governing New York State: The Rockefeller Years*, p. 199. Kristof was director of UDC's Division of Economics and Housing Finance.

169. Quoted in Alan S. Oser, "Logue Forecasts 1973 Slowdown in U.D.C. Pace," *New York Times*, Aug. 12, 1973.

170. The bond arrangements employed by UDC and other agencies in New York were devised as a means of circumventing a state constitutional requirement for public approval of bond issues backed by the full faith and credit of the state.

171. Rockefeller was succeeded in December 1973 by Malcolm Wilson, who had served as lieutenant governor throughout Rockefeller's thirteen years as governor.

172. Richard Ravitch, chairman, New York State Urban Development Corporation, quoted in Joseph P. Fried, "U.D.C.'s Ripple Effect," *New York Times*, Apr. 3, 1975.

Chapter Eleven: Whither an Open Society?

1. William K. Reilly and S. J. Schulman, "The State Urban Development Corporation: New York's Innovation," *Urban Lawyer* I (Summer, 1969), p. 144.

2. Daniel L. Miller, southern regional director, New York State Urban Development Corporation, "Remarks at the Westchester Municipal Planning Federation Annual Dinner," May 31, 1973, p. 4.

3. *Politics and the Housing Crisis Since 1930* (New York: Universe Books, 1973), pp. 224–25.

4. "The Coming Apart of Fortress Suburbia," *New York* 5 (Jan. 31, 1972), p. 24.

5. "Housing and Community Development: How Then and How Now?" Lecture, Woodrow Wilson School of Public and International Affairs and the

School of Architecture and Urban Planning, Princeton University, Princeton, N.J., Apr. 23, 1975.

6. "Opening Up the Suburbs: Notes on a Movement for Social Change," *Yale Review of Law and Social Action* 2 (Summer, 1972), p. 307.

7. *Ibid.*, pp. 307–8.

8. *Ibid.*, p. 312.

9. "On 'Opening Up' the Suburbs," *Public Interest*, No. 37 (Fall, 1974), p. 110.

10. *Low-Income Housing: A Critique of Federal Aid* (Baltimore: Johns Hopkins Univ. Press, 1970), pp. 126–27.

11. See, for instance, John M. Levy, "Exclusionary Zoning: After the Walls Come Down," *Planning* 38 (Aug., 1972), pp. 159–60.

12. Glazer, "On 'Opening Up' the Suburbs," p. 111.

13. Quoted in William E. Farrell, "Municipal Group Seeks Policy of 'Urban Conservation' to Save American Cities," *New York Times*, Dec. 4, 1974.

14. U.S. Department of Housing and Urban Development, *HUD News*, "Remarks Prepared for Delivery by Carla A. Hills, Secretary of Housing and Urban Development at the Forty-Third Annual Conference of the United States Conference of Mayors, Sheraton-Boston Hotel, Boston, Mass., July 8, 1975," (July 8, 1975), pp. 1–2.

15. Quoted in Monroe W. Karmin, "The Changing Aspirations of Cities," *Wall Street Journal*, Dec. 6, 1972.

16. "Squeezing Spread City," *New York Times Magazine*, Mar. 17, 1974, p. 44.

17. John Dyckman, professor of city and regional planning, University of California, Berkeley; see U.S. Commission on Civil Rights, *Hearing Held in Washington, D.C., June 14–17, 1971* (Washington: U.S. Government Printing Office, 1971), p. 182.

18. Jerome Showstack, board of directors, Southeastern Pennsylvania Transportation Authority, quoted in Lenora Berson, "A Closer Look: Philadelphia," *City* 5 (Jan. / Feb., 1971), p. 41.

19. *Opening Up the Suburbs: An Urban Strategy for America* (New Haven: Yale Univ. Press, 1973), p. 28.

20. "Opening the Suburbs: Towards Inclusionary Land Use Controls," *Syracuse Law Review* 22 (1971), p. 511.

21. Joseph D. Dorris, business administrator, Camden, N.J., quoted in Donald Janson, "Camden, Like Newark, to Seek State Aid to Avert Bankruptcy," *New York Times*, Dec. 11, 1972.

22. U.S. President's Task Force on Suburban Problems, *Final Report*, edited by Charles M. Haar (Cambridge, Mass.: Ballinger Pub. Co., 1974), pp. 17, 45.

23. *A Decent Home* (Washington: U.S. Government Printing Office, 1969), p. 13. For a thoughtful analysis of the broader implications of residential location, see David M. Trubek, "Law and the Politics of Justice: Rethinking the Open Suburbs Movement," in National Committee Against Discrimination in Housing, *Exclusionary Land Use Litigation: Policy and Strategy for the Future*, Papers presented at NCDH–Potomac Institute Exclusionary Land Use Litigation Con-

ference, Washington, D.C., Nov. 14–15, 1974 (Washington, n.d.), pp. 112–14.

24. Commissioner Robert C. Embry, Jr., Department of Housing and Community Development, Baltimore, quoted in Antero Pietila, "City Hints Court Action to Stop New Housing," *Baltimore Sun*, Nov. 20, 1972.

25. *Housing and Social Policy* (Englewood Cliffs, N.J.: Prentice-Hall, 1974), p. 159. Anthony Downs makes a strong case for combining housing allowances with subsidies for construction in *Federal Housing Subsidies: How Are They Working?* (Lexington, Mass.: Lexington Bks., 1973), pp. 59–61.

26. See Scott Jacobs, "The Housing Allowance Program in Kansas City Turns into a Notable Failure," *Planning* 39 (Oct., 1973), pp. 10–13. See also U.S. Department of Housing and Urban Development, Office of Policy Development and Research, *Second Annual Report of the Experimental Housing Allowance Program* (Washington: U.S. Government Printing Office, 1975), pp. 32–48.

27. Borough President Percy Sutton, New York City, quoted in Joseph P. Fried, "Nixon's Housing Policy," *New York Times*, Sept. 29, 1973. In a study conducted for HUD, the Urban Institute estimated that a full-scale housing-allowance program would lead to increases in the costs of housing of almost thirty percent in areas with tight housing markets; see Frank de Leeuw et al., *The Market Effects of Housing Policies* (Washington: Urban Inst., 1974), pp. 29–35.

28. "The Federal Government as 'Houser of Last Resort': A Policy for Democratic Urban Growth," *Urban Law Annual* (1972), p. 37.

29. See U.S. Commission on Civil Rights, *Hearing Held in Washington, D.C., June 14–17, 1971*, p. 848.

30. *In-Zoning: A Guide for Policy-Makers on Inclusionary Land Use Programs* (Washington: Potomac Inst., 1974), p. 94.

31. *Ibid.*, p. 5. Franklin, Falk, and Levin discuss these three factors in detail on pp. 94–106.

32. *Southern Burlington County N.A.A.C.P. v. Township of Mt. Laurel*, 67 N.J. 151, 336 A2d 713 (1975) at 733.

33. "The Ghost of U.D.C." (editorial), May 5, 1975.

34. *Exclusionary Zoning: Land Use Regulation and Housing in the 1970s* (New York: Praeger Publishers, 1973), p. 116.

35. See U.S. Commission on Civil Rights *Hearing Held in Washington, D.C., June 14–17, 1971*, p. 850.

36. *Opening Up the Suburbs*, pp. 94–95.

37. *Ibid.*, pp. 75–76.

38. *Ibid.*, p. 99.

39. See *Jones v. Mayer Co.*, 392 U.S. 409 (1968).

40. *Equal Opportunity in Suburbia* (Washington: U.S. Government Printing Office, 1974), p. 51.

41. *Understanding Fair Housing*, Clearinghouse Publication 42 (Washington: U.S. Government Printing Office, 1973), p. 7.

42. U.S. Commission on Civil Rights, *The Federal Civil Rights Enforcement Effort—1974*, Vol. II, To Provide . . . For Fair Housing (Washington: U.S. Government Printing Office, 1974), pp. 36–39.

43. *Ibid.*, pp. 48–49, 77–91.

44. See Peter H. Weiner, "Report: Sixth Conference on Exclusionary Land Use Policies," Clearinghouse on Exclusionary Land Use Problems, National Urban Coalition, New York, Apr. 15, 1971, p. 29.

45. *Opening Up the Suburbs*, p. 160.

46. William K. Reilly, ed., *The Use of Land: A Citizens' Policy Guide to Urban Growth*, A Task Force Report Sponsored by the Rockefeller Brothers Fund (New York: Crowell, 1973), p. 251.

47. See Robert W. Burchell with James W. Hughes, *Planned Unit Development: New Communities American Style* (New Brunswick, N.J.: Center for Urban Policy Research, Rutgers University, 1972), pp. 117–21. See also Jay C. Shaffer and Kenneth E. Meiser, "Exclusionary Use of Planned Unit Developments: Standards for Judicial Scrutiny," *Harvard Civil Rights–Civil Liberties Law Review* 8 (Mar., 1973), pp. 384–418.

48. See Edward P. Eichler and Marshall Kaplan, *The Community Builders* (Berkeley: University of California Press, 1967).

49. The Fairfax and Montgomery plans are summarized in Franklin, Falk, and Levin, *In-Zoning*, pp. 140–41. See also Ernest Erber and John Prior, *The Emergence of the "Housing Density Bonus,"* NCDH Information Series Number 4 (Washington: National Committee Against Discrimination in Housing, 1975); Ralph D. Fertig and Robert Cassidy, "Moderately Priced Housing Without Subsidy: the MPDU Proposal," *Planning* 39 (May, 1973), pp. 26–27; Thomas Kleven, "Inclusionary Ordinances—Policy and Legal Issues in Requiring Private Developers to Build Low Cost Housing," *UCLA Law Review* 21 (Aug., 1974), pp. 1432–1528; and Jerome G. Rose, "From the Legislatures: the Mandatory Percentage of Moderately Priced Dwelling Ordinance (MPMPD) Is the Latest Technique of Inclusionary Zoning," *Real Estate Law Journal* 3 (Fall, 1974), pp. 176–79.

50. The five communities were Flower Mound, Tex., Jonathan, Minn., Park Forest South, Ill., Riverton, N.Y., and Woodlands, Tex.; see Peter R. Morris, *State Housing Finance Agencies: An Entrepreneurial Approach to Subsidized Housing* (Lexington, Mass.: Lexington Bks., 1974), pp. 82–83.

51. Leonard Downie, Jr., *Mortgage on America* (New York: Praeger Publishers, 1974), p. 160.

52. Mark Freeman, executive director, League of New Community Developers, quoted in "New Towns in Trouble," *Time* 105 (Mar. 24, 1975), p. 70.

53. *Serrano* v. *Priest*, 5 Cal.3d 584, 487 P.2d 1241 (1971) at 1244.

54. See *Milliken* v. *Green*, 389 Mich. 1, 203 N.W.2d 457 (1972) and *Robinson* v. *Cahill*, 62 N.J. 473, 303 A2d. 273 (1973).

55. See *San Antonio Independent School District* v. *Rodriquez*, 411 U.S. 1 (1973).

56. See Eric J. Branfan, Benjamin I. Cohen, and David M. Trubek, "Measuring the Invisible Wall: Land Use Controls and the Residential Patterns of the Poor," *Yale Law Journal* 82 (Jan., 1973), pp. 483–508; and Eric J. Branfan, Benjamin I. Cohen, and David M. Trubek, *Fiscal and Other Incentives for Exclusionary Land Use Controls*, Working Paper W2-7 (New Haven: Institution for Social and Policy Studies, Yale University, 1972). This research did not estimate the direct

impact of restrictive local controls. Instead, "exclusion" was calculated by comparing the lower-income percentage of the population of each local jurisdiction with the hypothetical "norm" of a proportional distribution of lower-income individuals throughout the metropolitan area.

57. See William F. Highberger, "Limitation on Regional Land-Use Planning," (Senior Thesis, Princeton University, 1972), pp. 124–25.

58. "Opening the Suburbs: Toward Inclusionary Land Use Controls," p. 536.

59. See U.S. Commission on Civil Rights, *Hearing Held in Washington, D.C., June 14–17, 1971*, p. 862.

60. Quoted in William Lilley III, "Housing Report / Administration and Congress Follow Courts in Promoting Residential Integration," *National Journal* 3 (Nov. 12, 1971), p. 2439. As indicated in chapter 8, Agnew had supported dispersing the poor in 1970 before the Warren incident; after President Nixon's attacks on "forced integration," the vice president began inveighing against relocating the poor in suburbia.

61. "Segregation and the Suburbs" (editorial), Aug. 20, 1974.

62. *Housing and Social Policy*, p. 173.

63. Edmund Hume, executive director, Essex County Conference of Mayors, quoted in Leonard J. Fisher, "Trouble Expected for 'Open Zoning,' " *Newark Star Ledger*, Mar. 26, 1975. Hume, as indicated in chapter 10, was New Jersey's commissioner of community affairs during the first half of the Cahill Administration.

64. Representative Charles E. Wiggins, see U.S. Congress, House of Representatives, Committee on the Judiciary, *Federal Government's Role in the Achievement of Equal Opportunity in Housing*, Hearings before the Civil Rights Oversight Subcommittee, 92d Cong., 1st and 2d sess. (Washington: U.S. Government Printing Office, 1972), p. 407. Wiggins, a Republican, was a resident of suburban El Monte, where he had served as chairman of the planning commission, as a member of the city council, and as mayor before being elected to Congress.

65. *Exclusionary Zoning*, p. 50.

66. *Opening Up the Suburbs*, pp. 137–38.

67. *Ibid.*, p. 185.

68. Editorial in the *Cleveland Plain Dealer*, quoted in Robert Beckham, "Detour Ahead: That's the Message Coming to Public Agencies Attempting to Move Down the Road to Suburbia to Build Low-Income Housing," *Journal of Housing* 30 (May, 1973), p. 229.

69. *Exclusionary Zoning*, pp. 50, 48.

70. *Ibid.*, p. 49.

71. "Housing for Wyandanch" (editorial), Aug. 17, 1973.

72. "Statement About Federal Policies Relative to Equal Housing Opportunity," June 11, 1971, *Public Papers of the Presidents of the United States: Richard Nixon 1971* (Washington: U.S. Government Printing Office, 1972), p. 734.

73. *Opening Up the Suburbs*, p. 133.

74. See Leadership Conference on Civil Rights, "Response by Public Interest

Groups to Administration Pronouncement on Equal Housing Opportunity," in U.S. House of Representatives, *Federal Government's Role in the Achievement of Equal Opportunity in Housing*, p. 170.

75. See William Lilley III, "Housing Report / Romney Faces Political Perils with Plan to Integrate Suburbs," *National Journal Reports* 2 (Oct. 17, 1970), p. 2263.

76. *Exclusionary Zoning*, p. 90.

77. A. Russell Parkhouse, chairman, Montgomery County Commission, Morristown, Pa., quoted in Richard L. Papiernik, "5 Towns Oppose Housing Funds," *Philadelphia Inquirer*, Jan. 9, 1975. Refusal of a number of suburbs to participate in the block-grant program despite the assurances of county officials reduced the county's eligibility of federal funds from $1 million to $340,000; see "FH Groups Protest Grant Applications," *NCDH Trends in Housing* 19 (Spring, 1975), p. 2.

78. State of New Jersey, Governor, *New Horizons in Housing*, A Special Message to the Legislature by William T. Cahill, Governor of New Jersey (Mar. 27, 1972), p. 7.

79. U.S. Congress, Senate, Committee on Interior and Insular Affairs, *National Land Use Policy*, Hearings on S. 632 and S. 992, 92d Cong., 1st sess. (Washington: U.S. Government Printing Office, 1971), pt. 1, p. 162.

80. Representative George H. Mahon, *Congressional Record*, 89th Cong., 2d sess. 112:6 (Mar. 29, 1966), p. 7080.

81. Bernard F. Hillenbrand, executive director, National Association of Counties, quoted in William Lilley III, "Washington Pressures / Friendly Administration, Growth of Suburbs Boosts Counties' Influence," *National Journal* 3 (May 29, 1971), p. 1127.

82. "Suburbanization: Reviving the Town on the Metropolitan Frontier," *Publius* 5 (Winter, 1975), p. 56.

83. Review of *Opening Up the Suburbs* by Anthony Downs, *Planning* 40 (Jan., 1974), p. 27.

84. *Opening Up the Suburbs*, p. 85.

85. Jerome G. Rose, professor of urban studies, Rutgers University, New Brunswick, N.J., quoted in Donald Janson, "New Zoning Fight in State Forecast," *New York Times*, Nov. 16, 1973. Rose was appointed by a New Jersey judge to develop zoning recommendations in the case involving Washington Township; see chapter 7.

86. Leonard Millner, planning board, East Windsor, N.J., quoted in Mark Jaffe, "E. Windsor in Zoning Spotlight," *Trenton Evening Times*, June 1, 1975. Mt. Laurel itself eventually rezoned to permit the construction of 103 low- and moderate-income apartment units, with provision for future zoning changes to permit the community to meet its housing quotas as determined by the Delaware Valley Regional Planning Commission; see "Mt. Laurel Enlarges Zoning Plan," *Trenton Evening Times*, Feb. 14, 1976.

87. Alice Costello, director, Mercer County Legal Aid Society, quoted in *ibid*. The suit was brought by a local group, the Hightstown–East Windsor Human Relations Commission.

88. John Levy, associate planner, Westchester County, N.Y., quoted in "Multifamily Edges into Snob-Zoned Suburbs, but Civil Righters Aren't Happy," *House & Home* 44 (Oct., 1973), p. 58.

89. *Suburbia in Transition* (New York: Franklin Watts, 1974), p. 10.

90. See National Committee Against Discrimination in Housing, *Handbook for Citizen Fair Housing Advocacy under the Housing and Community Development Act of 1974* (Washington, 1974). Opportunities for open-housing litigation in the Housing and Community Development Act of 1974 are explored in Herbert M. Franklin, "Open Communities Litigation and the Housing and Community Development Act of 1974," in National Committee Against Discrimination in Housing, *Exclusionary Land Use Litigation*, pp. 83–107.

91. See "FH Groups Protest Grant Applications," p. 1. Parma was one of a handful of suburbs to have its application for community development assistance rejected by HUD in 1975; see Potomac Institute, Metropolitan Housing Program, *The Housing Assistance Plan: A Non-Working Program for Community Improvement? A Preliminary Evaluation of HUD Implementation of the 1974 Housing and Community Development Act* (Washington, 1975), p. 16.

92. See *City of Hartford* v. *Hills*, U.S. District Court, Dist. of Conn., Civil No. H-75-258, Jan. 28, 1976; and Lawrence Fellows, "Hartford Blocks Aid for Suburbs," *New York Times*, Jan. 29, 1976.

93. "Michigan Advocacy Model," *NCDH Trends in Housing* 17 (Spring, 1975), p. 2.

94. Miller, "Remarks at the Westchester Municipal Planning Federation Annual Dinner," p. 3.

95. Supervisor John Passidomo, Harrison, N.Y., quoted in Linda Greenhouse, "Westchester Towns Pressed on Housing," *New York Times*, Jan. 17, 1973.

96. Mayor Ralph H. Clarbour, Arlington Heights, Ill., quoted in Tom Jones, "Eligible Suburbs Slow to Apply for New HUD Grants," *Chicago Sun-Times*, Dec. 8, 1974.

97. *In-Zoning*, p. 52.

98. *Opening Up the Suburbs*, p. 137.

99. See *Gautreaux* v. *Chicago Housing Authority*, 503 F.2d 930 (1974).

100. Petition for a Writ of Certiorari to the United States Court of Appeals for the Seventh Circuit, Robert H. Bork, Solicitor General, *Mitchell* v. *Gautreaux*, U.S. Supreme Court, Oct. Term, 1974, No. 74-1074, p. 9.

101. The Supreme Court did not require the adoption of a metropolitan remedy. Instead, the Court ruled that the federal district court in the case had "the authority to direct HUD to engage in remedial efforts in the metropolitan area outside the city limits of Chicago"; see *Hills* v. *Gautreaux*, U.S. Sup. Ct. 74-1047 (Apr. 20, 1976), p. 21.

102. Quoted in "Mrs. Hills Say Suburbs Will See Housing Needs," *New York Times*, Apr. 29, 1976.

103. See, for example, Ernest Holsendolph, "Urban Crisis of the 1960s Is Over, Ford Aides Say," *New York Times*, Mar. 23, 1975; and Glazer, "On 'Opening Up' the Suburbs," *passim*.

104. *Understanding Fair Housing*, p. 17.

105. *Ibid.*

106. *Southern Burlington County N.A.A.C.P.* v. *Township of Mount Laurel*, 67 N.J. 151, 336 A2d 713 (1975) at 742.

107. "Statement about Desegregation of Elementary and Secondary Schools," Mar. 24, 1970. *Public Papers of the Presidents of the United States: Richard Nixon 1970* (Washington: U.S. Government Printing Office, 1971), p. 318.

108. Jimmy Carter, quoted in "Jimmy Carter Explains 'Ethnic Purity' Remark," *Trenton Evening Times*, Apr. 13, 1976. While opposed to forced integration and "black intrusion" into white neighborhoods, Carter condemned racial discrimination in housing; see Christopher Lydon; "Carter Defends All-White Areas," *New York Times*, Apr. 7, 1976.

109. Quoted in Howard Benedict, "Ford Says 'Heritage' the Word," *Trenton Evening Times*, Apr. 14, 1976.

Index

Acevedo v. *Nassau County* (1974), 392*n*
Advisory Commission on Intergovernmental Relations, 18, 44, 283
Agnew, Spiro T., 218-19, 229, 343, 423*n*
Alexander, Lee, 385-86*n*, 410*n*
Allan-Deane Corporation, 191-92
Allen, Frank, 125
Aloi, Frank, 390*n*
American Can Company, 143-45
American Civil Liberties Union, 114, 162, 190, 195, 393-94*n*
American Institute of Planners, 265
American Jewish Committee, 114-15, 125
American Society of Planning Officials, 248
American Telephone and Telegraph Company, 144
Americans for Democratic Action, 302
Amherst, N.Y., 312-13
Anderson, Richard, 368*n*
Annexation, 15-17, 30, 283
Apartments, 52, 55-56, 333-34, 350, 369*n*; and court rulings, 53, 175-77, 179, 183, 190, 194; opposition in suburbs, 53-55, 112; zoning restrictions, 52-59, 71, 73-74, 99, 127-28, 301
Appeal of Girsh (1970), 388*n*, 391*n*
Appeal of Kit-Mar Builders (1970), 391*n*
Arlington, Va., 65
Aronson, Robert, 416*n*
Ashley, Thomas L., 239, 403*n*; and metropolitan housing subsidies, 240, 275-76, 278, 346
Association of Bay Area Governments, 248, 264
Atherton, Howard, 367*n*

Atlanta Housing Authority, 94, 178, 185, 193
Atlanta metropolitan area, 92; subsidized housing in the suburbs, 94, 98, 161, 178, 185, 193, 197, 204
Atomic Energy Commission
Austin, Richard B., 195-96, 212, 234, 395*n*

Babcock, Richard F.: concentration of subsidized housing, 88, 336; conflict between environmental and open-housing groups, 128; courts and zoning, 169, 186-88, 198, 388*n*; local control of land use, 34, 347; rationale for lowering suburban housing barriers, 343-45; states and land-use control, 279, 286-87; weakness of metropolitan agencies in housing, 260, 274
Babylon, N.Y., 145, 321, 345, 384*n*
Badillo, Herman, 242
Baltimore County, Md., 29-30, 110; exclusionary policies, 43, 94; opposition to subsidized housing, 102, 220, 223
Baltimore metropolitan area, 29-30, 363*n*; subsidized housing in the suburbs, 83, 94, 102, 220, 223, 332
Banks v. *Perk* (1972), 373*n*, 391*n*
Barba, Louis R., 383*n*
Barraud, Charles W., 380*n*
Barrington, Ill., 44
Bass, Doris, 386*n*
Batch, Ralph F., 369*n*
Bates, Ted, 400*n*
Bay Area Rapid Transit District, 330
Becker, Robert, 374*n*
Bedford Hills, N.Y., 318

Bedford, N.Y., 320
Bedminster Township, N.J., 125, 146-48, 157, 191-92
Beecher, Mich., 88
Belle Terre, N.Y., 183-84
Bellman, Richard, 194-95, 198, 374n, 381n, 393n
Bergen County, N.J., 45-46, 53, 112
Berlin, Conn., 247, 406n
Bernards Township, N.J., 144
Berry, Brian J. L., 6-7
Berteau, George A., 406n
Bertsch, Dale F., 252-54, 269, 271-74, 339, 351, 376n
Berwyn, Ill., 242
Bettancourt, Phillip, 363n
Biertumpfel, F. Edward, 413n
Billerica, Mass., 305
Birbach, Jerry, 386n
Bisgaier, Carl S., 391n, 393n
Black, Hugo, 180-81
Black Jack, Mo., 31-33, 54, 99, 166-67; court challenges of zoning restrictions, 184-86, 190, 231-33, 393-94n; opposition to subsidized housing, 32-33, 84-85, 89-90, 184-86
Blackburn, Benjamin B., 237-38, 276, 387n
Blacks: desirability of opening the suburbs, 107, 124-25, 131, 150, 153-56, 254-55, 263-64, 325, 327; impact of local housing and zoning policies on residential location, 13, 43, 78, 89-92, 107, 172-74, 177-78, 301, 326; limited access to suburbia, 7-14, 89-92, 337-39, 360n
Bloomington, Minn., 48, 61
Blue Springs, Mo., 84
Board of Appeals of Hanover v. Housing Appeals Committee (1973), 416n
Board of County Supervisors of Fairfax County v. DeGroff Enterprises, Inc. (1973), 382n, 393n
Boca Raton, Fla., 66-67, 75
Bolton, Pamela, 410n
Bosselman, Fred P.: courts and zoning, 388n; development timing in Ramapo, 371n, 393n; local control of land use, 38, 140, 347; quotas for subsidized housing, 336; rationale for lowering suburban housing barriers, 343-45; states and land-use control, 286-88; weaknesses of metropolitan agencies in housing, 260

Boston Herald, 302
Boston, Mass., 16, 19, 302-3
Boston metropolitan area, 16, 19; subsidized housing, 96, 102, 117, 222-23, 305-6; suburban opposition to subsidized housing, 99-100, 166, 301-3, 305; zoning restrictions, 57, 63, 300-1
Boswell, Charles, 379n
Boulder, Colo., 67, 88
Bradley v. Milliken (1971), 362n, 387n
Bradley v. School Board of the City of Richmond, Virginia (1972), 362n
Bradley, Thomas, 328
Brennan, William, 389n
Bristow v. City of Woodhaven (1971), 390n
Brookhaven, N.Y., 174
Brooks, Mary E., 98
Brown Deer, Wis., 111
Brown, Garry, 403n
Brown, William H., III, 384n
Brownell, James F., 370n
Broyhill, Joel T., 276-77
Buchanan v. Warley (1917), 361n
Buffalo metropolitan area: development of new town in Amherst, 312-13; opposition to subsidized housing in Lackawanna, 99, 177, 185
Builders Institute of Westchester and Putnam Counties, 317
Building codes, 50, 76; and prefabricated housing, 62-63, 78; uniform state codes, 279, 286, 294, 297, 412n
Bukovinsky, John, 388n
Burlington County, N.J., 198
Burlington Development Corporation, 305
Buscher, Carl, 388n
Butler, Harry J., 365n, 366n
Byrne, Brendan T., 297-300, 387n

Cahill, William T., 163, 293-99, 346-47
California: courts and local zoning, 176; courts and school finance, 341; provision for local referenda on public housing, 99-100, 180-81; state role in housing and land use, 282, 286
California Council for Environmental and Economic Balance, 134
California Department of Housing and Community Affairs, 282
Callies, David L., 128, 287-88

Camden, N.J., 18-19
Carey, Hugh L., 322
Carter, Jimmy, 426n
Carter, Robert L., 402n
Caruso, Willis, 409n
Case, Clifford P., 397n
Caso, Ralph G., 43, 200, 396n
Cassidy, Robert, 348
Center for National Policy Review, 114, 212
Centerville, O., 271
Centex Homes Corporation, 191
Central Connecticut Regional Planning Agency, 247, 406n
Chandler, Gladstone L., Jr., 363n
Chappel, John, 414n
Chelmsford, Mass., 305
Chicago Heights, Ill., 103
Chicago Housing Authority, 95-96, 157, 178, 196, 212, 355
Chicago, Ill.: location of public housing, 82, 151, 157, 178, 195-96, 212, 234, 386n
Chicago metropolitan area: exclusionary zoning, 41, 97, 168, 170; home building scandals, 37, 86-87, 267; jobs and the suburbs, 3, 24; local autonomy and zoning, 31; metropolitan planning, 246, 266-68; open-housing groups, 162, 170, 265-69; racial segregation, 9, 102-3, 265-67; subsidized housing in the suburbs, 102-4, 178, 196, 266-69, 355, 425n; suburban opposition to subsidized housing, 94-97, 103-4, 242, 267-69
Cicero, Ill., 242
Cities: doubts about opening the suburbs, 131, 149-58, 325, 327-28, 354-55; future prospects in the segregated metropolis, 150-51, 155-56, 327-31; impact of suburban exclusion, 4-5, 18-19, 102, 331-32; political separation from suburbs, 15-21, 94-96, 156-58; support for opening the suburbs, 107, 129-31, 149-51, 155-57, 289-90, 302-3
Citizens Committee for Faraday Wood v. Lindsay (1973), 392n
Citizens for Local Control, Harrison, N.Y., 318
Citizens Housing and Planning Association, Boston, Mass., 302
City of Hartford v. Hills (1976), 425n
Civil Rights Act of 1964, 144, 264; federal aid

to exclusionary suburbs, 212-13, 219-20, 225, 227
Civil Rights Act of 1968: discrimination in the sale and rental of housing, 338; federal aid to exclusionary suburbs, 212-13, 219-20, 225, 227, 229; racially discriminatory zoning, 185, 231
Clarbour, Ralph H., 425n
Clark, Joseph S., 397n
Clark, Robert P., 415n
Clawson, Marion, 35, 69, 282
Cleghorn, Reese, 94, 397n
Cleveland metropolitan area: housing and zoning referendums in the suburbs, 38, 100-1, 164; metropolitan planning, 246-47; racial segregation, 8, 29, 91-92, 177-78, 182-83, 351; subsidized housing in the suburbs, 177-78, 182-83; suburban opposition to subsidized housing, 91-92, 95, 109; zoning restrictions, 61, 351
Cleveland Metropolitan Housing Authority, 95, 375n
Cleveland, O., 95, 109, 246-47; city officials and suburban exclusion, 149, 247, 263; location of public housing, 82, 152
Cleveland Plain Dealer, 423n
Clifton, N.J., 25
Cline, James, 400n
Clinkenbeard, Harlan, 407n
Coalition for Housing Action, Fairfax County, Va., 112, 118
Coalition on Block Grant Compliance, Detroit, Mich., 351
Cohen, David, 414n
Coke, James G., 34, 59
Colegrove v. Green (1946), 394n
Colored People's Civic and Political Organization, Lackawanna, N.Y., 99, 117
Columbia, Md., 339-40
Commission on Civil Rights: access of minorities to suburbs, 78, 204, 231, 338, 356; federal policies in the suburbs, 202, 213, 402n; jobs and housing in the suburbs, 146; on New York's Urban Development Corporation, 308; racial discrimination in housing, 12-13, 104-5
Commission on the Cities in the '70s, 233
Commonwealth v. County of Bucks (1973), 390n
Commonwealth of Pennsylvania v. County of Bucks (1972), 395n

Concord, Mass., 57, 305
Concord Township, Pa., 177, 196-97
Congress, 200-1, 236, 355; federal aid and
    suburban housing policies, 237-42; 1968
    housing legislation, 210-11; opposition to
    metropolitan housing plans, 242, 275-78;
    opposition to subsidized housing in the
    suburbs, 161, 207-9, 236-39; rent supple-
    ment program, 206-8
Connecticut: efforts to modify local zoning,
    290, 306; state role in subsidized housing,
    284, 289; zoning restrictions, 61
Constantine, Pano, 379n
Construction Industry Association of
    Sonoma County, Sonoma County, Cal.,
    191
Construction Ind. Assn. of Sonoma County v.
    City of Petaluma (1973) and (1974), 191,
    392n
Contra Costa County, Cal., 127-28
Cook County (Ill.) Housing Authority,
    95-96, 102-3, 157
Corman, Maurice, 416n
Costello, Alice, 424n
Cottingham, Phoebe, 10-11
Council of Housing Producers, 135
County government, 34, 48
Courts, 159-61, 174-75, 324-25, 348-49; ac-
    cessibility to open-housing interests, 159,
    167-69, 172, 292, 389-90n; attractions for
    interests lacking influence in other political
    arenas, 159-63, 198, 295-96, 327;
    beneficiaries of open-housing litigation,
    189-94; and economic exclusion, 173,
    178-81; impact of rulings on federal
    officials, 161, 163, 211-12, 214, 217-18,
    258; impact of rulings on local officials,
    100, 157, 267-68, 349; impact of rulings on
    metropolitan agencies, 198; impact of rul-
    ings on state officials, 161, 163, 294, 296,
    298-300; implementing rulings on housing
    and zoning, 160, 164, 169, 192-98, 349;
    location of subsidized housing, 176-78,
    180-85, 193, 195-97, 212; and metropoli-
    tan housing needs, 177-79, 187-89, 196,
    243, 268; obstacles for open-housing liti-
    gants, 164-69, 198, 222, 233, 304-5; and
    planners, 188-89, 193-95; and racial dis-
    crimination in housing and zoning, 172,
    177-78, 180-86, 233; and school desegrega-
    tion, 19, 161, 193, 362n

Cowley, Malcolm, 380n
Craig, Lois, 274
Cristiano, Peter, 400n
Crow v. Brown (1971), 387n, 391n, 392n, 394n
Crowell, H. Harland, Jr., 382-83n
Cuyahoga County, O., 61, 95
Cuyahoga Metropolitan Housing Authority,
    95, 177-78, 197

Daley, Richard J., 149, 157
Dannis, Lillian Klimecki, 400n
Danville, Ill., 146
Darke County, O., 273
Davidoff, Linda, 331, 342, 367n, 380n
Davidoff, Paul, 148, 194, 276, 312, 331, 342;
    and Suburban Action Institute, 188, 380n;
    views on suburban exclusion, 118-19,
    367n, 381n
Dayton Daily News, 251, 256, 271
Dayton Journal Herald, 256
Dayton metropolitan area, 250-53, 314, 351;
    business support for opening the suburbs,
    145, 255-56; fair housing in the suburbs,
    13; fair-share housing plan, 250-59,
    269-74, 277, 324, 351; opposition to sub-
    sidized housing in the suburbs, 83, 111,
    254, 256-57, 271-74; zoning and sub-
    sidized housing, 97, 271
Dayton, O., 251, 253, 255, 273
DeKorte, Richard, 297
Delaware Valley Regional Planning Com-
    mission, 198, 264, 424n
Deming, Donald, 418n
Demonstration Cities and Metropolitan De-
    velopment Act of 1966, 244-55
Denton, John H., 31, 361n, 375n
Denver metropolitan area: subsidized hous-
    ing, 82-83, 103-5
Department of Justice, 90-91, 101, 214,
    231-33
Derry Borough v. Shomo (1972), 390n
Detroit metropolitan area: opposition to sub-
    sidized housing in the suburbs, 223-25;
    racial segregation, 25, 92, 223; school de-
    segregation, 161, 362n; subsidized housing
    in the suburbs, 82-83, 86-87
Detroit News, 224
Development interests: and the courts, 161,
    165-66, 190-92; influence in suburbs,
    36-39, 47, 69-74, 131-34, 136-39; and

suburban exclusion, 131-41; *see also* Home builders
de Vise, Pierre, 9, 14
Dodd, Frank J., 415
Dorris, Joseph D., 420n
Douglas, Paul, 209-10, 397n, 398n; *see also* National Commission on Urban Problems
Douglas, William O., 183, 389n
Dover Township, N.J., 132
Downie, Leonard, Jr., 36-37, 88, 422n
Downs, Anthony: community quotas on subsidized housing, 336-37, 344, 354; metropolitan development patterns, 328, 360n; political support for opening the suburbs, 130-31, 345, 348; rationale for opening the suburbs, 150-51, 156, 243, 330-31; subsidized housing in the suburbs, 101-2, 339; suburban zoning and housing opportunities, 23, 42, 52, 76, 107-9
DuPage County, Ill., 97
DuPage County (Ill.) Housing Authority, 94
Dwyer, Florence P., 237
Dyckman, John, 420n

East Brunswick, N.J., 389n
East Chicago Heights, Ill., 103
East Cleveland, O., 29
East Windsor, N.J., 349
Eastlake, O., 38
East-West Gateway Coordinating Council, 260-61, 265
Edenfield, Newell, 197
Ehrlichman, John D., 226
El Monte, Cal., 423n
Elazar, Daniel J., 29, 348
Embry, Robert C., 421n
Engler, Robert, 303, 416n
English, John F., 365n
Environmental protection: state policies, 286-89; suburban concerns, 47, 60, 64-69, 72, 126-28; and suburban exclusion, 47-48, 68-69, 87-88
Epley, Mrs. Noah, 374n
Epstein, Hedy, 361n
Equal Employment Opportunities Commission, 119, 144, 214, 384n
Erber, Ernest, 48, 270
Essex County, N.J., 8-9
Euclid, O., 391n
Evans v. Buchanan (1975), 362n
Evans v. Lynn (1974) and (1975), 390n

Ewing, John H., 369n
Exclusionary Land-Use Practices Clearing House, 114

Fabricant, Herbert J., 388n
Fain, Jim, 251
Fair housing: federal role, 216, 338-39; in the states, 285-86; in the suburbs, 13, 105, 113-14, 116-17, 122
Fair Housing Congress of Southern California, 116-17
Fairfax County, Va., 120; fair-share housing, 259, 261; growth controls, 65-66, 68-70; zoning for subsidized housing, 110-12, 118, 124, 135-38, 261, 340, 422n
Fairfax County Police Association, 112
Falk, David, 334, 354
Farley, Reynolds, 10
Fauquier County, Va., 72
Federal-Aid Highway Act of 1962, 244
Federal aid to the suburbs, 201-3, 206; block grants for community development, 240-42, 275, 277-78, 351-52; penalizing exclusionary communities, 209-10, 212-13, 219-29, 233, 256, 270, 272, 279-80; rewarding inclusionary communities, 216, 238, 257, 276, 342
Federal Communications Commission, 144
Federal government, 199-201; locational policies for federal installations, 202, 231, 238, 402n; role in land-use control, 34, 138-39, 158, 200, 206, 210, 225, 229, 236-38, 404n
Federal Housing Administration, 203-4, 206-7, 238, 273
Federal housing programs, 79-83, 101-6, 202-6; moratorium on subsidized housing in 1972, 106, 231, 277; workable program requirement, 93-94, 96, 210; *see also* Public housing, Rent supplements, Section 8 leased-housing program, Section 221(d)3 moderate-income housing program, Section 235 homeownership program, and Section 236 moderate-income housing program
Federal planning assistance: and metropolitan housing, 244-45, 248-50, 258, 262-64, 266; to suburbs, 70-71, 202
Feibel, Alfred S., 372n, 382n
Field Foundation, 122
Finger, Harold B., 398n, 399n

Fino, Paul A., 207
Fitzpatrick, Paul, 388*n*
Florida Environmental Land and Water Management Act of 1972, 287
Foley, Donald L., 12, 186
Ford Foundation, 122, 266
Ford, Gerald, 350-52, 355, 357
Ford Motor Company: Mahwah, N.J., plant, 40-41, 142, 145
Forest Hills, Queens, N.Y., 151, 396*n*
Foundations, 122-23, 162, 266, 387-88*n*
Framingham, Mass., 99
Frank, George A., 381*n*
Frankfurter, Felix, 394*n*
Franklin, Herbert M., 186, 354; federal housing policies, 206, 241; local use of housing restrictions, 74, 94, 333-34
Franklin Lakes, N.J., 41, 143-44, 146-47, 171, 389*n*
Free, Lloyd A., 361*n*
Freeman, Mark, 422*n*
Fremont, Cal., 142-43
Fried, Joseph P., 225, 284, 376*n*
Fulton County, Ga., 98, 178, 185, 193
Fulton County Housing Authority, 94
Fund for New Jersey, 122-23
Fust, Robert, 395*n*

Gaithersburg, Md., 202
Garden Cities Development Corporation, 121-22
Garfield Heights, O., 391*n*
Gargan, John J., 34
Gallagher, Thomas, 415*n*, 416*n*
Gautreaux v. *Chicago Housing Authority* (1969), 212, 373*n*, 391*n*, 395*n*; (1974), 268, 395*n*, 425*n*
Gautreaux v. *Romney* (1973), 395*n*
G&D Holland Construction Co. v. *City of Marysville* (1970), 390*n*
Geauga County, O., 61
General Motors Corporation, 142-43
General Services Administration, 202, 231, 402*n*
Gerardi, Natalie, 371*n*
Germantown, Md., 202
Gibson, James, 396*n*
Girsh, Joseph, 165
Glassboro, N.J., 175, 178, 294
Glazer, Nathan, 327, 420*n*

Glickstern, Howard A., 385*n*
Godwin, Gerald C., 413*n*
Golar, Simeon, 158, 200, 396*n*
Gold, Neil, 118-22, 379*n*, 380*n*
Goldberg, Arthur Abba, 390*n*
Golden Valley, Minn., 270
Golden v. *Planning Board of Ramapo* (1972), 371*n*, 393*n*
Gordon, Bernard, 419*n*
Granirer, Martus, 371-72*n*
Great Neck Civic Association, Manhasset, N.Y., 125
Greater St. Louis Committee for Freedom of Residence, 13-14, 265
Greece, N.Y., 313-14
Greenburgh, N.Y., 320
Greenhouse, Linda, 385*n*
Greenwhich, Conn., 38, 46, 60, 78, 124, 143, 380*n*
Groves, Marvin, 386*n*
Growth controls: development timing, 67-69, 184, 187; moratoriums, 57, 66, 99, 133; population ceilings, 66-67, 75, 175
Grumman Corporation, 40, 145, 384*n*

Haar, Charles M., 367*n*, 388*n*
Hackensack Meadowlands Reclamation and Development Act (N.J.), 291, 413*n*
Hadden, Jeffrey K., 350
Hamilton, Charles S., 15⁻
Hanover, Mass., 305
Harrison, N.Y., 316, 320
Hart, Phillip A., 397*n*
Hartford, Conn., 119, 351
Hartman, Chester W., 12, 333, 343
Harvard Enterprises, Inc. v. *Board of Adjustment, Township of Madison, County of Middlesex* (1970), 389*n*
Harvey, Ill., 103
Harvey, James, 386*n*
Hawaii: state land-use controls, 286, 288
Heckler, Margaret M., 404*n*
Hempstead, N.Y., 83-84
Henry, Anthony R., 155
Hermalin, Albert I., 10
Hernandez, Aileen, 381*n*, 408*n*
Hesburgh, Theodore M., 213, 410*n*
Hillenbrand, Bernard F., 424*n*
Hills, Carla A., 242, 328, 355
Hills v. *Gautreaux* (1976), 391*n*, 395*n*, 425*n*

Hoffman Estates, Ill., 37
Hofstede, Albert J., 408n
Holland, Arthur J., 395n
Hollister, Eugene A., 406n
Holmdel, N.J., 389n
Holmgren, Edward L., 270, 386n, 408n
Holverstott, Carl, 361n
Home builders: corruption of local zoning, 37, 139; and the courts, 137, 140, 190-92, 197; and metropolitan housing plans, 255, 263, 270-71, 273, 278, 409n; and open-housing groups, 121-22, 134-36, 140-41; pressures on federal government, 134-36, 139-40, 211, 215, 217, 236; and state government, 292, 301-2; and subsidized housing, 80-81, 86-87, 93-100, 103-6, 112, 135-36, 139-41, 204, 210-11, 234, 241, 405n; and suburban exclusion, 107, 129-41, 325, 355
Home Builders Association of Massachusetts, 301-2
Homebuilders Association of Metropolitan Dayton, 255
Homeowner and neighborhood groups, 31, 37-38, 56, 365n
HOPE, Wheaton, Ill., 170
Hopkins, Gerald, 118
Horn, Stephen, 361n
House of Representatives, 201; Appropriations Committee, 207-8; Banking and Currency Committee, 239-40, 277; Housing Subcommittee, Banking and Currency Committee, 238, 240, 276
Housing: general features in metropolitan areas, 5-11, 332, 356, 420-21n
Housing Act of 1937, 182-83
Housing Act of 1949, 206, 212
Housing Act of 1954, 244
Housing Act of 1961, 373n
Housing allowances, 235-36, 332-33, 338, 421n
Housing and Community Development Act of 1974, 240-42, 277-78, 350, 404-5n, 425n; see also Section 8 leased-housing program
Housing and income, 5-7, 9-11, 78-79, 332
Housing and Urban Development Act of 1965, 207-9; see also Rent supplements
Housing and Urban Development Act of 1968, 135, 210-11, 335, 354, 373n; construction and financial problems with housing programs, 86-89, 235; housing planning requirements, 248, 351; impact on the production of subsidized housing, 81-83, 211, 215; see also Section 235 home-ownership program and Section 236 moderate-income housing program
Housing and Urban Development Act of 1970 (proposed), 237-38
Housing and Urban Development Act of 1972 (proposed), 275-78
Housing and Urban Development, Department of: and Black Jack, Mo., 32, 231; efforts to open the suburbs, 214, 217-28, 242, 248, 257-59, 262, 325, 398-99n, 408n; and housing discrimination, 34, 203-5, 212-13, 223-24, 338-39; locational policies for subsidized housing, 82, 154, 163, 178, 212, 222, 231-35, 395n, 402n; and metropolitan housing plans, 248-50, 257-62, 264, 268-75, 351, 408n; moratorium on federal housing subsidies, 235, 277, 321, 335; open communities program, 221-26, 231-37, 402n; proposed zoning legislation in 1970, 138-39, 222, 236-37, 399n
Housing authorities, 93-96, 157-58, 282-83
Housing costs, 79, 349; and local zoning restrictions, 57, 60-63, 73-78, 287-88
Housing for the elderly, 102, 239, 304, 315, 349-50, 353-55
Housing Opportunities Council of Metropolitan Washington, 114, 212
Houston metropolitan area, 217
HUD, see Housing and Urban Development, Department of
Hughes, Richard J., 291, 295-96
Hume, Edmund T., 293, 296, 413n, 423n
Hunterdon County, N.J., 72
Hutt, Stewart M., 382n
Hyde, Floyd H., 403n

Iatrides, Demetrius S., 388n
Illinois: state role in subsidized housing, 284, 289
In Re Bradley (1972), 362n
Interfaith Housing Corporation, Boston, Mass., 117
Internal Revenue Service, 120, 174
International Business Machines, 41, 143-44, 146-47

Irondequoit, N.Y., 313, 315
Irvine, Cal., 339
Islip, N.Y., 311-12

Jackson, Henry M., 238, 404n
Jackson, Samuel C., 398-399n
James v. Valtierra (1971), 169, 180-86, 191, 377n, 391n
Javits, Jacob K., 238, 397n
Jobs and housing in the suburbs, 23-25, 40-41, 46, 82, 119, 141-44, 329-31; federal policies, 202, 238; impact on blacks, 24-25, 142-45, 148, 153, 155-56, 202; suburban employees and local housing, 46-47, 129-31, 141-48, 325, 344, 350, 355, 383-84n
Johnson, Lyndon B., 206-7, 209-11, 331-32
Jonathan, Minn., 340
Jones v. Mayer Co., (1968), 421n
Jones, Nathaniel, 156
Jones, Sam H., 361n
Jones, Victor, 248

Kaden, Lewis, 415n
Kaiser, Edgar F., 210; see also President's Committee on Urban Housing
Kansas City metropolitan area, 84, 333
Kansas City, Mo., 154, 333
Kaplan, Nathan, 191
Karmin, Monroe W., 401n
Kaufman & Broad Homes, 37
Keith, Nathaniel S., 324, 397n
Kennedy, Edward M., 397n
Kennedy Park Homes Ass'n v. City of Lackawanna (1970), 391n, 392n
Kennedy, Robert F., 211, 397n
Kerrigan, John J., 362n
Kettering, O., 253, 271
King, Martin Luther, 265, 309
Kirkwood, Ga., 92
Klein, Woody, 368n
Kleina, Bernard J., 387n, 389n
Koch, Edward, 417n
Kodak Corporation, 314
Kotler, Milton, 15
Kraft, Joseph, 123, 324-25
Karmer, Lawrence, 296
Kristof, Frank S., 419n
Kuckuck, Francis E., 374n
Kugler, George F., Jr., 412n
Kula, Kathryn, 387n

Labor unions, 40, 117, 256, 285-86
Lackawanna, N.Y., 99, 117, 177, 185
Land: availability for housing in metropolitan areas, 2-4, 50, 74-75, 81-82, 331-32
Landrieu, Moon, 328
Landry, Clifford A., Jr., 406n
La Puente, Cal., 99
Lauber, Daniel, 389n, 390n
Lawrence Township, N.J., 105-6
Lawthur, Robert M., 376n, 378n
Lawyers' Committee for Civil Rights Under Law, 114, 162
Leadership Conference on Civil Rights, 114, 231, 401n
Leadership Council for Metropolitan Open Communities, Chicago, Ill., 265-69
League of Women Voters, 115, 125-26, 129; support for metropolitan housing plans, 255, 265; support for New York's Urban Development Corporation, 314, 317
Lefcoe, George, 392n, 401n
Leichter, Franz S. J., 413n
Lent, Norman F., 239
Lethbridge, George, 137-38
Levin, Arthur J., 334, 354
Levin, Melvin, 394n, 412n
Levitt and Sons, 66, 76, 132-33, 381n
Levitt, William, 132-33
Levy, John, 425n
Lewisboro, N.Y., 320
Lexington, Ky., 146
Lexington, Mass., 100, 305
Liebman, Charles S., 59
Lilley, William, III, 401n
Lindsay, John V., 149, 308-10
Lindsey v. Normet (1972), 392n
Linowitz, Sol M., 145, 384n
Little Rock metropolitan area: Section 235 homeownership program, 104-5
Livermore, Cal., 67-68
Livingston, N.J., 171, 389n
Local government in the suburbs, 17-22, 29-35, 48-49; role in land-use control, 1-2, 4, 27-52, 195, 229-30, 234, 275-76, 282, 300-5, 307-12, 333-35, 347, 353, 357; role in subsidized housing, 79-80, 92-106, 206-11, 238-39, 241-42, 269-72, 285, 303-4, 319-21; rulings by courts on housing and land use responsibilities, 168-69, 176-83, 195-97
Local taxes: and land use policies in the

suburbs, 43-47, 56-59, 70, 175-76, 341-42, 422-23*n*

Logue, Edward J., 307-8, 310-12, 315-22, 325

Lombard, Ill., 170

Los Altos Hills, Cal., 182

Los Angeles, Cal., 151

Los Angeles metropolitan area: opposition to subsidized housing, 99, 151, 392*n*

Loudoun County, Va., 66

Louisville metropolitan area: school desegregation, 362*n*

Lucey, Patrick, 280

Lustig, Morton, 372*n*

Lynn, James T., 242

Lysander, N.Y., 312-13

Macauley, Bonnie, 409*n*

Madison, O., 273

Madison Township, N.J., 59, 177, 188, 191, 294, 373*n*

Mahaley v. Cuyahoga Metropolitan Housing Authority (1973) and (1974), 391*n*, 392*n*; (1974) 395*n*

Mahon, George H., 208-9, 424*n*

Mahwah, N.J.: litigation against restrictive zoning, 164, 171; opposition to subsidized housing, 113, 121-22, 137-38; zoning restrictions, 40-41, 138, 142, 145

Maier, Henry W., 249, 263, 406*n*, 410*n*

Mandelker, Daniel R., 53, 282

Manhasset, N.Y., 125

Manhattanville College, Harrison, N.Y., 316

Maplewood, Minn., 87-88

Marshall, Thurgood, 180-81

Martin, Harold, 415*n*

Martin, James D., 207

Maryland: impact of state sewer moratorium on housing development, 288

Maryland Homebuilders Association, 191

Masotti, Louis H., 350

Massachusetts, 51, 300-1; state role in subsidized housing, 284-85, 289-90, 300-1, 303-6, 352; zoning appeals law, 286- 300-6

Massachusetts Federation for Fair Housing and Equal Rights, 302

Massachusetts Federation of Planning Boards, 302

Massachusetts General Court (legislature): Committee on Urban Affairs, 301

Massachusetts Housing Appeals Committee, 300, 303-4, 306, 416*n*

Massachusetts Housing Finance Agency, 285

Massachusetts Legislative Research Council, 301

Massachusetts Selectmen's Association, 302

Massachusetts Special Commission on Planning, Zoning, and Subdivision Control, 301

Maxwell, David O., 404*n*

Mayors' Steering Committee, Chicago, Ill., 267-69

McAlevey, John F., 371*n*, 378*n*, 383*n*

McCahill, Ed, 37

McDonnell Douglas Corporation, 146, 385*n*

McHarg, Ian, 127

McLinden, Joseph L., 373*n*, 380*n*

Merck, Albert N., 296-97, 299, 375*n*

Metropolitan agencies, 244-46, 251-53, 261-62, 274-78, 352; review of applications for federal aid, 244-46, 253-54, 256-58, 270, 272-75, 277-78; role of suburban interests, 246-47, 249-50, 252, 256-57, 260, 266-73, 278; *see also* Metropolitan councils of government, Metropolitan governments, and Metropolitan planning agencies

Metropolitan Council of the Twin Cities, 77, 259-62, 270, 277

Metropolitan councils of government, 245-49, 259-65, 270, 274-78, 355

Metropolitan differences: between city and suburbs, 15-29, 262, 283, 315, 324, 331, 341-42, 422-23*n*; racial separation, 8-14, 19-20, 155-56, 203-13, 331, 356-57; socioeconomic separation, 1, 17-26, 337, 356-57; variations among areas, 17, 352-53

Metropolitan government, 34, 155, 244

Metropolitan Housing Center, Milwaukee, Wis., 265

Metropolitan Housing Coalition, Chicago, Ill., 267-69, 353

Metropolitan Housing Corporation, St. Louis, Mo., 265

Metropolitan Housing Development Corporation, Chicago, Ill., 265-66

Metropolitan housing plans, 95-96, 157-58, 234-35, 238-40, 243-44, 247-50, 312-15; allocations to suburbs, 250, 253, 259-61, 268, 273, 275-78, 335-37; and central

Metropolitan housing plans (*Continued*) cities, 247, 261, 263, 278; and the courts, 187-89, 196; federal encouragement, 234-35, 244-50, 257-59, 262-64, 272-78; impact on segregated housing patterns, 252, 260-64, 267-70, 273-74, 278; implementation, 249, 252, 256, 260, 269-75, 277-78; political support, 254-56, 259-73; quotas for individual suburbs, 256, 258, 264, 296, 304, 336-37, 344; suburban attitudes, 250, 254, 256-57, 260-61, 267-69

Metropolitan planning agencies, 245-78, 355

Metropolitan Washington Council of Governments, 258-59, 261, 276-77, 408*n*

Mexican Americans: discrimination in the San Francisco metropolitan area, 100, 117, 142-43, 166, 176-77, 193

Meyerson, James, 389*n*

Meyner, Robert B., 293

Mezey, Frederick C., 393*n*, 394*n*

Miami Valley Regional Planning Commission, 250-59, 269-74, 351

Miamisburg, O., 254, 271

Michaelian, Edwin G., 316-17

Michigan: courts and school finance, 341; state role in housing and land use, 281

Middlesex County, N.J., 58-59, 73, 93-94, 171, 389-90*n*

Mid-Peninsula Citizens for Fair Housing, Santa Clara County, Cal., 116

Miller, Daniel L., 418*n*, 419*n*, 425*n*

Miller, David H., 382*n*

Miller, Newton, 379*n*

Miller, Richard A., 418*n*

Milliken v. *Bradley* (1974), 362*n*, 387*n*

Milliken v. *Green* (1972), 422*n*

Milliken, William G., 281

Millner, Leonard, 424*n*

Milwaukee Journal, 280

Milwaukee metropolitan area, 283; dispersing subsidized housing, 111, 249-50, 265; opposition to subsidized housing in the suburbs, 87; zoning restrictions on subsidized housing, 99

Milwaukee, Wis., 249-50

Minneapolis–St. Paul metropolitan area, 261-62; housing costs, 77; subsidized housing in the suburbs, 82, 87-88, 259-60, 270, 277; zoning restrictions, 61

Mitchell, James C., 405*n*

Mitchell, John C., 418

Mitchell, John P., 226-28, 398*n*

Mobile homes, 62-63, 333-35, 350; zoning restrictions, 52, 63-64, 75, 175-76

Mogulof, Melvin B., 245-46

Molino v. *Mayor and Council of Borough of Glassboro* (1971), 390*n*, 391*n*, 414*n*

Molnar, Robert S., 415*n*

Mondale, Walter F., 238, 346, 397*n*

Monmouth County, N.J., 62, 73

Monroe County, N.Y., 313

Montgomery County, Md., 103, 288; fair-share housing, 259, 261; zoning for subsidized housing, 110-12, 124, 137, 261, 340, 422*n*

Montgomery County (O.) Mayors and Managers Association, 254

Montgomery County, Pa., 424*n*

Moore, Audrey, 371*n*

Moorhead, William S., 404*n*

Moraine, O., 271

Morse, Wayne, 397*n*

Mount Laurel, N.J., 40, 365*n*; court rulings and zoning restrictions, 166, 179, 188, 294, 298-300, 349-50, 424*n*

Moynihan, Daniel P., 218, 226, 399*n*

Murphy, Walter F., 389*n*

Muskie, Edmund S., 397*n*

NAACP Legal Defense and Education Fund, 114, 174

Nardi, Joseph M., Jr., 362*n*

Nassau County, N.Y., 110, 182, 239; exclusion of nonresidents from public facilities, 41, 43

National Academy of Science–National Academy of Engineering, 243, 360*n*, 361*n*, 363*n*

National Advisory Commission on Civil Disorders, 7, 209

National Association for the Advancement of Colored People, 114-15, 125, 136, 255; and the courts, 128, 162, 164, 168, 170-71, 192, 389*n*; on the need to open the suburbs, 107, 150, 155-56

National Association of Building Manufacturers, 191

National Association of Counties, 403*n*

National Association of Home Builders, 132, 134-36, 138-39, 191, 278

National Association of Real Estate Boards, 138-39

National Bureau of Standards, 202

National Commission on Urban Problems, 209; federal housing policy, 203, 209-11; local housing and land-use policies, 34, 64, 73, 76; role of the states, 279-82, 284

National Committee Against Discrimination in Housing, 89, 114-16, 126-28; and the courts, 162, 171, 174, 192, 198; and federal policies in the suburbs, 200, 212, 231, 350-51; and home builders, 132-36; importance of suburban exclusion, 107, 150; and metropolitan housing plans in the San Francisco area, 264; and suburban employers, 144-45; use of state fair-housing laws to open suburbs, 285-86

National Housing and Economic Development Law Project, 114

National Housing Conference, 397n

National Job-Linked Housing Center, 114, 141

National Land and Investment Co. v. Kohn (1965), 390n

National League of Cities, 149, 403n

National Neighbors, 117, 379n

National Tenants Organization, 155

National Urban Coalition, 114, 144, 276, 317

National Welfare Rights Organization, 155

Neighborhood stabilization groups, 113, 117, 379n

Nelson, Gaylord A., 397n

Nether Providence Township, Pa., 165, 177

Neuberger, Maurine, 397n

New Britain, Conn., 247, 406n

New Canaan, Conn., 146, 388n

New Castle, N.Y., 174, 320, 390n

New Democratic Coalition, New York, N.Y., 290

New Fairfield, Conn., 120-21, 126

New Jersey, 290; courts and exclusionary zoning, 161, 165-66, 169, 175-76, 178-80, 188-89, 193-95, 197, 325, 334-35, 348-49, 391n; courts and racial discrimination in housing, 133; courts and school finance, 341; efforts to modify local zoning, 163, 291-300, 325; land-use controls and property taxes, 45; state assistance and housing, 300; state land-use powers, 286, 291-92, 295, 413n; zoning and state fair-housing

laws, 285-86, 412n; zoning restrictions, 41, 61-63, 71, 73-74, 290-91

New Jersey Builders Association, 76-77, 166

New Jersey Civil Liberties Union, 192

New Jersey Coastal Area Facility Review Act, 286

New Jersey Community Development Corporation (proposed), 294-95

New Jersey County and Municipal Government Study Commission, 289, 365n, 368n, 372n, 376n

New Jersey Department of Environmental Protection, 288

New Jersey Division of Civil Rights, 285-86

New Jersey Hackensack Meadowlands Development Commission, 33, 291, 413n

New Jersey Housing Finance Agency, 45, 105-6, 285, 294

New Jersey Land Use Planning and Development Law (proposed), 291-93, 295, 413n

New Jersey League of Municipalities, 195, 299

New Jersey Shore Builders Association v. Township of Ocean (1974), 395n

New towns, 312-13, 339-41, 422n

New York: courts and growth controls, 187, 189; efforts to modify local zoning, 289-90, 307-10, 312, 319-21; state role in subsidized housing, 284, 412n

New York Ad Hoc Legislative Committee on Exclusionary Suburban Zoning, 289-90

New York City: opposition to scatter-site housing, 151-52; support for opening the suburbs, 149, 156-58, 200, 289-90; and the Urban Development Corporation, 308-10

New York City Housing Authority, 158

New York Civil Liberties Union, 164

New York Medical College, Westchester County, N.Y., 316

New York metropolitan area: benefits and costs of economic development in the suburbs, 45-46; blacks and suburban exclusion, 125, 156; city interests and opening the suburbs, 149, 156-57; courts and exclusionary zoning, 164-65, 168, 171, 174, 177, 182-84, 188, 194-95, 294; exclusion of nonresidents from public facilities, 41-43; fiscal zoning, 43-45, 56-60; growth limita-

New York metropolitan area (Cont.) tions, 65, 67, 72, 128, 187; home builders and local zoning, 132-34, 137-38, 141, 191-92; housing costs, 77; jobs and housing in the suburbs, 40-41, 142-48, 157; local residents and zoning, 37-39, 56; open-housing efforts, 111, 119-22, 124-27; opposition to subsidized housing, 83-85, 91, 112-13, 121-22, 125-26, 151-52, 182, 311-12, 315-21, 345; racial patterns, 8-9, 25; subsidized housing in the suburbs, 93-94, 102, 108-11, 126, 316-19; suburban housing policies and the exclusion of blacks, 42-43, 78; zoning restrictions, 40-41, 51, 53-64, 72

New York State Urban Development Corporation, 307-8, 320-24, 351, 412n, 418n; development of new towns, 312-13; financing, 308, 320-22, 419n; housing in the suburbs, 311-22, 335; and local land-use controls, 33, 286, 307-12, 315-21, 416n; urban renewal in older cities, 308, 310-11, 316, 321; Westchester Nine-Towns Plan, 315-21, 353, 390n; Wyandanch project, 321, 345

New York Times, 230, 297, 309, 335, 345

Newburg Area Council, Inc. v. Board of Education of Jefferson County, Kentucky (1973), 362n

Newport Beach, Cal., 72

Newton, Mass., 166

Nickerson, Eugene H., 378n

Nixon, Richard M., 213-15, 217-18, 221, 295-96, 345-46, 357; and the courts, 160, 163, 387n; and federal-state-local relations, 214, 218; moratorium on federal housing subsidies, 106, 231, 235-36, 277, 321, 335; and school desegregation, 161, 213, 226-27; and the suburbs, 213-14, 221, 225-31, 257, 262, 345

Norman, Thomas, 190

North Castle, N.Y., 320

North Hempstead, N.Y., 125

Northeast Ohio Coordinating Agency, 246-47

Northeastern Illinois Planning Commission, 246, 266-70

Northern Virginia Builders Association, 133, 191

Nyland, Lawrence, 380n

Oak Brook, Ill., 41

Oakwood at Madison, Inc. v. Township of Madison (1971), 391n, 414n; (1974), 393n

Oakwood, O., 253, 271

Oettinger, George, 419n

Office of Management and Budget, 245

Olivette, Mo., 43

O'Neill, Kevin, 366n

Open-housing groups, 113-30, 140-41, 150, 154-55, 263, 265, 350, 379n; and the courts, 114-15, 119-21, 129, 159, 161-77, 181-82, 184-86, 188-98, 295-96, 349-50, 387n; and the development of subsidized housing, 31-32, 80, 117-18, 120-21, 166, 190, 206, 304-6; and the federal government, 199-200, 212-14, 217, 231, 236, 350-51; and metropolitan housing plans, 249-50, 263-69, 274-76, 278; and New York's Urban Development Corporation, 312, 314, 317; political support in the suburbs, 125-29, 325-27; and states, 280, 283, 285-86, 290, 296, 302

Operation Breakthrough, 216-17, 219

Orange County, N.Y., 66

Owens, Ronald, 412n

Oyster Bay, N.Y., 40, 48, 110, 128, 164, 168, 171, 388n, 394n

Packard, Jean R., 371n

Pahl, Jack D., 267-69

Palo Alto, Cal., 66, 110, 350

Park View Heights Corporation, St. Louis, Mo., 117

Park View Heights Corporation v. City of Black Jack (1972), 393-94

Parma, O., 95, 100-1, 164, 351, 425n

Parsippany-Troy Hills, N.J., 55, 368n

Pascack Association, Limited v. Mayor and Council of Township of Washington, Bergen County (1974), 394n

Pascack Association, Ltd. v. Township of Washington (1975), 394n

Pashman, Morris, 414-15n

Passidomo, John A., 418n, 425n

Pastore, John O., 208

Patton, D. K., 377n, 387n

Penfield, N.Y., 168, 313

Pennsylvania: courts and exclusionary zoning, 165, 176-77, 189-90, 197, 283; efforts

to modify local zoning, 289-90; state assistance and exclusionary zoning, 283
Pennsylvania Department of Community Affairs, 119, 283, 289-90, 411n
Pennsylvania State Association of Boroughs, 290
Pepsico, 143
Percy, Charles H., 211
Perez (Dr. and Mrs. Martin) Foundation, 122
Perinton, N.Y., 314
Perk, Ralph J., 95, 152, 263
Perry, Alfred A., 398n
Petaluma, Cal., 67, 184, 191, 392n
Petruska, John, 376n, 388n
Philadelphia metropolitan area: allocation of subsidized housing to suburbs, 188, 198, 263-64; efforts to link city residences and suburban jobs, 330; exclusionary zoning, 40, 165-66, 175, 177-79, 193-97; open-housing interests, 117, 264; racial discrimination in private housing, 132-33; racial patterns, 8, 10-11; subsidized housing, 82-83, 103-6, 110, 350
Philadelphia, Pa., 15; location of subsidized housing, 82, 152, 178, 212, 263
Philbin, James, 392n
Phillips, Kevin P., 226-27, 398n
Phoenix Gazette, 230
Pittsburgh metropolitan area, 283
Planned-unit developments, 54, 339
Plechner, Richard, 373n
Polikoff, Alexander, 196
Political decentralization in metropolitan areas, 15-22, 29-30, 47-49, 156, 261, 282-83; impact within suburbia, 21-22, 71, 113, 115-16, 169, 196
Poltzer, Robert, 363-64n
Pomona, Cal., 99
Post, George, 365n
Potter, John H., 418n
Powers, James, J., 418n
Pratter, Jerome, 364n
Prefabricated housing, 62-63, 216-17, 333-34
President's Committee on Urban Housing, 3, 76, 210, 280, 332
President's Task Force on Low-Income Housing, 219
President's Task Force on Suburban Problems, 210, 331-32

President's Task Force on Urban Renewal, 219
Price, James H., 408n
Prince Georges County, Md., 8, 66, 88, 99, 288
Princeton, N.J., 110, 350
Princeton (N.J.) Community Housing, 117
Public housing, 80-83, 102-3, 105, 157, 203, 206; local opposition, 83-86, 90, 94-96, 109-11, 151-52; use of referendums by local governments, 99-100, 180-81
Public Housing Act of 1937, 93
Purcell, Francis, 373n, 404n
Purchase, N.Y., 143

Quaker Oats, 146-47
Quigley, Jack L., 374-75n

Rabin, Yale, 366n
Racial covenants on deeds, 13, 204
Racial discrimination in housing, 9-14, 89-92, 100-1, 104-5, 132-33, 204, 333-39
Racial zoning, 13
Radio Corporation of America, 146
Ramapo, N.Y.: growth controls, 68, 187, 371n; subsidized housing, 102, 110-11
Ramsey, N.J., 171, 389n
Rausch, Edward, 256-57
Ravitch, Richard, 419n
Readington, N.J., 120
Realtors, 12, 138-40
Referendums: and subsidized housing, 33, 99-101, 169, 174, 180-82, 376n, 392n; and zoning, 38, 100, 292
Regional Plan Association, New York, N.Y., 43-44, 77, 125, 262, 317
Reilly, William K., 419n, 422n
Rent supplement program (Housing and Urban Development Act of 1965), 96, 206-9, 397n
Ribicoff, Abraham, 238, 346
Richmond metropolitan area: school desegregation, 362
Rimmel, Gerald, 363n
Rivkin, Malcolm D., 381n, 383n
Rizzo, Frank, 152, 263
Robinson v. Cahill (1973), 422n
Rochester metropolitan area, 145, 168, 312-15, 318, 351-52

Rockefeller, Nelson A., 307-10, 312, 316, 319-22, 419n
Rockland County, N.Y., 54, 67, 311
Rogers, Henrietta, 367n, 378n
Romney, George W., 217-18, 234, 295-96, 324-25, 346-47, 403n; federal aid to the suburbs, 223-25, 233; and housing production, 215-18, 235; local zoning and federal housing programs, 93, 96-97, 225, 234; metropolitan approaches, 234-35, 244-45, 248, 257-59, 262, 408n; and Nixon's suburban housing policies, 226-28, 401n; and racial segregation in the metropolis, 204-6, 233; shortcomings of the 1968 housing programs, 86, 235; subsidized housing in the suburbs, 81-83; Warren, Mich., 92, 223-26, 257
Roos, Lawrence K., 369n, 373n, 378n
Rose, Jerome G., 393n, 394n, 412n, 424n
Rosensteil, Lewis S., 380n
Roudebush, G. S., 385n
Rousselot, John H., 241-42
Rubinowitz, Leonard S., 97, 236, 409n, 412n, 416n
Rustin, Bayard, 155, 231
Rutledge, Edward, 395-96n
Ryan, William Fitts, 207-8, 410n

Saddle River, N.J., 171, 389
Sagalyn, Lynne B., 77
Sager, Lawrence G., 50-51, 393n, 405n, 411n
St. Louis County, Mo., 32-33, 60, 94, 102
St. Louis metropolitan area: exclusion of blacks, 13-14, 32, 43, 89-91, 104-5; metropolitan housing plan, 260-61, 265; open-housing groups, 31-32, 117, 166-67, 265, 385, 393-94; opposition to subsidized housing in the suburbs, 31-33, 84-85, 89-91, 184, 260-61; subsidized housing in the suburbs, 54, 94, 102, 104-5, 190; suburban attitudes toward city, 21, 84, 109; zoning restrictions, 33, 54, 60, 99
St. Louis, Mo.: subsidized housing, 102, 152
San Antonio Independent School District v. Rodriquez (1973), 422n
San Antonio metropolitan area, 83
San Francisco metropolitan area, 36-37; growth limitations, 64, 66-68, 127-28, 184, 191, 392n; jobs and housing in the suburbs, 142-44, 330; metropolitan planning,

248, 264; open-housing groups, 116; opposition to subsidized housing in the suburbs, 91, 100, 166; racial discrimination in housing and zoning, 12, 31, 91; subsidized housing in the suburbs, 110, 117, 176-77, 182, 193, 264, 350
San Mateo County, Cal., 64
Sander, Hans, 383n
Sandman, Charles W., Jr., 297, 387n
Santa Clara County, Cal., 36-37
Santa Rosa, Cal., 144
Scammon, Richard M., 251
Scarsdale, N.Y., 312
Schermer, George, 379n
Schmickley, Dennis, 368n
Schneider, Karen, 416n
Schoenbrod, David S., 71, 381n
Schools: impact of desegregation efforts, 19-20, 152-53, 161, 326; racial segregation in metropolitan areas, 4, 331
Schulman, S. J., 419n
Schumann (Florence and John) Foundation, 122
Schwelb, Frank F., 375n, 402n
Schwern, Gerald, 111
Scott, Randall W., 247, 389n
Seaver, Edward, 406n
Section 8 leased-housing program (Housing and Community Development Act of 1974), 241-42, 270, 278, 352, 354
Section 204 areawide review (Demonstration Cities and Metropolitan Development Act of 1966), 244-45
Section 221(d)3 moderate-income housing program (Housing Act of 1961), 80, 96, 99-100, 373n
Section 235 homeownership program (Housing and Urban Development Act of 1968), 80-83, 100-6, 181, 211, 241, 304, 331, 373n; and blacks, 104-5, 153, 204, 338; construction and financing problems, 86-89, 235; and home builders, 135-36, 140; zoning restrictions, 96-97, 99
Section 236 moderate-income housing program (Housing and Urban Development Act of 1968), 80-83, 101-6, 153, 167, 181-82, 211, 241, 270, 274, 331, 338, 373n; construction and financing problems, 86-89, 235; and home builders, 135-36, 140; local opposition, 31-32, 84-91, 99-101, 121, 184-85; and state housing

finance agencies, 284, 412*n*; zoning restrictions, 31-32, 96-97, 99, 121
Section 701 planning grants (Housing Act of 1954), 244, 248-50, 258, 262-64
Segal Construction Co. v. *Zoning Board of Adjustment, Borough of Wenonah* (1975), 391
Semer, Milton P., 383*n*
Serrano v. *Priest* (1971), 422*n*
Sewers: federal assistance, 220-23, 226, 233, 237-40; and suburban development, 50, 66, 288-89
Shafor, Ann M., 257, 407*n*
Shannon v. *U.S. Dept. of Housing & Urban Dev.* (1970), 373*n*, 391*n*, 398*n*
Sheilds, Geoffrey, 114, 140-41, 326, 381*n*, 382*n*, 387-88*n*
Sheldon, Ann, 375*n*
Shelley v. *Kraemer* (1948), 361*n*
Showstack, Jerome, 420*n*
Silver, Raphael D., 383*n*
Simmons v. *City of Royal Oak* (1972), 390*n*
Simmons, Samuel J., 398-99*n*
Sisters of Providence of St. Mary of the Woods v. *City of Evanston* (1971), 388*n*
Slavet, Joseph S., 412*n*
Smith, Jefferson S., 382*n*
Smith, Katherine B., 6-7
Solon, O., 391*n*
Somers, N.Y., 320
Somerset County, N.J., 61-62
Southampton, N.Y., 72
Southeast Michigan Council of Government, 351
Southeastern Pennsylvania Transportation Authority, 330
Southeastern Wisconsin Regional Planning Commission, 249-50, 265
Southern Alameda Spanish Speaking Organization, Alameda County, Cal., 100, 117, 166, 176-77, 193
Southern Alameda Spanish Speaking Organization v. *City of Union City, Cal.* (1970), 390*n*, 394*n*
Southern Burlington County NAACP v. *Township of Mount Laurel* (1972), 388*n*, 391*n*, 394-95*n*; (1975), 298-300, 334-35, 388*n*, 390*n*, 391*n*, 393*n*, 395*n*
Spector, L. Sanford, 114, 140-41, 326, 381*n*, 382*n*, 387-88*n*
Spirrizi, John, 414*n*
Stachweicz, Raymond, 375*n*

Stanton, J. William, 237
Stastny, John, 382*n*, 409*n*, 410*n*
State Farm Mutual Insurance Company, 144
State government, 199, 279-90; allocation of subsidized housing to local governments, 294-95, 299-300, 303-4; assistance to local governments, 280, 283, 300, 342; and housing, 158, 281-86, 293-94; housing and zoning reform, 289-304, 306, 309-10, 312, 315, 319-21; and local autonomy in the suburbs, 281-83, 290-93, 297-304, 309, 312, 317-20; and local land-use powers, 33-34, 51, 279-82, 285-313, 315-21; state land-use powers, 286-89, 291-92, 295, 300-1, 303-12, 315-21; and subsidized housing, 280, 284-85, 289-90, 300-1, 303-22, 352; urban development agencies, 306-23, 335
State housing finance agencies, 284-85, 307, 412*n*
Stephens, Robert G., 403*n*
Stern Foundation, 122
Sternlieb, George, 58, 77, 104, 150
Stevens, Bart, 385*n*
Stokes, Carl B., 263, 385*n*
Stoughton, Mass., 222-23
Subdivision regulation, 50, 62
Subsidized housing: allocation of federal subsidies between cities and suburbs, 149-50, 154, 234, 263, 278, 335, 351; concentration in cities, 82, 102, 211; development in suburbs, 81-83, 101-6, 126, 206-12; and local employees in the suburbs, 111-13; and local residents in the suburbs, 105-6, 111-15, 117-19, 122-23, 242, 274, 315-18, 321, 353-57; and local services in the suburbs, 84-92, 103-5, 313; and local taxes in the suburbs, 44-45, 85-89, 126, 313, 418*n*; opposition in cities, 151-52; opposition in suburbs, 32-33, 83-106, 109-11, 121-22, 139, 157-58, 182, 184-85, 217, 220, 223-25, 236, 239, 267-69, 271, 311-21, 351, 397*n*; and race, 89-92, 100-5, 151-54, 216-17, 262, 274, 313, 315, 318; and suburban concern with community character, 83-92, 126, 273-74, 313, 336-37, 342-44
Suburban Action Institute, 118-23, 126, 137-38, 150, 379*n*; and the courts, 119-20, 162, 177, 182, 390*n*; environment and exclusion, 127; and federal policies in the

Suburban Action Institute (*Continued*)
  suburbs, 174, 231, 351; and home builders, 134-36, 191-92; and states, 280, 283,
  312, 411*n*; and suburban employers, 119,
  144-46, 148; suburban reaction to zoning
  litigation, 164, 297
Suburban Maryland Homebuilders, 137
Suburbs, 2-4, 359*n*; attitudes toward cities,
  20-21, 53-54, 84, 109, 132, 302, 318, 324,
  342-45; desire for socio-economic homogeneity, 336-37, 342-45, 356; differences among local jurisdictions, 4, 21-22,
  27-31, 46-49, 91-92, 109-13, 124-26, 128;
  economic development, 3-4, 20, 45-47, 49,
  141-48, 155; exclusion of nonresidents
  from public facilities, 41-43; federal role in
  suburban development, 33-34, 201-5,
  212-13; future development, 328-29, 350;
  influence in American politics, 323-25,
  327, 344, 347-48; influence in federal politics, 140, 156, 200-1, 205-9, 214, 217,
  224-29, 234-42; influence on metropolitan
  agencies, 246-47, 249-50, 252, 254-57,
  260-61, 263, 266-73; influence on state
  governments, 140, 156, 281, 286, 288-304,
  308-21, 323; localistic perspectives, 39-49,
  108-29, 148; and lower-income families,
  11, 22-26, 43, 83-91, 108-9, 123-24, 128,
  131, 150-51, 153, 228-31; neighborhood
  interests, 37-38, 56, 365*n*; responsiveness
  of government to local residents, 4, 15-16,
  27-33, 37-42, 48-49, 70, 72, 111-13,
  121-22, 133-34, 214, 217; role of planners,
  70-71, 109-10; role of public employees,
  112-14, 124; state role in suburban development, 33, 39, 279, 282-89
Suffolk County (N.Y.) Defenders of the
  Environment, 65, 128
Suffolk County, N.Y., 102, 120-21; opposition to subsidized housing, 311-12
Suffolk (N.Y.) *Life*, 419*n*
Sullivan, Richard J., 413*n*
Summit, N.J., 110, 126
Sutton, Percy, 156, 290, 421*n*
Syracuse metropolitan area, 278; develop-
  ment of new town by the Urban Develop-
  ment Corporation, 312-13

Taconic Foundation, 122
Taggart, Robert III, 327, 397*n*
Tanenhaus, Joseph, 389*n*

Tappen, Mary F., 368*n*
Taylor, G. Tapley, 366*n*
Teichert, Robert, 409*n*
Tenafly, N.J., 191
Tennessee Homebuilders Association, 135
Texaco Corporation, 143
Thompson, Fletcher, 237, 387*n*
Thorsen, Thomas, 317*n*
Toledo, O., 223, 239
Torrance, Cal., 99, 392*n*
Trenton Evening Times, 415*n*
Trimble, John W., 365*n*
Trotwood, O., 256-57
Trubek, David M., 280-81, 311, 334, 336,
  342
Tydings, Joseph D., 397*n*

UDC-Greater Rochester, 312-15
Union City, Cal., 100, 166, 176-77, 193
United Automobile Workers (Region Nine)
  Housing Corporation, 40, 117, 285-86
United Citizens for Home Rule, Holmdel,
  N.J., 297
United States v. *City of Black Jack, Missouri*
  (1974), 392*n*
U.S. Conference of Mayors, 149, 403*n*
U.S. Court of Appeals: Second Circuit, 185,
  390*n*; Third Circuit, 212; Sixth Circuit,
  182-83, 197, 391*n*; Seventh Circuit, 395*n*;
  Eighth Circuit, 185; Ninth Circuit, 184
U.S. Supreme Court, 160-61, 172, 175, 193,
  325, 387*n*; equal protection and school
  finance, 341; and local zoning, 53, 168-69,
  183-184; location of subsidized housing,
  178, 355, 395*n*, 425*n*; and racial discrimination in housing, 13, 169, 180-186, 338;
  standing to challenge local zoning, 168,
  172; use of referendums on subsidized
  housing, 100, 169, 174
United Towns for Home Rule, Westchester
  County, N.Y., 317-18
Upper Saddle River, N.J., 171, 389*n*, 415*n*
Upper Saint Clair Township, Pa., 283
Upper St. Clair Township v. *Commonwealth,
  Department of Community Affairs* (1973),
  411*n*
Urban League, 114-15, 237, 255
Urban renewal, 240, 404*n*; role in reducing
  housing opportunities in suburbs, 42-43,
  205; suburban opposition, 92, 220, 223,
  225

Van Dusen, Richard C., 383*n*, 398*n*
Vermont: impact of state land-use controls on housing costs, 287
Veterans Administration, 204, 238
Village of Belle Terre v. *Borass* (1974), 183-84
Village of Euclid v. *Ambler Realty Co.* (1926), 368*n*, 389*n*
Virginia Builders Association, 137

Wade, Richard C., 16
Wall Street Journal, 343
Walsh, James, 365*n*
Waner, John L., 242, 377*n*
Warner, Sam Bass, Jr., 16, 360*n*
Warren, Mich., 25, 29, 48, 92; controversy with HUD over subsidized housing, 223-27, 236-37, 257, 262, 275, 295-96, 400*n*
Warth v. *Seldin* (1975), 389*n*, 394*n*
Washington, D.C., 202, 261
Washington metropolitan area, 8, 261; growth limitations, 65-66, 68-70, 72, 133-34, 191, 288; home builders and land-use controls, 133-38, 191; location of federal installations, 202; metropolitan housing plan, 258-59, 261; open-housing supporters, 112, 118, 120, 124; opposition to subsidized housing in suburbs, 90, 99; subsidized housing in the suburbs, 88, 103, 110-12, 189
Washington Township, N.J., 194-95, 394*n*
Wassung, John, 368*n*
Water supply: federal aid, 220-23, 226, 233, 237-40
Wattenberg, Ben J., 251
Watts, William, 361*n*
Wauwatosa, Wis., 99
Wayne, N.J., 46, 171, 367*n*, 389*n*
Weaver, Clifford L., 374*n*
Weber, Arnold R., 406*n*
Weicker, Lowell P., Jr., 290
Weinberg, Robert, 381*n*, 382*n*
Weiner, Leon, 136
West Carrollton, O., 271
Westchester County, N.Y., 41, 56; fiscal zoning, 43-44; housing needs, 108-9, 111, 316, 318, 353, 418*n*; opposition to subsidized housing, 83, 85, 91, 311, 315-21; urban renewal, 42-43; zoning restrictions, 61, 133-34

Western Electric Company, 125, 146-48, 157
Westlake, O., 391*n*
Westport, Conn., 54, 102, 112
Wheaton, William L. C., 64, 399*n*
White Plains, N.Y., 316
Widnall, William B., 237
Wiggins, Charles E., 423*n*
Wilcox, William, 283
Williams, Harrison A., 397*n*
Williams, Lucille, 415*n*
Williams, Norman, Jr., 189-90, 372*n*
Willis, Sidney L., 366*n*, 414*n*
Wilmington metropolitan area, 217; school desegregation, 362*n*
Wilson, Malcolm, 396*n*, 419*n*
Wilson, Robert W., 371*n*
Winchester, Mass., 305
Windsor, Charles L., 385*n*
Wisconsin: state role in local fiscal disparities, 283; state role in housing and land use, 280, 289
Wojtowicz, Raymond, 374*n*
Wood, Robert C., 27, 69-70, 72

Xerox Corporation, 46, 145, 314

Ybarra v. *Town of Los Altos Hills* (1973), 392*n*
Ylvisaker, Paul N., 71, 290-93, 295-97, 300, 307
Yonkers, N.Y., 316

Zoning, 36, 50-52, 367*n*; age and family size restrictions, 57-58, 63-64, 175; and community character, 52-56, 59-60, 64-69, 183-84; inclusionary zoning, 111-12, 118, 124, 135-38, 189, 334-35; informal negotiations with developers, 72-74, 132-33, 137-39, 166; large-lot zoning, 59-62, 65, 75, 175-77, 179, 301, 333-34, 350; minimum building size restrictions, 61, 76, 99, 170, 177, 179, 333-34, 350; for single-family homes, 53, 59-62; special permits and variances, 73-74, 97-99; and subsidized housing, 79, 87-88, 93-106, 121, 301, 333-34; suburban capabilities, 35-39, 69-74; and suburban parochialism, 40-49; *see also* Apartments and Mobile homes
Zoning Appeals Law (Massachusetts), 300-6